Strategic Marketing Management

Dedication

This book is dedicated to the authors' wives – Gillian and Rosie – and to Ben Gilligan for their support while it was being written.

Acknowledgements

Our thanks go to Janice Nunn for all the effort that she put in to the preparation of the manuscript.

Strategic Marketing Management

Planning, implementation and control

Third edition

Richard M.S. Wilson
Emeritus Professor of Business Administration
The Business School
Loughborough University

and

Colin Gilligan
Professor of Marketing
Sheffield Hallam University
and Visiting Professor, Northumbria University

ELSEVIER
BUTTERWORTH-
HEINEMANN

AMSTERDAM • BOSTON • HEIDELBERG • LONDON • NEW YORK • OXFORD
PARIS • SAN DIEGO • SAN FRANCISCO • SINGAPORE • SYDNEY • TOKYO

Butterworth-Heinemann is an imprint of Elsevier
Linacre House, Jordan Hill, Oxford OX2 8DP, UK
30 Corporate Drive, Suite 400, Burlington, MA 01803, USA

First edition 1992
Second edition 1997
Reprinted 1998, 1999, 2001, 2003
Third edition 2005
Reprinted 2007

Notice
No responsibility is assumed by the publisher for any injury and/or damage to persons
or property as a matter of products liability, negligence or otherwise, or from any use
or operation of any methods, products, instructions or ideas contained in the material
herein. Because of rapid advances in the medical sciences, in particular, independent
verification of diagnoses and drug dosages should be made

British Library Cataloguing in Publication Data
A catalogue record for this book is available from the British Library

Library of Congress Cataloging-in-Publication Data
A catalog record for this book is available from the Library of Congress

ISBN: 978-0-7506-5938-3

For information on all Butterworth-Heinemann publications
visit our website at books.elsevier.com

Printed and bound in China

07 08 09 10   10 9 8 7 6 5 4 3 2

Working together to grow
libraries in developing countries

www.elsevier.com | www.bookaid.org | www.sabre.org

ELSEVIER   BOOK AID International   Sabre Foundation

Contents

Preface

In writing the first edition of this book in the early 1990s, we were motivated by a concern to help improve the effectiveness of marketing practice. Twelve years and two editions later, our purpose is unchanged. In doing this, we have sought to address a number of key questions that logically follow each other in the context of strategic marketing management:

1 Where are we now?
2 Where do we want to be?
3 How might we get there?
4 Which way is best?
5 How can we ensure arrival?

The themes of planning, implementing and controlling marketing activities are reflected in the answers to these questions – as offered in the eighteen chapters which follow. The structure of the book is designed to take the reader through each of the questions in turn. The sequencing of the chapters is therefore significant. We have sought to build the book's argument in a cumulative way such that it will provide guidance in generating effective marketing performance within a strategic framework – once the reader has worked through each chapter in turn.

Against this background we can specify the book's aims as being:

➡ To make the readers aware of the major aspects of the planning and controlling of marketing operations
➡ To locate marketing planning and control within a strategic context
➡ To demonstrate how the available range of analytical models and techniques might be applied to marketing planning and control to produce superior marketing performance
➡ To give full recognition to the problems of implementation and how these problems might be overcome.

Since the appearance of the first edition in 1992, the marketing environment – and therefore the challenges facing marketing planners and strategists – have changed in a variety of often dramatic ways. Amongst some of the most significant of these changes has been the emergence of what within this book we refer to as 'the new consumer' and 'the new competition'. This new consumer is typically far more demanding, far more discriminating, much less loyal and more willing to complain than in the past, whilst the new competition is frequently far less predictable and often more desperate than previously. At the same time, the marketing environment has also been affected by a series of unpredictable events (SARS and the Iraq war are just two of the more recent of these), and by the emergence of new technologies and delivery systems. Together, these changes have led to a new type of marketing reality which has major implications for the marketing planning and strategy processes. The question of how marketing planners might respond or, indeed, have responded to the new marketing reality is therefore an underlying theme of this book.

In practice, many marketing planners have responded by focusing to an ever greater degree upon short-term and tactical issues, arguing that during periods of intense environmental change, traditional approaches to marketing planning and management are of little value. Instead, they suggest, there is the need to develop highly sensitive environmental monitoring systems that are capable of identifying trends, opportunities and threats at a very early stage, and then an organizational structure and managerial mindset that leads to the organization responding quickly and cleverly.

Within this book we question these sorts of assumptions and focus instead upon the ways in which the marketing planning process can be developed and managed effectively and *strategically*. We therefore attempt to inject a degree of rigour into the process, arguing that rapid change within the environment demands a *more* strategic approach rather than less. We have also introduced a considerable amount of material designed to reflect some of the areas that have emerged over the past few years and that currently are of growing importance. The most obvious of these are e-marketing, branding, the leveraging of competitive advantage and CRM.

It is not intended that this should be used as an introductory text: we have deliberately assumed that readers will have had some prior exposure to marketing principles, if not to marketing practice. The intended market of the book comprises the following segments:

➡ Students reading for degrees involving marketing (especially MBA candidates and senior undergraduates following business studies programmes)
➡ Students of The Chartered Institute of Marketing who are preparing for the Marketing Planning paper in the CIM's Diploma examinations
➡ Marketing practitioners who will benefit from a comprehensive review of current thinking in the field of strategic marketing planning, implementation and control.

Richard M S Wilson
Colin Gilligan

Overview of the book's structure

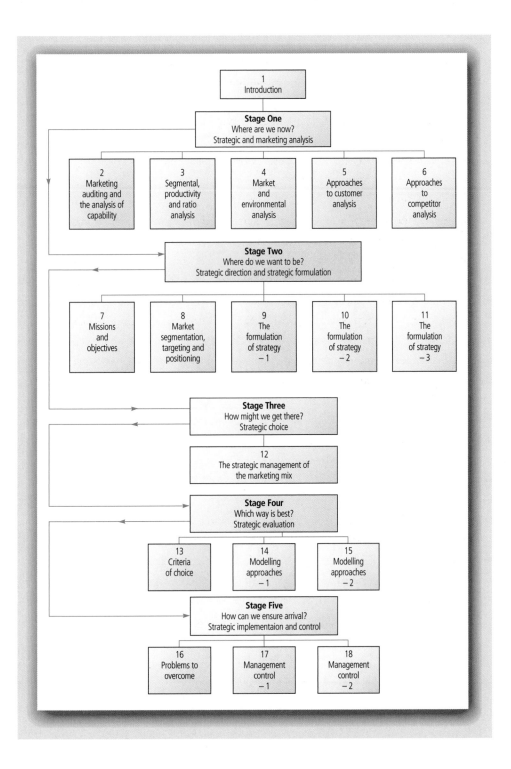

1
Introduction

Stage One
Where are we now?
Strategic and marketing analysis

| **2**
Marketing auditing and the analysis of capability | **3**
Segmental, productivity and ratio analysis | **4**
Market and environmental analysis | **5**
Approaches to customer analysis | **6**
Approaches to competitor analysis |

Stage Two
Where do we want to be?
Strategic direction and strategic formulation

| **7**
Missions and objectives | **8**
Market segmentation, targeting and positioning | **9**
The formulation of strategy − 1 | **10**
The formulation of strategy − 2 | **11**
The formulation of strategy − 3 |

Stage Three
How might we get there?
Strategic choice

12
The strategic management of the marketing mix

Stage Four
Which way is best?
Strategic evaluation

| **13**
Criteria of choice | **14**
Modelling approaches − 1 | **15**
Modelling approaches − 2 |

Stage Five
How can we ensure arrival?
Strategic implementaion and control

| **16**
Problems to overcome | **17**
Management control − 1 | **18**
Management control − 2 |

Chapter 1

Introduction

1.1 Learning objectives

When you have read this chapter you should be able to:

(a) define marketing in strategic terms;
(b) understand the basic structure of the book and how this chapter establishes the context for what follows;
(c) specify the characteristics of strategy and strategic decisions;
(d) understand the nature of the debate about the future role of marketing and its contribution to management;
(e) appreciate the changing emphases within marketing and the implications of these changes for the ways in which marketing strategies are developed.

1.2 The nature of marketing

The question of what marketing is and what it entails has been the focus of a considerable amount of work over the past 40 years. From this, numerous definitions have emerged, with differing emphases on the process of marketing, the functional activities that constitute marketing, and the orientation (or philosophy) of marketing. The Chartered Institute of Marketing, for example, defines it as:

" . . . the management process for identifying, anticipating and satisfying customer requirements profitably.**"**

A slightly longer but conceptually similar definition of marketing was proposed by the American Marketing Association (AMA) in 1985:

" Marketing is the process of planning and executing the conception, pricing, promotion and distribution of ideas, goods and services to create exchanges that satisfy individual and organizational objectives.**"**

Although this definition, or variations of it, has been used by a variety of writers (see, for example, McCarthy and Perreault, 1990; Kotler, 1991; Jobber, 2003), Littler and Wilson (1995, p. 1) have pointed to the way in which 'its adequacy is beginning to be questioned in some European textbooks' (e.g. Foxall, 1984; Baker, 1987). It could be said that the AMA definition is more of a list than a definition and is therefore clumsy and inconvenient to use; that it cannot ever be comprehensive; and that it fails to provide a demarcation as to what necessarily is or is not '*marketing*'.

They go on to suggest that the AMA definition presents marketing as a *functional* process conducted by the organization's marketing department, whereas the general thrust of the more recent literature on marketing theory is that marketing is increasingly being conceptualized as an organizational philosophy or 'an approach to doing business'. This strategic as opposed to a functional approach to marketing is captured both by McDonald (1989, p. 8):

"Marketing is a management process whereby the resources of the whole organization are utilized to satisfy the needs of selected customer groups in order to achieve the objectives of both parties. Marketing, then, is first and foremost an attitude of mind rather than a series of functional activities.**"**

and by Drucker (1973), who put forward a definition of marketing orientation:

"Marketing is so basic that it cannot be considered a separate function on a par with others such as manufacturing or personnel. It is first a central dimension of the entire business. It is the whole business seen from the point of view of its final result, that is, from the customers' point of view.**"**

A significant shift in emphasis since Drucker wrote this is to be found in the importance that is now attached to *competitive position* in a changing world. Thus, the marketing concept is that managerial orientation which recognizes that success primarily depends upon identifying changing customer wants and developing products and services which match these better than those of competitors (Doyle, 1987; see also Wilson and Fook, 1990).

The contrasting emphases on customers and competitors can be highlighted as in Figure 1.1. If an enterprise is managed a little better than customers expect, and if this is done in a slightly better way than competitors can manage, then the enterprise should be successful.

Within Figure 1.1 the customer-oriented and competitor-centred categories speak for themselves. The self-centred category is characterized by an introspective orientation

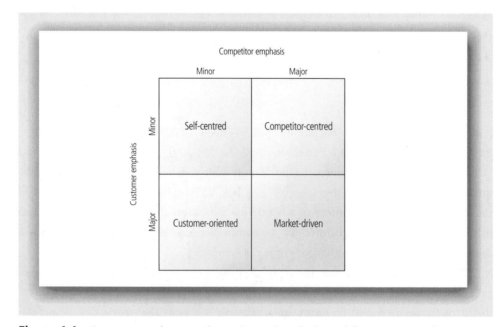

Figure 1.1 Customer and competitor orientations (adapted from Day, 1990)

that focuses on year-on-year improvements in key operating ratios, or on improvements in sales volume without making direct comparisons with competitors. Such an orientation is potentially disastrous when viewed in strategic terms. At the opposite extreme is a market-driven approach to marketing which seeks to balance a responsiveness to customers' requirements on the one hand with direct competitor comparisons on the other (see Illustration 1.1).

Illustration 1.1 But is your organization *really* market-driven?

When Peter Drucker first outlined the marketing concept 50 years ago, he equated marketing with customer orientation, arguing that for a firm to be market-driven meant always putting the customer first and innovating continuously to improve the delivered value. Subsequently, it has been recognized that Drucker's perspective lacked strategic content in that it gives emphasis to the organizational culture, but fails to provide guidance on *which* customers to serve and how to serve them. Equally, Drucker's initial views failed to take explicit account of competitors and the discipline of profit in the analysis of product and market opportunity. It is because of this that *customer* orientation has been replaced with the broader concept of *market* orientation.

Given this, we can see marketing operating at three levels:

1 Marketing as a *culture*, characterized by a set of values and beliefs that highlights the importance of the customer's interests

2 Marketing as a *strategy*, concerned with the choice of products, markets and competitive stance

3 Marketing as the set of *tactics* (essentially the seven Ps of the expanded marketing mix) that provides the basis for the imple-

mentation of the business and competitive strategy.

Recognition of this has led Webster (1999, pp. 239–40) to argue that the extent to which an organization is market-driven can be measured against eleven dimensions:

1 The extent to which a customer focus pervades the *entire* organization

2 The commitment to delivering value

3 The identification and development of distinctive competencies

4 The formation of strategic partnerships

5 The development of strong relationships with strategically important customers

6 The emphasis upon market segmentation, targeting and positioning

7 The use of customer information as a strategic asset

8 The focus on customer benefits and service

9 Continuous improvement and innovation

10 The definition of quality based on meeting customers' expectations

11 A commitment to having the best information technology available.

For Day (1990), the characteristics of a market-driven organization can be stated more succinctly:

➡ An externally orientated culture that emphasizes superior customer value
➡ Distinctive capabilities in market sensing as a means of anticipating the future
➡ Structures that are responsive to changing customer and market requirements.

The significance of being market-driven has, in turn, been highlighted by a series of studies, including one amongst 600 managers in France, the USA, Germany, Japan and the UK, which found that 'the single strongest influence on company performance is innovativeness. Further, a market-oriented company culture was found to have a positive impact in all five countries, while customer orientation, by itself, has virtually no influence on bottom line performance' (Webster, 1999, p. 241). It is the recognition of this that, as Webster suggests, highlights the need for firms to innovate continuously in order to exceed the customer's evolving definition of value.

Given the nature of these comments, the essential requirements of marketing can be seen to be (Wilson, 1988b, p. 259):

1 The identification of consumers' needs (covering *what* goods and services are bought, *how* they are bought, by *whom* they are bought, and *why* they are bought)
2 The definition of target market segments (by which customers are grouped according to common characteristics – whether demographic, psychological, geographic, etc.)
3 The creation of a *differential advantage* within target segments by which a distinct competitive position relative to other companies can be established, and from which profit flows.

The way in which a differential advantage might be achieved – and sustained – is through the manipulation of the elements of the *marketing mix*. This mix has traditionally been seen to consist of the 'four Ps' of marketing: product, price, place and promotion. Increasingly, however, but particularly in the service sector, it is being recognized that these four Ps are rather too limited in terms of providing a framework both for thinking about marketing and for planning marketing strategy. It is because of this that a far greater emphasis is now being given to the idea of an expanded mix which has three additional elements:

➡ People
➡ Physical evidence
➡ Process management.

The detail of both the traditional 'hard' elements of the mix and of the 'softer' elements appears in Figure 1.2; the individual elements of the mix are discussed in Chapter 12 of this book.

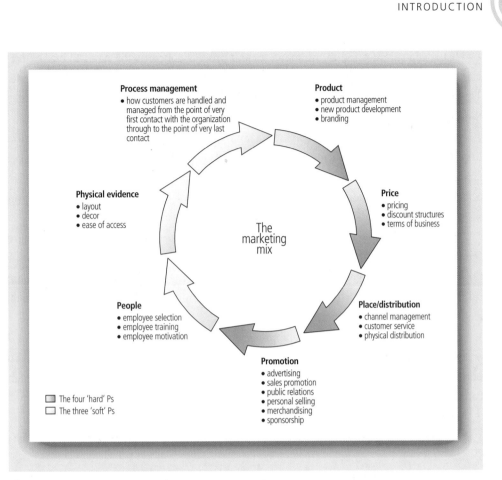

Figure 1.2   The elements of the marketing mix

1.3 The management process

Management can be looked at from a variety of viewpoints. It may be seen from one perspective as being largely an *attitude* that reflects a willingness to debate issues and
resolve them through the use of appropriate techniques and procedures. Alternatively,
management may be viewed in terms of its *responsibility for achieving desired objectives*
which requires the selection of means to accomplish prescribed ends as well as the articu-
lation of those ends. This view of management can be analysed further by focusing on
its *task orientation* (e.g. in the functional context of marketing) or on its *process orientation*
(i.e. the way in which the responsibility is exercised). In either case it has been suggested
that decision-making and management are the same thing (Simon, 1960, p. 1).

The process of decision-making is rendered problematic on account of the existence
of risk and uncertainty. In the face of risk or uncertainty, some managers postpone making a choice between alternative courses of action for fear of that choice being wrong.
What they typically fail to recognize in this situation is that they are actually making
another choice – they are deciding *not to decide* (Barnard, 1956, p. 193), which favours
the status quo rather than change. This is not a means of eliminating risk or uncertainty
since it seeks to ignore them rather than to accommodate them: the imperative to adapt
is one that cannot be ignored.

If the central question in the management process concerns the need to make decisions, we need to know *what* decisions should be made and *how* they should be made. This book is intended to deal with both these issues by following a sequence of stages that reflects a problem-solving routine. Figure 1.3 summarizes these stages.

Stage One (strategic and marketing analysis) raises the question of where the organization is now in terms of its competitive position, product range, market share, financial position, and overall levels of capability and effectiveness. In addressing this question we are seeking to establish a baseline from which we can move forward.

Stage Two (strategic direction and strategy formulation) is concerned with where the organization should go in the future, which requires the specification of ends (or objectives) to be achieved. While top management in the organization will have some discretion over the choice of ends, this is often constrained by various vested interests, as we shall see later in this book.

Stage Three of the management process deals with the question of how desired ends might be achieved, an issue that begs the question of how alternative means to ends might be identified. This strategy formulation stage requires creative inputs which cannot be reduced to mechanical procedures.

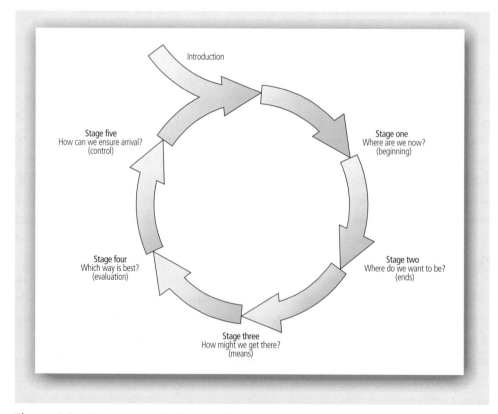

Figure 1.3 The framework of the book

Stage Four focuses on the evaluation of alternative means by which the most preferred (or 'best') alternative might be selected. The need to choose may be due to alternatives being mutually exclusive (i.e. all attempting to achieve the same end) or a consequence of limited resources (which means that a rationing mechanism must be invoked).

Stage Five covers the implementation of the chosen means, and the monitoring of its performance in order that any corrective actions might be taken to ensure that the desired results are achieved. Since circumstances both within the organization and in its environment are unlikely to stay constant while a strategy is being pursued, it is necessary to adapt to accommodate such changes.

Within these stages are to be found the main managerial activities of:

➡ Planning
➡ Decision-making
➡ Control.

The entire sequence of Stages One to Five constitutes control, within which the planning activities are to be found in Stages One to Four. At every stage it is necessary for decisions to be made, so you will see that these managerial activities are closely intertwined. Moreover, their links are spread across three different time dimensions which are not of equal significance: the past, the present and the futurre. Let us consider these in turn.

The *past* brought the organization (and its products, competitors, etc.) to their present positions. By gaining an understanding of how the organization arrived in its present position, the managers of that organization might develop some insights to help them in deciding how to proceed in the future. However, there is no way in which the past can be influenced, so the best one can do is to attempt to learn from it instead of being constrained by it. If an organization simply continues on unchanging routes its viability is almost certain to be endangered as the environment changes but it does not.

Stage One is concerned with establishing the ways in which the past brought the organization to its present position.

The *present* is transient: it is the fleeting moment between the past and the future when one must take one's understanding of the past and link this to the development of one's aspirations for the future. Decisions are made (with both planning and control consequences) in the present, but their impact is intended to be in the future.

The time dimension that is of major relevance in any planning exercise must be the *future* rather than the present or the past. There is nothing about an organization that is more important than its future, and the spirit of this was aptly summarized by C.F. Kettering: 'I am interested in the future because that is where I intend to live.' The past may help us in deciding how to proceed in the future, but there is no way in which we can influence the past, so there is a limit to the amount of effort that should be applied to it as opposed to planning for the future. This is especially relevant when we consider what a constraint to innovation the past might be: in Goethe's terms, we see what we know, and if we are obsessed with carrying on along unchanging routes we must expect our viability to become endangered as the environment changes but we fail to adapt to those changes.

On the other hand, the anticipation of the future should not become too fanciful. In a deliberately extreme mood, De Jouvenal (1967) has stated that:

". . . world population, and also the available labour force in industrial countries, is doubling every 50 years. The GNP is doubling every 20 years, and so are the number of major scientific discoveries. The whole scientific and engineering establishment, including, for example, the numbers of graduates, membership of learned societies, and scientific publications, is doubling every 15 years. The money spent on applied research is doubling every 7 years, and so also is the demand for electronics and aviation. If all these processes were to continue unchecked . . . within about 100 years every one of us would be a scientist, the entire national output would be absorbed in research, and we should be spending most of our lives airborne at 40 000 feet.*"*

This can be contrasted with a rather more serious comment made by Professor William H. Pickering of Harvard in a speech made during June 1908, in which his lack of imagination is as extreme as De Jouvenal's excess:

*"*The popular mind often pictures gigantic flying machines speeding across the Atlantic carrying innumerable passengers in a way analogous to our modern steamship. It seems safe to say that such ideas are wholly visionary, and, even if the machine could get across with one or two passengers, the expense would be prohibitive to any but the capitalist who could use his own yacht.*"*

With this uninspired perspective from a member of the establishment in the early twentieth century, it is not surprising that the vision of writers such as Jules Verne and H.G. Wells was mocked, yet their premonitions have often come to be justified, with surprising speed and accuracy in some instances. We did, for example, have Concorde, despite Professor Pickering's pessimism.

It should not be expected that any particular vision of the future will be correct in every detail, nor necessarily very detailed in its conception. Writing in 1959, Drucker made the rather careless statement that '. . . if anyone still suffers from the delusion that the ability to forecast beyond the shortest time span is given to us, let him look at the headlines in yesterday's paper, and then ask himself which of them he could possibly have predicted 10 years ago'. What Drucker does not take into account is the vital *level of resolution*: our interest over a 10-year period may be more in the continued existence of *The Times*, or even of a free press, than in specific headlines, because the level of resolution would have to be relatively low (i.e. broad horizons, broad view, little detail).

A balance must be maintained in dealing with the short-run future on the one hand and the long-run future on the other. Apart from headlines in *The Times* we can note the short-run preoccupation in the UK with financial results and contrast this with the longer-run relevance of market-building strategies, or the risk of being obsessed with tactics to the exclusion of a proper concern for strategy.

1.4 Strategic decisions and the nature of strategy

Strategic decisions are concerned with seven principal areas:

1 They are concerned with the scope of an organization's activities, and hence with the definition of an organization's boundaries.

2 They relate to the matching of the organization's activities with the opportunities of its substantive environment. Since the environment is continually changing it is necessary for this to be accommodated via adaptive decision-making that anticipates outcomes – as in playing a game of chess.

3 They require the matching of an organization's activities with its resources. In order to take advantage of strategic opportunities it will be necessary to have funds, capacity, personnel, etc., available when required.

4 They have major resource implications for organizations – such as acquiring additional capacity, disposing of capacity, or reallocating resources in a fundamental way.

5 They are influenced by the values and expectations of those who determine the organization's strategy. Any repositioning of organizational boundaries will be influenced by managerial preferences and conceptions as much as by environmental possibilities.

6 They will affect the organization's long-term direction.

7 They are complex in nature since they tend to be non-routine and involve a large number of variables. As a result, their implications will typically extend throughout the organization.

Decision-making (whether strategic or tactical) is but a part of a broader problem-solving process. In essence, this consists of three key aspects: analysis, choice and implementation.

Strategic analysis focuses on understanding the strategic position of the organization, which requires that answers be found to such questions as:

➡ What changes are taking place in the environment?
➡ How will these changes affect the organization and its activities?
➡ What resources does the organization have to deal with these changes?
➡ What do those groups associated with the organization wish to achieve?

Strategic choice has three aspects:

➡ The generation of strategic options, which should go beyond the most obvious courses of action
➡ The evaluation of strategic options, which may be based on exploiting an organization's relative strengths or on overcoming its weaknesses
➡ The selection of a preferred strategy which will enable the organization to seize opportunities within its environment or to counter threats from competitors.

Strategic implementation is concerned with translating a decision into action, which pre-supposes that the decision itself (i.e. the strategic choice) was made with some thought being given to feasibility and acceptability. The allocation of resources to new courses of action will need to be undertaken, and there may be a need for adapting the organization's structure to handle new activities, as well as training personnel and devising appropriate systems.

The elements of strategic problem-solving are summarized in Figure 1.4.

We have given some thought to strategic decisions, but what is meant by strategy?

Hofer and Schendel (1978, p. 27) have identified three distinct levels of strategy in a commercial context. These are:

1 Corporate strategy, which deals with the allocation of resources among the various businesses or divisions of an enterprise
2 Business strategy, which exists at the level of the individual business or division, dealing primarily with the question of competitive position
3 Functional level strategy, which is limited to the actions of specific functions within specific businesses.

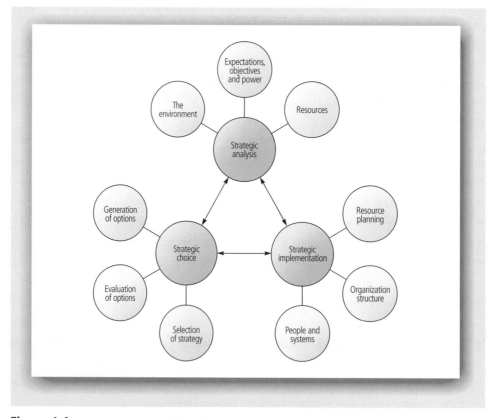

Figure 1.4 A summary model of the elements of strategic management (source: Johnson and Scholes, 1988, p. 16)

Our main concern is in relation to business strategy (i.e. level 2 above) and the way in which this links to marketing as a set of functional activities (i.e. level 3 above).

Different authorities have defined strategy in lots of different ways; there is no standard definition. However, a range of elements that most writers seem to subscribe to in discussing strategy have been put forward by Simmonds (1980, pp. 7–9), as follows:

➡ Strategy is applicable to business within defined boundaries. While the boundaries may change, the strategy applies at any one time to actions affecting a delimited area of demand and competition.

➡ There are specified direct competitors. These are competitors selling essentially the same products or services within the defined demand area. Indirect competitors are those operating outside the defined business and whose products are not direct substitutes. Indirect competition is usually ignored or covered by the concept of price elasticity of demand.

➡ There is zero-sum competition between the direct competitors for the market demand, subject to competitive action affecting the quantity demanded. Demand within the defined market varies over time. This variation in demand is largely independent of supplier strategies and is often referred to as the *product life cycle*. At its simplest it is depicted as a normal curve over time with regularly growing then declining demand.

➡ Strategy unfolds over a sequence of time periods. Competition evolves through a series of skirmishes and battles across the units of time covered by the product life cycle.

➡ Single-period profit is a function of:
  ➡ The price level ruling for the period
  ➡ The accumulated volume experience of the enterprise
  ➡ The enterprise's achieved volume as a proportion of capacity.

➡ Market share has intrinsic value. Past sales levels influence subsequent customer buying, and costs reduce with single-period volume and accumulated experience.

➡ Competitors differ in market share, accumulated experience, production capacity and resources. Competitors are unequal, identified and positioned. Objectives differ. Enterprises composed of ownership, management and employee factions and operating a range of different businesses have different objectives. Strategic business thinking, however, will usually express these as different time and risk preferences for performance within an individual business, measured in financial terms.

➡ Within a given situation there will be a core of strategic actions which will be the essential cause of change in competitive position. Non-strategic, or contingent, actions will support strategic actions and should be consistent with them, but will not change competitive position significantly.

➡ Identification of an optimal core of strategic actions requires reasoning, or diagnosis, is not attained through application of a fixed set of procedures and is situational. In short, thinking is required.

Taken together, these elements present a view of business strategy that sees it as a chosen set of actions by means of which a market position relative to other competing enterprises is sought and maintained. This gives us the notion of competitive position.

It needs to be emphasized that 'strategy' is not synonymous with 'long-term plan', but rather consists of an enterprise's attempts to reach some preferred future state by adapting its competitive position as circumstances change. While a series of strategic moves may be planned, competitors' actions will mean that the actual moves will have to be modified to take account of those actions.

We can contrast this view of strategy with an approach to management that has been common in the UK. In organizations that lack strategic direction there has been a tendency to look inwards in times of stress, and for management to devote their attention to cost cutting and to shedding unprofitable divisions. In other words, the focus has been on *efficiency* (i.e. the relationship between inputs and outputs, usually with a short time horizon) rather than on *effectiveness* (which is concerned with the organization's attainment of goals – including that of desired competitive position). While efficiency is essentially introspective, effectiveness highlights the links between the organization and its environment. The responsibility for efficiency lies with operational managers, with top management having the primary responsibility for the strategic orientation of the organization.

Figure 1.5 summarizes the principal combinations of efficiency and effectiveness.

An organization that finds itself in cell 1 is well placed to thrive, since it is achieving what it aspires to achieve with an efficient output/input ratio. In contrast, an organization in cell 4 is doomed, as is an organization in cell 2 unless it can establish some strategic direction. The particular point to note is that cell 2 is a worse place to be than

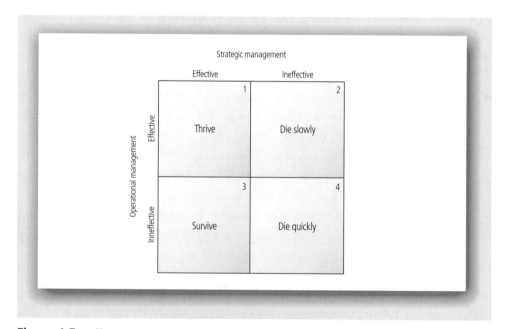

Figure 1.5 Efficiency versus effectiveness (adapted from Christopher et al., 1987, p. 80)

is cell 3 since in the latter the strategic direction is present to ensure effectiveness, even if rather too much input is currently being used to generate outputs. To be effective is to survive, whereas to be efficient is not in itself either necessary or sufficient for survival.

Effectiveness in marketing terms can therefore be seen to be the ability on the part of management to search out and embrace changing markets and structures and then reflect this in the marketing strategy.

In crude terms, to be effective is to do the right thing, while to be efficient is to do the (given) thing right. An emphasis on efficiency rather than on effectiveness is clearly wrong. But who determines effectiveness? Any organization can be portrayed as a coalition of diverse interest groups, each of which participates in the coalition in order to secure some advantage. This advantage (or inducement) may be in the form of dividends to shareholders, wages to employees, continued business to suppliers of goods and services, satisfaction on the part of consumers, legal compliance from the viewpoint of government, responsible behaviour towards society and the environment from the perspective of pressure groups, and so on. Figure 1.6 illustrates the way in which a range of interest groups come together to sustain (and, indeed, constitute) an organization. In so far as the inducements needed to maintain this coalition are not forthcoming, the organization ceases to be effective. Thus, for example, employees may go on strike in furtherance of a pay dispute; shareholders may be unwilling to subscribe further capital if the value of their shares has fallen due to bad management; consumers may have defected in the light of superior market offerings from competitors; and each of these will remove one vital element from the coalition.

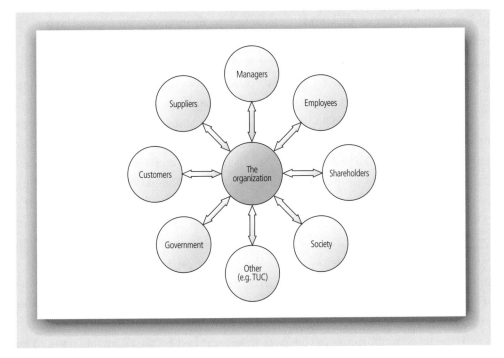

Figure 1.6 Interest groups

It should be apparent from this view of an organization that management's freedom of movement is constrained by virtue of the expectations of the various interest groups within the coalition. We are unable to assume that a clean slate exists on which any strategy might be drawn, since this may be against the interests of members of the coalition. What we can say, therefore, is that any strategy is potentially available in so far as it ensures that the interests of coalition members are protected. If this is not so the organization cannot be effective, and if it is not effective it will not survive.

The failure to achieve an appropriate balance between operational and strategic management has been illustrated by numerous organizations in recent years, including Marks & Spencer, the Post Office and BA. In the case of the Post Office, the British government set out its vision for the future of the organization in its report, *Counter Revolution: Modernizing the Post Office Network*. The report highlighted a variety of issues, including:

➡ The failure to come to terms with the service requirements of increasingly sophisticated and demanding customers
➡ The lack of any real competitive stance, with the result that other service providers such as Federal Express, DHL and UPS were able to capture a substantial share of the organization's most profitable business
➡ The slow adoption of new technologies
➡ A belief that the brand equals the branch network.

With approximately 18 500 branches or outlets in 1999/2000, compared with less than one-fifth of this number amongst its most obvious competitors, the organization had proved to be slow and monolithic in its response to the far more focused and agile behaviour of others. In order to overcome this – and indeed to survive – a number of significant changes were needed, the most obvious of which was to identify with a far greater clarity exactly where and how the Post Office brand could add to the communications chain for business customers and consumers alike.

The difficulties of balancing both the operational and the strategic dimensions of management was also highlighted at the beginning of the century by BA's poor performance at the time and, in particular, its failure to come to terms with the low-cost, no-frills entrants to the airlines market, such as Ryanair and easyJet. Having been hit by the low-cost carriers and then by a series of other factors – including the 2001 foot-and-mouth outbreak, the slowdown in the USA and global economy, and by the turmoil in the aviation industry after the terrorist attacks in the USA in September 2001 – the company then sold its own low(ish)-cost airline, Go!, in a management buyout for a little over £100 million. Eleven months later, Go! was taken over by easyJet for £374 million in a deal that strengthened BA's competitor yet further.

These sorts of difficulties have also been experienced by the car manufacturer Fiat (see Illustration 1.2).

Illustration 1.2 Balancing operational and strategic issues

With annual sales of more than two million units with over 30 billion euros, the family-dominated Fiat Group is the world's sixth largest manufacturer of cars and trucks. However, between 1990 and 2001, the company's share of the intensely competitive western European car market drifted from just under 14 per cent to a little over 9 per cent. In commenting on this, Martin (2002) suggests that:

> Survival in such a brutal environment depends on finding an upmarket niche, profitable business elsewhere, a hot-selling model or dominance of a domestic market.

> Past business decisions give Fiat no claim to the first two of these. Its new model, the Stilo, on which great hopes were pinned, is selling less well than had been hoped. And domestic dominance, once absolute, is under pressure. Though Fiat retains 35 per cent of the Italian market, it no longer does so effortlessly: it must offer price concessions and discounts. The fact that 57 per cent of Fiat's western European car and truck sales are made in Italy underscores the point. The car markets of Britain, Germany and France are all bigger than Italy's but Fiat's market share there is much smaller – nowhere higher than 5 per cent, too low to generate healthy profits in mass-market cars.

The sort of problems that are faced by Fiat are also faced by some of the other car manufacturers, including the European operations of Ford and General Motors (Martin, 2002).

> . . . relentless price and hence cost pressures, the need for irresistible new models, the imperative of establishing a premium position for the brand, the scramble to defend legacy market shares.

However, Martin goes on to suggest that Fiat can be criticized for failing to face up to some of the options that are open to it:

> . . . this is where the first issue – the difficult strategic position of European car-makers – collides with the second, the ownership structure of family empires.

> In effect, the Agnellis run a holding company with a core competence of politico-financial manoeuvring. To say this is not to denigrate them: success in this area is an essential skill in Italian business life. And the family also possesses a secondary competence, the appointment of loyal and largely effective managers. *Day-to-day, the companies are run well* [our emphasis].

> But difficult strategic decisions will always come second to the need to preserve the family's role. Even where there is no direct conflict between this aim and the needs of a subsidiary, the primacy of manoeuvring will always postpone difficult decisions that affect one of the operating businesses. That is, at least until there is a crisis, either at the operating level or in the overall stewardship of the group. The problem for Fiat is that both types of crises have arrived simultaneously.

The sort of issue highlighted above, that the business is run well on a day-to-day basis but has failed to come to terms with some of the broader – and arguably more fundamental – strategic issues, is one that has been faced by numerous organizations, including Royal Mail. The Post Office's operations have tradition- ally been run well on a day-to-day basis, but the management team, for a variety of reasons, failed to read the market suffi- ciently well and was hit hard by a series of competitors.

Given the nature of these comments, it should be apparent that achieving a consistent balance between operational and strategic issues is inherently problematic and it is the ability to do this that ultimately determines the organization's overall level of marketing effectiveness.

The question of what determines marketing effectiveness has been the subject of a considerable amount of research and is an issue to which we return at various points in the book (see, for example, Section 11.12). At this stage, therefore, we will limit ourselves to an overview of the sorts of factors that contribute to the effectiveness of marketing activity (see Illustration 1.3).

Illustration 1.3 The dimensions of marketing effectiveness

Although it is tempting to identify the characteristics of marketing effectiveness and to believe that the straightforward adoption of these will lead to business success, it is also potentially simplistic and dangerous, since it can lead to the view that this is the formula for success. Nevertheless, there are certain elements that appear to contribute to effectiveness and it is in this way that the list below should be seen:

➡ A strong sense of vision amongst the members of the senior management team

➡ A strong customer orientation across all aspects of the business and a fundamental recognition of the importance of the customer

➡ A detailed recognition of the relative value of different segments and customer groups, and a clear policy of targeting and positioning

➡ A clarity and ambition of marketing objectives

➡ A detailed understanding of the organization's assets and competencies

➡ A detailed understanding of the market

➡ A willingness to redefine the market and create and exploit windows of opportunity

➡ The creation of one or more market breakpoints

➡ An emphasis upon differentiation and the leveraging of strong selling propositions

➡ A fundamental understanding of the strategic importance of competitive advantage

➡ The innovative management of each of the elements of the marketing mix

➡ A balanced product portfolio

➡ A commitment to product and process innovation

➡ An emphasis upon the coordination of activities across the organization

➡ A recognition of the fundamental importance of implementation.

1.5 The marketing/strategy interface

On the basis of a literature review, Greenley (1986b, p. 56) has drawn some distinctions between marketing planning (seen as being an annual exercise) and strategic planning (seen as being of a long-term nature), including those listed in Table 1.1.

These differences indicate that strategic planning logically precedes marketing planning by providing a framework within which marketing plans might be formulated. As Cravens (1986, p. 77) has stated:

"Understanding the strategic situation confronting an organization is an essential starting point in developing a marketing strategy."

This understanding can be derived from an assessment of:

➡ Organizational capabilities
➡ Threats from environmental forces
➡ Competitors' strengths and weaknesses
➡ Customers' needs

and fits into an iterative setting as shown in Figure 1.7.

The strong interdependence of strategic and marketing planning is clearly seen in this diagram. We can use this interdependence to develop the marketing mix (of Figure 1.2 above) into a set of elements from which a competitive strategy might be developed (as in Figure 1.8). The aim should be to build strength in those elements that are critical to achieving superiority in areas deemed important by customers. In this way the organization should be able to challenge its competitors from a position in which it can use its relative strengths.

Table 1.1 Differences between strategic planning and marketing planning

Strategic planning	Marketing planning
Concerned with overall, long-term organizational direction	Concerned with day-to-day performance and results
Provides the long-term framework for the organization	Represents only one stage in the organization's development
Overall orientation needed to match the organization to its environment	Functional and professional orientations tend to predominate
Goals and strategies are evaluated from an overall perspective	Goals are subdivided into specific targets
Relevance of goals and strategies is only evident in the long term	Relevance of goals and strategies is immediately evident

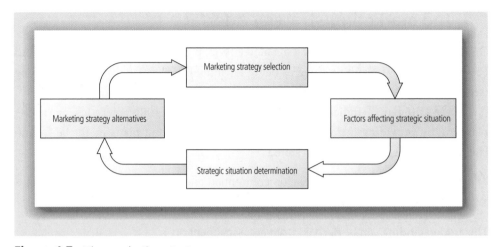

Figure 1.7 The marketing strategy process

The potential benefits of a strategic underpinning to marketing planning are probably apparent, but what about the problem of implementation? If implementation is ineffective, the carefully devised strategy will be unable to help in improving the organization's performance. The question becomes, therefore: 'given a specific type of strategy, what marketing structures, policies, procedures, and programmes are likely to distinguish high performing business units from those that are relatively less effective, efficient, or adaptable?' (Walker and Ruekert, 1987, p. 15). Part of the answer is undoubtedly the extent to which the organization reflects a customer orientation.

Figure 1.8 Elements of a competitive strategy (source: Milton and Reiss, 1985b)

Left-handed and right-handed organizations

The issue of customer orientation has been discussed by Doyle (1994, pp. 7–9) in terms of what he refers to as *left-handed* and *right-handed* organizations. For many senior managers, he argues, the principal business objectives are profitability, growth and shareholder value. There is, however, a danger in these, he suggests, in that they ignore the customer even though:

"... satisfied customers are the source of all profits and shareholder value. Customers can choose from whom they buy, and unless the firm satisfies them at least as well as competitors, sales and profits will quickly erode. Customer satisfaction should therefore be a prime objective and measure of the performance of managers.*"*

This leads Doyle to highlight the differences between the two types of organization. In the case of left-handed or financially-driven organizations, he suggests that the key planning mechanism is the financial plan or budget, with costs, expenses, debt and assets – and the elements of the marketing mix – all being controlled in order to achieve financial goals; this is illustrated in Figure 1.9. The consequence of this is that when sales begin to slip there is a tendency to cut back on areas such as advertising and R&D in order to maintain or boost profits.

By contrast, right-handed or market-driven organizations have as their primary focus the objective of satisfying customers. This involves defining and understanding market segments and then managing the marketing mix in such a way that customers' expectations are fully met or exceeded. The difference between the two approaches,

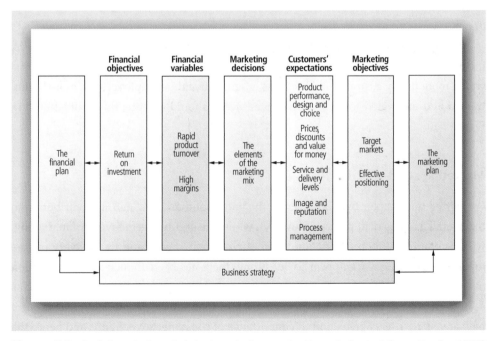

Figure 1.9 Left-handed and right-handed organizations (adapted from Doyle, 1994)

Doyle argues, is that 'Business decisions flow back from an understanding of customers rather than from a financial requirement'.

He goes on to suggest that the market-led approach, which is based on the idea of achieving market leadership through superiority in meeting customers' needs, has typically been associated with Japanese organizations. By contrast, the financially-driven approach has all too often been a reflection of British and US organizations. The idea of a left- versus right-handed orientation leads in turn to the notion of *wrong-side-up* and *right-side-up* organizations (see Figure 1.10). Given the importance to any organization of its customers, it follows that staff must be customer-led. Doyle argues that the *truly* fundamental importance of this has been recognized by relatively few organizations; those which have are the ones that achieve true customer delight.

Among those which have been forced to recognize the real significance of a customer orientation are McDonald's, Marks & Spencer and, in the 1980s, Scandinavian Airlines. Jan Carlzon, the airline's Chief Executive, recognized at an early stage the importance of what he referred to as 'moments of truth'; these are the occasions when the customer deals with the organization's staff and is exposed to the quality of service and type of personal contact. Carlzon's thinking in turning round and revitalizing what was at the time a poorly performing airline was therefore straightforward. Because the airline's frontline staff, many of whom are in relatively junior positions, are the customer's only really visible point of contact with the airline, managers need to ensure that all staff understand and act out the values that senior management claims are important. This means they need to be the most customer-oriented, best trained and most strongly motivated employees in the business. However, the reality in many cases is that these are the people who least understand the core values and are often only poorly trained. The net effect of this is that the organization fails to deliver to the customer what it promises.

In an attempt to overcome this, organizations have responded in a variety of ways, including downsizing, developing flatter structures and by empowering staff. In this way, a more firmly customer-led business in which frontline employees are more highly trained and motivated to satisfy customers' needs should emerge; this is illustrated in Figure 1.10.

Marketing's mid-life crisis

We started this chapter by talking about the nature of marketing and its contribution to the overall management process. However, whilst the arguments in favour of marketing, with its emphasis upon the identification of customers' needs and the delivery of customer satisfaction, are (or appear to be) strong, there has been an increasing recognition over the past few years that marketing is (or may be) facing what is loosely referred to as a 'mid-life crisis'. The basis for this comment is that, although a whole generation of management writers agree upon the importance of consumer sovereignty, and hence the apparent and pivotal importance of marketing, there is now a widespread and growing

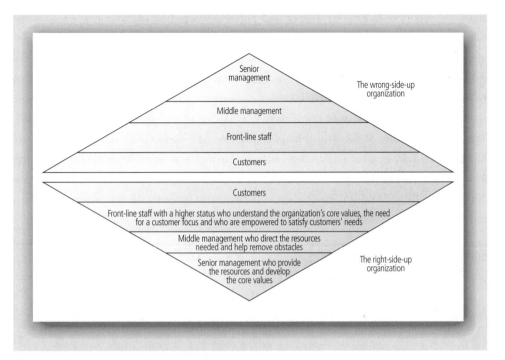

Figure 1.10 The two types of organization (adapted from Doyle, 1994)

concern that 'something is amiss, that the (marketing) concept is deeply, perhaps irredeemably, flawed, that its seemingly solid theoretical foundations are by no means secure and that the specialism is teetering on the brink of serious intellectual crisis' (Brown, 1995, p. 42).

In developing this argument, Brown makes reference to a variety of commentators:

➡ Piercy (1991, p. 15), for example, maintains that the traditional marketing concept 'assumes and relies on the existence of a world which is alien and unrecognizable to many of the executives who actually have to manage marketing for real'.

➡ Gummeson (1987, p. 10) states that 'the present marketing concept . . . is unrealistic and needs to be replaced'.

➡ Rapp and Collins (1990, p. 3) suggest that 'the traditional methods . . . simply aren't working as well any more'.

➡ Brownlie and Saren (1992, p. 38) argue that 'it is questionable whether the marketing concept as it has been propagated can provide the basis for successful business at the end of the twentieth century'.

➡ Finally, Michael Thomas (1993), who after 30 years of disseminating the marketing message, made the frank, and frankly astonishing, confession that he is having serious doubts about its continuing efficacy.

Hooley and Saunders (1993, p. 3), however, have pursued a rather different line of argument, suggesting instead that the marketing concept has come of age in that, whereas even 10 years ago, many senior managers did not *really* understand marketing, there appears now to be a far deeper and wider appreciation of the concept and of the benefits that it is capable of delivering. To a very large extent this is due to the succession of studies which have highlighted the contribution that effective marketing programmes are capable of making to organizational performance and success; a number of these are summarized in Illustration 1.4. However, despite this sort of evidence, there is still a question mark over the direction that marketing should take in the future. Without doubt, one of the triumphs of marketing as a discipline over the past decade has been the way in which it has been accepted in a host of areas by managers who previously had denied its value and scope for contributing to the sector's performance. Included within these are healthcare, not-for-profit organizations, leisure, religious movements, cultural organizations and the political arena.

Illustration 1.4 But does marketing work?

The question of whether marketing 'works' in the sense that it contributes to or is the principal influence upon higher and more sustained levels of business performance has been the subject of a number of studies. Some of the best known of these were conducted by:

➡ Hooley and Lynch (1985), who examined 1504 British companies and concluded that the high-performing organizations were characterized by a significantly greater market orientation, strategic direction and concern with product quality and design than the 'also rans'.

➡ Narver and Slater (1990), who focused upon the marketing orientation of the senior managers in 140 North American strategic business units (SBUs) and identified not only a very strong relationship between marketing orientation and profitability, but also that the *highest* degree of marketing orientation was manifested by managers of the *most profitable* companies.

➡ Kohli and Jaworski (1990), who conducted a series of semi-structed interviews with marketing practitioners in the USA and discovered a high degree of managerial understanding of the three key component parts of the marketing concept (*customer orientation*, *coordination* and *profitability*), and that the perceived benefits of the marketing philosophy included better overall performance, benefits for employees and more positive customer attitudes.

➡ Wong and Saunders (1993), who, as the result of a study of matched Japanese, American and British companies, demonstrated that organizations, classified as 'innovators', 'quality marketeers' and 'mature marketeers', were significantly more successful in terms of profits, sales and market share than those classified as 'price promoters', 'product makers' and 'aggressive pushers'.

Nevertheless, there is still a significant degree of scepticism about the value and future role of marketing. In discussing this, Brown (1995, p. 43) focuses upon four stages of marketing acceptance. The first of these, *realization*, is characterized by a general acceptance that the marketing concept is sound, but that there is often a problem with its implementation; the most common manifestation of this would be that of getting senior management to accept and embrace the concept. The net effect of this in many organizations has been 'a preoccupation with making marketing work through a heightened understanding of organizational politics and interfunctional rivalry . . . [and] a programme of internal marketing' designed to ensure that organizational transformation takes place. The second position is *retrenchment*, in which, again, the concept is seen to be sound, but there are certain circumstances in which it is either inappropriate or of little immediate relevance; many managers in the very fastest moving high-tech industries have, for example, argued that this is the case. Other sectors and markets in which its role and contribution is, it is argued, of little real value include commodity markets, public administration and poorly developed markets in which either there is a significant imbalance between demand and supply and/or an almost complete absence of infrastructure.

The third position, *rearrangement*, demands a far more fundamental reappraisal of marketing so that it can more easily and readily come to terms with the very different realities of today's markets. Webster (1988), for example, has argued for a move away from the position in which marketing and strategic management have, for many commentators, become synonymous. Instead of a myopic preoccupation with market share, competitor activity and so on, marketing should, he claims, return to its roots of a true customer focus. A broadly similar line of argument has been pursued by Christopher et al. (1991), who highlight the fundamental importance of marketing relationships rather than one-off transactions.

The fourth, final and most radical position is that of *reappraisal*, which, according to Brown (1995, p. 45), gives acknowledgement to:

" . . . the simple fact that the marketing concept has not succeeded and is unlikely to prove successful in its present form. Despite the latter-day 'triumph' of marketing, the failure rate of new products is as high as it ever was – possibly higher. Consumerism, the so-called 'shame of marketing', is still rampant, especially in its virulent 'green' mutation. Selling has not, contra to the marketing concept, been rendered redundant because few products actually sell themselves. Companies in countries where the marketing message has not been received loud and clear, such as Japan and Germany, continue to outperform their Anglo-American counterparts and, even in the latter milieux, businesses can still succeed without the aid of modern marketing (Piercy (1992) cites The Body Shop and Marks & Spencer as prime examples.)**"**

(Authors' note: Subsequently, of course, both The Body Shop and Marks and Spencer have experienced significant market pressures which, arguably, might have been avoided had their marketing been stronger.)

Redefining marketing: coming to terms with the challenges of the new millennium

Against the background of our comments so far, it is apparent that there is a strong case either for redefining marketing or, at the very least, thinking about the role that it should play in the twenty-first century. For many managers the need for this has been highlighted by the way in which a series of fundamental changes have taken place within many markets which demand a new and possibly radical rethinking of strategies. Prominent among these changes are:

➡ The decline of the megabrands as the result of attacks from low-branded, low-priced competitors
➡ The disappearance within many industrial organizations of staff marketing departments and their replacement by more focused functions with specific line responsibilities
➡ The decline in the demand for certain specialist marketing skills, including the collection and analysis of data
➡ The emergence of a 'new' type of consumer who demands a far higher value-added offer
➡ Markets which are characterized by infinitely more aggressive – and desperate – levels of competition.

It was against this background that Kashani (1996, pp. 8–10) conducted an international study of 220 managers with a view to identifying the challenges that marketing managers were facing, how these might best be met and what the implications for marketing might be. The findings suggested that, in order of importance, the principal challenges were seen to be:

➡ High and rising levels of competition across virtually all markets
➡ Far higher levels of price competition
➡ An increasing emphasis upon and need for customer service
➡ A demand for higher levels of product quality
➡ Higher rates of product innovation
➡ Changing and less predictable customer needs
➡ The emergence of new market segments
➡ The growing power of distribution channels
➡ Growing environmental ('green') concerns
➡ Increases in government regulations
➡ European integration
➡ Increasing advertising and promotional costs.

The principal implications of these were seen by managers to be: the need for constant improvements to product and/or service quality; the development of new products; keeping up with competitors; and adding to or improving customer service.

As part of the study, Kashani also asked managers about the sorts of changes that were most likely to affect their markets in the future. The three most significant of these proved to be:

➡ The consolidation of competition as fewer but larger players emerge
➡ Changing customers and their demands
➡ The globalization of markets and competition.

In order to cope with these sorts of changes, he suggests that marketing needs to respond in several ways. Perhaps the most obvious of these is that it needs to take on a *far more direct line responsibility* within the organization, with an emphasis upon segment or product management, where the focus is upon customer segments or particular products or technologies. The effect of this would be that marketing thinking and action would be better integrated into day-to-day business decisions.

Following on from this, marketing needs to become more strategic and less specialized in its nature, so that it becomes part of a more integrated process which might, for example, include upstream product development or downstream distribution management.

The third sort of change which is needed can in many ways be seen to be the underpinning that is needed for the future – that of a marketing or customer orientation becoming far more widespread. This would mean that marketing would no longer be the isolated concern of a few people, but of staff throughout the business. Thus:

"A widespread appreciation of market forces and customer needs and how parts of an organization may contribute to creating a superior customer value is a necessity if the entire organization is to become market responsive. In a fast changing market environment, such an appreciation can make the difference between success and failure."

(Kashani, 1996, p. 9)

Assuming changes such as these are made, the sorts of skills and competencies that managers will need in the future will differ from those which are needed today, with a far greater emphasis being placed upon strategic thinking, communication and customer sensitivity.

The increasing volatility of markets has also been referred to in a number of recent books, such as *The State We're In* (Hutton, 1995), *The End of Affluence* (Madrick, 1995) and *The End of Work* (Rivkin, 1995), all of which argue that the developed western economies are facing a major step change in their fortunes as unemployment levels rise, deficits persist and purchasing power declines. There appear to be two major forces that are contributing to these changes. The first is *globalization*, which leads to an opening up of domestic markets and to the threat of low-priced foreign entrants. The second contributory factor is that of the seemingly ever faster pace of *technological change*. Together, these demand not only that managers have a far more detailed understanding of their current and potential markets and of their organization's ability to capitalize upon the undoubted opportunities that exist, but also of the ways in which these threats might best be minimized; in essence, this is a case for marketers to recognize the fundamental need for their behaviour patterns to be what Ries and Trout (1986) discuss in terms of being faster, more focused and smarter. In the absence of this, an organization's ability to compete is reduced dramatically.

But although the new market environment demands more innovative thinking and more creative ways of tackling the market, there are, in many organizations, significant barriers to this; these are illustrated in Figure 1.11.

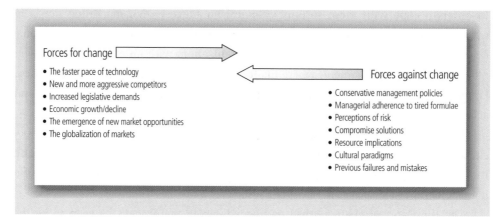

Figure 1.11 The conflicting environmental and organizational forces

Given the nature of these opposing forces and of the likelihood of those on the right-hand side leading to a failure on the part of the organization to change, the marketing planner needs to focus upon a number of issues, including what Hamel and Prahalad (1994, pp. 49–71) refer to in terms of 'learning to forget'. (This is an issue which is developed in detail on pages 467–74.) In arguing for this, they suggest that far too many managers, while acknowledging at an intellectual level the need for change, fail to accept it at an emotional level. In other words, while they are aware of the environmental changes taking place and accept the need to behave more proactively, they are often far too constrained by day-to-day pressures and the organizational culture to make the possibly radical shifts that the environment demands. Because of this, they remain wedded to old patterns of thought, believing that the current ways of doing things will ultimately prove to be adequate.

In order to overcome this myopia, Wind (1996, p. 7) argues that there needs to be a far greater emphasis upon being close to the customer, together with a far more fundamental recognition of the importance of customer satisfaction, the need for customer relationship building, an emphasis upon understanding customer value and the enhanced product offering, and that brand equity stems from a loyal customer base.

The implications of this can be seen to be far-reaching, including the way in which marketing needs to be looked at from a pan-organizational perspective rather than from the far narrower departmental perspective that predominates in many organizations. In turn, this different approach demands a rethinking of an organization's vision, objectives, strategies and structures, as well as of the sorts of skills that its staff need.

In discussing this, Wind (1996) argues that managers need to ask – and answer – twelve questions:

1 Is marketing and its focus on meeting and anticipating customers' needs widely accepted as a business philosophy?
2 Are the business and corporate strategies focused on creating value for all the stakeholders?

3 Do the objectives include customer satisfaction and the creation of value?

4 Is the marketing function integrated with the other functions of the company as part of the key value-creating process?

5 Are the key marketing positions market segment (or key account) managers?

6 Are products viewed as part of an integrated product and service offering which delivers the desired benefit positioning for the target segment?

7 Is the marketing strategy global in its scope?

8 Is full use being made of market research and modelling in generating and evaluating marketing and market-driven business strategies?

9 Is there an emphasis upon information technology as an integral part of the organization's marketing strategies?

10 Does a significant part of the marketing effort constitute innovative practices not previously used by the organization and its competitors?

11 Are strategic alliances for co-marketing activities being formed, and are marketing strategies based on the development of long-term relationships with clients?

12 Is there a sufficient focus of attention and resources upon message effectiveness (instead of media power) and value-based pricing (instead of discounting)?

Wind goes on to argue that it is not enough just to answer 'yes' to these twelve questions, but that there is also a need to recognize the interrelationships between many of the questions, and that the corporate vision and objectives *must* reflect a marketing orientation. This, in turn, highlights the critical importance of ensuring that the organizational architecture (this embraces the culture, structure, processes, technology, resources, people, performance measures and incentives) is focused upon the implementation of the new marketing paradigm. This paradigm, Wind suggests, can best be summed up in terms of building upon the historical role of marketing as the linkage between the organization and the environment, but which also focuses upon the twelve questions above and which, in turn, has implications for marketing as:

➡ The leading business philosophy
➡ The knowledge and wisdom centre of the company that provides all organizational members with concepts and findings about customers, tools for measuring and forecasting customer behaviour, and models and decision support systems for improving the quality of marketing and business decisions
➡ The growth engine which, through creative marketing strategies that utilize technology and mobilize the other business functions of the company, stimulates the top-line growth of the company.

Given the nature of these comments, it should be apparent that marketing is facing a series of fundamental challenges and that many planners are reappraising how marketing might best contribute to the overall management of an organization. As part of this debate, Figure 1.12 attempts to pull together the kinds of relationships that should

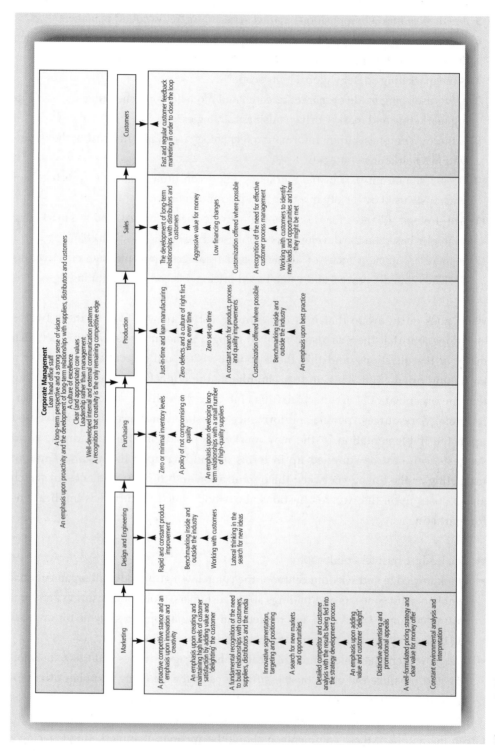

Corporate Management
Lean head office staff
A long-term perspective and a strong sense of vision
An emphasis upon proactivity and the development of long-term relationships with suppliers, distributors and customers
A culture of excellence
Clear (and appropriate) core values
Leadership rather than management
Well-developed internal and external communication patterns
A recognition that creativity is the only remaining competitive edge

Marketing	Design and Engineering	Purchasing	Production	Sales	Customers

Marketing
A proactive competitive stance and an emphasis upon innovation and creativity

An emphasis upon creating and maintaining high levels of customer satisfaction by adding value and 'delighting' the customer

A fundamental recognition of the need to build relationships with customers, suppliers, distributors and the media

Innovative segmentation, targeting and positioning

A search for new markets and opportunities

Detailed competitor and customer analysis with the results being fed into the strategy development process

An emphasis upon adding value and customer 'delight'

Distinctive advertising and promotional appeals

A well-formulated pricing strategy and clear value for money offer

Constant environmental analysis and interpretation

Design and Engineering
Rapid and constant product improvement

Benchmarking inside and outside the industry

Working with customers

Lateral thinking in the search for new ideas

Purchasing
Zero or minimal inventory levels

A policy of not compromising on quality

An emphasis upon developing long-term relationships with a small number of high-quality suppliers

Production
Just-in-time and lean manufacturing

Zero defects and a culture of right first time, every time

Zero set-up time

A constant search for product, process and quality improvements

Customization offered where possible

Benchmarking inside and outside the industry

An emphasis upon best practice

Sales
The development of long-term relationships with distributors and customers

Aggressive value for money

Low financing changes

Customization offered where possible

A recognition of the need for effective customer process management

Working with customers to identify new leads and opportunities and how they might be met

Customers
Fast and regular customer feedback marketing in order to close the loop

Figure 1.12 Marketing and its contribution to effective management

or might realistically exist between marketing and other areas of a marketing organization. Within this, there are several areas to which attention needs to be paid, but most obviously the characteristics of corporate management (the long-term perspective, a sense of vision, clear values, proactive patterns of thought and behaviour, and so on), the process linkages between marketing and the other functions, and the sorts of factors which characterize the effective management of each of the five functions identified.

Changing emphases within marketing

As the part of the organization which interacts most directly and immediately with the environment, there is an obvious need for the marketing planner to investigate, analyse and respond to any environmental changes that are taking place. If this is not done – or if it is done only poorly – not only will opportunities be missed, but potential and emerging threats are more likely to become actual threats, both of which will be reflected in a decline in performance. Because of this, the marketing planner needs to develop a clear vision of the future and of the ways in which the business environment is most likely to develop. In doing this, it is essential that the planner recognizes how patterns of marketing thinking are changing and how the organization might best come to terms with areas of growing importance.

Recognizing this, we can identify a number of marketing priorities for the new millennium:

➡ As the pace of change increases, the speed of anticipation and response will become ever more important and time-based competition more essential.
➡ As markets fragment, customization will become more necessary. With expectations rising, quality will become one of the *basic* rules of competition (in other words, a 'must have') rather than a basis for differentiation.
➡ Information and greater market knowledge will provide a powerful basis for a competitive advantage.
➡ Sustainable competitive advantage will increasingly be based upon an organization's core competencies. The consequences of a lack of strategic focus will become more evident and more significant.
➡ As market boundaries are eroded, the need to think globally will become ever more necessary. In this way, the marketing planner will be able to offset temporary or permanent declines in one market against growing opportunities in another. At the same time, of course, the need to recognize the strategic significance of size and scale is increasing. However, in going for size, the marketing planner should not lose sight of the need for tailoring products and services to the specific demands of markets by thinking globally, but acting locally.
➡ Differentiation will increasingly be based upon service.
➡ Partnerships with suppliers and distributors will become far more strategically significant.

➡ Strategic alliances will become more necessary as a means of entering and operating within markets, partly because they offer the advantages of access to greater or shared knowledge, but also because of the sharing of costs and risks.

➡ A far greater emphasis upon product, service and process innovation.

➡ A need to recognize the greater number and complexity of stakeholders' expectations.

In turn, these marketing priorities have substantial implications for organizational structures and cultures. Doyle (1994, pp. 384–6) identifies the ten most obvious of these as being the need to:

1 Break hierarchies and reorganize around flatter structures

2 Organize around small(er) business units

3 Develop self-managing teams

4 Re-engineer

5 Focus upon developing networks and alliances

6 Move towards transactional forms of organization

7 Become a true learning organization

8 Emphasize account management in order to integrate specialist expertise across the organization for the benefit of the customer

9 Recognize the importance of 'expeditionary marketing' so that, instead of focusing upon what Hamel and Prahalad refer to as *blockbuster innovation* designed to get it right first time, the organization concentrates upon developing a stream of low-cost, fast-paced innovative products

10 Rethink the way in which the board of directors operates so that it focuses to a far greater extent upon strategic direction rather than control and day-to-day management.

Marketing and a shift of focus

Many of the sorts of changes to which we have referred are reflected in the way in which we have seen a move from the sort of mass marketing that prevailed up until the mid-1970s, through just-in-time thinking and time-based competition, to the far greater emphasis today upon one-to-one marketing; this is illustrated in Figure 1.13. These changes are also reflected in Figure 1.14, which shows the emergence of different marketing paradigms, culminating in today's paradigm of electronic marketing (the role of the Internet in marketing is discussed in greater detail in Chapter 10 of the book).

Although the most obvious driver for this move towards the emerging paradigm of electronic marketing is the development of the technology itself, there are several underlying factors that have led analysts to question marketing practices and the need for a degree of rethinking. In 1993, for example, Coopers & Lybrand surveyed 100 companies and concluded that marketing departments were 'ill-focused and over-indulged'. In the same year, McKinsey released a report suggesting that 'marketing

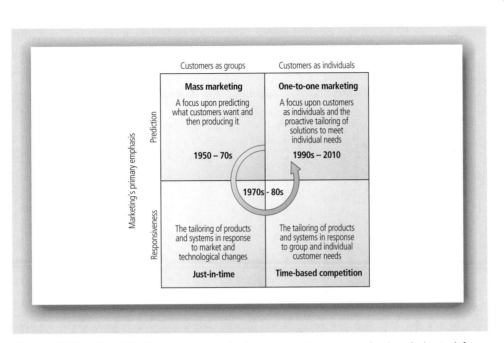

Figure 1.13 The shift from mass marketing to one-to-one marketing (adapted from Datamonitor Analysis, 1996)

departments have shown themselves to be "unimaginative", generating "few new ideas", and have simply stopped "picking up the right signals" . . . many consumer goods CEOs are beginning to think that marketing is no longer delivering'. A year later, Booz, Allen & Hamilton issued a report warning 'brand managers were failing to get to grips with commercial realities'.

Given the nature of these (and other) comments, a number of marketing strategists have come to recognize the need for a far stronger and tighter focus upon customers, far better and more effective feedback systems, and a generally more strategic approach to customer management, something that has helped in this movement away from the traditional mass marketing paradigm.

So why do great companies fail?

Long-term success is typically based on a combination of innovation, investment, the creation of value and – very importantly – a strong emphasis upon strategic management.

However, the quality and consistency of strategic thinking in many organizations has been severely criticized over the past few years. De Kare-Silver (1997), for example, highlights two studies, one from the consulting firm Kalchas CSC Index which suggested that 'only one in ten companies had the information or insight needed to make truly worthwhile strategic decisions' and one from *Business Week* (1996) which claimed that 'only 6% of executives rated their company highly for long term planning skills'.

This led Hamel and Prahalad (1994) to suggest that in many organizations there is an inherent tension between their past and their future which, unless it is addressed in

	Mass marketing (traditional paradigm)	Target marketing (transitional paradigm)	Customer marketing (the new paradigm)	Electronic marketing (the emerging paradigm)
Key characteristics, underlying assumptions and approaches	Mass selling ↑ Consumers are satisfied with a standard product ↑ Resellers are used to reach the consumer ↑ Heavy advertising will be successful	Market segmentation ↑ Markets consist of distinct and definable groups ↑ Success is gained from clear customer targeting and the development of a strong position within particular segments ↑ Targeting can be achieved through market analysis	A focus upon key customers and database management ↑ Databases enable organizations to store and interrogate customer information to provide insight ↑ Performance is improved by focusing on individual's needs ↑ The costs of customization are reducing all the time Technology now allows for direct marketing	The Internet ↑ Customers are more demanding, more discriminating and less loyal. They demand more information and are capable of processing this effectively ↑ Buyers want 24-hour access to develop a dialogue ↑ Markets are increasingly global in their nature
Weaknesses and failings	↑ A lack of focus and the subsequent waste of resources ↑ It ignores the demand for individual responses	↑ Large and profitable segments attract numerous players ↑ Customers shift from one segment to another and may belong to contradictory segments ↑ Segments may be illusory ↑ Some financial services organizations	'Databases' are often just lists of names and addresses rather than detailed customer profiles Database management and database mining skills are often more limited than is needed	↑ Customers may be concerned about security

Figure 1.14 Marketing's four paradigms: the shift from mass marketing to electronic marketing

a radical way, ultimately leads to the organization's decline and failure; this is illustrated in Figure 1.15.

In discussing this, De Kare-Silver (1997) suggests that those organizations that do manage to overcome this tension have several common features:

➡ A clear sense of purpose and direction
➡ Clearly articulated strategies
➡ Continuous investment
➡ A focus of resources and effort
➡ A commitment to the long term
➡ A determination to overcome roadblocks
➡ A relentless focus on *making* their future
➡ An emphasis on implementation.

In essence, he suggests they understand competitive advantage and what it takes to win. It is this sort of issue that effective strategic marketing planning is designed to address.

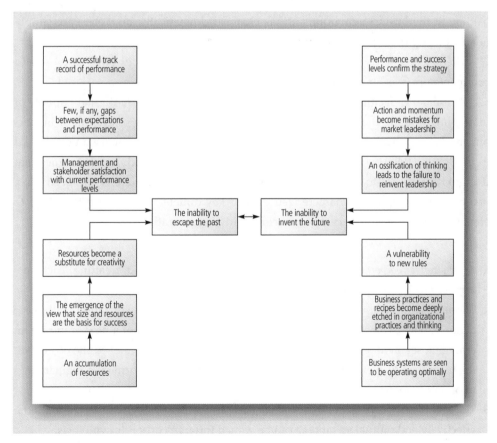

Figure 1.15 Escaping the past and inventing the future (adapted from Hamel and Prahalad, 1994)

The four horsemen of the corporate apocalypse and the emergence of the neo-marketing organization

Given what has been discussed so far within this chapter, it can be argued that there are two types of organization: those with a marketing department and those with a marketing soul. Those with a marketing department tend to believe still that the business models and formulae that have worked well in the past will continue to work well in the future, despite the sorts of often radical changes that have affected and still are affecting the vast majority of markets. Those with a marketing soul can be seen to be those organizations in which the senior management team has recognized that the way in which marketing had, for a long time, been interpreted was far too functional and far too limited. It is this that has led to the rise of what might be termed the neo-marketing organization.

One of the first highly credible criticisms of marketing came from Brady and Davies (1993), two consultants working for the management consultancy, McKinsey & Co. They argued that 'doubts are surfacing about the very basis of contemporary marketing'. They went on to say that 'costly brand advertising often dwells on seemingly irrelevant points of difference' and that 'marketing departments are often a millstone around an organization's neck' (p. 7). As evidence of this, they suggested that there were far too few examples of new marketing frameworks or fresh approaches: 'Although the business environment has changed dramatically, marketers are simply not picking up the right signals any more.'

These views have subsequently been echoed by a number of other authors and commentators (see, for example, Brannan, 1993; Thomas, 1994).

A number of factors appear to have conspired to invalidate traditional patterns of marketing thought, the four most significant of which were the saturation of numerous markets, globalization, market fragmentation and corporate downsizing. Referred to by Brown (1995) as the four horsemen of the corporate apocalypse, he argues that if organizations are to cope effectively with these pressures, there is the need for a neo-marketing approach, characterized by four key dimensions that, together, help to create a far more customer-centric and competitive organization:

1 *A far stronger corporate philosophy* in which emphasis is given to 'treat(ing) each customer as if they are the only one'.
2 *The much greater and more effective use of teams* from across the organization, with these teams having to meet specific targets such as the development of a new brand for an emerging segment or the re-launch of a product line. Having achieved the objectives, the team then disbands. Clusters therefore form, break and reform on a regular basis in order to move in time with the rhythm of the market.
3 *The better use of alliances* in areas such as R&D so that knowledge can be shared more effectively and mutual advantage can be gained through corporate symbiosis.
4 *IT-driven thinking* that provides a far greater insight to customers' patterns of thinking and behaviour, and helps to overcome the confusion caused by market fragmentation

and saturation. By using information technology *strategically*, the marketing planner gains a far greater understanding of buying habits, cross-brand elasticities, marketing sensitivities and market structures, and, in this way, can raise barriers to entry and move further towards 'owning the customer'.

1.6 Summary

This chapter seeks to offer some ideas constituting a framework for the rest of the book. It begins by considering the nature of management and of the management process. The process is often characterized in the following stages:

➡ Planning
➡ Decision-making
➡ Control.

These are related to a series of questions, around which the book is structured:

1 Where are we now?
2 Where do we want to be?
3 How might we get there?
4 Which way is best?
5 How can we ensure arrival?

Strategy can be seen as a normative matter concerning what an organization would like to achieve. As such it:

➡ Guides the organization in its relationship with its environment
➡ Affects the internal structure and processes of the organization
➡ Centrally affects the organization's performance.

Marketing, via its policies and programmes relating to the seven elements of the marketing mix, can provide the means to facilitate the attainment of a strategy.

The extent to which the strategy is achieved provides a measure of the organization's effectiveness. Any organization's effectiveness depends upon the balance between what is desired and what is achieved on the one hand, and by paying due regard to the requirements of all stakeholders, whether internal or external, on the other. It is through the process of organizational control that managers seek to achieve organizational effectiveness, and this gives a reference point for all that follows.

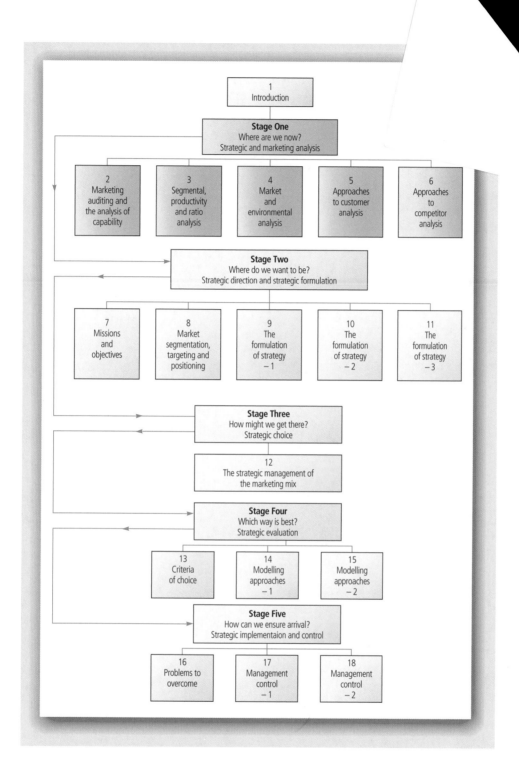

1
Introduction

Stage One
Where are we now?
Strategic and marketing analysis

2
Marketing auditing and the analysis of capability

3
Segmental, productivity and ratio analysis

4
Market and environmental analysis

5
Approaches to customer analysis

6
Approaches to competitor analysis

Stage Two
Where do we want to be?
Strategic direction and strategic formulation

7
Missions and objectives

8
Market segmentation, targeting and positioning

9
The formulation of strategy – 1

10
The formulation of strategy – 2

11
The formulation of strategy – 3

Stage Three
How might we get there?
Strategic choice

12
The strategic management of the marketing mix

Stage Four
Which way is best?
Strategic evaluation

13
Criteria of choice

14
Modelling approaches – 1

15
Modelling approaches – 2

Stage Five
How can we ensure arrival?
Strategic implementaion and control

16
Problems to overcome

17
Management control – 1

18
Management control – 2

Stage One: Where are we now? Strategic and marketing analysis

Our primary concern within this stage is with the ways in which organizations can most clearly identify their current position and the nature of their marketing capability. It is against the background of the picture that emerges from this analysis that the marketing planner should then be in a far better position to begin the process of deciding upon the detail of the organization's future direction and the ways in which strategy is to be formulated.

The starting point in this process of strategic and marketing analysis involves a detailed marketing audit and review of marketing effectiveness. Together, the two techniques are designed to provide the strategist with a clear understanding of:

➡ The organization's current market position
➡ The nature of environmental opportunities and threats
➡ The organization's ability to cope with the demands of this environment.

The results of this analysis are then incorporated in a statement of Strengths, Weaknesses, Opportunities and Threats (SWOT), and subsequently a measure of capability.

Although the marketing auditing process is, as we discuss in Chapter 2, a relatively under-utilized activity, a growing number of planners, strategists and writers have over the past few years highlighted the nature of its potential contribution to effective strategy formulation.

Although there is no single format for the audit, it is generally acknowledged that, if the process is to be worthwhile, account needs to be taken of six dimensions:

1 The marketing environment
2 The current marketing strategy
3 Organizational issues
4 The marketing systems in use
5 Levels of marketing productivity
6 Marketing functions.

Used properly, marketing auditing and a review of marketing effectiveness are recognized as potentially powerful analytical tools that are capable of providing the planner with a detailed understanding of the organization's marketing capability and the nature of the environment that it is likely to face.

This process of analysis is taken a step further in Chapter 3, in which we discuss the ways in which the planner can establish patterns of resource allocation and its productivity by relating inputs (resources or costs) to outputs (revenues and profits). By doing this, the process of cost-effective planning is capable of being improved significantly.

Against this background, we turn in Chapters 4–6 to the various ways in which external environment in general and then customers and competitors, in particular, can be analysed.

It has long been recognized that marketing strategy is, to a very large extent, driven by the strategist's perception of the environment as a whole and competitors and customers specifically. Because of this, the failure to analyse and understand the environment *in detail* will almost inevitably be reflected in strategies which lack an adequate underpinning.

In the case of competitors, our understanding of how competitive relationships develop and operate has increased greatly over the past few years, largely as the result of the work of Michael Porter. Porter's work is based on the idea that the nature and intensity of competition within an industry is determined by the interaction of five key forces:

1 The threat of new entrants
2 The power of buyers
3 The threat of substitutes
4 The extent of competitive rivalry
5 The power of suppliers.

Analysis of these allows, in turn, for the identification of strategic groups, and for a far clearer identification of the relative position, strengths and objectives of each competitor. In the light of this, the arguments in favour of a competitive intelligence system are compelling. However, as we point out in Chapter 6, the value (and indeed the existence) of such a system is determined to a very large extent by the belief in competitive monitoring on the part of top management. Without this, the evidence that emerges from the work of numerous writers suggests that the organization will be largely introspective, with competitive analysis playing only a minor role in the planning process.

Broadly similar comments can be made about the role and value of customer analysis. As with competitive behaviour, our understanding of how buyers behave has advanced significantly in recent years, largely as the result of the work of researchers such as: Foxall; Turnbull and Cunningham; Webster; Robinson, Faris and Wind; and Hakansson. All too often, however, evidence suggests that firms devote relatively little attention to detailed customer analysis, assuming instead that because they interact with customers on a day-to-day basis they have a sufficient understanding of how and why markets behave as they do. Only rarely is this likely to be the case and, recognizing that customer knowledge is a potentially powerful source of competitive advantage, the rationale for regular and detailed analyses of customers is therefore strong.

Chapter 2

Marketing auditing and the analysis of capability

2.1 Learning objectives

When you have read this chapter you should understand:

(a) the nature, structure and purpose of the marketing audit;

(b) the nature of the contribution made by the marketing audit to the overall management audit;

(c) the need for a regular review of marketing effectiveness and how such a review might be conducted;

(d) why a regular review of strengths, weaknesses, opportunities and threats is necessary;

(e) how the marketing effectiveness review, SWOT and TOWS analysis, and the marketing audit contribute to the marketing planning process.

2.2 Introduction

Although the process of marketing auditing is a fundamental underpinning for the marketing planning process, it is for many organizations still a relatively new and under-utilized activity. This is despite a substantial body of evidence which suggests that an organization's performance in the marketplace is directly influenced by the marketing planner's perception of three factors:

1 The organization's current market position

2 The nature of environmental opportunities and threats

3 The organization's ability to cope with environmental demands.

Given this, the marketing audit is designed to provide the strategist with a clear understanding of these three dimensions and in this way provide a firm foundation for the development of strategy, something that is reflected in a comment by McDonald (1995, p. 28):

*"*Expressed in its simplest form, if the purpose of a corporate plan is to answer three central questions:

Where is the company now?

Where does the company want to go?

How should the company organize its resources to get there?

then the audit is the means by which the first of these questions is answered. An audit is a systematic, critical and unbiased review and appraisal of the environment and of the company's operations. A marketing audit is part of the larger management audit and is concerned (specifically) with the *marketing environment and marketing operations.*"

[authors' emphasis]

What is a marketing audit?

The marketing audit is in a number of ways the true starting point for the strategic marketing planning process, since it is through the audit that the strategist arrives at a measure both of environmental opportunities and threats and of the organization's marketing capability. The thinking that underpins the concept of the audit is therefore straightforward: it is that corporate objectives and strategy can only be developed effectively against the background of a detailed and objective understanding both of corporate capability and environmental opportunity. The audit is, therefore, as McDonald (1995, p. 28) has suggested:

"The means by which a company can identify its own strengths and weaknesses as they relate to external opportunities and threats. It is thus a way of helping management to select a position in that environment based on known factors."

Definitions of the audit have also been proposed by a variety of authors, all of whom highlight the need for the audit to be a systematic, critical and impartial review of the total marketing operation. In essence, therefore, the audit *must* embrace the marketing environment in which the organization – or the business unit – is operating in, together with the objectives, strategies and activities being pursued. In doing this, the planner needs to take an objective view of the organization and its market and not be affected by preconceived beliefs. It follows from this that the audit must be *comprehensive, systematic, independent* and conducted on a *regular basis*.

Given this, the three major elements and potential benefits of the marketing audit can be seen to be:

1 The detailed analysis of the external environment and internal situation
2 The objective evaluation of past performance and present activities
3 The clearer identification of future opportunities and threats.

These three elements can then usefully be viewed against the background of comments made by Ansoff (1968), who has suggested that 'irrespective of the size of the organization, corporate decisions have to be made within the constraint of a limited total resource'. Recognizing this, the strategist is then faced with the task of producing 'a resource allocation pattern which will offer the best potential for meeting the firm's objectives'. The marketing audit can therefore be seen in terms of providing a sound basis for this process of resource allocation. In this way, any strategy that is then developed should be far more consistent both with the demands of the environment and the organization's true capabilities and strengths.

The rationale for the audit is therefore straightforward and in a number of ways can be seen to derive from the more commonly known and widely-accepted idea of the financial audit which, together with audits of other functional areas, is part of the overall management audit. The nature of this relationship is illustrated in Figure 2.1.

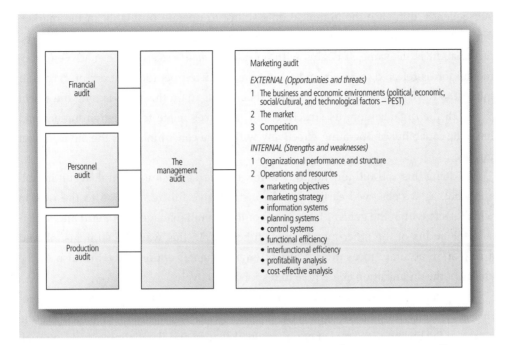

Figure 2.1 The place of the marketing audit in the overall management audit

The structure and focus of the audit

In terms of its structure, the marketing audit consists of three major and detailed diagnostic steps. These involve a review of:

1 The organization's environment (opportunities and threats)
2 Its marketing systems (strengths and weaknesses)
3 Its marketing activities.

The first of these is designed to establish the various dimensions of the marketing environment, the ways in which it is likely to change and the probable impact of these changes upon the organization. The second stage is concerned with an assessment of the extent to which the organization's marketing systems are capable of dealing with the demands of the environment. The final stage involves a review of the individual components of the marketing mix.

It should be apparent from this that, in conducting an audit, the strategist is concerned with two types of variable. First, there are the *environmental* or *market variables*, over which the strategist has little or no direct control. Second, there are the *operational variables*, which can be controlled to a greater or lesser extent. This distinction can also be expressed in terms of the *macro-environmental forces* (political/legal, economic/demographic, social/cultural, and technological) that affect the business, and *micro-environmental actors* (customers, competitors, distributors and suppliers) who subsequently influence the organization's ability to operate profitably in the market-place. Regardless of which approach to categorization is used, the process and purpose of the audit is the same. It begins with an *external audit* covering the macro-environmental forces referred to above and the markets and competitors that are of particular interest to the company. The *internal audit* then builds upon this by assessing the extent to which the organization, its structure and resources relate to the environment and have the capability of operating effectively within the constraints that the environment imposes.

In doing this, the auditor should not view the marketing audit and its result in isolation but, as we observed earlier, should instead give full recognition to the way in which it sits within the general framework of the overall management audit and alongside the audits of the other management functions. In this way, the strategist should arrive at an accurate measure not just of environmental opportunity, but also of the ability of the organization as a whole to respond effectively.

With regard to the question of how frequently the audit should be conducted, this is typically influenced by several factors, the most important of which are the nature of the business, the rate of environmental change and the planning cycle (annual, bi-annual). In so far as it is possible to provide a reasonably definitive guideline, it is that the organization should undertake a full audit at the beginning of each major planning cycle, supplemented by less intensive but more frequent reviews of specific or key areas as conditions change.

The stages of the audit

In conducting a marketing audit, the majority of planners adopt a stepwise procedure. In this way, it is argued, the approach ensures a degree of consistency that allows for a comparison from one period to another. In discussing this, Grashof (1975) advocated the following steps:

1 *Pre-audit activities* in which the auditor decides upon the precise breadth and focus of the audit
2 *The assembly of information* on the areas which affect the organization's marketing performance – these would typically include the industry, the market, the firm and each of the elements of the marketing mix
3 *Information analysis*
4 The formulation of *recommendations*
5 The development of *an implementation programme.*

A broadly similar approach has been outlined by Cannon (1968, p. 102); this is illustrated in Table 2.1.

Although for many organizations it is the assembly of information that proves to be the most time-consuming, it is (in terms of Grashof's suggested framework) steps 3 and 5

Table 2.1   Cannon's five stages of audit (Cannon, 1968)

Stage	Key elements
Step 1 Define the market	*Develop:* ➡ Statement of purpose in terms of benefits ➡ Product scope ➡ Size, growth rate, maturity state, need for primary versus selective strategies ➡ Requirements of success ➡ Divergent definitions of the above by competitors ➡ Definition to be used by the company
Step 2 Determine performance differentials	➡ Evaluate industry performance and company differences ➡ Determine differences in products, applications, geography and distribution channels ➡ Determine differences by customer set
Step 3 Determine differences in competitive programmes	*Identify and evaluate individual companies for their:* ➡ Market development strategies ➡ Product development strategies ➡ Financing and administrative strategies and support
Step 4 Profile the strategies of competitors	➡ Profile each significant competitor and/or distinct type of competitive strategy ➡ Compare own and competitive strategies
Step 5 Determine the strategic planning structure	*When size and complexity are adequate:* ➡ Establish planning units or cells and designate prime and subordinate dimensions ➡ Make organizational assignments to product managers, industry managers and others

that often prove to be the most problematic. In analysing information the auditor therefore needs to consider three questions:

1 What is the *absolute* value of the information?
2 What is its *comparative* value?
3 What *interpretation* is to be placed upon it?

It is generally acknowledged that, if these questions are answered satisfactorily, the recommendations will follow reasonably easily and logically. The only remaining problem is then the development of an effective implementation programme.

It should be apparent from the discussion so far that a marketing audit, if carried out properly, is a highly specific, detailed and potentially time-consuming activity. Because of this, many organizations often do not bother with a full audit, and opt instead for a less detailed, more general and more frequent *review of marketing effectiveness*, coupled with an analysis of strengths, weaknesses, opportunities and threats. Recognizing this, we focus initially upon one of the most typical ways of reviewing effectiveness as a prelude in the final part of the chapter to an examination of the more detailed marketing auditing processes.

2.3 Reviewing marketing effectiveness

Marketing effectiveness is, to a very large extent, determined by the extent to which the organization reflects the five major attributes of a marketing orientation, namely:

1 A customer-oriented philosophy
2 An integrated marketing organization
3 Adequate marketing information
4 A strategic orientation
5 Operational efficiency.

Each of these dimensions can be measured relatively easily by means of a checklist and an overall rating then arrived at for the organization: an example of this appears in Figure 2.2. It needs to be recognized, however, that an organization's marketing effectiveness is not always reflected in current levels of performance. It is quite possible, for example, for an organization to be performing well simply by force of circumstance rather than because of good management. In other words, good performance may be due to being in the right place at the right time as opposed to anything more fundamental. A change in strategy as the result of an effectiveness review might well then have the result of improving performance from good to excellent. Equally, an organization may be performing badly despite seemingly excellent marketing planning. Again, the explanation may well be environmental rather than poor management. Recognizing this, the purpose of going through the process of a marketing effectiveness rating review is to identify those areas in which scope exists for marketing improvement. Action, in the form of revised plans, can then be taken to achieve this.

With regard to the process of arriving at a measure of marketing effectiveness, the procedure is straightforward and involves managers from a number of departments – not just marketing – completing the checklists of Figure 2.2. Scores are then summarized in order to arrive at an overall perception of marketing effectiveness. In practice, and as might be expected, few companies achieve a score in the highest range; among the few to have done this are organizations such as Wal-Mart, Ikea, Starbucks, Amazon.com and a small number of airlines, such as Emirates, Cathay Pacific and Singapore Airlines. The majority of companies, however, cluster around the fair-to-good range, suggesting that scope exists for improvements in one or more of the five areas.

Customer philosophy   Score
1 *To what extent does management recognize the need to organize the company to satisfy specific market demands?*

The managerial philosophy is to sell existing and new products to whoever will buy them.   ☐ 0
Management attempts to serve a wide range of markets and needs with equal effectiveness.   ☐ 1

Having identified market needs, management focuses upon specific target markets in order to maximize company growth and potential.   ☐ 2

2 *To what extent is the marketing programme tailored to the needs of different market segments?*
Not at all.   ☐ 0
To some extent.   ☐ 1
To a very high degree.   ☐ 2

3 *Does management adopt a systems approach to planning, with recognition being given to the interrelationships between the environment, suppliers, channels, customers and competitors?*
Not at all; the company focuses solely upon its existing customer base.   ☐ 0
To some extent, in that the majority of its effort goes into serving its immediate and existing customer base.   ☐ 1

Yes. Management recognizes the various dimensions of the marketing environment and attempts to reflect this in its marketing programmes by taking account of the threats and opportunities created by change within the system.   ☐ 2

Marketing organization
4 *To what extent does senior management attempt to control and integrate the major marketing functions?*
Not at all. No real attempt is made to integrate or control activities, and conflict between areas of marketing exists.   ☐ 0
To a limited degree, although the levels of control and coordination are generally unsatisfactory.   ☐ 1
To a very high degree with the result that functional areas work together well.   ☐ 2

5 *What sort of relationship exists between marketing management and the management of the R&D, finance, production and manufacturing functions?*
Generally poor, with frequent complaints being made that marketing is unrealistic in its demands.   ☐ 0
Generally satisfactory, although the feeling exists that each department is intent on serving its own needs.   ☐ 1
Overall very good, with departments working together well in the interests of the company as a whole.   ☐ 2

6 *How well organized is the new product development process?*
Not very well at all.   ☐ 0
A formal new product process exists but does not work very well.   ☐ 1
It is well structured, professionally managed and achieves good results.   ☐ 2

Marketing information
7 *How frequently does the company conduct market research studies of customers, channels and competitors?*
Seldom, if ever.   ☐ 0
Occasionally.   ☐ 1
Regularly and in a highly structured way.   ☐ 2

8 *To what extent is management aware of the sales potential and profitability of different market segments, customers, territories, products and order sizes?*
Not at all.   ☐ 0
To some degree.   ☐ 1
Very well.   ☐ 2

9 *What effort is made to measure the cost effectiveness of different levels and types of marketing expenditure?*
None at all.   ☐ 0
Some, but not in a regular or structured way.   ☐ 1
A great deal.   ☐ 2

Figure 2.2 A marketing effectiveness rating instrument (adapted from Kotler, 1977)

The strategic perspective   **Score**

10 *How formalized is the marketing planning process?*
    The company does virtually no formal marketing planning.   ☐ 0
    An annual marketing plan is developed.   ☐ 1
    The company develops a detailed annual marketing plan and a long-range plan that is   ☐ 2
    updated annually.

11 *What is the quality of the thinking that underlies the current marketing strategy?*
    The current strategy is unclear.   ☐ 0
    The current strategy is clear and is largely a continuation of earlier strategies.   ☐ 1
    The current strategy is clear, well argued and well developed.   ☐ 2

12 *To what extent does management engage in contingency thinking and planning?*
    Not at all.   ☐ 0
    There is some contingency thinking, but this is not incorporated into a formal planning   ☐ 1
    process.
    A serious attempt is made to identify the most important contingencies, and contingency   ☐ 2
    plans are then developed.

Operational efficiency

13 *How well is senior management thinking on marketing communicated and implemented down the line?*
    Very badly.   ☐ 0
    Reasonably well.   ☐ 1
    Extremely successfully.   ☐ 2

14 *Does marketing management do an effective job with the resources available?*
    No. The resource base is inadequate for the objectives that have been set.   ☐ 0
    To a limited extent. The resources available are adequate but are only rarely applied in an   ☐ 1
    optimal manner.
    Yes. The resources available are adequate and managed efficiently.   ☐ 2

15 *Does management respond quickly and effectively to unexpected developments in the marketplace?*
    No. Market information is typically out of date and management responses are slow.   ☐ 0
    To a limited extent. Market information is reasonably up to date, although management   ☐ 1
    response times vary.
    Yes. Highly efficient information systems exist and management responds quickly and   ☐ 2
    effectively.

The scoring process

Each manager works their way through the 15 questions in order to arrive at a score. The scores are then aggregated and averaged. The overall measure of marketing effectiveness can then be assessed against the following scale:

  0–5   = None
  6–10 = Poor
 11–15 = Fair
 16–20 = Good
 21–25 = Very good
 26–30 = Superior

With a score of *10 or less* major questions can be asked about the organization's ability to survive in anything more than the short term, and any serious competitive challenge is likely to create significant problems. Fundamental changes are needed, both in the management philosophy and the organizational structure. For many organizations in this position, however, these changes are unlikely to be brought about by the existing management, since it is this group which has led to the current situation. The solution may therefore lie in major changes to the senior management.

    With a score of *between 11 and 15* there is again a major opportunity to improve the management philosophy and organizational structure.

    With a score of *between 16 and 25* scope for improvement exists, although this is likely to be in terms of a series of small changes and modifications rather than anything more fundamental. With a score of *between 26 and 30* care needs to be taken to ensure that the proactive stance is maintained and that complacency does not begin to emerge.

Figure 2.2 Continued

Having conducted a review of marketing effectiveness, the marketing planner may decide that the results provide sufficient insight into the organization's strengths and weaknesses. There is, however, a strong argument for viewing the marketing effectiveness rating review as the jumping-off point for a more detailed analysis of strengths, weaknesses, opportunities and threats.

2.4 The role of SWOT analysis

Although SWOT analysis is one of the best-known and most frequently used tools within the marketing planning process, the quality of the outputs often suffer because of the relatively superficial manner in which it is conducted. There are several ways in which SWOT analyses can be made more rigorous, and therefore more strategically useful, and this is something to which we will return at a later stage in this chapter. However, before we turn to the detail of the SWOT, it is perhaps worth summarizing the key elements of the four dimensions; these are illustrated in Figure 2.3.

Identifying opportunities and threats

Faced with a constantly changing environment, each business unit needs to develop a marketing information system (MkIS) that is capable of tracking trends and developments within the marketplace. Each trend or development can then be categorized as an *opportunity* or a *threat*, and an assessment made of the feasibility and action needed if the organization is either to capitalize upon the opportunity or minimize the impact of the threat.

STRENGTHS : Areas of (distinctive) competence that:
➡ Must always be looked at relative to the competition
➡ If managed properly, are the basis for competitive advantage
➡ Derive from the marketing asset base

WEAKNESSES : Areas of relative disadvantage that:
➡ Indicate priorities for marketing improvement
➡ Highlight the areas and strategies that the planner should avoid

THREATS : Trends within the environment with potentially negative impacts that:
➡ Increase the risks of a strategy
➡ Hinder the implementation of strategy
➡ Increase the resources required
➡ Reduce performance expectations

OPPORTUNITIES : Environmental trends with positive outcomes that offer scope for higher levels of performance if pursued effectively:
➡ Highlight new areas for competitive advantage

Figure 2.3   SWOT: a summary

SWOT analysis is therefore designed to achieve two principal objectives:

1 To separate meaningful data from that which is merely interesting
2 To discover what management must do to exploit its distinctive competencies within each of the market segments both now and in the longer term.

However, in examining opportunities and threats, the reader needs to recognize that they can never be viewed as 'absolutes'. What might appear at first sight to be an opportunity may not be so when examined against the organization's resources, its culture, the expectations of its stakeholders, the strategies available, or the feasibility of implementing the strategy. At the risk of oversimplification, however, the purpose of strategy formulation is to develop a strategy which will take advantage of the opportunities and overcome or circumvent the threats.

For our purposes, an opportunity can be seen as any sector of the market in which the company would enjoy a competitive advantage. These opportunities can then be assessed according to their *attractiveness* and the organization's *probability of success* in this area; this is illustrated in Figure 2.4.

The probability of success is influenced by several factors, but most obviously by the extent to which the organization's strengths, and in particular its distinctive competences, match the key success requirements for operating effectively in the target market *and* exceed those of its competitors. Competence by itself is rarely sufficient in anything more than the short term since, given time, competitive forces will erode this competence. Because of this the strategist needs to concentrate upon developing

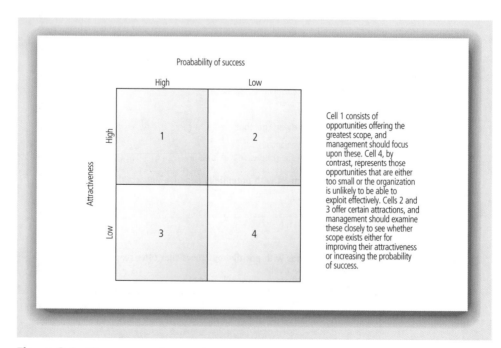

Figure 2.4 The opportunity matrix

competitive advantages which are sustainable over time; the bases of a sustainable competitive advantage are illustrated in Figures 2.5 and 2.6, and then discussed in greater detail in Chapter 10.

However, at the same time as generating opportunities, the external environment also presents a series of *threats* (a threat being a challenge posed by an unfavourable trend

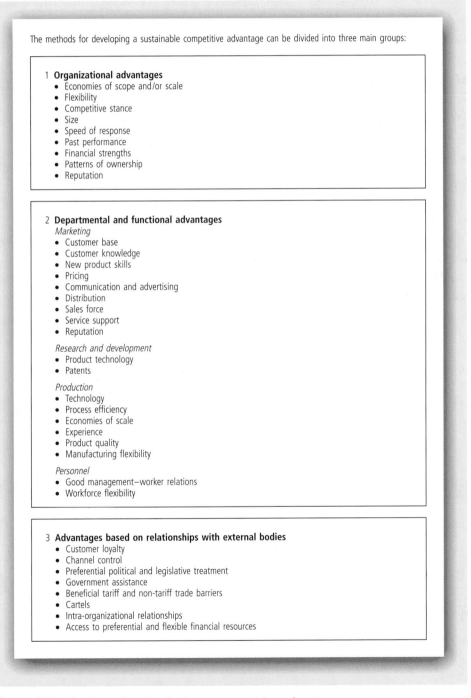

The methods for developing a sustainable competitive advantage can be divided into three main groups:

1 **Organizational advantages**
- Economies of scope and/or scale
- Flexibility
- Competitive stance
- Size
- Speed of response
- Past performance
- Financial strengths
- Patterns of ownership
- Reputation

2 **Departmental and functional advantages**
Marketing
- Customer base
- Customer knowledge
- New product skills
- Pricing
- Communication and advertising
- Distribution
- Sales force
- Service support
- Reputation

Research and development
- Product technology
- Patents

Production
- Technology
- Process efficiency
- Economies of scale
- Experience
- Product quality
- Manufacturing flexibility

Personnel
- Good management–worker relations
- Workforce flexibility

3 **Advantages based on relationships with external bodies**
- Customer loyalty
- Channel control
- Preferential political and legislative treatment
- Government assistance
- Beneficial tariff and non-tariff trade barriers
- Cartels
- Intra-organizational relationships
- Access to preferential and flexible financial resources

Figure 2.5 The bases for developing a competitive advantage

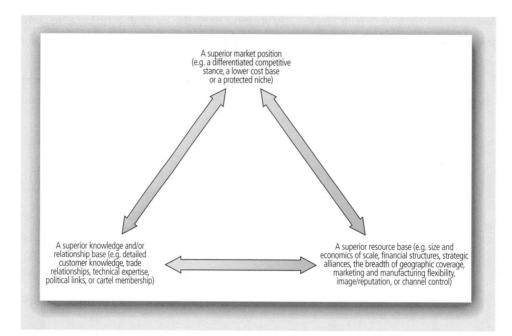

Figure 2.6 Sources of competitive advantage (adapted from McDonald, 1990)

or development in the environment, which, in the absence of a distinct organizational response, will lead to the erosion of the company's market position).

Threats can be classified on the basis of their *seriousness* and the *probability of their occurrence*; an example of how this can be done is illustrated in Figure 2.7.

Given the nature of these comments, it can be seen that by putting together a picture of the major opportunities and threats facing the business the marketing planner is

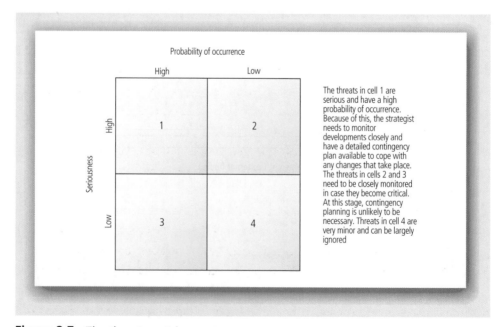

Figure 2.7 The threats matrix

attempting to arrive at a measure of *the market's overall attractiveness*. In essence, four possibilities exist:

1 An *ideal* business that is characterized by numerous opportunities but few, if any, threats

2 A *speculative* business that is high both in opportunities and threats

3 A *mature* business that is low both in opportunities and threats

4 A *troubled* business that is low in opportunities but high in threats.

Identifying strengths and weaknesses

Although in many markets it is often a relatively simple process to identify a whole series of environmental opportunities, few organizations have the ability or the competences needed to capitalize upon more than a small number of these. Each business needs therefore to evaluate on a regular basis its *strengths* and *weaknesses*. This can be done by means of the sort of checklist illustrated in Figure 2.8.

Each factor is rated by management or an outside consultant according to whether it is a fundamental strength, a marginal strength, a neutral factor, a marginal weakness, or a fundamental weakness. By linking these ratings, a general picture of the organization's principal strengths and weaknesses emerges. Of course, not all of these factors are of equal importance either in an absolute sense or when it comes to succeeding with a specific business opportunity. Because of this, each factor should also be given a rating (high, medium or low) either for the business as a whole or for a particular marketing opportunity. Combining performance and importance levels in this way injects a greater sense of perspective to the analysis and leads to four possibilities emerging; these are illustrated in Figure 2.9 in the form of a performance–importance matrix.

In Figure 2.9, cell 1 consists of those factors which are important but in which the organization is currently performing badly. Because of this the organization needs to concentrate on strengthening these factors. Cell 2 consists of unimportant factors. Cell 3 is made up of factors in which the business is already strong but in which it needs to maintain its strengths. Improvements here, while often desirable, have low priority. Cell 4 is made up of unimportant factors in which (possibly as the result of over-investment in the past) the business is unnecessarily strong.

Another way of looking at issues of performance and importance involves focusing specifically upon the organization's performance relative to the competition; the framework for this is illustrated in Figure 2.10.

On the basis of this sort of analysis it should be apparent that, even when a business has a major strength in a particular area, this strength does not invariably translate into a competitive advantage. There are several possible explanations for this, the two most prominent of which are that it may not be a competence that is of any real importance to customers, or that it is an area in which competitors are at least equally strong. It follows from this that, in order to benefit from the strength, it *must* be relatively greater than that of the competitor.

Strengths	Performance					Importance		
	Fundamental strength	Marginal strength	Neutral	Marginal weakness	Fundamental weakness	High	Medium	Low
Marketing factors								
1 Relative market share	——	——	——	——	——	——	——	——
2 Reputation	——	——	——	——	——	——	——	——
3 Previous performance	——	——	——	——	——	——	——	——
4 Competitive stance	——	——	——	——	——	——	——	——
5 Customer base	——	——	——	——	——	——	——	——
6 Customer loyalty	——	——	——	——	——	——	——	——
7 Breadth of product range	——	——	——	——	——	——	——	——
8 Depth of product range	——	——	——	——	——	——	——	——
9 Product quality	——	——	——	——	——	——	——	——
10 Programme of product modification	——	——	——	——	——	——	——	——
11 New product programme	——	——	——	——	——	——	——	——
12 Distribution costs	——	——	——	——	——	——	——	——
13 Dealer network	——	——	——	——	——	——	——	——
14 Dealer loyalty	——	——	——	——	——	——	——	——
15 Geographical coverage	——	——	——	——	——	——	——	——
16 Sales force	——	——	——	——	——	——	——	——
17 After sales service	——	——	——	——	——	——	——	——
18 Manufacturing costs	——	——	——	——	——	——	——	——
19 Manufacturing flexibility	——	——	——	——	——	——	——	——
20 Raw material advantage	——	——	——	——	——	——	——	——
21 Pricing	——	——	——	——	——	——	——	——
22 Advertising	——	——	——	——	——	——	——	——
23 Unique selling propositions	——	——	——	——	——	——	——	——
24 Structure of competition	——	——	——	——	——	——	——	——
Financial factors								
25 Cost of capital	——	——	——	——	——	——	——	——
26 Availability of capital	——	——	——	——	——	——	——	——
27 Profitability	——	——	——	——	——	——	——	——
28 Financial stability	——	——	——	——	——	——	——	——
29 Margins	——	——	——	——	——	——	——	——
Manufacturing factors								
30 Production facilities	——	——	——	——	——	——	——	——
31 Economies of scale	——	——	——	——	——	——	——	——
32 Flexibility	——	——	——	——	——	——	——	——
33 Workforce	——	——	——	——	——	——	——	——
34 Technical skill	——	——	——	——	——	——	——	——
35 Delivery capabilities	——	——	——	——	——	——	——	——
36 Supplier sourcing flexibility	——	——	——	——	——	——	——	——
Organizational factors								
37 Culture	——	——	——	——	——	——	——	——
38 Leadership	——	——	——	——	——	——	——	——
39 Managerial capabilities	——	——	——	——	——	——	——	——
40 Workforce	——	——	——	——	——	——	——	——
41 Flexibility	——	——	——	——	——	——	——	——
42 Adaptability	——	——	——	——	——	——	——	——

Figure 2.8 Strengths and weaknesses analysis (adapted from Kotler, 1988)

Having identified the organization's weaknesses, the strategist needs to return to Figure 2.8 and consider again the relative importance of these weaknesses. There is often little to be gained from overcoming all of the organization's weaknesses, since some are unimportant and the amount of effort needed to convert them to a strength would quite simply not be repaid. Equally, some strengths are of little real strategic value and to use

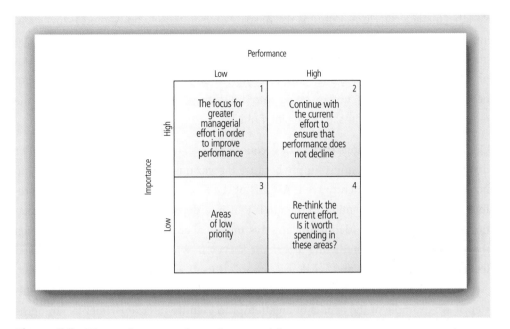

Figure 2.9   The performance–importance matrix

them in anything other than a peripheral way is likely to prove of little real value. Recognizing this, the marketing planner should focus upon those areas of opportunity in which the firm currently has major strengths or where, because of the size of the opportunity and the potential returns, it is likely to prove cost-effective in acquiring or developing new areas of strength. In commenting on this, Kotler (1987, p. 54) cites the example of Texas Instruments:

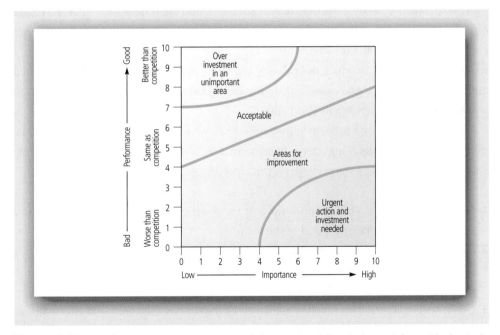

Figure 2.10   Performance–importance and the competition (adapted from Slack et al., 1998)

"[The] managers in Texas Instruments (TI) split between those who wanted TI to stick to industrial electronics where it had clear strength and those who urged the company to go into digital watches, personal computers, and other consumer products where it did not have the required marketing strengths. As it turned out, TI did poorly in these areas, but perhaps its mistake was not in going into these areas, but rather not acquiring the required marketing strengths to do the job right.**"**

On occasions, organizations suffer not because of a lack of individual, departmental or divisional strengths, but quite simply because the various departments or divisions do not work together sufficiently well. As part of the SWOT process, the strategist therefore should also pay attention to the quality of interdepartmental and divisional relationships with a view to identifying any dysfunctional areas. One of the ways in which this can be done is by conducting a periodic survey in which each department is asked to identify the strengths and weaknesses both of itself and of each other department. Action can then be taken to overcome areas of conflict, misunderstanding and inefficiency. An example of the results of an attempt to identify interdepartmental strengths and weaknesses appears in Figure 2.11. These are based on a consultancy project conducted by one of the authors several years ago. The client company operated in the engineering field and was a subsidiary of a far larger multinational organization. The company had a strong financial orientation and was rapidly being overtaken by its competitors: for obvious reasons, the client's name has been omitted.

Issues of capability

Although the analysis of strengths and weaknesses is a valuable step in the auditing process, the reader needs to recognize that strengths and weaknesses by themselves are of little real planning value. Instead, they should be seen as a step towards the planner coming to terms with the broader issue of capability. In doing this, the planner is giving recognition to the way in which the value of any strategy or plan is ultimately determined not by strengths and weaknesses, but by the organization's capability and the extent to which it is able to outperform its competitors.

Although capability has been defined in several ways it is, in essence, the ability of the management team to get things done. In arriving at a measure of capability, the marketing strategist needs to come to terms with six principal areas:

1 *Managerial capability.* This includes not just the abilities of individuals, but also – and perhaps more importantly – that of the team.
2 *Financial capability.* This is determined in part by the availability of money, but also the expectations of how it is used, the extent to which the management team is willing to take risks when investing, and the returns that are expected.
3 *Operational capability.* This involves the levels of day-to-day efficiency and effectiveness.
4 *Distribution capability.* This is determined by a combination of geographic reach or coverage, penetration (the proportion of possible outlets) and the quality of these distributors.

	Strengths	Weaknesses
Marketing	Market development Advertising Dealer development Competitor analysis	Long-term planning Liaising with sales Liaising with production Profitable new product development Identifying small but potentially profitable gaps in the market Expectations regarding quality and manufacturing capability Pricing Relations with corporate management
Sales	None identified	Expectations regarding delivery times Providing market feedback Often sell what can only be made with difficulty Little apparent awareness of costs Ignores small orders Patchy productivity Levels of training Sales staff turnover
Production	Quality	Slow to change Unwilling to cooperate with marketing and sales Often late in delivering Tend to want to make what they are good at A lack of flexibility caused by a strong trade-union presence Rising costs Lack of strong management Ageing plant Inadequate training in CAD/CAM
Personnel	Junior management and shop-floor training	Representation at board level Long-term senior management development Poor negotiating skills Willingness to give in to trade-union pressure Lack of real personnel management skills
Finance	Tight cost control Credit control Relationship with corporate management Access to significant financial resources	Over-emphasis on short-term returns Lack of vision Unwilling to cooperate with marketing and sales Unwilling to provide finance for major programmes of new product development Unrealistic reporting demands

Figure 2.11   Identifying interdepartmental strengths and weaknesses

5 *Human resource capability*. This is a reflection of the nature and experience of staff throughout the business.

6 *Intangible factors* (such as the brand). In the case of a powerful brand, capability is extended enormously, since it provides the opportunity not just for brand stretching, but also for pricing at a premium, gaining access to the strongest forms of distribution and increasing levels of customer loyalty.

At the same time, however, the planner also needs to understand these factors that inhibit capability. Typical examples of these include attitudes to risk and an adherence to a well-developed but increasingly tired business model.

Making SWOT analyses more effective

Although SWOT analysis is a potentially useful input to the strategic marketing planning process, in practice it often suffers from a number of weaknesses. Amongst the most common of these are that:

→ The planner fails to relate strengths and weaknesses to critical success factors
→ Strengths and weaknesses are seen in absolute terms rather than in relation to the competition
→ The elements of the analysis are insufficiently specific
→ Competitors' capabilities are underestimated and/or misunderstood
→ The focus is upon marketing-specific issues rather than reflecting a broader company perspective
→ Emphasis is placed largely upon the 'hard' or quantifiable elements and fails to take account of managerial attitudes, cultures, capabilities and competencies.

The implications of this have been highlighted by both Piercy (2002, pp. 539–46) and Weihrich (1982, pp. 54–66), who have argued that, as a result, its full potential is rarely realized.

In suggesting this, Piercy claims that 'the use of this tool has generally become sloppy and unfocused – a classic example perhaps of familiarity breeding contempt'. There are, he believes, several factors which have contributed to this, the most obvious of which are that:

"(a) because the technique is so simple it is readily accessible to all types of manager;

(b) the model can be used without a need for extensive information systems;

(c) it provides planners with a structure that allows for a mixture of the qualitative and quantitative information, of familiar and unfamiliar facts, of known and half-known understandings that characterize strategic marketing planning.*"*

In order to make better use of the SWOT framework, Piercy proposes five guidelines:

1 *Focus the SWOT* upon a particular issue or element, such as a specific product market, a customer segment, a competitor, or the individual elements of the marketing mix.

2 Use the SWOT analysis as a mechanism for developing a *shared vision* for planning. This can be done by pooling ideas from a number of sources and achieving a team consensus about the future and the important issues.

3 *Develop a customer orientation* by recognizing that strengths and weaknesses are largely irrelevant unless they are recognized and valued by the customer. One of the ways in which this can be done is by applying McDonald's 'so what?' test in which the planner looks at each of the claimed benefits from the viewpoint of the consumer and, by asking 'well, so what?', tries to assess its *true* significance (see pp. 405–6). By doing this, the

planner is also likely to move away from the trap of making a series of so-called *motherhood statements* (a motherhood statement is warm, reassuring and difficult to argue against). As an example of the most common of motherhood statements to emerge in analyses of strengths is the suggestion that 'we are committed to the customer'. The reality, Piercy argues, is often far removed from this.

4 In the same way that strengths and weaknesses must always be viewed from the viewpoint of the customer, so the analysis of opportunities and threats must relate to *the environment which is relevant to the organization's point of focus*. Anything else simply leads to a generalized – and largely pointless – set of comments.

5 The final guideline is concerned with what Piercy refers to as *structured strategy generation*. This involves:

- *Matching strategies*. Strengths *must* be matched to opportunities, since a strength without a corresponding opportunity is of little strategic value.
- *Conversion strategies*. While often difficult, these are designed to change weaknesses into strengths and threats into opportunities. As an example of this, competitors may well be growing and proving to be an increasing threat. However, by recognizing that a head-on battle is likely to prove expensive and counter-productive, the emphasis might shift to developing strategic alliances that then provide both organizations with a greater combined strength, which, in turn, allows them to capitalize upon growing opportunities.
- *Creative strategies*. These are necessary to develop the business and emerge as the result of a detailed analytical process rather than the vague and unfocused lines of thought to which we referred earlier.
- *Iteration*. As the planner goes through the process of identifying hidden strengths, matching strengths to opportunities, converting weaknesses to strengths, and so on, there is a periodic need to go back to the beginning of the process in order to identify how the situation that is emerging changes the SWOT model and any initial assumptions.

SWOT analysis can also be made more effective by thinking:

- To what extent has the relative importance of the various elements been identified?
- To what extent have the implications of each of the elements been examined?
- To what extent does the management team really recognize the significance of the elements?
- To what extent have attempts been made in the past to manage the SWOT analysis outcomes *proactively*?

SWOT to TOWS

The limitations that Piercy suggests typically characterize SWOT analyses have also been highlighted by Weihrich (1982). His principal criticism of SWOT is that, having conducted the analysis, managers frequently fail to come to terms with the strategic choices that the outcomes demand. In order to overcome this, he argues for the TOWS matrix, which, while making use of the same inputs (Threats, Opportunities, Weaknesses and Strengths), reorganizes them and integrates them more fully into the strategic planning process. To do this involves the seven steps that are illustrated in Figure 2.12. The TOWS matrix is then illustrated in Figure 2.13.

The matrix outlined in Figure 2.13 does, of course, relate to a particular point in time. There is therefore a need to review the various inputs on a regular or ongoing basis in order to identify how they are changing and the nature of the implications of these changes. It is also often useful if, when planning and having made particular assumptions, the planner then produces TOWS matrices for, say, three and five years ahead with a view to identifying how the strategic options and priorities may change.

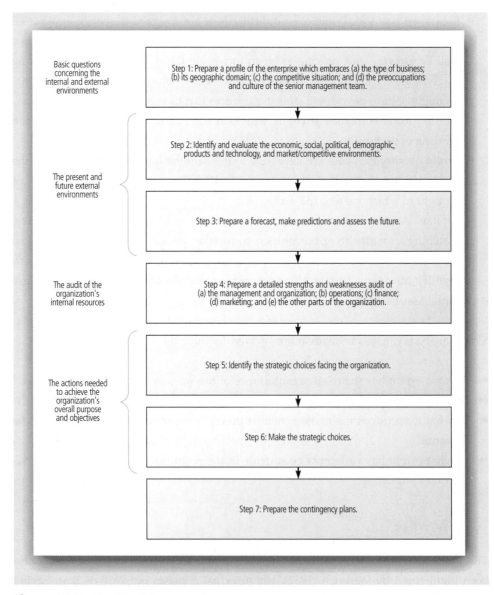

Figure 2.12 The TOWS framework

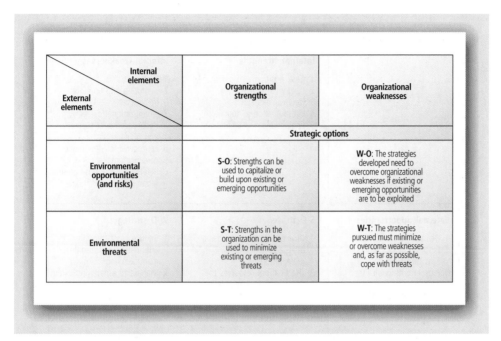

Figure 2.13 The TOWS matrix (adapted from Weihrich, 1982)

In this way there is a greater likelihood that the planning team will come to terms with what the future really demands.

An example of how Daimler-Benz used the TOWS matrix in its Mercedes cars division is illustrated in Figure 2.14.

But are SWOT and TOWS analyses of any real value?

Although TOWS analysis can be seen to add another dimension to the traditional thinking about strengths, weaknesses, opportunities and threats, a fundamental question can be raised about just how useful this sort of analysis is within today's markets. In commenting on this, Walton (1999, p. 33) argues that its value is limited, suggesting that '. . . compared with the steady state of the 1960s and 1970s, today's markets are characterized by an exponential increase in the rate of change, brought about by a combination of social, technological, legislative and other forces'. The implications of this are then reflected by the way in which 'as more organizations changed from portrait to landscape structures, the mayhem of the operational day-to-day often gets in the way – not only of a true understanding of the nature and pattern of competition, but also of the more added-value appreciation of the implications for business strategy'.

Amongst the sorts of factors that have contributed to this planning mayhem are mega-brands, mega-retailers (including category busters such as Toys 'R' Us and Wal-Mart) and convergence. For Walton (1999, p. 35), convergence has the effect of making competitive appraisal more difficult and can be the consequence of:

Strategies Tactics Actions	Internal strengths 1 Cash position 2 Luxury car image 3 New car models 4 Location dose to suppliers 5 Engineering and technology	Internal weaknesses 1 High costs 2 Venturing into unrelated businesses 3 Organizational diversity 4 Reliance on past successes and bureaucracy 5 Long cycle for new model development 6 Relatively weak position in Japan
External opportunities 1 Demand for luxury cars 2 Eastern Europe, especially East Germany 3 Prosperity through EC 1992 4 Electronics technology	S-O strategy 1 Develop new models (using high-tech) and charge premium prices 2 Use financial resources to acquire other companies or increased production capacity	W-O strategy 1 Reduce costs through automation and flexible manufacturing 2 Manufacture parts in Eastern Europe 3 Reorganizations 4 Daimler-Benz management holding companies
External threats 1 Decrease in defence needs because of easing of East–West tensions 2 BMW, Volvo, Jaguar, Lexus, Infinity in Europe 3 BMW in Japan 4 Diesel emissions 5 Renault/Volvo cooperation 6 Political instability in South Africa	S-T strategy 1 Transform defence sector to consumer sector 2 Develop new models to compete especially in Europe	W-T strategy 1 Retrench in South Africa 2 Form strategic alliance with Mitsubishi to penetrate the Japanese market

Figure 2.14 TOWS analysis for Daimler-Benz's Mercedes-Benz car division 1990 (source: Weihrich, 1993)

". . . industry boundaries blurring and turf disputes opening up between new competitors. Consider how the last decade has seen supermarkets move successfully into petrol, and petrol stations increasingly move into food. And how new markets attract players from all quarters. For example, the direct marketing industry has attracted creative agencies, computer software houses, fulfilment businesses and door-to-door distribution companies, each bringing different competencies and skill sets to the market opportunity.

Technological convergence can produce even more thrills and spills for marketers. The last two years have shown how digital technology has brought what we have traditionally known as the photographic, video and audio markets all closer together, with significant implications. For instance, for the consumer, who has the brand authority in digital cameras? A film brand like Kodak, a camera brand like Olympus, a video brand like JVC or an imaging brand like Canon?*"*

Given this and what might be seen to be the Pavlovian tendency in mature and highly competitive markets for firms to converge (this is discussed at a later stage of the book in terms of the phenomenon of strategic herding), the implications for competition – and therefore for market and competitive analysis – are significant. As organizations merge, the industry status quo changes dramatically and the idea of the traditional enemy being outside the gates begins to disappear and is replaced by higher levels of internal competition. This internal competition is often geographic in its nature and, for organizations operating across the EU, is typically made more difficult by the degree of cultural diversity that exists, something that Walton (1999, p. 36) suggests has 'created a kind of tragi-comic *Jeux Sans Frontières* assault course which can lead to "euromush" marketing resulting from conflicting harmonization demands'.

At the same time, with brand strategies now performing a far more pivotal role within marketing and as a greater number of management teams begin to copy what might loosely be termed the Virgin model of brand architecture that is characterized by a far greater degree of mobility across category boundaries, marketing planners need to adopt a far broader perspective of competition. The 'Maginot-line' approach to SWOT analysis that many planners have pursued in the past tends to be based on a functional rather than a brand view of competition and is likely to miss potential new market entrants. The likelihood of this has, in turn, been compounded by the way in which, because consumers today are far more familiar with brands and open to new patterns of brand thinking, the scope for moving into and out of markets has increased dramatically.

Given the nature of these changes, the implications for SWOT analysis are potentially significant and provide the basis for a number of modifications to the traditional approach; these are illustrated in Figure 2.15.

The rise of asset- and competency-based thinking

Although TOWS analysis undoubtedly represents an improvement upon the rather more mechanistic examination of strengths, weaknesses, opportunities and threats that underpins many marketing plans, Davidson (1998, pp. 17–21) has argued for an alternative way of diagnosing an organization's current position and way forward. His method of asset- and competency-based marketing (ACM) reflects the idea that any business consists only of *assets* (these are the 'things' that the organization owns, and typically include brands, property, databases, supply chains and cash) and *competencies* (these are the skills created by staff both individually and in groups, and might include brand development, database management, cost management or trade marketing). The challenge for the marketing planner is therefore one of how best to recognize the organization's *real* assets and then, through the competencies, how best to exploit them.

He argues that for each asset it is essential that there is a corresponding competency. Without this, it is unlikely that the asset will be exploited. For an asset such as a brand, the competency needed is brand management, while for databases it is database management and customer service. The issue for the planner is therefore initially that of the recognition

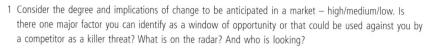

1 Consider the degree and implications of change to be anticipated in a market – high/medium/low. Is there one major factor you can identify as a window of opportunity or that could be used against you by a competitor as a killer threat? What is on the radar? And who is looking?

2 Within a market or category, what slots are already owned, being actively pursued and/or contested, and by whom?

3 What is the current phase of industry concentration? As we shift from 'middle game' to 'end game', what are the end game options? Does the industry leader have a future direction? What is our best long-term winning strategy or exit?

4 What industries and technologies are converging with our market? Can we zoom out and see proximate industries? For whom is our market an 'appetizing lunch'? Can the consumer value equation be met in a new and radical way?

5 What brand franchises are relevant to a category and can travel quickly and easily from, to and into it? What consumer-relevant brand properties are available to existing and potential market entrants? How robust is our brand architecture against the market and against the competition? Have we got some big guns?

6 How strong is the enemy within? What do we do about the 5th Column?

7 What is the 'diplomatic status' of the marketplace? What is the network of alliances? What extra problems and opportunities does this present? Who is tied up?

8 Who currently sets the industry agenda? How strongly is it controlled? How easy will it be to change the industry agenda?

9 Do the industry bandwagons have a role for us? Benchmark with caution!

10 Above all, can you identify a major disruption or a transformational initiative?

Figure 2.15 A checklist for the 'post-modern SWOT' (adapted from Walton, 1999, p. 37)

of the organization's asset and then, against the background of a detailed understanding of market needs and opportunities, how these can best be leveraged and exploited.

For Davidson, the advantage of ACM is that it 'divides the "strengths" into two key and separate elements – assets and competencies – and stresses the process of matching these both with each other, and with future opportunities'. He goes on to say that:

"Many successful marketers do this instinctively, but due to lack of systematic processes even they can miss big opportunities. Using ACM those opportunities which are best for a particular company can be revealed systematically. The company can exploit them better than others by capitalizing on its assets, and matching them to its distinctive competencies. The result is long-term competitive advantages that are exploitable and sustainable."

The application of ACM revolves around a six-step process that involves:

1 *Identifying the organization's exploitable assets and competencies.* To do this, the planner begins by listing all of the company's brand assets and competencies, and then focusing upon those that offer scope for competitive advantage and superior customer value.

2 *Reviewing the extent to which these assets and competencies are being exploited currently.* In doing this, Davidson highlights a series of action points that include:
   → Reprioritizing markets, channels, customers or brands, to generate the better utilization of assets

➡ Redeploying assets by buying, selling, developing and milking brands or physical assets

➡ Identifying the new competencies that are needed to exploit assets.

3 *Identifying the future shape of the industry and market.* By doing this, the planner can see more clearly how a market is likely to change and the sorts of assets and competencies that will be needed for the organization to compete effectively in the future.

4 *Deciding how the organization's assets need to change over the next five years.* As part of this, the planner needs to focus upon the prospects of current markets, brands and other assets with a view to identifying whether they will deliver the sorts of returns that the organization demands.

5 *Building and exploiting assets and competencies.*

6 *Matching assets and competencies with future opportunities.*

The outputs from ACM thinking should, Davidson argues, more easily enable the marketing planner to:

➡ Move assets into areas of higher return

➡ Fully exploit all assets and competencies

➡ Ensure they are well matched

➡ Identify new competencies which must be developed in the future

➡ Spread the marketing mindset by embracing efficient delivery of superior customer value throughout the company.

These ideas are summarized in Figure 2.16.

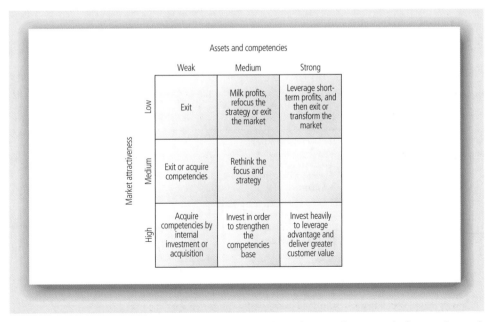

Figure 2.16 The asset- and competency-based marketing framework for market prioritization (adapted from Davidson, 1998, p. 21)

2.5 Competitive advantage and the value chain

Having analysed the strengths and resources of the organization, the marketing planner then needs to think about the ways in which these resources can best be used to contribute to the organization's performance. In other words, *how* might these resources best be used as a means of gaining and maintaining a competitive advantage? One of the ways in which this can be done is by means of the *value chain* and a detailed understanding of competitive advantage (in this chapter we highlight some of the issues associated with competitive advantage, but turn to a far fuller and more detailed analysis in Chapter 10).

Although value analysis has its origins in accounting and was designed to identify the profit of each stage in a manufacturing process, a considerable amount of work has been done in recent years in developing the concept and applying it to measures of competitive advantage. Much of this work has been conducted by Michael Porter, who suggests that an organization's activities can be categorized in terms of whether they are *primary activities* or *support activities*; this is illustrated in Figure 2.17.

The five primary activities identified by Porter (1985a) are:

1 *Inbound logistics*, which are the activities that are concerned with the reception, storing and internal distribution of the raw materials or components for assembly.
2 *Operations*, which turn these into the final product.
3 *Outbound logistics*, which distribute the product or service to customers. In the case of a manufacturing operation, this would include warehousing, materials handling and transportation. For a service, this would involve the way in which customers are brought to the location in which the service is to be delivered.
4 *Marketing and sales*, which make sure the customers are aware of the product or service and are able to buy it.
5 *Service activities*, which include installation, repair and training.

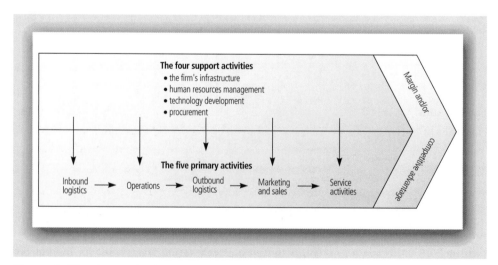

Figure 2.17 The value chain (adapted from Porter, 1985a)

Each of these primary activities is, in turn, linked to the support activities, which are grouped under four headings:

1 The *procurement* of the various inputs
2 *Technology development*, including research and development, process improvements and raw material improvements
3 *Human resource management*, including the recruitment, training, development and rewarding of staff
4 *The firm's infrastructure* and the approach to organization, including the systems, structures, managerial cultures and ways of doing business.

Porter suggests that competitive advantage is determined to a very large extent by how each of these elements is managed and the nature of the interactions between them. In the case of inbound logistics, for example, many organizations have developed just-in-time systems in order to avoid or minimize their stockholding costs. In this way, the value of the activity is increased and the firm's competitive advantage improved. Equally, in the case of operations, manufacturers are paying increasing attention to lean manufacturing processes as a means of improving levels of efficiency. Porter's message is therefore straightforward. Managers, he suggests, need to examine the nature and dimensions of each of the nine activities with a view to identifying how the value-added component can best be increased. He then goes on to argue that value chain analysis should not simply stop with the manager's own organization, but in the case of a manufacturer should also include the suppliers and distribution networks, since the value of much of what an organization does will be magnified or constrained by what they do.

2.6 Conducting effective audits

At an earlier stage in this chapter (see pp. 46–50) we made reference to the characteristics of effective audits, suggesting that if they are to be worthwhile they should be *comprehensive, systematic, independent* and conducted on a *regular basis*.

Comprehensive auditing

For the auditing process to be worthwhile it is essential that it covers *all* of the major elements of the organization's marketing activity, including those that seemingly are doing well, rather than just a few apparent trouble spots. In this way a distinction can be drawn between the *marketing audit* and a *functional audit*, which would focus far more specifically upon a particular element of marketing activity such as sales or pricing. As an example of this, a functional audit might well suggest that a high sales-force turnover and low morale is due to a combination of inadequate sales training and a poor compensation package. A more fundamental reason, however, might be that the company has a poor or inadequate product range and an inappropriate pricing and advertising strategy. It is the comprehensiveness of the marketing audit which is designed to reveal these sorts of factors and to highlight the *fundamental* causes of the organization's problems.

Systematic auditing

In carrying out the audit it is essential that a sequential diagnostic process is adopted, covering the three areas to which reference was made earlier: the external environment, internal marketing systems and specific marketing activities. This process of diagnosis is then followed by the development *and implementation* of both short-term and long-term plans designed to correct the weaknesses identified and, in this way, improve upon levels of marketing effectiveness.

Independent auditing

As with a financial audit, there are several ways in which the marketing audit can be conducted. These include:

➡ A self-audit in which managers use a checklist to assess their own results and methods of operation
➡ An audit by a manager of the same status but drawn from a different department or division within the organization
➡ An audit by a more senior manager within the same department or division
➡ The use of a company auditing office
➡ A company task force audit group
➡ An audit conducted by an outside specialist.

Of these, it is generally recognized that an audit conducted by an outside specialist is likely to prove the most objective and to exhibit the independence which any internal process will almost inevitably lack. Adopting this approach should also ensure that the audit receives the undivided time and attention that is needed. In practice, however, many large companies make use of their own audit teams (something which 3M, for example, has pioneered).

This question of *who* should conduct the audit has been the subject of a considerable amount of research and discussion in recent years with, as indicated above, the argument revolving around the issue of objectivity (in other words, how objective can a line manager be in conducting an evaluation of activities for which he has direct responsibility?). It is largely because of this that it has been suggested that outside consultants should be used to ensure impartiality. This is likely to prove expensive if done annually, and the answer is increasingly being seen to lie in a compromise whereby an outside consultant is used every third or fourth year, with line managers from different departments or divisions being used in the intervening periods. Alternatively, an organization might opt for what is in essence a composite approach, with an external auditor being used initially to validate line managers' self-audits, and subsequently to integrate them to produce an audit result for the marketing function as a whole.

To a large extent, however, it can be argued that the supposed difficulties of achieving impartiality are overstated, since a sufficiently well-structured and institutionalized auditing process can overcome many of these difficulties. There is a need, therefore, for managers to be trained in how best to use auditing procedures and, very importantly, for the audit process to be endorsed by senior management; without top management commitment to the audit process and, in turn, to the need to act on the results that emerge, the entire exercise is likely to prove valueless.

Regular auditing

If the company is to benefit fully from the auditing process, it is essential that it is carried out on a regular basis. All too often in the past companies have been spurred into conducting an audit largely as the result of poor performance. Ironically, this poor performance can often be traced to a myopia on the part of management, stemming from a failure to review activities on a sufficiently regular basis, something which has been pointed to by Shuchman (1950), who has commented that: 'No marketing operation is ever so good that it cannot be improved. Even the best *must* be better, for few if any marketing operations can remain successful over the years by maintaining the status quo.'

Why bother with a marketing audit?

Although we have so far argued the case for marketing auditing to be carried out on a regular basis, many organizations quite simply do not bother to do this until things go wrong. Most typically this would be manifested in terms of declining sales, a loss of market share, under-utilized production capacity, a demoralized sales force, reduced margins, and so on. Faced with these sorts of problems, the temptation for management is to firefight and hence fall into the trap of crisis management. In many cases this is characterized by the rapid launching and dropping of products, price cutting and attempts at drastic cost reduction. While this sort of response will often have an immediate and apparent pay-off, it is unlikely that it will solve any underlying and fundamental problems. The audit is designed to avoid the need for crisis management both by identifying and defining these fundamental problems *before they have any opportunity to affect the organization*. In this way, carrying out a regular and thorough marketing audit in a structured manner will go a long way towards giving a company a knowledge of the business, trends in the market, and where value is added by competitors as a basis for setting objectives and strategies. These points have been highlighted in a summary of the ten most common findings of marketing audits:

1 A lack of knowledge of customers' behaviour and attitudes
2 A failure to segment markets effectively
3 The absence of marketing planning procedures
4 Reductions in price rather than increases in volume
5 The absence of market-based procedures for evaluating products

6 Misunderstanding company marketing strengths

7 Short-term views of the role of promotion

8 A perception that marketing is limited just to advertising and sales activity

9 Inappropriate organizational structures

10 Insufficient investment in the future, particularly in the area of human resources.

The auditing process

The auditing process should begin with agreement being reached between the organization's marketing director and the marketing auditor – someone from inside or outside the organization – regarding the specific objectives, the breadth and depth of coverage, the sources of data, the report format and the time period for the audit. Included within this should be a plan of who is to be interviewed and the questions that are to be asked.

With regard to the question of *who* is to be questioned, it needs to be emphasized that the audit should never be restricted to the company's executives; it should also include customers, the dealer network and other outside groups. In this way, a better and more complete picture of the company's position and its effectiveness can be developed. In the case of customers and dealers, for example, the auditor should aim to develop satisfaction ratings which are capable of highlighting areas in need of attention.

Once the information has been collected, the findings and recommendations need to be presented with emphasis being given to the type of action needed to overcome any problems, the time scale over which remedial action is to be taken, and the names of those who are to be responsible for this.

Components of the audit

Within the general framework of the external and internal audits, there is the need to focus upon six specific dimensions. These are:

1 *The marketing environment audit.* This involves an analysis of the major macro-economic forces and trends within the organization's task environment, including markets, customers, competitors, distributors, dealers and suppliers.

2 *The marketing strategy audit.* This focuses upon a review of the organization's marketing objectives and strategy, with a view to determining how well suited they are to the current and forecasted market environment.

3 *The marketing organization audit.* This aspect of the audit follows on from point 2 above, and is concerned specifically with an evaluation of the structural capability of the organization and its suitability for implementing the strategy needed for the developing environment.

4 *The marketing systems audit.* This covers the quality of the organization's systems for analysis, planning and control.

5 *The marketing productivity audit.* This examines the profitability of different aspects of the marketing programme and the cost-effectiveness of various levels of marketing expenditure.

6 *The marketing functions audit.* This involves a detailed evaluation of each of the elements of the marketing mix.

How are the audit results used?

Having conducted the audit, the question that then arises is how best to use the results. In some companies a considerable amount of time, effort and expense is given over to the auditing process, but the corrective action that is then needed simply falls by the wayside. To ensure that the results are incorporated most effectively within the strategic planning process which forms the focus of the remainder of this book, the major findings of the audit need to be incorporated within an appropriate framework. This can be done in one of several ways, although undoubtedly the most useful are the SWOT and TOWS frameworks discussed earlier. This should focus on the *key* internal strengths and weaknesses in relation to the *principal* external opportunities and threats, and include a summary of the reasons for good or bad performance. It is then against the background of this document that the strategist should begin planning at both the functional and corporate levels. It is this process which provides the basis for much of the rest of this book.

2.7 Summary

Within this chapter we have focused upon the role and structure of marketing auditing and SWOT analysis. In doing this, we have highlighted the way in which the marketing audit represents an important first step in the marketing planning process and how, as a result, the value of much of what follows within this process is determined by the thoroughness of the audit procedure. It is therefore essential that the audit exhibits a number of characteristics, the four most significant of which are that it is:

1 Comprehensive in its coverage of the elements of the organization's marketing activity
2 Systematic
3 Independent
4 Conducted on a regular basis.

The purpose of the audit is to provide the strategist with a clear understanding both of environmental opportunities and threats, and of the organization's marketing capability. In doing this, the strategist begins by focusing upon the principal macro-environmental forces (political/legal, economic/demographic, social/cultural and technological) that affect the business. He or she then moves on to consider the micro-environmental actors (customers, competitors, distributors and suppliers) who influence the organization's ability to operate effectively in the marketplace. The internal audit builds upon this by providing an understanding of the extent to which the organization, its structure and resources relate to the environment and have the capability of operating effectively within the constraints that the environment imposes.

In addition to conducting the marketing audit, the strategist needs to carry out regular reviews of the organization's marketing effectiveness. This can be done most readily by means of a checklist which embraces five principal areas:

1 The nature of the customer philosophy
2 The marketing organization
3 Marketing information
4 The strategic perspective
5 Operational efficiency.

Against the background of the picture that emerges from the audit and the review of marketing effectiveness, the strategist should have a clear understanding both of the environment (opportunities and threats) and of the organization's marketing capability (strengths and weaknesses). It is this which then provides the basis for subsequent marketing planning.

Chapter 3

Segmental, productivity and ratio analysis

3.1 Learning objectives

When you have read this chapter you should be able to:

(a) understand how cost analysis can be applied to marketing segments;
(b) appreciate the role of marketing experimentation in improving the allocation of marketing effort;
(c) recognize the value of segmental productivity analysis;
(d) perceive critically how ratio analysis can be used in order to appreciate the current position;
(e) appreciate the relevance of strategic benchmarking.

3.2 Introduction

In relation to the question 'Where are we now?', it is useful to know how resources have been utilized and with what returns. To this end, it helps to think of the organization as a bundle of projects or activities. This is relevant whether the organization is large or small, commercial or non-commercial, engaged in manufacturing or service rendering. Typical projects might be defined as:

➡ Reformulation and relaunch of product X
➡ Continued market success with service Y
➡ The successful development and launch of project Z.

One might go further and define projects or activities in terms of *missions*: a mission in this context represents the provision of a product or range of products at a particular level of service to a particular customer or customer group in a particular area. Figure 3.1 illustrates this (see also Chapter 7).

An organization's mix of projects – or missions – will be constantly changing, and each has resource implications and profit consequences. For example, the scarcity of resources inevitably means that choices must be made in rationing available resources (whether in the form of funds, management time, etc.) among competing activities. It may be that new activities can only be adopted if old ones are deleted, thereby freeing resources. But how might a manager know which activities are worth retaining, which should be added to the portfolio and which should be deleted? One starting point is to establish the cost of each of the organization's existing activities.

We can think of cost as being equivalent in broad terms to *effort*, so what we are initially seeking to establish is how the available effort has been applied to the various activities in which the organization is engaged. Before we can really get to grips with this, however, we need to clarify our understanding of some important categories of cost.

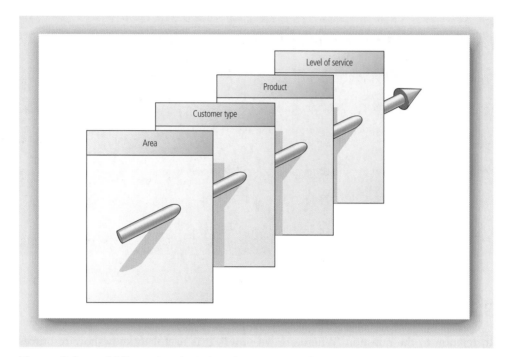

Figure 3.1 Multidimensional mission characteristics (source: Barrett, 1980, p. 143)

3.3 The clarification of cost categories

Many of the costs of marketing are not satisfactorily identified, since marketing *functions* are not always carried out by the marketing *department*. (It could be argued that any members of an organization who deal with customers, for example, are carrying out a marketing function even though they may not be recognized in any formal sense as members of the marketing staff.) This is one definitional problem, but not the only one.

Another definitional problem concerns the traditional focus that accountants have adopted, which puts product costing at the centre of their costing systems. This traditional preoccupation with the manufacturing costs of products and factory processes emphasizes the attributes of whatever is currently being made. Such an orientation fails to deal with patterns of consumer preferences and competitive positioning by market segment. The attributes of market segments – from which profit is derived – are fundamentally different from those attributes that characterize production processes. Any analysis based on product costing will generate insights that are limited by their origins, thereby failing to support marketing orientation.

Whatever cost object (or activity) is selected as the focus of attention, some costs will be *direct* (in the sense of being traceable to the activity – such as direct labour, and direct material inputs into a unit of manufactured output, or a salesperson's salary and expenses in relation to the sales territory), while others will be *indirect*. By definition, indirect costs cannot be traced directly to cost objects, so any procedure whereby these costs are assigned to cost objects will mean that the resulting full (or 'absorbed') cost is inaccurate to an unknown extent. The assigning of a 'fair share' of indirect costs, along with direct costs, to cost objects is at the heart of *absorption costing*.

A particular cost item can only be termed direct or indirect once the cost object has been specified. This could be, for example, a particular product, a product range, a brand, a customer or customer group, a channel, a sales territory, an order, and so on. Thus, a salesperson's salary will be indirect in relation to the individual product lines sold (assuming the salesperson carries a range of products), but it will be a direct cost of the territory in which that individual is operating. In the same way, the costs of distributing various products to wholesalers may be indirect with regard to the goods themselves, but direct if one is interested in costing the channel of distribution of which the wholesalers are part.

The same basic problems arise in attempting to determine the full cost of a cost object in every type of organization, whether a service company, a retailing enterprise, a factory or a non-commercial entity. For example, a garage (as one type of service organization) will treat the servicing of each customer's car as a separate job (or cost object), to which will be assigned the direct cost of the mechanic's time, materials and parts, plus an allowance (usually applied as an hourly rate and associated with the utilization of mechanics' time) for the use of indirect factors (which will include power, equipment, rent, rates, insurance, salaries of reception, supervisory and stores staff, etc.). A similar approach is applied by firms of solicitors or accountants, by consulting engineers, architects and management consultants. Non-commercial organizations typically provide services (such as health care, defence, education and spiritual guidance) and use resources in carrying out their various activities in much the same way as do commercial undertakings. The logic of absorption costing is equally applicable to non-commercial as to commercial enterprises.

3.4 Marketing cost analysis: aims and methods

Establishing a baseline for marketing planning can be seen to be concerned with the allocation of total marketing effort to cost objects (also known as segments), along with the profit consequences of these allocations. It is generally found, however, that companies do not know the profit performance of segments in marketing terms. Useful computations of marketing costs and profit contributions in the multi-product company require the adoption of analytical techniques which are not difficult in principle but which are not widely adopted in practice on account of, inter alia, the preoccupation with factory cost accounting that exists.

The fact that most companies do not know what proportion of their total marketing outlay is spent on each product, sales territory or customer group may be due to the absence of a sufficiently refined system of cost analysis, or it may be due to vagueness over the nature of certain costs. For instance, is the cost of packaging a promotional a production or a distribution expense? Some important marketing costs are hidden in manufacturing costs or in general and administrative costs, including finished goods inventory costs in the former and order-processing costs in the latter.

Since few companies are aware of costs and profits by segment in relation to sales levels, and since even fewer are able to predict changes in sales volume and profit contribution as a result of changes in marketing effort, the following errors arise:

1 Marketing budgets for individual products are too large, with the result that diminishing returns become evident and benefits would accrue from a reduction in expenditure

2 Marketing budgets for individual products are too small and increasing returns would result from an increase in expenditure

3 The marketing mix is inefficient, with an incorrect balance and incorrect amounts being spent on the constituent elements – such as too much on advertising and insufficient on direct selling activities

4 Marketing efforts are misallocated among missions and changes in these cost allocations (even with a constant level of overall expenditure) could bring improvements.

Similar arguments apply in relation to sales territories or customer groups as well as to products. The need exists, therefore, for planning and control techniques to indicate the level of performance required and achieved, as well as the outcome of shifting marketing efforts from one segment to another. As is to be expected, there exists great diversity in the methods by which managers attempt to obtain costs (and profits) for segments of their business, but much of the cost data is inaccurate for such reasons as those listed below:

➡ Marketing costs may be allocated to individual products, sales territories, customer groups, etc., on the basis of sales value or sales volume, but this involves circular reasoning. Costs should be allocated in relation to causal factors and *it is order-getting marketing expenditures that cause sales to be made* rather than the other way round: managerial decisions determine order-getting marketing costs. A different pattern typically applies to order-fitting (e.g. logistics) costs, since sales volume will cause (or *drive*) order-filling costs: order-getting → sales volume → order-filling. Furthermore, despite the fact that success is so often measured in terms of sales value achievements by product line, this basis fails to evaluate the efficiency of the effort needed to produce the realized sales value (or turnover). Even a seemingly high level of turnover for a specific product may really be a case of misallocated sales effort. (An example should make this clear: if a salesman concentrates on selling Product A, which contributes £50 per hour of effort, instead of selling Product B, which would contribute £120 per hour of effort, then it 'costs' the company £70 for each hour spent on selling Product A. This is the *opportunity cost* of doing one thing rather than another and is a measure of the sacrifice involved in selecting only one of several alternative courses of action.)

➡ General indirect and administrative costs are arbitrarily (and erroneously) allocated to segments on the basis of sales volume.

➡ Many marketing costs are not allocated at all as marketing costs, since they are not identified as such, but are classified as manufacturing, general or administrative costs instead.

Marketing cost analysis has been developed to help overcome these problems and aims to:

1 Analyse the costs incurred in marketing products (embracing order-getting and order-filling aspects), so that when they are combined with product cost data overall profit can be determined

2 Analyse the costs of marketing individual products to determine profit by product line

3 Analyse the costs involved in serving different classes of customers, different territories and other segments to determine their relative profit performance

4 Compute such figures as cost per sales call, cost per order, cost to put a new customer on the books, cost to hold £1's worth of inventory for a year, etc.

5 Evaluate managers according to their actual controllable cost responsibilities

6 Evaluate alternative strategies or plans with full costs.

These analyses and evaluations provide senior management with the necessary information to enable them to raise questions regarding which classes of customer to cultivate, which products to delete or encourage, which channels may be preferable, and so forth. Such analyses also provide a basis from which estimates may be developed of the likely increases in sales volume, value or profit (i.e. outputs) that a specified increase in marketing effort (i.e. input) might create. In the normal course of events, it is far more difficult to predict the outcome of decisions that involve changes in marketing outlays in comparison with changes in production expenditure. It is easier, for instance, to estimate the effect of a new machine in the factory than it is to predict the impact of higher advertising outlays. Similarly, the effect on productive output of dropping a production worker is easier to estimate than is the effect on the level of sales caused by a reduction in the sales force.

The basic approach of marketing cost analysis is similar to that of product costing. Two stages are involved (see Figure 3.2):

1 Marketing costs are initially reclassified from their *natural* expense headings (e.g. salaries) into *functional* cost groups (e.g. sales expenses) in such a way that each cost group brings together all the costs associated with a particular marketing activity

2 These functional cost groups are then apportioned to the cost object/segment of interest (e.g. product lines, customer groups, channels of distribution, etc.) on the basis of measurable criteria that bear as close an approximation as possible to a causal relationship with the total amounts of the functional cost groups.

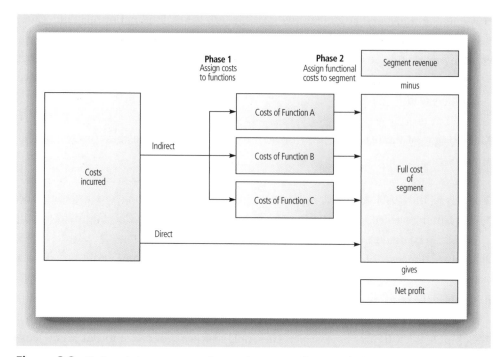

Figure 3.2 Determining segmental costs (source: Wilson and Chua, 1993, p. 87)

Once the natural indirect expenses have been reclassified on a functional basis, they are then charged to the segment in line with the usual benefit criterion (i.e. the segment is only allocated with that portion of each functional cost group that can be related to it on some approximation of a cause and effect basis). The logical basis of allocation may be apparent from an analysis of the underlying data, but it is important to observe that some costs vary with the characteristics of one type of segment only. Thus, inventory costs depend on the characteristics of products rather than on those of customers, whereas the cost of credit depends on the financial integrity and number of customers rather than on regional factors. Accordingly, not all functional costs should be allocated to products, customers and territorial segments. Allocation should only be made when an actual or imputed cause and effect relationship between an underlying activity and some resultant cost which is relevant to the segment(s) can be identified.

It must be remembered when using marketing cost analysis that any cost allocation involves a certain degree of arbitrariness, which means that an element of approximation is inevitably contained within the allocation. Furthermore, it remains necessary to supplement the analysis of marketing costs with other relevant information and with managerial judgement.

Marketing cost analysis is the joint responsibility of the controller and the marketing manager, with the controller supplying most of the information and the marketing manager supplying most of the judgement. Nevertheless, the marketing manager must be fully aware of the method and limitations of marketing cost analysis. The high cost of establishing and maintaining a marketing costing system is justified by the benefits derived from increasing the efficiency of marketing effort. The risks involved in adopting marketing cost analysis before the benefits have been demonstrated can be reduced by initially confining the analysis to a sample of products, customers or territories, and by making periodic rather than continuous analyses.

Since a fundamental objective of marketing cost analysis lies in increasing the productivity of expenditures and not necessarily in their reduction, the manager who wishes to introduce marketing cost analysis must emphasize the desire to make better use of existing resources rather than reducing future budgets. The integration of marketing costing with marketing research can assist in this matter. Confining any costing system to data provided from accounting records risks forcing that system to be historical, but marketing research can provide estimates of future outcomes resulting from variations in marketing effort (with or without experimentation and the building of complex models) which enable the efficiency of alternate expenditure patterns to be predetermined and evaluated in accordance with corporate aims.

See Illustration 3.1.

Illustration 3.1 My biggest mistake (David Bruce)

(David Bruce, 42, failed his maths 'O' level five times before leaving school to work for a brewery. In 1979, he came off the dole queue to open the Goose and Firkin pub in London after raising a loan against his home. By 1988, he had built a chain of eighteen pubs, which he sold for £6.6 million, intending to retire with his £2 million share. But he could not resist going back into business and is now trading as Inn Securities and building up a chain of Hedgehog and Hogshead pubs outside London.)

My biggest mistake was not paying proper attention to my accounts in the early days of the Firkin pubs. We had opened the Goose and Firkin in London in 1979 and I was working eighteen lousy hours a day, seven days a week, brewing the beer in the cellar and surviving on adrenalin. I had eight staff and a part-time book-keeper.

Everybody said the pub would not work, but people were queuing to get in. It was tremendously exciting and I was on a complete high. The tills were ringing, my break-even point was £2500 a week, but the pub never did less than £4500.

So why, I thought, if one has created this extraordinary thing, should one scuttle back home to Battersea and spend hours doing boring old paperwork? The turnover was so good I did not even bother with profit and loss accounts. (And you have to bear in mind that I did not have a natural aptitude for figures.)

In May 1980, I opened the Fox and Firkin in Lewisham. I trained a brewer to look after the Goose, but he promptly broke his leg, leaving me to deal with both pubs. There was even less time to do paperwork.

Then I opened another pub in London, and because the experts doomed us to failure I thought it would be easier if the pubs traded under separate companies. Each one had a different accounting year – it was a good lesson in how not to run a business.

By the time we had opened our fourth pub in 1981, our solicitors, Bishop and Sewell, had watched our progress with great interest and assumed we were incurring a hideous tax bill, so they suggested we met with accountants Touche Ross. My wife Louise and I went along with what little financial information we had, plus a couple of audits that showed we had traded at a loss from day one.

In fact, while the turnover for the first year was £1 million, we had made losses of £86 000. One of their corporate finance partners said that if I did not appoint a chartered accountant to the board as financial director immediately we would go bust within a couple of months. So I took on someone from a major brewery, who introduced systems such as stock control and weekly profit and loss accounts.

But that did not solve the immediate problems. Touche Ross also said I would have to sell one of the pubs, the Fleece and Firkin in Bristol, because it was costing too much time and money. Reluctantly I put it on the market.

By now it was obvious that I should have appointed a finance director at the beginning. The bank was getting nervous, my borrowings were rising and I was not producing a profit.

If the bank had pulled the rug we would have gone down personally for £500 000. Touche Ross advised me to sell a small percentage of the equity, which of course I did not want to do.

Eventually I struck a satisfactory deal with 3i (Investors in Industry), which bought 10 per cent of the business and gave us a loan. Better cash control enabled us to turn a loss into profit, and the following year, on a turnover of £1.6 million, we showed a profit of £47 000.

Touche Ross, who charged us under £5000 to sort the problem out, have done my audits ever since. Paul Adams, our managing director, is the resident chartered accountant. He has kept costs down and introduced budgets which the staff can stick to.

In hindsight the solutions were obvious, but I was a victim of my own success. If the turnover had not been so good, I would have realized a lot sooner how close I was to bankruptcy.

Source: As told to journalist Corinne Simcock, *The Independent on Sunday: Business*, 16 December 1990, p. 20.

3.5 An illustration of segmental analysis

As discussed above, a segment is any cost object which is of interest, and is synonymous with the notion of activity, project or mission as appropriate. Thus, for example, marketing segments may be one – or a combination – of the following:

➡ Product line or range
➡ Channel of distribution
➡ Sales representative or territory
➡ Customer or customer/industry group
➡ Size of order.

It is possible to vary the degree of aggregation of segments, as shown in Figure 3.3.

Initially one must select the segment in which one is interested (e.g. territory, customer, etc.). Then one must select the approach to costing that one prefers. Essentially, there are two major alternatives:

1 Absorption (or full) costing

2 Variable (or direct or marginal) costing.

Our earlier discussion dealt with the first of these, and we saw that this approach involves charging both direct and a portion of indirect costs to the segment in question. When set against the segment's revenue the result is a net profit figure.

Figure 3.4 shows an example of the net profit picture in an organization operating through three different channels of distribution.

The net profit figure reflects the result of the allocation of effort as shown by the total of:

➡ Cost of goods sold

➡ Direct marketing costs

➡ Indirect marketing costs.

Once this allocation has been set against the revenue figure, channel by channel, it is evident that the validity of the net profit figures that emerge depend critically upon the adequacy of the means by which indirect costs are apportioned.

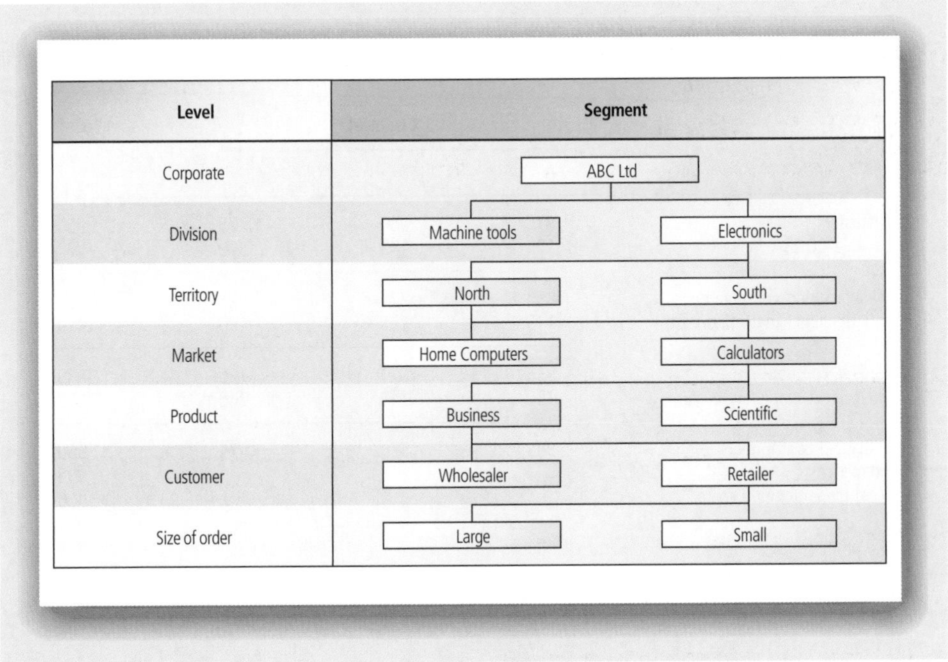

Level	Segment	
Corporate	ABC Ltd	
Division	Machine tools	Electronics
Territory	North	South
Market	Home Computers	Calculators
Product	Business	Scientific
Customer	Wholesaler	Retailer
Size of order	Large	Small

Figure 3.3   Segmental levels (adapted from Ratnatunga, 1983, p. 34)

£'000s	Channel						Total
	A		B		C		
Revenue	875		950		1,225		3,050
Cost of goods sold	325		285		490		1,100
Gross Profit	550		665		735		1,950
Direct marketing costs	265		245		450		960
Indirect marketing costs	330		275		250		855
Total marketing costs	595		520		700		1,815
Net profit	(45)		145		35		135

Figure 3.4 Profit analysis by channel

3.6 An alternative approach to segmental analysis

The alternative approach to segmental analysis is the variable costing approach, in which only direct costs are allocated to arrive at a measure of profit known as *marketing contribution*. Using the data from Figure 3.4, this has been reworked in Figure 3.5 to illustrate the variable costing approach.

It has been assumed that the cost of goods sold figures in Figure 3.4 included £700 000 of variable manufacturing costs and £400 000 of fixed manufacturing costs;

£'000s	Channel			Total
	A	B	C	
Revenue	875	950	1,225	3,050
Variable COGS	225	175	300	700
Manufacturing contribution	650	775	925	2,350
Variable direct marketing costs	115	105	190	410
Variable contribution	535	670	735	1,940
Fixed direct marketing costs	150	140	260	550
Marketing contribution	385	530	475	1,390
Indirect costs				855
Fixed manufacturing costs				400
Net profit				135

Figure 3.5 A direct costing profit statement

that the direct costs are all of a marketing nature and can be split into fixed and variable components as shown in Figure 3.5; and that the indirect costs are all non-allocable to channels. The result is a clear statement that sufficient revenue is being generated via each channel to cover the variable costs and the directly allocable fixed costs. Moreover, there is sufficient total contribution to cover the indirect costs and the fixed manufacturing costs while still making a net profit of £135 000.

3.7 Customer profitability analysis

An approach to segmental analysis that is of increasing interest is customer profitability analysis (CPA). If marketing effort is to be directed at customers or market segments with the greatest profit potential, it is essential that marketing managers have information showing both the existing picture with regard to customer profitability and prospects for the future.

Customer profitability analysis has been defined (Anandarajan and Christopher, 1987, p. 86) as:

" . . . the evaluation, analysis and isolation of:

➡ all the significant costs associated with servicing a specific customer/group of customers from the point an order is received through manufacture to ultimate delivery;
➡ the revenues associated with doing business with those specific customers/customer groups.*"*

The implementation of CPA can be achieved by a series of steps that parallel the steps suggested earlier for other types of segmental analysis. In outline, these steps are:

➡ *Step 1.* Clearly define customer groups and market segments in a way which distinguishes the needs of customers in one group from those of customers in another group.
➡ *Step 2.* For the customer groups or market segments of interest, identify those factors that cause variations in the costs of servicing those customers. This can be done by identifying the key elements of the marketing mix used for each customer group or segment, from which some indication of the costs of servicing each group should be drawn.
➡ *Step 3.* Analyse the ways in which service offerings are differentiated between customer groups. For example, terms of trade may vary between home-based and overseas customers, or between large and small customers, as might the level of service (i.e. speed of delivery) to key accounts.
➡ *Step 4.* Clearly identify the resources that have been used to support each customer group or segment – including personnel, warehouse facilities, administrative backup, etc.

➡ *Step 5.* Determine ways in which the costs of resources (step 4) can be attributed to customer groups.

➡ *Step 6.* Relate revenues and costs to each customer group, with profit emerging as the difference.

The total of the costs for a given customer group is a measure of the effort that has been allocated to that group, and the profit is a measure of the return from that effort. Until the existing pattern of allocation is known, along with its profitability, it is not possible to devise ways of improving that allocation.

See Illustration 3.2.

Illustration 3.2 Evolution

New technologies are beginning to make mass customization feasible and information systems are allowing us to identify the profitability of each customer.

Tower Records recently started offering its customers the top 40 lines of groceries. It was a publicity stunt, of course – a protest at the way supermarkets have started cherry-picking their business by selling records from the Top 40 chart.

Tower's initiative amounts to little more than a puff of hot air, but behind it lies an issue of growing importance. Cherry-picking is hardly new, but its extent and nature are changing. Increasingly, the most aggressive and successful cherry-pickers are coming from 'outside' the industry concerned – and as such these are invaders with a difference. They're changing the nature of the market itself.

To see what's happening we need to take a step back. Consider, for example, how people acquired their clothes, say, 50 years ago. Basically, they had three ways to do so. First, if they were rich, they could go to their tailor. His was a high-quality, high-convenience, high-service offer, with bespoke fitting at a high price. Second, you could buy mass manufactured garments. They offered standard quality and standard sizes at low prices but with low service and low convenience. Thirdly, you could make them yourself, buying cloth and thread and slaving over a hot sewing machine. This way you got bespoke fitting at a very low price, but the service and convenience elements were reduced.

Buying bespoke

Since then, mass manufacturing has swept nearly all before it. Its ongoing technological revolution has forced down prices and improved quality at such a rate that 'Royal' service and DIY have (in most sectors) become tiny niches for the very rich and the very poor respectively. Economies of scale were worth it, but came at a price. Everything was standardized and averaged and there was, to varying degrees, cross-subsidization between customers.

Today, that's changing. New technologies are beginning to make mass customization feasible and information systems are allowing us to identify the profitability of each customer – marketers are rightly questioning the validity of the mass production trade-off. Inspired by the total quality movement ('you can have better quality and lower prices'), they're racing to offer Royal, bespoke products and services at standard prices – an inspiring agenda that will keep them busy for decades.

At the same time, they're realizing that their customer base usually falls into three groups. The first group (let's call them the Superprofits) actually generates 150 per cent of their profits, even though it only accounts for, say, 60 per cent of customers and makes a crucial contribution to overheads even if its profitability is marginal. The third group actually costs money to serve.

De-averaging is now the order of the day. The big drive now is to 'fire' or otherwise lose the loss makers while going all out to deepen the relationship with the Superprofits.

So far, so good. This is classic segmentation taken to its next, logical, level. But de-averaging has a sting in the tail. In many a company it threatens to set off a chain reaction that unravels the ties that bound it together into a single entity in the first place. Instead of having one mass production business that dominates the market with its brands, de-averaging implies the return of a three-tiered business structure of Royals, standards and DIY, each with their own distinct brands and marketing strategies.

Cherry-picking costs

Without their mass markets and their economies of scale, the advantages that gave mass production its tremendous edge begin to go into reverse. Many of these businesses are, in effect, cross-subsidization businesses and if cross-subsidization falls apart, so do they.

Tower Records' beef is that sales of Top 40 records basically subsidize other titles, allowing it to offer a wider range and therefore a better service. If the Top 40 goes, the whole proposition goes. Ditto credit cards. Heavy borrowers who pay extortionate interest rates on high levels of rollover debt are subsidizing wily users who pay off their debts each month and get an excellent service for free. But a traditional credit card operator cannot cherry-pick its own Superprofits because ending the cross-subsidization would destroy the rest of its business.

Likewise banks. Current account holders whose balances are so low and transactions so frequent that they cost a fortune to serve are being subsidized by affluent customers with higher balances. Banking is ripe for a redivision into Royal, standard and DIY, but it's almost impossible for existing mass players to do so.

Or take insurance. It's all about averaging and cross-subsidization. Clever marketers have made good money by de-averaging – distinguishing high-risk customers from low-risk. But the better the match gets between premium and risk, the less incentive there is to bet: high-risk people won't be able to afford the premium, and very-low-risk types will realize they're better off investing their own premiums.

The real challenge comes when an outsider who hasn't got the same sort of cross-subsidizing structure targets another industry's Superprofits. Almost by definition, they can make a better offer – like the supermarkets and Tower Records. Or, perhaps, category killers poaching high-profit business from mass merchandisers. Or car companies and charities marketing credit cards. In each case, the victim company is no longer doing the segmenting, it is being segmented.

We can expect more of this as technological development reduces the volume a business needs to cover infrastructure costs (thereby lowering barriers to entry), or as specialist operators see big opportunities in creating cherry-picking platforms for 'outsider' brands.

> It's tempting to label the first type a niche player and the second type a brand extender, and to think that's the end of it. But beware: jargon suffocates thought. It may be just the beginning. Behind such brands and marketing strategies there might be much more than meets the eye. A completely new industrial – and brand – landscape may be emerging.
>
> Source: Mitchell (1997, p. 18)

An example, ABC Ltd, follows which illustrates in detail how the above approach might be implemented. This approach has been in existence for over 60 years, but renewed interest in it has been generated over the last 10 years or so under the banner of activity-based costing (ABC).

ABC Ltd: an exercise on segmental analysis

The profit and loss account for last month's operations of ABC Ltd is given in Figure 3.6, showing a net profit of £14 070. (The numbers in this example are only intended to show how the calculations can be done.)

Derek Needham, ABC's chief executive, is interested in knowing the profit from each of the company's three customers. Since this cannot be known from Figure 3.6 as it stands, he asks his management accountant, Philip Randall, to carry out the necessary analysis.

In addition to the five *natural* accounts shown in the profit and loss account, Mr Randall has identified four *functional* accounts:

1 Personal selling
2 Packaging and despatch
3 Advertising
4 Invoicing and collection.

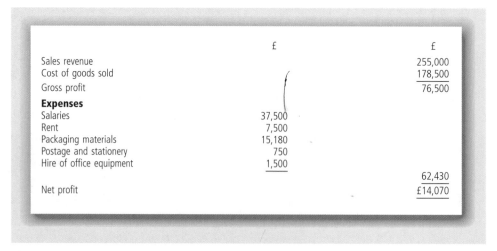

	£	£
Sales revenue		255,000
Cost of goods sold		178,500
Gross profit		76,500
Expenses		
Salaries	37,500	
Rent	7,500	
Packaging materials	15,180	
Postage and stationery	750	
Hire of office equipment	1,500	
		62,430
Net profit		£14,070

Figure 3.6 ABC Ltd: profit and loss account

His investigations have revealed that:

1 Salaries are attributable as follows:
   → Sales personnel £15 000
   → Packaging labour £13 500
   → Office staff £9000.
   Salesmen seldom visit the office. Office staff time is divided equally between promotional activities on the one hand and invoicing/collecting on the other.
2 The rent charge relates to the whole building, of which 20 per cent is occupied by offices and the remainder by packaging/despatch.
3 All the advertising expenditure is related to Product C.
4 ABC Ltd markets three products, as shown in Figure 3.7. These products vary in their manufactured cost (worked out on absorption lines), selling price and volume sold during the month. Moreover, their relative bulk varies: Product A is much smaller than Product B, which in turn is only half the size of Product C (see Figure 3.7).
5 Each of ABC's three customers requires different product combinations, places a different number of orders and requires a different amount of sales effort. As Figure 3.8

Product	Manufactured cost per unit	Selling price per unit	Number of units sold last month	Sales revenue	Relative bulk per unit
A	£105	£150	1,000	£150,000	1
B	£525	£750	100	£75,000	3
C	£2,100	£3,000	10	£30,000	6
			1,110	£255,000	

Figure 3.7 ABC Ltd: basic product data

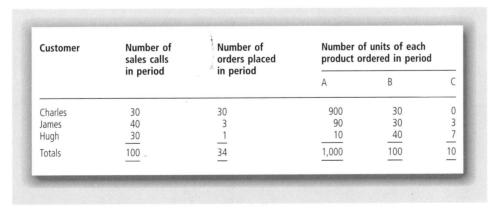

Customer	Number of sales calls in period	Number of orders placed in period	Number of units of each product ordered in period		
			A	B	C
Charles	30	30	900	30	0
James	40	3	90	30	3
Hugh	30	1	10	40	7
Totals	100	34	1,000	100	10

Figure 3.8 ABC Ltd: basic customer data

shows, James received more sales calls, Charles placed more orders and Hugh made up most of the demand for Product C.

Using the data that has been presented, and making various assumptions that we feel to be appropriate, we can apply absorption costing principles in order to determine the net profit or loss attributable to each of ABC's customers. On the basis of our analysis, we may be able to suggest what course of action be considered next.

Among the given data we are told that office staff divide their time equally between two functional activities:

1 Advertising (i.e. order-getting)
2 Invoicing and collections.

It seems reasonable to assume (in the absence of other guidance) that space, postage and stationery, and office equipment are used equally by these two functions. The calculations that follow are based on this assumption, but any other reasonable (and explicit) basis could be acceptable.

Rent is payable on the basis of:

➡ 20 per cent office space (i.e. £1500)
➡ 80 per cent packaging and despatch space (i.e. £6000).

All packaging materials are chargeable to packaging and despatch (which is a clear-cut example of a direct functional cost). Since packaging costs will vary with the bulk of the products sold rather than with, say, the number of units sold or sales revenue, we need to take note of the causal relationship between the bulk of sales and packaging costs (see Figure 3.9).

This can be done by computing (as in Figure 3.9) a measure termed 'packaging units', which incorporates both the number of units and their relative bulk. Even though only 10 units of Product C are sold during the month, the relative bulk of that product (with a factor of 6) ensures that it is charged with a correspondingly high amount of packaging effort (hence cost) per unit relative to Products A and B.

Product	Number of units sold		Relative bulk per unit		Packaging units
A	1,000	×	1	=	1,000
B	100	×	3	=	300
C	10	×	6	=	60
	1,110				1,360

Figure 3.9 ABC Ltd: packaging units

The bases for determining the rates to apply functional costs to segments can be built up in the following way:

1 *Assign natural expenses to functional activities* (see Figure 3.10).
2 *Select bases for assigning functional costs to segments.*

→ Sales calls can be used for personal selling expenses (although this assumes all calls took an equal amount of time)

→ The packaging costs vary in accordance with the number of packaging units handled, so a rate per product can be established by taking bulk and the number of units handled into account

→ Advertising can be related to the number of units of Product C sold during the period (which assumes that advertising was equally effective for all sales, and that all its benefits were obtained during the period in question)

→ The costs of invoicing can be assumed to vary in accordance with the number of orders (hence invoices) processed during the period.

Relevant calculations are given below:

$$\text{Cost per sales call} = \frac{\text{functional costs}}{\text{no. of sales calls}} = \frac{£15,000}{100} = £150.00$$

$$\text{Packaging costs} = \frac{\text{functional costs}}{\text{no. of packaging units}} = \frac{£34,680}{1,360} = £25.50$$

$$\text{Product A} = £25.50 \times 1 = £25.50$$
$$\text{Product B} = £25.50 \times 3 = £76.50$$
$$\text{Product C} = £25.50 \times 6 = £153.00$$

$$\text{Advertising cost} = \frac{\text{functional costs}}{\text{units of C sold}} = \frac{£6,375}{10} = £637.50$$

$$\text{Invoicing cost per order} = \frac{\text{functional costs}}{\text{no. of orders}} = \frac{£6,375}{34} = £187.50$$

Natural expense	Personal selling	Packaging and despatch	Advertising	Invoicing and collection
Salaries	£15,000	£13,500	£4,500	£4,500
Rent	–	£6,000	£750	£750
Packaging materials	–	£15,180	–	–
Postage and stationery	–	–	£375	£375
Hire of equipment	–	–	£750	£750
Total	£15,000	£34,680	£6,375	£6,375

Figure 3.10 ABC Ltd: assigning natural expenses

3 *Assign functional costs to segments.* Before this step can be executed fully, it is necessary to calculate the cost of goods sold (COGS) on a customer-by-customer basis. The data given in Figure 3.7 includes the manufactured cost per unit of each product, and from the data given in Figure 3.8 we can see how many units of each product are bought by each customer. From this, we can calculate the data given in Figure 3.11. We can now turn to the assigning of functional costs to segments. If we take the case of Charles, we know that he can be attributed with a total of £35,370 (see Figure 3.12). A similar computation needs to be carried out for James and Hugh, which gives us the data in Figure 3.13. Finally, the revenue generated from each customer must be calculated as in Figure 3.14.

4 *Compile a net profit statement.* All the pieces can now be put together to show the profit or loss of each customer account with ABC Ltd. The resulting figures (Figure 3.15) show that Charles and Hugh are profitable accounts, while James is marginally unprofitable.

		Customer					
		Charles		James		Hugh	
Product	Unit COGS	Units	COGS	Units	COGS	Units	COGS
A	£105	900	94,500	90	9,450	10	1,050
B	£525	30	15,750	30	15,750	40	21,000
C	£2,100	0	0	3	6,300	7	14,700
			£110,250		£31,500		£36,750

Figure 3.11 ABC Ltd: determining cost of goods sold by customer

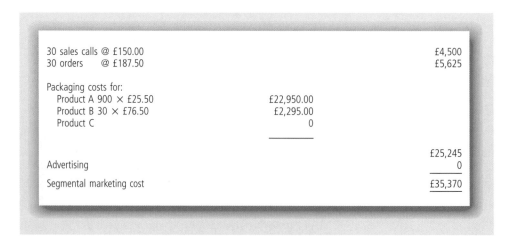

Figure 3.12 ABC Ltd: Charles's costs

James			Hugh		
40 sales calls @	£150.00	£6,000.00	30 sales calls @	£150.00	£4,500.00
3 orders @	£187.50	£562.50	1 order @	£187.50	£187.50
Packaging			Packaging		
A 90 × £25.50	£2,295		A 10 × £25.50	£255	
B 30 × £76.50	£2,295		B 40 × £76.50	£3,060	
C 3 × £153.00	£459		C 7 × £153.00	£1,071	
		£5,049.00			£4,386.00
Advertising 3 × £637.50		£1,912.50	Advertising 7 × £637.50		£4,462.50
Segmental marketing cost		£13,524.00	Segmental marketing cost		£13,536.00

Figure 3.13 ABC Ltd: costs of James and Hugh

		Customer					
	Unit selling price	Charles		James		Hugh	
Product		Units	Revenue	Units	Revenue	Units	Revenue
A	£150	900	135,000	90	13,500	10	1,500
B	£740	30	22,200	30	22,200	40	29,600
C	£3,000	0	0	3	9,000	7	21,000
			£157,200		£44,700		£52,100

Figure 3.14 ABC Ltd: revenue by customer

	Customer			
	Charles	James	Hugh	ABC Ltd
Sales revenue	£157,200	£44,700	£52,100	£254,000
COGS	110,250	31,500	36,750	178,500
Gross profit	46,950	13,200	15,350	75,500
Marketing expenses	35,370	13,524	13,536	62,430
Net profit	£11,580	£(324)	£1,814	£13,070

Figure 3.15 ABC Ltd: net profit by customer

In productivity terms (see pp. 102–4 below), it is evident that there are significant variations from one customer to another. Taking Charles first, we have:

Inputs	£	Outputs	£
COGS	110,250	Sales revenue	157,200
Marketing	35,370		
	£145,620		£157,200

$$\text{Productivity} = \frac{\text{Outputs}}{\text{Inputs}} = \frac{£157,200}{£145,620} = 1.08$$

This productivity index of 1.08 is better than the figure of 1.06 for ABC Ltd as a whole (as shown in Figure 3.16), and considerably in excess of the figures for James and Hugh. It is in excess of unity, which is, prima facie, a good thing.

Taking James next, we have:

Inputs	£	Outputs	£
COGS	31,500	Sales revenue	44,700
Marketing	13,524		
	£45,024		£44,700

$$\text{Productivity} = \frac{\text{Outputs}}{\text{Inputs}} = \frac{£44,700}{£45,024} = 0.99$$

Since this index is below unity, it follows that a loss is being made, and the loss (£324) is the amount by which the value of the inputs consumed in servicing James exceeds the output generated from his account.

Turning now to Hugh, we have the following picture:

Inputs	£	Outputs	£
COGS	36,750	Sales revenue	52,100
Marketing	13,536		
	£50,286		£52,100

$$\text{Productivity} = \frac{\text{Outputs}}{\text{Inputs}} = \frac{£52,100}{£50,286} = 1.04$$

The index is greater than unity, but not as large as that for Charles, or for that relating to ABC Ltd as a whole. This overall position is given below:

Inputs	£	Outputs	£
COGS	178,500	Sales revenue	254,000
Marketing	62,430		
	£240,930		£254,000

$$\text{Productivity} = \frac{\text{Outputs}}{\text{Inputs}} = \frac{£254,000}{£240,930} = 1.06$$

A summary is provided in Figure 3.16.

	Charles	James	Hugh	ABC Ltd as a whole
Outputs (£)	157,200	44,700	52,100	254,000
Inputs (£)	145,620	45,024	50,286	240,930
Productivity index	1.08	0.99	1.04	1.06

Figure 3.16 ABC Ltd: productivity by segment

Interpretation of data

A danger in using an absorption-based approach in segmental analysis is that the 'bottom line' might be taken as a criterion for *action*. It should not be – the aim is to determine the net profit as a criterion for *investigation*. (In a sense, of course, this is one type of action, but the type of action that should be avoided is the eliminating of James's account due to the loss revealed in Figure 3.15.)

Charles's account contributed almost 85 per cent of the total net profit, and he bought three times as much from ABC Ltd as did Hugh, and more than three times the purchases of James. However, the number of sales calls to Charles was fewer than to James, although Charles placed a much larger number of orders than both James and Hugh together.

The mix of products purchased clearly affects the profit performance of different customer accounts. While the COGS does not vary from one product to another (being 70 per cent of sales revenue for each product line), the variation in relative bulk of the product lines caused differences in packaging costs. Thus, Charles (whose orders were for 900 units of A, 30 of B and none of C) was charged with relatively less packaging cost than either James or Hugh due to the smaller packaging bulk of Product A. On a similar basis, since Charles bought no units of C his account was not charged with any advertising costs, so the profit performance of Charles's account would clearly be better than either of the others.

One possible way forward could be to consider calling less often on James, to encourage Charles to place fewer (but larger) orders, and to rethink the wisdom of the advertising campaign for Product C.

It is vital to recognize that this net profit approach to segmental analysis can only raise questions: it cannot provide answers. (The reason for this, of course, is that the apportionment of indirect costs clouds the distinction between avoidable and unavoidable costs, and even direct costs may not all be avoidable in the short run.)

The application of the above steps to a company's product range may produce the picture portrayed in Figure 3.17.

The segment could equally be sales territory, customer group, etc., and after the basic profit computation has been carried out it can be supplemented (as in Figure 3.18)

Product	% contribution to total profits
Total for all products	100.0
Profitable products:	
A	43.7
B	35.5
C	16.4
D	9.6
E	6.8
F	4.2
Sub-total	116.2
G	−7.5
H	−8.7
Sub-total	−16.2

Figure 3.17 Segmental profit statement

by linking it to an analysis of the effort required to produce the profit result. (Clearly this is a multivariate situation in which profit depends upon a variety of input factors – as suggested by Figure 3.1 – but developing valid and reliable multivariate models is both complex and expensive.) As a step in the direction of more rigorous analysis, one can derive benefits from linking profit outcome to individual inputs – such as selling time in the case of Figure 3.18.

Product	% contribution to total profits	% total selling time
Total for all products	100	100
Profitable products:		
A	43.7	16.9
B	35.5	18.3
C	16.4	17.4
D	9.6	5.3
E	6.8	10.2
F	4.2	7.1
Sub-total	116.2	75.2
Unprofitable products:		
G	−7.5	9.5
H	−8.7	15.3
Sub-total	−16.2	24.8

Figure 3.18 Segmental productivity statement

From Figure 3.18 it can be seen that Product A generates 43.7 per cent of total profits, requiring only 16.9 per cent of available selling time. This is highly productive. By contrast, Product E produces only 6.8 per cent of total profits but required 10.2 per cent of selling effort. Even worse, however, is the 24.8 per cent of selling effort devoted to Products G and H, which are unprofitable.

A number of obvious questions arise from this type of analysis. Can the productivity of marketing activities be increased by:

→ Increasing net profits proportionately more than the corresponding increase in marketing outlays?
→ Increasing net profits with no change in marketing outlays?
→ Increasing net profits with a decrease in marketing costs?
→ Maintaining net profits at a given level but decreasing marketing costs?
→ Decreasing net profits but with a proportionately greater decrease in marketing costs?

If these analyses are based purely on historical information, they will provide less help than if they relate to plans for the future. One way of overcoming the limitations of historical information is to plan and control the conditions under which information is gathered. This can be achieved through *marketing experimentation*.

3.8 Marketing experimentation

As we saw in Chapter 1 (see also Chapter 15), attempts are made in a marketing experiment to identify all the controllable independent factors that affect a particular dependent variable, and some of these factors are then manipulated systematically in order to isolate and measure their effects on the performance of the dependent variable.

It is not possible, of course, to plan or control all the conditions in which an experiment is conducted; for example, the timing, location and duration of an experiment can be predetermined, but it is necessary to measure such uncontrollable conditions as those caused by the weather and eliminate their effects from the results. Irrespective of these uncontrollable influences, the fact that experiments are concerned with the deliberate manipulation of controllable variables (i.e. such variables as price and advertising effort) means that a good deal more confidence can be placed in conclusions about the effects of such manipulation than if the effects of these changes had been based purely on historical associations.

Studies of marketing costs can provide the ideas for experiments. Questions such as the following can be answered as a result of marketing experimentation.

1 By how much (if any) would the net profit contribution of the most profitable products be increased if there were an increase in specific marketing outlays, and how would such a change affect the strategy of competitors in terms of the stability of, say, market shares?

2 By how much (if any) would the net losses of unprofitable products be reduced if there were some decrease in specific marketing outlays?

3 By how much (if any) would the profit contribution of profitable products be affected by a change in the marketing effort applied to the unprofitable products, and vice versa, and what would be the effect on the total marketing system?

4 By how much (if any) would the total profit contribution be improved if some marketing effort were diverted to profitable territories or customer groups from unprofitable territorial and customer segments?

5 By how much (if any) would the net profit contribution be increased if there were a change in the method of distribution to small unprofitable accounts, or if these accounts were eliminated?

Only by actually carrying out properly designed marketing experiments can management realistically predict with an acceptable degree of certainty the effects of changes in marketing expenditure on the level of sales and profit of each differentiated product, territory or customer segment in the multi-product company.

3.9 The nature of productivity

Productivity can be considered at either a macro level (i.e. in relation to entire industries or whole economies) or at a micro level (i.e. in relation to particular organizations, or in relation to particular activities within organizations). Our interest is in the latter – productivity at a micro level – although we must avoid being too introspective by focusing exclusively on one organization or function as if it were independent of its context.

At its simplest, productivity can be conceived of as the relationship between outputs and inputs. Thus, marketing productivity can be expressed as:

$$\frac{\text{marketing outputs}}{\text{marketing inputs}}$$

Sevin (1965, p. 9) has defined marketing productivity in more specific terms as:

" . . . the ratio of sales or net profits (effect produced) to marketing costs (energy expended) for a specific segment of the business.**"**

This equates productivity and profitability, which seems acceptable to some writers (e.g. Thomas, 1984, 1986), but not to others (e.g. Bucklin, 1978). The major objection to Sevin's definition is due to the effects of inflation, since sales, net profit and costs are all financial flows subject to changes in relative prices. For example, any increase in the value of sales from one period to another during inflationary times will be made up of two elements:

1 An increase due to a higher physical volume of sales
2 An increase due to higher prices.

If the value of the pound sterling were constant this would remove the problem, but since this is not the case it means that any financial data is necessarily suspect. The answer is to make some adjustments to ensure that measurement is made in *real* terms rather than simply in *monetary* terms – and to make these adjustments to both numerator and denominator in a way that allows for differential rates of inflation. Once measurement is made in real terms, it is possible to use the ratio that emerges as an index of efficiency. This can be used in relation to two types of question:

1 How much output was achieved for a given input?
2 How much input was required to achieve a given output?

These questions can be asked retrospectively (as above) or prospectively (for example, how much output should be achieved from a given mix and quantity of inputs?). The first relates to the notion of *technical efficiency*, whereby one seeks to maximize the output from a given input, whereas the second relates to the notion of *economic efficiency*, whereby one seeks to minimize the input costs for a given output.

Having specified in operational terms the numerator (output) and the denominator (input), and having eliminated the impacts of inflation, the result represents a measure of resource allocation (i.e. the pattern of inputs) and resource utilization (i.e. the generation of outputs), and these can be depicted via *ratio pyramids*, which we will look at later in this chapter. What we need to recognize at this point is that the array of ratios within a ratio pyramid can give us a vivid picture of the manner in which the organization has allocated its resources, and the efficiency with which those resources have been utilized. The next step, of course, is to consider how the allocation and its efficiency might be improved, which will mean changes in inputs and outputs. In turn, this requires an understanding of the causal relationships between inputs and outputs.

Let us be a little more specific and consider a particular productivity index from the distribution domain. The relevant output may be expressed in terms of the number of orders shipped during a given period, and the associated input may be the number of labour hours worked in the period. Thus:

$$\text{Productivity index} = \frac{\text{number of orders shipped}}{\text{number of labour hours worked}}$$

It will be apparent that this index relates one physical measure to another, hence there is no need to worry about inflationary distortions. However, had the numerator been expressed in terms of the *sales value* of orders shipped, and/or the denominator in terms of the *cost* of labour hours worked, it would have been necessary to adjust the figures to eliminate the effects of inflation – even though the index that results is a true ratio (i.e. it is not stated in terms of specific units).

It should also be apparent that any productivity index that is calculated is meaningless in isolation from some comparative figure. With what should an index be compared? There are a number of alternatives that will be examined later in more detail, but for the present we should be aware of the following:

➡ *Internal comparisons* can be made with figures from previous periods (which give a basis for trend analysis) or figures representing efficient or desired performance (which give a basis for budgetary control)
➡ *External comparisons* can be made with other organizations operating within the same markets.

The importance of external reference points cannot be overemphasized. As Christopher (1977) has stated:

"Business success is achieved where the client is, more than in our plants. External returns from the market are more appropriate measures than internal returns on investment. Success is more in manufacturing satisfied, repeat customers than in manufacturing products.**"**

3.10 The use of ratios

Whether one's primary interest is in the productivity of an organization as a whole, or in the productivity of a highly specific activity within an organization, ratios can be computed at a suitable level of aggregation. Their value lies in the relative measures (as opposed to absolute measures) on which they are based.

It is possible to calculate a great range of ratios, but a word of warning is needed to ensure that only useful ratios are calculated. Thus, for example, the ratio of

$$\frac{\text{advertising expenditure}}{\text{miles travelled by salesmen}}$$

within a given period is not likely to be very useful for at least two reasons:

1 It seeks to relate two input factors (rather than one input and one output)
2 The resulting ratio (of advertising expenditure per mile travelled by sales representatives) is not meaningful.

On the other hand, the ratio of

$$\frac{\text{incremental sales}}{\text{incremental promotion expenditure}}$$

relates one input to a relevant output and is potentially useful as a measure of promotional effectiveness. Discretion, therefore, is most important in choosing which ratios to calculate as a means towards assessing productivity within marketing.

Another warning needs to be given over the way in which ratios tend to average out any patterns in the underlying data. Consider the case of a seasonal business making 90 per cent of its sales in the first six months of every year and the remaining 10 per cent during the other six months. Average monthly sales over the whole year will differ significantly from the average monthly sales in each half year, so one must choose carefully the period over which one gathers data and the frequency with which one calculates ratios.

At an organizational level, the ultimate financial measure of short-term efficiency is the relationship between net profit and capital employed, typically expressed in percentage terms as the rate of return on capital employed or the rate of return on investment (ROI):

$$\text{ROI} = \frac{\text{net profit}}{\text{capital employed}} \times 100$$

This ratio shows the return (i.e. net output) that has been generated by the capital employed (i.e. input) during a given period of time. Problems exist in connection with the definitions, hence measurement, of both numerator and denominator, which highlights another note of caution in using ratios: always be sure to establish the definition of numerators and denominators. For example, is the net profit pre-tax or post-tax? Is the capital employed based on historic cost or replacement cost figures?

Given that profit is the residual once costs have been deducted from sales revenues, it is clear that ROI can be improved by either increasing sales revenues, decreasing costs or reducing capital employed – or by any combination of these. This gives us the basic idea underlying the ratio pyramid. At the apex is ROI, but this can be decomposed into two secondary ratios:

$$\text{Primary ratio: } \frac{\text{net profit}}{\text{capital employed}}$$

$$\text{Secondary ratios: } \frac{\text{net profit}}{\text{sales revenue}} \times \frac{\text{sales revenue}}{\text{capital employed}}$$

Each of the secondary ratios can help explain the ROI. The first is the profit rate on sales and the second is the capital turnover. Their interrelationship is such that:

$$\text{profit rate} \times \text{capital turnover} = \text{ROI}$$

Even the secondary ratios are highly aggregated, so it is necessary to proceed to measure tertiary ratios as one moves down the ratio pyramid using its structure as a diagnostic guide.

The general cause of any deviation in ROI from a target rate may be found by computing the profit ratio and the capital turnover ratio, but this is only a starting point. Before corrective action can be taken, a study of specific causes must be made, hence *tertiary ratios* need to be worked out.

Tertiary ratios are those that constitute the secondary ratios. The profit ratio reflects the relationship between the gross profit rate, the level of sales revenue, and operating costs (i.e. net profit + operating costs = gross profit), while the rate of capital turnover is affected by the level of sales revenue and the capital structure mix (of fixed and working capital, etc.). From these details it is a simple step to compute four tertiary ratios as follows (as shown in Figure 3.19):

1 $\dfrac{\text{Gross profit}}{\text{Sales revenue}}$

2 $\dfrac{\text{Sales revenue}}{\text{Operating costs}}$

3 $\dfrac{\text{Sales revenue}}{\text{Fixed assets}}$

4 $\dfrac{\text{Sales revenue}}{\text{Working capital}}$

Figure 3.19 also shows many other levels of the ratio pyramid that can be identified, and the process of decomposing broad ratios into their component parts can be continued further and further until the reasons for overall outcomes are known.

A variation on Figure 3.19, relating specifically to marketing, is provided by Figure 3.20.

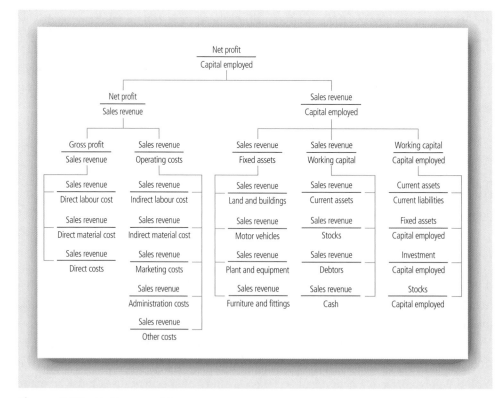

Figure 3.19 Ratio pyramid

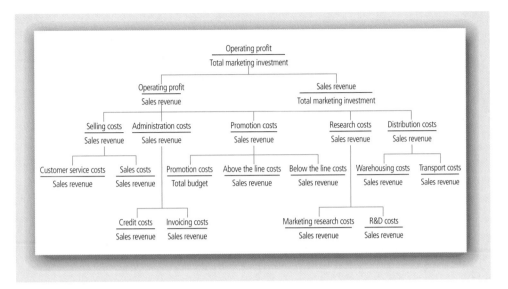

Figure 3.20 Marketing ratio pyramid

3.11 Analysing ratios and trends

It is possible to indicate trends in a company's performance over time by plotting successive ratios on a graph and thereby showing trends. Some important trends may only become apparent over a number of months (or even years), and ratio analysis can ensure that such trends do not develop unnoticed. Figure 3.21, for example, shows a continuing decline in a company's profitability. The causes for this trend may be found by breaking it down into its secondary components and so on through the ratio pyramid. These secondary trends – profit rate and capital turnover – are shown in Figure 3.22 and can be seen to be falling and rising respectively. Figure 3.23 then takes the former of these trends (falling profit rate) and decomposes it into a falling gross profit trend and a rising operating cost to sales revenue trend.

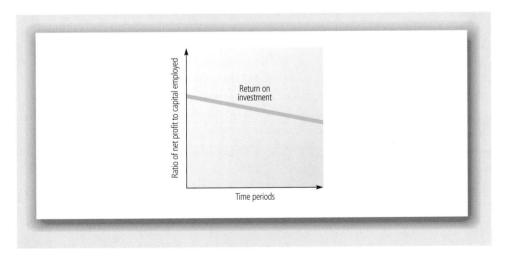

Figure 3.21 Primary trend

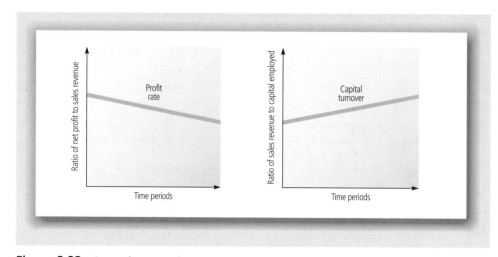

Figure 3.22 Secondary trends

It could prove necessary in a specific instance to work right through the ratio pyramid in plotting trends in order to isolate the causes of variations from the desired trend line in higher levels of the ratio hierarchy, and it may also be necessary to apply some imagination and common sense. This last-mentioned requirement can be illustrated in two ways. First, the declining ROI noted in Figure 3.21 may be thought, prima facie, to be due to the falling net profit to sales revenue trend shown in Figure 3.22, and so the rising capital turnover trend as in Figure 3.22 may be ignored. But ROI is clearly the combined outcome of a particular level of profit and a particular quantity of capital investment, so any variation in either will inevitably affect the ROI. Furthermore, a rising aggregate trend of capital turnover will almost certainly conceal many more compensating highs and lows in tertiary and subsequent levels of the ratio hierarchy. It follows that attention in the light of a falling ROI should not necessarily be focused

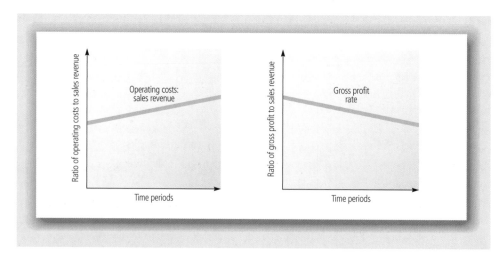

Figure 3.23 Tertiary trends

exclusively on the net profit trend, but some consideration should be given to the rate and trend of capital turnover.

The second common-sense point to note is that a rising operating cost to sales revenue trend, as in Figure 3.23, cannot be controlled until the specific items that cause the trend have been identified and appropriate steps taken to bring them under control. Of course, the extent to which the decline of the profit rate (a secondary trend) is caused by either of its constituent tertiary trends should be carefully established.

3.12 Ratios and interfirm comparison

In many industries – and especially in those in which operating methods, technology, product characteristics and general operating conditions are very similar – it is helpful to have comparative figures for one's own company and for other companies within the industry. From published accounts it is possible to see the primary, secondary and tertiary ratios (hence trends) of competing companies, but no reasons for divergences between one's own company's results and other companies' results can be discerned from such accounts due to a lack of detail relating to the lower part of the ratio pyramid (i.e. below the tertiary level) and so there is no guidance for future actions.

One major cause of divergence between the results of any two companies can be found in their use of differing accounting techniques and definitions. This will be seen, for example, if two companies purchase a similar asset each at the same point and one company chooses to depreciate the asset over four years while the other company chooses to take a 100 per cent depreciation allowance in the first year. It follows, therefore, that a meaningful comparison must be based on common definitions and usage. This can best be achieved (for comparative purposes) by a central organization and for this reason the Centre for Interfirm Comparison was set up.

While interfirm comparison figures are expressed in relation to quartiles and the median (i.e. if all results are ranked in descending order of size, the median is represented by the figure that comes halfway down, and the third quartile is three-quarters of the way down), the following example (OPQ Ltd) simplifies this by just giving the general approach to interfirm comparisons. The necessary steps in such an exercise are:

1 Ensure that the reports, etc., that are to be compared incorporate figures that have been prepared on a comparable basis
2 Compute the required ratios, percentages and key totals from submitted reports
3 Compare the results of each company with the aggregate results
4 Introduce intangible or qualitative factors that may aid in interpreting the results of each individual company in the light of the whole picture
5 Examine the numerator, denominator and lower ratios in instances where a ratio differs significantly from the external standard (or average, median or whatever)
6 Determine the adjustment (if any) that is required to bring a given company's divergent ratio into line with the aggregate norm.

OPQ Ltd: ratio analysis

The following is a simple example of interfirm comparison. Figure 3.24 shows the ratios of OPQ Ltd, a firm in a light engineering industry, for the two years 2002 and 2003.

	Ratio	Unit	2002	2003
1	$\dfrac{\text{Operating profit}}{\text{Assets employed}}$	%	8.25	10.0
2	$\dfrac{\text{Operating profit}}{\text{Sales revenue}}$	%	5.5	6.1
3	$\dfrac{\text{Sales revenue}}{\text{Assets employed}}$	times	1.5	1.65
3a	$\dfrac{\text{Assets employed}}{\text{Average daily sales revenue}}$	days*	249	222
4	$\dfrac{\text{Production cost of sales}}{\text{Sales revenue}}$	%	71.0	70.4
5	$\dfrac{\text{Distribution and marketing costs}}{\text{Sales revenue}}$	%	17.7	17.7
6	$\dfrac{\text{General and administrative costs}}{\text{Sales revenue}}$	%	5.8	5.8
7	$\dfrac{\text{Current assets}}{\text{Average daily sales revenue}}$	days*	215	188
8	$\dfrac{\text{Fixed assets}}{\text{Average daily sales revenue}}$	days*	34	34
9	$\dfrac{\text{Material stocks}}{\text{Average daily sales revenue}}$	days*	49	45
10	$\dfrac{\text{Work-in-progress}}{\text{Average daily sales revenue}}$	days*	53	46
11	$\dfrac{\text{Finished stocks}}{\text{Average daily sales revenue}}$	days*	52	39
12	$\dfrac{\text{Debtors}}{\text{Average daily sales revenue}}$	days*	61	54

* Days required to turn the asset item over once.

Figure 3.24 OPQ's own figures

This looks like a success story. Profit on assets employed has gone up from 8.25 to 10 per cent due to an increase in the firm's profit on sales (Ratio 2) and the better use it seems to have made of its assets (Ratios 3 and 3a). The higher profit on sales seems to have been achieved through operational improvements, which results in a lower ratio

Ratio		Firm				
		A	B	C	D	E
1	$\dfrac{\text{Operating profit}}{\text{Assets employed}}$	%	18.0	14.3	10.0	7.9	4.0
2	$\dfrac{\text{Operating profit}}{\text{Sales revenue}}$	%	15.0	13.1	6.1	8.1	2.0
3	$\dfrac{\text{Sales revenue}}{\text{Assets employed}}$	times	1.20	1.09	1.65	0.98	2.0
3a	$\dfrac{\text{Assets employed}}{\text{Average daily sales revenue}}$	days*	304	335	222	372	182
4	$\dfrac{\text{Production cost of sales}}{\text{Sales revenue}}$	%	73.0	69.4	70.4	72.5	79.0
5	$\dfrac{\text{Distribution and marketing costs}}{\text{Sales revenue}}$	%	8.0	13.1	17.7	13.7	15.0
6	$\dfrac{\text{General and administrative costs}}{\text{Sales revenue}}$	%	4.0	4.4	5.8	5.7	4.0
7	$\dfrac{\text{Current assets}}{\text{Average daily sales revenue}}$	days*	213	219	188	288	129
8	$\dfrac{\text{Fixed assets}}{\text{Average daily sales revenue}}$	days*	91	116	34	84	53
9	$\dfrac{\text{Material stocks}}{\text{Average daily sales revenue}}$	days*	45	43	45	47	29
10	$\dfrac{\text{Work-in-progress}}{\text{Average daily sales revenue}}$	days*	51	47	46	60	52
11	$\dfrac{\text{Finished stocks}}{\text{Average daily sales revenue}}$	days*	71	63	39	94	22
12	$\dfrac{\text{Debtors}}{\text{Average daily sales revenue}}$	days*	36	84	54	18	26

* Days required to turn the asset item over once.

Figure 3.25 The interfirm comparison

of cost of production (Ratio 4). The firm's faster turnover of assets (Ratio 3) is due mainly to a faster turnover of current assets (Ratio 7), and this in turn is due to accelerated turnovers of material stocks (Ratio 9), work in progress (Ratio 10), finished stock (Ratio 11) and debtors (Ratio 12).

The firm's illusion of success was shattered when it compared its ratios with those of other light engineering firms of its type. Figure 3.25 is an extract from the results – it gives the figures of only five of the twenty-two participating firms. OPQ Ltd's figures are shown under letter C.

In this year, the firm's operating profit on assets employed is well below that of two other firms, and this appears to be due to its profit on sales (Ratio 2) being relatively low. This in turn is mainly due to the firm's high distribution and marketing expenses (Ratio 5). In the actual comparison further ratios were given, helping Firm C to establish to what extent its higher Ratio 5 was due to higher costs of distribution and warehousing, higher costs of advertising and sales promotion, or higher costs of other selling activities (e.g. cost of sales personnel).

3.13 A strategic approach

A strategic-oriented approach to answering the question 'Where are we now?' can be provided from the PIMS database. PIMS stands for Profit Impact of Market Strategy and refers to an objective approach to analysing corporate performance using a unique database. Some 3000 strategic business units (SBUs) have contributed over 20 000 years' experience to this database.

PIMS research on what drives business profits has become more widely known over the last 25 years as more evidence has become available. We know that there is, in general, a range of factors which we can quantify and relate to margins or to return on capital employed (ROCE). But does the evidence show that these factors work in specific industries – do they actually explain the spread which dwarfs differences between industries?

PIMS results from examining real profits of real businesses suggest that the determinants of business performance can be grouped into four categories (see Figure 3.26):

1 Market attractiveness
2 Competitive strength
3 Value-added structure
4 People and organization.

The first category contains factors in the business situation which affect its performance. Customer bargaining power, market complexity, market growth and innovation are obvious examples.

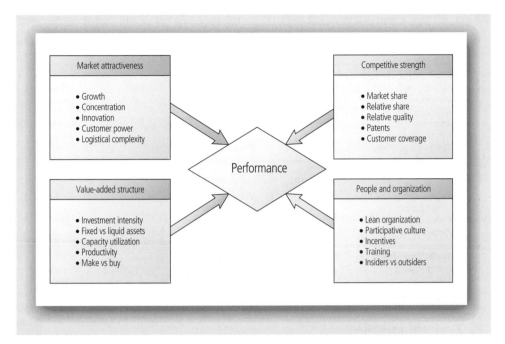

Figure 3.26 PIMS can quantify how strategic factors drive performance

The second group describes how a business differs from its competitors in its market. Share position, customer preference relative to competitors' offerings, market coverage and product range all have an effect.

The third category quantifies the way a business converts inputs into outputs; it includes investment intensity, fixed/working capital split, employee productivity, capacity use and vertical integration.

People and organization, an area in which PIMS has only recently built up comparable data, includes managers' attitudes, skill and training mix, personnel policies and incentives.

Figure 3.27 shows the impact of these factors on business profits tracked across PIMS' 3000 businesses. Some factors are more important than others, but each has an influence that is both measurable and explainable. The positioning of a business on the chart can be described as its 'profile'.

To test whether the profile of a business can explain its profits, irrespective of the industry in which it operates, PIMS looked at the performance of businesses with 'weak' and 'strong' profiles in each of five sectors. Weak and strong profiles were picked in terms of position on each of the fifteen variables in Figure 3.28. Factors related to people and organization were omitted from the exercise because the available sample at the time was not large enough to examine them by sector.

The results are startling! In every industry sector where there were enough observations to test, a business with a weak profit makes a 6 per cent return on sales (ROS) or 10 per cent return on capital employed (ROCE) over a four-year period. In contrast,

Factor	–	Effect on ROCE	+
Market attractiveness			
Market growth	Low		High
Innovation	Zero, very high		Moderate
R&D spend	Zero, very high		Moderate
Marketing spend	High		Low
Contract size	Large		Small
Customer complexity	Complex		Simple
Competitive strength			
Relative share	Low		High
Relative quality	Worse		Better
Differentiation	Commodity		Differentiated
Customer spread	Narrow		Broader
Product range	Narrow		Broader
Value-added structure			
Investment/sales	High		Low
Capacity use	Low		High
Vertical integration	Low		High
Employee productivity	Low		High
People and organization			
Attitudes	Restrictive		Open
Training	Little		Substantial
Incentives	Weak		Strong

Figure 3.27 Impact of strategic factors on performance (source: PIMS database)

a strong-profile business makes 11 per cent ROS or 30 per cent ROCE. The gap in profit performance between strong and weak businesses in each sector is bigger than the standard deviation in each group. So the profile does a better job of explaining differences in performance than the industry each business is in. The profile represents the strategic logic that shapes the real competitive choices facing managers in each business (see Figure 3.29).

These new results are critically important. Earlier studies have shown how margins are related to business characteristics, but this is the first time that businesses in different industries with similar profiles have been shown to have more in common when it comes to performance than businesses in the same industry with different profiles.

PIMS also tested the relationships between margins and profile variables in various subsectors in the chemical industry, which is particularly well represented in the PIMS database. In each case the determinants included in the profile have a powerful and consistent influence on profits. The effect of each determinant is similar irrespective of the product category. This is true even for what is probably the most subjective of the variables that PIMS measures: relative quality.

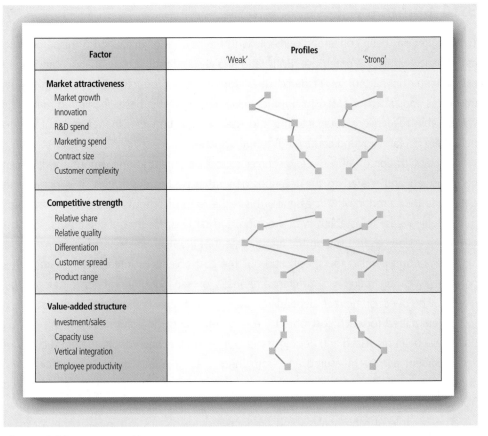

Figure 3.28 PIMS profiles 1

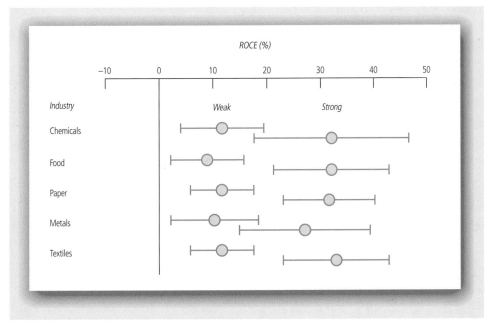

Figure 3.29 PIMS profiles 2 (source: PIMS database)

3.14 Summary

This chapter has been concerned primarily with the pattern of utilization of resources and its efficiency within the enterprise. Both ratio analysis and productivity analysis can help in establishing the pattern of resource utilization and its productivity by relating inputs (resources consumed or costs) to outputs (revenue). From this base, marketing managers will be able to derive greater insights into relationships between inputs and outputs to help them in planning (and controlling) future activities.

If the utilization of 'effort' (i.e. resources) across an organization's various activities can be measured and related to the revenues generated by those activities, it is possible to determine their productivity. In essence, this is the ratio of outputs/inputs. While the outputs are fairly easy to establish with precision, the same is not true of the inputs, so most of the discussion has focused on the measurement of inputs.

The starting point is the specification of the cost objects of interest, for example the productivity of operating via different channels, or serving different customer groups. Costs will be *direct* or *indirect*, depending upon the cost objects of interest. Full cost needs to be determined for each cost object (i.e. segment), and the ways in which this can be done have been discussed and demonstrated. Once this has been done, the productivity of each segment can be measured and from these measurements questions can be raised about the adequacy of each segment's productivity. For example, can effort be reallocated from Segment A to Segment B to improve these segments' productivity?

The key role of ratio analysis and productivity analysis lies in the basis they give for raising questions in the light of the existing state of play. Such techniques cannot generate answers as to what to do next.

A pyramid of marketing ratios was constructed to show the pattern of ratios (reflecting resource utilization and productivity) across relevant activities in a way that highlights interdependencies in an overall context.

Finally, the strategic approach provided by PIMS was outlined, which adds extra dimensions to the analysis of 'Where are we now?'

Chapter 4

Market and environmental analysis

4.1 Learning objectives

When you have read this chapter you should be able to understand:

(a) why a regular and detailed analysis of the organization's environment is important;
(b) the key elements of the environment;
(c) how firms go about analysing the environment;
(d) how environmental factors are changing;
(e) the dimensions of environmental scanning systems.

4.2 Introduction: the changing business environment (or the new marketing reality)

If there is a single issue or theme which now links all types and sizes of organization, it is that of the far faster pace of environmental change and the consequently greater degree of environmental uncertainty than was typically the case even a few years ago. This change and uncertainty has been manifested in a wide variety of ways, and has led to a series of environmental pressures and challenges with which managers need to come to terms: a number of these are illustrated in Figure 4.1. Although the fourteen points identified in Figure 4.1 are not intended either as a complete or a definitive list of the sorts of challenges that managers now face, they go some way towards illustrating the nature of the ways in which organizational environments are changing and how the pressures upon managers are increasing. They also illustrate the point made in Chapter 1 that strategic marketing planning is an essentially iterative process. It is iterative for a number of reasons, the most significant of which being that, as the company's external environment changes, so opportunities and threats emerge and disappear only to re-emerge perhaps in a modified form at a later stage. Because of this, the marketing planner needs to recognize the fundamental necessity both for an environmental monitoring process that is capable of identifying in advance any possible opportunities and threats, and for a planning system and organizational structure that is capable of quite possibly radical change to reflect the environment so that the effects of threats are minimized and that opportunities are seized.

In essence, therefore, in formulating the marketing plan, the planner is concerned with matching the *capabilities of the organization* with the *demands of the environment*. In doing this, the planner is faced with a difficult problem, since what we typically refer to as the environment encapsulates a wide variety of influences. The difficulty lies, therefore, in coming to terms with this diversity in such a way that it contributes to effective decision-making, since it is this that has a direct influence

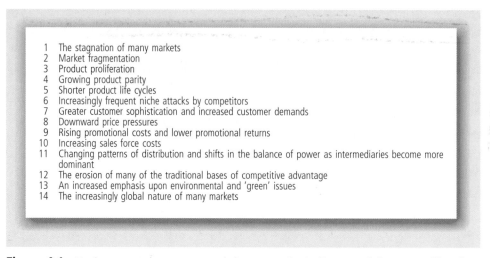

1 The stagnation of many markets
2 Market fragmentation
3 Product proliferation
4 Growing product parity
5 Shorter product life cycles
6 Increasingly frequent niche attacks by competitors
7 Greater customer sophistication and increased customer demands
8 Downward price pressures
9 Rising promotional costs and lower promotional returns
10 Increasing sales force costs
11 Changing patterns of distribution and shifts in the balance of power as intermediaries become more dominant
12 The erosion of many of the traditional bases of competitive advantage
13 An increased emphasis upon environmental and 'green' issues
14 The increasingly global nature of many markets

Figure 4.1 Environmental pressures and the strategic challenges of the new millennium

upon performance. This difficulty in coping with the environment can be viewed under two headings:

1 Understanding the *extent* to which the environment affects strategy
2 Understanding the ways in which environmental pressures can be *related* to the capabilities of the organization.

A possible danger that has been highlighted by several commentators is that of adopting a 'balance sheet' approach to environmental analysis – simply listing all possible environmental influences and then categorizing each as either an opportunity or a threat. If environmental analysis is limited to this alone, the strategist is left with far too broad and unsophisticated a picture of what really affects the organization. In addition, such an approach is likely to lead to the organization responding in a fragmented way rather than in a more integrated and strategic fashion.

This chapter therefore focuses on the various elements of the marketing environment with a view to illustrating the nature of their interaction and, subsequently, their effect on the organization. Against this background, we then move on to consider the ways in which an effective environmental monitoring process can best be developed and then, subsequently, how environmental forces are capable of determining the nature of the strategy pursued. We begin, however, by examining an approach to analysing the environment.

4.3 Analysing the environment

"When the rate of change inside the company is exceeded by the rate of change outside the company, the end is near."

Jack Welch, former Chief Executive Officer, General Electric

No organization exists in a vacuum. Marketing strategy must therefore develop out of a detailed understanding of the environment. Given this, the planner must:

➡ Know *what* to look for
➡ Know *how* to look
➡ Understand *what* he or she sees
➡ Develop the strategy and plan that takes account of this knowledge and understanding.

In analysing the environment, Johnson and Scholes (1988, p. 54) argue for a stepwise approach. This involves an initial audit of general environmental influences, followed by a sreies of increasingly tightly-focused stages that are designed to provide the planner with an understanding of the *key opportunities and threats* as a prelude to identifying the organization's *strategic position*. This process, which is illustrated in Figure 4.2, consists of five stages:

1 The starting point in this process is the *general audit of environmental influences*. The purpose of this is to identify the types of environmental factors that have influenced the organization's development and previous performance, and to arrive at an initial conclusion of the likely important influences in the future.

2 From here the strategist moves to an *assessment of the nature of the environment* and the degree of uncertainty and change that is likely to exist. If, from this, the strategist concludes that the environment is relatively static, then historical analysis is likely to

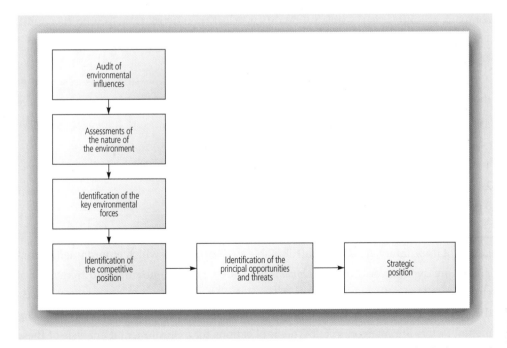

Figure 4.2 The five stages of environmental analysis (source: Johnson and Scholes, 1988)

prove useful. If, by contrast, the environment shows signs of instability, then a stronger emphasis upon the future is needed.

3 The third phase then involves focusing upon *specific environmental factors* such as the nature and structure of the market.

4 This in turn leads to an analysis of the firm's *competitive position*. A detailed discussion of how this can be done appears in Chapter 6. In essence, however, this involves a combination of *strategic group analysis* in which competitors are mapped in terms of their similarities, dissimilarities, their capabilities and the strategies they follow, and *market share analysis* to highlight their relative degrees of market power.

5 This information is then used as the basis for identifying *in detail* how environmental forces are likely to affect the organization and, in particular, the *opportunities and threats* that are likely to exist. This in turn provides the basis for a detailed understanding of the organization's strategic position and the degree to which there is match between strategy, structure and environment.

At this point we will examine the first three stages of this stepwise approach; the fourth stage is discussed at the end of this chapter, while the fifth stage was covered in some detail in Chapter 2.

Referring back to Figure 4.2, it can be seen that the first step in the process involves the *general audit of environmental influences*. The starting point for this involves the strategist in developing a list of those factors which are likely to have an impact on the organization and which will therefore need further analysis. In doing this, the purpose is to develop a detailed understanding of what environmental factors have influenced the organization in the past, and the degree to which any changes that are taking place are likely to increase or reduce in impact. Although quite obviously such a list has to be company specific, it is possible to identify a broad framework to help with this audit. This framework, which is typically referred to as PEST (Political, Economic, Social and Technological) analysis, is illustrated in Figure 4.3.

Against this background, the strategist can then move to an assessment of the *nature of the environment*. In essence, this is concerned with answering three questions:

1 How uncertain is the environment?
2 What are the sources of this uncertainty?
3 How should this uncertainty be dealt with?

Levels of uncertainty are directly attributable to the extent to which environmental conditions are dynamic or complex. *Dynamism* is due largely to the rates and frequency of change, while *complexity* is the result either of the diversity of environmental influences, the amount of knowledge required to cope with them, or the extent to which environmental factors are interconnected. The implications for environmental analysis of these different types of environmental condition are illustrated in Figure 4.4.

POLITICAL/LEGAL FACTORS
Political and legal structures
Political alliances
Legislative structures
Monopoly restrictions
Political and government stability
Political orientations
Taxation policies
Employment legislation
Foreign trade regulations
Environmental protection legislation
Pressure groups
Trades union power

ECONOMIC FACTORS
Business cycles
Money supply
Inflation rates
Investment levels
Unemployment
Energy costs
GNP trends
Patterns of ownership
The nature and bases of competition domestically and internationally
Trading blocks

SOCIO-CULTURAL FACTORS
Demographics
Lifestyles
Social mobility
Educational levels
Attitudes
Consumerism
Behaviour and behaviour patterns
Zeitgeists

TECHNOLOGICAL FACTORS
Levels and focuses of government and industrial R&D expenditure
Speed of technology transfer
Product life cycles
Joint ventures
Technological shifts
The direction of technological transfer
The (changing) costs of technology

Figure 4.3   The PEST framework for environmental auditing

	Conditions		
	Simple/static	**Dynamic**	**Complex**
Aims	To achieve thorough (historical) understanding of the environment	To understand the future rather than simply relying on past experiences	The reduction of complexity Greater structural understanding
Methods	Analysis of past influences and their effect on organizational performance Identification of key forces Analysis of existing relationships	Managers' sensitivity to change Scenario planning Contingency planning Sensitivity planning	Specialist attention to elements of complexity Model building
Dangers	The sudden emergence of unpredicted change Mechanistic organizational structures Lack of skills Focus on existing relationships Lack of willingness to accept that conditions are changing Stereotyped responses	Management myopia Mechanistic organizational structures Lack of skills Inappropriate forecasting Failure to recognize significant new players	Unsuitable organizational structure or control systems Inappropriate reactions Inappropriate focuses Over-reaction

Figure 4.4   Handling different environmental conditions (adapted from Johnson and Scholes, 1988)

Environment types

The question of *how* to categorize environments has been discussed in some detail by Miles (1980, Chapter 9), who developed a framework for a comprehensive and systematic analysis of environment types. The model calls for a 'measurement' response by those performing the analysis and is based upon the answers to six questions:

1 How complex is the environment? (Complexity is a measurement of the number of different environmental forces which have an impact, or potential impact, upon the organization.)
2 How routine and standardized are organizational interactions with elements of the environment?
3 How interconnected and how remote, initially, are the significant environmental variables?
4 How dynamic and how unpredictable are the changes taking place around the organization?
5 How receptive is management to the ways in which environmental pressures adversely affect the input and output processes of the organization?
6 How high is flexibility of choice and to what extent is the organization constrained from moving into new areas?

Using this checklist of questions, the strategist should then be able to establish the organization's environmental position on a number of continua:

Simple	↔	Complex
Routine	↔	Non-routine
Unconnected	↔	Interconnected
Proximate	↔	Remote
Static	↔	Dynamic
Predictable	↔	Unpredictable
High input receptivity	↔	Low input receptivity
High output receptivity	↔	Low output receptivity
High domain choice flexibility	↔	Low domain choice flexibility

Taken together, these elements can be incorporated into the matrix shown in Figure 4.5.

In turn, changes taking place within the environment can be plotted in Figure 4.6. Here, the two key dimensions are the immediacy of an event taking place and then its likely impact upon the organization.

The implications of environmental change

Undoubtedly one of the major problems faced by managers comes when the organization, having operated for some time in a largely predictable environment, is faced with having to come to terms with a far more complex, uncertain and possibly malevolent

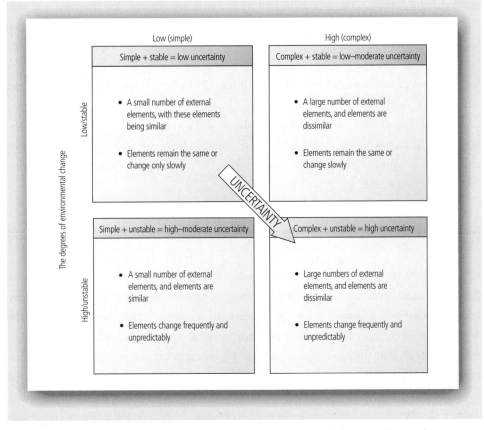

Figure 4.5 Degrees of environmental complexity (adapted from Daft, 1998)

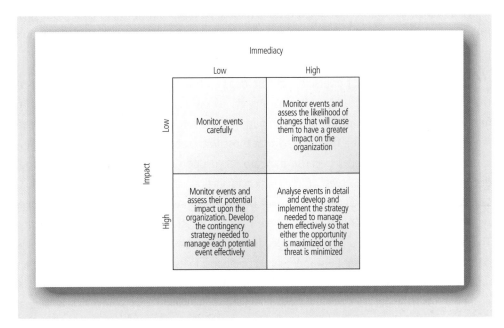

Figure 4.6 Issues of immediacy and impact

environment. Among those who have had to do this in recent years are the major clearing banks, which have been faced with a very different type of competition, initially from telephone banking and then, subsequently, from Internet banking. Equally, Hoover has had to come to terms with a very clever, fast-moving and unpredictable competitor in the fom of Dyson. Elsewhere, BA was challenged initially by Virgin and then by the low-cost airlines such as Ryanair.

The significance of changes such as these needs to be seen in terms of *how* the organization monitors the environment and, subsequently, *how* it *responds*. Quite obviously, what is appropriate to a static environment is not suited to either a dynamic or a complex environment.

Static, dynamic and complex environments

With regard to the question of how the organization monitors the environment, evidence suggests that, in *broadly static conditions*, straightforward environmental scanning is likely to be a useful and generally adequate process. In a *dynamic environment*, however, the organization is typically faced with major change in the areas of technology and markets, with the result that decisions can no longer be based upon the assumption that what broadly has happened in the past will continue in the future. As a consequence of this, the focus needs to be upon the future with a far greater degree of inspirational interpretation. Among the techniques that have been used to do this is Delphic forecasting. The results are then used as the basis for building alternative scenarios.

This idea of alternative futures can then be used to identify the likely impact upon consumers, suppliers, competitors, government, the financial institutions, their probable responses, and subsequently their impact upon the organization.

For organizations faced with a *complex* environment, many of the issues and problems to which reference has been made are exacerbated. In discussing how to cope with this, Johnson and Scholes (1988, p. 61) suggest that there are organizational and information processing approaches:

*"*Complexity as a result of diversity might be dealt with by ensuring that different parts of the organization responsible for different aspects of diversity are separate and given the resources and authority to handle their own part of the environment. Where high knowledge requirements are important it may also be that those with specialist knowledge in the organization become very powerful because they are relied upon, not only to make operational decisions, but are trusted to present information in such a way that a sensible strategic decision can be made: or indeed they themselves become responsible for the strategic decisions. As an information processing approach there may be an attempt to model the complexity. This may be done through a financial model, for example, which seeks to simulate the effects on an organization of different environmental conditions. In its extreme form there may be an attempt to model the environment itself. The Treasury Office draws on a model of the UK economy, for example. However, for most organizations facing complexity, organizational responses are probably more common than extensive model building.*"*

Regardless, however, of the degree of complexity in the environment, there appear to be certain common strands in the ways in which managers cope with their environments. The most significant of these is that managers develop over time what can loosely be referred to as the accepted wisdom of the industry and the workable solutions to the various situations that are likely to emerge. One consequence of this is that the major competitive threats to organizations often come from companies *outside* the industry, which, on entering the market, adopt a strategy that falls outside this area of standardized expectation, allowing for the conventional wisdom of response to change to be adopted.

A framework for analysing the environment is shown in Figure 4.7. Here, the planner begins by identifying a series of basic beliefs (these are the environmental changes and conditions that the planner believes fundamentally will characterize the market over the next 12, 24 and 36 months). Having identified these, the planner then takes each in turn and identifies the implications for the business as a whole and/or the brand. The final stage involves taking each of the implications and deciding how best they can be managed; the test here is that, if action is not taken, then either a significant opportunity will be missed or the organization will be hit hard by something within the environment.

Market change and the redefinition of the marketing mix : the role of partnerships (the fifth P of marketing)

As markets have become more competitive and customers far more demanding, many of the traditional bases of competitive advantage have, as we discuss on p. 6, been eroded. The implications of this for marketing planning have been seen by the way in which previously powerful elements of the marketing mix (such as the product, price and place) have become increasingly more standardized or commoditized across markets and, as a result, no longer act as a meaningful base for differentiation. In an attempt to overcome this, many marketing planners have shifted the focus for

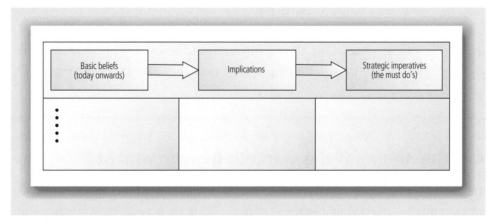

Figure 4.7 From basic beliefs to 'must do's'

differentiation away from the 'hard' elements of the mix (the product, price, place and promotion) to the 'softer' elements of people, physical evidence and process management (see pp. 6–7).

At the same time, in many particularly competitive markets, a further P – that of partnerships – has been added to the mix. The reason for this is that the rules of competition, insofar as they have ever existed, have for numerous organizations changed dramatically, with the result that marketing planners are no longer fighting on clearly delineated grounds where the competitor is obvious. In an attempt to come to terms with this, there has been an explosion in the number of strategic alliances that can cut across geographies and technologies. Although these alliances are not always necessarily comfortable, they are typically driven by expediency and represent an attempt either to reduce the costs of market entry, exploit economies of scale and scope, gain access to difficult markets, create new market knowledge, or leverage technological shifts. Although alliances are by no means new, the major change that took place at the end of the twentieth century and beginning of the twenty-first was the number and scale of these. The rationale in most cases is straightforward and relates to the ways in which alliances can cut the costs of market entry, exploit economies of scale and scope, either difficult and/or highly regulated markets, or provide access to new technologies and knowledge.

Amongst the industries in which this strategy has been pursued – with varying degrees of success – are cars and high technology. In the case of IBM, for example, in 1993 only 5 per cent of the firm's sales outside personal computers came from alliances. By 2001, the number of alliances had increased to almost 100 000 and contributed almost one-third of its turnover, boosting this by $10 billion (£6.3 billion). The significance of alliances as a basis for advantage has also been highlighted by the consultancy Ernst & Young, which, in an investigation of online retailing across twelve countries, found that 65 per cent of non-US and 75 per cent of US companies operated with some form of alliance. The driving force for this, the report argued, is the intensification of competition, which makes it impossible for firms to be managed properly unless alliances are used to leverage strengths in areas such as marketing, supply chain management and finance.

The implications for the marketing planner are significant and can be seen most obviously in the way in which alliances demand a greater degree of flexibility in thinking – both in terms of the alliances that need to be entered into and managed, and also in the ability to withdraw from them once they are no longer strategically valuable.

4.4 The nature of the marketing environment

The marketing environment has been defined in a variety of ways. Churchman (1968), for example, has referred to it in terms of factors that are outside the system's control but determine, in part at least, how the system performs. For our purposes, however, the definition that we will work with is that an organization's marketing environment is made up of those forces that lie outside the organization and that exert some degree of influence upon the ways in which marketing management develops relationship with the firm's target markets.

Within the environment there are two distinct components: the *micro-environment* and the *macro-environment*. These are illustrated in Figure 4.8.

The *micro-environment* is made up of those elements that are closest to the company and that exert the greatest and most direct influence over its ability to deal with its markets. This includes the organization itself, its suppliers, its distribution network, customers, competitors and the public at large. The *macro-environment* consists of the rather broader set of forces that have a bearing upon the company, including economic, demographic, technological, political, legal, social and cultural factors. Together, these elements of the environment combine to form what we can loosely refer to as the non-controllable elements of marketing, which in many ways act as a series of constraints on the parameters within which the marketing planner is required to operate.

In labelling these elements as non-controllable, the reader should recognize that, in some cases at least, the marketing planner may well adopt a highly proactive stance in an attempt to alter the nature and impact of the environment upon the organization – for example, by attempting a merger or takeover in order to minimize a competitive threat. Equally, a large organization may well lobby the government in order to have legislation developed or changed so that the company benefits in some way. The car, foodstuffs, cigarette and brewing industries, for example, all have powerful lobby groups that attempt to exert a degree of influence over government to ensure that any legislation is beneficial (or at least not harmful) to their interests. In other cases, however, the organization may adopt a rather more reactive stance and simply view the environment as something that has to be lived with and responded to.

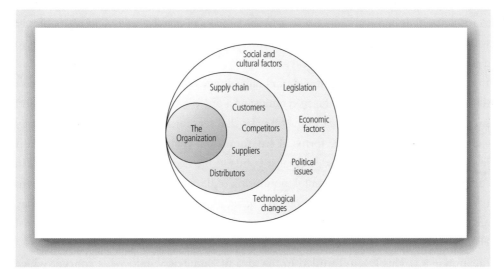

Figure 4.8   The organization's marketing environment

Regardless of which approach an organization adopts, it needs to be recognized that the environment is a significant determinant both of strategy and organizational performance, something which has been reflected in the work of a considerable number of writers, including Baker (1985, p. 85), who has described it as 'the ultimate constraint upon the firm's strategy'; Drucker (1969), who referred to the environment of the 1960s and 1970s as the 'age of discontinuity'; and Toffler (1970, p. 28), who, in looking ahead, referred to it as a time of 'future shock'. In making these comments, each author was giving recognition to the volatility, and indeed the potential malevolence, of environmental factors. As an example of this, the early 1970s witnessed an oil price crisis, which in turn precipitated an economic upheaval throughout the world. This was reflected for some considerable time in higher levels of unemployment, interest rates, the development of new economic thinking and, perhaps most importantly, levels of business confidence. More recently, of course, the bombing of the World Trade Center in September 2001 had major economic, political and social implications.

In the case of the oil crisis, although this was without doubt a significant environmental upset, its impact was obviously felt far more directly by some organizations than others. It should therefore be remembered that what is a key environmental issue for one organization is not necessarily a key environmental issue for another. For a multinational corporation, for example, the major areas of concern are likely to be government relations, spheres of influence and the various political complexions throughout the world. For a retailer, the more *directly* important environmental influences are likely to be customer tastes and behaviour, and interest rates, while for a manufacturer in the high-technology fields it is issues of technological development and speeds of obsolescence that are important.

The question of the extent to which environmental change, particularly of something as significant as the oil crisis, can be anticipated by business organizations has been the subject of considerable discussion and, in the case of the oil crisis, has led to both a 'yes' and a 'no' answer. 'Yes' in the sense that the techniques of environmental analysis undoubtedly existed at the time, but 'no' in that few people were willing, or indeed able, to recognize that one economic era was in the process of coming to an end, that another was about to start, and that balances of power throughout the world were beginning to change in a number of significant ways.

Although a number of commentators have suggested that environmental change of this magnitude is so rare as to be seen almost as a one-off, other writers' views differ and suggest that it is simply the *scale* of the oil crisis that separates it from the more commonly experienced and less dramatic forms of environmental change. The lesson to be learned in either case is straightforward, in that it points to the need for companies to engage in careful, continuous and fundamental monitoring of the environment with a view to identifying *potential* threats before they become *actual* threats, and opportunities before they are missed. In the absence of this, the organization runs the risk of falling victim to what Handy (1994, pp. 7–8) refers to as the 'boiled frog syndrome', which is discussed in Illustration 4.1. This has in turn led to the idea of 'strategic windows', a concept which has been discussed by Abell and Hammond (1979, p. 63).

Illustration 4.1 The parable of the boiled frog

All organizations are faced with a series of environmental changes and challenges. The principal difference between the effective and the ineffective organization is how well it responds, something that was encapsulated several years ago in one of the most popular of management fables, the parable of the boiled frog. What is now referred to as 'the boiled frog syndrome' is based on the idea that, if you drop a frog into a pan of hot water, it leaps out. If, however, you put a frog into a pan of lukewarm water and turn the heat up very slowly, it sits there quite happily not noticing the change in the water's temperature. The frog, of course, eventually dies.

The parallels with the management and development of any organization are – or should be – obvious. Faced with sudden and dramatic environmental change, the need for a response is obvious. Faced with a much slower pace of change, the pressures to respond are far less (this is the 'we are doing reasonably well and can think about doing something else at some time in the future' phenomenon), with the result that the organization becomes increasingly distant from the *real* demands of its customers and other stakeholders. Given this, think seriously about whether you are one of the frogs that is sitting quite happily in a pan of increasingly hot water. If so, why, what are the possible consequences and what, if anything, are you going to do about it?

Strategic windows

The term *strategic window* is used to describe the fact that there are often only limited periods when the 'fit' between the 'key requirements' of a market and the particular competences of a firm competing in that market is at an optimum. Investment in a product line or market area has to be timed to coincide with periods in which a strategic window is open, i.e. where a close fit exists. Disinvestment should be considered if, during the course of the market's evolution, changes in market requirements outstrip the firm's capability to adapt itself to the new circumstances.

The strategic window concept can be useful to incumbent competitors as well as to would-be entrants into a market. For the former, it provides a way of relating future strategic moves to market evolution and of assessing how resources should be allocated to existing activities. For the latter, it provides a framework for diversification and new entry.

The consequences of failing to identify strategic windows can, of course, be significant and are typically manifested in terms of a loss of opportunity, market share or competitive advantage. This was illustrated by the Swiss watch industry in the 1970s and 1980s, when it failed to recognize the significance of new, low-price market segments, new quartz technology, and a new, low-cost and aggressive form of competition from Japan and, subsequently, Hong Kong. The net effect of this was that the Swiss saw their share of the world watch industry drop from 80 per cent in 1948 to just 13 per cent in 1985; this is discussed in detail in Illustration 4.2.

That they have subsequently fought back with the Swatch watch is, in one sense at least, incidental. Perhaps the more important lesson to be learned from their experience is that a different approach to environmental monitoring might well have led to the industry avoiding the traumas that it undoubtedly faced.

Illustration 4.2 The Swiss watch industry and the consequences of new (and unexpected) competition

In 1948 the Swiss watch industry accounted for 80 per cent of all watches sold in the world. By 1985 its share of the market had dropped to just 13 per cent, with the Japanese, a relatively new entrant to the market, having taken over as market leader.

This surprising and remarkably rapid change in the market's structure was attributable to several factors, the most important of which can be identifed as:

1 A failure on the part of the Swiss to come to terms with the explosive growth in the less expensive sector of the market.
2 The speed of the switch away from mechanical (i.e. spring-powered) watches to the far more accurate quartz-powered watches. Whereas 98 per cent of all watches and movements produced in 1974 were mechanical and only 2 per cent were quartz, in 1984 the breakdown was 24 per cent mechanical and 76 per cent quartz. Ironically, in the light of the source and the technological base of the attack upon the Swiss watch industry, the quartz electronic watch was invented in Switzerland in 1968, but first marketed in the USA.
3 A failure to come to terms with the increasing Asian penetration of the large and lucrative American market. While Switzerland's estimated contribution to American import volume decreased from 99 per cent in 1950 to 4 per cent in 1984,

the percentage of import volume from Asia increased from 10 per cent in 1970 to 92 per cent in 1984.

The Japanese and subsequently the Hong Kong manufacturers owed their success to a combination of aggressive marketing, a high degree of production concentration and, perhaps most importantly, a relatively complacent competitor who was taken by surprise by the sudden inroads made by the Japanese and subsequently found it difficult to retaliate. With regard to the first two points, the nature of the challenge has been summed up in the following way.

The Japanese industry was highly concentrated, with the two major firms (Hattori Seiko and Citizen) stressing the development of automated production lines and maximum vertical integration of operations. Compared with the multitude of Swiss watch brands, the combined product lines of these two plus Casio, the third major Japanese watchmaker, did not exceed a dozen brands. In contrast, the industry in Hong Kong was highly fragmented, with several manufacturers producing 10–20 million watches per year and hundreds of small firms producing less than 1 million annually. These firms could not afford to invest in quartz analogue technology but, with virtually no barriers to entry for watch assembly, they produced complete analogue watches from imported movements and modules, often Swiss or Japanese. Design costs were also minimized by copying Swiss or Japanese products. The competitive advantages of the Hong Kong firms were low-cost labour, tiny margins and the flexibility to adapt to changes in the market.

The spectacular rise of Japan and Hong Kong, particularly in the middle- and low-price categories, was primarily due to their rapid adoption of quartz technology, a drive to achieve a competitive cost position through accumulation of experience, and economies of scale. Whereas in 1972 the digital watch module cost around $200, by 1984 the same module cost only $50. The Asian watchmaking industry had been ensuring a chronic state of world oversupply, mainly in the inexpensive quartz digital range. This had been the cause of a number of bankruptcies and had incited watch manufacturers to turn to the quartz analogue market, where added value was higher. Since, in contrast to quartz digital technology, quartz analogue technology was available only within the watch industry, the hundreds of watch assemblers scattered throughout the world were increasingly dependent on the three major movement manufacturers – Seiko, ETA and Citizen.

The fightback by the Swiss began at the beginning of the 1980s and was spearheaded by Dr Ernest Thomke. Thomke concluded that '. . . the future is in innovative finished products, aggressive marketing, volume sales and vertical integration of the industry'. Quartz analogue technology was more complex than digital but, because ETA was known for the technology it possessed for the production of the high-priced, ultra-thin 'Delirium' movement, Thomke decided to develop a 'low-price prestige' quartz analogue wristwatch that could be mass produced in Switzerland at greatly reduced cost. Two ETA micromechanical engineers specializing in plastic injection moulding technology, Jacques Muller and Elmar Mock, were given the challenge of designing a product based on Thomke's concept. This required inventing entirely new production technology using robots and computers for manufacture and assembly. By 1981, a semi-automated process had been designed to meet Thomke's goal of a 15 Swiss francs ex-factory price, and seven patents were registered. The watch's movement, consisting of only 51 instead of the 90–150 parts in other watches, was injected directly into the one-piece plastic case. The casing was sealed by ultrasonic welding instead of screws, precluding servicing. The watch would be simply replaced and not repaired if it stopped. The finished product, guaranteed for one year, was shock resistant, water resistant to 100 feet (30 metres) and contained a three-year replaceable battery.

Launched as the Swatch, the success of the marketing campaign is now legendary. However, the question that must be faced is to what extent might the problems faced by the Swiss watch industry have been avoided by a far more careful monitoring of the environment and the identification of a major competitive and technological threat?

Source: *I've Got a Swatch Case Study*, INSEAD, 1987.

The new marketing environment

It is suggested at the beginning of Chapters 5 and 6 that among the legacies of the economic and social turbulence of the late 1980s and then the whole of the 1990s has been the emergence of a new type of consumer and the development of a new type of competitive environment. Taken together, these changes have led to what is for many organizations a radically different and far more demanding marketing environment than has been the case in the past; this is illustrated in Figure 4.9, with organizations facing a general shift towards stages 3 and 4. The consequences of this shift have been felt in a variety of ways, but most obviously in terms of the need for a different approach to management; this would typically be discussed in terms of the need for managers to be more creative, innovative, flexible, dynamic, forward looking and willing to take risks. However, in making this comment and identifying the characteristics of a new approach, we run the risk of making a series of largely self-evident points, but then failing to develop the sort of culture in which these elements prosper.

In Figure 4.9, it is stages 3 and 4 which are of the greatest importance to us here. Environmental uncertainty and its implications have been discussed by numerous commentators over the past few years, including Charles Handy (1994) in *The Empty Raincoat* and Tom Peters (1992) who, in *Liberation Management*, referred to the extreme changes that some organizations now face as 'crazy days'. Crazy days, he argued, are increasingly being faced by managers, and call for responses which often fall outside the traditional, well-understood and well-rehearsed patterns of managerial behaviour. Often, he suggests, it is the case that if an organization is to survive, let alone prosper, managers need to pursue much more radical and truly innovative strategies than ever before. He refers to these new patterns of behaviour as 'crazy ways'. Thus, he argues, crazy days demand crazy ways.

Although others have suggested that Peters perhaps goes too far in his ideas of how to respond, it can be argued that they provide a useful starting point or underpinning of thinking about how best to manage the marketing process. In essence, what Peters is arguing for is a move away from the traditional to the more radical. This post-modern

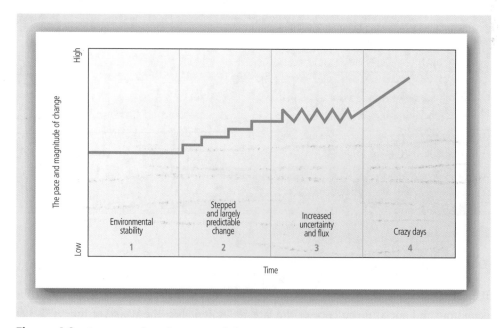

Figure 4.9 Patterns of environmental change

approach has, in turn, been developed by a wide variety of other commentators (see, for example, Brown, 1995; Nilson, 1995), all of whom have argued in one way or another for more innovative responses and patterns of managerial thinking and behaviour.

This theme has also been developed by Hamel and Prahalad (1994) who, in *Competing For The Future*, encapsulate many of these ideas in terms of what they label 'the quest for competitiveness'. This quest, they suggest, typically involves one or more of three possible approaches: *restructuring, re-engineering* and *reinventing the industry and/or strategies*; these are discussed in Chapter 11. In many cases, however, they claim that, whilst many managers over the past few years have placed emphasis upon the first two of these, they have failed to recognize the real significance – and, indeed, the strategic necessity in environments that are changing rapidly and unpredictably – of the third.

The implications of this are significant, and highlight one of the two key themes of this book: firstly, that in common with many other parts of a business, the marketing process needs to be managed in a truly strategic fashion and, secondly, that there is an ever greater need for innovation. These changes also highlight the need for organizations to be far closer to their markets than has typically been the case in the past and to have a far more detailed understanding of market dynamics. Without this, it is almost inevitable that any marketing programme will lack focus.

Responding to the changing market by coming to terms with the future

One of the principal themes that we pursue throughout this book is that the marketing environment is changing ever more dramatically and, for many organizations, ever more unpredictably. Faced with this, the marketing planner can take one of three approaches:

1 To ignore what is happening and accept the consequences of strategic drift and wear-out
2 To respond quickly or slowly, but largely reactively
3 To try to predict the nature of the changes and then manage them proactively.

The implications of the first of these in fast-moving markets are in most cases far too significant for this to be a realistic option for the majority of organizations, and so it is really only the second and third with which we need to be concerned here. In deciding whether to respond quickly or slowly, the planner needs to think about the opportunities or threats posed by the changes taking place, the time for which any window of opportunity is likely to be open, and the organization's ability to respond. Thus, the third option is in many ways the most desirable, but is typically dependent upon the quality of the environmental monitoring system that exists and the planner's ability to identify *how* to respond.

Although this third option is potentially the most difficult, it highlights a key issue for the marketing strategist: recognizing that an important part of planning and strategy is about the future; how can the organization get to the future first? It is the failure to do this and for external change to move ahead faster than management learning that typically creates significant problems for the marketing planner.

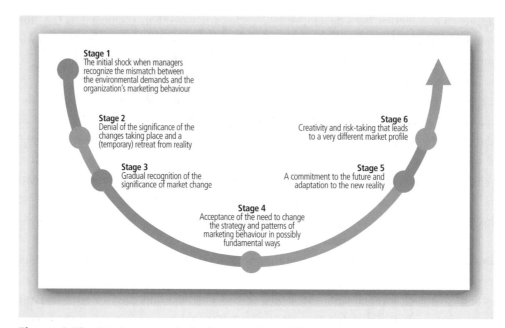

Figure 4.10 Moving towards the future (adapted from Fifield, 1997)

Recognizing this allows us to identify five types of manager:

1 Those who make it happen
2 Those who think they make it happen
3 Those who watch it happen
4 Those who wonder what happened
5 Those who fail to realize that anything has happened.

The likelihood of the last two of these occurring increases dramatically when the organization has a poorly developed or non-existent marketing information system, and can lead to managers suffering from psychological recoil when they finally do recognize the nature and significance of changes taking place. In these circumstances, the marketing planner can then either continue to deny the nature and significance of market changes or respond in one of a number of ways; this is illustrated in Figure 4.10.

Although the diagram shows the movement through the six stages, in practice of course many firms find such change to be difficult or impossible. In these circumstances, the organization will quite simply continue to drift further and further from what the market is demanding.

4.5 The evolution of environmental analysis

Recognition of the potential significance of environmental change highlights the need for a certain type of organizational structure and culture, which is then reflected both in a balanced portfolio of products and in an adaptive management style supported by a well-developed intelligence and information monitoring system. Without this, the likelihood of the firm being taken unawares by environmental changes of one sort or another increases dramatically. Against the background of these comments, the need for environmental analysis would appear self-evident. All too often, however, firms appear to pay only lip service to such need. In commenting on this, Diffenbach (1983) has identified three distinct stages in the evolution of corporate environmental analysis:

1 An *appreciation stage*, typically resulting from the emergence of books and articles that argue the case for looking beyond the short term and for considering the wider implications of the economic, technological, social and political factors that make up the business environment.
2 An *analysis stage*, which involves finding reliable sources of environmental data, compiling and examining the data to discuss trends, developments and key relationships. It also includes monitoring developments and anticipating the future. It was the emergence of this thinking which led to the appearance in the 1960s and 1970s of numerous books on environmental scanning, Delphic analysis and environmental forecasting.
3 The *application stage*, in which very real attempts are made to monitor the environment, assess the implications for change and incorporate staff evaluations into strategy and plans.

Assuming therefore that a firm intends to develop an effective system for environmental analysis, there is a need first to identify those dimensions that are likely to have the greatest impact upon the organization, and second to establish a mechanism whereby each of these elements is monitored on a regular basis. For most companies these elements are contained within the PEST analytical framework referred to earlier. Although in practice other factors can be added to this list, we will for convenience use this framework as a prelude to illustrating how environmental factors influence, and occasionally dictate, strategy. However, before examining these various dimensions, it is worth making brief reference to the ways in which organizations scan their environments.

In essence, there are three approaches to scanning, with these being characterized by an increasing degree of structure, systemization, sophistication and resource intensity (see Fahey et al., 1981):

1 *Irregular systems*, which predominate in companies with a poorly developed planning culture and in which the focus is upon *responding* to environmentally generated crises. The net effect of this is that emphasis is simply placed upon finding solutions to short-term problems, with little real attention being paid to identifying and assessing the likely impact of future environmental changes.
2 *Periodic models*, which represent a general development of the irregular system and which are more systematic, resource intensive and sophisticated. The environment is reviewed regularly and a longer-term perspective is developed.

3 *Continuous models*, which represent yet a further development and involve focusing upon the business environment generally and upon the long term as opposed to short-term and specific issues.

Fahey et al. (1981) went on to suggest that, although there is a general shift within American companies towards more sophisticated systems, this movement is slow and, compared with its apparent impact, has still to justify the level of resources required.

Nevertheless, the argument for continuous environmental monitoring in order to identify strategic issues and market signals in advance of their impact upon the company is a strong one, and has led Brownlie (1987, pp. 100–5) to identify the three basic premises upon which continuous environmental analysis is based:

1 The determinants of success are dictated by the business environment
2 The firm's response to environmental change therefore represents a fundamental strategic choice
3 A knowledge of the business environment must precede the acquisition of any degree of control over it.

Acknowledging the validity of these three assumptions leads to a recognition that effective management cannot take place in an information vacuum, or indeed in circumstances in which information is at best partial and poorly structured. There is therefore an obvious need for the organization to develop an effective information system that *collects*, *analyses* and then *disseminates* information both from within and outside the company.

There are, however, problems that are commonly associated with the first of these – information collection and the development of a worthwhile database. Brownlie identifies these as being that all too often the information is:

➡ Poorly structured
➡ Available only on an irregular basis
➡ Often provided by unofficial sources
➡ Qualitative in nature
➡ Ambiguous in its definitions
➡ Opinion based
➡ Poorly quantified
➡ Based on an insecure methodology
➡ Likely to change.

Because of problems such as these, the need to collect and analyse environmental information in a well-structured and usable fashion is essential, and it is this that frameworks such as PEST are designed to achieve. It must be emphasized, however, that the organization should avoid focusing just upon the immediate task environment, since all too frequently history has demonstrated that the most significant threats faced by companies often come from firms outside the task environment. We have already pointed to the example of the Swiss watch industry, which was significantly damaged by the introduction of microchips and digital technology on the part of firms that the Swiss did not see as competitors. Equally, companies in markets as prosaic as carbon paper were decimated by photocopying technology, while in the same period the British motorcycle manufacturers of the 1960s, seeing their competitors as being one another, were taken by surprise by the Japanese. In making these comments we are therefore arguing for a *breadth* of perspective within the general structure of PEST analysis.

However, although the environment exerts a significant and obvious influence upon the organization, it should not necessarily be seen as the most direct determinant of strategy. Porter (1980, Chapter 1), for example, has argued that industry structure is a more important factor than environmental conditions, since it typically exerts a strong influence in determining the competitive rules of the game, as well as the strategies potentially available to the firm. Recognizing this, the key issue for the planner lies in the developing the ability of the firm to deal with them.

However, before going on to consider some of the ways in which industry structure influences strategy, we need to examine the various dimensions of the political, economic, social and technological environments. It is this that provides the basis of the next section.

4.6 The political, economic, social and technological environments

At the beginning of this chapter we suggested that effective marketing planning is based on two important analytical ingredients. First, market opportunity must be analysed and, second, the company's ability to take advantage of these opportunities and cope with threats must be assessed.

Under the first heading, there are four basic building blocks:

1 Customers must be analysed to determine how the market can be segmented and what the requirements of each segment are
2 Competitors must be identified and their individual strategies understood
3 Environmental trends (social, economic, political, technological) affecting the market must be isolated and forecasted
4 Market characteristics in terms of the evolution of supply and demand and their interaction must be understood.

It is point 3 to which we now turn our attention. We do this by examining each of the elements of the PEST framework in turn, and then try to bring them together in Illustration 4.6, where we make reference to what we term world changing megatrends.

The political (and legal) environment

Marketing decisions are typically affected in a variety of ways by developments in the political and legal environments. This part of the environment is composed of laws, pressure groups and government agencies, all of which exert some sort of influence and constraint on organizations and individuals in society.

With regard to the legislative framework, the starting point involves recognizing that the amount of legislation affecting business has increased steadily over the past two decades. This legislation has been designed to achieve a number of purposes, including:

➡ Protecting companies from each other so that the size and power of one organization to damage another is limited
➡ Protecting consumers from unfair business practice by ensuring that certain safety standards are met, that advertising is honest, and that generally companies are not able to take advantage of the possible ignorance, naivety and gullibility of consumers
➡ Protecting society at large from irresponsible business behaviour.

It is important therefore that the marketing planner is aware not only of the current legislative framework, but also of the ways in which it is likely to develop and how, by means of industry pressure groups and lobbying of parliament, the direction of legislation might possibly be influenced so that it benefits the company. At a broader level, the strategist should also be familiar with the way in which legislation in other countries differs, and how this too might provide opportunities and constraints. The Scandinavian countries, for example, have developed a legislative framework to protect consumers that is far more restrictive than is generally the case elsewhere in Europe. Norway, for example, has banned many forms of sales promotion, such as trading stamps, contests and premiums, as being inappropriate and unfair methods for sellers to use in the promotion of their products. Elsewhere, food companies in India require government approval to launch a new brand if it will simply duplicate what is already on offer in the market, while in the Philippines food manufacturers are obliged to offer low-price variations of their brands so that low-income groups are not disadvantaged.

Although legislation such as this tends to be country-specific, examples such as these are potentially useful in that they highlight the need for marketing managers to be aware not just of the situation in their immediate markets, but also of how legislation might develop in order to restrict marketing practice. In a broader sense, marketing planners also need to monitor how public interest groups are likely to develop and, subsequently, influence marketing practice. In commenting on this in the context of American pressure groups, Salancik and Upah (1978) have said:

*"*There is some evidence that the consumer may not be King, nor even Queen. The consumer is but a voice, one among many. Consider how General Motors makes its cars today. Vital features of the motor are designed by the United States government; the exhaust system is redesigned by certain state governments; the production materials used are dictated by suppliers who control scarce material resources. For other products, other groups and organizations may get involved. Thus, insurance companies directly or

indirectly affect the design of smoke detectors; scientific groups affect the design of spray products by condemning aerosols; minority activist groups affect the design of dolls by requesting representative figures. Legal departments also can be expected to increase their importance in firms, affecting not only product design and promotion but also marketing strategies. At a minimum, marketing managers will spend less time with their research departments asking 'What does the consumer want?' and more and more time with their production and legal people asking 'What can the consumer have?'*"*

In the light of comments such as these, the need for careful and continual monitoring of the political and legal environment should be obvious, since at the heart of all such analysis is the simple recognition of the idea of political risk.

The economic and physical environments

Within the majority of small and medium-sized enterprises (SMEs), the economic environment is typically seen as a constraint, since the ability of a company to exert any sort of influence on this element of the environment is, to all intents and purposes, negligible. As a consequence, it is argued, firms are typically put into the position of responding to the state of the economy. Having said this, larger companies, and particularly the multinationals (MNCs), are perhaps able to view the economic environment in a rather different way, since they are often able to shift investment and marketing patterns from one market to another and from one part of the world to another in order to capitalize most fully on the global opportunities that exist. For a purely domestic operator, however, the ability to do this is generally non-existent. For both types of company there is still a need to understand *how* the economic environment is likely to affect performance, a need which received a significant boost in the 1970s in the wake of the oil crisis, when parallels were being drawn between that period and the Great Depression of the 1930s. More specifically, however, the sorts of changes that are currently taking place in the economic environment can be identified as:

1 An increase in real income growth
2 Continuing inflationary pressures
3 Changes in the savings/debt ratio
4 Concern over levels of Third World debt
5 Different consumer expenditure patterns.

The significance of changes such as these should not be looked at in isolation, but should be viewed instead against the background of changes in the *political/economic balances of power* (e.g. the rise and then the relative decline of Japan over the past 40 years, the opportunities today in Central and Eastern Europe, and the economic development of China), and major changes in the *physical environment*.

Concern with the physical environment has increased dramatically over the past few years, with the origins being traceable to the publication in the 1960s of Rachael Carson's book *Silent Spring* (1963). In this, Carson drew attention to the possibly irrevocable damage being done to the planet and the possibility that we would exhaust the world's resources. This concern was echoed in the coining of the phrase 'eco-catastrophe' and reflected subsequently in the formation of powerful lobby groups such as Friends of the Earth and Greenpeace, which have had an impact upon business practice. The five major areas of concern expressed by pressure groups such as these are:

1 An impending shortage of raw materials
2 The increasing costs of energy
3 Increasing levels and consequences of pollution
4 An increasing need for governments to become involved in the *management* of natural resources
5 The need for management teams to take a very much more informed view of sustainable development

The social, cultural and demographic environments

It should be apparent from what has been said so far that a broad perspective needs to be adopted in looking at the economic environment. From the viewpoint of the marketing planner, analysis of short-term and long-term economic patterns is of vital importance. In doing this, arguably the most useful and indeed logical starting point is that of demography, since not only is demographic change readily identifiable, but it is the size, structure and trends of a population that ultimately exert the greatest influence on demand. There are several reasons for this, the two most significant of which are, first, that there is a strong relationship between population and economic growth and, second, that it is the absolute size of the population that acts as the boundary condition determining potential or primary demand. A detailed understanding of the size, structure, composition and trends of the population is therefore of fundamental importance to the marketing planner. It is consequently fortunate that, in the majority of developed countries, information of this sort is generally readily available and provides a firm foundation for forecasting.

Illustration 4.3 The growth of the single-parent family

Between 1986 and 2001, the number of single-parent families in Britain doubled to the point at which they represented more than a quarter of families with children. These figures, published by the Office for National Statistics, also suggested that there were 1.75 million one-parent families and that almost 2.9 million, or 26 per cent, of children aged under 19 live in a one-parent family. The report highlighted the way in which virtually every kind of one-parent family had risen in relative numbers, but that the sharpest rise was the number of single lone mothers – women who had never married. The 26 per cent of families that lone parent units accounted for compared with just 14 per cent 15 years earlier.

At the same time, a variety of other equally important and far-reaching changes are currently taking place, including:

1 *The growth in the number of one-person households.* The size of this SSWD group (single, separated, widowed, divorced) has grown dramatically over the past few years, with 64 per cent of the UK's 24.4 million households consisting of just one or two people. Amongst the factors that have contributed to this are young adults leaving home earlier, later marriage, a rise in the divorce rate, a generally greater degree of social and geographic mobility, and higher income levels that give people the freedom to live alone if they wish to do so (see Illustration 4.3). The implications for marketing of changes such as these have already proved significant in a variety of ways and have been reflected in an increase in demand for more starter homes, smaller appliances, food that can be purchased in smaller portions, and a greater emphasis upon convenience products generally. (At this stage, the reader might usefully turn to the Appendix of Chapter 5 (p. 215), where some of the drivers of consumer change are discussed.)

2 *A rise in the number of two-person cohabitant households.* It has been suggested by several sociologists that cohabitation is becoming increasingly like the first stage of marriage, with more people of the opposite sex sharing a house. At the same time, the number of households with two or more people of the same sex sharing has also increased.

3 *An increase in the number of group households.* These are households with three or more people of the same or opposite sex sharing expenses by living together, particularly in the larger cities. These look set to increase yet further. The needs of these non-family households differ in a variety of ways from those of the more conventional family household, which in the past has typically provided the focus for marketing attention. By virtue of their increasing importance, non-family households are likely to require ever more different strategies over the next few years if full advantage of the opportunities they offer is to be realized.

4 *A much greater degree of social mobility.*

At the same time a variety of other significant demographic shifts are taking place throughout the world, all of which need to be reflected in the planning process. These include:

1 *An explosion in the world's population,* with much of this growth being concentrated in those nations that, by virtue of low standards of living and economic development, can least afford it.

2 *A slowdown in birth rates* in many of the developed nations. Many families today, for example, are opting for just one child and this has had significant implications for a variety of companies. Johnson & Johnson, for example, responded to the declining birth rate by very successfully repositioning its baby oil, baby powder and baby shampoo in such a way that the products also appealed to young female adults.

Similarly, cosmetics companies have placed a far greater emphasis on products for the over-50s. The implications of this slowdown in the birth rate are illustrated perhaps most graphically by the way in which, by 2025, the UK will have 1.6 million more people aged over 65 than under 16.

3 *An ageing population*, as advances in medical care allow people to live longer. One result of this trend, which has in turn been exacerbated by the slowdown in the birth rate, has been an increase in the number of empty nesters (see the section on the family life cycle on pp. 332–34) who have substantial sums of discretionary income and high expectations (see Illustration 4.4).

4 *Changing family structures* as a result of:
- Later marriage
- Fewer children
- Increased divorce rates
- More working wives
- An increase in the number of career women (see Illustration 4.5).

5 *Higher levels of education* and an increasing number of families in what has traditionally been seen as the middle class.

6 *Geographical shifts* in population and, in Britain at least, the emergence of a North–South divide characterized by radically different levels of economic activity and employment. In parallel with this, there has been the urbanization of society, with 33 per cent of the population now living in just 3 per cent of the UK land area.

7 *A growth in the number of people willing to commute long distances to work*, and an upsurge in the opportunities for telecommuting whereby people can work from home and interact with colleagues via computer terminals.

Illustration 4.4 The changing consumer: the growing power of the grey market

For many organizations, the over-50s market is seen to consist of largely passive consumers who are of little real interest to marketers. The reality, however, as a series of studies published at the end of the 1990s revealed, is often very different.

Prominent amongst the drivers of the growing importance of this market is the way in which the baby boomer generation is now moving into its 50s and that, in terms of size, the market is growing. The essentially active nature of the market is revealed by a variety of statistics, including the fact that 30 per cent of expenditure on household goods comes from households where the head is over 50 years old.

Undoubtedly one of the biggest mistakes that marketers have made in the past is to view the over-50s as a single consumer group. Given that the market now accounts for 40 per cent of the population, it is in reality a remarkably heterogeneous group. Recognition of this has led the specialist 50-plus advertising agency Millennium Direct to segment the market in terms of 'thrivers' (50–59), 'seniors' (60–69) and 'elders' (70-plus). By contrast with the typically time-poor thirtysomethings who have mortgages to pay and young children to look after, the over-50s market is frequently time-rich and, in many cases, has a high disposable income. It tends also to be a market in which levels of brand loyalty are high.

If anything, the significance of the over-50s market is likely to increase dramatically over the next few years, not just because of its greater size and higher total net worth, but also because the values of the baby boomer generation are very different from those that went before. The ways in which the expectations of the baby boomers have developed was touched upon by Robert Bork (1996) in his book *Slouching Towards Gomorrah*. Bork argues that the children of middle-class liber-als spent the 1960s questioning many of the traditional tenets of society and, in doing this, created fragmented markets in which the 'we' people become the 'me' people, who were far more demanding and far less tolerant. The baby boomer generation is also very different from its predecessors in one other very important way: it was the first generation in which the economics of scarcity were replaced by the economics of plenty and consumers were placed on a pedestal with companies setting out to satisfy their every whim.

Given this, the grey market (which includes both authors of this book) can only become far more powerful and demanding over the next few years.

Illustration 4.5 The changing face of women

The *Zeitgeist* of the late 1990s was captured by Helen Fielding (1997) in her highly successful book *Bridget Jones' Diary* (that was later made into a film). This depicted an angst-ridden woman obsessed with her single status and calorie intake. Given that 19.1 per cent of women describe themselves as single and that at any one time more than 80 per cent of women are concerned with their weight and/or shape, Fielding's book certainly seemed to ring true for many.

The march to affluence continued, with 19.6 per cent classified as ABs. More women worked: 28 per cent full time and 18 per cent part time. The TGI data shows that 15.6 per cent of women were educated beyond the age of 19, rising to 25 per cent among those aged 25–34 – with 7.4 per cent still studying.

The traditional family unit continued its decline. By 1999, sole-adult households had risen to 22 per cent, and those living alone were up from 13.8 to 17.2 per cent. The number of single parents had almost doubled, from 650 000 to 1.2 million – four times the level of 1969.

Home ownership has become more common: 26 per cent owned their home outright, while the proportion in the process of buying rose to 45 per cent.

Another change has been the increasing amount of weekly travel for many women, especially those in work. In 1969, only 5.2 per cent were 'heavily exposed' to poster advertising; by 1999, 25.7 per cent fell into this category.

In 1999 nearly half of all women (47.1 per cent) had a credit card, and four out of every five had a bank account. On the home front, 40 per cent of households had a separate freezer, 8.7 per cent a dishwasher and 30.5 per cent a tumble dryer.

Anyone with more than a passing acquaintance with modern car advertising – 'Nicole', 'Size Matters', etc. – will have noticed that a significant proportion is now targeted at women. More women are driving and more women are making car purchasing decisions. Back in 1969, only 32 per cent of women held a driving licence; in 1979 it was 42.2 per cent; last year it was up to 58 per cent.

The renaissance in cinema-going during the 1990s, driven by British-made hits such as *Four Weddings and a Funeral* and *Trainspotting*, as well as improved cinema complexes, showed up in an increase in women going to the movies – 57 per cent against just 40 per cent a decade earlier.

Source: *Marketing*, 18 May 2000, p. 35.

The net effect of changes such as these has been significant, and is continuing to prove so, with the marketing strategies of nearly all companies being affected in one way or another. At their most fundamental, these changes have led to a shift from a small number of mass markets to an infinitely larger number of micromarkets differentiated by age, sex, lifestyle, education and so on. Each of these groups differs in terms of its preferences and characteristics, and as a consequence requires different, more flexible and more precise approaches to marketing that no longer take for granted the long-established assumptions and conventions of marketing practice. The implications of these trends are therefore of considerable significance and, from the viewpoint of the strategist, have the advantage of being both reliable and largely predictable, at least in the short and medium term. There is thus no excuse either for being taken unawares by them or for ignoring them.

Social and cultural change: an overview

Taken together, the changes that we have pointed to in this section can be seen as fundamental, and have been described by Albrecht (1979) in the following ways:

*"*The period from 1900 until the present stands apart from every other period in human history as a time of incredible change. Mankind, at least in the so-called 'developed' countries, has lost its innocence entirely. The great defining characteristics of this period – the first three-quarters of the twentieth century – have been change, impermanence, disruption, newness and obsolescence, and a sense of acceleration in almost every perceptible aspect of American society.

Philosophers, historians, scientists, and economists have given various names to this period. Management consultant Peter F. Drucker (1968) has called it the Age of Discontinuity. Economist John Kenneth Galbraith (1977) has called it the Age of Uncertainty. Media theorist Marshall MacLuhan (1964, 1968) called it the Age of the Global Village. Writer and philosopher Alvin Toffler (1970, 1975) called it the Age of Future Shock. Virtually all thoughtful observers of America, Americans, and American society have remarked with some alarm about the accelerating pace with which our life processes and our surrounds are changing within the span of a single generation. And this phenomenon is spreading all over the industrialized world. I call this the Age of Anxiety.*"*

The technological environment

The fourth and final strand of the environment considered here is that of technology. Seen by many people as the single most dramatic force shaping our lives, technological advance needs to be seen as a force for 'creative destruction' in that the development of new products or concepts has an often fatal knockout effect on an existing product. The creation of the xerography photocopying process, for example, destroyed the market for carbon paper, while the development of cars damaged the demand for railways. The implications for the existing industry are often straightforward: change or die. The significance of technological change does, however, need to be seen not just at the corporate or industry level, but also at the national level, since an economy's growth rate is directly influenced by the level of technological advance.

Technology does, therefore, provide both opportunities and threats, some of which are direct while others are far less direct in their impact. As an example of this, the development of the contraceptive pill led to smaller families, an increase in the number of working wives, higher levels of discretionary income, and subsequently to a greater emphasis on holidays, consumer durables, and so on. Recognizing then that the impact of technology is to all intents inevitable, the areas to which Kotler (1988, pp. 154–6) suggests the marketing planner should pay attention include:

1 *The accelerating pace of technological change.* In his book *Future Shock*, Toffler (1970) makes reference to the accelerative thrust in the invention, exploitation, diffusion and acceptance of new technologies. An ever greater number of ideas are being developed, and the time period between their development and implementation is shortening. This theme was developed further by Toffler (1980) in *The Third Wave*, in which he forecast the rapid emergence and acceptance of telecommuting (the electronic cottage) with direct implications for such things as family relationships, home entertainment and, less directly, levels of car exhaust pollution.

2 *Unlimited innovational opportunities*, with major advances being made in the areas of solid-state electronics, robotics, material sciences and biotechnology.

3 *Higher research and development budgets*, particularly in the United States, northern Europe and Japan. One implication of this is that organizations are likely to be forced into the position of spending ever greater amounts on R&D simply to stay still.

4 *A concentration of effort in some industries on minor product improvements* that are essentially defensive, rather than on the riskier and more offensive major product advances.

5 *A greater emphasis upon the regulation of technological change* in order to minimize the undesirable effects of some new products upon society. Safety and health regulations are most evident in their application in the pharmaceutical, foodstuffs and car

industries, although across the entire spectrum of industry far more emphasis today is being given to the idea of technological assessment as a prelude to products being launched commercially.

A broadly similar view of the major changes taking place within the environment appears in Illustration 4.6, which highlights what have been termed 'world-changing megatrends'. From the viewpoint of marketing, the implications of each of these areas are potentially significant, and argues the case for careful technological monitoring in order to ensure that emerging opportunities are not ignored or missed. This, in turn, should lead to more market-oriented, rather than product-oriented, research and to a generally greater awareness of the negative aspects of any innovation.

Underlying all of these points is, of course, a recognition of the product life cycle (PLC) concept. The pros and cons of the PLC are detailed elsewhere in this book, and at this stage we are therefore concerned with the way in which simple recognition of the concept argues the case for the development of a formal technological forecasting system, which then acts as an input to the process of developing marketing strategy.

Illustration 4.6 World-changing megatrends

It should be apparent from what has been said so far that the marketing planner is faced with an increasingly volatile – and malevolent – environment. However, underpinning this are a number of what might be termed 'megatrends' that have a long-term and, in many cases, fundamental effect upon the pattern, structure and practices of business. These include:

1 The explosive and accelerating power of information and communication technologies
2 The globalization of markets, patterns of competition and innovation
3 The fundamental shifts from a world economy based on manufacturing and the exploitation of natural resources to one based on knowledge, information, innovation and adding value
4 The accelerated decoupling of the 'real' global economy from the 'virtual' economy of financial transactions
5 Geographic rebalancing and the emergence of a new world economic order
6 The twilight of government
7 Sector convergence
8 The emergence of unprecedented new forms of business organization, both within and between firms
9 A shift in the economic 'centre of gravity' of the business world from large multinationals to smaller, nimbler and more entrepreneurial companies
10 The increase in the social, political and commercial significance of environmental considerations
11 An exponential increase in the velocity, complexity and unpredictability of change.

Source: Lewis, K (1997).

4.7 Coming to terms with industry and market breakpoints

A fundamental element of any competitive marketing strategy should be the anticipation – or precipitation – of major environmental or structural change. Sometimes referred to as *industry breakpoints*, the consequences of major change are seen in a variety of ways, but most obviously in terms of how a previously successful strategy is made obsolete. An understanding of how breakpoints work and how they might best be managed is therefore an essential part of strategic marketing.

In discussing industry breakpoints, Strebel (1996, p. 13) defines them as:

" . . . a new offering to the market that is so superior in terms of customer value and delivered cost that it disrupts the rules of the competitive game: a new business system is required to deliver it. The new offering typically causes a sharp shift in the industry's growth rate while the competitive response to the new business system results in a dramatic realignment of market shares.*"*

There are numerous examples of industries in which the phenomenon has been experienced (see, for example, the discussion of the Swiss watch industry in Illustration 4.2 and the launch of Häagen-Dazs ice-cream in Illustration 11.7), although in many instances it appears that managers have learned little from the lessons of other markets in which traumatic change has already taken place. However, given the seemingly ever greater pace of competition, shorter product, market and brand life cycles, and the consequently more intensive search for competitive advantage, it is almost inevitable that at some stage a majority of managers will be faced with the problems that breakpoints create. The experiences of the personal computer industry are discussed in Illustration 4.7. A breakpoint on a slightly smaller scale was illustrated in 2002/2003 by the popularity of the Atkins Diet. The high-protein regime that the diet demands was reflected in significant shifts in demand for food products, with sales of meat increasing substantially and sales of carbohydrates such as bread and pasta falling.

Illustration 4.7 Industry breakpoints and the personal computer industry

When Apple launched its first PC, it provided the market with a low-cost product that was infinitely more convenient than traditional centralized computing systems. However, few, if any, of the established players appear to have seen Apple as any sort of threat. By contrast, numerous small firms recognized the opportunities that Apple's simplicity offered, with the result that competition in the PC market escalated as firms tried to define the form and content of a PC.

With IBM's entry to this part of the market, an industry standard began to emerge, production volumes grew, prices dropped and the pace of technological change escalated. Many of the smaller players were unable to match the shifts that took place and were shaken out of the market. Indeed, even Apple was hit hard by the changes that were taking place and eventually responded by ousting its founders in favour of a consumer marketing expert.

Levels of competition continued to increase dramatically as firms focused upon expanding the market and capturing market share by offering the product at even lower prices. The intensity of this price competition created major difficulties as more and more firms tried to find a way out of the downward spiral.

However, it was not until Apple launched the Macintosh, with its much higher levels of user-friendliness, that things really began to change. Amongst the numerous competitors, it was only those who recognized that customers' values had changed – in that they were ready for hard disks, better graphics, faster operating speeds and new software – who managed to cope with this new breakpoint. Others, however, were quickly forced out. It was therefore something of an irony that Apple appear not to have recognized the real value of the shift they had generated and, as a consequence, failed to capitalize upon it

to the extent that they might have done. By contrast, Bill Gates of Microsoft saw the opportunities of graphics software and began creating the equivalent for the IBM standard.

The next breakpoint was created by the recession of the late 1980s. Given the size of the market, it was inevitable that it would be affected by the downturn in spending and so, as sales dropped, each company's cost base became crucial. Those who were best placed to benefit from this were the firms in the Far East and companies such as Compaq.

As the recession eased, the industry was affected by yet another breakpoint as more powerful chips and software emerged, and the market shifted towards laptops, integrated networks and workstations (see Figure 4.11). At the same time, there was a major shift in the supplier base, with Intel and Microsoft having emerged as the dominant suppliers of chips and software respectively. Meanwhile, the fortunes of IBM, Apple and many of the Far Eastern manufacturers had all declined dramatically.

Source: Strebel (1996).

According to Strebel (1996, p. 13), there are two basic types of breakpoint:

1 *Divergent breakpoints*, which are associated with sharply increasing variety in the competitive offerings and consequently higher value for the customer
2 *Convergent breakpoints*, which are the result of improvements in the systems and processes used to deliver the offerings, with these then being reflected in lower delivered costs.

These are illustrated in Figure 4.12.

With regard to the specific causes of breakpoints, it appears that they can be created by a variety of factors, including:

➡ Technological breakthroughs that provide the innovative organization with a major competitive advantage but, in turn, put competitors at a disadvantage

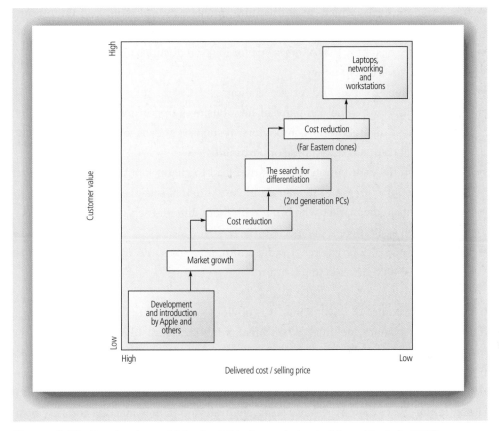

Figure 4.11 Breakpoints within the PC industry (adapted from Strebel, 1996)

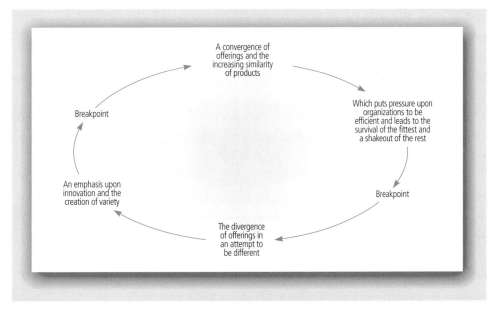

Figure 4.12 The evolutionary cycle of competitive behaviour (adapted from Strebel, 1996)

➡ The economic cycle, which, in a downturn, forces a radical rethink of the product and how it is to be marketed

➡ A new source of supply that offers scope for major reductions in cost

➡ Changes in government policy

➡ Shifts in customer values and/or expectations

➡ The identification by one company of new business opportunities, with the result that there is a divergence in competitors' responses and behaviour as they try to work out how best to exploit these opportunities

➡ Shifts within the distribution network that lead to changes in the balance of power between manufacturers and retailers, and very different sets of expectations

➡ New entrants to the market who bring with them different sets of skills and expectations, as well as a different perspective

➡ Declining returns, which force a radical rethink of how the company is operating and how it should develop in the future.

Given the significance of breakpoints, it is obviously essential that, wherever possible, the marketing planner identifies when breakpoints are most likely to occur and the form they will take. In the absence of this the organization will be forced into a reactively responsive mode. However, it can be argued that a majority of managers are particularly badly equipped to identify breakpoints, especially in organizations with a closed culture, since their experience is largely irrelevant in new markets and new business systems. As an example of this, the established players in the computer industry focused much of their effort upon their existing products, markets and technologies, and had little cause or incentive to look at a redefinition of the product and market in the way that Apple did.

Nevertheless, planners need to come to terms with the dynamics of their industry and, in particular, with the sorts of pressures that we referred to earlier and that, sooner or later, lead to breakpoints occurring. In so far as a framework for this can be identified, it stems from the way in which there is a tendency for the competitive cycle to fluctuate between *divergence* (variety creation) and *convergence* (the survival of the fittest).

Faced with what, on the face of it, appears to be ever more rapid environmental change, marketing planners need to address a series of issues. Amongst the most prominent of these are:

➡ How to best balance short-run and long-run goals and actions

➡ How to become more firmly market focused and customer driven

➡ How to manage customers more effectively and, in particular, ever higher expectations and lower levels of loyalty

➡ How to segment markets more creatively and strategically

➡ How best to achieve leadership in selected market segments

➡ How best to add value and differentiate the company's offer

➡ How to price in order to gain competitive advantage

➡ How to develop an effective distribution strategy

➡ How to deal most effectively with new technologies

➡ How to cope with shifting market boundaries and the globalization of markets

➡ How to improve the marketing information, planning and control systems.

4.8 Coming to terms with the very different future: the implications for marketing planning

*"*Predicting the future is the easy part. It's knowing what to do with it that counts.*"*

(Faith Popcorn, 2001)

Given the nature of our comments so far, it should be apparent that the marketing planner must be concerned with the future. A fundamental consideration for many firms is therefore the question of how the organization can get to the future before its competitors. In discussing this, and how, by getting to the future first, organizations can create a possibly significant competitive advantage, Hamel and Prahalad (1994) suggest that: 'Companies that create the future are rebels. They break the rules. They are filled with people who take the other side of an issue just to spark a debate.'

They go on to suggest that, because so many markets are now dramatically more competitive than in the past, the traditional idea of being better, faster and smarter (which has led to the three words running together in the form of the management mantra 'betterfastersmarter') is no longer enough. Instead, there is the need for managers to recognize the fundamental importance of innovation and creativity being in many markets the only truly sustainable forms of competitive advantage. However, if this is to be achieved, run-of-the-mill large companies need to take on many of the mindsets of smaller organizations that are characterized by a far greater degree of flexibility and speed of response. It was this pattern of thinking and the difficulties of achieving it that led Kanter (1989) to refer to the idea of getting elephants to dance. In the absence of this, managers face the danger of simply drifting into the future. In order to avoid this, Hamel and Prahalad (1994) argue that managers need to recognize the importance of three rules:

1 *Step off the corporate treadmill.* To do this, managers need to avoid an over-preoccupation with day-to-day issues and to focus instead upon the smaller number of issues that are *really* important and will contribute to competitive advantage.

2 *Compete for industry foresight and learn to forget.* This involves spending time identifying how the market will or can be encouraged to move and then quite deliberately forgetting some of the traditional rules of competition and patterns of behaviour.

3 *Develop the (new) strategic architecture,* and concentrate upon leveraging and stretching the strategy in such a way that far greater use is made of the organization's marketing assets.

In coming to terms with these areas, the marketing planner needs to understand which of the factors that are typically taken for granted (the conventional wisdoms), both within the organization and the market as a whole, can either be questioned or eliminated. The planner also needs to identify the two or three strategic actions that, if taken, would make a real difference to the organization's performance in the marketplace.

Looking to the future

There is in many organizations a temptation to focus upon the short term. There are several obvious explanations for this, the most obvious of which stems from the (greater) feeling of security that managers derive from concentrating upon the comfort zone of the areas and developments that are essentially predictable. A more fundamental explanation, however, emerged from a survey in the *Asian Wall Street Journal*. The study, which covered large firms and multinational corporations, illustrated the extent to which many senior managers are forced to demonstrate higher and more immediate short-term results than in the past. The implications for strategic marketing planning are significant, since strategic planners have little incentive to think and act long term if they know that they will be evaluated largely on the basis of short-term gains and results. The sorts of trade-offs that emerge from this have, in turn, been heightened as the pace of change within the environment, and the need to manage ambiguity, complexity and paradox, has increased.

Nevertheless, the strategic marketing planner must, of necessity, have some view of the longer term and of the ways in which markets are likely to move. In discussing this, Doyle (2002) identifies ten major trends within the environment:

1 The move towards what he terms the *fashionization of markets*, in which an ever greater number of products and markets are subject to rapid obsolescence and unpredictable and fickle demand
2 The *fragmentation* of previously homogeneous markets and the emergence of micro-markets
3 The *ever higher expectations* of customers
4 The greater pace of *technological change*
5 *Higher levels of competition*
6 The *globalization* of markets and business
7 Expectations of *higher service*
8 The *commoditization* of markets
9 The *erosion of previously strong and dominant brands*
10 A series of new and/or greater governmental, political, economic and social *constraints*.

Although the list is by no means exhaustive (it fails, for example, to come to terms with the detail of a series of major social and attitudinal changes) and, in a number of ways, focuses upon the broadly obvious in that much of what he suggests is simply a continuation of what exists currently, it does provide an initial framework for thinking about the future.

A somewhat different approach has been taken by Fifield (1998), who has focused upon tomorrow's customer. He suggests that this customer will not simply be a replication of the customer of the past, but will instead be characterized by a series of traits that include being:

➡ Inner-driven and less susceptible to fashion and fads
➡ Multi-individualistic and multifaceted
➡ Interconnected, with a far stronger awareness of different facets of their lives
➡ Pleasure seeking
➡ Deconstructed, in that they will view work, family and society in a very different way than in the past
➡ Unforgiving, in that will not expect more, but they will demand more and retaliate if and when this is not provided.

A slightly different and more focused view of the future has been spelled out by Hill and Lederer (2002), who in their book *The Infinite Asset* map out a future of world brand domination. In 10 years, they suggest, we will see brand-based business models become the dominant corporate life form. The implication of this is that the successful twenty-first century corporation will not be a collection of buildings, equipment and products, but a collection of brands and the activities that support them. In short, brands will exceed marketing. However, in making out this case, they argue that there is a need to forget about conventional notions of a brand simply being a name or a term that identifies a company or product. Instead, they suggest that there is the need to think about 'intersections' – points where two (or more) brands might meet. As an example of this, they talk about branding dream teams (e.g. Apple and Microsoft) and highlight the marketing potential of liaisons such as this.

The emergence of hypercompetition and the erosion of traditional competitive advantage

Since the early 1990s, a wide variety of markets have witnessed an increase in the nature and intensity of competition. Referring to this as the 'era of hypercompetition', D'Aveni (1999, p. 57) suggests that 'domestic upstarts and foreign entrants have entered markets with a ferocity that has toppled national oligopolies and well-established industry leaders'. As just one example of this, he points to the way in which Microsoft, Intel, Compaq, Dell and a host of clone manufacturers from Asia have battered the once invincible IBM.

D'Aveni (1999) suggests that:

" . . . hypercompetition is characterized by constantly escalating rivalry in the form of rapid product innovation, shorter design and product life cycles, aggressive price and competence-based competition, and experimentation with new approaches to serving

customer needs. Hypercompetitors engage in an unrelenting battle to re-position themselves and to outmanoeuvre their competitors. By being customer-oriented, by turning suppliers into alliance partners and by attacking competitors head on, global hypercompetitors destroy the existing norms and rules of national oligopolies.*"*

Given this, the implications for how firms operate are significant. If an organization is to win an advantage, it must seize the initiative. It 'must serve customers better than its competitors and must do things that competitors cannot or will not react to or even understand' (D'Aveni, 1999, pp. 57–8). To rely upon traditional thinking and defensive strategies as opposed to attempting to disrupt and unsettle the competition will almost inevitably lead to the firm's position being eroded. It is because of this that a number of commentators now believe that the idea that competitive advantages based upon the traditional ideas of quality, competencies, entry barriers and economies of scale is rapidly losing validity. Instead, success is far more likely to come from a reinvention of the rules of competition within the marketplace.

This move towards hypercompetitive markets appears to have been driven by four factors:

1 *The demand by customers throughout the world for higher quality at lower prices.* In the USA, for example, numerous low-cost foreign competitors have entered price-sensitive market sectors with a higher value for money offer than the well-entrenched players. Having established a foothold in the market, they have gone on to expand the market and capture significant share.
2 *The speed of technological change and the information revolution* that has led to the traditional 'owners' of markets being outsmarted by new players who move faster and in very different ways. As an example of this, First Direct rewrote some of the rules of banking by being the first in the UK to offer 24-hour telephone banking.
3 *The emergence of aggressive and well-funded competitors* who take a long-term view and are willing to lose possibly substantial sums of money in the early years in order to dominate a market with long-term strategic potential and significance.
4 *Changes in government policies that have led to the collapse of traditional entry barriers.* Examples of this include legislation on competition within the EU, the reduction of tariffs, and the trend worldwide towards privatization and deregulation that has allowed non-traditional competitors to break up long-standing oligopolies.

Competing (effectively) in hypercompetitive markets

Faced with an increasingly hypercompetitive market, the marketing strategist is faced with a number of options. However, underpinning all of these has to be the recognition that the traditional competencies are likely to become increasingly less relevant as the rules of the competitive game change. The astute competitor therefore plays upon this by disrupting the product market and/or the factor (input) market.

In order to disrupt the product market, D'Aveni (1999, p. 60) suggests that there are several possibilities, the most obvious of which involve:

➡ *Changing the bases of competition* by redefining the meaning of quality on the product and then offering it at a lower price, a strategy that was pursued by easyJet when it entered the airlines market.

➡ *Modifying the boundaries of the market* by bundling and splitting industries. In the mobile phone market, for example, the astute competitors recognized that it is the air time that offers the greatest opportunities to make money, not the hardware. Because of this, the major players, particularly in the early years, focused upon building the customer base by offering cellular phones at very low prices. Equally, Microsoft and Intel split the personal computer business by capturing the value that at one stage was held by the PC manufacturers.

To disrupt the factor or input market, the strategist needs to focus upon one or more of three possibilities:

1 *Redefining the knowledge that is critical to success.* Dell, for example, by opting for direct selling through the Internet and telephone ordering, assembly to order and out-sourced delivery, undercut players such as IBM.

2 *Applying competencies developed outside the industry.* This approach is illustrated by First Direct's use of IT and telephone selling expertise developed in other sectors.

3 *Altering the sums of money needed to survive within a particular sector.* The so-called 'category killers', such as Toys 'R' Us, Wal-Mart and Car Supermarket, are all examples of this sort of approach.

Given the nature of these comments, it is apparent that, within hypercompetitive markets, the rules of competition change dramatically. In order to survive and prosper, firms need to behave in a very different way, characterized by far more rapid innovation, aggressive price- and competence-based competition, new approaches to meeting customers' needs, and very different mindsets.

Market domination and third-wave companies

For many organizations faced with or facing massively changed environments and ever greater customer expectations, the nature of the strategic marketing planning challenges with which they need to come to terms are radically different from those of the past. The implications of this, according to Vollman (1996, p. 5), are that organizations generally, but manufacturing firms in particular, need to recognize the need to dominate their markets. It is the failure to do this, he argues, which will almost inevitably lead to the decline and probable death of the organization. In making this comment, he believes that the nature and scope of change over the past few years has led to such a change in the competitive environment that what contributed towards the profile of a winning organization in the past does not necessarily apply today.

These 'third-wave' companies differ from their predecessors in a variety of ways, although in nearly every instance, he suggests, they reached their current position not by a series of evolutionary moves, but by a transformative leap which gave them a profile of dominance. However, it needs to be recognized that domination is not necessarily about *size* (General Motors, for example, despite being the biggest automotive company, does not dominate the industry. Instead, it is the smaller organizations such as Toyota that set the pace of competition), *monopolistic competition* or *profitability*. Rather it is the degree of influence they exert within their market sector(s).

The alternative to market domination, Vollman argues, is death, with this happening quickly or, more frequently, very slowly (see Chapter 1, Figure 1.5 and the supporting discussion). The signs of organizational decay are often identifiable long before crises become apparent. Included within these are a loss of market share, possession of the wrong set of competencies, slow(er) or slowing growth patterns, a loss of employee morale, poor product and process development, and the failure to recognize competitors' true capabilities (see Figure 4.13).

Faced with problems such as these, organizations typically respond in one of a number of ways, including:

➡ Improvement programmes such as time-based competition, quality and flexibility. However, in many markets these sorts of initiatives no longer provide the basis for competitive advantage, but are instead 'commodities of process'. In other words, without them you will not survive, but with them you are simply a player in the market.

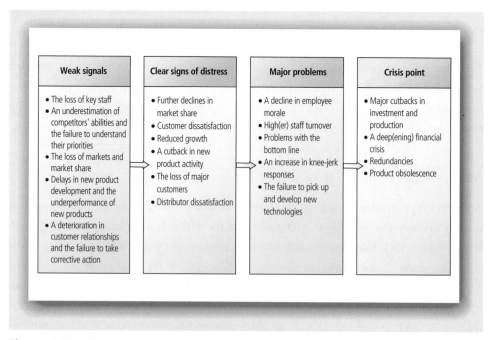

Figure 4.13   The signs of impending doom

➡ Financial restructuring and downsizing which, whilst apparently helpful in the short term, often do little to change the organizational culture.

➡ Management changes, which are characterized by a reshuffling of job titles, responsibilities and structures, rather than any real change in focus and direction.

By contrast, dominant organizations typically exhibit a very different set of characteristics and responses, including:

➡ Paradigm shifts that reflect a recognition that the old set of operating assumptions is no longer valid.

➡ Proactive rather than reactive changes, with these being made possible because of:
   ➡ High levels of responsiveness and flexibility
   ➡ A high degree of anticipation and forecasting of how the market is likely to develop
   ➡ The creation of change in the marketplace as the result of a series of marketing initiatives.

➡ Enterprise transformation that, because of a fundamental recognition on the part of management of the significance of environmental change and the consequent inadequacy of current structures and systems, leads to radically different ways of doing business.

The combined effect of these sorts of initiatives is that, in the successful organizations (Vollman, 1996, p. 7):

" . . . the very shape and structure of the enterprise have had to change, their competencies and capabilities have changed, their resources have changed, their outputs have changed, their attitude to customer service has changed and their fundamental *raison d'être* has changed.

In the unsuccessful, their missions have reverted back to 'doing core business', crisis management has replaced strategy and 'passengers' (such as cost) replace 'drivers' (such as customer satisfaction). They certainly are not the companies they once were – they have indeed been transformed. But no one was steering the change towards dominance.**"**

4.9 Approaches to environmental analysis and scanning

Against the background of our discussion so far, it should be clear that environmental analysis and forecasting are capable of making a major contribution to the formulation of strategy. Indeed, it has been argued by a number of strategists that environmental analysis and forecasting is the true starting point of any effective planning system, since strategy is based not only on a detailed understanding of the firm's capacity, but also on a full knowledge and appreciation of environmental forces and changes that are likely to have an impact on the firm. At its most extreme, the failure to do this is highlighted by Theodore Levitt's ideas of 'Marketing Myopia', which he discussed in his now classic *Harvard Business Review* article (1960, pp. 45–56).

In this article, Levitt argued that declining or defunct industries generally reached this position because of a product rather than a marketing orientation. In other words, they focused too firmly on products rather than the environment in which they operated. As a consequence, these companies were often taken by surprise by environmental change, found it difficult to respond and, in many cases, either lost significant market shares or were forced into liquidation.

A system of environmental analysis and forecasting consists of two elements: the first of these is concerned with the *generation* of an up-to-date database of information, while the second involves the *dissemination* of this information to decision-makers and influencers. The effectiveness of such a system, and in particular of this second part, is in practice likely to be influenced by a variety of factors, including:

➡ The technical skills of those involved in the process of analysis and forecasting
➡ The nature of the managerial environment that exists within the company.

The significance of this second point is, in many companies, all too often ignored, but highlights the importance of a planning culture that is both endorsed and promoted by top management. In addition, the managerial environment affects the process in the sense that, in large companies at least, those who are involved in the mechanics of analysis and forecasting are rarely the decision-makers themselves. Instead, they are generally in an advisory role. This role can lead to the emergence of an important political process within the system, whereby the analyst presents information in such a way that the decision-maker's perception of the environment and, in turn, the options open to the company, are distorted in a particular way. By the same token, the decision-maker will often place a particular interpretation on the information presented by the analyst, depending on his or her perception of the analyst's track record. In commenting on this political process, Brownlie (1987, p. 99) suggests that:

❞ . . . students of history will recognize that many a bloody political intrigue was spawned by the jealously guarded, and often misused, privilege of proximity to the seat of power which was conferred on privy counsellors and advisors. Thus in addition to the technical skills demanded of environmental analysts and forecasters, astute political skills could be said to be the hallmark of an effective operator. *❞*

It should therefore be recognized that the effectiveness of a planning system is not determined solely by its methodology, but that it is also affected by several other factors, including the willingness and ability of a management to recognize and subsequently respond to the indicators of coming environmental change.

Taken together, these comments argue the case for what we can refer to as *formal environmental scanning*, a process which covers the full spectrum of activities firms use in order to understand environmental changes and their implications. The essential element of formal environmental scanning is that it should be seen as an activity that becomes an *integral* part of the ongoing process by which companies develop, implement, control and review strategies and plans at both the corporate and the business unit levels.

In practice, the precise role of an environmental scanning process is influenced by a variety of factors, the most significant of which is typically that of management expectations. This, in turn, is often a function of the size of the organization and managerial perceptions of the complexity of its environment. Thus, in the case of many small firms, the focus is likely to be on the general trends that are likely to influence short- and medium-term levels of performance. In large firms, however, and in particular the multinationals, the focus tends to be far broader, with a greater emphasis being placed upon longer-term and more fundamental issues, including possible changes in the political, economic, social and technological variables that provided the focus for the first part of this chapter.

With regard to the specific benefits of environmental scanning, Diffenbach (1983), in a study of ninety American corporations, has suggested that there are seven principal pay-offs:

1 An increased general awareness by management of environmental changes
2 Better planning and strategic decision-making
3 Greater effectiveness in government matters
4 Better industry and market analysis
5 Better results in foreign business
6 Improvements in diversification and resource allocations
7 Better energy planning.

It should be noted that from this study Diffenbach found that, although environmental scanning is widely practised and generally considered to be important by the majority of those firms that do it (73 per cent), a sizeable number of companies (27 per cent) simply did not bother with scanning, or did it but found it to be of only limited value (28 per cent).

These benefits of environmental scanning have also been expanded upon by Jain (1990, p. 250), who has listed the major attractions to be that the process:

1 Helps firms to identify and capitalize upon opportunities rather than losing out to competitors
2 Provides a base of objective qualitative information
3 Makes the firm more sensitive to the changing needs and wishes of customers
4 Provides a base of 'objective qualitative information' about the business environment that can subsequently be of value to the strategist
5 Provides a level of intellectual stimulation for strategists
6 Improves the image of the firm with the public by illustrating that it is sensitive to its environment
7 Provides a continuing broad-based education for executives in general, and the strategist in particular.

Having said this, the complexity of the scanning process varies greatly from one company to another. In commenting on this, Ansoff (1984) has suggested that it is determined by two factors:

1 Perceptions within the company of the degree of environmental uncertainty (most typically this is a function of the rate of environmental change)
2 Perceptions of the degree of environmental complexity (this is generally influenced by the range of activities and markets in which the firm is currently and prospectively involved).

The significance of this second factor needs to be seen in terms of the implications for the structure of the scanning process that the firm then develops. Recognizing the dangers of overload within a system, there is a need for those involved in scanning to organize the process in such a way that the environment can be reduced to something manageable, while at the same time ensuring that extraneous factors are not ignored. What this means in practice is that a process of filtration generally operates in which the full breadth of environmental stimuli is reduced to something more manageable.

The question of who should decide on these elements has been referred to by Ansoff (1984), who has argued that it is the *user* of the information who should exert the major influence. In practice, however, it is often the scanner who determines the choice of approach.

Returning for a moment to the filtration process through which a structure is imposed upon the full breadth and complexity of the environment, Brownlie (1987, pp. 110–12) identifies three levels:

1 *The surveillance filter*, which provides a broad and generally unstructured picture of the business environment. However, although this picture is broad it will, by virtue of the perceptions of those involved, 'be selective and partial'.
2 *The mentality filter*, which emerges as the result of past successes and failures, and in turn leads to the idea of bounded rationality (by which a manager's ability to make optimal decisions is constrained by factors such as complexity and uncertainty), allowing those involved to cope with the volume and complexity of the information being generated. However, while this mentality filter is undoubtedly useful in helping to provide a structure, bounded rationality can create problems in that environmental signals that are extreme in nature and outside the manager's historical experience are likely to be perceived as being of little significance and subsequently screened out. There is a need, therefore, to balance the benefits of the mentality filter with a willingness to assess and possibly incorporate novel and perhaps extreme signals.
3 *The power filter*, which is essentially an attitude of mind on the part of top management and reflects a willingness to incorporate material in the strategic decision-making process that falls outside the bounds of previous practice and preconceived notions. Recognition by the scanner of the existence of an attitude such as this is

then likely to be reflected in the scanner's own willingness to build into the process a breadth of perspective rather than a straightforward identification and assessment of largely predictable environmental changes.

Against the background of comments such as these, it is possible to identify the features that are most likely to lead to an effective environmental scanning system. These include:

➡ Top management involvement and commitment
➡ A detailed understanding of the dimensions and parameters of the scanning model that it is intended should operate
➡ An established strategic planning culture.

In addition, attention needs to be paid to the *boundaries of the firm's environment* and hence to those areas that are deemed to be either relevant or irrelevant, and to the *time horizon* that is felt to be meaningful. In the case of the chemicals and pharmaceuticals industries, for example, the planning time horizon – and hence the scanning period – may easily be in excess of 30 years, while in the clothing industry it may be a year or less.

Brownlie's work (1983, 1987) suggests that environmental scanning is typically the responsibility of one of three levels of management:

1 *Line management*, with one or more line managers being given the task of scanning in addition to their normal responsibilities. In practice, however, such an approach typically suffers from limitations, the most obvious of which is that it is an additional responsibility and may not therefore get the attention it deserves. On top of this, the perspective is likely to be at best medium term, since the manager is unlikely to have the full range of specialist skills needed for the task to be performed effectively.
2 *Strategic planning*, in which environmental scanning is made part of the overall process of strategic analysis. While this is arguably more likely to succeed than is the case if responsibility is passed to line management, other problems are likely to emerge, largely because corporate staff may not necessarily understand the detail of the firm's business on a day-to-day basis. Because of this, it is argued, they are unlikely to be able to define and interpret the relevant parameters of the environment any more effectively than a line manager.
3 *A specialist organizational unit* with specific responsibilities for environmental monitoring.

Of these, the third approach may be seen as an ideal that few firms have yet to embrace. As a result, it is a mixture of the first two that predominates in business today. Most typically the mixture operates on a largely unstructured basis, with corporate planners focusing upon the general environment, while line managers focus upon the product market. The two perspectives, together with the general forecasts that can be bought from consultants and organizations such as the Henley Centre, are then assessed before the overall picture is developed.

Recognizing these sorts of organizational problems has led Diffenbach (1983) to identify the specific difficulties of environmental analysis that act as deterrents to the development and implementation of an effective scanning system:

1 The interpretation of results and the assessment of their specific impact upon the organization is rarely clear-cut
2 The output of environmental analysis may be too inaccurate, general or uncertain to be taken seriously
3 A preoccupation with the short term pre-empts attention being paid to longer-term environmental issues
4 Long-term environmental analyses are often treated sceptically
5 In diversified businesses the amount of analysis needed is likely to be both considerable and complex, particularly when interrelationships are considered
6 Perceptions and interpretations of scenarios identified may differ significantly between one manager and another.

For many marketing managers, one of the biggest and most enduring problems is that of understanding their markets. Without this understanding, they lose touch with the market, are taken by surprise by shifts in customer expectations, are slow to react to competitors, and fail to make full use of their distribution channels. The net effect of this is that they then fail to anticipate the nature and direction of changes within the market, constantly miss opportunities and, when they do respond, typically behave slowly and counter-productively. By contrast, managers within the truly market-driven organization are notable for the way in which they sense how their markets are likely to change, the nature of the opportunities that this is likely to create and how these opportunities can then best be exploited.

In discussing the difference between the two types of organization and what determines whether an organization is market driven, Day (1996a, p. 12) highlights the importance of market learning:

"Market learning involves much more than simply taking in information. The learning process must give managers the ability to ask the right questions at the right time, absorb the answers into their mental model of how the market behaves, share the new understanding with others in the management team and act decisively. Effective learning about markets is a continuous process that pervades all decisions. It cannot be spasmodic."

This effective learning process, which is illustrated in Figure 4.14, consists of several distinct stages:

➡ *Open-minded enquiry* based on the belief that decisions need to be based on a detailed and broad understanding of the market, and that conventional wisdoms and preconceived notions and beliefs are dangerous

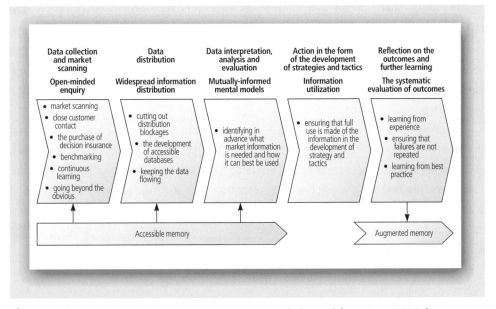

Figure 4.14 The organizational learning process (adapted from Day, 1996a)

➡ *Widespread information distribution* to ensure that managers across the organization develop a greater market understanding

➡ *Mutually-informed mental models*, which are used in the interpretation of information and ensure that issues that are deemed to be strategically important are examined

➡ *An accessible organizational memory* to ensure that the organization keeps track of what has been learned so the information and knowledge can continue to be used.

The process is then reinforced by a deliberate reflection on the outcomes of the strategies and tactics that have been developed and, by means of integrated databases, the augmentation of the organizational memory.

4.10 Summary

Marketing strategy is concerned with matching the capabilities of the organization with the demands of the environment. There is therefore a need for the strategist to monitor the environment on an ongoing basis so that opportunities and threats facing the organization are identified and subsequently reflected in strategy.

In analysing the environment a stepwise approach is needed. This begins with an initial audit of general environmental influences, followed by a series of increasingly tightly-focused stages designed to provide the strategist with a clear understanding of the organization's strategic position.

Although a variety of approaches can be used for analysing the environment, arguably the most useful is the PEST framework. This involves the strategist focusing in turn upon the Political/legal, Economic, Social/cultural and Technological elements of the environment. Each of these elements has been discussed in detail.

The environmental conditions faced by an organization are capable of varying greatly in their complexity, and need to be reflected both in the ways in which environmental analysis is conducted and in the ways in which strategy is subsequently developed. The consequences of failing to take account of a changing environment have, as discussed, been illustrated by a wide variety of organizational experiences, including those of the Swiss watch industry in the 1970s.

It is widely recognized that the pace of environmental change is increasing and that the need for organizations to develop a structured approach to environmental analysis, with the results then being fed into the strategic marketing planning process, is greater than ever. Despite this, the evidence suggests that in many organizations environmental scanning systems are only poorly developed. If this is to change, top management commitment both to the development of a scanning system and to the incorporation of the results into the planning process is essential.

Chapter **5**

Approaches to customer analysis

5.1 Learning objectives

When you have read this chapter you should be able to understand:

(a) the factors that influence consumer behaviour;
(b) the structure of the consumer buying decision process;
(c) the nature of organizational buying;
(d) how an understanding of buying processes can be used in the development of marketing strategy;
(e) why relationship marketing is becoming an increasingly important strategic marketing tool and how a relationship marketing programme can be developed.

5.2 Introduction

It has long been recognized that marketing planning is ultimately driven by the marketing planner's perception of how and why customers behave as they do, and how they are likely to respond to the various elements of the marketing mix (see Illustration 5.1).

Illustration 5.1 The advantages of understanding customer needs

Although the arguments for constant and detailed customer analysis have been well rehearsed, numerous organizations fall into the trap of believing that, because they deal with their customers on a day-to-day basis, they have a clear understanding of their needs and motivations. The reality is, however, often very different, as is shown for example by the ways in which companies are seemingly taken by surprise by the decline of major market sectors, the loss of long-standing accounts, and by the way in which some 80 per cent of all new products launched fail. There is therefore an overwhelming argument for regular assessments (and reassessments) of what customers *really* want, their current levels of satisfaction, and the scope that exists for developing new products and services that existing customers might buy. In discussing

this, Davidson (1987a, p. 60) cites a number of examples, including:

➡ Accounting firms which having been heavily committed to a mature product – the annual company audit – used this as the entry point for developing a wide range of consultancy services. They are now firmly positioned in the highly profitable management consultancy market, having retained their stable core auditing business.

➡ One of the great success stories of the 1980s was the Sony Walkman. Its development was brought about as the result of Sony's Chairman, Akio Morita, observing that the quality of stereo on planes was poor. The Sony Walkman technology was therefore developed initially for global travellers. Once the technology was available, Sony recognized the product's potential for a younger and far larger market.

➡ Dulux Solid Emulsion Paint, which overcame the perennial problem faced by the DIY decorator, that of paint spattering over the floor. The advantages of the product were capitalized upon in an intensive advertising campaign and confirmed Dulux's position as the market leader.

By contrast, when the American motorcycle manufacturer Harley Davidson threw a party in September 2003 to celebrate the 100th anniveresary of its foundation, it chose as its leading act Elton John, only to find the crowd leaving in droves. According to Jim Stingl of the *Milwaukee Journal*: 'It was the wrong choice. These guys – the dealers and the hardcore hairy road warriors – like ZZ Top and Cream. It was as if Harley was saying, "You think you know our customer? Think again."'

In the majority of markets, however, buyers differ enormously in terms of their buying dynamics. The task faced by the marketing planner in coming to terms with these differences is consequently complex. In consumer markets, for example, not only do buyers typically differ in terms of their age, income, educational levels and geographical location, but more fundamentally in terms of their personality, their lifestyles and their expectations. In the case of organizational and industrial markets, differences are often exhibited in the goals being pursued, the criteria employed by those involved in the buying process, the formality of purchasing policies, and the constraints that exist in the form of delivery dates and expected performance levels.

Despite these complexities, it is essential that the marketing planner understands in detail the dynamics of the buying process, since the costs and competitive implications of failing to do so are likely to be significant. In the case of new product development, for example, it is generally recognized that some 80 per cent of all new products launched fail, a statistic that owes much to a lack of understanding of customers' expectations. It is for these sorts of reasons that a considerable amount of research has been conducted in the post-war period in order to provide us with a greater understanding of buying patterns, and to enable us to predict more readily *how* buyers will behave in any given situation. Within this chapter we therefore focus upon some of the factors which influence behaviour and how subsequently they influence marketing strategy. It does need to be emphasized, however, that a series of interrelationships exist between this material and the areas covered in Chapter 8, in which we examine approaches to segmentation, targeting and positioning. The reader might therefore find it useful at this stage to turn briefly to Chapter 8 to identify the nature of these interrelationships before continuing.

5.3 Coming to terms with buyer behaviour

Irrespective of whether the marketing planner is operating in a consumer, industrial or organizational market, there are eight questions which underpin any understanding of buyer behaviour:

1 Who is in the market and what is the extent of their power with regard to the organization?

2 What do they buy?

3 Why do they buy?

4 Who is involved in the buying?

5 How do they buy?

6 When do they buy?

7 Where do they buy?

8 What are the customers' 'hot' and 'cold' spots? ('Hot' spots are those elements of the marketing offer that the customer sees to be particularly important and reassuring – and on which the organization delivers. 'Cold' spots are those elements that alienate the customer. An example of this might be poor or inconsistent service.)

It is the answers to these questions which should provide the marketing planner with an understanding of the ways in which buyers are most likely to respond to marketing stimuli. It then follows from this that the organization that makes the best use of the information should be in a position to gain a competitive advantage. For this reason, a considerable amount of time, effort and money has been spent over the past few decades in attempting to provide the marketing planner with a series of answers.

The starting point for much of this work has been a straightforward stimulus–response model of the sort illustrated in Figure 5.1.

Here, stimuli in the form both of the external environment and the elements of the marketing mix enter the buyer's 'black box' and interact with the buyer's characteristics and decision processes to produce a series of outputs in the form of purchase decisions. Included within these is the question of whether to buy and, if so, which product and brand, which dealer, when, and in what quantities. The task faced by the marketing

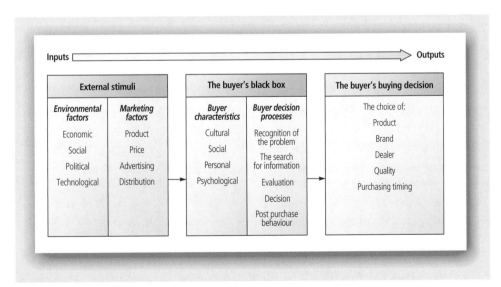

Figure 5.1 A stimulus–response model of buyer behaviour

planner therefore involves understanding how this black box operates. To do this, we need to consider the two principal components of the box: firstly, the factors that the individual brings to the buying situation; secondly, the decision processes that are used. We will therefore begin by focusing upon these background factors – cultural, social, personal and psychological – as a prelude to examining the detail of the decision process itself.

However, before doing this, we need to highlight just one of the major changes of the past few years, that of the emergence of what might loosely be termed 'the new consumer'. The new consumer is typically far more demanding and far more discriminating than consumers of the past, as well as being far less brand loyal and much more willing to complain. In many ways, the emergence of this new type of consumer represents one of the biggest challenges for marketers, since their expectations of organizations and their relationships that they demand are very different from anything previously. The characteristics and marketing implications of the new consumer are examined in some detail at a later stage in the chapter (see pp. 188–92), although Illustration 5.2 provides the reader with an overview of some of their key features.

Illustration 5.2 The emergence of the new consumer

In many ways, the most significant and far-reaching legacies for marketing of the economic and social changes and turbulence of the late 1980s and early 1990s are reflected in what we might loosely refer to as the emergence of the 'new' consumer and the 'new' competitor (the dimensions of the new competitor are discussed in Chapter 6). Although neither is necessarily new in any absolute sense, they differ in a series of ways from traditional consumers and competitors in that their expectations, values and patterns of behaviour are all very different from that with which marketing planners traditionally had to come to terms. The consequences of this are manifested in several ways but, in the case of the new consumer, by the way in which the degree of understanding of customers' motivations must be far greater and the marketing effort tailored more firmly and clearly to the patterns of specific need. We can therefore see the new consumer as being characterized by:

➡ The development of new value systems
➡ A greater emphasis upon value for money
➡ Higher levels of price awareness and price sensitivity
➡ An increased demand for and a willingness to accept more and exciting new products
➡ Less technophobia
➡ Lower levels of brand and supplier loyalty, and the development of what might be referred to as customer and brand promiscuity
➡ A greater willingness to experiment with new products, ideas and delivery systems
➡ A generally far more questioning and sceptical attitude towards government, big business and brands
➡ Higher levels of environmental awareness
➡ Fundamental changes in family structures and relationships
➡ The changed and changing roles of men and women.

In essence, therefore, one can see the new consumer to be very different from consumers of the past in that they are typically:

1 Far more demanding
2 Far more discriminating

3 Much less brand loyal
4 Much more willing to complain than customers in the past.

These themes are explored in greater detail in the Appendix to this chapter.

Taking just one of these twelve characteristics listed in Illustration 5.2 – the changed and changing roles of men and women – its significance can perhaps be appreciated by the fact that more than 40 per cent of new cars that are bought privately are now bought by women; this compares with less than 6 per cent in 1970. From the viewpoint of the car manufacturers, the implications have been enormous and have had to be reflected not just in terms of the design of cars, but also the nature of the market research that is conducted, the advertising and promotion that is carried out, and the approach to selling.

The new consumer and the youth market

The differences that exist between the new consumer and the old are even more apparent – and more extreme – in the case of young(er) consumers (for our purposes here, we see these to be aged between 4 and 19), in that this segment, when compared with other customer groups, is also typically:

➡ Far more media literate
➡ Infinitely more advertising literate
➡ Much more brand literate, brand sophisticated and brand discriminating
➡ Far more technologically literate.

To a large extent, these higher levels of media advertising, brand and technological literacy can be seen to be the direct result of having been exposed to a far greater number and a much larger variety of media than any previous generation. Included within this are 24-hour television, satellite broadcasting, and a huge upsurge in the numbers of newspapers and ever far more finely targeted magazines. The advertising literacy then follows directly from this in that the sheer number of advertisements to which they have been exposed is higher than ever before. Brand literacy emerges from brands having been an integral part of lifestyles for as long as this generation has been alive, something that was not always the case with older consumers. Equally, the technological literacy follows from their exposure to technologies such as information technology from a very early age. The combined effect of this is the emergence of a very different type of young buyer who has very different and often much more unpredictable patterns of buying, and who is typically very aware of the subtleties of brand differences.

In many ways, the emergence of this new type of consumer, be it in the teen market or those aged 20–55, represents one of the biggest challenges for marketers, since their expectations of organizations and the nature of the relationships that they demand are very different from anything previously. Recognizing this, if marketers fail to come to terms with this development, the implications for organizational performance and marketing planning are significant, something that is discussed at a later stage in the chapter.

5.4 Factors influencing consumer behaviour

From the viewpoint of the marketing planner, the mix of cultural, social, personal and psychological factors that influence behaviour (illustrated in Figure 5.2) is largely non-controllable. Because of the influence they exert upon patterns of buying, it is essential that as much effort as possible is put into understanding *how they interact* and, ultimately, *how they influence* purchase behaviour. In doing this, it is important not to lose sight of the differences that exist between customers and consumers, and the implications of these differences for strategy. The term 'consumer' is typically taken to mean the final user, who is not necessarily the customer. In the case of foodstuffs such as breakfast cereals, for example, the buyer (generally still the housewife) acts on behalf of her family. For the marketing mix to be effective, it is quite obviously essential that the strategist therefore understands not just what the *customer* wants (e.g. value for money), but also what the *consumer* wants (e.g. taste, free gifts, image).

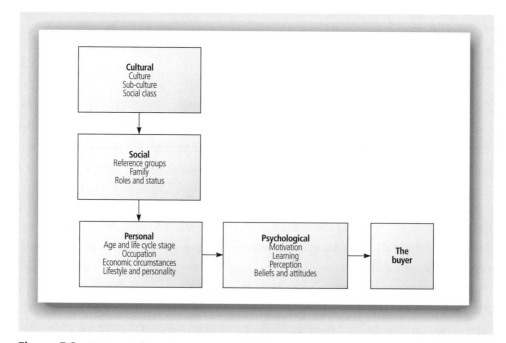

Figure 5.2 Factors influencing consumer behaviour

The significance of culture

The most fundamental of the four influencing forces, and hence the logical starting point for any analysis of behaviour, is the buyer's set of *cultural* factors. These include culture, subculture and social class. Of these, it is the culture of the society itself that typically proves to be the most fundamental and enduring influence on behaviour, since human behaviour is very largely the result of our socialization, initially within the family and then, increasingly, within a series of other institutions such as schools, friendship groups, clubs, and so on. It is from this that we learn our set(s) of values, perceptions, preferences and behaviour patterns. Schiffman and Kanuk (1983, pp. 404–20) suggest that, in the western world at least, these include achievement, success, efficiency, progress, material comfort, practicality, individualism, freedom, humanitarianism, youthfulness and practicality. It is these which, to a very large extent, determine and drive our patterns of behaviour.

This broad set of values is then influenced in turn by the subcultures in which we develop. These include nationality groups, religious groups, racial groups and geographical areas, all of which exhibit degrees of difference in ethnic taste, cultural preferences, taboos, attitudes and lifestyle.

The influence of subcultures is subsequently affected by a third set of variables: that of *social stratification* and, in particular, *social class*. The significance of social class as a determinant of behaviour is discussed in some detail in Chapter 4. At this stage, we will therefore simply highlight its key characteristics, which, traditionally at least, have been suggested to be as follows:

1 People within a particular social class are more similar than those from different social classes
2 Social class is determined by a series of variables, such as occupation, income, education and values, rather than by a single variable
3 Individuals can move from one social class to another.

Although research in recent years has led to a modification of these ideas as the degree of social mobility has increased, the most important single implication of social class is the still valid assumption that it exerts a significant degree of influence in areas such as clothing, cars, leisure pursuits and media preferences.

Social factors

Against this background of cultural forces, the strategist needs then to turn to an examination of the influence exerted by a series of social factors, including reference groups, family, social role and status.

Reference groups can be divided into four types:

1 *Primary membership groups*, which are generally informal and to which individuals belong and within which they interact. These include family, neighbours, colleagues and friends.

2 *Secondary membership groups*, which tend to be more formal than primary groups and within which less interaction typically takes place. Included within these are trade unions, religious groups and professional societies.

3 *Aspirational groups*, to which an individual would like to belong.

4 *Dissociative groups*, whose values and behaviour the individual rejects.

The influence exerted by reference groups tends to vary considerably from one product and brand to another, as well as at different stages of the individual's life stage. Among the products and brands that typically have been found to be influenced most directly by reference group behaviour are cars, drinks, clothing and cigarettes. The influence of reference groups does, however, change over the course of the product life cycle. In the introductory stage, for example, the question of *whether* to buy is heavily influenced by others, although the influence upon the choice of brand is not particularly significant. In the growth stage, the group influences both product and brand choice, while in maturity it is the brand but not the product that is subject to this influence. The influence of reference groups in the decline stage is almost invariably weak in terms of both the product and brand choice.

The implications of these findings are significant and provide the marketing planner with a series of guidelines, the most important of which centres around the need to identify the *opinion leaders* for each reference group. Our understanding of opinion leadership has developed considerably over the past few years, and whereas at one time it was believed that opinion leadership was limited primarily to prominent figures within society, this is no longer seen to be the case. Rather, it is recognized that an individual may well be an opinion leader in certain circumstances, but an opinion follower in others. Quite obviously, this makes the task of identifying opinion leaders more difficult and gives emphasis to the need to understand not just the demographic but particularly the psychographic characteristics of the group that the strategist is attempting to influence.

For many products, however, it is the family that exerts the greatest single influence on behaviour, even though, as we suggest elsewhere in this chapter, the size and structure of the family unit has changed considerably over the past 20 years. This includes both the *family of orientation* (parents, brothers and sisters) and the *family of procreation* (spouse and children). The significance of the family as a determinant of buying behaviour has long been recognized, and for this reason it has been the subject of a considerable amount of research in order to identify the roles and relative influence exerted by different family members. Although it is not our intention to examine this area in detail, there are several general conclusions that have emerged from this research and that merit emphasis at this stage:

➡ The involvement of both partners within a relationship upon purchase decisions varies greatly from one product category to another, with women still playing the principal role in the purchasing of food and clothing. Although this has changed somewhat over the past few years as the proportion of working women has increased and divorce rates have escalated, the Institute of Grocery Distribution has estimated that, in the UK, women still account for some 80 per cent of food purchases.

➡ Joint husband and wife (or partner) decision-making tends to be a characteristic of more expensive product choices, where the opportunity cost of a 'wrong' decision is greater.

At a more general level, however, research in the USA has identified three patterns of decision-making within the family and the sorts of product category with which each is typically associated. These are:

1 Husband-dominant – life insurance, cars and consumer electronics
2 Wife-dominant – washing machines, carpets, kitchenware and non-living-room furniture
3 Equal – living-room furniture, holidays, housing, furnishings and entertainment.

Although this research is useful in that it distinguishes between the different decision-making patterns, the results need to be treated with a degree of caution, if only because of the ways in which roles within the family have changed (and indeed still are changing) significantly.

The final social factor that typically influences purchase behaviour consists of the individual's actual and perceived *roles* and *statuses*, both within society in general and within groups in particular. The significance of status symbols and the messages they communicate has long been recognized. The obvious implication, however, for the marketing strategist is to position products and brands in such a way that they reinforce the messages suited to particular individuals and groups.

Personal influences on behaviour

The third major category of influences upon behaviour is made up of the buyer's set of *personal characteristics*, including age and life-cycle stage, occupation, economic circumstances, lifestyle and personality. The majority of these factors have been used extensively by marketing strategists in segmenting markets; this is discussed further on pp. 328–45.

Psychological influences

The fourth and final set of influences upon behaviour consists of the four principal *psychological factors* – motivation, perception, learning, and beliefs and attitudes. The first of these, motivation, is in many ways both the most important to understand and the most complex to analyse. The starting point involves recognizing the differences between *biogenic* needs, which are physiological (hunger, thirst and discomfort), and *psychogenic* needs, which are essentially psychological states of tension (these include the need for esteem and the desire for recognition or belonging). It is these needs which, when they become sufficiently intense, create a motivation to act in such a way that the tension of the need is reduced. The search to understand the detail of this process has led to a considerable amount of research over the past 100 years and, in turn, to a variety of theories of human motivation. The best known of these are the theories of Marshall, Freud, Veblen, Herzberg, Vroon and Maslow.

The first of these, the Marshallian model, is in many ways the most straightforward and is based on the idea that a person's behaviour is inherently rational and motivated by economic factors. The economic individual therefore attempts to maximize total satisfaction by buying goods and services from which the marginal utility is, in theory at least, equivalent to the marginal utility of the alternatives. Although such an overtly rational view of behaviour has long been criticized as being too partial and inadequate an explanation, it has been argued that the Marshallian model contributes the following to our understanding of buyer behaviour:

1 It is axiomatic that every buyer acts in the light of his own best interest. The question is whether an economist would describe these actions as 'rational'.
2 The model is normative in the sense that it provides a logical basis for purchase decisions, i.e. how one *should* decide rather than how one *actually* decides.
3 The model suggests a number of useful behavioural hypotheses, e.g. the lower the price, the greater the sales; the lower the price of substitute products, the lower the sales of this product; the lower the price of complementary products, the higher the sales of this product; the higher the real income, the higher the sales of this product, provided that it is not an 'inferior' good; the higher the promotional expenditure, the higher the sales.

Freud's work, by contrast, suggests that the psychological factors that influence behaviour are for the most part unconscious, and that as a consequence we can only rarely understand our true motivations. Equally, in the process of growing up and conforming to the rules of society, we repress a series of urges. The obvious implication of this for marketing is that a consumer's *stated* motive for buying a particular brand or product may well be very different from the more fundamental *underlying* motive. Thus, in the case of a fast car, the stated motive might be the ability to get from A to B quickly. The underlying motive, however, might well be the desire for status and to be noticed. Similarly, with an expensive watch the stated motive might be the product's reliability, while the real – and unconscious – motive might again be status and the desire to impress others.

The best-known exponent of Freudian theory in marketing was Ernest Dichter, who, in the 1950s, developed a series of techniques, under the general heading of *motivational research*, designed to uncover consumers' deepest motives. Motivational research was subjected to a considerable amount of criticism on the grounds that buyers were subsequently being manipulated and persuaded to act against their own interests. Two of the most vociferous opponents of motivational research proved to be Galbraith and Packard. Galbraith (1958), for example, levelled a series of criticisms against the development of the consumer society, arguing that consumers were being persuaded to act against their true interests. Packard's criticisms, in his book *The Hidden Persuaders* (1957), were aimed even more specifically at techniques of motivational research and raised the spectre of the wholesale manipulation of society by marketing people for their own ends. Largely because of the subsequent publicity, motivational research became a less acceptable research technique and this, coupled with a whole series of problems experienced in its use, led to its gradual decline.

The Freudian view that a consumer's stated motives may well be very different from the true motives is echoed in Veblen's (1899) socio-psychological interpretations of behaviour. Many purchases, he argued, are motivated not by need but by a desire for prestige and social standing. Although Veblen's views, and in particular his emphasis upon conspicuous consumption, have subsequently been modified by research findings, his contribution to our understanding of buyer behaviour is significant, not least because it stresses the importance of social relationships as an influence upon choice.

The fourth major theory of motivation, one which has received considerable attention from marketing analysts over the past 30 years, was developed by Herzberg. Labelled the 'two-factor theory' of motivation, it distinguishes between *satisfiers* (factors that create satisfaction) and *dissatisfiers* (factors that create dissatisfaction). In the case of a car, for example, the absence of a warranty would be a dissatisfier. The existence of a warranty, however, is not a satisfier since it is not one of the principal reasons for buying the product. These are more likely to be the car's looks, its performance and the status that the buyer feels the product confers upon the driver.

There are several implications of this theory for marketing, of which two are particularly significant. First, the seller needs to be fully aware of the dissatisfiers, which, while they will not by themselves sell the product, can easily 'unsell' it. The second implication, which follows logically from this, is that the strategist needs to understand in detail the various satisfiers and then concentrate not just upon supplying them, but also giving them full emphasis in the marketing programme.

The fifth and final principal theory of motivation was put forward by Maslow, who suggested that behaviour can be explained in terms of a hierarchy of needs; this is illustrated in Figure 5.3.

The model suggests that a person begins by concentrating upon satisfying the most important and most basic physiological needs before moving on to the higher levels of need. Thus, as each level is satisfied, the next level is likely to become the focus of attention.

Although, from the viewpoint of the marketing strategist, Maslow's theory is arguably of less direct value than that of, say, Herzberg, it is of value in that it provides yet another insight into the ways in which products fit into the goals and lives of consumers.

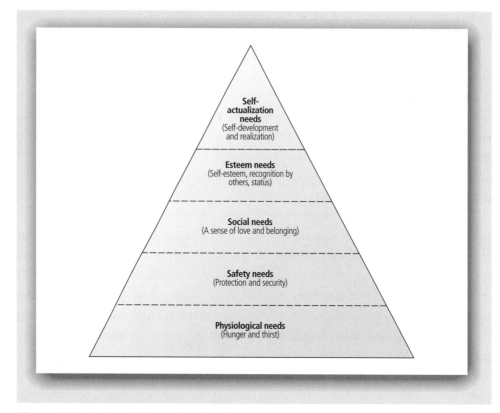

Figure 5.3   Maslow's hierarchy of needs

Issues of perception

Against the background of an understanding of the factors influencing motivation, the marketing strategist needs then to consider the influence of *perception*, since it is the way in which motivated individuals perceive a given situation that determines precisely how they will behave. It has long been understood that because of the three elements of the perceptual process – selective attention, selective distortion and selective retention – individuals can perceive the same object in very different ways. It is the failure to recognize and take account of this that often leads to a confusion of, for example, advertising messages. Research in this area has provided a series of insights into the perceptual process, and subsequently to a series of guidelines for marketers. In the case of *selection attention*, for example, simply because of the enormous number of stimuli that we are exposed to each day (more than 2200 advertisements alone), a substantial number are either ignored or given only cursory attention. If a marketing message is to succeed, it therefore has to fight against this screening process. This can be done in one of several ways, including:

1 The use of black and white advertisements when others are in colour, or vice versa.

2 The use of shock messages – in 1990, for example, the RSPCA drew attention to the number of stray dogs being destroyed each year by showing a mountain of bodies. Equally, Benetton has over the years run a series of highly controversial advertisements, while French Connection UK coveted controversy with the ambiguity of the FCUK logo.

3 The sheer size of the advertisement.

4 Substantial money-off offers.

5 The unexpected – a glue manufacturer used his product to stick a car to a hoarding in London some 15 feet above the pavement.

However, even when a message does reach the consumer, there is no guarantee that it will be interpreted in the way that was intended. Each person modifies information in such a way that it fits neatly into the existing mindset. This process of *selective distortion* means that messages that confirm preconceived notions are far more likely to be accepted than those that challenge these notions. Although a mindset can be changed, this is typically both costly and time-consuming. However, one example of where this has been done with considerable success is with Japanese products. The image and reputation of the majority of Japanese products in the 1960s was generally poor, a factor that had implications for, among other things, distribution and pricing. Throughout the 1970s, 1980s and 1990s, however, the Japanese concentrated on quality and product innovation to the point at which even the most die-hard and conservative European or American was forced to admit that in many markets it is now the Japanese who set the lead.

A similar example is that of the car manufacturer, Skoda. Long seen as rugged, cheap and utilitarian, their takeover by Volkswagen in the 1990s and a heavy investment in new product development, manufacturing and marketing has led to a radical repositioning of the brand; this is discussed in Illustration 5.3.

Illustration 5.3 The repositioning of Skoda

Throughout the 1980s and into the early 1990s, Skoda was a byword for everything that was wrong with east European products in general and their cars in particular. With a reputation for being ugly, unreliable and for rusting away, the brand had little credibility in western markets. Following the collapse of communism and the Socialist Republic of Czechoslovakia in 1989, the new government immediately embarked on a programme of industrial privatization. Among the companies put up for sale was Skoda.

In 1990, Volkswagen Group, intent on expanding into eastern Europe, took a 30 per cent share of the company and gained managerial control (it subsequently increased its shareholding to 70 per cent and then total ownership). Specialists from Germany were sent to the main Skoda factory to re-engineer the production line, retrain the workers, update the designs, and encourage suppliers to adopt just-in-time practices.

Within the first 10 years of VW's control and with an investment of £1 billion and a further £1 billion planned, Skoda launched three new models and invested heavily in an advertising campaign designed to reposition the brand in consumers' minds. In doing this, the company decided to confront the problem head-on. Typical of the poster campaign was a sleek image of a shadowy, powerful car with a Skoda badge and the line 'No, really . . .'. In a television campaign, three stooges – a politician, a self-important car show official and a car park attendant – all mistake the gleamingly up-to-date new Skoda for something else. The pay-off line is, 'It's a Skoda. Honest.'

Underpinning the campaign was the fundamental recognition that any attempt at repositioning had to be based upon a series of radical changes and improvements to the product itself. In the absence of this, any attempt at repositioning would undoubtedly fail. The new Skoda models therefore emphasized quality, the driving experience, the Volkswagen link/heritage and value for money.

Previously, the traditional Skoda driver was a 56-year-old man with little interest in design or performance, and who wanted basic low-cost and no-frills transport. Although the company was intent on repositioning the brand by appealing to a younger market and more women (young, middle-class women make up the largest single group of customers for small cars), it also recognised it could not afford to alienate its traditional markets, which had a 76 per loyalty/repurchase rate.

Source: *Weekend FT Magazine, Financial Times*, 29 April 2000, pp. 22–3, 40.

The third element of perception is that of *selective retention*. Quite simply, individuals forget much of what they learn. Therefore, to ensure that a message is retained, it needs to be relevant, generally straightforward, one which reinforces existing positive attitudes and that, in the case of certain products, is catchy. Many people, for example, still remember simple advertising slogans such as 'Beanz Meanz Heinz', 'Drinka Pinta Milk a Day', 'Go to work on an egg' and 'Guinness is good for you', even though, in some cases, the message has not been used for well over 30 years.

Once individuals have responded to an advertisement, they go through a process of learning. If the experience with the product is generally positive, the likelihood of repeat purchase is obviously increased. If, however, the experience is largely negative, not only is the likelihood of repeat purchase reduced, but the negative attitude that develops is likely to be extended to other products from the same manufacturer and possibly the country of origin. It is the set of *beliefs* and *attitudes* that emerge both from our own experiences and from those of individuals in our reference groups that build up a set of product and brand images. These, in turn, lead us to behave in relatively consistent ways. An obvious problem that can therefore be faced by a manufacturer stems from the difficulties of changing attitudes and images once they have been established.

5.5 The buying decision process

Having identified the various factors that influence behaviour, the marketing strategist is then in a position to examine the buying process itself. This involves focusing on three distinct elements:

1 The buying roles within the decision-making unit

2 The type of buying behaviour

3 The decision process.

The five buying roles

In the majority of cases and for the majority of products, identifying the buyer is a relatively straightforward exercise. In some instances, however, the decision of what to buy involves several people, and here we can identify five distinct roles:

1 The *initiator*, who first suggests buying the product or service

2 The *influencer*, whose comments affect the decision made

3 The *decider*, who ultimately makes all or part of the buying decision

4 The *buyer*, who physically makes the purchase

5 The *user(s)*, who consume(s) the product or service.

Identifying who plays each of these roles, and indeed *how* they play them, is important since it is this information which should be used to determine a wide variety of marketing decisions. In the case of advertising, for example, the question of who plays each of the buying roles should be used to decide on who the advertising is to be aimed at, the sort of appeal, the timing of the message, and the placing of the message.

Different types of buying behaviour

So far in this discussion, we have referred simply to 'buying behaviour'. In practice, of course, it is possible to identify several types of buying decision and hence several types of buying behaviour. The most obvious distinction to make is based on the expense, complexity, risk and opportunity cost of the purchase decision – the process a consumer goes through in deciding on a new car or major holiday, for example, will be radically different from the process in deciding whether to buy a chocolate bar. Recognition of this has led Assael (1987, Chapter 4) to distinguish between four types of buying behaviour, depending on the degree of buyer involvement in the purchase and the extent to which brands differ. This is illustrated in Figure 5.4.

Understanding the buying decision process

The third and final stage that we are concerned with here is the structure of the buying decision process that consumers go through. In other words, precisely *how* do consumers buy particular products? Do they, for example, search for information and make detailed comparisons, or do they rely largely upon the advice of a store assistant? Are they influenced significantly by price or by advertising? Questions such as these have led to a considerable amount of research into the buying process and subsequently to consumers being categorized either as deliberate buyers or compulsive buyers.

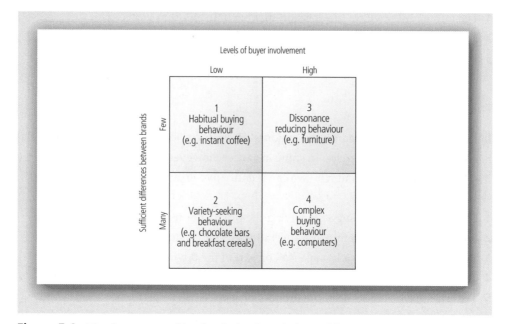

Figure 5.4 The four types of buying behaviour (adapted from Assael, 1987)

To help in coming to terms with this, a series of models have been proposed that focus not simply upon the purchase *decision*, but upon the *process* leading up to this decision, the decision itself, and then subsequently post-purchase behaviour. An example of this sort of model is illustrated in Figure 5.5.

Here, the process begins with the consumer's *recognition of a problem*, or perhaps more commonly, a want. This may emerge as the result of an internal stimulus (hunger or thirst) or an external stimulus in the form of an advertisement or a colleague's comment. This leads to the *search for information*, which might be at the level simply of a heightened awareness or attention to advertising, or at the deeper level of extensive information searching. In either case, the search process is likely to involve one or more of four distinct sources:

1 *Personal sources*, such as family, friends, colleagues and neighbours
2 *Public sources*, such as the mass media and consumer organizations – a typical example would be the Consumers' Association's *Which?* magazine

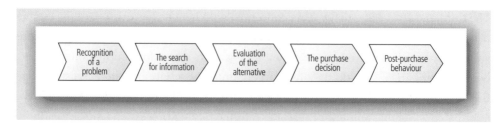

Figure 5.5 A sequential model of the buying process

3 *Commercial sources*, such as advertising, sales staff and brochures

4 *Experimental sources*, such as handling or trying the product.

The relative importance of each of these varies greatly from person to person and product to product. Typically, therefore, the consumer might gain the greatest amount of information from commercial sources such as newspapers and advertisments. However, the information that is most likely to influence behaviour comes from personal sources such as friends. Each type of source plays a different role in influencing the buying decision. Commercial information, for example, plays an informing function, while personal sources perform a legitimizing and/or evaluation function.

By gathering information in this way, consumers develop an awareness, knowledge and understanding of the various brands in the market. An obvious task then faced by marketing strategists is how best to ensure that their brand stands out from the others available and is subsequently purchased. In essence, this involves moving the product or brand from the *total set* available, through to the consumer's *awareness set* and *consideration set* to the *choice set*, from which the consumer ultimately makes the buying decision; this is illustrated diagrammatically in Figure 5.6.

However, for this to be done effectively, the strategist needs to have a clear understanding of the criteria used by consumers in comparing products. Much of the research in this area has focused primarily upon the cognitive element, suggesting that consumers make product judgements on a rational basis (see Illustration 5.4). Whether this is the case in practice is, of course, highly debatable and contradicts much of what we have already said.

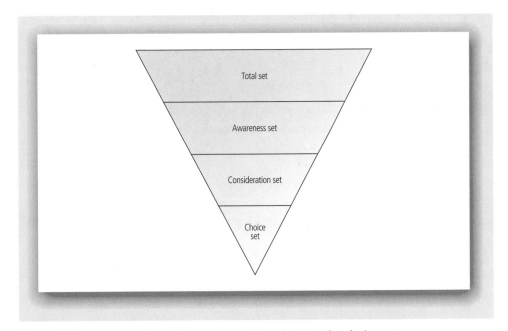

Figure 5.6 The move from the consumer's total set to the choice set

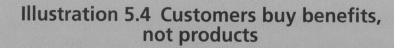

Illustration 5.4 Customers buy benefits, not products

Recognition of the idea that customers do not buy products but are instead interested in the benefits gained from using the product has long been at the heart of successful marketing. This has been commented on by, among others, McDonald (1995, pp. 102–3):

> The difference between benefits and products is not just a question of semantics. It is crucial to the company seeking success. Every product has its features: size, shape, performance, weight, the material from which it is made, and so on. Many companies fall into the trap of talking to customers about these features rather than what those features mean to the customer. This is not surprising. For example, if, when asked a question about the product, the salesman could not provide an accurate answer, the customer might lose confidence and, doubting the salesman, will soon doubt his product. Most salesmen are therefore very knowledgeable about the technical features of the products they sell. They have to have these details at their fingertips when they talk to buyers, designers and technical experts.

However, being expert in technical detail is not enough. The customer may not be able to work out the benefits that particular features bring and it is therefore up to the salesman to explain the benefits that accrue from every feature he mentions.

A simple formula to ensure that this customer-oriented approach is adopted is always to use the phrase 'which means that' to link a feature to the benefit it brings:

> 'Maintenance time has been reduced from 4 to 3 hours, which means that most costs are reduced by . . .'

> 'The engine casing is made of aluminium, which means that six more units can be carried on a standard truck load, which means that transport costs are reduced by . . .'

McDonald goes on to argue that companies should undertake detailed analyses to identify the full range of benefits *they are able to offer* the customer as a prelude to identifying the range of benefits that *customers actually want* or will respond to. Benefits typically fall into four categories:

1 *Standard benefits*, which arise from the company and its products
2 *Double benefits*, which bring a benefit to the customer and subsequently, through an improvement in the customer's product, to the end-user
3 *Company benefits*, which emerge as the result of a relationship that develops by virtue of having bought a particular product – a typical example would be world-wide service backup
4 *Differential benefits*, which distinguish the product from those offered by competitors.

Nevertheless, there are several interesting factors that have emerged from this research that merit consideration. These include the need to think about:

1 The *product's attributes*, such as its price, performance, quality and styling
2 Their *relative importance* to the consumer

3 The consumer's perception of each *brand's image*

4 The consumer's *utility function* for each of the attributes.

By understanding consumers' perceptions in this way, the strategist can then begin modifying the product offer. This can be done in one of six ways:

1 Changing the physical product by, for example, adding features (real repositioning)

2 Changing beliefs about the product by giving greater emphasis to particular attributes (psychological repositioning)

3 Changing beliefs about competitors' products by comparative advertising and 'knocking copy' (competitive depositioning)

4 Changing the relative importance of particular attributes – as a product moves through the product life cycle, for example, and consumers become more familiar with the concept and the technology, the emphasis in the advertising can be shifted from, say, reassuring consumers about reliability and service backup, to a range of additional uses

5 Emphasizing particular product features that previously have been largely ignored

6 Changing buyers' expectations.

Against the background of these comments, the strategist should then be in a position to consider the act of purchase itself, and in particular *where* the purchase will be made, the *quantities* in which it will be made, the *timing*, and the *method* of payment.

An overview of models of consumer behaviour

Throughout the 1960s attempts were made to integrate a variety of theories, research findings and concepts from the behavioural sciences into a general framework that could be used to explain and predict consumer behaviour. In doing this, the principal writers (such as Nicosia, 1966; Engel et al., 1968; Sheth, 1969) moved away from the general perspective that had previously been adopted by economists and which in a number of ways is typified by Marshall's work and the Marshallian model of 'economic man'. Instead of viewing consumer behaviour simply as a single act made up of the purchase itself and the post-purchase reaction, a far greater recognition was given to the consumer's psychological state before, during and after the purchase.

But although these so-called 'comprehensive models' of consumer behaviour have been of value in extending our understanding of the decision process, their value has been questioned in recent years. One of the first to do this was Foxall (1987, p. 128), who suggested:

➡ The models assume an unrealistic degree of consumer rationality

➡ Observed behaviour often differs significantly from what is described

➡ The implied decision process is too simplistic and sequential

➡ Insufficient recognition is given to the relative importance of different types of decisions – each decision is treated by comprehensive models as significant and of high involvement, but the reality is very different and by far the vast majority of decisions made by consumers are relatively insignificant and of low involvement

➡ The models assume consumers have a seemingly infinite capacity for receiving and ordering information – in practice, consumers ignore, forget, distort, misunderstand or make far less use than this of the information with which they are presented

➡ Attitudes towards low-involvement products are often very weak and only emerge after the purchase, not before as comprehensive models suggest

➡ Many purchases seem not to be preceded by a decision process

➡ Strong brand attitudes often fail to emerge even when products have been bought on a number of occasions

➡ Consumers often drastically limit their search for information, even for consumer durables

➡ When brands are similar in terms of their basic attributes, consumers seemingly do not discriminate between them, but instead select from a repertoire of brands.

In the light of these criticisms, it is perhaps not surprising that the results that have emerged from attempts to test the models have proved disappointing.

5.6 The rise of the new consumer and the implications for marketing planning

We suggested in Illustration 5.2 that the 1990s saw the emergence of a very different type of consumer. This theme has been developed by Lewis and Bridger (2000), who, in their book *The Soul of the New Consumer*, suggest that consumers have evolved from being conformist and deferential children, reared on the propaganda of the post-Second World War era and prepared to trust mass advertising, into free-thinking, individualistic adults, who are sceptical of figures of authority and believe in what Sigmund Freud called 'the narcissism of small differences' (see Figure 5.7).

Reflecting the change from an era of austerity to one of affluence, these consumers have largely exhausted the things they *need* to purchase and are now concentrating on what they *want* to buy. In this sense, shopping is not merely the acquisition of things but the buying of identity.

While 'old consumers' were typically constrained by cash, choice and the availability of goods, 'new consumers', Lewis and Bridger suggest, are generally short of time, attention and trust (this is the cash-rich/time-poor generation that we discuss in greater detail on p. 218). Mass society has shattered and been reduced to a mosaic of minorities:

❝In a hypercompetitive world of fragmented markets and independently-minded, well-informed individuals, companies that fail to understand and attend to the needs of New Consumers are doomed to extinction. Currently, the average life of a major company only

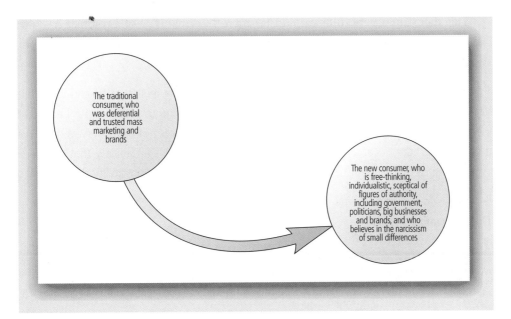

Figure 5.7 The shift from the old to the new consumer

rarely exceeds 40 years. In the coming decade, any business that is less than highly successful will find that lifespan reduced by a factor of at least 10.*"*

Even though such a drastic picture and such short time scales can be questioned, the overall picture that emerges is significant and has major implications for the marketing planner. Perhaps the first of these is the need for organizations to reconnect with their customers. Even giant consumer products companies with powerful brands and long trading histories – such as Levi Strauss, Kellogg's, Marks & Spencer and Coca-Cola – can lose touch with the new consumers, whose behaviour often transcends the traditional categories such as age, ethnic identity and even income.

The second main implication of the new consumer is that consumer products companies must become much better at directing their messages to increasingly critical audiences who have access to technology. The proliferation of Internet sites, for example, has enabled groups of consumers to publicize instantaneous and often highly critical reviews of new products, services or films that can be far more influential than the formal advertising campaigns. However, from the company's point of view, improving technology and growing consumer sophistication also enable them to become smarter. New advertising channels, such as Internet sites, video screens at supermarket checkouts and interactive television all enable suppliers to find more willing buyers. Companies are also becoming better at stimulating a street 'buzz' about their products by influencing select opinion formers, rather than by focusing largely upon mass advertising hype. Amongst those to have done this are companies such as Disney, Apple, Virgin, and Starbucks, all of which have caught the *Zeitgeist* and created innovative means such as viral marketing to deliver their message to new consumers.

This theme of a very different and far more assertive type of consumer has also been developed by the advertising agency Publicis, who, in their report *The New Assertiveness* (2002), suggest that this new type of consumer:

" . . . infuriated by the pressures of 21st-century living and a feeling of having little control over many aspects of their lives, consumers are attempting to regain control and vent their frustration through their buying habits . . . Seventy per cent of those surveyed believe the future is more uncertain than it was in their parents' day – an anxiety that has been increased since September 11. Many now feel vulnerable to the possibility that anything could happen, at any time."

The study argues that:

" This insecurity and frustration is breeding a new generation of consumer. Increasingly, we are buying products or services to cheer ourselves up – 31 per cent of adults surveyed said their consumption was motivated by this, a figure that rose to 50 per cent among 15- to 24-year-old respondents."

The report also highlighted the way in which consumers' expectations of product quality and levels of service are outstripping satisfaction. Ninety-six per cent of respondents made a complaint about a product or service during the previous 12 months.

The findings of the study were seen by the agency to present both a warning and an opportunity to brand owners.

Competitive intensity, the new consumer and the rise of complicated simplicity (or the law of increasing individuality)

With markets becoming ever more competitive and consumers more demanding, organizations can respond in any one of a number of ways. However, underpinning many of these is the need to individualize and tailor services to the consumers' needs to a far greater extent than has typically been the case in the past. This sort of response, which can be labelled 'complicated simplicity', means the end of a mass audience-oriented approach and the far greater acceptance of an audience-of-one approach. This shift is likely to be driven, in part at least, by the consumer empowerment movement, which (amongst other things) demands a far greater degree of price transparency. The implications of this are potentially significant, since organizations face the pressure of cutting costs and maintaining profitability, while having little opportunity to raise prices.

Complicated simplicity also highlights the need for organizations to take greater account of the 'ninety-nine lives' trend first identified by Faith Popcorn, the American trend forecaster. This involves recognizing that a consumer can play a variety of roles (e.g. mother, wife, manager, outdoor enthusiast) and that typecasting under a single broad heading is likely to be of little real value. This expectation of individual attention is, of course, at odds with the general trend of the past 30 years of mega-mergers and conglomeration. Amongst those to have used technology to come to terms with this individualization is Amazon.com, which outmanoeuvred the established market leader, Barnes & Noble, partly by developing a new business model but also by tailoring its message and response to consumers as individuals.

Another contributor to complicated simplicity is the move across society to Me, Myself and I Inc. With government as well as organizations across Europe, the United States and Japan slowly dismantling the cradle-to-grave welfare state, levels of corporate loyalty are declining rapidly. At the same time, long-term permanent employment is disappearing and greater numbers of people are beginning to work for themselves. Faced with this, the implications for marketing are potentially significant, and are likely to be seen most obviously in terms of consumers' far higher expectations and demands for individual treatment.

The genie of the super-powered consumer

Arguably, one of the most significant and far-reaching legacies for marketing of the social and economic turbulence of the late 1980s and early 1990s was the emergence of what we have termed 'the new consumer'. This new consumer exhibits a number of characteristics that as we suggested earlier, can perhaps best be summarized in terms of buyers who are now far more demanding, far more discriminating, much less loyal and far more willing to complain. This type of consumer has, over the past few years, developed even further, with the emergence of what might loosely be termed the 'super-powered consumer'. The super-powered consumer is typically media-literate, has access to his/her own mass-media channel of communication (the web), has a number of tools for a fast response to problems (the mobile phone), and often has a public relations strategy and an ability to hurt companies. They are also often well informed and frequently politicized in their behaviour patterns. Examples of the super-powered consumer in action include the anti-global brand demonstrations in Seattle in 1999, French farmers attacking the 'imperialism' of McDonald's, European and North American customers asking questions of Nike about their manufacturing policies in South-East Asia, and the green lobby forcing the British government to change its policy on genetically modified foods.

In a number of ways, the emergence of the super-powered consumer represents something of a paradox. Marketers have worked hard to create this type of consumer by giving them greater access, more information and more influence over how business is done, and how brands communicate. Having been encouraged to ask questions, consumers have become far more discriminating and cynical, with the result that marketing planners are now under far greater pressure and need to respond with communication that is far more open.

The new consumer and the new radicalism

In her book *The Customer Revolution* (2001), Patricia Seybold argues that because of the Internet, customers are more easily able to influence a company's behaviour. Web sites such as TheCorporateLibrary.com, for example, have an extensive list of articles and reports on the behaviour of companies, and this, she argues, provides the basis for small shareholders to begin exerting a greater power and influence than in the past. The implication of this is that a company can be measured not just through the traditional measures of profit and loss, return on assets and the price/earnings ratio, but also on the quality of customer relationships. To help with this, Seybold has developed a 'customer value index' that gives investors a way to measure company performance by looking at the present and future value of its customer base. The net effect of this is that measures such as customer satisfaction, customer retention and share of wallet become easier and more meaningful.

In many markets, she suggests, there are now three types of customer: those who are *price sensitive* and concerned about costs; those who are *service sensitive* and who focus upon areas such as quality and delivery; and those who are *commitment sensitive* and look for long-term relationships.

5.7 Organizational buying behaviour

Although there are certain factors common to both consumer and organizational buying behaviour, there are also numerous points of difference. Perhaps the most obvious feature of commonality in approaching the two areas is the fundamental need to understand how and why buyers behave as they do. There are, however, certain features of organizational buying which are not found in consumer markets. These typically include the following:

➡ Organizations generally buy goods and services to satisfy a variety of goals such as making profits, reducing costs, meeting employees' needs, and meeting social and legal obligations.

➡ A greater number of people are generally involved in organizational buying decisions than in consumer buying decisions, especially when the value of the purchase is particularly high. Those involved in the decision usually have different and specific organizational responsibilities and apply different criteria to the purchase decision.

➡ The buyers must adhere to formal purchasing policies, constraints and requirements.

➡ The buying instruments, such as requests for quotations, proposals and purchase contracts, add another dimension not typically found in consumer buying.

Although quite obviously, as with consumers in consumer markets, no two companies behave in the same way, both research and experience have demonstrated that patterns of similarity do exist in the ways in which organizational buyers approach the task of buying, and that they are sufficiently uniform to simplify the task of strategic marketing planning.

In analysing patterns of organizational buying, the starting point is in many ways similar to that for consumer markets, with the strategist posing a series of questions:

➡ *Who* makes up the market?
➡ What *buying decisions* do they make?
➡ Who are the *key participants* in the buying process?
➡ What are the *principal influences* upon the buyer, and what organizational rules and policies are important?
➡ What *procedures* are followed in selecting and evaluating competitive offerings, and how do buyers arrive at their decisions?

The three types of buying decision

Much of the research conducted over the past 35 years into the nature of the industrial buying process has made either explicit or implicit use of a categorization first proposed in 1967 by Robinson, Faris and Wind. There are, they suggested, three distinct buying situations or buy classes, each of which requires a different pattern of behaviour from the supplier. They are the straight rebuy, the modified rebuy and the new task.

Of these, the *straight rebuy* is the most straightforward and describes a buying situation where products are reordered on a largely routine basis, often by someone at a fairly junior level in the organization. Among the products ordered in this way is office stationery. Here, the person responsible for the ordering simply reorders when stocks fall below a predetermined level and will typically use the same supplier from one year to another until either something goes wrong or a potential new supplier offers a sufficiently attractive incentive for the initial decision to be reconsidered. The implications of this sort of buying situation are for the most part straightforward, and require the supplier to maintain both product and service quality. Perhaps the biggest single problem in these circumstances stems from the need on the part of the supplier to avoid complacency setting in and allowing others to make an approach that causes the customer to reassess the supplier base.

The second type of buying situation – the *modified rebuy* – often represents an extension of the straight rebuy and occurs when the buyer wants to modify the specification, price or delivery terms. Although the current supplier is often in a relatively strong position to protect the account, the buyer will frequently give at least cursory consideration to other possible sources of supply.

The third type of buying situation – the *new task* – is the most radical of the three, and provides the marketing strategist with a series of opportunities and challenges. The buyer typically approaches the new task with a set of criteria that have to be satisfied, and in order to do this will frequently consider a number of possible suppliers, each of whom is then faced with the task of convincing the buyer that his product or service will outperform or be more cost-effective than the others. The buyer's search for information is often considerable and designed to reduce risk. Where the costs are high there will typically be several people involved in the decision, and the strategist's task is therefore complicated by the need not just to identify the buying participants, but also their particular concerns and spheres of influence. In doing this, the strategist should never lose sight of the significance of attitudes to risk and the ways in which individuals may work to reduce their exposure to it. Chisnall (1989, p. 72), for example, has commented that: 'A buyer's professional activities may be tempered by the fundamental instinct he has for survival and for enhancing his career.' This point has also been made by McClelland (1961): 'A great part of the efforts of business executives is directed towards minimizing uncertainties.'

Who is involved in the buying process?

A major characteristic of organizational buying is that it is often a group activity, and only rarely does a single individual within the organization have sole responsibility for making all the decisions involved in the purchasing process. Instead, a number of people from different areas and often with different statuses are involved either directly or indirectly. Webster and Wind (1972, p. 6) were the first to refer to this group as the decision-making unit (DMU) of an organization and as the buying centre, and defined it as 'all those individuals and groups who participate in the purchasing decision-making process, who share some common goals and the risks arising from the decisions'. There are, they suggest, six roles involved in this process, although on occasions all six may be performed by the same person:

1 *Users* of the product or service, who in many cases initiate the buying process and help in defining the purchase specifications
2 *Influencers*, who again help to define the specification, but who also provide an input to the process of evaluating the alternatives available
3 *Deciders*, who have the responsibility for deciding on product requirements and suppliers
4 *Approvers*, who give the authorization for the proposals of deciders and buyers
5 *Buyers*, who have the formal authority for selecting suppliers and negotiating purchase terms (a summary of the different types of buyer that have been identified appears in Illustration 5.5)
6 *Gatekeepers*, who are able to stop sellers from reaching individuals in the buying centre – these can range from purchasing agents through to receptionists and telephone switchboard operators.

Illustration 5.5 The seven different types of buyer

The issue of the buyer's style and its implications for marketing strategy has been the subject of research in the USA by Dickinson (1967, pp. 14–17), who identified seven types of buyer:

1 *Loyal* buyers, who remain loyal to a source for considerable periods
2 *Opportunistic* buyers, who choose between sellers on the basis of who will best further their long-term interests

3 *Best deal* buyers, who concentrate on the best deal available at the time

4 *Creative* buyers, who tell the seller precisely what they want in terms of the product, service and price

5 *Advertising* buyers, who demand advertising support as part of the deal

6 *Chisellers*, who constantly demand extra discounts

7 *Nuts and bolts* buyers, who select products on the basis of the quality of their construction.

Although Webster and Wind's categorization of buying centre roles is the best known and the most widely used, a variety of other analytical approaches have been developed. Hill (1972), for example, has argued the case for analysing the buying centre not on the basis of the participants' roles, but on the basis of functional units. There are, he suggests, five such units:

1 *Control units*, which are responsible for the policy-making which influences buying and which imposes certain constraints – these might include buying where possible only from British suppliers or from local small firms

2 *Information units*, which provide information relating to the purchase

3 *The buying unit*, which consists of those with formal responsibility for negotiating the terms of the contract

4 *User units*, consisting of anyone in the organization who will be involved in using the product or service

5 *The decision-making unit*, which consists of those in the DMU who will make the decision.

Of these, it is only the control, information and decision-making units that he believes are of any real importance in influencing buying decisions.

Although the size, structure and formality of the buying centre will quite obviously vary depending both upon the size of the organization and the product decision involved, the strategist needs always to consider five questions:

1 Who are the principal participants in the buying process?

2 In what areas do they exercise the greatest influence?

3 What is their level of influence?

4 What evaluative criteria do each of the participants make use of and how professional is the buying process?

5 To what extent in large organizations is buying centralized?

The principal influences on industrial buyers

Much of the early research into industrial buying processes was based on the assumption that industrial buyers, unlike consumers, are wholly rational. More recently it has been recognized that, while economic factors play a significant role, a variety of other elements also needs to be taken into account. Chisnall (1989, p. 71), for example, in recognizing this, suggested that:

*"*Organizational buyers do not live like hermits; they are influenced by the personal behaviour of their colleagues, by the trading practices of other enterprises, and by the standards of the society to which they belong.

It is unrealistic, therefore, to approach the study of buying behaviour – personal or organizational – without an appreciation of the multiplexity of buying motivations. A balanced view is necessary; explanations of buying behaviour should not go from the one extreme of regarding 'rational' economic factors as solely responsible to the equally extreme view that emotional or 'irrational' influences entirely account for the purchase of products and services.*"*

A similar view was expressed by Harding (1966), who has argued that:

*"*Corporate decision-makers remain human after they enter the office. They respond to 'image'; they buy from companies to which they feel 'close'; they favour suppliers who show them respect and personal consideration, and who do extra things 'for them'; they 'over-react' to real or imagined slights, tending to reject companies which fail to respond or delay in submitting requested bids.*"*

Webster and Wind's model classifies the influences on industrial buyers under four headings: environmental, organizational, interpersonal and individual influences. These are illustrated in Figure 5.8.

The question of what influences buyers and how various sources of information are perceived has also been examined by a variety of writers, including Webster (1970). He was particularly interested in the relative importance of formal and informal information sources, and how they differ from consumer markets. His findings suggest that informal sources tend to be used far less frequently in industrial markets than in consumer markets, and that salespeople are often regarded as highly reliable and useful sources of information. By contrast, opinion leadership, which often plays a significant role in consumer markets, was found to be largely ineffective; a possible explanation of this is the perception that no two companies experience the same problem and that there is therefore little to be gained. Perhaps the most significant single finding to emerge from Webster's research was the significance of the role that the industrial salesperson is capable of playing *throughout* the buying process.

The relative importance of sources of information has also been examined by Martilla (1971) and Abratt (1986). Martilla's work led to a series of conclusions that are broadly similar to those of Webster, although in addition he highlighted the importance of word-of-mouth communication within firms, particularly in the later stages of the adoption process. Abratt's research, which focused on high-technology laboratory instrumentation, adds a further dimension to our understanding of the buying process, suggesting that, in markets such as these, buying personnel often have 'only a token administrative function'. Instead, the question of what to buy is the responsibility of

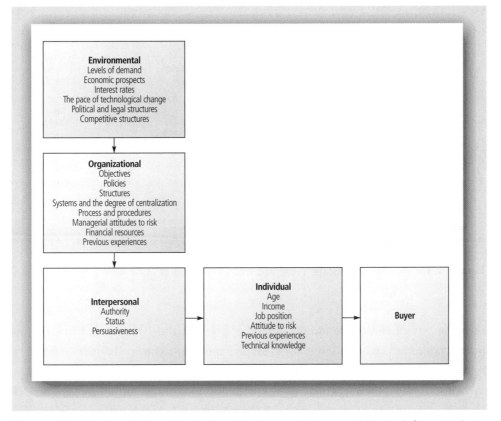

Figure 5.8 Factors influencing industrial buying behaviour (adapted from Webster and Wind, 1972)

groups of two to three people, with the most significant purchasing criteria proving to be product reliability and technical and sales service backup, while price was relatively unimportant.

However, perhaps the most underestimated and, in research terms, ignored elements of the buying process is that of the *gatekeeper*. Although the identity of the gatekeeper is often difficult to determine, it is the gatekeeper who in many organizations either blocks or facilitates access and who can therefore play a pivotal role in determining which products are considered. This has been recognized by Pettigrew (1975), who, in a study of the way in which a computer system was purchased, demonstrated how the gatekeeper is capable of filtering the information flow to suit his own objectives.

How do industrial buyers arrive at their decisions?

One of the major differences between consumer and industrial buying decisions is the buying motive. Whereas the majority of consumer purchases are made for the individual's personal consumption or utility, industrial purchases are typically designed to reduce operating costs, satisfy legal obligations, provide an input to the manufacturing process, and ultimately to make money. In order to provide a greater understanding of this process, Robinson et al. (1967) of the Marketing Science Institute identified eight

		Buy classes		
		Straight rebuy	Modified rebuy	New task
Buy phases	1 Problem recognition	No	Possibly	Yes
	2 Determination of the general need	No	Possibly	Yes
	3 Specific description of the required product	Yes	Yes	Yes
	4 Search for potential suppliers	No	Possibly	Yes
	5 Evaluation of suppliers	No	Possibly	Yes
	6 Selection of a supplier	No	Possibly	Yes
	7 Order-routine established	No	Possibly	Yes
	8 Review of performance and feedback	Yes	Yes	Yes

Figure 5.9 The buy-grid model (adapted from Robinson et al., 1967)

stages or buy-phases of the industrial buying process. They then related these to the three types of buying situation that we discussed earlier to form what they referred to as the *buy-grid framework*. This is illustrated in Figure 5.9.

This buying process, which begins with the recognition of a problem, can be sparked off by either internal or external stimuli. Internal stimuli typically include: the decision to develop a new product, and the recognition that this will require new equipment or materials; machine breakdowns; the belief on the part of the purchasing manager that better prices or quality can be obtained from an alternative supplier; curiosity; and organizational policy decisions. External stimuli include: the launch of a new product by a competitor; advertisements; sales representatives; and ideas that emerge as the result of trade shows.

This recognition of a problem is then followed by a *general need description*, in which the buyer identifies the characteristics and quantity of the products required to overcome the problem. This leads to the development of *product specifications* and subsequently to a *search for suppliers*.

The question of precisely *how* buyers select suppliers has been the subject of a considerable amount of research. However, in so far as it is possible to identify a common theme in this process of deciding between suppliers, it is the reduction, containment and management of risk. In commenting on this, Chisnall (1989, p. 83) suggested that:

*"*The element of risk in buying decisions could be considered along a continuum ranging from routine (low risk purchases) at one extreme to novel (high risk) purchases at the other end of the scale. In the centre would fall many industrial transactions where the hazards could reasonably be calculated sufficiently to allow decisions of tolerable risk to be made.*"*

This is illustrated in Figure 5.10.

It appears that buyers typically cope with these risks in several ways, including:

➡ Exchanging technical and other information with their customers and prospects

➡ Dealing only with those suppliers with whom the company has previously had favourable experiences

➡ Applying strict (risk-reducing) decision rules

➡ Dealing only with suppliers who have a long-established and favourable reputation

➡ The introduction of penalty clauses relating to, for example, late delivery

➡ Multiple sourcing to reduce the degree of dependence upon a single supplier.

Although for many buyers the pursuit of a risk-reducing strategy has a series of attractions, it needs to be recognized that such a strategy can also possess drawbacks. The most obvious of these stems from the way in which it is likely to lead to the company becoming and remaining a follower rather than becoming a leader. Developments both in product and process technology on the part of a supplier often provide significant opportunities for the development of a competitive edge, and unless this is recognized by the company it runs the risk of adopting new ideas only when they have been well tried by others.

Perhaps the final aspect of risk that needs to be considered here stems from the significance of post-purchase dissonance. Undoubtedly the best-known writer on dissonance is Festinger (1957), who has referred to it as a state of psychological discomfort. This discomfort is, in essence, the result of the individual questioning whether the decision made is correct. According to Festinger, a buyer will try to reduce this discomfort by seeking reassurance for the decision. This can be done by, for example, seeking the support of others, avoiding conflicting messages such as competitive advertising, and searching for editorials and advertisements that state how good the product just purchased is. The more expensive and significant the purchase, the greater the dissonance is likely to be. The implications for a supplier in these circumstances should be obvious: buyers need reassurance and this can best be provided by continuing to 'sell' the product and providing supporting evidence of the wisdom of the decision even after the sale itself has been made. Other ways in which dissonance can be reduced include giving emphasis to the quality of the after-sales service, maintaining regular contact

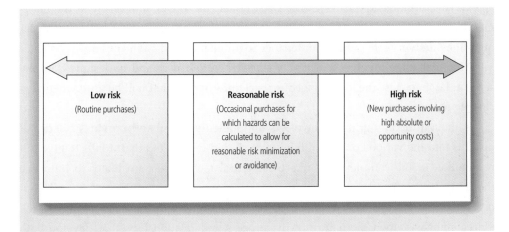

Figure 5.10 The buying risk continuum (adapted from Chisnall, 1989)

with customers, and giving prominence in advertising to the market leaders who have also bought the product. One example of an organization that recognizes the need for managing dissonance is IBM, the experiences of which are discussed in Illustration 5.6.

Illustration 5.6 IBM and its development of the total sales programme

IBM says that it sells solutions, not products. In doing this, the company concentrates upon gaining – and retaining – the customer's confidence from the moment of contact through until well after the sale has been made. One result of this is that long-term relationships are established, repeat purchases are guaranteed, and the likelihood of post-purchase dissonance is reduced so that it is to all intents meaningless. Some of the ways in which this is done are listed below:

➡ Inviting the customer contact and other members of the company to conferences and seminars that may be useful to them. Often these seminars feature major international figures.

➡ Inviting the contact to visit prestigious customers who have successful IBM installations.

➡ Inviting the contact and others in the company to visit IBM's factories to look at projects that may be of interest.

➡ Sending out articles, newsletters and house magazines.

➡ Ensuring that IBM's service engineers and systems specialists channel back information gained when working at the customer's plant so that as full a picture as possible is built up of the client's needs.

➡ The development of 'account planning sessions' in which IBM, together with the customer, draw up an action plan for the next few years, covering the systems and products that the customer may need.

➡ Ensuring a regular and worry-free relationship is developed and maintained.

Source: adapted from Düro (1989).

Having decided upon the choice of supplier, the buyer moves on to the *order-routine specification* by identifying such features as the technical specification, the order quantities, delivery schedules, maintenance requirements and payment terms.

The final stage involves a *review of suppliers' performance* and is designed, in one sense at least, to close the loop by feeding back information that will be used when purchasing in the future.

Although the buy-grid framework is undoubtedly useful and provides a series of insights into the various phases of buying, it should be realized that it fails to give full recognition to the complexity of the behavioural factors that are likely to influence those involved in making specific purchase decisions. Because of this, other models of organizational buying have been proposed, including *the interaction approach*, which places emphasis upon the nature of the process and relationships that develop both within and between buying and selling organizations. Thus:

→ Buyers and sellers are both seen to be active participants, and buyers often attempt to influence what they are offered

→ Relationships are often long term and based on mutual trust rather than any formal commitment

→ Patterns of interaction are frequently complex and extend within the organizations as well as between organizations

→ Emphasis is given to supporting these relationships as well as to the process of buying and selling

→ Links between buyers and sellers often become institutionalized.

This approach to modelling industrial buying has in turn provided one of the foundations for the work of Hakansson and the IMP (International Marketing and Purchasing of Industrial Goods) group. Their research focused upon industrial buying and selling behaviour in five European countries – West Germany (as it was at the time), the UK, France, Italy and Sweden – and led to the development of a model that views this behaviour as a process in which both sides play active roles within a given environment. They suggest that four elements influence the patterns of buyer–seller interaction. These elements, which are illustrated in Figure 5.11, are:

1 The interaction process

2 The participants in this process

3 The interaction environment

4 The atmosphere created by this interaction.

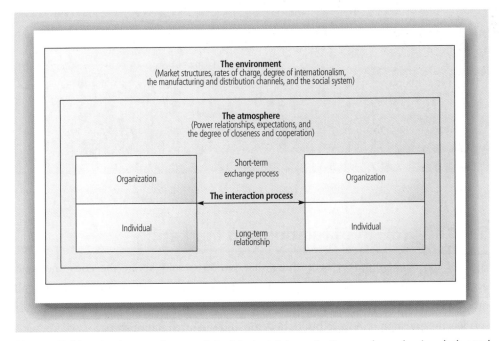

Figure 5.11   The interaction model of industrial marketing and purchasing (adapted from Hakansson, 1981)

The real value of this model, which makes use both of interorganizational theory and new institutional economic thinking, is that it gives far greater emphasis than earlier work to the idea that industrial buying and selling is concerned with the management of relationships.

The industrial buying process and issues of corruption

A somewhat different approach to thinking about the nature of the industrial buying process has been highlighted by the work of the research group Transparency International; a summary of their study of corruption appears in Illustration 5.7.

Ilustration 5.7 Corruption and business culture

It has long been recognized that incentives ranging from corporate entertainment through to out-and-out bribery and corruption are important – and sometimes essential – steps to doing business in certain parts of the world. The extent to which this is so was highlighted in a study conducted by the Berlin-based research group, Transparency International. The study revealed that Nigeria, Indonesia and Russia all scored badly on their corruption index, whilst Singapore emerged as the least corrupt (see Figure 5.12).

In commenting on this, *The Economist* pointed to the way in which, in Indonesia:

> President Suharto's family dominates the economy, owning huge chunks of

business, including power generation, an airline, construction, telecoms, toll roads, newspapers, property and cars. Family members and their cronies get first pick of government contracts and licences, so it helps to have one of their names on the company letterhead. Paying off family members or well-connected officials can add up to 30 per cent to the cost of a deal. Foreigners have long realized that Indonesia was corrupt but wrongly thought that it did not affect its economic effeciency. Yet in effect corruption is a form of tax.

Source: *The Economist* (1998), 'East Asian Economies Survey', 7–13 March, p. 12.

5.8 The growth of relationship marketing

Against the background of everything that we have said about the consumer and organizational buying processes, we can now turn to an issue that affects virtually all marketers, regardless of the nature of their customer base or indeed their product or service: the question of how to build, develop and nurture relationships.

A major focal point for a considerable amount of marketing thinking over the past 15 years has been the notion of loyalty and how long-term, cost-effective

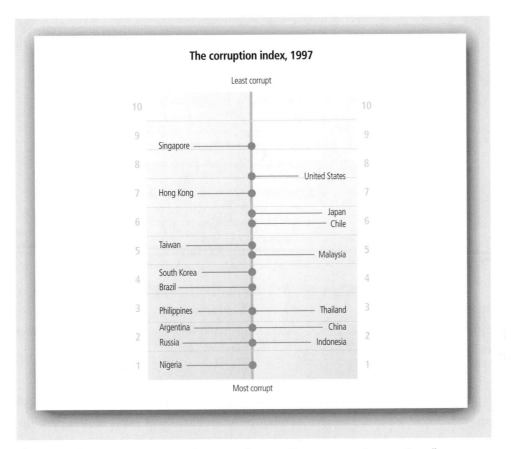

Figure 5.12 The corruption index, 1997 (source: Transparency International)

relationships might be developed with customers. In many ways, the idea of relationship marketing can be seen to be a logical development of the way in which the focus of marketing has changed from the early 1980s view that marketing is essentially a business function to the idea that, more realistically, it is – or should be – an organizational attitude, ethos and culture (see Chapter 1). Given this, it follows that the nature of any relationship between an organization and its markets should be based on a recognition of their fundamental interdependence, something that, in turn, has major implications for the ways in which the organization interacts with the customer base.

One of the most powerful drivers for relationship marketing has been what is in many ways the straightforward recognition of the fact that the costs of gaining a new customer, particularly in mature and slowly-declining markets, are often high. Given this, the marketing planner needs to ensure that the existing customer base is managed as effectively as possible. One way of doing this is to move away from the traditional and now largely outmoded idea of marketing and selling as a series of activities concerned with transactions, and to think instead of their being concerned with the management of long(er)-term relationships. This is illustrated in Figure 5.13.

Transaction marketing	Relationship marketing
A focus on single sales	A focus on customer retention and building customer loyalty
An emphasis upon product features	An emphasis upon product benefits that are meaningful to the customer
Short timescales	Long timescales, recognizing that short-term costs may be higher, but so will long-term profits
Little emphasis on customer retention	An emphasis upon high levels of service that are possibly tailored to the individual customer
Limited customer commitment	High customer commitment
Moderate customer contact	High customer contact, with each contact being used to gain information and build the relationship
Quality is essentially the concern of production and no-one else	Quality is the concern of all, and it is the failure to recognize this that creates minor mistakes which lead to major problems

Figure 5.13 Transaction versus relationship marketing (adapted from Christopher et al., 1991)

The potential benefits of this sort of approach are considerable and can be seen not just in terms of the higher returns from repeat sales, but also in terms of the opportunities for cross-selling, strategic partnerships and alliances. Clutterbuck and Dearlove (1993), for example, cite a study by Bain & Co., who suggest that, depending upon the type of business, a 5 per cent increase in customer retention can result in a profitability boost of anywhere from 25 to 125 per cent. The advantages are, of course, then increased further when the potential lifetime value of the customer is taken into account. In essence, therefore, the attractions of a loyal customer base can be seen in terms of the greater scope for profit from four main areas:

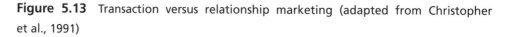

1 The price premium that loyal customers are or may be willing to pay
2 Customer referrals
3 A reduction in marketing costs
4 The value of a greater number of purchases.

The need for the proactive management of relationships has also been highlighted by a study of why industrial organizations lose customers that was conducted by Ashridge Management College (1993). By far the most important element was company indifference, characterized by the failure of managers to work with the customer sufficiently closely, the failure to communicate regularly, and the development of an attitude that led to customers feeling they they were being taken for granted. With company indifference accounting for 68 per cent of defections, the next most important factor was the 14 per cent of customers dissatisfied with the product. This was then followed by defection as the result of competitors offering lower prices (9 per cent), the appointment of a new manager within the customer organization who had existing relations with other suppliers (5 per cent), relocation (3 per cent) and death (1 per cent).

Developing the relationship strategy

In developing the relationship strategy, the marketing planner needs to focus upon five steps:

1 Analysing the gap between target and existing behaviour
2 Identifying what needs to be done to close the gap
3 Formulating a programme of benefits that satisfy customers' needs in order of importance of each within the segment
4 Formulating a communications plan to modify the behaviour of target groups
5 Monitoring performance and then, if necessary, changing the strategy being pursued.

However, before doing this, there is the need to:

→ Identify the *key* customers, since it is with these, particularly in the early stages, that the most profitable long-term relationships can be developed.
→ Determine which customers *want* a relationship. Although it is easy to assume that customers will benefit from – and will therefore want – a relationship, the reality is that not all customers want to move beyond anything more than a straightforward transaction. The normal reason for this is that, for a relationship to work, there is the need for an investment of time and effort from both sides. Although the organization may be willing to do this, it does not necessarily follow that the customer has the same commitment.
→ Following on from this, categorize customers in terms of their current or future potential (a framework for this appears in Figure 5.14). Here, the customer base is categorized as platinum, gold, silver or bronze customers, with a view to the nature of any relationship then being tailored to their potential.

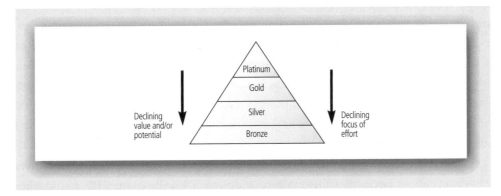

Figure 5.14   The categorization of customers

➡ Examine in detail the expectations of each segment for both sides.

➡ Identify how, if at all, the two can work together more closely in a cost-effective and profitable way.

➡ In the case of relationships in the commercial sector, appoint a relationship manager in each of the two organizations so that there is a natural focal point and think about how operating processes on both sides might need to be changed so that cooperation might be made easier.

➡ Go for a series of small wins in the first instance and then gradually strengthen the relationship.

➡ Recognize from the outset that different customers have very different expectations and that these need to be reflected in the way in which the relationship is developed.

As part of this, there is also the need to think about how customers can be managed and how the customer database might be used. As the prelude to this, six questions need to be posed:

1 How much do you know about the current customer base?

2 How good is the database?

3 How good is the management of the database?

4 What needs to be done to exploit it further?

5 What else does the organization need to know about customers?

6 How can this be achieved?

The position of relationship marketing within the customer loyalty chain is illustrated in Figure 5.15. The ways in which it was used strategically by SAS is then discussed in Illustration 5.8.

Although it might be argued that the movements of a buyer through the various stages from prospects to partners in Figure 5.15 should be straightforward and seamless, the reality in many instances is that organizations unwittingly erect a series of barriers that slow down or stop this movement. The first can be seen to be that of the way in which, in many cases, organizations make it difficult to do business with them. While this might seem to be something of a paradox, these barriers often exist in terms of inappropriate opening hours, unhelpful sales staff, uncompetitive prices, poor product configurations, slow delivery, and so on. The second barrier occurs at a later stage, when the customer deals with the organization on a regular basis, but no real effort is made to get close to the customer by building a relationship. Instead, each sale takes the form of a one-off transaction, an approach which goes at least part of the way towards explaining why long-standing customers 'suddenly' move to another supplier.

Given this, the arrow on the right-hand side of Figure 5.15 shows how customers can – and almost inevitably will – move back down the loyalty chain if the relationship is not managed proactively.

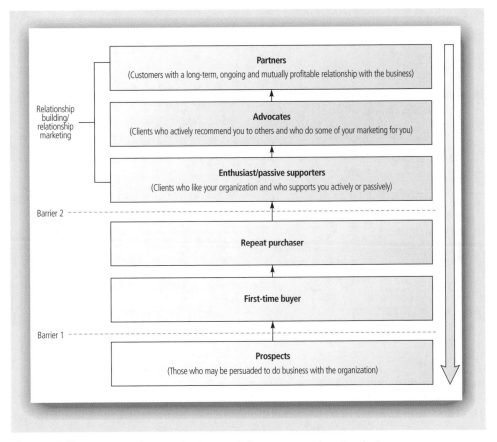

Figure 5.15 Relationship marketing and the customer loyalty chain

Illustration 5.8 Building relationships and the moments of truth

Jan Carlzon, president of Scandinavian Airlines System (SAS), achieved fame as the result of the way in which he turned SAS from heavy losses to healthy profit in the mid-1980s. In his book, Carlzon (1987, p. 3) says that each of his 10 million customers came in contact with approximately five SAS employees for an average of 15 seconds each time. He referred to these contacts as *moments of truth*, suggesting that, for SAS, these were 'created' 50 million times a year, 15 seconds at a time.

It is statistics such as these that indicate the scale of opportunity for managing and building relationships, or, as Clutterbuck and Dearlove (1993, p. 101) define these critical encounters, OTSUs (Opportunities To Screw Up).

When things do go wrong – and almost inevitably they will sooner or later in any long-term relationship – the question is how well the organizations handle the complaint. In examining this, the TARP organization in the USA concluded that when a customer complains and feels that the complaint is handled properly, he or she comes away satisfied and is likely to be *more loyal* to that brand or supplier than a customer who has never experienced a problem. Related to customer segment brand loyalty, the findings were as follows:

Experienced no problem	87 per cent
Satisfied complainant	91 per cent
Dissatisfied complainant	41 per cent
Non-complainant	59 per cent

Two key issues emerge here: firstly, dissatisfied customers should be encouraged and assisted to complain, but secondly, the complaint must be resolved to the customer's complete satisfaction.

Where customers remain dissatisfied, the implications are significant because not only will they fail to buy again, they tend not to keep quiet about their experiences. Statistics surrounding this issue are quoted ubiquitously, but all tend to tell the same story. Gerson (1992), for example, states that a dissatisfied customer will tell ten people about his experiences; approximately 13 per cent of dissatisfied customers will tell up to twenty people. Customers who are satisfied or have had their complaints satisfactorily resolved will tell between three and five people about their positive experience.

The stark reality of these statistics is that three to four customers have to be satisfied for every one who remains dissatisfied – a 4:1 ratio against.

Relationship marketing and the marketing mix

There are numerous ways in which relationships can be managed proactively, including by redefining and extending the marketing mix. As markets have become more competitive, the extent to which the marketing planner can differentiate purely on the basis of the traditional four Ps has become increasingly more difficult and more questionable. To overcome this, as we mentioned in Chapter 1, the focus in many markets has moved to the 'softer' elements of markets and the additional three Ps of People, Physical evidence and Processes that include proactive customer service; these are developed in detail by Adrian Payne (see Peck et al., 1999). In emphasizing the softer elements of marketing, the marketing planner is giving explicit recognition to the way in which the product or service is typically delivered through people and that it is the organization's staff who have the ability to make or break the relationship. This, in turn, is influenced either positively or negatively by organizational processes and the effectiveness of process management (which is concerned with the ways in which the customer is handled, from the point of very first contact with the organization through to the last). The third of the soft Ps (Process Management) is interpreted by Payne as that of proactive customer service and the ways in which levels of customer satisfaction can be leveraged by proactive rather than reactive service standards and initiatives.

The development of relationship marketing concepts and the emphasis placed upon the organization's staff has led, in turn, to a greater clarity of thinking about the differences that exist between what might loosely be termed the three dimensions of marketing: *external marketing*, which is concerned with the traditional four Ps of marketing and how they contribute to the development of the external profile of the organization or brand; *internal marketing*, which is concerned with the ways in which senior management communicate the organizational values and priorities to their staff; and *interactive marketing*, which is concerned with the ways in which staff then interact with the customer or client base (this is illustrated in Figure 7.5).

Relationship building and the growth of loyalty marketing

For many customers in the consumer goods sector, the most obvious manifestation of relationship marketing over the past few years has been the growth of customer loyalty schemes. The rationale for many of these has been the straightforward recognition that, particularly in mature markets, the costs to an organization of recruiting a new customer are typically far greater than those associated with keeping an existing one. Because of this, marketing campaigns that are designed to build customer loyalty offer – or appear to offer – considerable strategic benefits. Recognizing this, the mid-1990s saw an upsurge in the number of organizations developing loyalty marketing programmes. Amongst the most proactive in this were the major food retailers.

However, calculating the *potential* value of a customer, as opposed to the value of each transaction, involves a very different approach to marketing and customer service, something that has forced many organizations to rethink how they use their internal accounting and data management systems. Having done this, they should then be in a far better position to communicate with customers in a more focused and strategic way, and apply the 80:20 rule (Pareto's Law) in order to target the 20 per cent of customers who generate the largest revenues and/or the greatest profits. The value of loyalty schemes can therefore be seen to lie in *how* the knowledge gained from customer databases is used.

There are, however, questions that can be raised about the long-term benefits of loyalty schemes. In the case of the food retailers, for example, it might be argued that the cards are a zero-sum game in that, ultimately, the total amount of food bought will remain the same and that the discounts that the cards give to customers will translate into lower gross margins for supermarkets. In commenting on this, Denison (1994) has suggested that, in the long term:

❝ . . . loyalty schemes are not particularly effective. As schemes proliferate, what began as a 'reward' turns into an 'incentive' – or bribe. As companies try to outbid each other's incentives they risk slipping into loyalty wars – price wars by another name. And as consumers learn to shop around for the best schemes, marketers risk fuelling the very promiscuity they set out to combat. Until companies invent a means of introducing switching costs for customers, the future benefits of many loyalty schemes will be very marginal. They could end up in a lose–lose situation.

If this happens, it could be the result of a certain amount of muddled thinking as marketers confuse retention with loyalty: a customer may return again and again, not out of any loyalty but out of sheer habit. Others assume that greater customer satisfaction must bring increased loyalty. But as British Airways' head of customer relations, Charles Weiser, has pointed out, this isn't necessarily the case. Defection rates among BA passengers who declare themselves satisfied are the same as among those who make complaints.❞

Relationship marketing myopia

Although relationship marketing and relationship management has an obvious attraction, Piercy (1999) has identified what he terms 'relationship marketing myopia', or the naive belief that every customer wants to have a relationship with its suppliers. He goes on to suggest that 'customers differ in many important ways in the types of relationship they want to have with different suppliers, and that to ignore this reality is an expensive indulgence'.

This, in turn, leads him to categorize customers in terms of those who are:

➡ *Relationship seekers* – customers who want a close and long-term relationship with suppliers
➡ *Relationship exploiters* – customers who will take every free service and offer, but will still move their business elsewhere when they feel like it
➡ *Loyal buyers* – those who will give long-term loyalty, but who do not want a close relationship
➡ *Arm's-length, transaction buyers* – those who avoid close relationships and move business based on price, technical specification or innovation.

This is illustrated in Figure 5.16.

In categorizing customers in this way, Piercy gives recognition to the need for relationship strategies to be based upon the principles of market segmentation and customers' relationship-seeking characteristics:

*"*Relationship investment with profitable relationship seekers is good. Relationship investments with exploiters and transactional customers are a waste. The trick is going to be developing different marketing strategies to match different customer relationship needs.*"*

Piercy's comments are interesting for a variety of reasons, and raise the question of whether there is a direct link between customer satisfaction and customer loyalty (the nature of this relationship – if it exists – is illustrated in Figure 5.17). Although intuitively a link between the two might appear obvious, the reality is that there is little hard evidence to suggest that anything more than an indirect relationship exists. Instead, it is probably the case that it is customer *dissatisfaction* that leads to customer disloyalty, although even here the link may be surprisingly tenuous. Whilst this might at first sight seem to be a strange comment to make, the reality in many markets is that there is often a surprisingly high degree of inertia within the customer base (Hamel refers to this in terms of customer friction being a potentially major source of profits for many companies). Given this, the customer or consumer may be in a position where they simply cannot be bothered to change their source of supply until levels of dissatisfaction reach a very high level.

Piercy's ideas about the need to rethink approaches to relationship marketing have, in turn, been taken a step further by Frederick Newell (2003), who in his book *Why CRM Doesn't Work* highlighted many of the failures of the numerous customer relationship

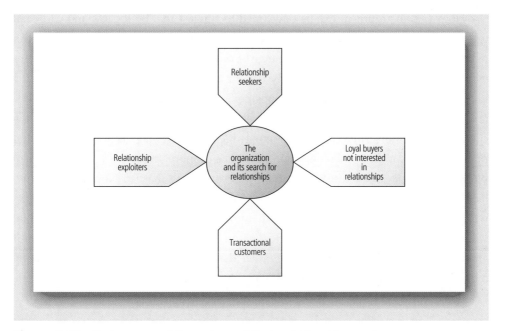

Figure 5.16   Customers and the nature of their relationship needs

management (CRM) initiatives. With Frost & Sullivan having estimated that spending on CRM now exceeds \$12 billion worldwide and is expected to double again in the next four years, the costs of a radical rethink are high. For Newell, there is now the need to move away from CRM to what he refers to as CMR, the customer management of relationships. Arguing that this is more than just a matter of semantics, Newell suggests the need for a new balance of power that allows 'the customer to tell us what she's interested in, what kind of information she wants, what level of service she wants to receive, and how she wants us to communicate with her – where, when and how often'.

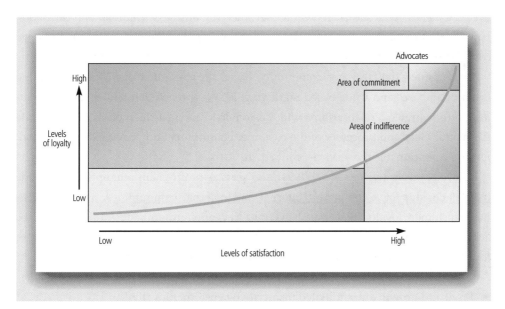

Figure 5.17   Customer loyalty and customer satisfaction

However, an argument can be developed to suggest that both CRM and CMR fail to come to terms with the real complexities of consumer choice, something that can only become more problematic as the range of products and services available becomes ever wider. In these circumstances, any benefit to the customer that then justifies the idea of a relationship diminishes a proposition. As an example of this, loyalty cards – one of the original drivers of CRM – were seen at one stage as a way of engaging the customer's attention, but as Newell acknowledges, the advantage is marginal now that practically every airline and retail chain offers one or more. In the USA, 60 million people now belong to frequent-flyer programmes, something that led Newell to acknowledge that 'half of all members of loyalty programmes are free riders, enjoying benefits without spending more at the business that provides them'. Recognizing this, the real value of cards to the issuer is to provide data on customers' purchasing patterns, but if an organization is to pursue the CMR rather than the CRM philosophy, the company must use the information not just to sell more, but to 'make their lives easier and create emotional loyalty to the business relationship'.

Developing the customer community

Given some of the problems faced with the now traditional approach to relationship marketing campaigns (e.g. a survey undertaken in 2001 by Bain & Co. concluded that one in five executives believe that CRM initiatives had damaged customer relationships), Hunter (1997) has argued that, although marketing success needs to be based on the development of a loyal customer base, ensuring that product or service offerings meet customers' needs, having an ongoing competitive intelligence system, effective and efficient sales channels and – most importantly from our standpoint at this stage – building new business around current customers, the ways in which this is done need to be rethought. Amongst the ways in which he believes this can be done is by building an interdependent relationship with the customer in which each relies on the other for business solutions and successes. Hunter refers to this in terms of building a customer community that – given the average company loses 20–40 per cent of its customer base each year – is strategically important.

For Hunter, the customer community, based on integrated one-to-one marketing contact databases and value-based marketing, is an approach that allows for the building of truly strategic relationships with customers. Amongst the models that illustrate the central ideas and processes of the customer community and provide the framework for implementing it is the service–profit chain.

Developed by Heskett et al. (1994), the service–profit chain attempts to show the interrelationship of a company's internal and external communities, and highlights how customer loyalty that translates into revenue growth and profits might be achieved. It does this by establishing relationships between profitability, customer loyalty and employee satisfaction. The links in the chain are as follows:

➡ Profit and growth are stimulated primarily by customer loyalty
➡ Loyalty is a direct result of customer satisfaction

➡ Satisfaction is largely influenced by the value of services provided to customers

➡ Value is created by satisfied, loyal and productive employees

➡ Employee satisfaction, in turn, results primarily from high-quality support services and policies that enable employees to deliver results to customers.

The significance of customer promiscuity

One of the principal themes pursued throughout this book is that many of the traditional assumptions that have been made about customers and that have driven thinking on marketing strategy are quite simply no longer appropriate. Rather than being able to take customer loyalty for granted, the reality for many planners is that, as customers have become more demanding, more discriminating, less loyal and more willing to complain, levels of customer promiscuity have increased dramatically. In a number of ways, this can be seen to be the logical end point of the sorts of ideas discussed in 1970 by Alvin Toffler in his book *Future Shock*; he predicted that we would be living in a world of accelerating discontinuities where 'the points of a compass no longer navigated us in the direction of the future'.

Amongst Toffler's predictions was that, as the pace of change accelerates, so the nature of relationships becomes much more temporary. For marketers, the most obvious manifestation of this is a fracturing of the relationship between the organization and its markets and the decline of brand loyalty. This disconnection between consumers and brands is then exacerbated by vicarious living, a phenomenon that has been explored by Crawford Hollingworth (2001) of Headlight Vision. Hollingworth has argued that 'We live in a world where there is so much choice and information and so many different experiences that we believe that we have had, but in fact we haven't actually had.'

With customers now faced with so many stimuli in the form of advertising, promotions, point-of-sale offers, poster sites and sponsorship, the danger is that of a considerable amount of marketing activity simply becoming white noise. Given this, there is a need to rethink the nature of the relationship between the consumer and the brand. Amongst the ways in which this can be done is by focusing upon added value and the extra value proposition (EVP), customer-driven strategies and permission marketing (see Figure 10.15). In the absence of this, there is the very real danger of competitive oblivion, particularly as web-based strategies reduce market entry barriers and costs.

An additional problem stems from what Hamel (2001) has referred to as the end of friction as a reliable service of profits (friction is defined by Hamel as customer ignorance or inertia). For many banks, for example, a substantial part of their revenue is often derived from the problems that customers face in identifying and/or choosing alternatives. However, with a generally greater degree of customer scepticism or cynicism, far higher expectations, increasing levels of customer promiscuity and the ease of access to alternatives via the web, friction is likely to become a far less common phenomenon.

Relationship marketing: the next stage of thinking

Although relationship marketing has undoubtedly had a major impact upon marketing thinking and upon the ways in which organizations interact with their customers, relationship marketing should not be seen as an end in itself. Instead, the marketing planner should think about how this sort of thinking might be moved ahead yet further, something that is made possible by the better management of databases, far more effective targeting, and the greater scope for one-to-one marketing; this is illustrated in Figure 5.18.

Here, the marketing planner focuses not just upon getting even closer to the customer, but also upon the development of a series of far more strategic and inherently cleverer interactions that are based upon true customer insight. However, in doing this, the planner needs to understand in detail the potential that each customer offers, since this then provides the basis for far better approaches to market segmentation.

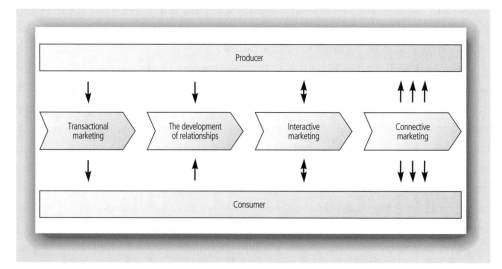

Figure 5.18   The move from transactional to connective marketing

5.9 Summary

Within this chapter we have focused on the detail of consumer and industrial buying structures and processes, and on the ways in which an understanding of these contributes to effective marketing planning.

A variety of factors influence consumer behaviour, the most significant of which are a network of cultural, social, personal and psychological forces. Each of these was discussed in some detail and the nature of their interrelationships explored. Against this background we then considered the structure of buying decision processes, and in particular:

➡ The buying roles within the decision-making unit
➡ The different types of buying behaviour
➡ The process through which a consumer goes in making a decision.

A variety of attempts have been made over the past 40 years to model the complexities of the buying process, the best known of which are those proposed by Nicosia, Engel et al., and Sheth. These models have been the subject of a certain amount of criticism, one consequence of which has been that the strategist's ability to predict with any real degree of accuracy the probable response of consumers to marketing behaviour is still relatively limited.

Research into organizational buying behaviour has pursued broadly similar objectives to that in the consumer field, with attention being paid to the questions of:

➡ Who makes up the market?
➡ What buying decisions do they make?
➡ Who are the key participants in the buying process?
➡ What influences the buyer?
➡ How do buyers arrive at their decisions?

Each of these areas was examined in some detail and the best known of the models of organizational buying behaviour were reviewed. As with models of consumer behaviour, the majority of these have been heavily criticized, largely because of their poor analytical or predictive ability. There are, however, exceptions to this, as discussed, including Robinson et al.'s buy-grid model and Hakansson's interaction approach, in which use is made of interorganizational theory and new institutional economic thinking. It is in these areas that future developments in our understanding of organizational buying processes are most likely to be made.

Appendix: The drivers of consumer change

A variety of studies have been conducted over the past few years in an attempt to identify the principal drivers of change amongst twenty-first century consumers. There are several features that are common to virtually all of these studies and suggest that western societies are increasingly being characterized by:

1 Changing demographics
2 Changing family relationships
3 A significant cash-rich/time-poor segment
4 A search for (greater) value
5 The rise of ethical consumerism
6 An emphasis upon health and healthy lifestyles
7 A desire for indulgence and small treats as a reward for working hard and/or as a retreat from the pressures of the world.

Changing demographics

The youthful elderly

Although it has long been recognized that changing demographics in many countries are leading to increasingly elderly populations, less emphasis has been given to the characteristics of these people. The notion of the youthful elderly is based on the way in which, as the children of the 1960s move into middle age/late middle age, they are increasingly retaining their youthful lifestyles and attitudes (see, for example, Richardson, 2001). Benefiting from higher levels of health and fitness and having more money than previous generations, the youthful elderly expect – and are able – to live life to the full. In these circumstances, age largely becomes an attitude of mind.

Although this market has often been largely ignored by planners, its real size and value is shown by the way in which, in the UK, more than 44 per cent of the population is currently over 50. In 20 years, one in two adults will be over 50.

However, it needs to be recognized that, within the over-50s segment, major differences do exist. Although a growing number of retired people are healthier, more active, more affluent, want to have more fun, eat out more often, travel, and as a result are more experimental with food and are open to new technology (including the Internet), those dependent on state pensions are now having to pay more for their healthcare and becoming more entrenched in terms of attitude to new ideas and products. There is therefore a growing polarization within the group.

Ageing children (the under 14s)

At the same time that we are seeing the elderly becoming more youthful, we also have a series of changes that are affecting the children's market. In the case of the under 14s, numbers are currently declining. Between 2000 and 2005, for example, the 5–9 years age segment will have declined by 6 per cent, the 10–14s will remain static and 15–19s will increase by 5 per cent. By 2010, 5–9s will have declined by 11 per cent, 10–14s will have declined by 5 per cent and 15–19s will increase by 6 per cent. The widening availability of technology and media means that children are exposed to the adult world much earlier and are now aware of advertising and its role by the age of 3. One result of this is that they are more demanding of brands and their environment, with this being due in part to more spoiling by time-pressured parents and the easy availability of luxuries. They are also more sophisticated and far more unforgiving with regard to brands. They expect entertainment and have low boredom thresholds.

Ageing children (the teens)

Although the teenage market has traditionally been seen to be amongst the fastest changing segments of consumer markets, a strong case can be made to suggest that this segment is now changing even faster than in the past. In part, this is because of the ways in which teenagers today have been exposed to a greater number of stimuli than those previously, and it is this that has led to a generation that is now far more advertising media, technologically and brand literate than any of those that have gone before. However, the 'teen' world is characterized by a series of paradoxes, with a continual seeking of new youth world/escapism (as adults invade their space) and for excitement, as well as increasing insecurity and the need to belong.

This manifests itself in a teen world that is characterized by:

➡ Living for today, with a heavy emphasis upon individual self-expression, mobility, freedom and hedonism
➡ A commercial and marketing overload that has led to those within this group being media literate, cynical and more demanding
➡ A group that has a strong appreciation of brands and their heritage; where there is a superficial idealism for the brand, the market has a tendency to reject it.

Changing family relationships

With the breakdown of the traditional family structure, a decline in the number of births to 1.64 per woman and a growth in the number of working women (refer to the discussion on p. 145), family decision-making structures have undergone a series of fundamental changes. There is therefore a big question over who within the redefined family makes decisions and how these are arrived at. In essence:

➡ Democracy and individualism have replaced traditional family hierarchies and children play a far greater role. They are no longer protected from the adult world in the way they were previously.
➡ Because the number of working and career women has increased dramatically, male/female/family dynamics have changed. Independence is now an economic possibility for a greater number of women – with the economics of divorce having contributed to this. However, a number of commentators have identified a culture of guilt surrounding the question of how to be a good mother, whilst at the same time working full time and pursuing a career.

There are now no set life-stages and less age-appropriate behaviour. Children are exposed to a greater number of stimuli (half of all four-year-olds have a television in their bedroom) and are far more brand conscious. Adults stay young longer. The age at which many have children is getting later as they concentrate on having 'fun' (this is the rise of 'middle youth' – people in their 30s and 40s who still haven't 'settled down', something that has been manifested in the rise of adventure holidays targeted at this group).

The rise of the cash-rich/time-poor segment

Because more and more people are working longer hours, the service sector has grown enormously to fill the time gap. The idea of getting someone to do something for you is no longer unacceptable (laziness/snobbery). Instead, it is a sign of valuing your life. Other factors that have led to the growth of the service sector to serve this market include:

➡ Seventy-two per cent of women of working age are now employed and whilst statistics show that women still do the majority of housework, young women are less inclined to do it than their mothers. The number of single-person households is also increasing and so these people have no one else to do it for them.

➡ The desire to fully exploit the little time people do have. They are therefore willing to pay for time, quality and simplicity – life is too short to do it yourself. This is not a return to Edwardian hierarchy (i.e. 'I am too good to clean'), but rather 'I don't have enough time to clean, so I will pay someone to do it for me'.

➡ The 24-hour society that has been driven by:
  ➡ The Internet being 'open' 24 hours, helping to confirm this notion of the 24-hour society
  ➡ Home delivery and combination of products when and where you want them
  ➡ An increase in stress-related diseases.

However, at the same time that we have seen the rise of the cash-rich/time-poor segment, there has also been a growth in the time-rich/money-poor segment, a factor that has implications for the value-for-money offer.

A search for (greater) value

Against the background of the factors discussed in the above section, there is increasingly the emergence of two (or three) nations within society (see Illustration 5.9), characterized by:

➡ Forty per cent of households are affluent, but one in three is poor and getting poorer

➡ The wealthiest 5 per cent of UK society own 42 per cent of the total national wealth, whilst the bottom 50 per cent own just 6 per cent of national wealth (the top 25 per cent own 74 per cent of the wealth)

➡ High levels of price consciousness continue to thrive, and retailers are set to capitalize on this with the growth of retailers such as Wal-Mart, Aldi and Netto

➡ Even the wealthier, older households will feel squeezed as more of their discretionary income goes on health, education and private insurance

➡ Consumers are becoming even more demanding of quality and see price/value solutions more than price per se to be important

➡ Home shopping, with much more prominent pricing cues, will help to fuel the price mentality.

Illustration 5.9 The rise of the three-nation society

In the mid-1990s, the Henley Centre highlighted the ways in which there is an interaction of time and money and how this has led to the emergence of a sizeable time-poor/cash-rich segment in society. The profile of this segment, which they referred to as 'the first nation', differs sharply from those segments labelled the second and third nations; the characteristics of the three segments are illustrated in Figure 5.19. The 20 per cent of the people in this first nation segment are characterized by being willing to spend money to save time, something that distinguishes them from the other 80 per cent of society. By virtue of their income levels, this segment of society also has open to it a greater spectrum of product choices and has responded by being more willing than other segments to pass on to others some aspects of life management.

The first nation	The second nation	The third nation
20% of the population	50% of the population	30% of the population
40% of consumer spending	50% of consumer spending	10% of consumer spending
Cash-rich	Cash constrained	Cash-poor
Time-poor	Time-constrained	Time-rich

Figure 5.19   The three-nation society

The rise of ethical consumerism

Because of the large numbers of financial, food, health and environmental scares over the past decade, a greater cynicism about government, politicians, big business and brands has emerged.

Ethical consumerism has been a response to this and reflects the desire to gain control over one's life. Buying ethical products from a supermarket, for example, involves no major life changes, but is an easy way to make the consumer feel he or she is making a difference. In these circumstances, prices are often of less importance than how the product is positioned.

An emphasis upon health and healthy lifestyles

Because of the growing awareness of the ability and personal responsibility for individuals to influence their own health, the greater evidence regarding links between diet and disease, and the shift from the welfare state to the individual, there has been an upsurge in the emphasis given to lifestyle management. Underpinning this is the recognition that diet is an important contributor to healthiness ('I am more concerned about what I eat and drink than I used to be'), and that children today are increasingly exposed to smoking, pollution, drugs, stress and a lack of exercise. There is, though, a general confusion over how to eat healthily, 'the advice given on healthy eating is always changing' and a (growing?) body of consumers who just opt out or cannot afford to participate ('I would like to eat healthier foods but it costs a lot more to buy the right things').

The desire for indulgence and small treats

With society generally becoming wealthier, the rises in consumers' disposable income and the number of people considering themselves 'middle class', tastes and aspirations are changing. Stressful lifestyles and time famine means there is a greater need for pampering and enhanced leisure time. Even in times of economic hardship small indulgences remain intact; in fact, these are increasingly seen as essentials.

Chapter **6**

Approaches to competitor analysis

6.1 Learning objectives

When you have read this chapter you should be able to understand:

(a) the importance of competitor analysis;

(b) how firms can best identify against whom they are competing;

(c) how to evaluate competitive relationships;

(d) how to identify competitors' likely response profiles;

(e) the components of the competitive information system and how the information generated feeds into the process of formulating strategy.

6.2 Introduction

We suggested in Chapter 5 that the last 10 years have seen the emergence of a new type of consumer who is characterized by a very different type of value system and far higher expectations. At the same time, a new type of competitor appears to have emerged along with a different type of competitive environment. This new environment is characterized by:

➡ Generally higher levels and an increasing intensity of competition

➡ New and more aggressive competitors who are emerging with ever greater frequency

➡ Changing bases of competition as organizations search ever harder for a competitive edge

➡ The wider geographic sources of competition

➡ More frequent niche attacks

➡ More frequent and more strategic alliances are necessary

➡ A quickening of the pace of innovation

➡ The need for stronger relationships and alliances with customers and distributors

➡ An emphasis upon value-added strategies

➡ Ever more aggressive price competition

➡ The difficulties of achieving long-term differentiation, with the result that a greater number of enterprises are finding themselves stuck in the marketing wilderness with no obvious competitive advantage

➡ The emergence of a greater number of 'bad' competitors (i.e. those not adhering to the traditional and unspoken rules of competitive behaviour within their industries).

The implications of these changes, both individually and collectively, are significant and demand far more from an enterprise if it is to survive and grow. Most obviously, there is a need for a much more detailed understanding of who it is that the enterprise is competing against and their capabilities. However, in coming to terms with this, the marketing planner needs to focus not just upon the 'hard' factors (e.g. their size, financial resources, manufacturing capability), but also upon the 'softer' elements (such as their managerial cultures, their priorities, their commitment to particular markets and market offerings, the assumptions they hold about themselves and their markets, and their objectives). Without this, it is almost inevitable that the marketing planner will fail to come to terms with any competitive threats. Given the nature of these comments, the need for, and advantages of, detailed competitive analysis should be apparent and can be summarized in terms of how it is capable of:

➡ Providing an understanding of your competitive advantage/disadvantage relative to your competitors' positions
➡ Helping in generating insights into competitors' strategies – past, present and potential
➡ Giving an informed basis for developing future strategies to sustain/establish advantages over your competitors.

Although the vast majority of marketing planners and strategists acknowledge the importance of competitive analysis, it has long been recognized that less effort is typically put into detailed and formal analysis of competitors than, for example, of customers and their buying patterns. In many cases this is seemingly because marketing managers feel that they know enough about their competitors simply as the result of competing against them on a day-by-day basis. In other cases there is almost a sense of resignation, with managers believing that it is rarely possible to understand competitors in detail and that, as long as the company's performance is acceptable, there is little reason to spend time collecting information (see Figure 6.1). In yet others, there is only a general understanding of who it is that the company is competing against. The reality, however, is that competitors represent a major determinant of corporate success, and any failure to take detailed account of their strengths, weaknesses, strategies and areas of vulnerability is likely to lead not just to a sub-optimal performance, but also to an unnecessarily greater exposure to aggressive and unexpected competitive moves. Other probable consequences of failing to monitor competition include an increased likelihood of the enterprise being taken by surprise, its relegation to being a follower rather than a leader, and to a focus on short-term rather than more fundamental long-term issues.

Figure 6.1 Attitudinal barriers to undertaking competitor analysis

There are numerous examples of organizations having been taken by surprise by new competitors who introduce and then play by very different rules of the game (think, for example, of the way in which BA and the other major European flag carriers have been hit by new entrants such as easyJet and Ryanair; how Hoover and Electrolux were hit by Dyson; and how the major clearing banks were seemingly taken by surprise by the telephone and Internet bankers). It is apparent from these sorts of examples and the points made above that competitor analysis is not a luxury but a necessity in order to:

➡ Survive
➡ Handle slow growth
➡ Cope with change
➡ Exploit opportunities
➡ Uncover key factors
➡ Reinforce intuition
➡ Improve the quality of decisions
➡ Stay competitive
➡ Avoid surprises.

(See Kelly, 1987, pp. 10–14.)

It follows from this that competitive analysis should be a central element of the marketing planning process, with detailed attention being paid to each competitor's apparent objectives, resources, capabilities, perceptions and competitive stance, as well as to their marketing plans and the individual elements of the marketing mix. In this way, areas of competitive strength and weakness can more readily be identified, and the results fed into the process of developing an effective marketing strategy. Better and more precise attacks can then be aimed at competitors and more effective defences erected to fight off competitors' moves. An additional benefit of competitor analysis, in certain circumstances at least, is that it can help in the process of understanding buying behaviour by identifying the particular groups or classes of customer to whom each competitor's strategy is designed to appeal. This can then be used as the basis for determining the most effective probable positioning strategy for the organization.

Recognition of these points leaves the strategist needing to answer five questions:

1 Against whom are we competing?
2 What strengths and weaknesses do they possess?
3 What are their objectives?
4 What strategies are they pursuing and how successful are they?
5 How are they likely to behave and, in particular, how are they likely to react to offensive moves?

Taken together, the answers to these five questions should provide the marketing strategist with a clear understanding of the competitive environment and, in particular, against *whom* the company is competing and *how* they compete. An example of this appears in Figure 6.2.

Kodak's products	Principal competitor(s)	Kodak's market position	Intensity and bases of competition	Likelihood of new entrants	Kodak's core strategy
Instant cameras and instant film	Polaroid	Challenger to a well-established leader	High and increasing with greater emphasis being placed on innovation	High	Penetration pricing to sell cameras as fast as possible to build a base for the sales of film
Photographic paper	Fuji Photo Film Co	Leader but being threatened by Fuji and other Japanese companies	High – the attack is based on lower prices and statements of quality	Medium	Share maintenance by emphasizing the quality of Kodak paper and making consumers aware that some processors do not use Kodak paper
Office copiers	Xerox, IBM, 3M	Late entrant to a highly competitive market in which Xerox held a 75 per cent share	Very high with ever greater emphasis being given to innovation, cost and service	Very high (particularly from Japanese firms)	The establishment of a separate sales and service network utilizing the firm's image and marketing capabilities in the microfilm equipment area

Figure 6.2 The competitive environment for selected Eastman Kodak products in the late 1970s (adapted from *Business Week*, 20 June 1977)

It is then against the background of the picture that emerges from this sort of analysis that the marketing strategist can begin to formulate strategy. In the example cited in Figure 6.2, for example, the central issue for Kodak revolved around the costs, risks, and possible long-term returns from penetrating new markets in instant cameras and office copiers, as opposed to sustaining and defending the company's position as the market leader in the photographic paper market. The principal environmental inputs to the company's strategic planning process at this time were therefore competitive forces and new technology.

Having developed a picture of the market in this way, the analysis can then be taken a step further by a compilation of each competitor's likely response profile; the various inputs needed for this are illustrated in Figures 6.3–6.5.

The analysis in Figure 6.3, in turn, provides the basis for completing the framework that appears in Figure 6.4. Here, each competitor's particular strengths and weaknesses can be shown and their competitive profiles developed.

This information is then used to develop a competitive response profile for each competitor: the framework for this is illustrated in Figure 6.5.

In using this model, the strategist begins by focusing upon the competitor's current strategy, and then moves successively through an examination of competitive strengths and weaknesses; the assumptions that the competitor appears to hold about the industry and itself; and then, finally and very importantly, the competitor's probable future goals and the factors that drive it. It is an understanding of these four dimensions which then allows the marketing strategist to begin compiling the detail of the response profile and to answer four principal questions:

1 Is the competitor satisfied with its current position?
2 What future moves is the competitor likely to make?

The strength of the competitors' positioning	What market share does each competitor have? How strong is each competitor's image What is their position within the trade? Is there a particular focus in certain markets?
The strength of the competitive offerings	In relative terms, how good is each element of each competitor's marketing mix? How satisfied is each competitor's customer base? What levels of customer loyalty exist? How satisfied are each competitor's distributors?
The strength of the competitors' resources	How profitable is each competitor? What is the size of each firm's resource base? How big and efficient is the production base? How fast and effective are the product development processes?
Understanding the competitors' strategies	What is each competitor's strategic intent? What are their actions and probable reactions?

Figure 6.3 Competitor analysis: step 1 – developing a general picture of the competition

Competencies/capabilities	Competitors' position				
	Competitor 1	Competitor 2	Competitor 3	Competitor 4	Competitor 5
Competitive stance					
Price levels					
Brand recognition					
Distribution network					
After sales service					
Promotion/public relations					
Strategic focus					
Manufacturing skills					
Financial stability					
Technology skills					
New product innovations					

Strong/high	Above average	Average	Less average	Weak/low

Figure 6.4 Competitor analysis: step 2 – developing an overview of competitors' strengths

3 In which segments or areas of technology is the competitor most vulnerable?

4 What move on our part is likely to provoke the strongest retaliation by the competitor?

Against the background of the answers to those questions, the marketing strategist needs then to consider two further issues: where are we most vulnerable to any move on the part of each competitor, and what can we realistically do in order to reduce this vulnerability?

Porter's approach to competitive structure analysis

Undoubtedly one of the major contributions in recent years to our understanding of the ways in which the competitive environment influences strategy has been provided by Porter (1980, Chapter 1). Porter's work, which is discussed in greater detail in Chapter 10, is based on the idea that 'competition in an industry is rooted in its underlying economics, and competitive forces that go well beyond the established combatants in a particular industry' (Porter, 1979, p. 138). He has also emphasized that the first determinant of a firm's profitability is the attractiveness of the industry in which it operates. The second determinant is competition:

"The second central question in competitive strategy is a firm's relative position within its industry. Positioning determines whether a firm's profitability is above or below the industry average . . . The fundamental basis of above average performance in the long run is sustainable competitive advantage."

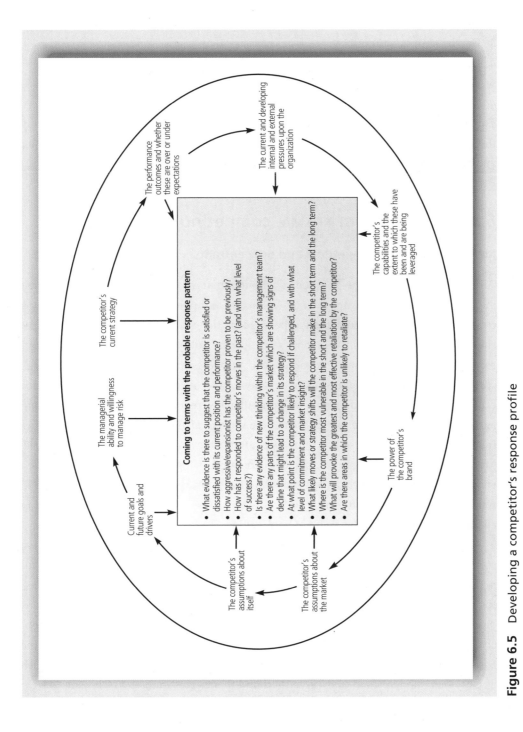

Figure 6.5 Developing a competitor's response profile

This leads Porter to suggest that the nature and intensity of competition within any industry is determined by the interaction of five key forces:

1 The threat of new entrants
2 The power of buyers
3 The threat of substitutes
4 The extent of competitive rivalry
5 The power of suppliers.

This work is, as we commented above, examined in Chapter 10 and the reader may therefore find it of value to turn to the first part of that chapter before going any further and attempting to answer the five questions referred to on p. 225.

6.3 Against whom are we competing?

Identifying present competitors and new entrants

Although the answer to the question of who it is that a company is competing against might appear straightforward, the range of actual and potential competitors faced by a company is often far broader than appears to be the case at first sight. The strategist should therefore avoid competitive myopia both by adopting a broad perspective and recognizing that, in general, companies tend to overestimate the capabilities of large competitors and either underestimate or ignore those of smaller ones. In the 1970s, for example, the large manufacturers of computers were preoccupied with competing against one another and failed for some time to recognize the emergence and growing threat in the PC market posed by what were at the time small companies such as Apple. More recently, we have seen companies such as BA being taken by surprise by much smaller organizations such as easyJet. Equally, book retailers have been forced to rethink their strategies, often in a radical way, as the result of Amazon.com having changed the competitive dynamics of book selling.

In a more general sense, business history is full of examples of companies that have seemingly been taken by surprise by organizations they had failed to identify as competitors, or whose competitive capability they drastically underestimated. In Chapter 4, for example, we discussed the experiences of the Swiss watch industry, which was brought to its knees in the late 1960s and early 1970s by new manufacturers of inexpensive watches that incorporated digital technology, a technology that, ironically, the Swiss themselves had developed. Equally, in the reprographic market, companies such as Gestetner suddenly and unexpectedly found themselves in the 1970s having to fight aggressive new entrants to the market such as Xerox. Xerox entered this market with a new, faster, cleaner and infinitely more convenient product to which Gestetner, together with a number of other companies in the market at the time, experienced difficulties in responding. Similarly, the British and US television and motorcycle manufacturers either failed to recognize the Japanese threat or underestimated their expansionist objectives. The result today is that neither country has a domestic manufacturing industry of any size in either of these sectors. Less drastic, but in many ways equally fundamental, problems have been experienced in the car industry.

It is because of examples such as these that astute strategists have long acknowledged the difficulties of defining the boundaries of an industry, and have recognized that companies are more likely to be taken by surprise and hit hard by *latent* competitors than by *current* competitors whose patterns of marketing behaviour are largely predictable. It is therefore possible to see competition operating at four levels:

1 Competition consists only of those companies offering a similar product or service to the target market, utilizing a similar technology, and exhibiting similar degrees of vertical integration. Thus, Nestlé (which makes Nescafé) sees General Foods, with its Maxwell House brand, as a similar competitor in the instant coffee market, while Penguin sees its direct competitors in the chocolate snack bar market to be Kit-Kat's six pack, Twix and Club.

2 Competition consists of all companies operating in the same product or service category. Penguin's indirect competitors, for example, consist of crisps and ice-creams.

3 Competition consists of all companies manufacturing or supplying products that deliver the same service. Thus, long-distance coach operators compete not just against each other, but also against railways, cars, planes and motorcycles.

4 Competition consists of all companies competing for the same spending power. An example of this is the American motorcycle manufacturer, Harley Davidson, which does not necessarily see itself as competing directly with other motorcycle manufacturers. Instead, for many buyers it is a choice between a Harley Davidson motorcycle and a major consumer durable such as a conservatory or a boat: this is discussed in greater detail in Illustration 6.1.

Illustration 6.1 Harley Davidson and its perception of competition

Harley Davidson, the last remaining American motorcycle, is seen by many as one of the icons of the design world. As a symbol of freedom and adventure, the socio-economic profile of Harley Davidson owners differs significantly from that of virtually all other motorcycle riders. The late Malcolm Forbes, the owner of *Forbes* magazine, for example, rode Harleys with his 'gang' called the Capitalist Tools and did much to promote the bike among clean-cut executives known as Rich Urban Bikers (RUBs). This image has been reinforced by the bike's appearance in numerous commercials, including a Levi's advertisement in which a monstrous Harley is ridden on to a Wall Street dealing-room floor.

Although it is acknowledged that the bikes are technically antiquated, few current or aspiring owners see this as a drawback. Most Harley owners do not actually ride them a great deal. They are, as one commentator has observed, social statements rather than forms of transport. One consequence of this is that Harley Davidson, at least in the UK, competes only very indirectly with other motorcycle manufacturers. Instead, as Steve Dennis of Harley Street, a dealership specializing in used and customized bikes, puts it: 'We're competing against conservatories and swimming pools, not other bikes.'

Source: *Sunday Times*, 23 September 1990.

It should be apparent from this that the marketing strategist needs not only to identify those competitors who reflect the same general approach to the market, but also to consider those who 'intersect' the company in each market, who possibly approach it from a different perspective, and who ultimately might pose either a direct or an indirect threat. As part of this, the strategist needs also to identify potential new entrants to the market and, where it appears necessary, develop contingency plans to neutralize their competitive effect. Newcomers to a market can, as Abell and Hammond (1979, p. 52) have pointed out, enter from any one of several starting points:

➡ They already sell to your customers, but expand their participation to include new customer functions which you currently satisfy (e.g. they initially sell a component of a computer system and expand into other system components that you supply)
➡ They already satisfy customer functions that you satisfy but expand their participation into your customer market from activities in other customer markets (e.g. they initially sell pumps for oil exploration only and then expand into the marine pump business, where you are active)
➡ They already operate in an 'upstream' or 'downstream' business (e.g. Texas Instruments entered calculators from its position as a semiconductor manufacturer, while some calculator manufacturers have integrated backwards into the manufacture of semiconductors)
➡ They enter as a result of 'unrelated' diversification.

Taken together, these comments lead to two distinct viewpoints of competition: the *industry point of view* and the *market point of view*.

The industry perspective of competition

The industry perception of competition is implicit in the majority of discussions of marketing strategy. Here, an industry is seen to consist of firms offering a product or class of products or services that are close substitutes for one another; a close substitute in these circumstances is seen to be a product for which there is a high cross-elasticity of demand. An example of this would be a dairy product such as butter, where if the price rises a proportion of consumers will switch to margarine. A logical starting point for competitor analysis therefore involves understanding the industry's competitive pattern, since it is this that determines the underlying competitive dynamics. A model of this process appears in Figure 6.6.

From this it can be seen that competitive dynamics are influenced initially by conditions of supply and demand. These in turn determine the *industry structure*, which then influences *industry conduct* and, subsequently, *industry performance*.

Arguably the most significant single element in this model is the structure of the industry itself, and in particular the number of sellers, their relative market shares, and the degree of differentiation that exists between the competing companies and products; this is illustrated in Figure 6.7.

The interrelated issue of the number of sellers and their relative market shares has long been the focus of analysis by economists, who have typically categorized an industry in terms of five types:

1 An absolute monopoly, in which, because of patents, licences, scale economics or some other factor, only one firm provides the product or service

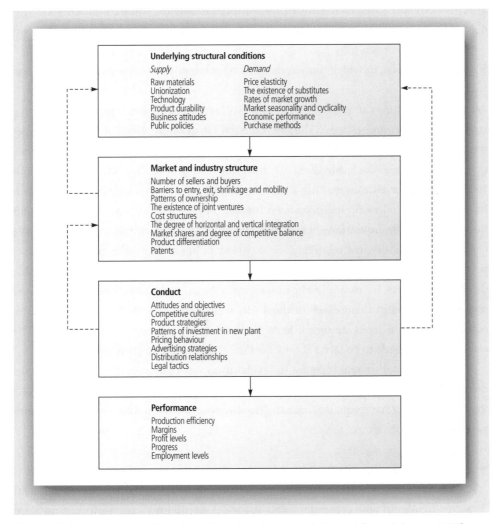

Figure 6.6 The competitive dynamics of an industry (adapted from Scherer, 1980)

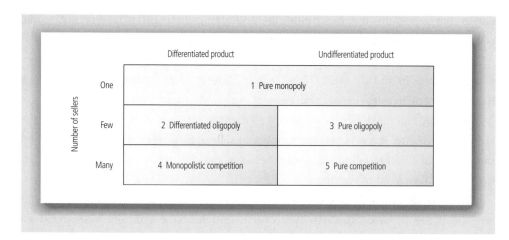

Figure 6.7 Five industry structure types

2 A differentiated oligopoly, where a few firms produce products that are partially differentiated

3 A pure oligopoly, in which a few firms produce broadly the same commodity

4 Monopolistic competition, in which the industry has many firms offering a differentiated product or service

5 Pure competition, in which numerous firms offer broadly the same product or service.

Although industries can at any given time be categorized in these terms, competitive structures do of course change. The rail industry, for example, faced significant competition initially from bus companies such as National Express coaches, and then subsequently from Stagecoach and First Group after deregulation within the industry in 1980, and was forced into making a series of changes to its marketing strategy, which have continued following the privatized break-up of BR. Equally, patterns of competition in many other industries, such as cars, consumer electronics and white goods, have changed dramatically in a relatively short period as the result of the growth of import penetration. In the case of white goods such as refrigerators, washing machines, tumble driers and freezers, for example, the domestically-based manufacturers such as Hoover and Hotpoint found themselves in the 1970s facing new, aggressive and often price-based competition from, among others, Zanussi, Indesit, Electrolux and Candy. The issue that then needs to be faced is how best the challenged company can respond.

Although a substantial increase in levels of import penetration are in many ways the most conspicuous causes of a change in competitive structures, a series of other factors exist that can have equally dramatic implications for the nature and bases of competition. These include:

➡ Changes within the distribution channels – the emergence of very powerful retail chains such as Tesco and Sainsbury with groceries, B&Q in the DIY (do-it-yourself) sector, PC World with computers, and Toys 'R' Us with toys – has led to a significant shift in the balance of power between manufacturers and retailers, with the retailers adopting an ever more proactive stance regarding product acceptance, new product development, price points, promotional activity and advertising support

→ Changes in the supplier base

→ Legislation

→ The emergence of new technology.

The market perspective of competition

As an alternative to the industry perspective of competition, which takes as its starting point companies making the same product or offering the same service, we can focus on companies that try to satisfy the same customer needs or that serve the same customer groups. Theodore Levitt has long been a strong advocate of this perspective and it was this which was at the heart of his classic article 'Marketing Myopia'. In this article, Levitt (1960), pointed to a series of examples of organizations that had failed to recognize how actual and potential customers viewed the product or service being offered. Thus, in the case of railways, the railway companies concentrated on competing with one another and in doing this failed to recognize that, because customers were looking for transport, they compared the railways with planes, buses and cars. The essence of the market perspective of competition therefore involves giving full recognition to the broader range of products or services that are capable of satisfying customers' needs. This should, in turn, lead to the marketing strategist identifying a broader set of actual and potential competitors, and adopting a more effective approach to long-run market planning (see Illustration 6.2).

Illustration 6.2 Substitutes for aluminium

The need to have a clear understanding of who exactly your competitors are and the nature of their strengths and weaknesses is illustrated below. In this we list some of the alternatives to aluminium. Although not all of the materials listed in the left-hand column are alternatives in each and every situation in which aluminium is used, the table goes some way towards illustrating how an overly narrow competitive perspective could well lead to an organization being taken by surprise as customers switch to the alternatives.

Material	Advantages	Drawbacks
Mild steel	Very cheap Widely available	Weight Rust easily
Low-chrome ferritic stainless steel	Similar price Widely available	Weight Rusts in sea water
Titanium	Strength (especially at temperature) Corrosion resistance	Cost Processing (not easily extrudable)

Material	Advantages	Drawbacks
Magnesium	Very lightweight	Vulnerable to fire
Polystyrene	Lightweight	Low strength
Unplasticated PVC	Reasonably cheap	No temperature/fire resistance
ABS, nylon engineering plastics	Lightweight Strong	Cost
Wood	Cheap Widely available	Variable quality Rots
Composites		
Aluminium MMCs	Stronger Stiffer Harder	Extra cost Processing difficulties
Fibre-reinforced plastics	Lighter for quality Stiffness/strength	Can lack toughness Extra cost

6.4 Identifying and evaluating competitors' strengths and weaknesses

By this stage it should be apparent that the identification and evaluation of competitors' strengths, weaknesses and capabilities is at the very heart of a well-developed competitive strategy. The marketing planner should, as a first step, therefore concentrate upon collecting information under a number of headings as a prelude to a full comparative assessment. These include:

➡ Sales
➡ Market share
➡ Cost and profit levels, and how they appear to be changing over time
➡ Cash flows
➡ Return on investment
➡ Investment patterns
➡ Production processes
➡ Levels of capacity utilization
➡ Organizational culture
➡ Products and the product portfolio
➡ Product quality
➡ The size and pattern of the customer base
➡ The levels of brand loyalty
➡ Dealers and distribution channels

➡ Marketing and selling capabilities
➡ Operations and physical distribution
➡ Financial capabilities
➡ Management capabilities and attitudes to risk
➡ Human resources, their capability and flexibility
➡ Previous patterns of response
➡ Ownership patterns and, in the case of divisionalized organizations, the expectations of corporate management.

The signs of competitive strength in a company's position are likely to be:

➡ Important core competences
➡ Strong market share (or a leading market share)
➡ A pace-setting or distinctive strategy
➡ Growing customer base and customer loyalty
➡ Above-average market visibility
➡ Being in a favourably situated strategic group
➡ Concentrating on fastest-growing market segments
➡ Strongly differentiated products
➡ Cost advantages
➡ Above-average profit margins
➡ Above-average technological and innovational capability
➡ A creative, entrepreneurially alert management
➡ In a position to capitalize on opportunities.

Obtaining this sort of information typically proves to be more difficult in some instances than in others. Industrial markets, for example, rarely have the same wealth of published data that is commonly available in consumer markets. This, however, should not be used as an excuse for not collecting the information, but rather emphasizes the need for a clearly developed competitive information system that channels information under a wide variety of headings to a central point. This information needs to be analysed and disseminated as a prelude to being fed into the strategy process.

The sources of this information will obviously vary from industry to industry, but will include most frequently the sales force, trade shows, industry experts, the trade press, distributors, suppliers and, perhaps most importantly, customers. Customer information can be gained in several ways, although periodically a firm may find it of value to conduct primary research among customers, suppliers and distributors to arrive at a profile of competitors within the market. An example of this appears in Figure 6.8, where current and potential buyers have been asked to rate the organization and its four major competitors on a series of attributes. A similar exercise can then be conducted among suppliers and distributors in order to build up a more detailed picture.

Significant buying factors	Our company	Competitors		
		1	2	3
Products				
Product design	Good	Exc	Fair	Good
Product quality	Good	Exc	Fair	Exc
Product performance	Good	Good	Fair	Good
Breadth of product line	Fair	Fair	Poor	Good
Depth of product line	Fair	Fair	Poor	Good
Reliability	Good	Exc	Fair	Exc
Running costs	Fair	Good	Equal	Good
Promotion and pricing				
Advertising/sales promotion	Fair	Exc	Fair	Good
Image and reputation	Fair	Exc	Fair/Poor	Exc
Product literature	Poor	Exc	Poor	Good
Price	Equal	Fair	Good	Equal
Selling and distribution				
Sales force calibre	Fair	Good	Poor	Good
Sales force experience/knowledge	Fair	Good	Fair	Exc
Geographical coverage	Good	Good	Poor	Good
Sales force/customer relations	Fair	Exc	Poor	Exc
Service				
Customer service levels	Fair	Exc	Poor	Exc
Performance against promise	Fair	Exc	Poor	Exc

The classification of factors from excellent (Exc) to poor should be determined by marketing intelligence, including studies of the perceptions of current and potential buyers, as well as those of suppliers and distributors.

Figure 6.8 The comparative assessment of competitors

A variation on this approach is shown in Figures 6.9 and 6.10. In the first of these, a list of characteristics that can be associated with success in the sector in question has been identified and each main competitor (including ourselves – ABC Co) has been evaluated on each of the characteristics. From the total scores it appears that

Key success factor/strength measure	ABC Co	Rival 1	Rival 2	Rival 3	Rival 4
Quality/product performance	8	5	10	1	6
Reputation/image	8	7	10	1	6
Raw material access/cost	2	10	4	5	1
Technological skills	10	1	7	3	8
Advertising effectiveness	9	4	10	5	1
Distribution	9	4	10	5	1
Financial strength	5	10	7	3	1
Relative cost position	5	10	3	1	4
Ability to compete on price	5	7	10	1	4
Unweighted overall strength rating	61	58	71	25	32

Rating scale: 1 = Very weak; 10 = Very strong

Figure 6.9 Unweighted competitive strength assessment

Key success factor/ strength measure	Weight	ABC Co	Rival 1	Rival 2	Rival 3	Rival 4
Quality/product performance	0.10	8/0.80	5/0.50	10/1.00	1/0.10	6/0.60
Reputation/image	0.10	8/0.80	7/0.70	10/1.00	1/0.10	6/0.60
Raw material access/cost	0.10	2/0.20	10/1.00	4/0.40	5/0.50	1/0.10
Technological skills	0.05	10/0.50	1/0.05	7/0.35	3/0.15	8/0.40
Advertising effectiveness	0.05	9/0.45	4/0.20	10/0.50	5/0.25	1/0.05
Distribution	0.05	9/0.45	4/0.20	10/0.50	5/0.25	1/0.05
Financial strength	0.10	5/0.50	10/1.00	7/0.70	3/0.30	1/0.10
Relative cost position	0.30	5/1.50	10/3.00	3/0.90	1/0.30	4/1.20
Ability to compete on price	0.15	5/0.75	7/1.05	10/1.50	1/0.15	4/0.60
Sum of weights	1.00					
Weighted overall strength rating		5.95	7.70	6.85	2.10	3.70

Rating scale: 1 = Very weak; 10 = Very strong

Figure 6.10 Weighted competitive strength assessment

Rival 2 is the strongest competitor, with Rival 1 being only marginally weaker than ABC Co. However, while the relative strengths of each competing enterprise are clearly visible in Figure 6.9, there is no indication of the relative importance of each of the key success factors. For example, it may be that relative cost position and ability to compete on price are the most important factors for competitive success within this sector, with technological skills, advertising effectiveness and distribution being relatively unimportant. These priorities can be indicated by weights, as in Figure 6.10. From this it is now evident that Rival 1 is the market leader, followed by Rival 2, which is ahead of ABC Co. These profiles indicate quite clearly the relative importance of key success factors and the relative strength of each competitor on each of those factors.

Competitive product portfolios

In many cases, one of the most useful methods of gaining an insight into a competitor's strengths, weaknesses and general level of capability is by means of portfolio analysis. The techniques of portfolios analysis, which include the Boston Consulting Group matrix, are by now well developed and are discussed in detail in Chapter 9. It might therefore be of value at this stage to turn to pp. 367–70 in order to understand more fully the comments below.

Having plotted each major competitor's portfolio, the marketing strategist needs to consider a series of questions:

1 What degree of internal balance exists within each portfolio? Which competitors, for example, appear to have few, if any, 'cash cows' but a surfeit of 'question marks' or 'dogs'? Which of the competitors appears to have one or more promising 'stars' that might in the future pose a threat?

2 What are the likely cash flow implications for each competitor's portfolio? Does it appear likely, for example, that they will be vulnerable in the near future because of the cash demands of a disproportionate number of 'question marks' and 'stars'?

3 What trends are apparent in each portfolio? A tentative answer to this question can be arrived at by plotting the equivalent growth-share display for a period three to five years earlier, and superimposing on this the current chart. A third display that reflects the likely development of the portfolio over the next few years, assuming present policies are maintained, can in turn be superimposed on this to show the direction and rate of travel of each product or strategic business unit (SBU).

4 Which competitors' products look suited for growth and which for harvesting? What are the implications for us and in what ways might we possibly pre-empt any competitive actions?

5 Which competitor appears to be the most vulnerable to an attack? Which competitor looks likely to pose the greatest threat in the future?

In plotting a competitor's portfolio the marketing strategist is quite obviously searching for areas of weakness that subsequently can be exploited. A number of the factors that contribute to vulnerability are identified in Illustration 6.3.

Illustration 6.3 What makes a competitor vulnerable?

A knowledge of a competitor's weaknesses can often be used to great effect by an astute marketing strategist. Amongst the factors that make a competitor vulnerable are:

Financial factors

➡ Cash flow problems
➡ Under funding
➡ Low margins
➡ High-cost operations and/or distribution.

Market and performance-related factors

➡ Slow/poor growth
➡ An overdependence on one market
➡ An overdependence on one or a small number of customers

➡ Strength in declining market sectors
➡ Little presence in growing and high margin markets
➡ Low market share
➡ Distribution weaknesses
➡ Weak segmentation of the market
➡ Poor/confused and/or unsustainable positioning
➡ A weak reputation and/or poorly defined image.

Product-related factors

➡ Outdated products and a failure to innovate
➡ Product weaknesses
➡ Weak or non-existent selling propositions.

Managerial factors	➡ An over- and ill-justified confidence
	➡ Managerial arrogance and a belief that the organization has an inalienable right to a place in the market
➡ A short-term orientation	
➡ The poor management of staff	
➡ The failure to focus upon what is important	➡ Competitive arrogance, competitive myopia and competitive sclerosis
➡ Managerial predictability and the adherance to well-tried formulae	
➡ Product or service obsolescence/weaknesses	➡ Bureaucratic structures
	➡ A fiscal year short-term fixation

At this point it is perhaps worth uttering a word of caution. The marketing strategist should not of course limit competitive analysis just to a series of marketing factors, but should also focus upon other areas, including financial and production measures. In this way it is possible to identify far more clearly which competitors within the industry are relatively weak and might therefore be vulnerable to a price attack or a takeover. Equally, it can identify which competitors within the industry should, by virtue of their financial strength or production flexibility, be avoided.

6.5 Evaluating competitive relationships and analysing how organizations compete

In essence, five types of relationship can develop between an organization and its competitors:

1 *Conflict*, where the firm sets out to destroy, damage or force the competitor out of the market.
2 *Competition*, where two or more firms are trying to achieve the same goals and penetrate the same markets with broadly similar product offers.
3 *Coexistence*, where the various players act largely independently of others in the market. This may in turn be due to the marketing planner being unaware of the competition; recognizing them but choosing to ignore them; or behaving on the basis that each firm has certain territorial rights that, tacitly, each player agrees not to infringe.
4 *Cooperation*, where one or more firms work together to achieve interdependent goals. Typically, this is done on the basis of exchanging information, licensing arrangements, joint ventures and through trade associations.
5 *Collusion*, which, although typically illegal, has as its purpose that of damaging another organization or, more frequently, ensuring that profit margins and the status quo are maintained.

Given this, any analysis of *how* firms compete falls into four parts:

1 What is each competitor's current strategy?
2 How are competitors performing?

3 What are their strengths and weaknesses?

4 What can we expect from each competitor in the future?

However, before moving on to the detail of these four areas, the strategist should spend time identifying what is already known about each competitor. There are numerous examples of companies that have collected information on competitors only to find out at a later stage that this knowledge already existed within the organization but that, for one reason or another, it had not been analysed or disseminated. In commenting on this, Davidson (1987a, p. 133) has suggested that:

*"*Recorded data tends not to be analysed over time, and often fails to cross functional barriers. Observable data is typically recorded on a haphazard basis, with little evaluation. Opportunistic data is not always actively sought or disseminated.*"*

This failure to collect, disseminate or make full use of competitive information is, for the majority of organizations, a perennial problem and often leads to the same information being collected more than once. It is, however, an issue that we discuss in greater detail at a later stage, and at this point we will therefore do no more than draw attention to it.

In attempting to arrive at a detailed understanding of competitive relationships, it is essential that each competitor is analysed separately, since any general analysis provides the strategist with only a partial understanding of competitors, and tells little either about potential threats that might emerge or opportunities that can be exploited. It is worth remembering, however, that what competitors have done in the past can often provide a strong indication of what they will do in the future. This is particularly the case when previous strategies have been conspicuously successful. Companies such as Mars, for example, have traditionally pursued an objective of market leadership, while the Japanese are often willing to accept long payback periods. Recognition of points such as these should then be used to guide the ways in which strategy is developed.

Other factors that need to be borne in mind include:

➡ Patterns of investment in plant

➡ Links with other competitors

➡ Patterns of advertising expenditure

➡ Relative cost positions

➡ Major changes in the senior management structure, but particularly the appointment of a new chief executive who might act as an agent for change.

Identifying strategic groups

In the majority of industries competitors can be categorized, at least initially, on the basis of the similarities and differences that exist in the strategies being pursued. The strategist can then begin to construct a picture of the market showing the strategic groups that exist; for our purposes here, a strategic group can be seen to consist of those firms within the market that are following a broadly similar strategy. An example of how strategic groupings can be identified is illustrated in Figure 6.11.

Having identified strategic groups in this way, the strategist then needs to identify the relative position and strength of each competitor. This can be done in one of several ways, including the categorizing of firms on the basis of whether their position within the market overall and within the strategic group is dominant, strong, favourable, tenable, weak or non-viable. Having done this, the strategist needs to consider the bases of any competitive advantages that exist; this is illustrated in Figure 6.12.

The experiences of many companies suggest that the easiest starting point from which to improve an organization's competitive position is Level 3, since this can often be achieved by good management. One example of a company that did this with considerable success was Beecham with its Lucozade brand, which it repositioned over a number of years in order to take advantage of a growing market for energy drinks.

There are several points that emerge from identifying strategic groups in this way. The first is that the height of the barriers to entry and exit can vary significantly from one group to another. The second is that the choice of a strategic group determines which companies are to be the firm's principal competitors. Recognizing this, a new entrant would then have to develop a series of competitive advantages to overcome, or at least to neutralize, the competitive advantages of others in the group.

There is, of course, competition not just *within* strategic groups but also *between* them, since not only will target markets develop or contract over time and hence prove to be either more or less attractive to other firms, but customers might not fully recognize major differences in the offers of each group. One consequence of this is that there

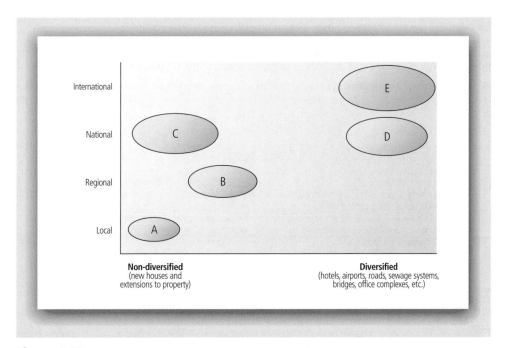

Figure 6.11 Strategic groups in the construction industry

Level	Competitive status	Examples
1	One or more sizeable advantages	Honda, Sony, Seiko, Coca-Cola and Microsoft
2	A series of small advantages that combine to form one large advantage	McDonald's
3	Advantages exist but these are either not recognized or not exploited fully	
4	No obvious or sustainable competitive advantages	Petrol retailers, estate agents and high street banks
5	Competitive disadvantages because of the organization's limited size, inflexibility, inefficient manufacturing practices, distribution networks, cost structures, culture, lack of skills, or poor image	Eastern European car manufacturers before the expansion of the E.U.

Figure 6.12 The five types of competitive status and the implications for competitive advantage (adapted from Davidson, 1987a)

is likely to be a degree of comparison buying across groups, something which again argues the case for the marketing strategist to adopt a market, rather than an industry, perspective of competition.

Although in Figure 6.11 we have made use of just two dimensions in plotting strategic groupings, a variety of other factors can typically be expected to be used to differentiate between companies and to help in the process of identifying group membership. A summary of these characteristics appears in Figure 6.13.

The particular relevance to any given industry of these characteristics is in practice influenced by several factors, the most significant of which are the history and development of the industry, the types of environmental forces at work, the nature

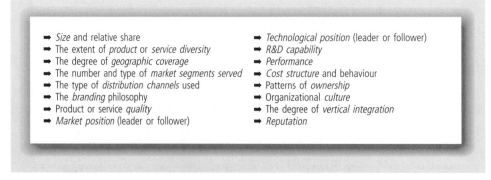

➡ *Size* and relative share
➡ The extent of *product* or *service diversity*
➡ The degree of *geographic coverage*
➡ The number and type of *market segments served*
➡ The type of *distribution channels* used
➡ The *branding* philosophy
➡ Product or service *quality*
➡ *Market position* (leader or follower)
➡ *Technological position* (leader or follower)
➡ *R&D capability*
➡ *Performance*
➡ *Cost structure* and behaviour
➡ Patterns of *ownership*
➡ Organizational *culture*
➡ The degree of *vertical integration*
➡ *Reputation*

Figure 6.13 Some characteristics for identifying strategic groups (adapted from Johnson and Scholes, 1988)

of the competitive activities of the various firms, and so on. It should be evident from this that each company does therefore have a different strategic make-up that needs to be profiled separately. Often, however, a strategy proves difficult to describe since it encompasses so many different dimensions, but Abell and Hammond (1979, p. 53) have outlined a useful framework for thinking about the strategic decision process:

➡ How does the competitor define the business in terms of customer groups, customer functions and technologies, and how vertically integrated is this competitor? And at a lower level of aggregation, how is the competitor segmenting the market and which segments are being pursued?

➡ What mission does this business have in its overall portfolio of businesses? Is it being managed for sales growth, market share, net profit, ROI or cash? What goals does it appear to have for each major segment of the business?

➡ What is the competitor's marketing mix, manufacturing policy, R&D policy, purchasing policy, physical distribution policy, etc.?

➡ What size are its budgets and how are they allocated?

In so far as it is possible to generalize, it is the third of these areas in which marketing managers find it most easy to collect information. This should not, however, be seen as a reason for ignoring the other three areas, since it is here that insights into what really drives the competition can best be gained.

This leads us to a position in which we are able to begin to construct a detailed list of the areas in which we need to collect competitive information. In the case of each competitor's current performance, this list includes sales, growth rates and patterns, market share, profit, profitability (return on investment), margins, net income, investment patterns and cash flow. Other areas to which attention needs to be paid include the identification of the importance of each market sector in which the competitor is operating, since this allows the marketing strategist to probe the areas of weakness or least concern at the minimum of risk.

The character of competition

The final area that we need to consider when examining how firms compete is what can loosely be termed 'the character of competition'. Because competition within a market is influenced to a very high degree by the nature of customer behaviour, the character of competition not only takes many forms, but is also likely to change over time. One fairly common way of examining the character of competition is therefore by means of an analysis of the changes taking place in the composition of *value added* by different firms. (The term 'value added' is used to describe the amount by which selling prices are greater than the cost of providing the bought out goods or services embodied in market offerings.) An analysis of changes in the value-added component can therefore give the strategist an understanding of the relative importance of such factors as

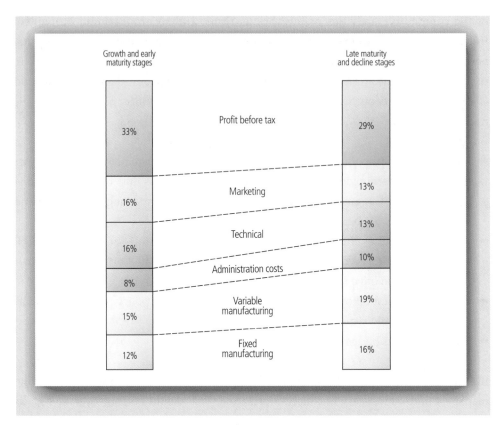

Figure 6.14 A comparison of the value-added components across the product life cycle (adapted from Abell and Hammond, 1979)

product and process development, selling, after-sales service, price, and so on, as the product moves through the life cycle. See Figure 6.14 for an example of this for a hypothetical product.

The marketing planner can also arrive at a measure of the character of competition by considering the extent to which each competitor develops new total industry demand (primary demand) or quite simply competes with others for a share of existing demand (selective demand). When a competitor's objective is the stimulation of primary demand, it is likely that efforts will focus upon identifying and developing new market segments. Conversely, when a competitor concentrates upon stimulating selective demand, the focus shifts to an attempt to satisfy existing customers more effectively than other companies. The obvious consequence of this is that the intensity of competition on a day-to-day basis is likely to increase significantly.

6.6 Identifying competitors' objectives

Having identified the organization's principal competitors and their strategies, we need then to focus upon each competitor's objectives. In other words, what drives each competitor's behaviour? A starting point in arriving at an answer to this is to assume that each competitor will aim for profit maximization either in the short term or the long term. In practice, of course, maximization is an unrealistic objective, which for a wide variety of reasons many companies are willing to sacrifice. A further assumption can be made – that each competitor has a variety of objectives, each of which has a different weight. These objectives might typically include cash flow, technological leadership, market share growth, service leadership or overall market leadership. Gaining an insight into this mix of objectives allows the strategist to arrive at tentative conclusions regarding how a competitor will respond to a competitive thrust. A firm pursuing market share growth is likely to react far more quickly and aggressively to a price cut or to a substantial increase in advertising than a firm that is aiming for, say, technological leadership.

In a general sense, however, company objectives (as pointed out in Chapter 7) are influenced by a wide variety of factors, but particularly the organization's size, history, culture and the breadth of the operating base. Where, for example, a company is part of a larger organization, a competitive thrust always runs the risk of leading to retaliation by the parent company on what might appear to be a disproportionate scale. Conversely, the parent company may see an attack on one of its divisions as being a nuisance but little more, and not bother to respond in anything other than a cursory fashion. This has been discussed in some detail by Rothschild (1989), who argues that the potentially most dangerous competitive move involves attacking a global company for which this is the only business.

It follows that the marketing strategist should give explicit consideration to the relative importance of each market to a competitor in order to understand the probable level of commitment that exists. By doing this, it is possible to estimate the level of effort that each competitor would then logically make in order to defend its position. Several factors are likely to influence this level of commitment, the five most important of which are likely to be:

1 The proportion of company profits that this market sector generates
2 The managerial perceptions of the market's growth opportunities
3 The levels of profitability that exist currently and that are expected to exist in the future
4 Any interrelationships between this and any other product or market sector in which the organization operates
5 Managerial cultures – in some companies, for example, any threat will be responded to aggressively almost irrespective of whether it is cost-effective.

As a general rule of thumb, therefore, competitive retaliation will be strong whenever the company feels its core business is being attacked. Recognizing this, the marketing planner should concentrate on avoiding areas that are likely to lead to this sort of response, unless of course the target has a strong strategic rationale. This sort of issue is discussed in detail in Chapter 11.

6.7 Identifying competitors' likely response profiles

Although a knowledge of a competitor's size, objectives and capability (strengths and weaknesses) can provide the strategist with a reasonable understanding of possible responses to company moves such as price cuts, the launch of new products and so on, other factors need to be examined. One of the most important of these is the organization's culture, since it is this that ultimately determines how the firm will do business and hence how it will act in the future.

The issue of how a competitor is likely to behave in the future has two components. Firstly, how is a competitor likely to respond to the general changes taking place in the external environment and, in particular, in the marketplace? Secondly, how is that competitor likely to respond to specific competitive moves that we, or indeed any other company, might make? For some companies at least, there is also a third question that needs to be considered: how likely is it that the competitor will initiate an aggressive move, and what form might this move be most likely to take? In posing questions such as these we are trying to determine where each competitive company is the most vulnerable, where it is the strongest, where the most appropriate battleground is likely to be and how, if at all, it will respond. In doing this, a potential starting point involves identifying each competitor's most probable reaction profile, the four most common of which are:

1 *The relaxed competitor*, who either fails to react or reacts only slowly to competitive moves. There are several possible reasons for this, the most common of which are that the management team believes that their customers are deeply loyal and are therefore unlikely to respond to a (better) competitive offer; they may fail to see the competitor's move or underestimate its significance; they may not have the resources to respond; the market might be of little real importance; or the focus may be upon harvesting the business. However, whatever the reason, the marketing strategies must try to understand why the competitor is taking such a relaxed approach.

2 *The tiger competitor*, who responds quickly and aggresively almost regardless of the nature and significance of any competitive move. Over time, firms such as this develop a reputation for their aggression and in this way create Fear, Uncertainty and Despair (FUD marketing) amongst other players in the market.

3 *The selective competitor*, who chooses carefully – and often very stategically – how, where and with what level of aggression they will respond to any competitive move. Such an approach is generally based not just on a clear understanding of the relative value of the organization's markets, but also on the costs of responding and the likelihood of the response proving to be cost-effective.

4 *The unpredictable competitor*, for whom it proves difficult or impossible to identify in advance how – or, indeed, if – they will respond to any particular move. The unpredictability of competitors such as this comes from the way in which in the past they may have responded aggressively on one occasion, but not at all on another when faced with what appears to be a broadly similar attack.

This general theme has, in turn, been developed by Bruce Henderson (1982) of the Boston Consulting Group who, in discussing competition, argues that much depends on the competitive equilibrium. Henderson's comments on this have been summarized by Kotler (1997, pp. 239–40) in the following way:

1 If competitors are nearly identical and make their living in the same way, then their competitive equilibrium is unstable.

2 If a single major factor is the critical factor, then competitive equilibrium is unstable. This would describe industries where cost differentiation opportunities exist through economies of scale, advanced technology, experience curve learning, etc. In such industries, any company that achieves a cost breakthrough can cut its price and win market share at the expense of other firms that can only defend their market shares at great cost. Price wars frequently break out in these industries as a function of cost breakthroughs.

3 If multiple factors may be critical factors, then it is possible for each competitor to have some advantage and be differentially attractive to some customers. The more the multiple factors that may provide an advantage, the more the number of competitors who can coexist. Each competitor has its competitive segment defined by the preference for the factor trade-offs that it offers. This would describe industries where many opportunities exist for differentiating quality, service, convenience and so on. If customers also place different values on these factors, then many firms can coexist through niching.

4 The fewer the number of competitive variables that are critical, the fewer the number of competitors. If only one factor is critical, then no more than two or three competitors are likely to coexist. Conversely, the larger the number of competitive variables, the larger the number of competitors, but each is likely to be smaller in its absolute size.

5 A ratio of 2:1 in market share between any two competitors seems to be the equilibrium point at which it is neither practical nor advantageous for either competitor to increase or decrease share.

The significance of costs

In attempting to come to terms with the structure of competition, the marketing planner should also take account of *cost structures* and *cost behaviour*. Cost structure is usually defined as the ratio of variable to fixed costs and is typically capable of exerting a significant influence upon competitive behaviour. In businesses where, for example, the fixed costs are high, profits are sensitive to volume. Companies are therefore forced to behave in such a way that plants operate as near to full capacity as possible. An example of this would be aluminium smelting. Where demand is price sensitive, the industry is likely to be characterized by periodic bouts of aggressive price wars. Where, however, it is the case that variable costs are high, profits are influenced far more directly by changes in margins. Recognizing this, the marketing strategist needs to focus upon differentiating the product in such a way that prices and hence margins can be increased.

The second cost dimension is that of its behaviour over time and, in particular, how the organization can make use of learning and experience effects, as well as scale effects.

The influence of the product life cycle

Competitive behaviour is typically affected in several ways by the stage reached on the product life cycle (PLC). Although the PLC (see Chapter 11) is seen principally as a model of product and market evolution, it can also be used as a framework for examining probable competitive behaviour. Used in this way, it can help the strategist to anticipate changes in the character of competition. In the early stages of the life cycle, for example, advertising and promotion are generally high, and prices and margins are able to support this. The natural growth of the market allows firms to avoid competing in an overtly direct way. As maturity approaches and the rate of growth slows, firms are forced into more direct forms of competition, a situation that is in turn exacerbated by the often generally greater number of companies operating within the market. This greater intensity of competition manifests itself in several ways, but most commonly in a series of price reductions. The role of advertising changes as greater emphasis is placed upon the search for differentiation. In the final stages, some firms opt to leave the market, while others engage in perhaps even greater price competition as they fight for a share of a declining sales curve. It follows from this that the PLC is yet one more of the myriad of factors that the marketing strategist needs to consider in coming to terms with competitors.

6.8 Competitor analysis and the development of strategy

Given the nature of our comments so far, how then does the analysis of competitors feed in to the development of a strategy? Only rarely can marketing strategy be based just on the idea of winning and holding customers. The marketing strategist also needs to understand how to win the competitive battle. As the first step in this, as we have argued throughout this chapter, the planner must understand in detail the nature and bases of competition, and what this means for the organization. In the absence of this, any plan or strategy will be built upon very weak foundations. This involves:

➡ Knowing the strength of each competitor's position
➡ Knowing the strength of each competitor's offering
➡ Knowing the strength of each competitor's resources
➡ Understanding each competitor's strategy.

Against this background, the planner needs then to think about how this information can best   ~gues for a focus upon four areas; these are

1. The market's key factors for success	➡ Identify the KFSs for industry ➡ Inject resources where you can gain a competitive advantage
2. Relative superiority	➡ Exploit differences in competitive conditions between company and rivals using technology and the sales network
3. Developing aggressive initiatives	➡ Challenge assumptions about the way of doing business ➡ Change the rules of the game ➡ Challenge the status quo ➡ Develop a fast-moving and unconventional strategy
4. Developing strategic degrees of freedom	➡ Be innovative ➡ Open up new markets or develop new products ➡ Exploit market areas untouched by competitors ➡ Search for 'loose bricks' in their position

Figure 6.15 Linking competitor analysis to strategy

It can be seen from this that it is through understanding the nature of the market's key success factors and issues of relative strength and weakness that the planner can start to move towards the development of the sorts of marketing initiatives and degrees of freedom that will underpin the strategy.

6.9 The competitive intelligence system

It should be apparent from everything that has been said in this chapter that the need for an effective competitive intelligence system (CIS) is paramount. In establishing such a system, there are five principal steps:

1 Setting up the system, deciding what information is needed and, very importantly, who will use the outputs from the system and how
2 Collecting the data
3 Analysing and evaluating the data
4 Disseminating the conclusions
5 Incorporating these conclusions into the subsequent strategy and plan, and feeding back the results so that the information system can be developed further.

A framework for developing a CIS is given in Figure 6.16.

The mechanics of an effective CIS are in many ways straightforward and involve:

➡ Selecting the key competitors to evaluate. However, in deciding who these competitors should be, the planner should never lose sight of the point that we make about the way in which, in many markets, the *real* competitive threat comes not from the established players but from new and often very unexpected players who operate with different rules.

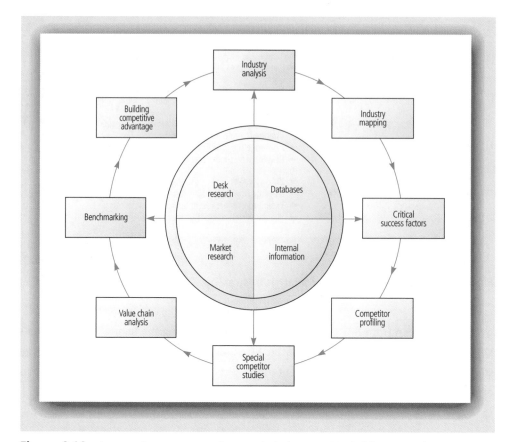

Figure 6.16   Approaches to competitor analysis (source: Harbridge House)

➡ Being absolutely clear about what information is needed, *how* it will be used and by whom.

➡ Selecting and briefing those responsible for collecting the information.

➡ Allocating the appropriate level of resource to the collection and evaluation processes.

➡ Publishing regular tactical and strategic reports on competition.

➡ Ensuring that the outputs from the process are an integral part of the planning and strategy development processes rather than a series of reports that are rarely used.

The sources of data are, as we observed at an earlier stage, likely to vary significantly from one industry to another. However, a useful framework for data collection involves categorizing information on the basis of whether it is recorded, observed or opportunistic. The major sources of data under each of these headings are shown in Figure 6.17.

With regard to the question of precisely what information is needed, this will of course vary from one industry to another and from one company to another. It is, nevertheless, possible to identify with relative ease the sorts of headings under which information should be gathered; these are identified in Figure 6.18.

Recorded data	Observable data	Opportunistic data
Market research	Competitors' pricing	Raw material suppliers
Secondary data sources, e.g. Mintel	Promotions	Equipment suppliers
Business press	Patent applications	Trade shows
Trade press	Competitive advertising	Customers
Technical journals	Planning applications	Packaging suppliers
BRAD (British Rate & Data)	Sales force feedback	Distributors
Government sector reports, e.g. Monopolies Commission	Buying competitors' products and taking them apart to determine costs of production and manufacturing methods	Sub-contractors
Stockbrokers' reports		Internal newsletters
Credit reports		Disgruntled employees
Annual reports		Poaching competitors' employees
Public documents		Conferences
		Placing advertisements and holding interviews for jobs that do not exist in order to entice competitors' employees to spill the beans
		Private investigators

Figure 6.17 The major sources of competitive data (adapted from Davidson, 1987b)

Deciding who to attack: coming to terms with 'good' and 'bad' competitors

Given the sort of information that we refer to above, the strategist should be able to determine far more precisely which competitors are operating in the same strategic group. From here, he or she can then go on to decide far more readily which competitors to attack and when, and the basis on which this should be done. Equally, he or she is also able to decide which competitors are to be avoided. Although these issues are discussed in detail in Chapter 11, there are several points that can usefully be made at this stage.

Assuming that the company is to go on the offensive, the strategist needs to begin by deciding *which* competitors to attack. In essence, this represents a choice between strong and weak competitors, close and distant competitors, and good and bad competitors.

Although *weak competitors* are by their very nature the most vulnerable, the potential pay-off needs to be examined carefully. It may be the case, for example, that the share gained, while useful, is of little long-term strategic value, since it takes the company into segments of the market offering little scope for growth. Equally, these segments may require substantial long-term investment. By contrast, competing against *strong competitors* requires the firm to be far leaner, fitter and more aggressive, a point that has been argued in some considerable detail for more than two decades by Porter, and which was developed further in his book *The Competitive Advantage of Nations* (Porter, 1990).

The second decision involves deciding between *close* and *distant* competitors. We have already commented that the majority of companies compete against those within the strategic group they most resemble. Thus, as we observed earlier, Nestlé's Nescafé

Although it is not possible to develop an exhaustive list of headings under which competitive information should be collected, these are nine principal areas to which the strategist should pay attention on a regular basis:

1 **Sales**
Number of units sold
Sales by product line
Sales trends
Market shares
Share trends

2 **Customers**
Customer profiles
Buying motives
Patterns of usage
New accounts/buyers
Lost accounts/buyers
Proportion of repeat business/degree of brand loyalty
Depth of brand loyalty
Identity and image among buyers
Satisfaction levels with the product's design, performance, quality and reliability
The existence of special relationships

3 **Products**
Breadth and depth of the product range
Comparative product performance levels
New product policies
Investment in R&D
New product introduction and modifications
Size assortments
New packaging

4 **Advertising and promotion**
Expenditure levels and patterns
Effectiveness
Product literature
Sales promotions
Customers' brand preferences
Image and levels of recognition

5 **Distribution and sales force**
Types of distribution network used
Relationships and the balance of power
Cost structures
Flexibility
Special terms and the existence of agreements
Dealer objectives
Distributors' performance levels

Size, calibre and experience of the sales force
Sales force customer coverage
Levels of technical assistance available
Dealer support levels and capabilities
Stock levels
Shelf facings
After-sales service capabilities
Customer service philosophy
Location of warehouses
Degree of customer satisfaction

6 **Price**
Cost levels
Cost structure
List prices and discounts by product and customer type
Special terms

7 **Finance**
Performance levels
Margins
Depth of financial resources
Patterns of ownership and financial flexibility

8 **Management**
Objectives (short and long term)
Philosophy and culture
Expectations
Attitudes to risk
Identity of key executives
Skills and special expertise
Competitive strategies
'Ownership' of strategies and the commitment to them
Organizational structures
Investment plans
Key success factors

9 **Other**
Sales per employee
Plant capacity utilization
Type of equipment used
Labour rates and relationships
Raw material purchasing methods
Principal suppliers
Degree of vertical and horizontal integration
Commitment to market sectors

Figure 6.18   What companies need to know about their competitors

is in direct competition with General Foods' Maxwell House. The strategist needs, in certain circumstances at least, to beware of destroying these close competitors, since the whole competitive base may then change. In commenting on this, Porter (1985a, pp. 226–7) cites some examples:

➡ Bausch & Lomb in the late 1970s moved aggressively against other soft lens manufacturers with great success. However, this led one competitor after another to sell out to larger firms such as Revlon, Johnson & Johnson and Schering-Plough, with the result that Bausch & Lomb now faced much larger competitors.

➡ A speciality rubber manufacturer attacked another speciality rubber manufacturer as its mortal enemy and took away market share. The damage to the other company allowed the speciality divisions of the large tyre companies to move quickly into speciality rubber markets, using them as a dumping ground for excess capacity.

Porter expands upon this line of argument by distinguishing between 'good' and 'bad' competitors. A good competitor, he suggests, is one that adheres to the rules, avoids aggressive price moves, favours a healthy industry, makes realistic assumptions about the industry growth prospects, and accepts the general status quo. Bad competitors, by contrast, violate the unspoken and unwritten rules. They engage in unnecessarily aggressive and often foolhardy moves, expand capacity in large steps, slash margins and take significant risks.

The implication of this is that good competitors should work hard to develop an industry that consists only of good companies. Amongst the ways in which this can be done are coalitions, selective retaliation and careful licensing. The pay-off will then be that:

➡ Competitors will not seek to destroy each other by behaving irrationally
➡ They will follow the rules of the industry
➡ Each player will be differentiated in some way
➡ Companies will try to earn share increases rather than buying them.

It follows from this that a company can benefit in a variety of ways from competitors, since they often generate higher levels of total market demand, increase the degree of differentiation, help spread the costs of market development, and may well serve less attractive segments.

6.10 The development of a competitive stance: the potential for ethical conflict

A key element of any marketing strategy involves the development of a clear, meaningful and sustainable competitive stance that is capable of providing the organization with an edge over its competitors. In doing this, organizations have responded in a variety of ways, ranging from, at one extreme, a series of actions that are both legally and ethically questionable through to, at the other extreme, an approach that discourages or prohibits doing business with particular customer groups. In the case of the Co-operative Bank, for example, their highly publicized competitive stance has been based on an ethical platform that led the bank to stop dealing with customers deemed to be involved in 'unethical' activities. This policy, which was formulated in 1992, led in the first year to the bank severing its ties with twelve corporate customers, including two fox-hunting associations, a peat miner, a company that tested its products on animals, and others where it took the view that the customer was causing unreasonable environmental damage. The bank has also taken a stand against factory farming.

An ethical dimension – albeit one with an element of self-interest – was also at the heart of a strategy developed by British Alcan in 1989 to recycle used beverage cans. With the industry suffering in the late 1980s from problems of overcapacity, the price of aluminium on the world markets had dropped significantly and Alcan, in common with other aluminium producers, began searching for ways in which costs might be reduced. The aluminium recycling process offers a number of advantages, since not only are the capital costs of investing in a recycling operation as little as one-tenth of investing in primary capacity, but recycled aluminium also requires only one-twentieth of the energy costs. An additional benefit is that, unlike steel recycling, the recovery process does not lead to a deterioration in the metal. At the same time, however, the company was acutely aware of a series of environmental pressures and concerns and, in particular, the greater emphasis that was being given both by governments and society at large to the issue of finite world resources and to the question of recycling.

Faced with this, Alcan developed a highly proactive stance that involved the development of an infrastructure that was capable of collecting and recycling aluminium beverage cans. The success of the campaign was subsequently reflected by the way in which, between 1989 and 1994, the UK's recycling rate of aluminium cans, largely as the result of the Alcan initiative, increased from less than 2 per cent to more than 30 per cent.

However, for many other organizations the implications of an increasingly demanding and apparently competitively malevolent environment has led to the search for a competitive stance and a competitive edge almost irrespective of the cost. In doing this, the problem that can then be faced concerns the stage at which the need for managers to deliver seemingly ever higher levels of performance leads to actions that subsequently are deemed to be unacceptable, something which the senior management of British Airways was faced with in the early 1990s (see Illustration 6.4).

Illustration 6.4 British Airways versus Virgin Atlantic

At the beginning of the 1990s, British Airways was heavily criticized for its supposed 'dirty tricks' campaign against its far smaller competitor, Virgin Atlantic. Virgin, which had been set up by Richard Branson several years previously, had achieved a number of publicity coups, including no-frills, low-cost flights to the United States and then, spectacularly and under the gaze of the world's media, fly-ing out of Baghdad a planeload of British hostages at the outbreak of hostilities between the western world and Iraq.

Perhaps because of Virgin's small size (it had just eight planes at the time, compared with BA's 250) and Richard Branson's apparently relaxed management style, British Airways had seemingly underestimated the company and the threat that it was capable of posing. However, these became apparent when, in 1991, the Civil Aviation Authority recommended that Heathrow Airport be opened up to a larger number of airlines than had previously been the case. For Virgin, which had been flying from Gatwick, the implications were significant and led Branson to suggest not only that he would be able to cut his already low prices by 15 per cent, but that by 1995 he hoped to capture 30 per cent of the transatlantic market.

Faced with this challenge, BA went on to the offensive with a strategy that involved their Helpline team gathering intelligence on Virgin, pursuing a highly proactive public relations campaign that highlighted Virgin's apparent failings, targeting specific routes and, according to Gregory (*Sunday Times*, 13 March 1994, p. 10), obtaining information on Virgin 'by extracting it from BA's own computer reservation system, known as BABS, which it shares with other airlines'. This information was seemingly then used for several purposes, including switch-selling, whereby passengers already booked on to a Virgin flight would be approached and encouraged to switch to BA. The ethical significance of using the reservation system in this way was highlighted by Gregory:

> The confidentiality of the information in that system is vital – so much so that it was enshrined in commitments the company had given to the House of Commons transport committee when the system was set up. As it set about using BABS to capture data about

Virgin, BA knew that it was straying into the twilight zone of sharp practice and anti-competitive behaviour.

As the details of the British Airways approach gradually became public, the company was forced on to the defensive as a series of increasingly unsympathetic and revealing articles appeared in the press. This then came to a head when, in 1993, British Airways was forced into making a humiliating apology in open court to Richard Branson and his company, Virgin Atlantic. Included within this were the words '. . . they wish to apologize for having attacked the good faith and integrity of Richard Branson', that 'hostile and discreditable stories' had been placed in the press, and that BA's approach gave 'grounds for serious concern about the activities of a number of BA employees . . . and their potential effect on the business interests and reputation of Virgin Atlantic and Richard Branson' (*Sunday Times*, 27 March 1994, p. 7).

The British Airways/Virgin Atlantic story is an interesting one for several reasons, not least because of the way in which it highlights the position that managers can find themselves in when faced with real or imaginary competition. Whilst an aggressive competitive response in these circumstances is both realistic and to be expected, the danger is that of one or more managers resorting to an approach that subsequently becomes difficult to justify either ethically or legally.

A far more detailed treatment of the British Airways/Virgin Atlantic conflict can be found in Gregory (1994).

Ethics and market intelligence: the growth of corporate espionage

With many markets having grown enormously in their complexity in recent years, so the demand for increasingly detailed and effective market intelligence systems has escalated. Although many of the inputs to a market intelligence system can be obtained through relatively straightforward and conventional market research routines, the much more strategically useful – and indeed more necessary – information on competitors' intentions, capabilities and strategies can, as we saw in the British Airways example, often only be obtained by radically different approaches. Although the legality of many of these approaches has been called into question, the law, both in Europe and the USA, has in many instances failed to keep pace with the developments that have taken place in information technology and electronic data distribution.

The implication of this is that whilst the techniques used to gain the more confidential forms of competitive information may not in the strictly legal sense be wrong, the ethics of the approach are arguably rather more questionable. The net effect of this is that in many companies the search for a competitive edge has led managers to enter what has been referred to as 'the twilight zone of corporate intelligence', in which the traditional boundaries of legal and ethical behaviour are blurred; this is illustrated in Figure 6.19, which represents a continuum of the types of competitive intelligence that are available, their sources and the difficulties of gaining access to them.

For many organizations, much of the market research effort over the past two decades, particularly in Europe, has been concentrated towards the upper part of the continuum. However, as competitive pressures grow, so the need for more and more confidential competitive intelligence increases. One consequence of this in the USA, and now increasingly in Europe, has been a growth in the number of agencies that specialize in obtaining the sorts of competitive information that, whilst increasingly being seen to be necessary, can only be obtained through what might loosely be termed as unconventional methods. Amongst the more extreme of these is what is referred to in the USA as 'doing trash', something which involves sifting through competitors' rubbish bins, using hidden cameras and listening devices, intercepting fax lines, bugging offices and planting misinformation. Although the leading competitive intelligence agencies have been quick to condemn this sort of approach – and indeed several agencies now publish codes of ethics – the ever greater pressures upon managers, particularly in international markets, demand ever more detailed competitive information, little of which may be obtained by adhering to traditional legal and ethical principles.

Because of this, managers are faced with what is possibly a dilemma, since whilst competitive pressures demand the information, traditional and ethical patterns of behaviour argue against the actions that will provide it. In these circumstances managers can respond in one of several ways, ranging from an adherence to truly ethical behaviour (and then living with the competitive consequences) through to a pragmatically straightforward belief that the ends justify the means and that without the information the organization will be at a competitive disadvantage.

Intelligence gathering and corporate culture

The work practices of competitive intelligence agencies have highlighted a series of differences between managerial cultures in Europe and the USA, with the general approach of European managers having proved to be far less aggressive and proactive

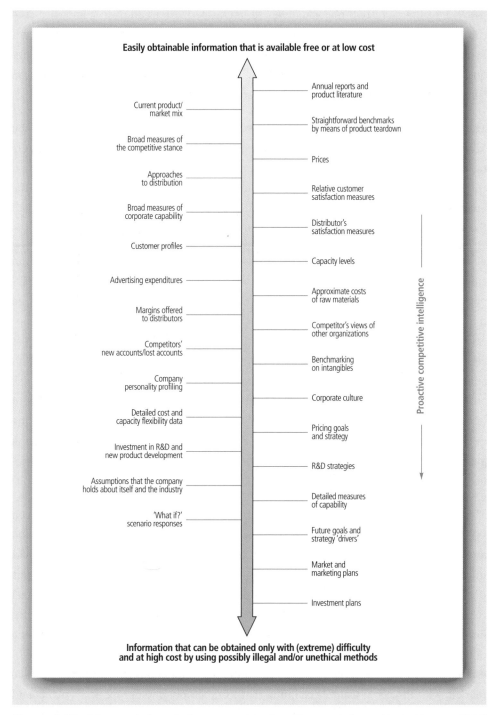

Figure 6.19 Managerial needs for competitive intelligence (adapted from Button, 1994)

than that of their American counterparts. A Conference Board report in 1988, for example, suggested that only 50 per cent of British managers view the monitoring of competitors' activities as 'very important'. This has, in turn, led to the suggestion by Button (1994, pp. 3–4):

". . . that there are two major differences between US and European companies. The culture is different, obviously. But also there is a greater degree of loyalty to the corporation in Europe than in the US. One consequence of this, together with the greater frequency of job-moving in the States, is that the incidence of security leaks is greater and US companies are more vulnerable to the corporate spy.*"*

The differences and implications of the two cultures have also been highlighted by McGonagle and Vella (1993), who have suggested that the ethics of senior UK managers make them reluctant to engage in 'shady practices or covert operations'. By contrast, corporate intelligence agencies and their clients in the USA, whilst often stressing the ethical and legal standards to which they adhere, are rarely willing to discuss in detail the techniques they adopt (Button, 1994, p. 9):

*"*Although 'data detectives' don't necessarily lie, they tend not to tell the whole truth either. On the telephone, they regularly identify themselves as industry researchers, without disclosing their affiliation to a specific client. By focusing their introduction on the type of information they need rather than who they are and why they need it, plus an upfront statement that they are not interested in anything confidential or proprietary, interviewees are lulled into a false sense of security. Industry jargon is used with care so as not to appear overly knowledgeable and questions are carefully phrased to avoid suspicion. Ask an interviewee about their employer's weaknesses and they are liable to clam up. But when the victim is protected by their visual anonymity and physical distance from the caller, a question such as 'If you had a magic wand, which three things would you change about your manufacturing/distribution/pricing policy?' often produces the same information, without raising the alarm.*"*

The significance of industrial espionage and the possible scale of the problem has been highlighted by a series of studies, one of the most useful being that of Johnson and Pound (1992), who found that 40 per cent of large US and Canadian firms had uncovered some form of espionage costing some $20 billion annually. The problems proved to be at their most acute in the high-technology industries, where the commercial returns between the leaders and the followers are potentially considerable. Hitachi, for example, pleaded guilty to obtaining confidential documents from IBM dealing with one of its computer systems. However, Berkowitz et al. (1994, p. 97) also cite the example of espionage occurring in other less esoteric industries, including the American cookie market, with Procter & Gamble claiming that 'competitors photographed its plants and production lines, stole a sample of its cookie dough, and infiltrated a confidential sales presentation to learn about its technology, recipe and marketing plan'. Procter & Gamble took action against the competitor and won $120 million in damages.

In an attempt to overcome the criticisms that have been made of industry practices, a number of competitive intelligence (CI) agencies have published ethics statements that emphasize that they will not lie, bribe or steal in the information gathering process. However, with levels of competition increasing at an ever greater rate, the pressures upon managers, and hence the CI agencies they employ, will invariably become greater.

These problems have in turn been highlighted by a series of newspaper revelations concerning the ways in which a number of governmental security services have been involved in commercial espionage for many years. In the case of the old Iron Curtain countries, for example, many of the security agencies, having lost much of their previous role, have now turned their attention to the commercial sector.

A high profile – and highly embarrassing – example of corporate espionage came to light in 2000 when Harry Ellison, the chief executive of Oracle, was found to have hired a private detective agency to spy on corporate supporters of Microsoft. Amongst the approaches used by the agency was the bribing of cleaning staff at one of the target organizations, something that some corporate detectives suggest is an unnecessary expense – in many cases employees further down the corporate ladder can be coerced into parting with secrets simply because they do not understand the value of the information.

Sifting through a rival's rubbish bins has been used by numerous firms and is helped by the way in which, in Britain at least, information is not regarding as property under UK theft law. Although the law may change, under the current system, if a person can prove they will return the discarded paper to the local council – the legal owner of the rubbish – they cannot be charged.

For many firms, however, there is a more fundamental problem that has been highlighted by the Risk Advisory Group, a London-based specialist investigation agency. Their research suggests that some 80 per cent of all leaked company secrets can be traced to senior management, who are either aggrieved because they may have been overlooked for promotion, are preparing to set up on their own, or have found someone prepared to pay a large sum for the information. This is more likely in industries such as construction and oil and gas, where large contracts are at stake and where a relatively small piece of intelligence can boost a company's chances of winning a multimillion pound tender.

6.11 Summary

Within this chapter we have emphasized the need for constant competitor analysis and for the information generated to be fed into the strategic marketing planning process.

Although the need for competitor analysis has long been acknowledged, a substantial number of organizations still seemingly fail to allocate to the process the resources that are needed, relying instead upon a far less detailed understanding of competitive capabilities and priorities. It does therefore need to be recognized that, if an effective system of competitive monitoring is to be developed, and the results used in the way intended, it is essential that there is top management commitment to the process.

In developing a structured approach to competitive analysis, the strategist needs to give explicit consideration to five questions:

1 Against whom are we competing?
2 What are their objectives?

3 What strategies are they pursuing and how successful are they?

4 What strengths and weaknesses do they possess?

5 How are they likely to behave and, in particular, how are they likely to react to offensive moves?

Taken together, the answers to these five questions can be used to develop a detailed response profile for each competitive organization, and the probable implications for competitive behaviour fed into the planning process.

Several methods of categorizing competitors have been discussed, including Porter's notion of strategic groups. We then examined the ways in which these ideas can be taken a step further by focusing upon the character of competition and how this is likely to change over the course of the product life cycle.

Particular emphasis was given to the need for the strategist to take account of each competitor's probable objectives, its competitive stance, and the relative importance of each market sector. Again, a variety of frameworks that can help in this process of understanding have been discussed, including portfolio analysis.

Against this background, we discussed the ways in which an effective competitive intelligence system (CIS) might be developed and the nature of the inputs that are required. Much of the information needed for such a system is often readily available, and emphasis therefore needs to be placed upon developing a framework which will ensure that this information is channelled, analysed and disseminated in the strategically most useful way.

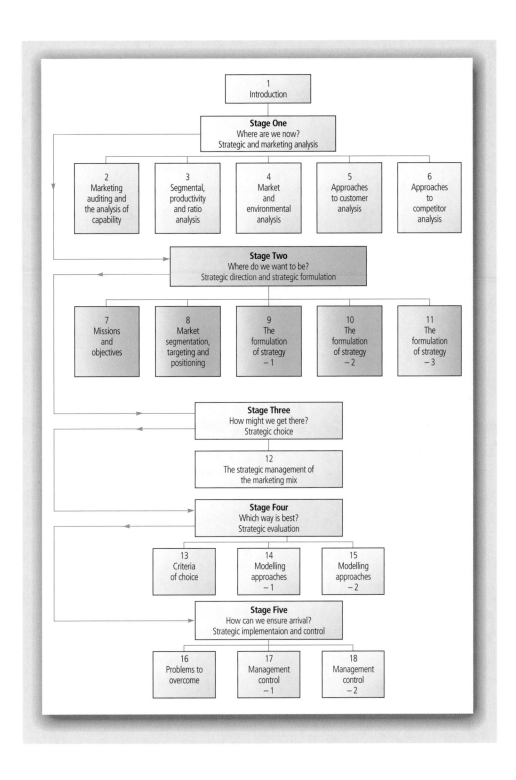

Stage Two: Where do we want to be?
Strategic direction and strategy formulation

Within this stage we focus on where the organization wants to go. In doing this we take as our foundation the material of Stage One, in which we examined where the organization is currently, the characteristics of its markets and the nature of its marketing capability.

We begin by considering the organizational mission and the nature of marketing objectives (Chapter 7). We then turn to an examination of the approaches that might be adopted when segmenting the market (Chapter 8). In Chapter 9 we examine a number of the models that have been developed to help in the process of strategy formulation, as a prelude – in Chapter 10 – to a discussion of the factors that influence the nature of the strategy to be pursued.

Mission statements have been the subject of considerable discussion in recent years, with the majority of commentators pointing to their potential for providing employees with a clear understanding of core corporate values. Although many organizations still lack a mission statement, while others have statements that reflect a degree of wishful thinking rather than reality, the guidelines for developing a meaningful corporate mission are now well developed. The significance of the mission statement can be further highlighted by recognizing that it is against the background of the mission statement that the strategist should set objectives at both the corporate and functional levels (in the case of marketing, these objectives revolve around two major dimensions: products and markets). It follows from this that a poorly developed mission statement is likely to have consequences for the nature and appropriateness of any subsequent objectives.

Following on from the discussion of mission statements, we turn our attention to the idea of vision and how the vision or picture of how the organization should look in three to five years' time helps to drive objectives and the marketing planning process.

As well as being influenced by the corporate mission, organizational objectives are typically influenced by a wide variety of other factors, including the nature and demands of the environment. The marketing strategist typically analyses the environment within the PEST (Political, Economic, Social and Technological) framework, the individual elements of which are – in the majority of markets – undergoing a series of significant and often unprecedented changes, each of which needs to be taken into account both when setting objectives and formulating strategies. It might therefore be of value to return to Chapter 4, to the discussion of some of the key changes that are taking place within the marketing environment, before proceeding.

The changing environment also has consequences for methods of segmentation. Effective segmentation is at the heart of a well-developed marketing strategy, and has implications for virtually everything else that follows in the strategy-making process. It is therefore a source of concern that work by a variety of writers (e.g. Saunders, 1987) has highlighted the fact that senior managers in many British organizations seemingly fail to recognize this, and pay little or no attention either to the need for segmentation or to the ways in which it can be carried out most effectively.

The strategic significance of segmentation is reinforced by the way in which decisions on how the organization's markets are to be segmented subsequently has implications for targeting and market positioning. The failure to segment effectively is therefore likely to weaken much of the marketing process.

In Chapters 9–11 we focus upon approaches to the formulation of marketing strategy. In the first of these chapters we consider some of the developments that have taken place over the past 30 years in techniques of portfolio analysis. The portfolio approach to management emerged largely as a result of the turbulence of the early 1970s and is based on the idea that an organization's businesses should be viewed and managed in a similar way to an investment portfolio, with a strategic perspective being adopted in the management of each major element.

Although a wide variety of portfolio techniques have been developed and have contributed to a greater understanding on the part of management of what is meant by strategy, research findings are beginning to emerge which suggest that usage levels of even the best-known methods are low. Several explanations for this have been proposed, including unrealistic expectations on the part of managers, difficulties with the data inputs, and an overzealous adherence to the strategic guidelines that typically accompany the models. Nevertheless, models of portfolio analysis need to be seen as one of the major developments in strategic thinking over the past 30 years and, if used wisely, are capable of contributing greatly to a structured approach to marketing management.

The type of marketing strategy pursued by an organization is often the result of the interaction of a series of factors, including past performance, managerial expectations and culture, competitive behaviour, the stage reached on the product life cycle, and the firm's relative market position. Porter (1980) has attempted to provide a structure for examining the strategic alternatives open to an organization and suggests that, in order to compete successfully, the strategist needs to select a generic strategy and pursue it consistently. The three generic strategies that he identifies are:

1 Cost leadership
2 Differentiation
3 Focus.

Dangers arise, Porter suggests, when the firm fails to pursue one of these and instead is forced or drifts into a 'middle-of-the-road' position, where the message to the market is confused and the likelihood of a successful competitive attack is increased.

A considerable amount of work has been done in recent years in drawing parallels between military warfare and marketing strategy, with a view to identifying any lessons that the marketing strategist might learn. A number of general lessons have emerged from this, and guidelines on how best either to defend a market position or attack other organizations are now well developed. Within Chapter 11 we have attempted to draw upon the experiences of successful organizations and to highlight particular dangers. Included within these is the danger of adhering to a particular strategy for too long a period, labelled 'strategic wear-out'. There is an obvious attraction in sticking to a well-proven strategy, although evidence exists to suggest that even the best formulated strategy has a limited life. The marketing strategist should therefore closely monitor the effectiveness of any given strategy, and be willing to change it in order to reflect the environment, different managerial expectations, and the progression through the product and market life cycles.

7

Missions and objectives

7.1 Learning objectives

When you have read this chapter you should be able to understand:

(a) the purpose of planning;
(b) the nature of the corporate mission and how a mission statement can best be developed;
(c) the significance of vision;
(d) the factors influencing objectives and strategy;
(e) the nature of corporate objectives;
(f) the nature of marketing objectives.

7.2 Introduction

To be effective, a strategic planning system must be goal driven. The setting of goals or objectives is therefore a key step in the marketing planning process since, unless it is carried out effectively, everything that follows will lack focus and cohesion. In terms of its position within the overall planning process, which forms the basis of this book, objectives setting can be seen to follow on from the initial stage of analysis and, in particular, the marketing audit, which provided the focus of Chapter 2 (see Figure 7.1).

By setting objectives, the planner is attempting to provide the organization with a sense of direction. In addition, however, objectives provide a basis for motivation, as well as a benchmark against which performance and effectiveness can subsequently be measured. The setting of objectives is thus at the very heart of the planning process, and is the prelude to the development of strategies and detailed plans. (For a discussion of the interrelationships between objectives, strategies and plans, see Illustration 7.1.) Perhaps surprisingly therefore, in view of its fundamental importance, the literature on *how* to set marketing objectives is surprisingly thin, something that is reflected in a comment made 20 years ago by McDonald (1984, p. 82):

''The literature [on marketing planning] is not very explicit, which is surprising when it is considered how vital the setting of marketing objectives is. An objective will ensure that a company knows what its strategies are expected to accomplish and when a particular strategy has accomplished its purpose. In other words, without objectives, strategy decisions and all that follow will take place in a vacuum.**''**

Although the situation has undoubtedly improved since McDonald made this comment, the reality is that marketing planning appears in many ways to be one of those areas that is seen to be important, but which is subjected to relatively little fundamental scrutiny.

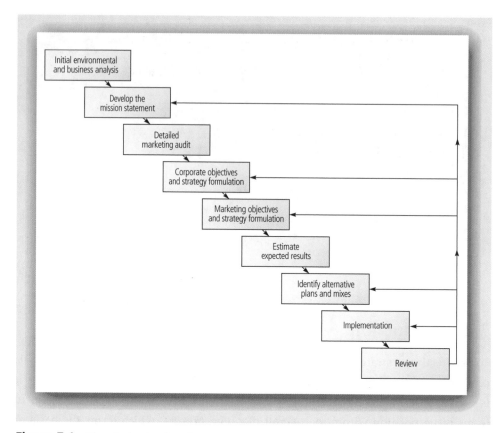

Figure 7.1 The strategic planning process

There are several possible explanations for this, the most obvious of which is that, in principle at least, the process of setting objectives is relatively straightforward and, as such, merits little discussion. The rest of the planning and strategy development process is then seen by some to follow easily and logically. In practice, however, the process is infinitely more difficult, particularly in divisionalized organizations, or where the company has an extensive product range being sold across a variety of markets. Regardless of whether we are talking about principles or practice, the sequence should be the same, beginning with an identification of the organization's current position and capabilities, a statement of assumptions about environmental factors affecting the business, and then agreement among stakeholders as to the objectives themselves.

In moving through this process, the majority of commentators recommend that the planner moves from the general to the specific and from the long term to the short term. This frequently translates into statements on three aspects of the business:

1 The nature of the current business (what business *are* we in?)

2 Where it should go (what business *should* we be in?)

3 How we should get there.

Identifying where the company is currently is often far more difficult than it might appear, something which is reflected in a comment by the ex-Chairman of ICI, Sir John Harvey-Jones (1988):

*"*There is no point in deciding where your business is going until you have actually decided with great clarity where you are now. Like practically everything in business this is easier said than done.*"*

Recognizing the validity of this point should encourage the marketing planner to focus not just upon the business's current position, but also *how* and *why* it has achieved its current levels of success or failure. Having done this, he or she is then in a far better position to begin specifying the *primary* or *most important* corporate objectives, as well as a series of statements regarding the key results areas, such as sales growth, market penetration and new product development, in which success is essential to the organization. Following on from this, the planner should then begin developing the *secondary* or *sub-objectives*, such as geographical expansion and line extension, which will need to be achieved if the primary objectives are to be attained.

This process of moving from the general to the specific should lead to a set of objectives that are not just attainable within any budgetary or other constraints that exist, but that are also compatible with environmental conditions as well as organizational strengths and weaknesses. It follows from this that the process of setting objectives should form what is often referred to as an internally consistent and mutually reinforcing hierarchy. As an illustration of this, if we assume that corporate management is concerned first and foremost with, say, long-term profits and growth, it is these objectives that provide the framework within which the more detailed subset of operational objectives, including market expansion and product-specific increases in sales and share, are developed. Taken together, these then contribute to the achievement of the overall corporate objectives.

It is these operational objectives that are the principal concern of those in the level below corporate management. Below this, managers are concerned with objectives that are defined even more specifically, such as creating awareness of a new product, increasing levels of distribution, and so on. This hierarchy points in turn to the interrelationship, and in some cases the confusion, that exists between corporate objectives and marketing objectives. The distinction between the two is an important one and is discussed at a later stage in this chapter. However, as a prelude to this, and indeed to the process of objectives setting, there is a need for the strategist to decide upon the business mission. We therefore begin this chapter with a discussion of the role and purpose of planning as the background against which we can more realistically examine approaches to the development of the mission statement and, subsequently, corporate and marketing objectives (see Illustration 7.1).

Illustration 7.1 Objectives, strategies and plans

The interrelationships between objectives, strategies and plans have been spelled out by Davidson (1987a, p. 122), who, in discussing BMW's recovery efforts in Germany in the 1960s, made the following comments.

BMW was on the verge of bankruptcy. It was producing motorcycles for a dwindling market, and making a poor return on its bubble cars and six-cylinder saloons. A takeover bid by Daimler-Benz, the makers of Mercedes, was narrowly avoided, and the group was rescued by a Bavarian investment group.

Paul G. Hahnemann, Opel's top wholesale distributor, was appointed Chief Executive. His first objective was obviously to get BMW back on an even keel, where it was sufficiently profitable to survive in the long term. Having got there, he would then move to a more ambitious objective of challenging Mercedes for leadership of the market for high-quality executive cars.

He was convinced that there was an unexploited market for a sporty saloon car, which Mercedes was not tapping. As he pointed out, 'If you were a sporty driver and German, there was no car for you. The Mercedes is big, black and ponderous. It's for parking, not driving.'

Consequently, he evolved a strategy for producing a range of high-quality cars with better performance and a more sporty image than any other saloon. This strategy has remained broadly unchanged since. But the plans for executing it have evolved and been refined.

The successful rebirth of BMW is now a matter of history. The company sells over 1.1 million cars a year and has annual revenues above £20 billion.

Source: Davidson (1997, pp. 180–1).

7.3 The purpose of planning

In discussing the nature and role of the planning process, Jackson (1975) comments that:

"Planning attempts to control the factors which affect the outcome of decisions; actions are guided so that success is more likely to be achieved. To plan is to decide what to do before doing it. Like methods, plans can be specially made to fit circumstances or they can be ready made for regular use in recurrent and familiar situations. In other words, a methodical approach can be custom built or ready made according to the nature of the problems involved."

The purpose of planning can therefore be seen as an attempt to impose a degree of structure upon behaviour by allocating resources in order to achieve organizational objectives. This is reflected in a somewhat cumbersome but nevertheless useful comment by Drucker (1959), who suggests that:

"... business planning is a continuous process of making present entrepreneurial decisions systematically and with best possible knowledge of their futurity, organizing systematically the effort needed to carry out these decisions against expectations through organized feedback."

While not particularly succinct, this definition has a certain value in that it highlights the three major elements of planning:

1 The need for systematic decision-making
2 The development of programmes for their implementation
3 The measurement of performance against objectives, as a prelude to modifications to the strategy itself.

It follows from this that if the planning process is to be effective, then the planner needs to give full recognition to the changing nature and demands of the environment, and to incorporate a degree of flexibility into both the objectives and the plan itself. Any failure to do this is likely to lead to a plan that quickly becomes out of date. Simmons (1972) pointed to the dangers of this both in the planning carried out by the Eastern bloc countries and by American business. In the case of the Eastern bloc countries in the 1940s, 1950s and 1960s, for example, he suggests that:

"They tried to impose a fixed five-year plan on changing conditions. Unfortunately, some American businesses are still making this mistake . . . frequently a well constructed plan only six months old will be found to be very much out-of-date."

If planning is to prove effective, there is an obvious need for a regular review process, something that is particularly important when the environment in which the organization is operating is changing rapidly. As an example of this, Chisnall (1989, pp. 133–4) has pointed to the Post Office and the increasingly competitive environment it faced following the Post Office Act of 1969, which:

" . . . transformed the Post Office from a Department of State into a State Corporation that had to achieve a predetermined level of profits. The establishment of a marketing department in 1972 added to the keen commercial awareness and new professional skills which were needed to tackle, for instance, the fast-growing and aggressive competition in parcels traffic from several new market suppliers."

[*Authors' note*: Subsequently, of course, The Post Office has been hit hard by a series of competitive moves and, according to its critics, a focus upon short-term operational issues rather than longer-term strategic planning, something to which reference was made in Chapter 1.]

The principal purpose and indeed benefit of planning can therefore be seen in terms of the way in which it imposes a degree of order upon potential chaos and allocates the organization's resources in the most effective way. Among the other benefits are the ways in which the planning process brings people together and, potentially at least, leads to 'a shared sense of opportunity, direction, significance and achievement'. The planning process can therefore be seen to consist of four distinct stages:

1 Evaluation (where are we now, where do we want to go, and what level of resource capability do we have?)

2 Strategy formulation (how are we going to get there?)
3 Detailed planning
4 Implementation and review.

For many organizations, it is the implementation stage that proves to be the most difficult, but which paradoxically receives the least attention. There are several possible explanations for this. Peters and Waterman (1982, pp. 9–12), for example, suggest that all too often emphasis is placed upon what they refer to as the 'hard-ball' elements of strategy, structure and systems, with too little recognition being given to the significance of the 'soft-ball' elements of style, skills, staff and subordinate systems.

The problems of marketing planning

Although marketing planning has an inherent logic and appeal, McDonald (1995, p. 64) suggests that the vast majority of organizations experience significant problems in developing truly effective planning systems and cultures. There are, he believes, ten factors that contribute to this:

1 Too little support from the chief executive and top management. As a result, the resources that are needed are not made available and the results are not used in a meaningful way.
2 A lack of a plan for planning. As a consequence, too few managers understand how the plan will be built up, how the results will be used, the contribution that they are expected to make and the time scales that are involved.
3 A lack of support from line managers.
4 A confusion over planning terms – remember that not everyone is familiar with Ansoff and the Directional Policy matrix.
5 Numbers are used instead of written objectives and strategies.
6 The emphasis is on too much detail, too far ahead.
7 Planning becomes a once-a-year ritual instead of an integral part of the day-to-day management process.
8 Too little thought or attention is given to the differences between operational or short-term planning and strategic planning.
9 There is a failure to integrate marketing planning into the overall corporate planning system.
10 The task of planning is left to a planner who fails to involve those who are actually managing the business.

McDonald goes on to suggest that far too many plans also fail to take sufficient account of the issues associated with the plan's implementation. The consequences of this, which have also been discussed by Bonoma (1985), are illustrated in Figure 7.2.

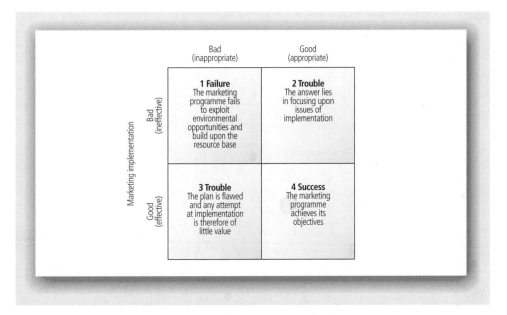

Figure 7.2   The planning and implementation matrix (adapted from Bonoma, 1985)

7.4 Establishing the corporate mission

Referring to Figure 7.1 it can be seen that, following an initial environmental and business analysis, the development of a mission statement is the starting point both for corporate and marketing planning, since it represents a vision of what the organization is or should attempt to become. This is typically expressed in terms of the two questions to which we have already referred: 'What business are we in?' and 'What business should we be in?' It is the answer to this second question in particular that sets the parameters within which objectives are subsequently established, strategies developed and action programmes implemented (see Illustration 7.2). It is also the question that many organizations, when faced with a rapidly changing market environment, find difficult to answer. In the case of the high street retailer W.H. Smith, for example, the question of what business the organization should be in was thrown into sharp relief at the beginning of 2004, as it became increasingly evident that many of the company's core product lines, such as CDs, DVDs and even books, were being targeted by other Internet retailers such as Amazon, as well as seemingly very different types of retail organization such as Tesco. Equally, at the same time Boots found its core lines under attack both from the low-price retailers such as Superdrug and the large supermarket chains such as Tesco and Sainsbury's, both of which offered convenience and relatively low prices.

Given these sorts of issues, the role of the mission statement should be seen in terms of the way in which it is – or should be – capable of performing a powerful integrating function, since it is in many ways a statement of core corporate values and is the framework within which individual business units prepare their business plans, something that has led to the corporate mission being referred to as an 'invisible hand' that guides geographically scattered employees to work independently and yet collectively towards the organization's goal. A similar sentiment has been expressed by Ouchi (1983, p. 74), who suggests that the deliberate generality of the mission statement performs an integrating function of various stakeholders over a long period of time. This is illustrated in the case of the earth-moving equipment manufacturer J.C. Bamford, which has a clearly stated policy of quality and product improvement, something of which everyone in the organization is fully aware and which acts as a consistent guideline in determining behaviour at all levels, but particularly within the planning process.

Illustration 7.2 Whitbread and the question of what business we are in and what we should be in

Founded in 1742, Whitbread was the UK's first purpose-built mass-production brewery. Having become a public company in 1948, the organization grew rapidly throughout the 1960s with a series of mergers and acquisitions, and by 1971 owned ten breweries and 9000 – some 10 per cent – of the country's pubs. During this period, the company also signed a series of licensing deals, including Heineken in 1968 and then Stella Artois. In 1974, they opened their first Beefeater restaurant and, although the company went on to buy the Boddington's brewery in Manchester, the 1980s saw an increasing focus on leisure, with the establishment of a Pizza Hut joint venture, the UK TGI Friday's franchise and the opening of the first Travel Inn. This move into the leisure industry gathered speed throughout the 1990s, with the purchase of Berni Inns, David Lloyd Leisure, the Costa coffee chain, Swallow Group and the UK Marriott Hotels franchise.

In 1999, the company tried to buy Allied Domeq's pub estate, but after a bitter battle lost out to Punch Taverns. Having conceded defeat, the brewing arm, which had been the foundation of the business, was sold off to Interbrew in 2000 and a year later the management team called time on 258 years of brewing heritage and withdrew completely from the pub business. By the beginning of 2004, the business had more than 360 hotels, 1500 restaurant outlets and 55 tennis-based leisure clubs.

For a mission statement to be worthwhile, it should be capable of providing personnel throughout the company with a shared sense of opportunity, direction, significance and achievement, factors which are particularly important for large organizations with divisions that are geographically scattered.

The potential benefits of a strong binding statement of fundamental corporate values and good communication have been highlighted by a variety of writers, including Collins and Porras (1998), who have highlighted the importance of a powerful vision that is then driven throughout the organization. Equally, a study of European managers by Management Centre Europe found that what gave highly successful companies an edge over their competitors was the importance they attached to basic corporate values. In commenting on these findings, Chisnall (1989, pp. 138–9) has said:

*"*As with comparable studies in the United States, there often seemed to be a rather curious inverse relationship between those companies which emphasized profitability as

a primary corporate value and the actual profitability achieved. On the other hand, companies generally ranking customer satisfaction as the most important corporate value were highly profitable. It is important to note, however, that professed commitment to high corporate values needs to be translated into practice: strong declarations themselves may sound impressive, but implementation has to be effected by management at every level of organization and expressed in many ways, such as high standards of customer service, good teamwork between executives in different departments as well as in the same section, keeping promised delivery dates, etc. Clearly, these duties should always be undertaken by those responsible for them but, too often, such everyday tasks are just not well done."

In many ways, therefore, the mission statement, the position of which within the overall planning process is illustrated by the acronym MOST (Mission, Objectives, Strategy, Tactics), represents a visionary view of the overall strategic posture of an organization and, as Johnson and Scholes (2002, p. 239) comment, 'is a generalized statement of the overriding purpose of an organization. It can be thought of as an expression of its *raison dêtre*.' Richards (1983, p. 104) has referred to the mission in much the same way, calling it 'the master strategy' and suggesting that it is a visionary projection of the central and overriding concepts on which the organization is based. He goes on to suggest that 'it should not focus on what the firm is doing in terms of products and markets currently served, but rather upon the services and utility within the firm.'

It follows from this that any failure to agree the mission statement is likely to lead to fundamental problems in determining the strategic direction of the firm. Recognizing this, the managment teams of The Body Shop and easyJet have both concentrated upon developing *and communicating to their staff* their mission statements. The rationale in each case is straightforward and is a reflection of the fact that a mission statement is of little value unless it is understood by everyone in the organization and *acted upon*.

In the case of easyJet, for example, the mission statement is:

" . . . to provide our customers with safe, low-cost, good value, point-to-point air services . . . to offer a consistent and reliable product at fares appealing to leisure and business markets from our bases to a range of domestic and European destinations. To achieve this we will develop our people and establish lasting partnerships with our suppliers."

For The Body Shop, the mission is:

" *To dedicate* our business to the pursuit of social and environmental change.

To creatively balance the financial and human needs of our stakeholders, employees, franchisees, customers, suppliers and shareholders.

To courageously ensure that our business is ecologically sustainable, meeting the needs of the present without compromising the future.

To meaningfully contribute to local, national and international communities in which we trade, by adopting a code of conduct which ensures care, honesty, fairness and respect.

To passionately campaign for the protection of the environment, human and civil rights and against animal testing within the cosmetics and toiletries industry.

To tirelessly work to narrow the gap between principle and practice, whilst making fun, passion and care part of our daily lives. **"**

For Marks & Spencer, the vision is 'to be the standard against which all others are measured'. The company's mission is 'to make aspirational quality accessible to all'.

In each case the mission statement represents a reflection of basic corporate values, and in doing this provides an overall purpose and sense of direction.

The characteristics of good mission statements

Good mission statements can be seen to exhibit certain characteristics, the most notable being that they are, as Wensley (1987, p. 31) has commented, 'short on numbers and long on rhetoric while (still) remaining succinct'. Having said this, Toyota's mission statement, expressed in 1985, did contain a useful and significant number. Sometimes called the Global 10 mission, it expressed Toyota's intention to have 10 per cent of the world car market by the 1990s. In many cases, however, the mission statement emerges as little more than a public relations exercise. In making this comment we have in mind the temptation that exists for overambition, which is typically reflected in the too frequent use of phrases such as 'first in the field', 'excellent', and so on. For a mission statement to be worthwhile, it is essential that it is realistic and specifies the business domain in which the company will operate. According to Abell (1980, Chapter 3), this domain is best defined in terms of three dimensions:

1 The *customer groups* that will be served
2 The *customer needs* that will be met
3 The *technology* that will satisfy these needs.

Given the nature of Abell's comments, the six tests for a successful mission statement are that it must:

1 Be sufficiently specific to have an impact on the behaviour of staff throughout the organization
2 Be founded more on customer needs and their satisfaction than on product characteristics
3 Reflect the organization's core skills
4 Reflect opportunities and threats
5 Be attainable
6 Be flexible.

These factors can be brought together in the framework shown in Figure 7.3.

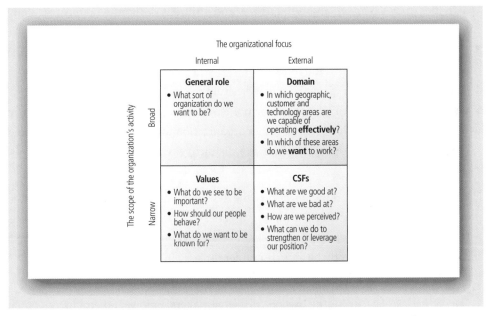

Figure 7.3 Developing the mission statement (adapted from Piercy, 1997)

Modifying the mission statement over time

Having developed a mission statement, it should not be seen as a once-and-for-all expression of the organization's purpose, but rather as something that changes over time in response to changing internal conditions, and external environmental opportunities and threats. A mission statement developed in the 1970s, for example, is unlikely to be appropriate today, when issues such as environmentalism and the green consumer are of considerably greater importance. Equally, the mission statement needs to reflect changing emphases as the organization grows, adds new products and moves into new markets. Over the past decade, for example, many of the drinks companies have moved away from the focus upon brewing that dominated for several decades to a far broader focus upon leisure, and in doing this have redefined their mission statements on several occasions.

Influences on the mission statement

In developing the mission statement for a company, there are likely to be five major factors that need to be taken into account:

1 The company's history and in particular its performance and patterns of ownership.
2 The preferences, values and expectations of managers, owners and those who have power within the organization. In commenting on this in the context of the nature of strategic decisions, Johnson and Scholes (1988, p. 7) suggest that 'strategy can be thought of as a reflection of the attitudes and beliefs of those who have the most influence in the organization. Whether an organization is expansionist or more concerned with consolidation, or where the boundaries are drawn for a company's

activities, may say much about the values and attitudes of those who most strongly influence strategy.'

3 Environmental factors, in particular the major opportunities and threats that exist and are likely to emerge in the future.

4 The resources available, since these make certain missions possible and others not.

5 Distinctive competences. While opportunities may exist in a particular market, it would not necessarily make sense for an organization to enter the market if it would not be making the fullest use of its areas of distinctive competence.

However, for the majority of organizations, the development of a mission statement often proves to be a difficult process, involving a series of decisions on strategic trade-offs between different groups of stakeholders both inside and outside the organization. These stakeholders can conveniently be grouped under three main headings:

1 *Internal stakeholders*, including owners, decision-makers, unions and employees

2 *External stakeholders*, such as the government, the financial community, trade associations, pressure groups and society

3 *Marketplace stakeholders*, including customers, competitors, suppliers and creditors.

Of these three groups it is the internal stakeholders who undoubtedly exert the greatest and most immediate effect upon the mission and subsequently the objectives pursued, since it is their expectations and patterns of behaviour that influence the organization most directly on a day-to-day basis.

The impact of external stakeholders is by contrast less direct, although still felt in a variety of ways. The implications of legislation, for example, in the form of, say, compulsory seat belts in the rear of cars have an effect both upon the manufacturers of cars and seat belts. Equally, the financial community represents a significant influence in that the availability and cost of finance, as well as financial expectations in terms of returns, will all force the planner to behave in particular ways. In the case of pressure groups, the most obvious factor in recent years has been the emergence of environmental issues, with the 'greening' of business policies having subsequently been felt across a wide spectrum of products, including petrol, foodstuffs and white goods such as refrigerators.

The third category of stakeholders is made up of those in the marketplace. Of the four major types of marketplace stakeholder, it is customers and competitors who have the most obvious and direct impact upon planning since, in order to succeed, the company needs to understand in some detail their expectations and likely patterns of behaviour. It follows from this that both the organizational mission and the objectives pursued must of necessity be a direct reflection of both elements. By contrast, the influence of suppliers is generally seen to be less direct. There is, however, an obvious need for planning to take account of issues of supply availability, consistency and quality, since without this problems of shortfall or irregular supply are likely to be experienced.

Mission statements: the starting point

Before attempting to write a mission statement the strategist needs to spend time preparing a meaningful statement about the purpose of the firm. In doing this, it is important to recognize the organization's capabilities, the constraints upon it both internally and externally, and the opportunities that exist currently and those that might feasibly develop.

For a mission statement to be useful, it therefore needs to exhibit certain characteristics. It should, for example, focus upon *distinctive values* rather than upon every opportunity that is likely to exist. A statement that includes comments on producing the highest-quality product, offering the most service, achieving the widest distribution network and selling at the lowest price is both unrealistic and too ambitious. More importantly, it fails to provide the sorts of guidelines needed when trade-offs are necessary. Equally, the mission statement must define what we can refer to as the *competitive domain* within which the organization will operate. This competitive domain can be classified by a series of statements on scope:

1 *Industry scope*. This is the range of industries that are of interest to the organization. Some organizations, for example, will operate in just one industry sector, while others are willing to operate in a series. Equally, some organizations will only operate in an industrial or consumer goods market, while others are willing to operate in both.

2 *Geographical scope*. The geographical breadth of operations in terms of regions, countries or county groupings is again part of the mission statement, and varies from a single city right through to multinationals, which operate in virtually every country of the world.

3 *Market segment scope*. This covers the type of market or customer that the company is willing to serve. For a long time, for example, Johnson & Johnson sold its range of products only to the baby market. Largely because of demographic shifts, the company redefined its market segments and, with considerable success, moved into the young adult market.

4 *Vertical scope*. This refers to the degree of integration within the company. Thus, Ford, as part of its car manufacturing operations, also owns rubber plantations, glass manufacturing plants and several steel foundries. Others, by contrast, buy in everything and simply act as middlemen.

It should be apparent, therefore, that in developing the mission statement a variety of considerations need to be borne in mind. The end purpose, however, should be that of *motivation* by ensuring that stakeholders recognize the significance of their work in a far broader sense than simply that of making profits.

The third aspect of the mission statement is that it should only give emphasis to the *major policies* that the organization wishes to pursue. These policies are designed to narrow the range of individual discretion, with the result that the organization should operate in a more consistent manner.

The danger of bland mission statements: rethinking the approach by developing 'the awesome purpose'

Although mission statements have a potentially valuable role to play in clarifying what an organization stands for (its singular purpose), far too many mission statements have proved to be bland and meaningless. The extent to which this is the case was high-lighted by Abrahams (1999), who in *The Mission Statement Book* analyses 301 corporate mission statements from America's top companies. The words used most frequently were: service (230 times); customers (211); quality (194); value (183); employees (157); growth (118); environment (117); profit (114); shareholders (114); leader (104); and best (102). Many of the 301 statements proved to be interchangeable and gave no real indica-tion of the nature of the organization from which it emerged or any insight to what might make the organization distinctive. First-generation companies know instinctively what they stand for, but after several generations of management, the singular purpose to which we referred above becomes far harder to identify. One of the few vary large organizations not to have lost sight of this in its mission statement is Chrysler, which has as its mission 'To produce cars and trucks that people will want to buy, will enjoy driving, and will want to buy again.'

Mission statements have also been criticized by Piercy (1997, p. 181), who has sug-gested that numerous organizations are guilty of a 'holier than thou' posturing in which the mission statement is full of phrases such as 'we will be a market leader . . . A total quality supplier . . . A socially responsible producer . . . A green/environmentally friendly firm, . . . A global player . . . A good corporate citizen . . . a responsible partner with distributors . . . (and) a caring employer'.

It was in an attempt to overcome this that the management consultant Nigel MacLennan (2000, p. 13) has argued that what companies need instead is an 'awe-some purpose'. Awesome purpose, he suggests, is the framework into which every element of the organization's culture should be aligned. Examples of an awesome purpose include that of the Toyota 10, to which reference was made earlier, and companies such as Ryanair and easyJet deciding to redefine the airlines market and, in this way, hitting hard and/or beating the established market players. Others who have taken a similar and seemingly impossible approach include the management team of Toyota, who pursued a vision of creating a car that would allow them to undercut the prices of German luxury cars while at the same time beating them on quality. The result was the Lexus.

The need for communication and the growth of visioning

Once a mission has been developed it is, of course, imperative that it is communicated to employees so that everyone in the organization is aware of it, since (as we suggested earlier) the statement is designed to provide a sense of vision and direction for the organization over the next 10–20 years. A mission statement is therefore of little value if employees are either not made aware of it or misunderstand it, or if it is revised every few years in response to minor environmental changes. There is, however, a need for it to be redefined either when it has lost its appropriateness or when it no longer defines the optimal course for the organization.

However, although mission statements have an undoubted value in that they are capable of highlighting an organization's core values, many mission statements have, as suggested above, been criticized in recent years on the grounds that they are far too general ('to be the best'), too ambitious ('to be the world leader') and too similar. Therefore, if a mission statement is to be meaningful, it is essential that it is firmly rooted in organizational realities, capabilities and competences. Without this, it is quite simply empty rhetoric.

It is partly in recognition of this that a greater emphasis is now being given to the idea of *visioning*. The thinking behind visioning is straightforward and designed to encourage management teams at the corporate level, the business unit or the brand level to think in detail about what they are trying to create. The vision can therefore be seen to be the picture that the planner has of what exactly the organization will look like in three or five years' time. In developing this picture of the future size and profile of the organization, there is an obvious need for a clear understanding both of the ways in which the environment might develop (or be encouraged to develop) and of the organization's competences. Against this background, an initially broad but then an increasingly detailed vision of the organization or brand in, say, three, five and ten years' time can be developed (an example of the Swatch vision appears in Illustration 7.3).

Where visioning has been successful, it has therefore tended to reflect a clarity of managerial thinking about several areas, including:

➡ The size of the organization, business unit or brand in three, five or ten years' time
➡ The image and reputation that will have been created
➡ The corporate and brand values that will be developed
➡ The nature of the customer base and the customer segments that will be served
➡ How these customers should perceive the organization or brand
➡ The geographic coverage that will have been achieved
➡ The overall position within the market and the competitive stance
➡ The links with other organizations.

The significance of vision has been highlighted by a variety of writers over the past few years, but most notably by Collins and Porras (1998), who argue the case not just for corporate (or brand) vision, but also for visionary product concepts and visionary market insights. However, vision cannot be developed in isolation, but needs to be based on the planner's clarity of thinking and understanding of organizational values. The ways in which the two dimensions come together and contribute to performance are illustrated in Figure 7.4.

Illustration 7.3 The Swatch vision

One of the major successes of the 1980s and 1990s has been the Swiss Corporation for Microelectronics and Watchmaking (SMH). The company was formed in 1983 by the merger of two of Switzerland's biggest watchmakers, both of which were insolvent. The new company, under the leadership of Nicholas Hayek, developed the Swatch watch, which, Hayek openly admits, was the result not of detailed financial analysis but of a burning desire to rebuild the Swiss watch industry and a vision of how this might be done.

Hayek recognized that in order to beat his Asian competitors he would have to produce something distinctive. In the event, this was a watch with a European sense of style that, despite being built in a high-labour-cost environment, was able to compete against – and beat – watches from SMH's Japanese competitors such as Seiko.

In commenting on this, Hayek said:

Everywhere children believe in dreams. And they ask the same question: Why? Why does something work a certain way? Why do we behave in certain ways? We ask ourselves those questions every day.

People may laugh – the CEO of a huge Swiss company talking about fantasy. But that's the real secret of what we've done.

Ten years ago, the people on the original Swatch team asked a crazy question: Why can't we design a striking, low-cost, high-quality watch and build it in Switzerland? The bankers were sceptical. A few suppliers refused to sell us parts. They said we would ruin the industry with this crazy product. But this was our vision and we won!

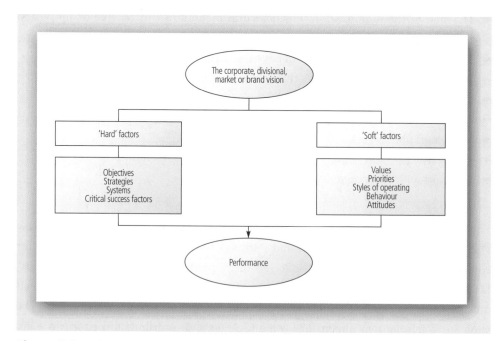

Figure 7.4 Influences on the vision

Having created the mission and the vision, the management team can then begin to focus upon the development of the specific objectives and the detail of the strategy. However, it is not enough for this strategy to be appropriate in that it builds upon organizational capabilities and environmental demands, it must also be implementable. The reader needs to recognize at this stage that there are numerous barriers to the effective implementation of any strategy, and that good leadership and well-developed patterns of communication are a fundamental part of overcoming these barriers. Without these, it is almost inevitable that the staff will have little real understanding of the core values or what is expected of them.

It is because of this that considerable emphasis in recent years has been given to the idea of *internal marketing*. This term, which is used to describe the work that is done within the organization in terms of training, motivating and communicating with the employees, was developed largely within the service sector. Increasingly, however, it is becoming recognized that it is a fundamental part of the marketing equation for any organization, since in its absence the ways in which employees interact with customers will lack true focus (see Figure 7.5).

Vision, commitments and leadership principles

Having developed the vision, be it at corporate, divisional, brand or market level, there is then the need to link this to a series of what might be referred to as inspiring commitments

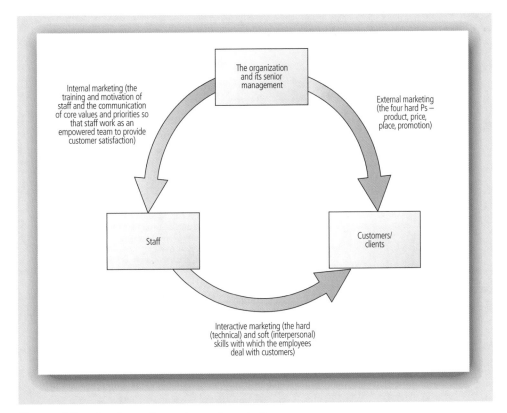

Figure 7.5   The three dimensions of marketing

and then, in turn, to leadership principles; this is illustrated in Figure 7.6 and reflects how Shell Oils operated at the end of the 1990s.

Although it has often been argued that a fundamental underpinning for any marketing strategy, be it at the corporate, divisional or brand level, is a shared vision of what the management team is trying to achieve, research at Cranfield School of Management (see Kakabadse, 1999) has highlighted the degree of dissension that often exists within senior management teams. His findings suggested:

" . . . the (senior) management of 20% of Swedish, 23% of Japanese, 30% of British, 31% of Austrian, 32% of German, 39% of French, 42% of Finnish, 46% of Spanish, 68% of Irish companies and 56% of top civil servants in the Australian Commonwealth government, report that the members of the top team hold *deeply* different views concerning the shape and direction of their organization – in effect differences of vision.*"*

The common retort is that differences such as these are only to be expected and can be seen to be the sign of a healthy organization characterized by a degree of creative tension. However, the research suggests that this is not in fact the case and those differences in vision manifest themselves in a number of ways, including:

➡ Organizational turbulence
➡ An emphasis upon the short term
➡ Infighting
➡ Staff keeping their heads down.

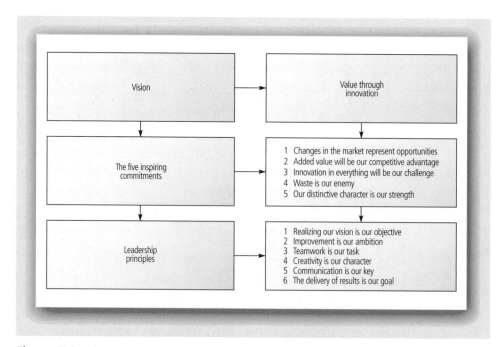

Figure 7.6 The vision, inspiring commitments and leadership principles

In order to overcome this, Kakabadse argues for more open communication amongst senior management; the promotion of a stronger feedback culture from further down the organization; the development of more overtly shared values; attention to be paid to the detail of the differences in ambitions and goals that each person has for their own department, division or function; and for the (revised) vision then to be established and driven throughout the organization.

Although vision is an important early stage in the planning process, a series of studies suggest that staff are only rarely included in discussions about corporate brand and reputation. The consultants ORC, for example, found that only 6 per cent of European employees are involved in discussions at departmental level, compared with 12 per cent in the US and 17 per cent in the Pacific Rim. In addition, 13 per cent of European employees do not know their employer's brand mission, vision or values.

Given that a considerable amount of emphasis has been given in recent years to the idea that there is a need for staff to 'live the brand', the failure to understand it has potentially significant implications for the process of planning and implementation. Recognizing this, BBC Worldwide has spent a considerable time ensuring that the organization's vision, strategy and values are family integrated and then communicated throughout the organization (see Illustration 7.4).

Illustration 7.4 Vision, strategy and values

BBC Worldwide is the BBC's international marketing arm, with a brief for marketing and selling BBC programmes overseas. The vision, strategy and values represent the framework within which marketing planning takes place.

The vision

To be recognized as one of the UK's leading international consumer media companies, admired around the world for its outstanding products and exceptional commercial performance, thereby bringing substantial and growing benefit to the BBC – not just commercially but also creatively.

The strategy

BBC Worldwide aims to become a world-class marketing organization, able to understand, respond to and anticipate market needs better than its competitors. In particular, it will develop outstanding skills in driving value from major brands across media and markets. It will continue to focus on developing the most creative, cost-effective and high-quality range of consumer media products on the market. It will build lasting partnerships with the BBC and independents that ensure unique access to the best of BBC brands and properties. And it will help make the BBC the natural first choice for talent.

Our UK strategy is to be the first choice provider of quality media products for many 'communities of interest' by exploiting the BBC's unique broadcast strengths across all media platforms, past and future, and in the majority of genres.

Our international strategy is to focus on fewer market segments, where the BBC has clear competitive advantage. It will understand these target segments better than its competitors, and will seek to build a robust cross-media business around major BBC brands.

The values

We have worked to identify the key behaviours which characterize successful performance at BBC Worldwide. We believe that these should define 'the way we do things around here'. Therefore, BBC Worldwide embraces these values and guiding behaviours:

➡ *Clarity* – we have a clarity of direction, purpose and goals

➡ *Responsibility* – we are responsible for creating our own success

➡ *Excellence* – we foster and encourage innovation and creativity as the life-blood of our business

➡ *Appreciation* – we fully appreciate and respect each other

➡ *Teamwork* – we are team players and believe in cooperation and collaboration at all levels

➡ *Effective* – we are committed to delivering high-quality products that delight our partners and customers.

7.5 Influences on objectives and strategy

Having developed the mission statement and the vision, the planner is then in a position to turn to the objectives and strategy. It has long been recognized that any organization represents a complex mix of cultural and political influences, all of which come to bear in some way on the objectives that are pursued. It follows from this that objectives and strategy are not simply set in a vacuum or just by reference to environmental factors, but rather that they emerge as the product of a complex interaction at various levels of the organization. This is reflected in Figure 7.7, which illustrates the various layers of cultural and political influences on objectives (and subsequently strategy), ranging from the values of society to the far more specific influences such as organizational objectives, individuals' expectations, and indeed the power structures that exist within and around the organization.

It logically follows that, if we are to understand fully the process of setting objectives, we need to recognize the complexities of these interrelationships.

These have been commented on by Johnson and Scholes (1988, pp. 113–15), and it is worth quoting them at some length:

"

➡ There are a number of cultural factors in an organization's *environment* which will influence the internal situation. In particular the values of society at large and the influence of organized groups need to be understood.

➡ The *nature of the business*, such as the market situation and the types of product and technology are important influences not only in a direct sense but in the way they affect the expectations of individuals and groups.

➡ Most pervasive of all these general influences is the organizational *culture* itself.

➡ At a more specific level, individuals will normally have shared expectations with one or more groups of people within the organization. These shared expectations may be concerned with undertaking the company's tasks and reflect the formal structure of the organization, e.g. departmental expectations. However, *coalitions* also arise as a result of specific events, and can transcend the formal structure.

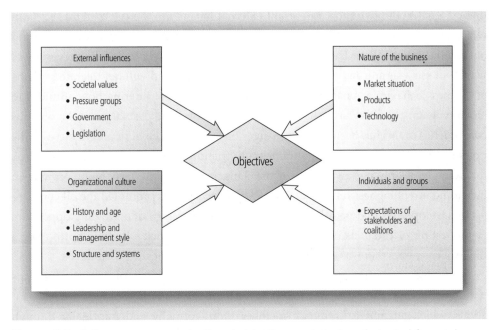

Figure 7.7 Influences on organizational objectives and strategy (adapted from Johnson and Scholes, 1988)

➡ Internal groups and individuals are also influenced by their contacts with *external stakeholders* – groups which have an interest in the operation of the company such as customers, shareholders, suppliers or unions. For example, sales staff may be pressurized by customers to represent their interests within the company.

➡ Individuals or groups, whether internal or external, cannot influence an organization's strategies unless they have an influencing mechanism. This mechanism is called *power*, which can be derived in a variety of ways.

➡ Organizational *objectives* traditionally have been afforded a central/dominant role in influencing strategy, i.e. strategy is seen as the means of achieving preordained and unchangeable objectives. That is not our view. Whereas organizations do have objectives, which are often valuable in strategy formulation, they should not be regarded as an unchangeable set of expectations. They should be viewed as an important part of the strategic equation, and open to amendment and change as strategies develop.

➡ Objectives tend to emerge as the wishes of the most dominant coalition, usually the management of the organization, although there are notable exceptions. However, in pursuing these objectives the dominant group is very strongly influenced by their reading of the political situation, i.e. their perception of the power struggle. For example, they are likely to set aside some of their expectations in order to improve the chance of achieving others." **″**

External influences on objectives

By referring to Figure 7.7 it can be seen that the most general of the influences upon individuals and groups, and hence on organizational objectives and strategy, are external factors, the nature of the business and the organizational culture. Taking the first of these, arguably the two most important external factors are the *values of the society* in which the organization is operating and the *behaviour of organized groups* both inside and outside the organization. The influence of social values is likely to be felt in a variety of ways, but most significantly in terms of what society will and will not tolerate in terms of business behaviour. As an example of this, it is worth considering how attitudes to environmental pollution have changed dramatically over the past 20 years. An obvious consequence of this has been to force changes on business behaviour and to increase the pressures for safer and more environmentally friendly products. In the case of petrol, for example, a growing awareness of the dangers of airborne lead pollution and an increasing unwillingness on the part of society to accept this prompted the oil companies to develop unleaded petrols. Equally, it was an awareness of a growing opposition to the testing of products on animals that led Anita Roddick's Body Shop to offer a range of cosmetics that was developed without the need for testing on animals.

Objectives and strategy are also affected by the behaviour of organized groups within the organization. The most obvious of these are trade unions and trade associations, which attempt to influence members both formally and informally through codes of conduct and norms of behaviour. In the case of the travel industry, for example, ABTA (the Association of British Travel Agents) has, over the past few years, worked hard to monitor and improve the standards within the industry so that clients receive better and more professional standards of service.

The nature of the business

The second general influence on objectives and strategy is the *nature of the business itself* and, in particular, the market situation faced by the organization, the life-cycle stages of its products, and the types of technology being used. The influence of market situation can perhaps best be understood by referring back to the mid-1980s, when much of British industry was undergoing fundamental restructuring in order to survive in the face of increasing globalization. The markets in which the industries were operating had changed dramatically over a 20-year period, with an upsurge in the market of often low-priced foreign competition that made operating profitably difficult. Faced with this, the steel, coal and shipbuilding industries were forced into the position of massive restructuring, changed working practices and radically different product/market strategies in order to survive. This, in turn, was reflected in the type of technology that could be used, attitudes within the industry, and subsequently in the ways in which employees viewed policy.

The significance and implications of the organizational culture

The third general influence on objectives and strategy is *organizational culture*. Culture has been defined in a variety of ways over the past few years but, for our purposes here, it can be seen as the commonly held core beliefs of the organization. As such, it determines how people within the organization behave and respond. In examining and trying to understand organizational culture, Johnson and Scholes (2002, pp. 230–6) argue the case for what is referred to as the 'cultural web'. This web, they suggest, is made up of six major dimensions:

1 Stories and myths
2 Rituals and routines
3 Symbols
4 Power structures
5 Organizational structures
6 Control systems.

Together, these four factors determine the type and profile of the organization, and hence how it is likely to behave in the marketplace. Factors such as these led Miles and Snow (1978) to identify three types of organization: defenders, prospectors and analysers. The implications of each type for objectives, strategies, and planning and control systems appear in Figure 7.8.

Individual and group expectations

The fourth and final influence on objectives and strategy is that of the *expectations of individuals, stakeholders and coalitions*. In most cases it is the expectations of coalitions

Organization type and dominant objectives	Characteristics of policy making (preferred strategy)	Nature of the planning and control systems
1 *Defenders* Desire for stability	Specialization with cost efficient production; a marketing emphasis on price and service to defend current business A tendency for vertical integration	Generally, centralized with detailed control and an emphasis on cost-efficiency Extensive use of formal planning procedures
2 *Prospectors* Search for and exploitation of new product and market opportunities	Growth through product and market development Constant monitoring of environmental change Multiple technologies	Emphasis on flexibility and decentralization with use of *ad hoc* measurements
3 *Analysers* Desire to match new ventures to present shape of business	Steady growth through market penetration Exploitation of applied research Followers in the market	Often extremely complicated Coordinating roles between functions Intensive planning

Figure 7.8 Different types of organizational culture and their influences on policy-making (adapted from Miles and Snow, 1978)

that exert the greatest influence on the organization, in that while individuals may well have a variety of personal aspirations, they often share expectations with a number of others. This, together with the relative inability of any single individual to exert a major influence upon the organization, leads to the emergence of groups within departments, regions and levels of the hierarchy, all of which attempt in one way or another to influence the direction of the organization. In practice, however, and particularly in the case of a multinational or large divisionalized organization, the ability of any one group to exert any significant degree of influence may well be limited. Almost inevitably, of course, conflicts between the expectations of different groups are likely to exist and this, in turn, leads to a series of trade-offs. This was referred to in a slightly different context at an earlier stage in this chapter when talking specifically about marketing objectives. More generally, the sorts of conflicts that are likely to emerge are between growth and profitability; growth and control/independence; cost efficiency and jobs; and volume/mass provision versus quality/specialization.

7.6 Guidelines for establishing objectives and setting goals and targets

Few businesses pursue a single objective; instead they have a mixture, which typically includes profitability, sales growth, market share improvement, risk containment, innovativeness, usage, and so on. Each business unit should therefore set objectives under a variety of headings and then *manage by objectives*. In other words, it is the pursuit of these objectives that should provide the framework both for the planning and control processes. However, for this to work, several guidelines must be adhered to, with objectives being:

1 *Hierarchical*: going from the most important to the least important
2 *Quantitative*: in order to avoid ambiguity – the objective 'to increase market share' is not as satisfactory a guideline as 'to increase market share by 5 per cent' or indeed 'to increase market share by 5 percentage points within 18 months'
3 *Realistic*: it is only too easy for objectives to reflect a degree of wishful thinking; instead they should be developed as the result of a detailed analysis of opportunities, corporate capability, competitive strengths and competitive strategy
4 *Consistent*: it is quite obviously unrealistic to pursue incompatible objectives; as an example of this, to aim for substantial gains in both sales and profits simultaneously is rarely possible.

It is also essential that they satisfy the SMART criteria of being Specific rather than general in their nature, Measurable, Actionable, Realistic and Time-based. In the case of marketing objectives, there is also the need for them to be related to or fall out of the corporate objectives.

Primary and secondary objectives

Although for a long time economists argued that firms aimed to maximize profits, it is now generally recognized that the modern large corporation, managed by professionals, pursues a far broader and infinitely more diverse set of objectives. As a consequence, traditional views of profit maximization as the principal objective have been challenged by the reality of the behaviour of corporate management. With this in mind, two types of objective can be identified: *primary* and *secondary*.

Traditionally the primary objective was, as observed above, profit maximization. Other objectives are, however, often seen by managers to be of more immediate relevance and, as Chisnall (1989, p. 137) points out, may affect the organization's profit-earning ability:

*"*These secondary objectives, which are not in any way inferior to the primary objective, are necessary if a company is to plan effectively for its future progress. In the short term, for instance, a profit maximization policy may be affected by changes in economic conditions which demand some restructuring of corporate resources to meet new levels of competition. Survival or market share defences may, in fact, become primary objectives.*"*

This issue of the multiplicity of objectives has also been discussed by Drucker (1955), who isolated eight areas in which organizational objectives might be developed and maintained:

1 Market standing
2 Innovation
3 Productivity
4 Financial and physical resources
5 Manager performance and development
6 Worker performance and attitude
7 Profitability
8 Public responsibility.

Rethinking business objectives: the significance of the triple bottom line and the alternative three Ps

The eighth of Drucker's objectives, public responsibility, has received far greater attention over the past few years than at any time since he first identified them almost 50 years ago. With a far greater emphasis having been given in recent years to the impact upon society of marketing behaviour, issues of sustainable development have led to the emergence of the triple bottom line and the alternative three Ps.

The triple bottom line is based on the idea that business should not simply pursue economic objectives, but that decisions should also reflect social and ecological considerations. This has, in turn, led to the three Ps of People, Planet and Profit, in which environmental quality and social equity are seen to be just as important as profit. Amongst the advocates of such an approach is Anita Roddick, the founder of The Body Shop. The Body Shop's corporate philosophy is that social justice, human rights and spirituality are integral parts of modern business practice. With business and marketing decision-making having long been based on quantifiable measures such as efficiency, proponents of the triple bottom line argue that highlighting social issues and taking responsibility for business practice will increasingly prove to be the way in which firms will gain a competitive advantage.

Objectives and time horizons

It should be apparent by this stage that, in setting objectives, the marketing planner needs to take account of a wide variety of factors. Perhaps the final influence that we need to examine here before focusing upon the detail of corporate and marketing objectives is that of the time horizons involved. In the case of those industries that are highly capital-intensive, for example, the planning horizons tend to be considerably longer than is the case in faster-moving consumer goods markets. We can therefore usefully distinguish between the short, medium and long terms.

From the planner's point of view, the short term is concerned essentially with issues of tactics, while the long term is concerned with the major issues of strategy and the allocation and reallocation of resources. The medium term then sits neatly between these in that it provides the focus for determining how effectively resources are being used. Although there is perhaps an understandable temptation to tie each of these phases to specific periods of time (e.g. up to one year in the case of the short term, one to five years for the medium term and over five years for the long term), such an exercise is generally only useful when carried out in relation to a specific industry or company.

At a more general level, the significance of planning time horizons relates rather more to the degree of environmental change being experienced and the ability of the organization to respond by reallocating resources. A useful distinction (derived from economics) between long term and short term focuses on *capacity*. Within the short run capacity is given, hence the aim should be to make the best use of available capacity – whether this is defined in terms of sales personnel, productive facilities, distribution systems or any other resource constraint. One moves from the short run to the long run when capacity is increased (or reduced). Making extra capacity available involves capital expenditure/investment, and its existence – in whatever time frame – is usually associated with fixed (or establishment) costs. The significance of this from the point of view of establishing objectives can therefore be seen in terms of the need to identify objectives both for the short term and the long term. The long-term objectives will then be concerned with the direction in which the organization is heading, while the short-term objectives will be allied far more closely with the stages through which the organization will have to move in order to achieve this position.

The nature of corporate objectives

In the light of our discussion here and in Chapter 1, it should be apparent that corporate management, having established the corporate mission and vision, then has to take these a stage further by developing a series of specific objectives for each level of management. Most typically these objectives are expressed in terms of sales growth, profitability, market share growth and risk diversification. Because the majority of organizations generally pursue a number of objectives, it is, as we have seen, important that they are stated in a hierarchical manner, going from the most important to the least important, with this hierarchy being both internally consistent and mutually reinforcing. By doing this, the strategist is clarifying priorities so that if, at a later stage, a conflict of objectives emerges, a decision can then be made as to which particular objective is to dominate. At the same time it is essential that the objectives established are realistic both in terms of their magnitude and the time scale over which they are to be achieved. Almost invariably, however, organizations experience difficulties and conflicts in establishing objectives, problems that are in turn compounded by the need to establish multiple objectives. For example, it is seldom, if ever, possible for an organization to satisfy concurrently objectives of rapid growth *and* risk aversion, or to maximize both sales *and* profits. Recognizing this, Weinberg (1969) has identified eight basic strategic trade-offs facing firms:

1 Short-term profits versus long-term growth
2 Profit margins versus competitive position
3 Direct sales effort versus market development effort
4 Penetration of existing markets versus the development of new markets
5 Related versus non-related new opportunities as a source of long-term growth
6 Profit versus non-profit goals
7 Growth versus stability
8 A 'riskless' environment versus a high-risk environment.

It follows from this that the strategist has to decide upon the relative emphasis that is to be given to each of these dimensions. Any failure to do this is ultimately likely to lead to conflict and reduce the extent to which the objectives provide useful strategic guidelines.

However, while the need for clear objectives may well be self-evident, it is relatively unusual to find explicit references as to just *how* managers should go about developing these objectives in the first place. One of the few who has attempted to provide guidelines for formulating objectives is McKay (1972), who suggests that it is possible to identify two categories of issues that should be considered: the general issues that apply to all organizations, and the more specific, which force a more detailed examination. These general issues are:

➡ *Business scope* – what business should we be in?
➡ *Business orientation* – what approach is most appropriate for our business scope and to our purposes of survival, growth and profit?

➡ *Business organization* – to what extent is our organizational style, structure and staff policy suited to the orientation chosen?

➡ *Public responsibility* – is there a match between our selection of opportunities and the existing and future social and economic needs of the public?

➡ *Performance evaluation* – is there a match between our appraisal and planning systems?

The *specific* areas that then follow from this, he suggests, relate to each strategic business unit (SBU) and include:

➡ Customer classes
➡ Competitors
➡ Markets and distribution
➡ Technology and products
➡ Production capability
➡ Finance
➡ Environment.

Taking account of competitors' objectives

Objectives should never be set in a vacuum. Instead they should be set against the background of a detailed understanding of environmental demands and opportunities. In doing this, particular attention needs to be paid to the objectives that are likely to be pursued by competitors, since these will often have a direct impact upon subsequent levels of performance.

A competitor's objectives are likely to be influenced by many factors, but particularly by its size, history, managerial culture and performance. They are also affected by whether the company is part of a larger organization. If this is the case, the strategist needs to know whether it is being pressured to achieved growth or whether it is viewed by the parent as a 'cash cow' and is being milked. Equally, we need to know just how important it is to the parent: if it is central to the parent company's long-term plans, this will have a direct influence upon how much money will be spent in fighting off an attack. As mentioned earlier, Rothschild (1984, Chapter 6), for example, argues that the worst competitor to attack is the competitor for whom this is the sole or principal business, and who has a global operation.

There is therefore, as discussed in Chapter 6, a strong argument for the strategist to develop a detailed competitive map in which issues of competitive capability and priority figure prominently. In doing this, a useful assumption, at least initially, is that competitors will aim for profit targets and choose their strategies accordingly. Even here, however, organizations differ in the emphasis they put on short-term as opposed to long-term profits. In reality, of course, few organizations aim for profit maximization, be it in the short or long term, but instead opt for a degree of *satisficing* (a term coined by Simon (1960) to refer to an acceptable level of performance, typically across multiple objectives, rather than an optimal performance on just one). They have target profit figures and are satisfied to achieve them, even if greater profits could have been achieved by other strategies with perhaps a greater degree of risk.

An alternative approach is to assume that each competitor has a variety of objectives, each of which is of different importance and which has therefore a different weight in the minds of the members of the management team. Recognizing this, the marketing strategist needs to determine, at least in broad terms, the relative weighting that each competitor gives to areas such as current and long-term profitability, market share retention and gowth, risk avoidance, technological leadership, distribution dominance, service, and so on. Knowing this provides an insight into whether each competitor is broadly satisfied with its current strategy and results, whether – and how – it will respond to different forms of competitive movement and attack, and so on. The competitor who, for example, is pursuing a service-based strategy is far more likely to respond aggressively to a similar competitive move than if the move is based on, say, an advertising-led attack by the same competitor.

The argument for looking in detail at your competitors as a prelude to developing your own objectives is, in many ways, self-evident, since what a competitor has done in the past will typically provide potentially strong insights to what the competitor is likely to do in the future. This is particularly the case when the organization has been performing strongly and the managerial priorities and mindsets have become well established. The management team will have developed a business model and, although it would be foolish to suggest that this is never reviewed or questioned, its success is likely to lead to its continued pursuit. Given this, a competitor's marketing strategists should, within certain parameters, be able to predict future patterns of behaviour. Firms such as GE, Mars, P&G and Kellogg's all have a focus upon brand leadership, whilst hotel chains such as Four Seasons have a focus on the premium end of the business market, an approach that is unlikely to change.

Having said this, competitive attitudes, objectives and strategies, but especially approaches to implementation, do of course change over time, even when a particular strategy is proving to be successful. History has shown though that the probability of change is far greater when a particular strategy is not working, or when there is a change in management at the top of the organization. There are therefore several specific factors that should be taken into account, as well as the rather more general issue of competitive posture referred to above. These include:

➡ *Each competitor's previous successes and failures.* It is quite normal to continue with a successful formula and to change one that is not working.
➡ *The volume and direction of investment in advertising and plant.* A rational competitor will concentrate advertising effort on the products and markets that appear to offer the greatest scope. Monitoring patterns of competitive advertising spend can therefore provide the strategist with a good indication of the directions in which to concentrate. Equally, a knowledge of competitors' investment in plant, which can often be picked up from equipment suppliers, planning applications and the trade press, provides an invaluable guide to profitable future plans.

➡ *Each competitor's relative cost position.* The starting point for this is to arrive at an assessment of each competitor's relative cost position in each major market sector. Working on the assumption that each competitor will have conducted a similar exercise, it is reasonable to suppose that they will give priority to cost-reduction strategies in those markets in which they are currently high-cost operators.

By focusing upon areas such as these, the strategist should be in a far better position to answer four fundamental questions:

1 What is each competitor seeking?
2 What is it that drives each competitor?
3 What is each competitor's potential competitive capability?
4 In what ways might this capability be translated into objectives and strategy?

It is against this background that the strategist can then define and perhaps redefine his or her own organization's objectives.

Developing offensive corporate objectives

Firms can be broadly classified as *proactive* or *reactive*. The former are characterized by an entrepreneurial and highly positive attitude to their markets, with a constant searching and pursuit of new business opportunities; in essence they try to shape the environment to fit the organization's resources and objectives. By contrast, reactive firms adopt a far more passive and less entrepreneurial posture, responding to rather than initiating environmental change. These contrasting styles have an obvious effect upon the sorts of objectives pursued and indeed, in most cases, upon subsequent levels of trading performance.

The implications of this for the way in which marketing objectives are set are reflected in the way in which there are few incentives for the marketing strategist to take an offensive approach within the marketplace unless ambitious marketing objectives have been set and a proactive and aggressive and high-performing marketing culture established.

With regard to the specific objectives that an offensive or proactive organization might pursue, these will depend to a large degree upon the organization's market position. If, for example, it is intent on increasing its market share, the starting point involves deciding upon which competitor(s) to attack. The options open to it are essentially:

1 *To attack the market leader.* This is typically a high-risk but potentially high-return strategy and one which makes sense if the leader is generally complacent or not serving the market as well as it might – Xerox, for example, chose to attack 3M by developing a cleaner, faster and more convenient copying process (dry copying rather than wet). Equally, Dyson attacked Hoover with a technologically different product, whilst Airbus Industries attacked Boeing.

2 *To attack firms of its own size.* These firms may be either underfinanced or undermanaged.

3 *To attack local and regional firms.* This strategy was pursued with considerable success in the 1960s and 1970s by a small number of large brewers who gobbled up the small, regional brewers in the UK. It has been adopted subsequently by some of the major car producers such as Ford, who have bought some of the smaller and specialist manufacturers such as Volvo and Aston Martin, and Volkswagen, who bought Skoda and Seat.

4 *To ignore the major players.* The organization could pursue a flanking strategy that leads to the development and growth of a new market sector, something that has been done with considerable success by Ryanair and easyJet, both of whom sidestepped the major flag carriers.

Given the nature of these comments, it should be apparent that this question of *who* to attack is therefore at the very heart of an effective offensive strategy, since to make the wrong choice is likely to prove immensely costly.

Setting truly ambitious objectives: the significance of BHAGs

In discussing goals, Collins and Porras (1998) argue the case for what they term Big Hairy Audacious Goals (BHAGs). As examples of BHAGs, they point to a variety of organizations, including Boeing, which in the 1950s gained a significant advantage over its principal competitor Douglas aircraft (later to become McDonnell-Douglas) by establishing itself as the dominant player in the commercial aircraft industry with its 707, despite having little experience in that sector of the market. It then followed this in quick succession with the 727 (Douglas launched the DC-9 more than two years later), the 737 and then the 747 jumbo jet.

For Collins and Porras (1998, p. 94):

" . . . a BHAG engages people – it reaches out and grabs them in the gut. It is tangible, energizing, highly focused. People 'get it' right away; it takes little or no explanation.*"*

Amongst the other organizations they cite as having or having had BHAGs are the cigarette manufacturer Philip Morris, which in 1961 was a sixth-place also-ran with less than 10 per cent of the tobacco market. The BHAG that the management team set themselves was that of replacing RJ Reynolds as the market leader, something that they achieved largely through their Marlboro brand. Other BHAGs include Sam Walton's objective of becoming the world's largest retailer (Wal-Mart), Walt Disney's ideas for the new type of amusement park that became Disneyland, IBM's reshaping of the computer industry in the 1960s, and Jack Welch's reshaping of General Electric.

In doing this, Welch stated that the first step – before all other steps – is for the company to 'define its destiny in broad but clear terms. You need an overarching message, something big, but simple and understandable.' In the case of GE, Welch developed the BHAG of 'To become number 1 or number 2 in every market we serve and revolutionize this company to have the speed and agility of a small enterprise.' Employees throughout

GE fully understood – and remembered – the BHAG. The compelling clarity of GE's BHAG can be contrasted with the difficult-to-understand, hard-to-remember 'vision statement' articulated by Westinghouse in 1989 (see Figure 7.9).

The point that the reader needs to take from this is not that GE had the 'right' goal and Westinghouse had the 'wrong' goal. Rather, it is that GE's goal was clear, compelling and more likely to stimulate progress. Similar BHAG thinking was at the heart of the Amazon.com strategy, with Jeff Bezos becoming the biggest Internet bookseller by pursuing his GBF (Get Big Fast) philosophy.

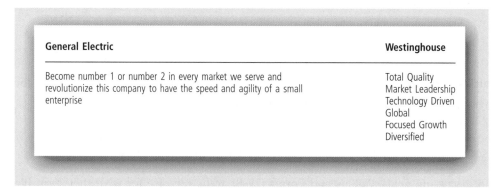

General Electric	**Westinghouse**
Become number 1 or number 2 in every market we serve and revolutionize this company to have the speed and agility of a small enterprise	Total Quality Market Leadership Technology Driven Global Focused Growth Diversified

Figure 7.9 General Electric's BHAG and Westinghouse's vision statement

Establishing the marketing objectives

Against the background of the comments made so far, we can identify a firm's competitive situation and hence its marketing decisions as being concerned with just two major elements: products and markets. This has been discussed by a variety of writers, but most obviously by McKay (1972), Guiltinan and Paul (1988), and Ansoff (1968). McKay, for example, identifies just three fundamental marketing objectives:

1 To enlarge the market
2 To increase market share
3 To improve profitability.

McKay's ideas of three principal marketing objectives have been taken several steps further by Guiltinan and Paul, who argue that there are six objectives that should be given explicit consideration:

1 Market share growth
2 Market share maintenance
3 Cash flow maximization
4 Sustaining profitability
5 Harvesting
6 Establishing an initial market position.

In many ways, however, the thinking underpinning both approaches can be seen to come together in Ansoff's ideas of a product/market matrix. This is illustrated in Figure 7.10.

The matrix in Figure 7.10, which focuses upon the product (what is sold) and to whom it is sold (the market), highlights four distinct strategic alternatives open to the marketing strategist:

1 Selling more existing products to existing markets
2 Extending existing products to new markets
3 Developing new products for existing markets
4 Developing new products for new markets.

Although in practice there are of course *relative* degrees of newness both in terms of products and markets – and hence the number of strategies open to the organization is substantial – Ansoff's matrix is useful in that it provides a convenient and easily understood framework within which marketing objectives and strategies can be readily developed, something that is reflected in Figure 7.11.

⫽ It follows from this that setting objectives and strategies *in relation to products and markets* is a fundamental element of the marketing planning process. These marketing objectives then represent performance commitments for the future, and are typically stated in terms of market share, sales volume, levels of sterling distribution, and profitability. For these to be worthwhile, however, they need to be stated both quantitatively and unambiguously. In this way they are capable of measurement, something which is not possible if they are stated only in broad directional terms. ⟍⟍

The argument for explicit and quantitatively expressed objectives is therefore overpowering, since any failure to do this simply offers scope for confusion and

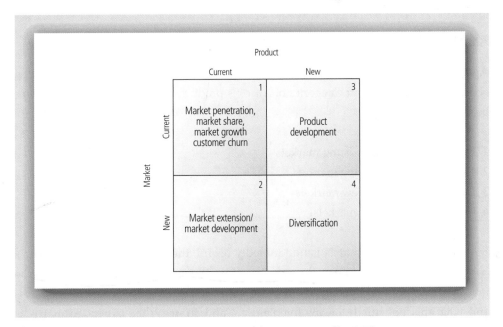

Figure 7.10 Ansoff's growth vector matrix (source: Ansoff, 1957)

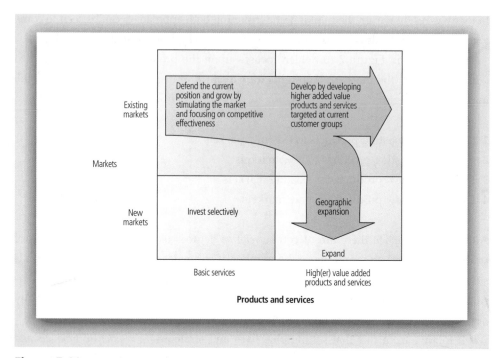

Figure 7.11 Developing strategic direction

ambiguity at a later stage, not just in terms of the sort of action required, but also in terms of the performance measurement standards that are to be used. In stating objectives they also need to be related to the fundamental philosophies and policies of a particular organization, something which again argues the case for a clear and well-communicated mission statement. The *process* of setting objectives is therefore central to its effectiveness.

Ansoff's matrix revisited and expanded

Against the background of the comments so far, it should be apparent that marketing objectives relate to the four categories of Ansoff's product/market matrix, with decisions being needed on:

1 Existing products in existing markets
2 New products in existing markets
3 Existing products in new markets
4 New products in new markets.

But, although Ansoff's matrix is undoubtedly useful, the simplicity of a 2 × 2 matrix has a number of limitations. Recognizing this, Wills et al. (1972) have taken the matrix a step further by highlighting the degree of product and market newness and what this potentially means for planning and strategy; the expanded matrix is illustrated in Figure 7.12.

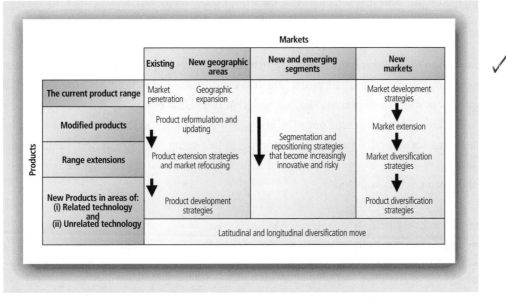

Figure 7.12 Developing the Ansoff matrix

The general nature and direction of the choices between these strategic alternatives is influenced both by the product life cycle and the current shape of the company's product portfolio. This in turn leads to a series of choices for each product/market condition, choices that can be expressed in terms of five types of strategy:

1 *Maintenance* of the current competitive position.

2 *Improvement* of the current competitive position.

3 *Harvesting*, which involves reducing or relinquishing the current competitive position in order to capitalize upon short-term profit and improve cash flow.

4 *Exiting*, which typically occurs when the company is suffering from a weak competitive position or recognizes that the cost of staying in the market and/or improving upon the position is too high. As an example of this, ICI sold its loss-making European fertilizer business to Europe's second largest fertilizer producer, the Finnish company Kemira Oy. The decision to withdraw from this market sector was made after ICI had experienced losses for four years, despite having made major attempts to improve the business, including vigorous cost reductions and investment in new technology.

5 *Entry* to a new sector.

However, while considering either the need or the feasibility of each of these strategies, the marketing planner needs to recognize the danger of adhering slavishly to any particular set of rules relating to the five categories and to be fully aware of the major constraints within which he or she is operating. Among the most commonly used and useful frameworks for identifying these is the concept of the limiting factor (a limiting factor might include costs of distribution that limit the market to a small geographic region, limitations on production capacity, and so on) and techniques of gap analysis, which are designed to highlight any gaps that exist between long-term forecasts of performance and the sales or financial objectives that have been set (see Figure 7.13).

In the case of Figure 7.13(a), the lowest curve represents a projection of expected sales from the organization's current portfolio of businesses. The highest curve traces the sales targets for the next 10 years, which, as can be seen, are more ambitious than the current portfolio will permit. The question that then quite obviously follows is how best to fill this strategic planning gap. The courses of action open to the strategist can then be examined in several ways. The first involves subdividing the gap into the *operations gap* and the *new strategies gap*. In the case of the *operations gap*, the approaches to reducing or eliminating it totally include:

➡ Greater productivity by means of reduced costs
➡ Improvements to the sales mix or higher prices
➡ Higher levels of market penetration.

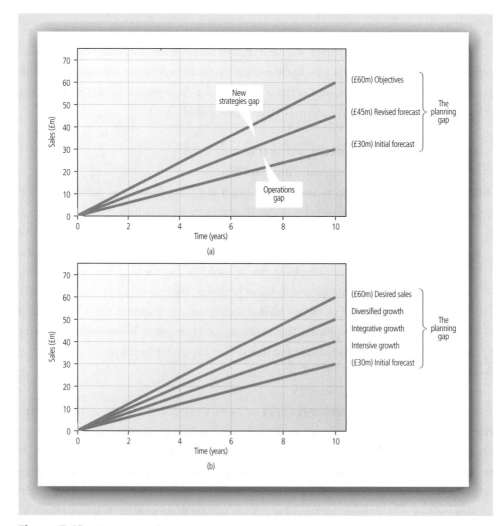

Figure 7.13 The strategic planning gap

In the case of the *new strategies gap*, the courses of action include:

➡ A reduction in objectives
➡ Market extension in the form of new market segments, new user groups or expansion geographically
➡ Product development
➡ Diversification by selling new products to new markets.

An alternative way of looking at the strategic planning gap is illustrated in Figure 7.13(b). Here, the solutions to the shortfall have been categorized as:

➡ Identifying further opportunities to achieve growth within the company's current business (intensive growth)
➡ Identifying opportunities to build or acquire businesses related to the current sphere of operations (integrative growth)
➡ Adding businesses that are unrelated to current operations (diversification).

In weighing up which of these alternatives to pursue, the planner needs to give consideration to a variety of issues. For many companies the most attractive option proves to be greater market penetration, since this is concerned with existing products and markets, and typically therefore involves less cost and risk than would be incurred by moving outside existing areas of knowledge. Equally, it generally pays an organization to search for growth within existing and related markets rather than moving into new markets, since by doing this it is more readily able to build upon its reputation. If, however, the company decides to move into new and possibly unrelated areas, there is then a need not only to establish itself against a new set of competitors, but also to build new distribution networks and come to terms with a different technology. This should not in itself be seen as an argument against moving into new markets with new products, but rather an argument for the planner to develop objectives and strategies against the background of a firm understanding of the organization's strengths, weaknesses and overall corporate capability, all of which should emerge clearly from the marketing audit.

The levels of risk associated with each of the strategic alternatives identified in the Ansoff matrix can perhaps be better understood by considering an extension to the basic model. While undoubtedly useful as a framework, Ansoff's four-cell matrix is not able to reflect different *degrees* of technological or market newness, or indeed of the risk associated with the four alternatives. By returning for a moment to Figure 7.10, it should be apparent that, all other things being equal, the lowest level of risk is associated with the market penetration strategy of cell 1. This then increases through cells 2 and 3, peaking in cell 4 with a strategy of diversification. The matrices in Figures 7.14 and 7.15 are both designed to add a further dimension to Ansoff's original model.

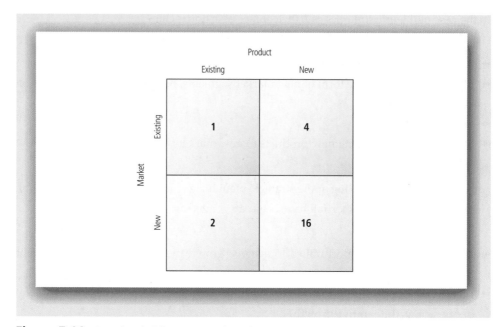

Figure 7.14 Levels of risk associated with various product/market combinations – 1 (adapted from Ward, 1968)

Figure 7.14, for example, gives recognition to the fact that strategies involving new products (hence new technology) generally entail a greater degree of risk than those limited just to new markets.

Figure 7.15 takes this model somewhat further by distinguishing between the different types and degrees of market and product development, and in doing this

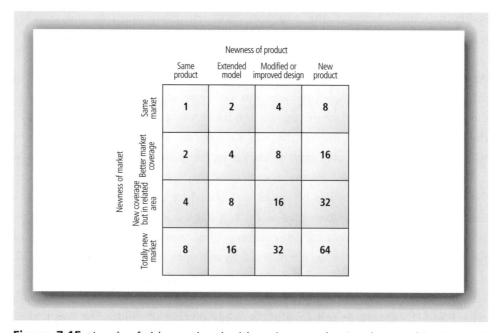

Figure 7.15 Levels of risk associated with various product/market combinations – 2 (adapted from Ward, 1968)

illustrates the relative degrees of risk more precisely. It can be seen from this how risk levels escalate as the organization moves away from its existing product and market base. It then follows that the issue of corporate capability, and in particular the ability of the organization to cope with risk, needs to be understood in some detail by the marketing planner. Without this understanding there is a very real danger that the organization will move too far and too fast into areas in which it will find difficulties in operating effectively. Again, however, this should not be seen simply as an argument for the company to stay where it is currently, since the product life cycle alone necessitates changes both to products and markets if sales and profits are to be maintained or increased. Rather it is an argument for strategic development to reflect objectives, opportunities and capabilities, together with an understanding of the entry and exit barriers to possible market areas. The implications of entry and exit barriers for a market's attractiveness are illustrated in Figure 7.16.

The most attractive segment from the viewpoint of profit is one in which entry barriers are high and exit barriers are low. Few new firms are able to enter, and the poor performers can exit easily. When both entry and exit barriers are high the profit potential is high, although this is generally accompanied by greater levels of risk as the poorer performers, finding it difficult to leave, are forced to fight for share. When both entry and exit barriers are low, firms find it easy both to enter and leave, and returns tend to be stable and low. The worst-case scenario is when barriers to entry are low but exit barriers are high: here firms enter when the market is buoyant, but then find it difficult to leave when there is a downturn. The result is overcapacity, which affects all the players.

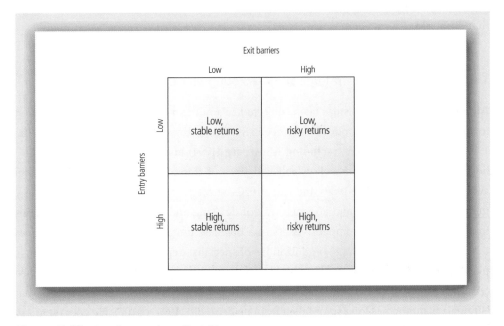

Figure 7.16 Barriers and profitability

7.7 The development of strategies

In the light of what has been discussed so far, it should be apparent that a marketing objective is what the organization wants to achieve in terms of sales volume, market share, and so on (i.e. the ends). How the organization then sets out to achieve these objectives is the *strategy* (i.e. the means). An effective strategy statement should therefore make reference not just to the allocation of resources but also to time scales; inevitably it is broad in scope. Following on from this, the planner then moves to develop the *tactics* and *programme for implementation*. From the viewpoint of the marketing planner, the major aspects of strategy are the individual elements of the marketing mix. Before moving on, however, it is worth focusing on one of the other major influences upon strategic success. Although decisions are typically taken against a background of resource constraint, their effects can often be minimized by the strategist giving full recognition to the importance of the *leverage* that can be gained by the development of one or more *distinctive competences* to gain a comparative marketing advantage. Although the importance of distinctive competences has long been recognized, their strategic significance was highlighted by the results of a study carried out by the American management consultants, McKinsey & Co. Prominent among their findings was that:

" . . . the distinguishing characteristic shared by (successful companies) was that they did one particular thing well. They had developed significant strength in one feature of their business which gave them a comparative advantage over their competitors.*"*

It follows from this that, in developing strategies, the planner needs to identify these distinctive competences and build on them. As an example of how this can be done, the Dominos Pizza chain in the USA developed as its USP (unique selling proposition) rapid delivery times with a refund to the customer if delivery of the pizza took longer than it should.

The changing focus of strategic and marketing planning

Although portfolio analysis has been subjected to a number of criticisms, its contribution to strategic planning has undoubtedly been significant. However, at the beginning of the 1990s, a number of writers, including Mintzberg (1994) and Stacey (1991), began questioning the traditional and well-established lines of thinking about strategic planning. With its origins in the late 1960s and early 1970s, strategic planning had been held up by many as the most logical and effective way of devising and implementing the strategies that would improve the competitiveness of a business unit. However, Mintzberg argues that the creation in many large organizations of specialist departments staffed by strategic planners who were involved in the thinking but not the doing or the implementation has created a series of difficulties and tensions. The net effect of this, he suggests, is that 'strategic planning has long since fallen from its pedestal' (1994, p. 107). He goes on to say that:

"But even now, few people really understand the reason: *strategic planning* is not *strategic thinking*. Indeed, strategic planning often spoils strategic thinking, causing managers to confuse real vision with the manipulation of numbers. And this confusion lies at the heart of the issue: the most successful strategies are visions, not plans.**"**

In making this comment, Mintzberg highlights the way in which the traditional approach to strategic planning is, in essence, *strategic programming*, an activity that involves articulating strategies or visions that already exist. What is needed, he believes, is that managers should understand the differences between planning and strategic thinking so that they can then focus upon what the strategy development process should really be. This process, he suggests, involves capturing what the manager learns from all sources (the soft insights from his or her personal experiences, the experiences of others throughout the organization, and the hard data from market research and the like) and then synthesizing that learning into a vision of the direction that the business should pursue.

Recognition of this means that the role of the planner changes significantly and, for Mintzberg, highlights the way in which the planner's contribution should be *around* rather than *inside* the strategy-making process. In other words, the planner should provide the analyses and data inputs that strategic thinkers need and not the one supposedly correct answer to the strategic challenge being faced.

This redefinition of roles illustrates, in turn, the distinction that needs to be made between the analytical dimension of planning and the synthesis, intuition and creativity that characterize effective strategic thinking. It also goes some way towards highlighting the way in which the formal and traditional approach to planning (Mintzberg, 1994, p. 109):

" . . . rests on the preservation and rearrangement of established categories, the existing levels or strategy [corporate, business, functional], the established types of products (defined as 'strategic business units'), and overlaid on the current units of structure [divisions, departments, etc.].

But real strategic change requires not merely rearranging the established categories, but inventing new ones. Search all those strategic planning diagrams, all those interconnected boxes that supposedly give you strategies, and nowhere will you find a single one that explains the creative act of synthesizing experiences into a novel strategy. Strategy making needs to function beyond the boxes, to encourage the informal learning that produces new perspectives and new combinations. As the saying goes, life is larger than our categories. Planning's failure to transcend the categories explains why it has discouraged serious organizational change. This failure is why formal planning has promoted strategies that are extrapolated from the past or copied from others. Strategic planning has not only amounted to strategic thinking but has often impeded it. Once managers understand this they can avoid other costly misadventures caused by applying formal technique, without judgement and intuition, to problem-solving.**"**

These criticisms of the traditional logical and sequential approach to planning have, in turn, been developed by Stacey (1992), who in his book *Managing Chaos*, argues for a managerial emphasis upon adaptability, intuition, paradox and entrepreneurial creativity in order to cope with an unpredictable and, indeed, inherently unknowable future.

In many ways, Stacey's ideas are a reflection of chaos and complexity theories ('chaos' in these terms refers not to muddle and confusion, but to the behaviour of a system that is governed by simple physical laws but is so unpredictable as to appear random) in which the complexity of interaction between events is so great that the links between cause and effect either disappear or are so difficult to identify as to be meaningless. The implication of this for strategic planning is potentially far-reaching and, according to Stacey, highlights the importance of intuition and the need for managers to deal with problems in a truly holistic fashion. He goes on to suggest that managers 'must learn to reason through induction rather than deduction; and to argue by analogy, to think in metaphor and to accept paradox' (Stacey, 1994, p. 64).

Like Mintzberg, Stacey (1994, p. 65) argues for a greater creativity within organizations and refers to the scientific concept of the 'edge of chaos' as a metaphor for more independence of managerial thought:

*"*Tucked away between stability and instability, at the frontier, non-linear feedback systems generate forms of behaviour that are neither stable nor unstable. They are continuously new and creative. This property applies to non-linear feedback systems no matter where they are found. All human organizations, including businesses, are precisely such non-linear feedback systems; and while it is not necessary or indeed desirable for all organizations to be chaotically creative all the time those that do should not think in terms of stability and adapting to their environment but in terms of using amplifying feedback loops or self-reinforcing mechanisms to shape customer needs.*"*

With regard to the detail of planning and strategy, Stacey's views rest upon the idea that, because of the nature and complexity of the business system, anything useful about the future is essentially unknowable, something which negates the value of the conventional planning wisdom that success depends upon developing a vision of where the company wants to be in five, ten or twenty years' time, the strategy that will achieve this, and a shared culture. Instead, he believes that:

" . . . managers should recognize that these strategic planning meetings every Monday morning serve a ritual rather than a functional purpose rather like the ceremonial laying of the foundation stone on a building. They should recognize too that those elaborate computer-modelled forecasts presented to the board to convince them of the wisdom of a proposed business venture are a fiction, and that their purpose is to allay anxiety rather than perform any genuinely predictive purpose. Real strategy is not derived from this sort of planning. No, real strategy emerges from group dynamics, from the politicking and informal lobbying in the corridors, from the complicated patterns of relationships and interplay of personalities, from the pressure groups that spring up after the formal meeting is over and real success lies not in total stability and 'sticking to your knitting', but in the

tension between stability (in the day-to-day running of the business) and instability (in challenging the status quo). Instability is not just due to ignorance or incompetence, it is a fundamental property of successful business terms.*"*

Given this, he suggests that creative organizations deliberately set out to encourage counter-cultures and subversion. Among the examples that he cites of organizations that have done this with a high degree of success is Honda, which, during the past decade, has hired large numbers of managers in mid-career from other organizations as a means of introducing a series of pressures, challenges and contention into the organization. The effect of this has been to encourage a culture of creative destruction, greater learning and an increase in flexibility (see also Stacey, 1996).

7.8 Summary

In this chapter we have focused on four main areas:

1 The nature and purpose of planning
2 The significance of vision, and the corporate mission and vision
3 The nature and purpose of corporate and marketing objectives
4 How the thinking about the development of the marketing strategy might begin.

The starting point in the planning process involves the strategist in identifying where the organization is currently (where are we now?), and the short- and long-term direction for the organization (where do we want to be?). In addressing this second question, a variety of issues need to be considered, including:

➡ Environmental opportunities and threats (see Chapter 2)
➡ The organization's strategic capability (again, see Chapter 2)
➡ Stakeholders' expectations.

Having done this, it then becomes possible to give far more explicit and realistic consideration to the question of how the organization should go about achieving its objectives.

As a background to the planning process there needs to be agreement on the corporate mission, the mission being an aspirational statement of what the organization is or should attempt to become. The significance of the mission statement has been highlighted by a wide variety of writers, most of whom have given emphasis to its integrating role and to the way in which it provides a strong binding statement of fundamental corporate values – so long as it avoids platitudinous statements.

In developing a mission statement, the strategist needs to take account of a variety of factors, including:

➡ The organization's history, performance and patterns of ownership
➡ Managerial values and expectations

➡ The environment
➡ Resource availability
➡ The existence of any distinctive competences.

Having developed a mission statement and then the vision, the planner is in a far stronger position to begin the process of establishing corporate and marketing objectives. Objectives are typically influenced by several issues, including:

➡ The nature of the business (products, markets and technology)
➡ External factors (societal values, pressure groups, government and legislation)
➡ Organizational culture
➡ Individuals and groups within the organization.

Having identified the organization's corporate and marketing objectives, the marketing planner needs to ensure that they satisfy certain criteria, the four most significant of which are that they are arranged hierarchically, that they are expressed quantitatively, that they are realistic and that there is internal consistency. It is at this stage also that the planner is in a position to identify the nature and size of any gaps that are likely to emerge between where the organization wants to go and where in practice it is capable of going. Once this has been done, it then becomes possible to begin the process of developing the strategies that are to be used to achieve the agreed objectives.

Chapter 8

Market segmentation, targeting and positioning

8.1 Learning objectives

When you have read this chapter you should be able to understand:

(a) the nature and purpose of market segmentation;

(b) the contribution of segmentation to effective marketing planning;

(c) how markets can be segmented, and the criteria that need to be applied if segmentation is to prove cost-effective;

(d) how product positioning follows from the segmentation process;

(e) the bases by which products and brands can be positioned effectively.

8.2 Introduction

In Chapters 4–6, we focused on approaches to environmental, customer and competitor analysis, and the frameworks within which strategic marketing planning can best take place. Against this background we now turn to the question of market segmentation, and to the ways in which companies need to position themselves in order to maximize their competitive advantage and serve their target markets in the most effective manner. It does need to be recognized, however, that for many organizations the strategic issues of market segmentation, market targeting and positioning often take on only a minimal role. Saunders (1987, p. 25), for example, points to research that suggested that a substantial proportion of British companies still fail to segment their market. He quotes the marketing director of one consumer durables company as saying:

"We have not broken the customers down. We have always held the opinion that the market is wide ... and the product has wide appeal, therefore why break the market down at all?"

A similar comment emerged from a sales director, who stated:

"We do not see the market as being made up of specific segments. Our market is made up of the whole industry."

There are several possible reasons for views such as these, although, in the case of companies with a broadly reactive culture, it is often due largely to a degree of organizational inertia, which leads to the firm being content to stay in the same sector of the market for some considerable time. It is only when the effects of a changing environment become overwhelmingly evident that serious consideration is given to the need for repositioning in order to appeal to new sectors of the market. For other organizations, however, a well-thought-out policy of segmentation plays a pivotal role in the determination of success. It is the recognition of this that has led to the suggestion in recent years that the essence of strategic marketing can be summed up by the initials STP – segmentation, targeting and positioning. This is illustrated in Figure 8.1.

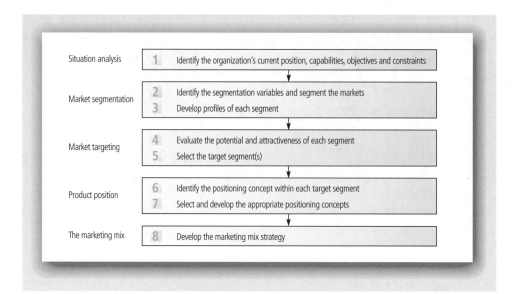

Figure 8.1   The eight stages of the segmentation, targeting and positioning process

Not all writers are in favour of segmentation so before we examine the methods used to segment markets, it is worth looking briefly at their views. Bliss (1980), for example, has suggested that, while many marketing managers acknowledge the rationale of segmentation, many are dissatisfied with it as a concept, partly because it is inapplicable or difficult to apply in many markets, but also because emphasis is too often given to the techniques of segmentation at the expense of the market itself and the competitive situation that exists. Equally, Resnik et al. (1979) have suggested that changing values, new lifestyles, and the rising costs of products and services argue the case for what they call 'counter-segmentation'; in other words, an aggregation of various parts of the market rather than their subdivision. The majority of writers, however, acknowledge the very real strategic importance of segmentation and, in particular, the ways in which it enables the organization to use its resources more effectively and with less wastage.

8.3 The nature and purpose of segmentation

During the past 30 years, market segmentation has developed and been defined in a variety of ways. In essence, however, it is the process of dividing a varied and differing group of buyers or potential buyers into smaller groups, within which broadly similar patterns of buyers' needs exist. By doing this, the marketing planner is attempting to break the market into more strategically manageable parts, which can then be targeted and satisfied far more precisely by making a series of perhaps small changes to the marketing mix. The rationale is straightforward and can be expressed most readily in terms of the fact that only rarely does a single product or marketing approach appeal to the needs and wants of all buyers. Because of this, the marketing strategist needs to categorize buyers on the basis both of their characteristics and their specific product needs, with a view then to adapting either the product or the marketing programme, or both, to satisfy these different tastes and demands.

The potential benefits of a well-developed segmentation strategy can therefore be considerable, since an organization should be able to establish and strengthen its position in the market and, in this way, operate more effectively. Not only does it then become far more difficult for a competitor to attack, but it also allows the organization to build a greater degree of market sector knowledge and customer loyalty.

Although the arguments for segmentation appear strong, it is only one of three quite distinct approaches to marketing strategy which exist. These are:

1 Undifferentiated or mass marketing
2 Product-variety or differentiated marketing
3 Target or concentrated marketing.

These are illustrated in Figure 8.2.

Undifferentiated, differentiated and concentrated (or atomized) marketing

A policy of *undifferentiated* or *mass marketing* emerges when the firm deliberately ignores any differences that exist within its markets and decides instead to focus upon a feature that appears to be common or acceptable to a wide variety of buyers. Perhaps the earliest, best-known and most frequently quoted example of this is Henry Ford's strategy with the Model T, which buyers could have 'in any colour as long as it is black'. A more

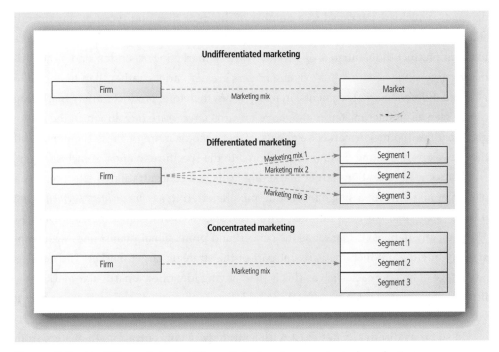

Figure 8.2 Undifferentiated, differentiated and concentrated marketing

recent example of undifferentiated marketing is provided by Black & Decker, which in the late 1970s was faced with a drop in its worldwide market share of the power tool market from 20 to 15 per cent as Japanese firms began marketing their brands in a far more aggressive manner. In an attempt to counter this, Black & Decker moved away from a policy of customizing products for each market and concentrated instead on making a smaller number of products that could be sold everywhere with the same basic marketing approach. The success of this undifferentiated global marketing strategy was subsequently reflected in the fact that, by the mid-1980s, Black & Decker had more than regained its 20 per cent share of the market.

The obvious advantage of an undifferentiated strategy such as this is that it offers scope for enormous cost economies in production, promotion and distribution, since the organization is dealing with a standardized product. At the same time it needs to be recognized that undifferentiated marketing is becoming increasingly rare, largely because of ever greater degrees of competition and the increasingly sophisticated and fragmented nature of the majority of developed markets. In these circumstances, the scope that exists for marketing a product aimed at a broad sector of the market is reduced significantly.

This de-massification of markets has led many organizations towards strategies of *product-variety marketing* and, ultimately, target marketing. As an example of this, Coca-Cola for many years produced only one type of drink for the entire market in the expectation that it would have a mass-market appeal. The success of the strategy is now part of marketing folklore. The company's strategy was changed, however, partly to cope with an increasingly aggressive competitive environment and partly to develop and capitalize on different patterns of consumer demand. As a result, the company's marketing effort today now reflects buyers' needs for a far wider variety of tastes and demands, which are packaged in a number of different sizes and types of container. It should be emphasized that the move on the part of many organizations in recent years towards product-differentiated or product-variety marketing has often had as its primary purpose the need to offer existing buyers greater variety, rather than to appeal to new and different market segments. In many ways, therefore, product-variety marketing can be seen as an interim step in the move towards *target marketing*, in which the strategist identifies the major market segments, targets one or more of these segments, and then develops marketing programmes tailored to the specific demands of each segment.

For some organizations target marketing leads to a concentration of effort on a single target market with a single marketing mix. Referred to as *concentrated segmentation*, it is a strategy that has been pursued with great success by the piano makers Steinway. The company defines its market as the concert and professional pianist and, while others may buy the product, they are not part of the strategic target market. The obvious advantage of an approach such as this is that, having identified a particular market, the firm can then control costs by advertising and distributing *only* to the market segment it views as its primary target.

In so far as disadvantages exist with a strategy of concentration, they stem from the possibility of missed opportunities; it may be the case, for example, that significant opportunities exist elsewhere but that the firm's single-minded approach to just one part of the market fails to recognize this. Equally, the organization can prove vulnerable either to a direct and sustained attack by a competitor or to a downturn in demand within the target market. Because of this, many marketing strategists pursue a policy of *multiple segmentation*, in which the firm focuses upon a variety of different segments and then develops a different marketing mix for each. This is often described as a 'rifle' rather than a 'shotgun' approach, in that the company can focus on buyers they have the greatest chance of satisfying rather than scattering the marketing effort. An example of its use is that of the Burton Group (now renamed Arcadia), which throughout the 1980s and 1990s developed and refined a highly segmented strategy with a series of retail concepts such as Top Shop, Top Man, Burton Menswear, Dorothy Perkins and Principles. In doing this, specific attention was paid to a variety of distinct customer groups by means of different types of retail outlet, each with its own distinct target market, image and customer appeal.

The ways in which a segment's characteristics influence the allocation of marketing effort is illustrated in the case of the retail banking sector, where there are four customer groups:

1 The very rich – a small but strategically significant group with substantial assets
2 The rich
3 High net worth individuals (HNWIs) – a semi-mass market with significant assets available for investment
4 Medium net worth individuals (MNWIs) – the bulk of the market both for the high street banks and building societies.

Each of these groups has very different sets of expectations, which need to be reflected in the organization's marketing strategy.

The rationale for target marketing and multiple segmentation can be seen to be straightforward, and stems from an expectation on the part of the organization that it will be able to generate a higher total level of sales by making specific appeals to a variety of different target groups. At the same time, however, a strategy of multiple segmentation almost invariably leads to cost increases in several areas, including production, promotion, distribution, inventory and administration. The choice between undifferentiated marketing, product-variety marketing and target marketing therefore involves a series of trade-offs, the most obvious of which is an increase in cost against an expectation of higher total returns. As a prelude to deciding which of these three approaches to adopt, the strategist needs to identify clearly the organization's capability, the opportunities that exist and the level of market coverage that is possible or realistic.

Perhaps the most extreme example of a trade-off is to be seen in *customized* or *atomized marketing*, where the product or service is modified to match the specific demands of each buyer. This is discussed in Illustration 8.1.

Illustration 8.1 Levi's and its use of one-to-one marketing

The idea of one-to-one marketing in the high street clothing market reached a peak in the 1950s and 1960s, when Burton's the Tailors developed a large and loyal customer base who often saved weekly through clothing accounts to buy several suits during the year, each of which was made to order. The customer went into the local Burton's for a fitting and the size, style and details of the chosen cloth were sent off to the company's factory. Several weeks later the suit arrived. The measurements were then stored so that they could be used the next time the customer wanted a suit.

Although bespoke tailoring still exists at the top end of the market, a combination of rising costs and more varied customer demands for off-the-peg led Burton's to begin pursuing a very different mass-market strategy in the 1970s. However, the thinking behind one-to-one marketing is potentially attractive and led to its trial in 1994 by the jeans manufacturer Levi's.

Levi's 'Personal Pair' trial was tested in four sites across America: New York; Cincinnati; Columbus, Ohio; and Peabody, Massachusetts.

It used customized clothing softwear developed by a specialist American company to fit a pair of tapered-leg jeans precisely to the body. Customers are measured for their jeans by a trained sales assistant, who feeds details into the computer. The PC then generates the code number of a pair of trial jeans with the correct measurements, which the customer tries on. From this point, small changes, as little as half an inch, can be made to perfect the fit.

Levi says that, on average, it takes two to three prototypes before a customer is totally satisfied. When the buyer is happy, the coordinates of the final prototype are sent by modem over ordinary phone lines to the Levi jeans factory in Mountain City, Tennessee, where a dedicated team of sewing operators makes the final pair, delivering them within three weeks. Sewn into the waistband of the jeans is a barcode with an individual customer number kept on computer by the company. The owner of the jeans can call Levi's at any time and order a new pair, in a range of colours and finishes, using the barcode.

Source: *Sunday Times*, 11 June 1995, p. 6.

Where there are no apparent natural segments, a more formal procedure needs to be adopted. Several approaches exist, the most popular of which consists of three steps:

1 *The survey stage*, where the researcher conducts informal interviews and focus group discussions in order to gain insight into motivations, attitudes and behaviour. Following this, the researcher then takes a formalized approach designed to identify:
   - Attributes and their importance ratings
   - Brand awareness and brand ratings
   - Product usage patterns
   - Attitudes toward the product and brand category
   - Respondents' demographics, psychographics and mediagraphics.

2 *The analysis stage*, where the researcher attempts to identify clusters within the market. In doing this, the aim is to identify those clusters that are internally homogeneous but externally very different from all other clusters.

3 *The profiling stage*, where each cluster is profiled in terms of attitudes, behaviour, demographics, psychographics and media consumption habits. Each segment can then be given a name based on a dominant distinguishing characteristic. In a study of the leisure market, for example, Andreasen and Belk (1980, pp. 112–20) found six market segments:

- The passive homebody
- The active sports enthusiast
- The inner-directed self-sufficient
- The culture patron
- The active homebody
- The socially active.

The development of segments over time

Having identified segments within a market, the strategist needs to recognize that this is not a once-and-for-all exercise, but rather one that needs monitoring and updating if it is to maintain its usefulness. This is illustrated by the ways in which attitudes to a given product's country of origin can change, possibly dramatically, over time. Thirty years ago, for example, attitudes in Britain to Japanese products were generally negative, largely because of perceptions of poor quality and inadequate levels of after-sales support. These attitudes began changing in the 1970s and today Japanese products are generally perceived very differently. The implications of this for preference patterns is significant and does, of course, need to be reflected in methods of segmentation. By the same token, Skoda for many years targeted a relatively poor segment of the market, but over the past decade has increasingly moved into a series of very different target markets (here, it might be useful to refer to Illustration 5.3, in which Skoka's changed approach is discussed).

8.4 Approaches to segmenting markets

The majority of markets can be segmented in a variety of ways. For the marketing strategist, the process of identifying the potentially most effective way begins with an initial examination of the market, with a view to identifying whether 'natural segments' already exist.

In the USA in the 1960s, for example, both Volkswagen and Toyota identified the growth potential of a market sector that was concerned with car size and fuel economy, a segment that the three major domestic manufacturers had either failed to identify or had chosen to ignore. Following the Arab–Israeli conflict of the early 1970s and the subsequent oil crisis, consumers became far more energy conscious and this part of the market grew dramatically. It was several years before domestic manufacturers were able to capitalize on these opportunities. Equally, Honda in the 1960s and 1970s identified and then targeted a young(er) and essentially middle-class market for small and medium-sized motorcycles in the United States that the other players within the market, such as Harley Davidson, had traditionally ignored. The advertising campaign featured college students riding the smaller Honda bikes and used the strapline 'You meet the nicest people on a Honda'. More recently, Mercedes, Porsche and BMW have all targeted the ageing baby boomer generation whose children have left home, have insurance policies maturing, are downsizing and rethinking their priorities, and who are not only searching for their lost youth, but more importantly have the money to indulge themselves.

There are several lessons to be learned from these sorts of examples, including the ways in which new segments can be identified by examining the sequence of variables that consumers consider when choosing a product. One way of doing this involves categorizing current consumer segments on the basis of a hierarchy of attributes. There are those, for example, whose major preoccupation is price (price-dominant), while others are more concerned with the brand (brand-dominant), quality (quality-dominant) or country of origin (nation-dominant).

In the case of hi-fi and audio equipment, for example, a buyer might only be willing to consider products from a Japanese manufacturer – this would be the first-level preference. The second-level preference may then be for, say, Sony followed by Panasonic. After this, issues of the price range and choice of outlet begin to emerge.

Recognition of hierarchies of attitudes such as these has led to the emergence of *market-partitioning theory*, with segments being determined on the basis of particular combinations such as quality/service/brand, price/type/brand, and so on. Underlying this is the belief that each combination will then reflect distinct demographic and psychographic differences.

The question of *how* to segment the market provides the basis for much of the remainder of this chapter. In essence, however, this involves deciding between *a priori* and *post hoc* methods. An a priori approach is based on the notion that the planner decides in advance of any research the basis for segmentation he or she intends to use. Thus, typically the planner will categorize buyers on the basis of their usage patterns (heavy, medium, light and non-users), demographic characteristics (age, sex and income) or psychographic profiles (lifestyle and personality). Having decided this, the planner then goes on to conduct a programme of research in order to identify the size, location and potential of each segment as a prelude to deciding on which of the segments the marketing effort is to be concentrated.

Post hoc segmentation, by contrast, involves segmenting the market on the basis of research findings. Thus, research might highlight particular attitudes, attributes or benefits with which particular groups of customers are concerned. This information can then be used as the basis for deciding how best to divide the market. One of the best-known – if oldest – examples of this is Haley's research into the toothpaste market in the early 1960s, which highlighted levels of concern among mothers about tooth decay in their children (Haley, 1963). Although a number of brands claiming decay prevention existed at the time, the size and potential for the growth of this segment had not previously been recognized. One result of Haley's work was to increase the number of companies that recognized the value of targeting this segment.

In making these comments, it must be emphasized that both a priori and post hoc approaches to segmentation have their place, and that their real value to the strategist depends largely on how much knowledge of the market the strategist has. If, for example, previous research or experience has enabled the planner to identify key segmentation dimensions within the market, then an a priori approach is likely to be adequate. When, however, the market is new, changing or unrelated to the planner's experience, a post hoc approach to determine the key segmentation variables is likely to prove more valuable (see Illustration 8.2).

Illustration 8.2 The changing nature of segmentation

Thinking on segmentation is changing in a variety of ways. In discussing this, Fifield and Gilligan (1996, p. 97) highlight a number of issues, arguing that far too many organizations base their approaches to segmentation on the sort of thinking that is reflected in the left-hand column rather than in the right.

Past	Future
Correlation	Causality
Description	Motivation

Past and future. When asked how they segment what they are doing in the area, almost invariably managers will start to describe their past experiences with customers; how people reacted; what they did; and even an analysis of where the last three years' sales have come from. As we all know, the future is unlikely to be a straight-line extrapolation from the past, much as we might like it to be so.

As marketers trying to put together a marketing strategy which will deliver what the business needs, our concerns must be for the future. Our attention must centre on where we should invest our marketing spend and our energy for both short- and long-term returns from the marketplace. The past has gone. There is some value to be gained from understanding the lessons of the past, but only if they can improve our future activity.

Correlation and causality. The second problem is that, when your managers are pressed to explain the rationale behind their segments, you are often presented with a whole series of correlations. What we need to uncover is some degree of causality. There may be some relationships which an in-depth study of our existing customers could expose. However, it is dangerous to build a strategy on relationships which lack an identifiable cause. In other words, is there an underlying motivational reason why people act in a certain way that we can understand from their circumstances?

Description and motivation. Finally, there is a general misunderstanding between description and motivation. An in-depth description of our existing customer base and our existing 'segments' in terms of age profiles, sex, income, occupation, education, family life stage or even socio-economic grouping is only really valid if we believe that these characteristics are motivational. Descriptors tend to come from the past. 'This is how last year's customers looked.' Only very rarely will a customer group described in these terms surprise us by acting in a way which is unique relative to the rest of the market.

The only thing we know for sure about the future is that our ideas and predictions will be wrong, but it is still worthwhile working to reduce the margin of error. It is our job to ensure that we make the best possible return on the resources or effort which the organization invests in its markets. Returns are based upon informed judgement of how a segment will respond to our offer and what will motivate it to buy.

8.5 Factors affecting the feasibility of segmentation

Market segmentation works at two levels, the strategic and the tactical. At a strategic level it has a direct link to decisions on positioning. At a tactical level it relates to the question of which customer groups are to be targeted. However, for a market segment to justify attention, six conditions typically need to be satisfied. The segment must be:

1 *Measurable*. Although in many consumer markets measurement is generally a relatively straightforward exercise, it is often a more difficult process with industrial or technical goods. This is due largely to the relative lack of specific published data.
2 *Accessible*. In some cases it may be possible to identify a sizeable and potentially profitable segment but then, either because of a lack of finance or in-house expertise, this potential may be difficult to exploit.
3 *Substantial*. If the strategist is to justify the development of a segment, the exercise must be cost-effective. The size and value of the segment is therefore an important determinant of this decision. Size should, of course, be seen in relative rather than absolute terms, since what may be too small to be considered by one organization may be appropriate to another, smaller, company. Morgan, for example, has concentrated on a very small and specialized part of the car market that is of no interest to the larger firms such as Ford, Toyota and Volkswagen.
4 *Unique* in its response, so that it can be distinguished from other market segments.
5 *Appropriate* to the organization's objectives and resources.
6 *Stable*, so that its behaviour in the future can be predicted with a sufficient degree of confidence.

Against the background of these six conditions, it should be possible to evaluate segments on the basis of two criteria: the attractiveness of the segment and the organization's ability to exploit the value of the segment. The framework for this is illustrated in

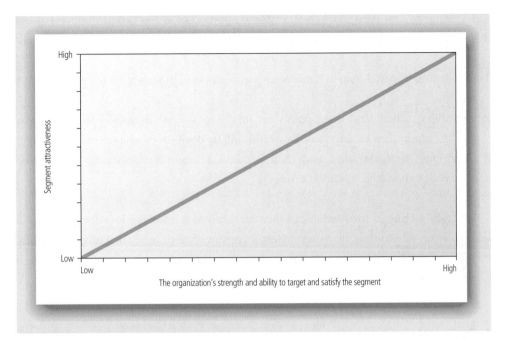

Labels on the figure: High; Low (y-axis "Segment attractiveness"); Low; High (x-axis "The organization's strength and ability to target and satisfy the segment")

Figure 8.3 The evaluation of segments (segment attractiveness is determined by factors such as the segment's size; growth potential; the intensity, bases and costs of competition; and opportunities for profit)

Figure 8.3. Here, the planner begins by plotting where on the attractiveness scale each segment might be positioned. Attention then turns to the question of the organization's ability to target and satisfy each segment's demands.

8.6 Approaches to segmentation

Although a wide variety of methods of segmentation have been developed over the past 40 years, their real value to the strategist in any given situation depends to a very large extent on the nature and characteristics of the product, and the market in which the company is operating. The task with which the strategist is faced involves deciding upon the most appropriate single method or combination of methods for dividing up the market. In the case of consumer goods, for example, the most commonly used methods have typically been geographic, demographic and benefit measures, while in the industrial sector they have typically been usage rate, source loyalty and location. Most of these measures, however, are at best partial, and the past few years have witnessed a growing willingness on the part of many companies, particularly in the consumer sector, to make greater use of more complex methods of segmentation in order to build up more detailed and useful pictures of their target markets. One result of this has been an upsurge of the interest expressed in behavioural and psychographic techniques as a means of gaining a greater insight into the question of *why* people behave in particular ways.

The thread that runs through all of these approaches is the need to understand in detail the structure of the market. This is most typically done by focusing on three areas:

1 Developing a spatial map of consumers' perceptions of brands within a given market sector
2 Identifying consumers' ideal points on this map so that demand for a particular product might then be estimated by examining its position in relation to the ideal
3 Developing a model that will then provide a basis for predicting consumers' responses to new and modified products.

This sort of picture of the market can then be taken a step further by superimposing a second map illustrating in greater detail consumer profiles. This might typically include sex (male versus female), age (young, middle-aged, old), income group (high earners versus low earners) and marital status.

8.7 The bases for segmentation

In 1978, Wind (1978, p. 317) commented that 'over the years almost all variables have been used as bases for market segmentation'. There are several possible explanations for this, the most significant of which is the difficulty that is typically encountered in putting into practice the normative theory of segmentation. In other words, while the marketing planner might well recognize that customer characteristics should determine strategy, all too often this is reversed, with managers focusing on the probable response of different segments to a previously determined strategy. Whilst, in the majority of circumstances, feedback will ensure that changes are subsequently made to the strategy to take account of the response received, it is often the case, as Baker (1985, p. 142) has pointed out, that 'the managerial approach is more closely akin to product differentiation than a normative approach to market segmentation'.

Although, as we observed earlier, a wide variety of variables have been used to segment markets, the majority of these can be grouped into four categories (see Figure 8.4):

1 Geographic and geodemographic
2 Demographic
3 Behavioural
4 Psychographic.

Only rarely, however, can just one of these dimensions be used to segment a market effectively, something that is reflected both in Illustration 8.3 and in a comment by Wind (1978, p. 318):

*"*In contrast to the theory of segmentation that implies that there is a single best way of segmenting a market, the range and variety of marketing decisions suggest that any attempt to use a single basis for segmentation (such as psychographic, brand reference, or product usage) for all marketing decisions may result in incorrect marketing decisions as well as a waste of resources.*"*

Geographic and geodemographic
Geographic: region, climate, population density.
Geodemographic: ACORN, MOSAIC, PiNPOINT, SUPERPROFILES, DEFINE, PiN, FiNPiN

Demographic
Age, sex, education, occupation, religion, race, nationality, family size, family life cycle, SAGACITY

Behavioural
Attitudes, knowledge, benefits, user status, usage rate, loyalty status, readiness to buy, occasions

Psychographic
Personality, lifestyle, VALS, AIO, 4Cs, Monitor

Figure 8.4 The major bases for segmenting consumer markets

Illustration 8.3 Recommendations for the bases of segmentation

Some of the most interesting work on market segmentation has been carried out in the USA by Yoram Wind (1978). One of the undoubted attractions of his work is its strong element of pragmatism and the recognition that he gives to the problems typically experienced by marketing managers in trying to develop and implement an effective segmentation strategy. This has led him to a series of recommendations for the bases of segmentation, which Baker (1985, pp. 142–3) has neatly summarized:

For general understanding of a market
➡ Benefits sought (in industrial markets, the criterion used is purchase decision)
➡ Product purchase and usage patterns
➡ Needs
➡ Brand loyalty and switching pattern
➡ A hybrid of the variables above.

For positioning studies
➡ Product usage
➡ Product preference

➡ Benefits sought
➡ A hybrid of the variables above.

For new product concepts (and new product introduction)
➡ Reaction to new concepts (intention to buy and preference over current brand)
➡ Benefits sought.

For pricing decisions
➡ Price sensitivity
➡ Deal proneness
➡ Price sensitivity by purchase/usage patterns.

For advertising decisions
➡ Benefits sought
➡ Media usage
➡ Psychographic/lifestyle
➡ A hybrid of the variables above and/or purchase/usage patterns.

For distribution decisions
➡ Store loyalty and patronage
➡ Benefits sought in store selection.

8.8 Geographic and geodemographic techniques

Geographic approaches

Geographic segmentation – one of the earliest and still most commonly used methods of segmentation, within both the consumer and the industrial sectors – involves dividing markets into different geographical units such as countries, regions, counties and cities. The strategist then chooses to operate either in just a few or in all of these. Typically, however, if a company pursues this second approach, minor modifications are often made to the marketing mix used for different geographical areas in order to take account of different regional tastes and preferences. In the case of the car industry, for example, the majority of manufacturers, while selling a particular model throughout Europe, will typically make a series of minor changes to the design and to the way in which the product is promoted and sold in order to reflect local differences, preferences and legislative demands. Similarly, food manufacturers modify the taste of the product to cater for regional taste differences. Across Europe, for example, companies such as Nestlé vary the strength and flavour of coffee to reflect regional preferences for stronger or weaker coffees. With other products, such as consumer electronics, geographical differences also need to be reflected in strategy. Makers of stereo equipment, for example, offer products that vary by region. Europeans tend to want small, unobtrusive, high-performance equipment, while many Americans prefer large speakers that, as one anonymous commentator said, 'rise from the floor of living rooms like the columns of an ancient temple'.

Among the undoubted attractions of geographic segmentation to the strategist is its flexibility and its apparent simplicity. It is the combination of these, together with its broad applicability, that has led to its widespread use. At the same time, however, it is a relatively unsophisticated approach to categorization and one that at best gives only a partial view of buying motives.

Geodemographic approaches

Largely because of the limitations of geography, a considerable amount of work has been done in Britain over the past few years in an attempt to improve on the traditional methods of geographic segmentation. One outcome of this has been the development of a variety of geodemographic systems such as ACORN (A Classification Of Residential Neighbourhoods), which classify people by where they live. Based on the idea that 'birds of a feather flock together', it gives recognition to the fact that people with broadly similar economic, social and lifestyle characteristics tend to congregate in particular neighbourhoods and exhibit similar patterns of purchasing behaviour and outlook.

The essential purpose of geodemographics is therefore to provide the base for targeting customers in particular areas who exhibit similar behaviour patterns.

The first attempt to formalize this and demonstrate its potential to the strategist was carried out in Liverpool in 1973 by Richard Webber. Working subsequently with the Census Office at a national level, Webber applied techniques of cluster analysis to identify thirty-eight separate neighbourhood types, each of which was different in terms of its population, housing and socio-economic characteristics. The potential value of this to the market research industry was subsequently recognized by Kenneth Baker (1982) of the British Market Research Bureau, who identified the scope that the system offered for controlling the fieldwork of the bureau's Target Group Index (TGI). The respondents in the TGI survey were categorized on the basis of Webber's neighbourhood groups, and illustrated graphically 'that respondents in different neighbourhood groups displayed significantly different propensities to buy specific products and services'.

Following this, Webber subsequently joined Consolidated Analysis Centres Inc. (CACI) and concentrated on developing the technique further in order to achieve higher levels of discrimination. The result was a classification of households that included agricultural areas, modern family housing owned by people with high incomes, older housing of intermediate status multiracial areas, high status non-family areas, and so on, that is used as a major method of market location. Specific applications of the technique include:

1 The identification of new retail sites
2 The selection of sales territories
3 The allocation of marketing resources
4 Media selection
5 Leaflet distribution
6 Decisions on which products and services to promote in particular retail outlets.

Using this profile, specific areas of high and low consumption can be identified from the ACORN 'buying power' indices. An example of this is ACORN type J35, which consists of 'villages with wealthy older commuters, have 2.4 times the national average proportion of households with two cars, and 2.7 times the proportion of those living in seven or more rooms'. Using information such as this, market targeting becomes both easier and far more accurate.

This work on the ACORN system of classification has led subsequently to a major reassessment of the ways in which geographic techniques might be used in the most effective way. One result of this has been the development of a variety of other geodemographic forms of classification, the common element of which is their use of census enumeration district (ED) data. ACORN, for example, uses regularly updated census variables that take account of the demographic, housing and social aspects of EDs. Their clustering techniques then enable customers to be matched to an ACORN type and, by the postcode, to the relevant ED.

Other geodemographic systems are broadly similar to this, although each uses a variety of other variables. MOSAIC, for example, includes financial data at postcode level and then relies on aggregated individual addresses within a postcode to reduce the errors encountered in matching postcodes to EDs. Other systems, such as PiNPOINT, base their clustering techniques on a larger sample and improvements to the grid referencing of EDs so that they more accurately match postcodes. Such developments represent a very real attempt to overcome some of the inevitable problems and inaccuracies of geodemographic analysis. However, in commenting on this, Joseph and Yorke (1989, p. 12) have said:

*"*It must be recognized that despite claims from commercial companies, there are inaccuracies within all the geodemographic systems. Many of the errors are bound up firstly with the difficulty of matching EDs to postcodes and secondly trying to reflect as far as possible the changes in housing since the last census.*"*

8.9 Demographic segmentation

The second major method of segmentation, and probably the one most frequently used, rests on the assumption that markets can be subdivided into groups on the basis of one or more demographic variables such as age, sex, income, education, occupation, religion, race, nationality, family size and stage reached in the family life cycle. Here, we will concentrate on just three of these variables: age and the family life cycle; income and occupation; and sex.

An undoubted attraction of demographic segmentation is the wide availability and easy interpretation of the data, and it is this – together with the fact that not only can most consumer markets generally be divided relatively easily along these lines, but also that purchase behaviour often correlates highly with demographic segmentation – that have combined to make it such a convenient, easily understood and frequently used approach. In recent years, considerable attention has been paid to the ways in which specific demographic variables can be used more effectively, with the result that variables such as age and life cycle, income, and sex have all been greatly refined. As an example of this, firms such as Lego, Toys 'R' Us and the Early Learning Centre give full recognition to the differences that exist between children of various ages, with the result that toys are now designed to fall into highly specific age categories. In this way, not only is the development potential of the child maximized, but the task of choosing toys by parents, friends and relatives is made infinitely easier. A similar, if perhaps rather more esoteric, recognition of the importance of age and life cycle is reflected in the marketing strategies of various petfood manufacturers who, over the past few years, have developed different dog foods for puppies, adult dogs, older dogs, overweight dogs and dogs with 'sensitive stomachs'. More frequently, however, the significance of life cycle is reflected in the notion of a *family life cycle* (FLC), the details of which are illustrated in Figure 8.5.

The family life cycle

The idea of a family life cycle can be traced back to Rowntree's work in the early part of the twentieth century, and while changes have occurred since then to the pattern through which the family passes, the concept is still the same. Today, the nine-stage

Stages in the family life cycle	Buying patterns
1 Bachelor stage: young, single people living at home	Few financial commitments. Recreation and fashion orientated Buy: cars, entertainment items, holidays
2 Newly married couples: young, no children	Better off financially than they are likely to be in the near future; high purchase rate of consumer desirables Buy: cars, white goods, furniture
3 Full nest 1: youngest child under six	House buying is at a peak; liquid assets are low Dissatisfied with level of savings and financial position generally Buy: medicines, toys, baby food, white goods
4 Full nest 2: youngest child six or over	Financial position is improving; a higher proportion of wives are working Buy: wider variety of foods, bicycles, pianos
5 Full nest 3: older married couples with dependent children	Financial position is improving yet further; a greater proportion of wives work and some children get jobs. Increasing purchase of desirables Buy: better furniture, unnecessary appliances and more luxury goods
6 Empty nest 1: older married couples, no children at home, head of household still in the workforce	Home ownership is at a peak; the financial situation has improved and savings have increased. Interested in travel, recreation and self-education. Not interested in new products Buy: holidays, luxuries and home improvements
7 Empty nest 2: Older married, no children living at home, head of household retired	Substantial reduction in income Buy: medical products and appliances that aid health, sleep and digestion
8 Solitary survivor in the workforce	Income still high but may sell home
9 Solitary survivor, retired	Same medical and product needs as group 7 Substantial cut in income. Need for attention and security.

Figure 8.5 The family life cycle and its implications for buying behaviour (adapted from Wells and Gubar, 1966)

FLC that was developed by Wells and Gubar (1966) is still the one to which reference is made most frequently. The potential strategic value of the FLC stems from the way in which it highlights the different and changing financial situation and priorities of the family as it moves through the nine stages. By recognizing and taking account of these differences, the strategist should be more easily able to develop a marketing programme that satisfies the *specific* rather than the general demands of target groups.

Despite its apparent attractions, the FLC has been subjected to a series of criticisms in recent years. For the most part, these stem from the significance and implications of changes taking place within society that are at best reflected only marginally in the basic FLC model (refer back to pp. 142–7, in which we discussed some of the changes taking place within society). Implicit in FLC thinking, for example, is a particular view of the role of women that is some way removed from today's reality, where the proportion of women working even during the early stages of their children's lives is high. Equally, the model fails to reflect high divorce rates and the large numbers of single-parent families. Because of criticisms such as these, fundamental questions have been raised about the model's validity and usefulness. However, defenders of the model have argued that it is simply a summary demographic variable that combines the effects of age, marital status, career status (income), and the presence or absence of children. This can then be used *together* with other variables to reflect reality. Reading (1988, p. 9), for example, has pointed out that:

" There is a distinctive life time pattern to saving and spending when we are in our twenties and thirties – getting married, buying houses, having children – we borrow and spend. When we are old and retired, we 'dissave' and spend. In middle age, therefore, we have to save like blazes to repay debts and build up capital for our old age.*"*

A slightly different version of the family life cycle has in recent years been proposed by Research Services in the form of SAGACITY. The basic thesis of the SAGACITY grouping is that people have different aspirations and behaviour patterns as they go through their life cycle. Four main stages of the life cycle are defined (dependent, pre-family, family and late), which are then subdivided by income and occupation groups.

The psychological life cycle

As an extension both to the traditional thinking about the family life cycle and as a recognition of a number of fundamental – and increasingly evident – weaknesses of the FLC model, work recently has focused upon the idea of a *psychological life cycle*, in which chronological age by itself is not necessarily the factor of greatest significance in determining consumption patterns. Rather it is the transformation of attitudes and expectations that becomes a more important factor, something which is reflected in Neugarten's (1968) research in the USA:

" Age has become a poor predictor of the timing of life events, as well as a poor predictor of a person's health, work status, family status, and therefore, also of a person's interests, pre-occupations, and needs. We have multiple images of persons of the same age: there is the 70-year-old in a wheelchair and the 70-year-old on the tennis court. Likewise, there are 35-year-olds sending children off to college and 35-year-olds furnishing the nursery for newborns, producing in turn, first-time grandparenthood for persons who range in age from 35 to 75.*"*

The significance of the psychological life cycle is also illustrated by the emergence of the 'kidults' segment, to which we made brief reference earlier (see the Appendix to Chapter 5), and by the way in which important target markets for Microsoft's X Box and Sony's Playstation are young adults as well as teenagers. Equally, Reebok and Adidas brands are owned by as many 25- to 44-year-olds as 15- to 24-year-olds.

Income and occupation

The second major category of demographic variable focuses upon *income* and *occupation*, the combination of which is reflected in the JICNARS approach to social classification.

Developed in the immediate post-war period, the JICNARS classification of A, B, C1, C2, D and E social classes proved for many years to be a popular, enduring and easily understood method of classification. Increasingly, however, it was seen to be an imprecise method of segmenting a market, since social class today is a far less accurate predictor of income and spending patterns than was once the case. It has also been argued that social class gives little *real* insight into a household's level of disposable income, particularly where there are several wage earners. Largely because of this, a considerable amount of work has been done in recent years in an attempt to develop it further and to identify better alternative methods of discrimination. It was this that led in 1999 to the revised JICNARS approach to social classification that appears in Figure 8.6.

The problems of the early thinking on social class as a basis for segmentation have also been highlighted by O'Brien and Ford (1988, pp. 289–332), who commented:

" The trends today are towards a more disparate family group, less inclined to share their meals and leisure time as a household unit, but following their own interests and tastes with like-minded peers. Whether peer groups share the same 'social' background is less important than their shared pursuit. Equally, Social Class does not act as an accurate gauge of disposable income. A C2 or D may not intellectually be performing the same role in the job market as a B or C1, but may well have more cash with which to acquire the trappings of our society. The financial chains of private education are likely to constrain the AB as

	NS-SEC	The old JICNARS	and the new
Class 1a	Large employers, higher level managers: company directors, senior police/fire/prison/military officers, newspaper editors, football managers (with squad of 25 plus), restauranteurs	A Professional	Class 1
Class 1b	Professionals: doctors, solicitors, engineers, teachers, airline pilots	B Managerial/technical	Class 2
Class 2	Associate professionals: journalists, nurse/midwifes, actor/musicians, military NCO/junior police/fire/prison officers, lower managers (fewer than 25 staff)	C1 Skilled (non-manual)	Class 3
Class 3	Intermediate occupations: secretaries, air stewardesses, driving instructors, footballers (employee sportsmen), telephone operators	C1 Skilled (non-manual)	Class 3
Class 4	Small employers/managers, non-professional self-employed: publicans, plumbers, golfer/tennis players (self-employed sportsmen), farm owner/managers (fewer than 25 employees)	C2 Skilled (manual)	Class 3
Class 5	Lower level supervisors, craft and related workers: electricians, mechanics, train drivers, building site/factory foremen, bus inspectors	D Partly skilled	Class 4
Class 6	Semi-routine occupations: traffic wardens, caretakers, gardeners, supermarket shelf-stackers, assembly-line workers	D Partly skilled	Class 4
Class 7	Routine occupation: cleaners, waiters/waitresses/bar staff, messengers/couriers, road workers, dockers	E Unskilled	Class 5
Class 8	Excluded: long-term unemployed, never worked, long-term sick	Other	Class 6

Figure 8.6 The JICNARS and NS-SEC approaches to social classification

much as the black economy and overtime can enhance the apparently lower wage of the C2 and D. From a different standpoint, social class categories are difficult to apply consistently. The variety and complexity of people's jobs make many social classifications inherently subjective rather than objective.*"*

Recognition of the problems of defining social class and of the limitations of traditional methods of social classification led the Market Research Society in the 1990s to publish an up-to-date guide to socio-economic status. The guide, which defines the pecking order of 1500 jobs, is based not on earnings, but on qualifications and responsibility. A summary of this appears in Figure 8.7.

NS-SEC

The weaknesses of the JICNARs approach to social classification and, in particular, its inability to reflect the complexity, differences and subtleties of what we referred to earlier as 'the new consumer', led the government at the beginning of the 1990s to fund the search for an alternative approach. Developed by Professor David Rose of

A: admiral, advocate, air marshal, ambassador, archbishop, attorney, bank manager, bishop, brigadier, chemist shop manager (more than 25 staff); chief constable, chief engineer, chief fire officer, chief rabbi, chiropodist (more than five staff); national orchestra conductor, coroner, university dean, dental surgeon with own practice, chartered estate agent, self-employed farmer (more than 10 staff), financier, general practitioner (own practice/partner), school head-teacher (more than 750 pupils), homoeopath, insurance underwriter, magistrate, hospital matron, judge, MP, professor and town clerk.

B: advertising account director, archdeacon, area sales manager, ballistics expert, qualified brewer, bursar, church canon, chef (more than 25 staff), police chief inspector, computer programmer, stock exchange dealer, deputy power station manager, drawing office manager, fund manager, master mariner, orchestra leader, parish priest, parson, prison governor, probation officer, rabbi, senior buyer, senior engineer, qualified social worker, secondary-school teacher, television newscaster, lecturer and nursing sister.

C1: advertising account executive, accounts clerk, announcer (television, radio or station platform), art buyer, articled clerk, athlete, band master, bank cashier, boxer, bus inspector, calligrapher, campanologist, telephone canvasser, cardiographer, cartographer, chef (5 to 24 staff), chemist dispenser, chorister, chorus girl, clown, sports coach, coastguard, computer operator, skilled cook, police constable, advertising copywriter, travel courier, curate, cricketer, dancer, dental hygienist, private detective, dietician, driving examiner/instructor, estate agent (not chartered), fashion model, film projectionist, golfer, hospital houseman, book illustrator, disc jockey, juggler, domestic loss adjuster, magician, maître d'hôtel, masseur/masseuse, midwife, monk, nun, staff nurse, non-manual office worker, pawn-broker, plant breeder, RSPCA inspector, receptionist, secretary, telephone operator, sports umpire, youth worker.

C2: AA patrolman, self-employed antique dealer, boat builder, bus driver, shoe-maker, bricklayer, carpenter, chimney sweep, bespoke tailoring cutter, deep-sea diver, dog handler, hair-dresser, skilled electrician, fireman, thatcher, train driver, Rolls-Royce trained chauffeur, skilled miner.

D: au pair, bingo caller, dustman, bodyguard, bus conductor, chauffeur, croupier, dog breeder, lumberjack, unskilled miner, nursemaid and ratcatcher.

E: anyone brave enough to admit it.

Figure 8.7 The Market Research Society's occupation groupings (source: Market Research Society, 1990)

the University of Essex, the new system – known as NS-SEC (National Statistics Socio-Economic Classification) – was designed to provide a far stronger base for the classification and tracking of today's consumers, who have many more facets to their lives than was the case when JICNARs was first developed. At the heart of the system is an essentially classless view of the consumer that reflects three profound shifts in society: the growth of the middle class, the emergence of a new petit bourgeoisie, and the very different role within the workforce played by women. Although it is similar to JICNARs in that it is occupation-based, NS-SEC gives far greater emphasis to people's purchasing power in the labour market. In doing this, it is designed to be a far more accurate tool with which to draw distinctions between purchasing habits.

The initial reaction from the market research industry to the new classification, which is shown in Figure 8.6 alongside the JICNARs approach, was somewhat sceptical. Despite this, there was a widespread recognition that JICNARs, which is essentially a definition of wealth rather than attitude, although adequate for broad consumer definitions, fails to reflect the ways in which consumers have become better educated, move jobs more frequently, and have higher levels of disposable income. It is these sorts of changes that have led to the recognition that class, income and gender are no longer accurate predictors of consumer behaviour.

In Rose's system, consumers are divided into seventeen narrow classifications by occupation that take account of employment relationships between managers and the managed. These seventeen classifications are then grouped into the eight broad categories that appear in Figure 8.6.

The need for an alternative to classification has also been highlighted by the Future Foundation, which has developed a method designed to capture changing values and systems. Based on the ideas of fuzzy logic, the technique – called 'fuzzy clustering' – allows consumers to be recognized and defined in different ways according to the time of day. Recognition of the complexity of modern society has also led The Henley Centre (2000) to a form of fuzzy clustering. In *Planning for Consumer Change*, the Centre reflected the dimensions of the complex consumer in a classification referred to as *polyglotting*. The thinking behind polyglotting is based not so much on consumer identity as upon modes of acting and behaviour at different times.

Sex

The third demographic category is that of sex. While this variable has obvious applications to such products as clothes, cosmetics, magazines and so on, ever greater attention has been paid in recent years to the ways in which it can be used as a key element in the strategies to market a far wider range of products. In part, this has been brought about by a series of fundamental changes that are taking place within society, including a greater number of working women and the generally higher levels of female independence. One result of this has been an increase in the number of marketing campaigns targeted specifically at women: examples include cigarettes, cars and hotels.

8.10 Behavioural segmentation

The third major approach to segmentation is based on a series of behavioural measures, including attitudes, knowledge, benefits sought by the buyer, a willingness to innovate, loyalty status, usage rates, and response to a product. Of these, *benefit segmentation* (in other words, reasons to believe) is probably the best known and most widely used, and is based on the assumption that it is the benefits that people are seeking from a product that provide the most appropriate bases for dividing up a market.

In applying this approach, the marketing planner begins by attempting to measure consumers' value systems and their perceptions of various brands within a given product class. The information generated is then used as the basis for the marketing strategy. One of the earliest and best-known examples of this is the work conducted on the watch market by Yankelovich (1964). His findings that 'approximately 23 per cent of the buyers bought for lowest price, another 46 per cent bought for durability and general product quality, and 31 per cent bought watches as symbols of some important occasion' were subsequently used by the US Time Company, which created its Timex brand to capitalize on the first two of these segments. The majority of other companies at this stage focused either largely or exclusively on the third segment and Timex therefore faced little direct competition in the early years.

Benefit segmentation begins therefore by determining the principal benefits customers are seeking in the product class, the kinds of people who look for each benefit, and the benefits delivered by each brand. Apple, for example, based its initial strategy, at least in part, on appealing to those looking for a more user-friendly system.

One of the first major pieces of benefit research was the work conducted by Russell Haley (1963), to which we made brief reference earlier. On the basis of his work in the toothpaste market, Haley identified four distinct segments, which, he argued, were sufficiently different to provide a platform for selecting advertising copy, media, commercial length, packaging and new product design. The four segments he identified were: seeking economy, decay prevention, cosmetic and taste benefits respectively.

Haley demonstrated that each group exhibited specific demographic, behavioural and psychographic characteristics. Those concerned primarily with decay prevention, for example, typically had large families, were heavy toothpaste users and were generally conservative in their outlook. By contrast, the group that was more concerned with bright teeth (the cosmetic segment) tended to be younger, were more socially active and in many cases were smokers. Each of these groups, he then demonstrated, exhibited preferences for particular brands: Crest in the case of those concerned with decay prevention, and Macleans and Ultra-Brite for those preoccupied with bright teeth.

The information generated by studies such as these can, as we observed earlier, be used in a variety of ways. Most obviously they prove useful in classifying the specific benefits being sought by particular customer groups, the segment's behavioural, demographic and psychographic characteristics, and the major competitive brands. An additional by-product of this sort of research can also be that it highlights a benefit that customers are seeking, but which currently is not being satisfied. As examples of this:

→ In the 1990s, Lucozade developed Lucozade Sport to cater for the fast-growing sports market, while Red Bull developed its product as a functional energy drink targeted at 16–34 sports enthusiasts, students, clubbers and people who need a pick-me-up during the day.

→ In the car market, Renault developed one of the first people carriers, the Espace, in the 1980s in response to the increasingly different ways in which people were using their cars and what they wanted from them.

→ In the cereals market, Kellogg's developed Special K many years ago as a product to help a predominantly female market with what is referred to as weight and shape management. More recently, the company developed cereal bars such as Nutri-Grain to meet the demand from people who skipped more traditional forms of breakfast.

→ In the glass market, Pilkington developed Pilkington Activ, a glass that has a coating that, through the action of sunlight and rainwater, leads to it being self-cleaning.

In many markets, benefit segmentation results in the company focusing upon satisfying just one benefit group, with the benefit offered being the unique selling proposition (USP). This is, however, just one of four choices that exist:

1 Single benefit positioning
2 Primary and secondary benefit positioning
3 Double benefit positioning
4 Triple benefit positioning.

These will be discussed in greater detail at a later stage in the chapter.

User status

As an alternative to benefit segmentation, markets can be subdivided on the basis of what is referred to as *user status*. Thus, a number of segments can typically be identified, including non-users, ex-users, potential users, first-time users and regular users. These final two categories can then be subdivided further on the basis of *usage rate* (this is sometimes referred to as *volume segmentation*).

For many firms the marketing task is seen in terms of moving buyers and potential buyers along the buying continuum; thus, non-users and potential users all need to be persuaded to try the product, while first-time users need to be persuaded to become medium users, and medium users to become heavy users. The essence of this approach is reflected in the strategies of a variety of organizations, including those of a number of cigarette companies, which, having been affected by changing smoking habits over the past two decades, have targeted particular user status groups. Across Europe, for example, young females in particular have been identified as a potentially valuable segment and a variety of brands developed to appeal specifically to this part of the market.

The attraction of different user status groups tends to vary from one type of organization to another. High market share companies, for example, typically focus on converting potential users into actual users, while smaller and lower share firms will often concentrate upon users of competitive brands with a view to persuading them to switch brands.

Loyalty status and brand enthusiasm

The third technique encompassed by behavioural segmentation is that of *loyalty status*, in which buyers are categorized on the basis of the extent and depth of their loyalty to particular brands or stores. Most typically this leads to the emergence of four categories: hard-core loyals, soft-core loyals, shifting loyals, and switchers. In the case of the airlines, for example, the past few years have seen an enormous investment in frequent flyer schemes that are designed to build loyalty. However, as we suggest in Section 5.8, loyalty and the relationships upon which they are supposedly built are not necessarily as straightforward or as deep as they might appear at first sight. It is for this reason that customer promiscuity has become a far more significant and costly issue for many organizations (see p. 213).

The implications of loyalty are, of course, significant since, in the case of those markets in which high patterns of loyalty exist, the ability to persuade buyers to shift from one brand to another is likely to be limited, even in the face of high levels of marketing expenditure. Thus, in these circumstances, a share-gaining or market-entry strategy may well prove to be at best only marginally cost-effective. However, the process of categorization referred to above is not by itself sufficient for the strategist. Rather it is the starting point from which the specific characteristics of each category then need to be examined. It may be the case, for example, that those buyers with the highest degrees of loyalty exhibit certain common characteristics in terms of age, socio-economic profile and so on, while those with lower degrees of loyalty exhibit a very different but common set of characteristics. Research designed to identify these differences may well then provide the planner with a far greater understanding and insight into the ways in which patterns of loyalty may prove vulnerable to attack. Equally, analysis of this sort can provide an insight into the ways in which a competitor's products are vulnerable to attack. In the case of soft-core loyals, for example, the strategist needs to identify the brands that compete either directly or indirectly with its own. By doing this, it can then strengthen its position, possibly by means of knocking copy or direct comparison advertising.

Analysis of the final group – the switchers – is also of potential strategic value, since this can provide the basis for understanding in greater detail the brand's weaknesses and the basis for attack.

As an alternative or addition to loyalty status, consumers can often be categorized on the basis of their *enthusiasm* for the product, the five categories that are used most frequently being *enthusiastic, positive, indifferent, negative* and *hostile*. Its major value as a technique is principally as a screening step in that, having identified the category within which the consumer falls, the organization can then focus its energies on the most likely prospects. This process can then be taken a step further by focusing on the *occasions* on which consumers develop a need, purchase or use a product.

Greeting cards companies, for example, have concentrated on increasing the number of occasions on which cards are given in relation to what was the case, say, 30 years ago. A glance at the shelves of any newsagent will reveal the enormous variety of cards that now exist, ranging from Father's Day and Mother's Day through to Get Well and Congratulations on Your Examination Success/New Baby/Moving House/New Job/ Passing Your Driving Test, and so on. Ice-cream manufacturers have pursued a broadly similar strategy in order to move away from a pattern of sales that was overly dependent on hot, sunny weather. The result in this case has been the development of a whole series of ice-cream-based desserts and cakes that can be used throughout the year.

Critical events

As a further development of occasion-related segmentation, the past few years have been the emergence of what is usually referred to as *critical event segmentation* (CES). This is based on the idea that major or critical events in an individual's life generate needs that can then be satisfied by the provision of a collection of products and/or services. Typical examples of these critical events are marriage, the death of someone in the family, unemployment, illness, retirement and moving house. Among those who have recognized the potential of CES are estate agents who, during the past decade, have moved away from simply selling houses to providing the whole range of legal and financial services surrounding house sale and purchase. The idea of critical events has also underpinned the marketing approach used by some of the chocolate companies, such as Thorntons, who have focused upon dates such as Valentine's Day, Mother's Day, Christmas, and so on.

8.11 Psychographic and lifestyle segmentation

The fourth and increasingly popular basis of consumer segmentation stems from work by Riesman et al. (1950), which led to the identification of three distinct types of social characterization and behaviour:

1 *Tradition-directed behaviour*, which changes little over time and, as a result, is easy to predict and use as a basis for segmentation
2 *Other directedness*, in which the individual attempts to fit in and adapt to the behaviour of his or her peer group
3 *Inner directedness*, where the individual is seemingly indifferent to the behaviour of others.

Although this relatively simplistic approach to categorization has subsequently been subjected to a degree of criticism, it has provided the basis for a considerable amount of further work, all of which has been designed to provide the strategist with a far more detailed understanding of personality and lifestyle.

The attempts to use personality to segment markets began in earnest in the USA in the late 1950s, when both Ford and Chevrolet gave emphasis to the brand personalities of their products in order to appeal to distinct consumer personalities (see Illustration 5.2). Buyers of Fords, for example, were identified as 'independent, impulsive, masculine, alert to change, and self-confident, while Chevrolet owers were conservative, thrifty, prestige-conscious, less masculine, and seeking to avoid extremes'. The validity of these descriptions was subsequently questioned by Evans (1959), who, by using a series of psychometric tests, argued that Ford and Chevrolet owners did not in fact differ to nearly the extent that had been suggested. More recent research has, with just one or two possible exceptions, been equally inconclusive. Among these exceptions is the work of Westfall (1962) and Young (1972). Westfall, for example, has reported finding evidence of personality differences between the buyers of convertible and non-convertible cars, with the former seemingly being 'more active, impulsive and sociable', while Young has pointed to the successful development of personality trait-based segmentation strategies in the cosmetics, drinks and cigarettes markets.

Largely because of the difficulties encountered in using personality as an easy, consistent and reliable basis for segmentation, attention in recent years has switched to *lifestyle* and to the ways in which it influences patterns of consumer demand. Lifestyle has been defined in a variety of ways, but is in essence *how* a person lives and interacts with their environment. As such, it is potentially a long way removed from social class and personality, and instead is a reflection of a person's way of being and acting in the world. An example of how psychographics and lifestyle can be used is that of Gap Inc., which owns the Gap, Banana Republic and Old Navy store chains. Gap customers are categorized as either 'style-conscious' or 'updated classics'. The style-conscious customers are 20- to 30-year-olds, while updated classics are older and more conservative customers (this is the group that felt disenfranchised by Gap's move into younger and edgier designs in 2001). Banana Republic targets sophisticated fashion leaders who want quality clothes and accessories and are not price sensitive. The 811-strong Old Navy chain consists of large (14 000 square feet) stores with value-priced clothing that attracts young families.

Because of the *apparent* insights offered by lifestyle analysis, a variety of models for categorizing consumers has emerged over the past few years. Prominent among these are the VALS framework, Young & Rubicam's 4Cs, and Taylor Nelson's Monitor.

The VALS framework

Developed in the USA by Arnold Mitchell of the Stanford Research Institute, the VALS framework used the answers of 2713 respondents to 800 questions to classify the American public into nine value lifestyle groups:

1 *Survivors*, who are generally disadvantaged and who tend to be depressed, withdrawn and despairing
2 *Sustainers*, who are again disadvantaged but who are fighting hard to escape poverty

3 *Belongers*, who tend to be conventional, nostalgic, conservative and generally reluctant to experiment with new products or ideas

4 *Emulators*, who are status conscious, ambitious and upwardly mobile

5 *Achievers*, who make things happen and enjoy life

6 *'I-am-me' people*, who are self-engrossed, respond to whims and are generally young

7 *Experientials*, who want to experience a wide variety of what life can offer

8 *Societally conscious people*, who have a marked sense of social responsibility and want to improve the conditions of society

9 *Integrated people*, who are psychologically fully mature and who combine the best elements of inner and outer directedness.

The thinking that underpins the VALS framework is that individuals pass through a series of developmental stages, each of which influences attitudes, behaviour and psychological needs. Thus, people typically move from a stage that is largely need-driven (survivors and sustainers) towards either an outer-directed hierarchy of stages (belongers, emulators and achievers) or an inner-directed hierarchy (I-am-me, experientials, societally conscious); relatively few reach the nirvana of the integrated stage.

From the marketing point of view, the need-driven segments have little apparent appeal, since it is this part of society that lacks any real purchasing power. Outer-directed consumers, by contrast, represent a far more attractive part of the market and in general buy products with what has been described as 'an awareness of what other people will attribute to their consumption of that product'. Typically, therefore, brand names such as Rolex, Gucci, Benetton, Chanel and Cartier will prove to be important. Inner-directed consumers, by contrast, are those people who in their lives place far greater emphasis on their individual needs as opposed to external values. Although in terms of overall numbers this group represents only a small part of the total market, it is often seen to be an important sector in terms of its ability to set trends. It is this group also that is currently showing the fastest growth rate within society, while the number of need-driven consumers declines and outer-directed remains about the same.

Young & Rubicam's 4Cs and Taylor Nelson's Monitor

Developed by the advertising agency, Young & Rubicam, 4Cs (a Cross-Cultural Consumer Characterization) divides people into three main groups, each of which is further subdivided along the following lines:

1 *The constrained*
    (i) the resigned poor
    (ii) the struggling poor.

2 *The middle majority*
    (i) mainstreamers
    (ii) aspirers
    (iii) succeeders.

3 *The innovators*
  (i) transitionals
  (ii) reformers.

The largest single subgroup in the UK is the mainstreamers, said to account for between 30 and 35 per cent of the population.

The principal benefit of 4Cs is that it defines in a fairly precise manner individual or group motivational needs. It does this by acknowledging the multidimensional nature of people and groups by taking the key motivational factors (e.g. success in the case of a succeeder) and overlaying this with other important motivational values to develop a motivational matrix. This can then be used to construct strategic frameworks for marketing and advertising campaigns both domestically and internationally.

A similar framework, labelled Monitor, has been developed by the UK-based market research agency, Taylor Nelson. The Monitor typology again divides people into three main groups, which are again subdivided:

1 *Sustenance-driven*. Motivated by material security, they are subdivided into:
  (i) the aimless, who include young unemployed and elderly drifters (5 per cent of the UK population)
  (ii) survivors, traditionally minded working-class people (16 per cent of the population)
  (iii) belongers, who are conservative family-oriented people (18 per cent of the population, but only half of them are sustenance driven).
2 *Outer-directed*. Those who are mainly motivated by the desire for status. They are subdivided into:
  (i) belongers
  (ii) conspicuous consumers (19 per cent of the population).
3 *Inner-directed*. This group is subdivided into:
  (i) social resisters, who are caring and often doctrinaire (11 per cent of the population)
  (ii) experimentalists, who are hedonistic and individualistic (14 per cent of the population)
  (iii) self-explorers, who are less doctrinaire than social resisters and less materialistic than experimentalists.

The development of approaches such as these has also led to the emergence of a wide variety of acronyms and labels; an example of this in the grocery retailing market appears in Illustration 8.4. Prominent among these are Yuppies (Young Upwardly Mobile Professionals), Bumps (Borrowed-to-the-hilt, Upwardly Mobile Professional Show-offs), Jollies (Jet-setting Oldies with Lots of Loot), Woopies (Well-Off Older Persons), Glams (Greying Leisured Affluent Middle-Aged) and Kippers (Kids in Parent's Pockets Eroding Retirement Savings). Although a number of these labels are now rather passé – Yuppies, for example, proved to be a phenomenon of the 1980s and the Big Bang – they have proved to be useful in that they characterize in an easily-understood fashion a particular style of life.

Illustration 8.4 Consumer profiling and shopping habits

In an attempt to reflect the diversity of society – and to determine our response to certain stimuli – the market research company AC Nielsen has separated shoppers into six categories:

1 *Habit-bound diehards*. These tend to be older people for whom routine and loyalty are important. They have limited funds and are cautious, with an eye for a bargain.
2 *Self-indulgent shoppers*. These are younger professionals, with no money worries or commitments and a fondness for the exotic and unusual. They are confident, self-assured and eager to experiment with a multiplicity of foods.
3 *Struggling idealists*. Not much respected or desired by supermarkets, they are pedantic and particular, favouring organic and 'natural' ingredients. They never spend much.

4 *Comfortable and contenteds*. Loosely called Middle Englanders, they are the most sought-after shopper, encompassing young comfortable mothers and housewives to middle-aged couples with disposable income. They tend to be admirers of Delia Smith and luxuriate in abundance and surplus.
5 *Frenzied copers*. Professional without much time, or mothers juggling a career and family, they spend freely but move quickly. They return to the same supermarkets, especially if they offer crèche facilities and consistent layouts.
6 *Mercenaries*. These are fickle, transient, often impoverished. They favour own-brand goods, promotions, discounts and damaged goods – anything cheap.

Source: *The Times*, 1 February 1997, p. 17.

8.12 Approaches to segmenting industrial markets

Although much of the work that has been done on segmentation analysis over the past 40 years has focused on consumer markets, many of the variables, such as benefits sought, geography and usage rates, can be applied with equal validity to industrial markets. Recognizing this, a number of writers, including Cardozo (1980) and Bonoma and Shapiro (1983), have concentrated on demonstrating, developing and refining their applicability. Cardozo, for example, has identified four dimensions that can be used either separately or collectively to classify organizational buying situations:

1 Familiarity with the buying task and in particular whether it is a new task, modified rebuy or straight rebuy
2 The type of product and the degree of standardization
3 The significance of the purchase to the buying organization
4 The level of uncertainty in the purchase situation.

Of these, it is arguably the last two factors that are of particular significance, as they reflect the fact that buyers also try to segment potential suppliers by developing assessment criteria and establishing formal vendor rating systems. This general line of thinking has been developed by Johnson and Flodhammer (1980), who, in arguing that the need to understand buyers' needs is as important in industrial markets as in consumer markets, have suggested that: 'Unless there is knowledge of the industrial users' needs the manufactured product usually has the lowest common denominator – price. Quality and service are unknown qualities.'

A slightly different line of argument has been pursued by Bonoma and Shapiro (1984), who have concentrated on developing a classification of industrial segmentation variables and listing the questions that industrial marketers should pose in deciding which customers they want to serve. A summary of these questions, in declining order of importance, appears in Figure 8.8.

From this it can be seen that the starting point is the question of which industry to serve, followed by a series of decisions on customer size and purchase criteria.

This method has been employed to great effect by, among others, IBM. IBM's starting point for segmentation has always been the idea that the company sells solutions rather than products. They therefore segment the market by commercial type: banking, transportation, insurance, processing industry and so on, in order to be able to tailor

---

Demographic

Industry: on which industries that use this product should we concentrate?

Company: on what size of company should we concentrate?

Location: in which geographical areas should we concentrate our efforts?

Operating variables

Technology: which customers technologies are of the greatest interest to us?

User status: on which types of user (heavy, medium, light, non-user) should we concentrate?

Customer capabilities: should we concentrate on customers with a broad or a narrow range of needs?

Purchasing approaches

Buying criteria: should we concentrate on customers seeking quality, service, or price?

Buying policies: should we concentrate on companies that prefer leasing, systems purchases, or sealed bids?

Current relationships: should we concentrate on existing or new customers?

Situational factors

Urgency: should we concentrate on customers with sudden delivery needs?

Size of order: should we concentrate on large or small orders?

Applications: should we concentrate on general or specific applications of our product?

Personal characteristics

Loyalty: should we concentrate on customers who exhibit high or low levels of loyalty?

Attitudes to risk: should we concentrate on risk taking or risk avoiding customers?

Figure 8.8 The major industrial market segmentation variables (adapted from Bonoma and Shapiro, 1984)

solutions to specific problem areas. Each segment is then divided into a series of sub-segments. Transportation, for example, can be divided into road, air, sea and rail.

Market segmentation and the dialogue of the deaf

The need for the planner to understand markets in detail and to avoid falling into the trap of blindly accepting the market and organizational preconceptions was highlighted by the American futurologist Faith Popcorn. In her book *Eve-olution* (2001), she argues that many (male) marketing planners fail to understand the real differences between men and women and, as a consequence, have been unable to capitalize upon them. To illustrate this, she points to the buying power of women (in the USA, it is estimated that women are responsible for or influence 80 per cent of all consumer, healthcare and vehicle purchases, 60 per cent of all electronic purchases, and represent 48 per cent of stock market investors) and to the biological differences that lead to women processing information differently.

Although Popcorn's critics have argued that these differences are not as significant or as far-reaching as she suggests, this can be seen to be part of a more fundamental issue about the relationship between companies and their customers. Almost irrespective of the sector, marketers are finding the gaps between what they think they know and actual buying behaviour are getting bigger. In an attempt to overcome this, marketing planners are spending ever more on technologies that, it is claimed, overcome the problems and imprecision of current segmentation models.

However, in many cases this is likely to have little effect, since there is often a fundamental misunderstanding at the heart of the customer/company dialogue. One example of this was the way in which Monsanto misread the issues surrounding genetically modified (GM) foodstuffs. The company was mesmerized by what it saw as a great scientific revolution and viewed the world through this one framework. How, its planners wondered, could there be objections to developments that had the potential to make food production so much more efficient? What it seemingly could not understand was that consumers viewed the situation very differently, were concerned for their safety and wanted information to make informed choices. The result was a dialogue of the deaf between manufacturer and consumer. It was, instead, the supermarkets that responded to these concerns by launching organically produced and GM-free ranges of foodstuffs.

8.13 Market targeting

Having decided how best to segment the market, the strategist is then faced with a series of decisions on how many and which segments to approach. Three factors need to be considered:

1 The size and growth potential of each segment
2 Their structural attractiveness
3 The organization's objectives and resources.

The starting point for this involves examining each segment's size and potential for growth. Obviously, the question of what is the 'right size' of a segment will vary greatly from one organization to another. The specialist car manufacturer Morgan has, for example, chosen to concentrate on a very small and specialized segment of the car market. Its customers are seeking the nostalgia of a pre-war sports car and the company has tailored its marketing mix accordingly. In commenting on this, *What Car?* said:

" The ride's as hard as a rock, comfort and space minimal, noise levels deafeningly high, and overall the sports car has about as much refinement as a tractor. Wonderful! *"*

This is neither a specification nor a segment that has any appeal for, say, Volkswagen or Jaguar, but Morgan operates within it with a high degree of success.

In so far as it is possible to develop broad guidelines, we can say that large companies concentrate on segments with large existing or potential sales volumes and quite deliberately overlook or ignore small segments, simply because they are rarely worth bothering with. Small firms, by contrast, often avoid large segments, partly because of the level of resource needed to operate in them effectively and partly because of the problems of having to cope with a far larger competitor.

With regard to the question of each segment's *structural attractiveness*, the strategist's primary concern is profitability. It may be the case that a segment is both large and growing but that, because of the intensity of competition, the scope for profit is low. Several models for measuring segment attractiveness exist, although arguably the most useful is Michael Porter's five-force model. This model, which is discussed at the beginning of Chapter 10, suggests that segment profitability is affected by five principal factors:

1 Industry competitors and the threat of segment rivalry
2 Potential entrants to the market and the threat of mobility
3 The threat of substitute products
4 Buyers and their relative power
5 Suppliers and their relative power.

Having measured the size, growth rate and structural attractiveness of each segment, the strategist needs then to examine each one in turn against the background of the organization's objectives and resources. In doing this, the strategist is looking for the degree of compatibility between the segment and the organization's long-term goals. It is often the case, for example, that a seemingly attractive segment can be dismissed either because it would not move the organization significantly forward towards its goals, or because it would divert organizational energy. Even where there does appear to be a match, consideration needs to be given to whether the organization has the necessary skills competences, resources and commitment needed to operate effectively. Without these, entry is likely to be of little strategic value.

There are therefore two questions that need to be posed:

1 *Is the segment growing or declining?* Here we are interested in two broad aspects of growth and decline. What is the projected future of the segment in terms of volume sales and profit? Despite much argument to the contrary, there need not be a link between volume sales and profit. Declining volumes in certain market segments can still be extremely profitable for the organizations that service them. It is therefore often more a question of how the segment is managed rather than what the segment is doing.

2 *Is the segment changing?* There are three aspects to this question of change. First, we need to understand how the structure and make-up of the segment are likely to change over time. Is the segment starting to attract new and slightly different members to its centre? What effect will this have on the segment's needs? The second aspect of change relates to the nature of the products and services that we would expect this segment to be demanding in the future. In other words, do we see any significant change in the way in which the members of the segment are likely to translate their needs into buying behaviour? Will they want different products or services in three years' time? The third area of segment change must consider the movements of the segments over time. Do we, for example, see the overall array of segments changing? There are two ways in which this structural change can occur. Segments may merge and combine to create larger, more 'shallow' segments. Alternatively, larger segments may fragment over time into smaller, more precise market targets for the organization to approach, something which led to Cafédirect's decision to target a particular type of consumer (this is discussed in Illustration 8.5).

Illustration 8.5 Charity coffee aims for a richer blend

In 1995, Cafédirect launched its first major advertising campaign under the heading 'Richer, mellower and distinctly less bitter'. With this, the company was not talking just about the taste of its coffee, but also its Latin American and African growers.

The company, which is backed by four charities (Oxfam, Traidcraft, Twin Trading and Equal Exchange Trading), started life in 1991, when it began selling coffee through the charities' mail-order catalogues. Its selling proposition is:

> . . . that it guarantees to pay farm cooperatives a minimum of 10 per cent

above the world coffee price for their produce and to ship the product directly to the UK where it is marketed. The farmers use the money they receive to benefit their communities and provide health care and education. The long-term basis of Cafédirect's relationship means farmers can make plans for the future rather than survive from one harvest to the next.

With the strong Central and South American heritage of the coffee, the traditional customer base for the product proved to be consumers who had above-average levels of political awareness, and church groups that sold the product to the members. However, in 1995 the company faced a classic marketing dilemma – how to move the brand on and attract new customers without alienating its core market.

The solution was seen to lie in the targeting of 'semi-ethical' women: these are defined in terms of those who have a reasonable interest in green and world issues and feel that they want to do the right thing, but only if it is not too difficult or too painful.

In order to capture this market, the advertising focused primarily on the quality of the product, something which had been made possible by the advice on growing and quality control techniques that had been given to the farmers, and only in a secondary way upon the background to the product.

Source: *Financial Times*, 12 November 1995, p. 8.

8.14 Deciding on the breadth of market coverage

The final segmentation decision faced by the strategist is concerned with which and how many segments to enter. In essence, five patterns of market coverage exist:

1 *Single segment concentration*. Here, the organization focuses on just one segment. Although a potentially high-risk strategy in that the firm is vulnerable to sudden changes in taste or the entry of a larger competitor, concentrated marketing along these lines has often proved to be attractive to small companies with limited funds. Left to itself, an organization that opts to concentrate upon a single segment can develop a strong market position, a specialist reputation, and above-average returns for the industry as a whole.

2 *Selective specialization*. As an alternative to concentrating upon just one segment, the strategist may decide to spread the risk by covering several. These segments need not necessarily be related, although each should be compatible with the organization's objectives and resources. One organization that has done this with a high degree of success is Land Rover. Launched at the end of the 1940s as a rugged, utilitarian and easily maintained off-road vehicle, the Land Rover was targeted at a wide variety of geographically dispersed agricultural and military markets. Having dominated these markets for a considerable time, the company subsequently developed the far more luxurious (and expensive) Range Rover, which proved to have an immediate appeal to a very different type of market altogether. Their strategy was then developed further in 1990 by the launch of the Land Rover Discovery and then, a few years later, the Freelander.

3 *Product specialization*. Here, the organization concentrates on marketing a particular product type to a variety of target markets. Examples of this include the Burton Group (now renamed Arcadia) and Next, both of which have concentrated upon selling fashion clothing to a predominantly young market.

4 *Market specialization.* Here, the organization concentrates on satisfying the range of needs of a particular target group. An example of this would be an agrochemicals manufacturer, whose principal target market is farmers.

5 *Full market coverage.* By far the most costly of the five patterns of market coverage, a strategy of full market coverage involves serving all (or most) customer groups with the full range of products needed. Two companies that have increasingly moved towards this position over the past few years are Volkswagen (the small VW Lupo through to the premium-priced VW Phaeton) and Mercedes-Benz (the A–Class through to premium-priced saloons and sports cars).

In deciding which of these five approaches to adopt, the marketing planner needs to take account of two interrelated issues:

1 *The nature of the current strategy.* In discussing this, Fifield and Gilligan (1996, p. 98) suggest that 'market segments ought to be selected according to the broader strategic decisions taken by the company'. For example, the organization aiming for a 'differentiated' position in the marketplace will need to retain a certain degree of flexibility, which will allow it to operate in a number of related market segments while still retaining its differentiated market position. The 'focused' organization, on the other hand, will necessarily have to get much, much closer to its fewer market segments, and will have to predict fragmentation and merging long before this phenomenon arises. It must be prepared and be able to continue to service changing segment needs as they arise. Failure to do this by the focused organization will leave it very vulnerable to competitive attack in its core markets.

2 *Organization resources and capability.* These need to be harnessed so that the customers' needs within the segments that are chosen are capable of being properly served.

Against the background of the answers to these two questions, the planner can then begin the process of ordering the segments so that a measure of their relative attractiveness across a series of dimensions can be arrived at; a framework for this appears in Figure 8.9.

Market niching and focusing

For small companies in particular, market niching offers a degree of security that is often denied to them if they try to compete in segments which, by virtue of their size, appeal to larger and better-funded organizations (market niching and the characteristics of the supernichers are also discussed in Section 11.8).

An undoubted attraction of many niche markets is the scope they offer for premium pricing and above-average profit margins. In addition, an effective niche strategy has for many firms provided a convenient jumping-off point for entry into a larger market. Both Volkswagen and Toyota, for example, niched when they first entered the North American car market. Their strategies, together with the subsequent growth of the small car market,

Criteria	Weight	Segments				
		1	2	3	4	5
1 Long-term volume growth 2 Long-term profit growth 3 Short-term volume growth 4 Short-term profit growth 5 Organizational image 6 Offensive strategic reasons 7 Defensive strategic reasons 8 Internal resource/capability 9 Relative competitive strength 10 Competitive vulnerability 11 Legislative constraints 12 Technological change 13 New product demands 14 Levels of price competition 15 Advertising levels 16 Distributor power 17 Life cycles						
Total						
Priority						
(Ratings 1–10, 10 = highly attractive)						

Figure 8.9 Identifying segment attractiveness (adapted from Fifield and Gilligan, 1996)

combined to change what had previously been a niche into a sizeable segment, which the American big three (Ford, General Motors and Chrysler) found difficult to attack because of the entrenched positions of VW and Toyota. Elsewhere, the Japanese have often used a niche as the entry point to a larger market. In the case of motorcycles, for example, 50 cc 'toys' proved to be the niche that gave Honda, in particular, the basis for expansion. Similarly, Volvo developed what was previously a niche that wanted a safe, functional and long-lasting car into a relatively large market. Amongst the others to have started with a strong niching strategy within a specialized, and initially small, market but who have subsequently developed the niche into a sizeable market segment are Body Shop, Harley Davidson, and Häagen-Dazs and Ben & Jerry ice-creams.

There is, however, a hidden danger in looking at what appear to be niche markets. Many strategists with small brands often deceive themselves by believing they have a niche product. The reality may in fact be very different, with the product being a vulnerable number four or number five brand in a mass market. To clarify whether a brand is a true market nicher, three questions can be posed:

1 Do consumers and distributors recognize the niche or is it simply a figment of the over-active imagination of a marketing planner?

2 Is the niche product or service *really* distinctive and does it have a strong appeal to a specific customer group?

3 Is the product capable of being priced at a premium and does it offer the scope for above-average profit margins?

Unless the answer to all three of the questions is 'yes', it is unlikely that the brand is a true nicher, but is instead simply a poor performer in a far larger market segment, something that leads to the idea that, although it is relatively easy to find a niche, the real secret is to ensure that it is of the right size – large enough to be profitable, but not sufficiently large to attract the far larger players, at least in the early days when the organization is trying to establish a market position.

Although there is a temptation to see niche marketers as small companies, the reality is that many niches are occupied by far larger organizations that have developed the skills of operating with small-volume products.

Given this, the characteristics of the ideal niche are:

1 It should be of sufficient size to be potentially profitable

2 It should offer scope for the organization to exercise its distinctive competences

3 It should/must have the potential for growth.

Other characteristics that favour niching would be patents, a degree of channel control, and the existence of customer goodwill.

8.15 Product positioning

Positioning: the battle for the mind

The third strand of what we referred to at the beginning of this chapter as STP marketing (segmentation, targeting and positioning) involves deciding on the position within the market that the product is to occupy. In doing this, the strategist is stating to customers what the product means and how it differs from current and potential competing products. Porsche, for example, is positioned in the prestige segment of the car market, with a differential advantage based on performance; Patek Phillipe is positioned as one of the highest quality watches available and for which the 'owner' is simply the product's custodian for the next generation; Mothercare is positioned to appeal to mothers of young children, with its differential advantage being based on the breadth of merchandise for that target group; Duracell is positioned as the longer-life and hence better value battery; brands such as Quicksilver are positioned to appeal to the urban street warrior; while Ryanair and easyJet are positioned as low-cost airlines.

The way in which an organization or a brand is perceived by its target markets (this is not just the existing customers, but also includes those who do not buy currently, might never buy, and so on) is determined by a series of factors, a number of which appear in Figure 8.10.

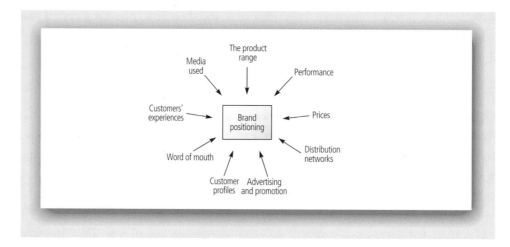

Figure 8.10 Influences on positioning

Positioning is therefore the process of designing an image and value so that customers within the target segment understand what the company or brand stands for in relation to its competitors. This can perhaps best be understood by considering an example such as grocery retailing, where the major UK retailers have set out to establish distinct market positions. Waitrose, for example, occupies a service and quality position. Aldi and Netto, by contrast, have pursued the low-price/no-frills position, while Sainsbury and Tesco occupy the quality, breadth of range, and convenience position. In doing this, the organization is sending a message to consumers and trying to establish a competitive advantage that it hopes will appeal to customers within a subsegment of the target segment. In the case of Waitrose, therefore, the company hopes that its quality/service position will appeal to the customer to whom these two dimensions are far more important than low prices. In the drinks market, Castlemaine XXXX is positioned as the genuine Australian lager, while in the banking sector the Co-op Bank is positioned on the basis of an ethical proposition. Given this, the reader needs to recognize that positioning is a battle for the customer's mind, since it is how the customer perceives the company or brand that determines success or failure. As an example of this, in the breakfast cereals market we can see the very different positions occupied by Kellogg's Corn Flakes, All Bran and Special K (see Figure 8.11).

It should be apparent from this that positioning is a fundamental element of the marketing planning process, since any decision on positioning has direct and immediate implications for the whole of the marketing mix. In essence, therefore, the marketing mix can be seen as the tactical details of the organization's positioning strategy. Where, for example, the organization is pursuing a high-quality position, this needs to be reflected not just in the quality of the product that is to be sold, but in every element of the mix, including price, the pattern of distribution, the style of advertising and the after-sales service. Without this consistency, the believability of the positioning strategy reduces dramatically.

For some organizations the choice of a positioning strategy proves to be straightforward. Where, for example, a particular positioning strategy and image has already been

	Corn Flakes	All Bran	Special K
Core target markets	Adults and children who need help to get started in the morning	Adults 30+	Women (25–39)
Functional promise	Wake-up food	Helps to keep you regular	Helps you to look good by helping you to manage your weight and shape
Emotional promise	Ready to begin the day	Peace of mind	The ally who helps you to feel good about yourself

Figure 8.11 Positioning and breakfast cereals

established in a related market, there are likely to be synergistic benefits by adopting the same approach in a new market or with a new product. For other organizations, however, the choice of position proves to be more difficult or less clear and the firm ends up by pursuing the same position as several others in the market. Where this happens, the degree and costs of competition increase dramatically. There is a strong case, therefore, for the strategist to decide in detail on the basis of differentiation: in other words, the organization must identify and build a collection of competitive advantages that will appeal to the target market and then communicate these effectively.

In the light of these comments, it should be apparent that the process of positioning involves three steps:

1 Identifying the organization or brand's possible competitive advantages
2 Deciding on those that are to be emphasized
3 Implementing the positioning concept.

Points 1 and 2 are discussed in detail in Chapter 10; therefore, only point 3 will be considered here.

Capitalizing on the competitive advantage

Having identified the competitive advantage (see Chapter 10) that appears to offer the greatest potential for development, the final step in the process involves communicating this to the market. Ries and Trout (1982), who in the eyes of many are the founding fathers of positioning theory, argue that positioning is first and foremost a communication strategy (this is the issue of the battle of the mind referred to earlier) and that any failure to recognize this will undermine the whole of the marketing mix. All too often, however, and despite having identified potentially valuable competitive advantages, organizations fail to signal these advantages sufficiently strongly. This then leads to one of three errors:

1 *Confused positioning*, where buyers are unsure of what the organization stands for (refer to the comments below about Gap's misjudgement of the market in 2001)
2 *Over-positioning*, where consumers perceive the organization's products as being expensive and fail to recognize the full breadth and value of the range
3 *Under-positioning*, where the message is simply too vague and consumers have little real idea of what the organization stands for or how it differs from the competition.

In order to select the most effective market position, the strategist needs to begin by identifying the structure of the market and the positions currently held by competitors. This can be done in a variety of ways, including by means of the sort of brand map to which we referred to earlier. With maps such as these the planner sets out firstly to plot where the product lies in relation to competitive products and, secondly, to identify those areas in which marketing opportunities might exist either for a new brand or for the existing brand if it was to be repositioned. In taking this second step, the strategist is setting out to position the product in such a way that its marketing potential is fully realized. A slightly unusual example of this appears in Illustration 8.6.

Illustration 8.6 A billion housewives every day . . . Positioning baked beans in China

At the beginning of 1998, Heinz, the world's leading supplier of baked beans, announced that it was launching them into China, the world's largest consumer market. With a retail price of about 60p a can, the company's strategy was very different from that used in the UK and the majority of its sixty or so other markets. Targeted very firmly at China's emerging middle classes and positioned as something of a status symbol, baked beans were positioned to be 'the kind of exotic dish served up to impress the boss when he comes to dinner'.

Source: *The Times*, 23 March 1998, p. 5.

As an example of how the greater potential of a different market sector might be realized, the German car manufacturer Audi set out in the 1980s and 1990s to reposition its range of products in order to move further up-market. In doing this, the company recognized that the organizations against which it would be competing would change and that, in this particular case, it would bring itself into more direct competition with both BMW and Mercedes-Benz. At the same time, numerous other car manufacturers have pursued repositioning strategies, with Jaguar targeting a younger market than in the past and Porsche pursuing a (relatively) less affluent sector.

In electing for a positioning or repositioning strategy, strategists therefore need to feel confident that, first, they will be able to reach the new market position for which they are aiming, and second, that they will be able to operate and compete effectively and profitably in this new position, something that was clearly understood by the Mini's marketing team (see Illustration 8.7).

For many organizations, however, repositioning proves to be a less than successful exercise. In 2001, for example, Gap reported an $8 million loss against net earnings of $877 million in 2000 and $1.1 billion in 1999, a problem that seemingly had emerged as the result of the way in which they had moved from their previously very clear market position to one that was far more edgy, fashion-forward and less appealing to its traditional markets.

The San Francisco-based company, which had grown dramatically for a decade, was accused by analysts of having alienated its Generation X market by trying to appeal to younger shoppers. However, in doing this, not only did Gap lose some of its traditional and highly loyal customer base, but failed to achieve the penetration of its new target market for which it was hoping. Subsequently, of course, the company has successfully moved back to its core markets.

Illustration 8.7 Positioning the new Mini

First launched in 1959, production of the original Mini finally ceased in 1998. As one of the original and best-loved motoring icons of the twentieth century, the brand's heritage offered enormous opportunities for BMW, the new owners. Recognizing that the new car was being launched into one of the most crowded parts of the intensively competitive European small car market, with competitors that included Renault, Volkswagen, Nissan, Peugeot, Citroen, Ford and Toyota, as well as some of the luxury brands such as the Mercedes A-Class and the Audi A2, the management team recognized that clear and clever positioning of the car was at the very heart of the company's marketing strategy. To do this and capture 4.6 per cent of the 'supermini' sector, a brand strategy was developed that deliberately set out to distance the Mini from what was considered to be the relatively bland competition. This strat-

egy was designed to position the car in such a way that it would appeal to two main groups. The younger of these, aged 25–35, was expected to buy the Mini as their main car and were expected to do this in preference to a similarly priced Toyota, Volkswagen, Renault or Smart. Older buyers in their 40s with grown-up children were expected to buy it as their second or third car.

An important element of the innovative and high-profile strategy that emerged was designed to differentiate the Mini from the competition and featured a £14.4 million television and cinema advertising campaign based around a series of 'Mini adventures' that included finding lost cities and helping to save the world from a Martian invasion. In the USA, the company ignored television and cinema advertising and opted instead for a guerrilla marketing campaign, which included mounting Minis on top of a fleet of Ford Excursions, one of the world's largest sports utility vehicles. The company also played to the growing backlash against the fuel-hungry SUV (Sports Utility Vehicle) sector. With these vehicles accounting for almost 27 per cent of total US vehicle sales, the Mini ads featured the line 'Let's not use the size of our vehicle to compensate for other shortcomings'. The positioning of the brand was then reinforced by the use of the BMW dealer network and an aggessive pricing strategy that learned from the mistakes made by Volkswagen when they launched their retro design Beetle.

The success of the strategy was reflected by the way in which global sales were 144 000 cars, compared with a target of 100 000. In the USA, the Mini's largest market outside Britain, the response to the car was equally strong, with 25 000 Minis being sold in the first 12 months compared with a target of 18 000.

Against the background of these comments, it should be recognized that very different positioning strategies need to be followed depending upon whether the firm is a market leader, follower or challenger and that, as a general rule, market followers should try to avoid positioning themselves too closely or directly against the market leader. The reasoning behind this is straightforward, since a smaller firm is most likely to succeed if it can establish its own position within the market and develop its own customer base. To compete head-on against an aggressive market leader such as Wal-Mart with a very clear position is to invite retaliation and a costly marketing war (see Illustration 8.8).

Illustration 8.8 Wal-Mart and its positioning by price

With more than 3000 stores serving 60 million people a week and annual revenues in excess of $140 billion, Wal-Mart is the world's largest retailer. The company's positioning statement is simple and unambiguous: 'We sell for less.' In order to achieve this, the founder, Sam Walton, rationalized and controlled costs to such an extent that he was able to undercut every one of his competitors. In commenting on this, Ritson (2002) suggests that:

> Walton achieved this control through a revolutionary approach to distribution and inventory management. Taking the company public in 1970 enabled him to use the subsequent funds to build

his own distribution network of giant warehouses that each had its own transportation system, linked up with 175 Wal-Mart stores. This network ensured that Wal-Mart handled its own distribution, saving millions of dollars on freight costs. The distribution network also had tremendous bargaining power because of the number of stores served. Walton underlined this power by ensuring that no supplier provided more than 3 per cent of the total Wal-Mart inventory. The message: if you don't price it as low as possible, we'll switch our business elsewhere.

Source: Ritson (2002).

Repositioning strategies

Having developed a position for a brand, there is frequently the need to reposition as the market develops, competitors enter or exit, and customers' expectations and needs change. In thinking about repositioning, the marketing planner has four strategic options:

1 *Gradual repositioning*, which involves a planned and continuous adaptation to the changing market environment. An example of this would be Skoda's move from an essentially utilitarian offer to one that is far more firmly mid-market.

2 *Radical repositioning*, where an increasing gap between what the brand offers and what the market wants leads the management team to think about a major strategic change. As an example of this, Lucozade moved from a position where its primary appeal was to the sick and the old to one where its major appeal is as a lifestyle and health drink.

3 *Innovative repositioning*, where the planner finds a new strategic position that offers market opportunities that have not so far been identified by competitors. Häagen-Dazs recognized the potential of the premium-quality, premium-priced adult ice-cream market, and throughout the 1990s successfully developed this.

4 *Zero positioning*, where the organization maintains an unchanged face to the market over a long period of time and/or it communicates very poorly with the target market, with the result that potential customers have little idea of what the organization stands for.

8.16 Summary

Within this chapter we have focused upon the ways in which a well-developed strategy of market segmentation, targeting and positioning contributes to effective marketing planning.

The rationale for segmentation is straightforward, and is based on the idea that only rarely can a single product or marketing approach appeal to the needs and wants of a disparate group of potential customers. Because of this there is a need for the marketing strategist to categorize buyers on the basis both of their characteristics and their specific product needs, with a view then to adapting either the product and the marketing programme, or both, to satisfy more specifically these different tastes and demands. An effective policy of segmentation is therefore a key contributory factor to the development of a competitive advantage.

A wide variety of approaches to segmentation have been developed, and these were discussed in some detail in the text. Many of the early approaches to segmentation are unidimensional and are incapable of providing the marketing planner with a sufficiently detailed picture of buyers' motives to be of real value. A considerable amount of work has therefore been conducted over the past 30 years to improve segmentation techniques, with the greatest emphasis being placed upon geodemographics and psychographics.

Work within the industrial products sector has, for the most part, tended to lag behind that in the consumer goods field, although the work of Cardozo, and Bonoma and Shapiro, has gone some way towards rectifying this.

Having segmented the market, the strategist should then be in a position to identify those segments which, from the organization's point of view, represent the most attractive targets. In deciding where to focus the marketing effort, the strategist needs to give consideration to three elements:

1 The size and growth potential of each segment
2 The structural attractiveness of different segments
3 The organization's objectives and resources.

Once a decision has been made on the breadth of market coverage, the strategist needs then to consider how best to position the organization, the product range and the brand within each target segment. A number of guidelines for market positioning have been discussed, and emphasis was placed upon the need to avoid making any one of the three most common positioning errors:

1 Confused positioning
2 Over-positioning
3 Under-positioning.

We concluded by returning to the significance of competitive advantage and to the ways in which a well-conceived and properly implemented strategy of segmentation, targeting and positioning can contribute to a highly effective marketing programme.

Chapter 9

The formulation of strategy – 1: analysing the product portfolio

9.1 Learning objectives

When you have read this chapter you should be able to understand:

(a) how strategic perspectives have developed over the past 35 years;
(b) how the responsibilities for planning vary throughout the organization;
(c) how portfolio analysis has developed and how it can be used in the development of strategy;
(d) the limitations and current status of portfolio analysis.

9.2 Introduction

Against the background of the material covered so far, we are now in a position to turn our attention to the ways in which organizations approach the development of a marketing strategy. In this, the first of three chapters on strategy, we begin by examining how strategic perspectives have developed over the past 35 years. We then turn our attention to a variety of models of portfolio analysis. In Chapters 10 and 11 we concentrate upon the issues surrounding growth, the approaches that are most typically used to achieve it, methods of developing a sustainable competitive advantage, and the ways in which market position influences strategy.

9.3 The development of strategic perspectives

Although a considerable amount has been written about strategic planning, it should be recognized that, as a discipline, strategic planning and the associated concepts and techniques did not emerge fully until the early 1970s. There are several reasons for this, perhaps the most significant of which stems from the way in which many companies throughout the 1950s and 1960s prospered largely as the result of the growing and continuously buoyant markets that characterized western economies at the time. In these circumstances, short-term operational planning was often seemingly all that was required. The turbulence of the early 1970s, which followed a series of crises, including oil supply restrictions, energy and material shortages, high inflation, economic stagnation, labour unrest, increased unemployment and then recession, caused many managers to search for a radically different approach to the running of their businesses. At the same time, an influx of low-price but relatively high-quality products from countries such as Japan began to flood Western markets, changing drastically the economics of manufacturing. The revised approach to management planning that emerged was designed to provide organizations with a far stronger and more resilient framework that would enable managers both to recognize opportunities more readily and overcome threats more easily. This new planning process was based on three central premises:

1 The company's business should be viewed and managed in a similar way to an investment portfolio, with each aspect of the business being closely monitored and decisions subsequently made on which products or specific parts of the business should be developed, maintained, phased out or deleted.

2 Emphasis should be placed upon identifying in detail the future profit potential of each aspect of the business.

3 A strategic perspective to the management of each major element of the business should be adopted. This notion of what has sometimes been referred to as a 'game plan' for achieving long-term objectives required the strategist to plan on the basis of industry position, objectives, opportunities and resources.

It needs to be recognized, however, that for the strategist to be able to adopt this approach to management, there is a need to understand in detail the complexities of the interrelationships that exist between different parts of the organizational structure. In the majority of businesses, three different organizational levels can be identified: the corporate level, the business unit level and the product level.

At the corporate level, the decisions made are concerned principally with the corporate strategic plan and how best to develop the long-term profile of the business. This, in turn, involves a series of decisions on the levels of resource allocation to individual business units, be it a division, subsidiary or brand, and on which new potential business should be supported. Following on from this, each business unit should, within the resources allocated by corporate headquarters, then develop its own strategic plan. Finally, marketing plans need to be developed at the product level. Plans at all three levels need then to be implemented, the results monitored and evaluated, and, where necessary, corrective action taken; this cycle of planning, implementation and control, which underpins the structure of this book, is illustrated in Figure 9.1.

Strategic planning and issues of responsibility

It should be apparent from what has been said so far that the ultimate responsibility for the planning process rests firmly with corporate management. This process, which involves statements of vision, mission, policy and strategy, establishes the broad framework within which plans at the business unit level are then developed. In practice, of course, organizations differ greatly both in how they go about this and in the degree of freedom given to the managers of individual business units. Some organizations, for example, allow the managers of business units considerable scope in developing their own objectives and strategies, requiring only that the promised levels of performance are then obtained – this is typically referred to as *bottom-up planning*. Others, by contrast, adopt an approach that is diametrically opposed to this in that they not only establish the objectives, but also subsequently insist on being involved in the development and implementation of strategy (*top-down planning*). Still others are content to establish the goals and then leave the business unit to develop the strategies for their achievement (*goals down/plans up*). However, irrespective of which approach is adopted,

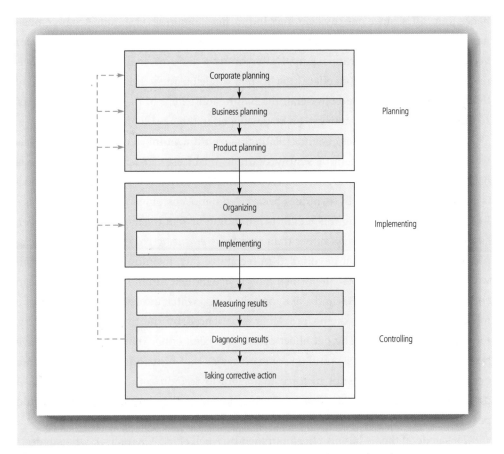

Figure 9.1   The strategic planning, implementation and control cycle

corporate management has the ultimate responsibility for the four major dimensions of planning:

1 The definition of the vision and business mission
2 Establishing the company's strategic business units (SBUs)
3 Evaluating the existing business portfolio
4 Identifying new areas for the business to enter.

The first of these – the definition of the vision and business mission – provided the focus for Chapter 7 and, as we emphasized at that stage, is designed to provide the organization with an overall sense of purpose. Once this has been done, the strategist is then in a position to move on and identify the organization's strategic business units (SBUs).

Planning with SBUs

The idea of SBUs as the basis for planning first emerged in the 1960s and gave recognition to the fact that the majority of companies operate a number of businesses, not all of which will necessarily be immediately apparent or identifiable. It does not follow, for example, that a company with four operating divisions will have four businesses and hence four SBUs, since one division may in practice contain several quite separate businesses. This typically comes about when the division produces different products for very different customer groups. Equally, two or three divisions may overlap or be interrelated in such a way that, in effect, they form a single business. It is therefore important that the planner understands in detail the nature and extent of these interrelationships so that the organization's strategy can be developed in the most logical way.

In commenting on this, Levitt (1960), along with a number of other writers, has warned against the dangers of simply defining businesses in terms of the products being made. Doing this, he argues, is myopic, since the demand for a particular product is likely to be transient. By contrast, basic needs and customer groups are far more likely to endure. In arguing this, Levitt is reminding us that businesses need to be seen as a *customer-satisfying process* rather than as a *goods-producing process*. Numerous examples exist of industries that have failed to recognize this, including the American railway companies in the 1950s, the British motorcycle industry in the 1960s, the European cutlery industry in the 1980s and 1990s, and the Swiss watch industry in the 1970s (for a more detailed discussion of the problems experienced by the Swiss watch industry, refer to Illustration 4.2). The net effect of this has been either that opportunities have been missed or the business – and on some occasions the entire industry – has gone into decline. It was in an attempt to force managers to recognize the transient nature of demand that Drucker (1973, Chapter 7) recommended that periodically they should pose the questions 'What business are we in?' and 'What business should we be in?'

This general theme has also been pursued by Abell (1980, Chapter 4), who suggests that businesses should be defined in terms of three elements:

1 The customer groups that will be served
2 The customer needs that will be satisfied
3 The technology that will be used to meet these needs.

Having done this, the planner can then move on to consider how best to manage each business strategically. A variety of frameworks to help with this have emerged over the past 25 years, although at the heart of virtually all of them is the concept of the *strategic business unit* or *strategy centre*. The term 'strategy centre' was first used by the American management consultants Arthur D. Little (1974), who defined it as:

*"*A business area with an external marketplace for goods or services, for which management can determine objectives and execute strategies independently of other business areas. It is a business that could probably stand alone if divested. Strategic Business Units are the 'natural' or homogeneous business of a corporation.*"*

It follows from this definition that SBUs exhibit a number of characteristics, the three most important of which are that an SBU:

1 Is a single business or a collection of related businesses that offer scope for independent planning and might feasibly stand alone from the rest of the organization

2 Has its own set of competitors

3 Has a manager who has responsibility for strategic planning and profit performance, and control of profit-influencing factors.

The idea of planning based on SBUs developed throughout the 1970s and has subsequently proved to be useful, not least because for many managers it has, to a very large extent, clarified what is meant by strategic marketing planning. The identification of SBUs is therefore a convenient starting point for planning since, once the company's strategic business units have been identified, the *responsibilities* for strategic planning can be more clearly assigned. In practice, the majority of companies work on the basis that strategic planning at the SBU level has to be agreed by corporate management. Thus, plans are typically submitted on an annual basis, with corporate management then either agreeing them or sending them back for revision.

In going through this process of review, corporate management attempts to identify future potential and hence where investment can most profitably be made. This has in turn led to the development of a variety of frameworks in which products are categorized on the basis of their potential. One of the best known of these was put forward by Drucker (1963), who labelled products as:

1 Tomorrow's breadwinners

2 Today's breadwinners

3 Products that are capable of making a contribution assuming drastic remedial action is taken

4 Yesterday's breadwinners

5 The also-rans

6 The failures.

By categorizing products or SBUs in this way, corporate management is moving towards a position where decisions regarding patterns of investment in the overall portfolio can be made with a far higher degree of objectivity than is typically the case when each SBU is viewed in partial or total isolation. To help with this and in order to ensure that the process is analytical rather than impressionistic, a number of models of portfolio evaluation have been developed. Among the best known of these are the Boston Consulting Group's growth–share and growth–gain matrices.

9.4 Models of portfolio analysis

The Boston Consulting Group's growth–share and growth–gain matrices

Undoubtedly the best-known approach to portfolio analysis, the Boston Consulting Group's (BCG) growth–share model involves SBUs being plotted on a matrix according to the *rate of market growth* and their *market share relative to that of the largest competitor*. This is illustrated in Figure 9.2.

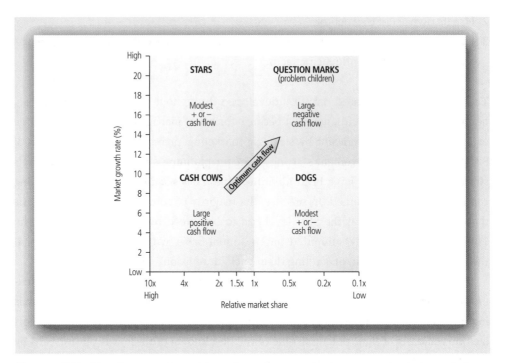

Figure 9.2 The Boston Consulting Group's growth–share matrix (adapted from Hedley, 1977)

In using these dimensions as the basis for evaluating the product portfolio, the Boston Consulting Group forces management to give explicit consideration both to the *future potential of the market* (i.e. the annual growth rate) and to the *SBU's competitive position*. Within the model, competitive position is measured on a logarithmic scale against the share of the firm's largest competitor; thus, a relative market share of 0.3 in Figure 9.2 signifies that the SBU's sales volume is 30 per cent of the leader's sales volume, while 4.0 would mean that the company's SBU is the market leader and has four times the market share of the next largest company in the market. A ratio of 1.0 signifies joint leadership. The vertical axis is then used to illustrate the largely uncontrollable annual rate of market growth in which the business operates. In Figure 9.2 this ranges from 0 to 20 per cent, with a growth rate in excess of 10 per cent being seen as high.

The 2 × 2 matrix that emerges from this is based on four assumptions:

1 Margins and the funds generated increase with market share largely as the result of experience and scale effects
2 Sales growth demands cash to finance working capital and increases in capacity
3 Increases in market share generally need cash to support share-gaining tactics
4 Growth slows as the product reaches life-cycle maturity and, at this stage, a surplus of cash can often be generated without the organization experiencing any loss of market share; this can then be used to support products still in the growth stages of their life cycles.

The matrix itself is divided into four cells, each of which indicates a different type of business with different cash-using and cash-generating characteristics; the characteristics of each of these cells are discussed in Figure 9.3.

Having plotted the position of the organization's SBUs, the balance and health of the portfolio can be seen fairly readily. A balanced portfolio typically exhibits certain characteristics, including a mixture of cash cows and stars. By contrast, an unbalanced and potentially dangerous portfolio would have too many dogs or question marks, and too few stars and cash cows. The likely consequence of this is that insufficient cash will be generated on a day-to-day basis to fund or support the development of other SBUs.

Having identified the shape of the portfolio, the planner needs then to consider the objectives, strategy and budget for each SBU. In essence, four major strategies can be pursued:

1 *Build*. In following a building strategy, the primary objective is to increase the SBU's market share in order to strengthen its position. In doing this, short-term earnings and profits are quite deliberately forsaken in the expectation that long-term returns will be far greater. It is a strategy that is best suited to question marks, so that they become stars.

Dogs (low share, low growth)
Dogs are those businesses that have a weak market share in a low-growth market. Typically they generate either a low profit or return a loss. The decision faced by the company is whether to hold on to the dog for strategic reasons (e.g. in the expectation that the market will grow, or because the product provides an obstacle, albeit a minor one, to a competitor). Dog businesses frequently take up more management time than they justify and there is often a case for phasing out (shooting) the product.

Question marks (low share, high growth)
Question marks are businesses operating in high-growth markets but with a low relative market share. They generally require considerable sums of cash since the firm needs to invest in plant, equipment and manpower to keep up with market developments. These cash requirements are, in turn, increased significantly if the company wants to improve its competitive position. The title of **question mark** comes about because management has to decide whether to continue investing in the SBU or withdrawing from the market.

Stars (high share, high growth)
Stars are those products which have moved to the position of leadership in a high growth market. Their cash needs are often high with the cash being spent in order to maintain market growth and keep competitors at bay. As stars also generate large amounts of cash, on balance there is unlikely to be any positive or negative cash flow until such time as the state of market growth declines. At this stage, provided the share has been maintained, the product should become a cash cow.

Cash cows (high share, low growth)
When the rate of market growth begins to fall, stars typically become the company's cash cows. The term **cash cow** is derived from the fact that it is these products which generate considerable sums of cash for the organization but which, because of the lower rate of growth, use relatively little. Because of the SBU's position in the market, economies of scale are often considerable and profit margins high.

Two further groups of SBUs have been identified by Barksdale and Harris (1982). These are **war horses (high market share and negative growth)** and **dodos (low share, negative growth)**.

Figure 9.3   The Boston Consulting Group's SBU classification

2 *Hold*. The primary objective in this case is to maintain the current share. It is the strategy that typically is used for cash cows to ensure they continue to generate the maximum amounts of cash.

3 *Harvest*. By following a harvesting strategy, management tries to increase short-term cash flows as far as possible, even at the expense of the SBU's longer-term future. It is a strategy best suited to cash cows that are weak or are in a market with seemingly only a limited future life. It is also used on occasions when the organization is in need of cash and is willing to mortgage the future of the product in the interests of short-term needs. Harvesting is also used for question marks when there appear to be few real opportunities to turn them into stars, and for dogs.

4 *Divest or terminate*. The essential objective here is to rid the organization of SBUs that act as a drain on profits or to realize resources that can be used to greater effect elsewhere in the business. It is a strategy that, again, is often used for question marks and dogs.

Having decided which of these four broad approaches to follow, the strategist needs then to give consideration to the way in which each SBU is likely to change its position within the matrix over time. SBUs typically have a life cycle that begins with their appearance as question marks and their progression through the stages of star, cash cow and, finally, dog. It is essential therefore that the BCG matrix is used not simply to obtain a snapshot of the portfolio as it stands currently, but rather that it is used to see how SBUs have developed so far and how they are likely to develop in the future. In doing this, it is possible to gain an impression of the probable shape and health of the portfolio in several years' time, any gaps that are likely to exist, and hence the sort of strategic action that is needed in the form of decisions on new products, marketing support and indeed product deletion. This process can then be taken a step further if similar charts are developed for each major competitor, since by doing this the strategist gains an insight into each competitor's portfolio strengths, weaknesses and potential gaps. The implications can then be fed back into the organization's own strategy.

The pitfalls of portfolio analysis

Although portfolio analysis is capable of providing a picture of the organization's current position, strategists need to adopt a degree of care in their interpretation and when developing future policy. A common mistake in portfolio analysis is to require each SBU to achieve an unrealistic growth rate or level of return: the essence of portfolio analysis involves recognizing that each SBU offers a different potential and as such requires individual management. Other typical mistakes include:

➡ Investing too heavily in dogs, hoping that their position will improve, but failing.

➡ Maintaining too many question marks and investing too little in each one, with the result that their position either fails to change or deteriorates. In the case of question marks, for example, they should either be dropped or receive the level of support needed to improve their segment position dramatically.

➡ Draining the cash cows of funds and weakening them prematurely and unnecessarily. Alternatively, investing too much in cash cows, with the result that the funding available for question marks, stars and dogs is insufficient.

➡ Seeing models of portfolio analysis as anything more than a *contributor* to decision-making. When the planner begins to use models such as the BCG growth–share matrix to replace evaluation and judgement by relying upon the essentially prescriptive ideas associated with each cell (e.g *always* milk cash cows, *always* shoot dogs, and so on) as the basis for action, there is the potential for disaster. Given this, a summary of the pros and cons of the Boston matrix – and, by extension, a number of the other models of portfolio analysis that we examine later in this chapter – appears in Figure 9.4.

It should be apparent from the discussion so far that cash cows are essential to the health and long-term profitability of the organization, since they provide the funds needed if it is to develop and realize its full potential. The reality in many companies, however, is that cash cows are often in short supply and may already have been too vigorously milked. In 1988, for example, Booz, Allen & Hamilton estimated that, in traditional portfolio analysis terms, 72 per cent of business units in the USA were dogs, 15 per cent cash cows, 10 per cent question marks and only 3 per cent stars. There is little evidence to suggest that the proportions in the UK at the time were radically different or, indeed, that they have changed a great deal since then. Recognizing this, the strategist needs to focus upon the long term and consider how best to manage the portfolio and ensure that the organization benefits from a *succession* of cash cows. Any failure to do this is likely to lead to suboptimal management and the sorts of disaster sequences that are illustrated in Figure 9.5.

Pros

➡ It is an easy-to-use guide that helps managers to think about the investment needs of a portfolio of businesses

➡ It provides a useful basis for thinking about priorities across a spread of activities

Cons

➡ It is a guide to **investment** rather than strategy

➡ It rests on the implicit assumption that business planning is driven by just two factors, growth rate and market share, and in doing this ignores the spectrum of factors that influence profitability, such as competitive intensity, competitive advantage and customer needs

➡ Cash flow is seen to be dependent upon market growth and market share. In practice, this is not necessarily the case

➡ Market share is rarely as easily defined as the model suggests. With the erosion of geographic boundaries and the emergence of a radically different competitive environment, share is often far more fluid and difficult to measure

➡ The model fails to come to terms with the nature of the strategy and form of competitive advantage that will lead to success

Figure 9.4 The pros and cons of the Boston matrix

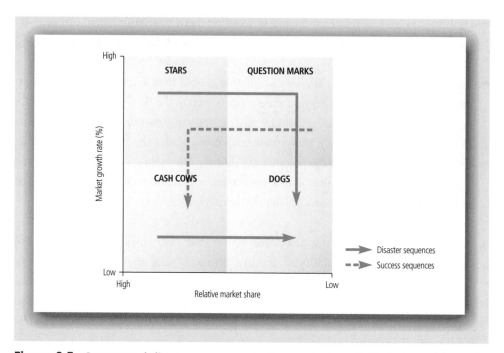

Figure 9.5 Success and disaster sequences in the product portfolio (adapted from the Boston Consulting Group, 1971)

A second model developed by the Boston Consulting Group – the growth–gain matrix – can go some way towards helping the strategist avoid problems such as those shown in Figure 9.5. The alternative matrix, which is often used in conjunction with growth–share analysis, illustrates the extent to which the growth of each product or SBU is keeping pace with market growth. The matrix, which is illustrated in Figure 9.6(a), features the growth rate of the product (or of its capacity) on the horizontal axis and the growth rate of the market on the vertical axis. Products with a growth rate just equal to the market growth rate are located on the diagonal. Share losers therefore appear above the diagonal, while share gainers are below.

Figure 9.6(b) shows the ideal location of products within a portfolio. Here, the dogs are clustered along or near the market growth axis, a position that reflects zero capacity growth. Cash cows are concentrated along the diagonal, showing that market share is being maintained. Stars should appear in the high-growth sector since they should be gaining, or at the very least holding, market share. Question marks then appear in two clusters, with one group receiving little support while the other is receiving the considerable support needed to maximize its chances of producing stars.

In discussing how best to use and interpret the growth–gain matrix, Alan Zakon (1971) of the Boston Consulting Group has highlighted the significance of the firm's *maximum sustainable growth*; this is plotted as a solid vertical line on the matrix. 'The weighted average growth rate of the products within the portfolio cannot', he emphasizes, 'exceed this maximum sustainable rate.' Where, however, the 'centre of gravity' (i.e. the weighted average growth rate) is to the left of this line, scope exists for further

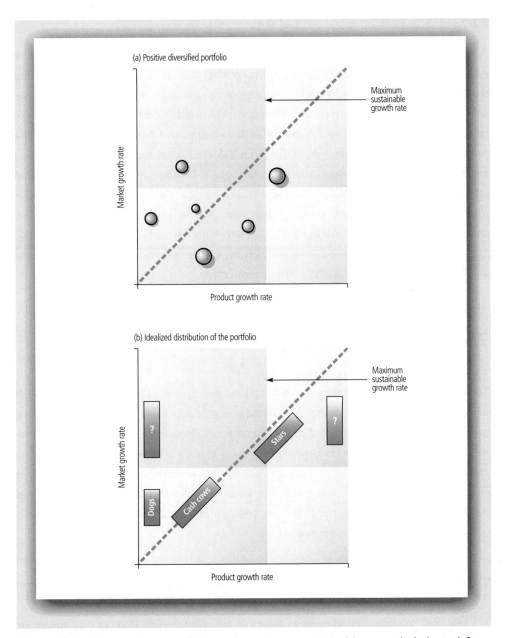

Figure 9.6 The product portfolio and maximum sustainable growth (adapted from the Boston Consulting Group, 1971)

growth. This would typically be achieved by a series of strategy changes to reposition products. As an example of this, extra funds might be shifted to one of the stars in order to achieve even higher rates of growth.

Used in this way, the growth–gain matrix provides a basis for moving the portfolio closer to the 'ideal' position of maximum sustainable growth. Equally, by plotting growth–gain matrices for each major competitor, the strategist can, as with growth–share analysis, gain an insight into the areas of competitive emphasis and react accordingly.

Portfolio analysis: an initial assessment

Although the BCG matrices have a number of obvious attractions, a word of caution needs to be uttered, since they do not represent the ultimate management panacea that many of their advocates in the early days argued. It should be recognized that the practical value of portfolio analysis is influenced significantly both by the quality of the basic data inputs, many of which are difficult to define and measure, and the broader political and social environments within which decisions are made. It was therefore in an attempt to give greater specific recognition to a broader spectrum of factors that other approaches to portfolio analysis, including the General Electric multifactor matrix, the Shell directional policy matrix, the Arthur D. Little strategic condition matrix, and Abell and Hammond's 3×3 relative investment opportunity chart have been developed. It is to these models, which are concerned with market attractiveness and business position, that we now turn our attention.

9.5 Market attractiveness and business position assessment

The two BCG matrices we have discussed so far are capable of providing the strategist with an understanding of several important strategic relationships, including internal cash flows, and market share and growth trajectories. However, it is generally acknowledged that, while the insights provided by these models is undoubtedly of significant value, they are in the majority of cases insufficient if worthwhile investment decisions affecting the future of the business are to be made. More specifically, critics such as Abell and Hammond (1979, pp. 211–12) have highlighted the three major shortcomings of relying simply on growth–share analysis:

1 Often, factors other than relative market share and industry growth play a significant role in influencing cash flow.
2 Cash flow may well be viewed as being of less significance than rate of return on investment (ROI) as a means of comparing the attractiveness of investing in one business rather than another.
3 Portfolio charts provide little real insight into how one business unit compares with another in terms of investment opportunity. Is it the case, for example, that a star is always a better target for investment than a cash cow? Equally, problems are often encountered in comparing question marks when trying to decide which should receive funds to make it a star and which should be allowed to decline.

Recognition of these sorts of problems has led to the development of an approach that is labelled '*market attractiveness–business position assessment*', the best known of which is the General Electric model.

The General Electric multifactor portfolio model

The thinking behind General Electric's multifactor model is straightforward and based on the argument that it is not always possible or appropriate to develop objectives or to make investment decisions for an SBU solely on the basis of its position in the growth–share matrix. The General Electric model therefore takes the general approach a step further by introducing a greater number of variables against which the position of SBUs might be plotted. This model, which appears in Figure 9.7, involves SBUs being rated against two principal dimensions: *industry attractiveness* and *competitive position*.

The circles then represent not the size of the SBU, but rather the size of the market in question, with the shaded part of the circle representing the SBU's market share. The thinking behind the choice of the two axes is based on the notion that the success of a company is determined, first, by the extent to which it operates in attractive markets and, second, by the extent to which it possesses the sorts of competitive business strengths needed to succeed in each of these markets. The failure on the part of the planning team to acknowledge this is likely to lead to long-term problems, since strong companies that operate in an unattractive market and weak companies operating in an attractive market will almost invariably underperform.

Recognizing this requires the planner to measure each of the two dimensions. In order to do this, the factors underlying each dimension must be identified, measured and then combined to form an index. Although within each dimension the list of factors that combine to form a measure of attractiveness will be specific to each company, it is possible to identify the sorts of factor that will, in nearly every instance, be of relevance. *Industry attractiveness*, for example, is determined to a very large extent by the market's size, its rate of growth, the nature, degree and bases of competition, the pace of technological change,

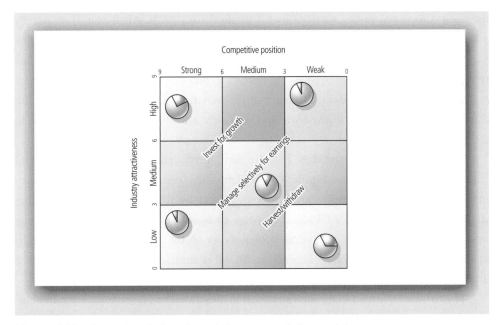

Figure 9.7 The General Electric multifactor portfolio model

the extent to which it is constrained by government or legislative regulations, the opportunities for profit that exist, and so on. Equally, *business strength* is influenced by such factors as market share, product quality, brand image and reputation, levels of management and operational capability, production capabilities, cost factors, the organization's distribution reach and strength, and the nature of the customer base and levels of loyalty.

It can be seen from Figure 9.7 that the nine cells of the General Electric matrix fall into three distinct areas, each of which requires a different approach to management and investment. The three cells at the top left of the matrix are the most attractive in which to operate and require a policy of investment for growth. The three cells that run diagonally from the top right to the bottom left have a medium attractiveness rating – the management of the SBUs within this category should therefore be rather more cautious, with a greater emphasis being placed upon selective investment and earnings retention. The three cells at the bottom right of the matrix are the least attractive in which to operate and management should therefore pursue a policy of harvesting and/or divestment.

As with the BCG matrix, it needs to be recognized that the General Electric approach to portfolio analysis also needs to take account of the probable future of each SBU. The planner should therefore attempt to look ahead by considering life cycles, new forms of technology and their probable impact, likely competitive strategies, and so on. Likely future changes can then be reflected in the matrix by adding a series of arrows showing how each SBU is likely to move over the next few years.

Other portfolio models

Although the BCG and GE models are undoubtedly the best-known approaches to portfolio analysis, a variety of other models have appeared over the years, including the Shell directional policy matrix (Shell Chemical Co., 1975), Abell and Hammond's 3×3 matrix (1979), and the Arthur D. Little strategic condition model (1974).

Shell's directional policy matrix (DPM), which is illustrated in Figure 9.8, again has two key dimensions: the company's *competitive capabilities* and the *prospects for sector profitability*. As with the General Electric matrix, each dimension is then subdivided into three categories. SBUs are located within the matrix and the strategic options open to the company then identified.

The directional policy matrix has, in turn, provided the basis for Abell and Hammond's 3×3 chart (see Figure 9.9), which is designed to depict relative investment opportunities. Although the terminology used by Abell and Hammond differs slightly from that of Shell's DPM – company competitive capability, for example, is referred to as business position, while prospects for sector profitability is termed market attractiveness – the thinking behind the model is similar and indeed can be seen to link back to the General Electric approach.

The Arthur D. Little (ADL) model, which is illustrated in Figure 9.10, is again similar in concept, although here the two dimensions used are the firm's *competitive position* and the *stage of industry maturity*.

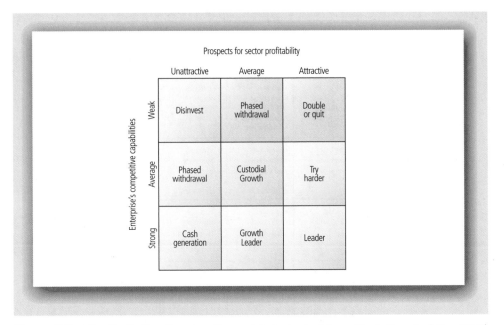

Figure 9.8 The Shell directional policy matrix (adapted from Shell Chemical Co., 1975)

Competitive position, it is suggested, is influenced by the geographical scope of the industry and the specific product–market sectors in which the SBU operates. It is not therefore simply market share that influences competitive position, but also competitive economics and a series of other factors, including technology. This led ADL to the recognition of five main categories of competitive position:

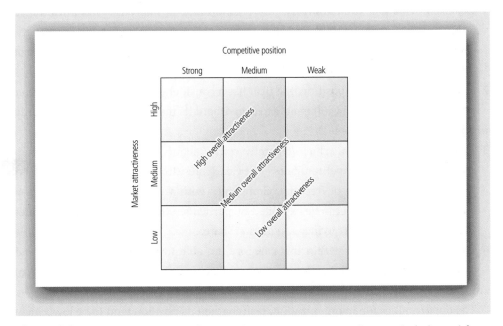

Figure 9.9 Abell and Hammond's 3 × 3 investment opportunity matrix (adapted from Abell and Hammond, 1979)

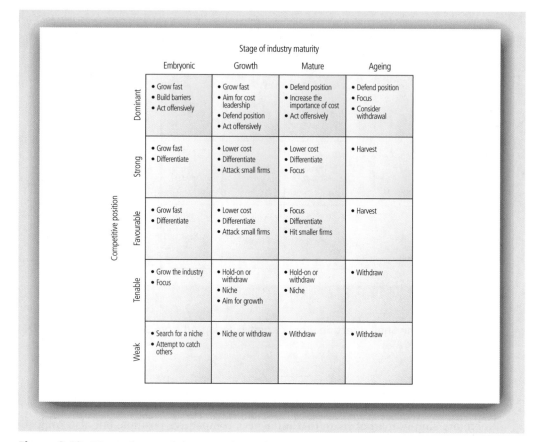

Figure 9.10 The Arthur D. Little strategic condition matrix (adapted from Arthur D. Little, 1974)

1 *Dominant.* This is a comparatively rare position and in many cases is attributable either to a monopoly or a strong and protected technological leadership. The implications are that the firm is able to exert considerable influence over the behaviour of others in the industry and has a wide variety of strategic options open to it.

2 *Strong.* By virtue of this position, the firm has a considerable degree of freedom over its choice of strategy and is often able to act without its market position being unduly threatened by competitors.

3 *Favourable.* This position, which generally comes about when the industry is fragmented and no one competitor stands out clearly, results in the market leaders having a reasonable degree of freedom. Companies with a favourable market position often have strengths that can be exploited by particular strategies and hence a greater than average opportunity to increase market share.

4 *Tenable.* Although firms within this category are able to perform satisfactorily and can justify staying in the industry, they are generally vulnerable in the face of increased competition from stronger and more proactive companies in the market. The opportunities for an organization to strengthen its position tend to be lower than average. The profitability of the tenable firm is best achieved and sustained through a degree of specialization.

5 *Weak.* The performance of firms in this category is generally unsatisfactory, although opportunities for improvement do exist. Often, however, the firm is either too big and inefficient to compete with any real degree of effectiveness, or it is too small to cope with competitive pressures. Unless the firm changes, it is ultimately likely to be forced out of the market or to exit of its own accord.

A sixth position, that of *non-viability*, can be added to this list and applies when the firm's performance is unsatisfactory and there are few, if any, opportunities for improvement. In these circumstances it is essentially a case of the strategist recognizing the reality of the situation and withdrawing from the market in the least costly way.

The second dimension of the model – the *stage of industry maturity*, ranging from embryonic to ageing – has, ADL argue, significant implications for the strategies open to the organization. Thus, once a basic strategy has been identified, there are certain things the strategist must do, might do and should not do if consistency is to be maintained.

This combination of competitive position and industry maturity provides the basis for determining the SBU's strategic condition and, subsequently, the identification and evaluation of the strategic options open to the company. This typically is a choice between investing in order to strengthen or maintain position, spending in order to maintain the status quo, harvesting, or exiting from the industry. In commenting on this, ADL state that 'there is a finite set of available strategies for each Business Unit' and that these can be seen in terms of six generic strategic groups:

1 Market strategies (domestic and international)
2 Product strategies
3 Technology strategies
4 Operations strategies
5 Management and systems strategies
6 Retrenchment strategies.

In choosing among these, ADL identify several guiding principles, the most important of which is that 'strategy selection (should) be driven by the condition of the business, not the condition of its managers'. In making this comment, ADL are arguing for realism in strategic planning and that it is this that should prevail if the organization is not to overreach itself.

9.6 Criticisms of portfolio analysis

Despite the rapid growth, adoption and indeed the apparent attractions of the underlying logic of portfolio analysis, it has been subject to a considerable and growing volume of criticism over the past 20 years. Although it is acknowledged by its critics that the sort of models referred to here have encouraged managers to think strategically, consider the economics of their businesses in greater detail, examine the nature of inter-relationships, and adopt a more proactive approach to management, many writers have argued that the models are generally too simplistic in their structure. In commenting on this, Kotler (1997, p. 77) suggests that:

*"*Portfolio analysis models must be used cautiously. They may lead the company to place too much emphasis on market-share growth and entry into high growth businesses, or to neglect its current businesses. The model's results are sensitive to the ratings and weights and can be manipulated to produce a desired location in the matrix. Furthermore, since these models use an averaging process, two or more businesses may end up in the same cell position but differ greatly in the underlying ratings and weights. Many businesses will end up in the middle of the matrix as the result of compromises in ratings, and this makes it hard to know what the appropriate strategy should be. Finally, the models fail to delineate the synergies between two or more businesses, which means that making decisions for one business at a time may be risky.*"*

These sorts of criticisms have been echoed by others, who have pointed to the way in which many firms managed to cope with the recession of the 1970s and early 1980s not because of a portfolio of products or even a high market share, but rather as the result of a strategy of concentrating upon a single product and market. Equally, many other firms, and especially those in mature markets, he suggests, have not only survived but have also prospered despite having products that, in portfolio analysis terms, would be universally classified as dogs. Brownlie (1983) also discusses these criticisms in some detail, and is worth quoting at length. He suggests that:

*"*Additional criticism of the BP [business portfolio] approach tends to focus on its over-simplified, and somewhat misleading, representation of possible strategy positions; and its use of the dimensions growth rate and market share, which are themselves considered to be inadequate measures of, respectively, industry attractiveness and competitive position. As Wensley concludes, this approach to strategy development 'encourages the use of general rather than specific criteria as well as implying assumptions about mechanisms of corporate financing and market behaviour which are rather unnecessary or false'. Indeed, it has been observed that market leadership does not always offer the benefits of lower costs, more positive cash flow and higher profits. On the contrary: the number of highly viable companies occupying market 'niches' is legion, and growing by the day. Recent trends that have favoured the development of greater specialization in some markets include the growth of private label consumer products and the emergence of differential preferences in some industrial markets, for example computers, as customers become familiar with product, or develop relevant in-house expertise.*"*

The business portfolio approach also tends to overlook other important and strategic factors that are more a function of the external competitive environment – for example, technological change; barriers to entry; social, legal, political and environmental pressures; union and related human factors; elasticity of demand; and cyclicality of sales. The application of business portfolio analysis to strategic decision-taking is in the manner of a diagnostic rather than a prescriptive aid in instances where observed cash flow patterns do not conform with those on which the four product–market categories are based. This commonly occurs where changes in product–market strategies have short-term transient effects on cash flow.

The limitations and problems of portfolio analysis have also been highlighted by McDonald (1989, p. 2), albeit from a rather different viewpoint from that of most writers. McDonald suggests that the gap between theory and practice is greater in the case of marketing than in any other discipline. One consequence of this, according to McDonald, is that little evidence exists to show that some of the more substantive techniques, such as the Ansoff matrix, the Boston matrix and the directional policy matrix, are used in practice. This is supported by research findings not just in the UK, but also in Australia and Hong Kong. Reid and Hinckley (1989, p. 9), for example, concluded:

*❝*Respondents were asked which techniques they were familiar with. The results were skewed towards ignorance of all the techniques to which they were exposed. The majority were not familiar with any by name.*❞*

Similarly, from a study of Australian management practice, McColl-Kennedy et al. (1990, p. 28) stated that 'The awareness and usage of planning tools is low'.

McDonald suggests that there are three possible explanations for this:

1 Companies have never heard of them
2 Companies have heard of them, but do not understand them
3 Companies have heard of them, have tried them and found that they are largely irrelevant.

More fundamentally, however, he argues that the gap between theory and practice is due to the failure of most writers' attempts to explain the strategic thinking underpinning such techniques. He illustrates this by discussing the directional policy matrix which, he suggests, is a well-known but under-utilized and misunderstood planning tool. This misunderstanding is, in one form or another, common to virtually all approaches to portfolio analysis. However, in the case of the DPM, the problems stem from the complexity of the analytical process that is needed if the model is to be used effectively. Thus:

*❝*The criteria for the vertical axis (market attractiveness) can only be determined once the population of 'markets' has been specified. Once determined, those criteria cannot be changed during the exercise. Another common mistake is to misunderstand that unless the exercise is carried out twice – once for t0 and once for t + 3 – the circles cannot move vertically. Also, the criteria have to change for *every* 'market' assessed on the horizontal axis each time a company's strength in that market is assessed. Some way has also to be found of quantifying the horizontal axis to prevent every market appearing in the left-hand box of the matrix. If we add to this just some of the further complexities involved, such as the need to take the square root of the volume or value to determine circle diameter, the need to understand that the term 'attractiveness' has more to do with future *potential*

than with any externally-derived criteria, and so on, we begin to understand why practising managers rarely use the device.*"*

Despite criticisms such as these, portfolio analysis has many defenders, including Day (1983), who suggests that:

*"*Current criticisms (of portfolio analysis) are unwarranted because they reflect a serious misunderstanding of the proper role of these analytical methods . . . what must be realized is that these methods can facilitate the strategic planning process and serve as a rich source of ideas about possible strategic options. But on their own, these methods cannot present the appropriate strategy or predict the consequences of a specific change in strategy.*"*

In many ways, Day's comments help to put the true role and value of portfolio analysis into perspective. It is not (as some managers appeared to believe in the early days) a set of techniques that guarantees greater success. Rather it is an approach to the formulation of strategy that, if used in the way intended, should force a deeper analysis and give far greater recognition to the interrelationships and implications of these interrelationships to the portfolio of brands or businesses being managed by the company. This, in turn, should lead to a far firmer base for effective decision-making.

This final point in particular was highlighted in 1979 by the results of a *Harvard Business Review*-sponsored study of strategic portfolio planning practices in *Fortune*'s 1000 companies. The study, by Haspelagh (1982), found that portfolio planning helped managers to strengthen their planning processes, particularly in divisionalized and diversified organizations. The secret to success, however, was found to lie not just in the techniques themselves, but also in the challenge of incorporating the theory of the techniques into managerial practice. The findings of the study did highlight several problems of portfolio planning, including the following:

➡ If done properly, the process is time-consuming and firms often experience difficulties of implementation
➡ If the techniques are seen simply as analytical tools, the company sees only limited benefits
➡ All too often, the strategist focuses upon factors that are in a sense inappropriate, e.g. levels of cost efficiency rather than organizational responsiveness
➡ The techniques are of only limited value in addressing the issue of new business generation.

Despite problems such as these, the techniques were found to be popular for a number of reasons:

1 They were felt to lead to improvements in strategies
2 The allocation of resources was improved
3 They provided an improved base for adapting planning to the needs of individual businesses
4 Levels of control improved.

9.7 Summary

In this, the first of three chapters on strategy, we have taken as our primary focus the nature and development of portfolio analysis. As a prelude to this we examined the development of strategic perspectives over the past 35 years, highlighting the way in which the environmental turbulence that characterized the early 1970s led to many managers rethinking their approaches to running their businesses. The new planning perspective that emerged was, we suggested, based on three central premises:

1 A need to view and manage the company's businesses in a similar way to an investment portfolio
2 An emphasis upon each business's future profit potential
3 The adoption of a *strategic* perspective to the management of each business.

The starting point for portfolio analysis involves identifying the organization's *strategic business units*, an SBU being an element of the business as a whole that:

➡ Offers scope for independent planning
➡ Has its own set of competitors
➡ Has a manager with direct profit responsibility who also has control over the profit-influencing factors.

A variety of approaches to portfolio analysis and planning have been developed, the best known of which are:

➡ The Boston Consulting Group's growth–share matrix
➡ The General Electric multifactor matrix
➡ The Shell directional policy matrix
➡ The Arthur D. Little strategic condition matrix
➡ Abell and Hammond's 3 × 3 investment opportunity chart.

The conceptual underpinnings in each case are broadly similar, with consideration being given in one form or another to the SBU's *competitive position* and *market attractiveness/ potential*. Each of the portfolio models also encompasses a series of strategic guidelines and these were examined.

Against this background we focused upon the limitations of portfolio analysis. Although it is acknowledged that these models have encouraged managers to think strategically, to consider the economics of their businesses in greater detail, and to adopt a generally more proactive approach to management, critics have argued that the models are overly simplistic in their structure and often require data inputs that are complex and difficult to obtain. Because of this, it is suggested, usage levels are generally low.

10

The formulation of strategy – 2: generic strategies and the significance of competitive advantage

10.1 Learning objectives

When you have read this chapter you should be able to understand:

(a) the need for a clear statement of marketing strategy;
(b) the types of marketing strategy open to an organization;
(c) the forces that govern competition within an industry and how they interact;
(d) the sources of competitive advantage and how competitive advantage might be leveraged.

10.2 Introduction

Having used the techniques discussed in Chapter 9 to identify the strengths and weaknesses of the product portfolio, the strategist should be in a far stronger position to focus upon the ways in which the organization is most capable of developing. Against this background, we now turn our attention to an examination of some of the principal factors that influence marketing strategy. We begin by examining Michael Porter's work, in which emphasis is given to the need for a clear statement of a generic strategy and for this to be based upon a detailed understanding of corporate capability and competitive advantage. The remainder of the chapter then focuses upon the nature, significance and sources of competitive advantage, the ways in which, in many markets, competitive advantage is being eroded, and how competitive advantage might possibly be leveraged. We then build upon this in Chapter 11, with an examination of the ways in which market leaders, followers, challengers and nichers might make use of this thinking.

However, before doing this it needs to be emphasized that, although a great deal of thinking on strategy revolves around the idea of a (high) degree of competitive antagonism, the reality in many markets is that a competitive complacency emerges, and indeed is encouraged, so that the status quo remains unchanged. In those markets where major changes in competitive position do occur, this may be the result of fat, lazy complacent and arrogant managerial thinking that leads to the firm losing its position. Amongst those to have fallen victim of this are Marks & Spencer in the mid to late 1990s, and the major flag carriers in the airlines market. More often though, it is because the management team of a competitor desperately wants to improve its position. It is this mindset of a quiet desperation and a commitment either to exploiting competitors' vulnerabilities or to redefining the market that is an important characteristic of firms that strengthen their position.

10.3 Types of strategy

Throughout this book we have tried to give full emphasis to the need for objectives and strategy to be realistic, obtainable and based firmly on corporate capability. In practice, of course, this translates into an almost infinite number of strategies that are open to an organization. Porter (1980) has, however, pulled them together and identified three generic types of strategy – *overall cost leadership*, *differentiation* and *focus* – that provide a meaningful basis for strategic thinking (see Figure 10.1). In doing this, he gives emphasis to the need for the strategist to identify a clear and meaningful selling proposition for the organization. In other words, what is our competitive stance, and what do we stand for in the eyes of our customers? Any failure on the part of the strategist to identify and communicate the selling proposition and strategy is, he suggests, likely to lead to a dilution of the offer and to the company ending up as stuck in the middle or, as it appears in Figure 10.1, a middle-of-the-roader heading into the marketing wilderness.

Porter's thesis is therefore straightforward: to compete successfully the strategist needs to select a generic strategy and pursue it consistently. The ways in which this might be done and the benefits and the problems that might possibly be encountered are referred to in Figure 10.2. Obviously, there is no single 'best' strategy even within a given industry, and the task faced by the strategist involves selecting the strategic approach that will best allow it to maximize its strengths vis-à-vis its competitors.

This needs to be done, Porter (1979) suggests, by taking into account a variety of factors, the five most significant of which are:

1 The bargaining power of suppliers
2 The bargaining power of customers
3 The threat of new entrants to the industry
4 The threat of substitute products or services
5 The rivalry among current competitors.

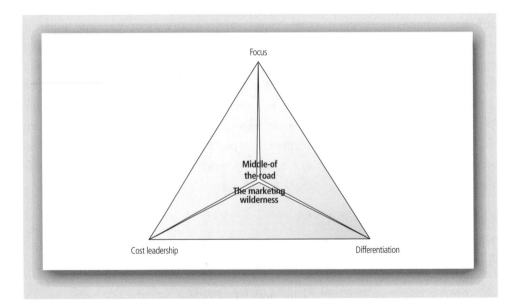

Figure 10.1   Porter's three generic strategies (adapted from Porter, 1980)

Type of strategy	Ways to achieve the strategy	Benefits	Possible problems
Cost leadership	Size and economies of scale Globalization Relocating to low-cost parts of the world Modification/simplification of designs Greater labour effectiveness Greater operating effectiveness Strategic alliances New sources of supply Learning Cost linkages Integration Timing Superior labour and management Advanced technology Smart buying	The ability to: ➡ outperform rivals ➡ erect barriers to entry ➡ resist the five forces	Vulnerability to even lower cost operators Possible price wars The difficulty of sustaining it in the long term
Focus	Concentration upon one or a small number of segments The creation of a strong and specialist reputation	A more detailed understanding of particular segments The creation of barriers to entry A reputation for specialization The ability to concentrate efforts	Limited opportunities for sector growth The possibility of outgrowing the market The decline of the sector A reputation for specialization which ultimately inhibits growth and development into other sectors
Differentiation	The creation of strong brand identities The consistent pursuit of those factors which customers perceive to be important High performance in one or more of a spectrum of activities The creation of strategic breakpoints The achievement of cost parity or cost proximity relative to its competitor in all areas that do **not** affect differentiation Additional features Packaging innovation Distribution innovation Speed of distribution Distribution breadth and/or depth Higher service levels Better after sales service Superior financing deals Greater flexibility Focused relationship building	A distancing from others in the market The creation of a major competitive advantage Flexibility	The difficulties of sustaining the bases for differentiation Possibly higher costs The difficulty of achieving true and meaningful differentiation Creating differences that customers do not value Focusing too much on the core product in developing bases for differentiation Differentiating on dimensions that become less important to customers over time Losing competitive cost proximity Failing to develop barriers to deter imitation and customer switching

Figure 10.2 Selecting and pursuing a generic strategy

Taken together, these factors represent the forces governing the nature and intensity of competition within an industry, and they are the background against which the choice of a generic strategy should be made.

In identifying the three specified generic strategies, Porter suggests that the firms that pursue a particular strategy aimed at the same market or market segment make up a *strategic group*. It is the firm that then manages to pursue the strategy most effectively that will generate the greatest profits. Thus, in the case of firms pursuing a low-cost strategy, it is the firm that ultimately achieves the lowest cost that will do best.

10.4 Porter's three generic competitive strategies

Overall cost leadership

By pursuing a strategy of cost leadership, the organization concentrates upon achieving the lowest costs of production and distribution so that it has the *capability* of setting its prices at a lower level than its competitors. Whether it then chooses to do this depends on its objectives and its perception of the market. Saunders (1987a, p. 12), for example, points to IBM and Boeing, both of which were for many years cost leaders who chose to use their lower costs not to reduce prices but rather to generate higher returns, which were then invested in marketing, R&D and manufacturing as a means of maintaining or strengthening their position. More commonly, however, firms that set out to be cost leaders then use this lower cost base to reduce prices and in this way build market share. Amongst those to have done this are Amstrad (now trading as Viglen) in the 1980s and, more recently, supermarkets such as Netto, Lidl, Asda and Aldi, and the low-cost airlines such as easyJet (see Illustration 10.3) and Ryanair.

Although cost reduction has always been an important element of competitive strategy, Porter (1980, p. 35) has commented that it became increasingly popular in the 1970s, largely because of a greater awareness of the experience curve concept. For it to succeed, he suggests that:

*"*Cost leadership requires aggressive construction of efficient-scale facilities, vigorous pursuit of cost reductions from experience, tight cost and overhead control, avoidance of marginal customer accounts, and cost minimization in areas like R&D, service, sales force, advertising, and so on.*"*

In tackling costs the marketing planner therefore needs to recognize in advance the potential complexity of the task, since the evidence suggests that true cost leaders generally achieve this by very tight and consistent control across *all* areas of the business, including engineering, purchasing, manufacturing, distribution and marketing. An important additional element, of course, is the scale of operations and the scope that exists for economies of scale. However, scale alone does not necessarily lead to lower costs; rather it provides management with an *opportunity* to learn how the triad of technology, management and labour can be used more effectively. Whether these opportunities are then seized depends on the management stance and determination to take advantage of the *potential* that exists for cost cutting. Research has shown, for example, that the Japanese are most adept at gaining experience, doing so at a faster rate than the Americans, who in turn are faster than the Europeans.

While the experience curve can provide the basis for cost reductions, manufacturers can also turn to a variety of other areas, including:

➡ *The globalization of operations*, including brands, in order to benefit from the economies that are not possible by operating purely on a regional basis
➡ *Concentrating the manufacturing effort* in one or two very large plants in countries such as South Korea, Taiwan and the Philippines, which (currently at least) offer a low-cost base
➡ *Modifying designs* to simplify the manufacturing process and make use of new materials
➡ *Achieving greater labour effectiveness* by investing in new plant and processes.

The potential benefits of being a low-cost producer are quite obviously significant, since the organization is then in a far stronger position to resist all five competitive forces, outperform its rivals and erect barriers to entry that will help protect the organization's long-term position. In practice, however, many organizations find the long-term pursuit and maintenance of a cost-leadership strategy to be difficult. The Japanese, for example, based much of their success in the 1960s on aggressive cost management but then found that, because of a combination of rising domestic costs and the emergence of new and even lower-cost competitors such as Taiwan, the position was not necessarily tenable in the long term. Although this realization coincided in many cases with a desire on the part of firms to move further up-market, where the scope for premium pricing is greater, the Japanese experience helps to illustrate the potential danger of an over-reliance upon cost leadership. It is largely because of this that many organizations opt sooner or later for an alternative policy, such as that of differentiation.

The difficulties of maintaining a cost-leadership position were also illustrated in the late 1980s and early 1990s in the UK grocery retailing sector, where the low-cost position had been occupied with some considerable success for a number of years by Kwik Save. The organization came under attack from an aggressive new German entrant to the market, Aldi, and from the Danish company, Netto. Faced with this, Kwik Save was forced into deciding whether to place greater emphasis on differentiation.

The effect of Aldi's entrance was not felt just by Kwik Save. Others, such as Sainsbury's and Tesco, both of which had for a number of years pursued with considerable success a strategy of differentiation, were also forced to respond, albeit in a less direct way. In part, this need to respond can be seen as virtually inevitable in any mature market where the opportunities for substantial growth are limited and a new entrant is therefore able to gain sales only at the expense of firms already in the market. (This is sometimes referred to as a zero-sum game, in that one organization's gain is necessarily another organization's loss.)

It is largely because of the difficulties of maintaining the lowest cost position over time and the vulnerability to a price-led attack that many organizations view cost leadership with a degree of caution and opt instead for one or other of Porter's generic strategies. Most frequently this proves to be differentiation.

Differentiation

By pursuing a strategy of differentiation, the organization gives emphasis to a particular element of the marketing mix that is seen by customers to be important and, as a result, provides a meaningful basis for competitive advantage. The firm might therefore attempt to be the quality leader (Mercedes-Benz with cars, Bang & Olufsen with hi-fi, and Marks & Spencer with food), service leader (Ritz–Carlton), marketing leader (the Japanese with cars), or the technological leader (Makita with rechargeable power tools in the early 1980s and Dolby with noise suppression circuits for tape decks). Other potential bases for differentiation include:

➡ Speed, by being the first into new market segments
➡ Levels of reliability that are higher than those of the competition
➡ Design
➡ Levels of service and delight
➡ Unique product features
➡ The brand image and personality
➡ New technologies
➡ A greater number and/or more relevant product features
➡ Stronger and more meaningful relationships.

Differentiation can also be achieved by means of the brand image and packaging, a ploy that is particularly suited to mature markets in which the products are for the most part physically indistinguishable. This might arguably include cigarettes and beer, where blind tests have shown that even highly brand-loyal customers experience difficulties in identifying their favourite brand. The significance of labels and brand images, and hence their potential for differentiation, is also shown in the fashion clothing industry, where brand names and logos such as Benetton, Nike and Lacoste are often prominently displayed and, by virtue of the images associated with them, used as the basis for premium pricing. The fundamental importance of differentiation has been highlighted by Trout and Rifkin (2000), who argue that far too often planners misunderstand what exactly the term means; this is discussed in Illustration 10.1.

Illustration 10.1 Differentiate or die

Over the past 10 years the word 'unique' has become one of the most frequently used – and abused – words in the marketing lexicon. At the same time, 'unique selling proposition' has become an ever more tired phrase that is deployed more in hope than expectation. It is because of this that Jack Trout, seen by many to be the father of positioning, argues that, in a world in which everything can be copied, it is the company's intangible assets that provide the basis for real differentiation. In his book *Differentiate or Die*, he suggests that marketing planners should not bother extolling the traditional virtues of quality, customer orientation or even creativity, since these are too easily copied. Instead, he suggests that what really matters are the points of difference rooted in areas such as ownership, leadership, heritage and topicality. Being different on the surface is simply not enough any more. Instead, it needs to be based on issues that are far more fundamental.

This focus upon differentiation is of course not new. But the sheer proliferation of products and services is making it imperative to determine just what, if anything, really does make a company different. Trout argues that

difference is only real if its essence can be expressed in just one word.

In the case of Microsoft, the company could, throughout the 1990s, claim that its describing word was 'innovative'; with its problems with American anti-trust legislation, this is no longer the case. Equally, Marks & Spencer used to be synonymous with 'value' whilst BA was 'British' and Gap was 'cool'. All three have, however, lost sight of their core differentiation. By contrast, easyJet is value, Virgin is 'flair', Nike is 'heroism', Sony is 'miniaturized perfection' and Disney is 'fun'.

Source: 'Can You Sum Up Your Brand With A Single Word?', *Marketing*, 20 April 2000, p. 20.

As an example of how a strategy of differentiation can be developed and used as the basis of competitive advantage, some of the major airlines such as Emirates, Singapore Airlines and Cathay Pacific have all used service to distance themselves from many of the other major flag carriers. In the case of first-class and, increasingly, business-class travellers, the fight for long-haul travellers at the beginning of the twenty-first century revolved around the introduction of beds that folded flat so that passengers could sleep more easily.

Differentiation can, however, prove costly if the basis for differentiation that is chosen subsequently proves to be inappropriate. Sony, for example, developed the Betamax format for its video recorders, but ultimately found that the market preferred JVC's VHS system. Despite this, differentiation is potentially a very powerful basis for strategic development, as companies such as Bang & Olufsen, Bose and Tesco have all demonstrated. Its potential is also illustrated by a McGraw-Hill study of industrial buying, which estimated that most buyers would require incentives that equated to a price reduction of between 8 and 10 per cent before considering a switch to a new supplier. In commenting on this, Baker (1985, p. 110) suggests that:

❝Assuming this applies to the average product with a minimum of objective differentiation, it is clear that sellers of highly differentiated products can require an even larger premium. Given higher margins the firm following a differentiated strategy is able to plough back more into maintaining the perception of differentiation through a policy of new product development, promotional activity, customer service, etc., and thereby strengthen the barriers to entry for would-be competitors.❞

It should be apparent from this that, if a strategy of differentiation is to succeed, there is a need for a very different set of skills and attitudes than is suited to cost leadership. Instead of a highly developed set of cost control skills, the strategist needs to be far more innovative and flexible so that me-too companies are kept at a distance.

Focus

The third of the generic strategies identified by Porter involves the organization in concentrating its efforts upon one or more narrow market segments, rather than pursuing a broader-based strategy. By doing this the firm is able to build a greater in-depth knowledge of each of the segments, as well as creating barriers to entry by virtue of its specialist reputation. Having established itself, the firm will typically then, depending upon the specific demands of the market, develop either a cost-based or differentiated strategy. Among those that have used this approach successfully, at least in the short term, at various stages are Laura Ashley, Thorntons (the chocolate manufacturers) and Land Rover. Other firms that have used a focused strategy are Morgan with cars, Steinway with pianos and, perhaps to a lesser degree, Apple with an emphasis upon the design world.

One of the biggest problems faced by companies adopting this approach stems paradoxically from its potential for success since, as the organization increases in size, there is a tendency both to outgrow the market and to lose the immediacy of contact that is often needed. As a general rule, therefore, a focused strategy is often best suited to smaller firms, since it is typically these that have the flexibility to respond quickly to the specialized needs of small segments. (At this stage, it may be useful to refer to the discussion of the supernichers on pp. 464–5.)

Specializing in this way also enables the organization to achieve at least some of the benefits of the other two strategies since, although in absolute terms the scale of operations may be limited, the organization may well have the largest economies of scale *within* the chosen segment. Equally, the greater the degree of concentration upon a target market, the more specialized is the firm's reputation and hence the greater the degree of perceived product differentiation.

Although Porter presents competitive strategies in this way, many companies succeed not by a blind adherence to any one approach, but rather by a combination of ideas. For many years, for example, the buying power and expertise of Marks & Spencer made it a (relatively) low-cost operator, whilst at the same time it differentiated itself on the basis of service and quality. Equally, Porsche pursues a strategy that combines both focus and differentiation.

It follows from this that the identification, development and maintenance of a competitive advantage, and hence a strong selling proposition, is at the very heart of an effective marketing strategy. In practice though, many organizations find this to be a difficult exercise, something that Levi's learned in the 1990s (see Illustration 10.2).

Illustration 10.2 The fall and rise of Levi's – the long-term problems of market fragmentation

For eleven consecutive years between 1985 and 1996, Levi's saw its global sales rise, culminating in a peak that year of $7.1 billion. Two years later, with sales in the UK having dropped by 23 per cent, Levi's was forced to rethink its strategy. Having relied for too long upon 501s and a mass-market strategy that allowed a number of fashion brands such as Diesel and YSL to erode its share in a declining or fragmenting market, the company fought back with a radically different approach.

In commenting on this, Ellsworth (2000) highlights the way in which:

> The company decided that innovation was the key and in October 1998 shifted its focus from individual product lines to a portfolio of brand bases – aligned with consumer segments – with particular emphasis on the 15- to 24-year-old youth sector. This enabled Levi's to take on smaller brands such as Diesel, own labels such as Gap and some designer ranges. But, like others, Levi's also faced competition from retail areas such as mobiles, CDs and DVDs.

Levi's further rationalized its lines by pulling out of the European children's jeans market to concentrate on 15- to 24-year-olds.

At the same time, the company also launched three premium sub-brands (Levi's Vintage, based on the original Levi's jeans from the 1850s; Red, a 'luxury' sub-brand; and ICD+, a joint initiative with Philips that incorporates 'wearable electronics' such as mobile phones into its design) and its Advanced Retail Concept (ARC), which replaced the traditional American theme with a lighter store design that included specific youth-oriented areas. The company also attacked the youth market through the sponsorship of live music events.

But although the strategy and the fight-back has been successful, the question of whether it is capable of achieving its high point of a 21.5 per cent share of the UK market is debatable. At the heart of Levi's problems is that the jeans market, in common with many brand-driven markets, has fragmented. Faced with fifteen rather than five other players, the fight for share becomes ever more desperate.

Source: Ellsworth (2000).

Without an advantage, however, the stark reality is that the organization runs the risk of drifting into the strategic twilight zone of being a middle-of-the-roader or, in Porter's terms, 'stuck in the middle'.

Porter's generic strategies: a brief comment

Although Porter believes strategy needs to be thought about in terms of these three generic approaches, this thinking has been the subject of a considerable amount of criticism in recent years. Given this, Figure 10.3 summarizes the pros and cons of the approach.

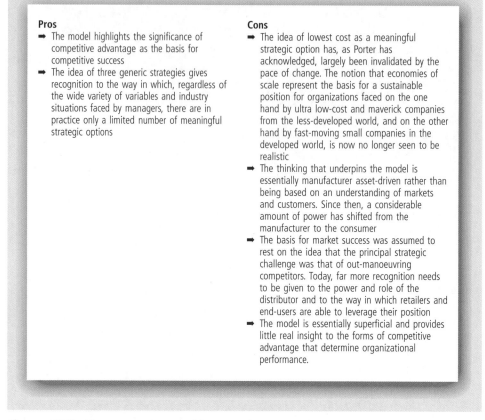

Pros
→ The model highlights the significance of competitive advantage as the basis for competitive success
→ The idea of three generic strategies gives recognition to the way in which, regardless of the wide variety of variables and industry situations faced by managers, there are in practice only a limited number of meaningful strategic options

Cons
→ The idea of lowest cost as a meaningful strategic option has, as Porter has acknowledged, largely been invalidated by the pace of change. The notion that economies of scale represent the basis for a sustainable position for organizations faced on the one hand by ultra low-cost and maverick companies from the less-developed world, and on the other hand by fast-moving small companies in the developed world, is now no longer seen to be realistic
→ The thinking that underpins the model is essentially manufacturer asset-driven rather than being based on an understanding of markets and customers. Since then, a considerable amount of power has shifted from the manufacturer to the consumer
→ The basis for market success was assumed to rest on the idea that the principal strategic challenge was that of out-manoeuvring competitors. Today, far more recognition needs to be given to the power and role of the distributor and to the way in which retailers and end-users are able to leverage their position
→ The model is essentially superficial and provides little real insight to the forms of competitive advantage that determine organizational performance.

Figure 10.3 The pros and cons of Porter's three generic strategies

10.5 Competitive advantage and its pivotal role in strategic marketing planning

Making use of the value chain

"The most successful species are those which adapt best to the changing environment. The most successful individuals are those with the greatest competitive advantage over the others."

> Charles Darwin, *The Origin of Species by Means of Natural Selection*, 1859

In discussing competitive advantage, Porter (1985a, Chapter 2) suggests that it:

". . . grows out of the value a firm is able to create for its buyers that exceeds the firm's cost of creating it. Value is what the buyer is willing to pay, and superior stems from offering lower prices than competitors for equivalent benefits or providing unique benefits that more than offset a higher price. There are two basic types of competitive advantage: cost leadership and differentiation."

He goes on to suggest that a convenient tool for identifying and understanding the potential competitive advantages possessed by a firm is by means of value chain analysis. In making this comment, Porter gives recognition to the way in which a firm is a collection of activities that are performed to design, produce, market, deliver and support its product.

The value chain (introduced in Chapter 2, pp. 70–1) disaggregates a firm into nine strategically significant activities so that the strategist is more easily able to understand the source and behaviour of costs in the specific business and industry, and the existing and potential sources of differentiation. These nine value activities consist of five primary activities and four support activities.

The five *primary* activities to which Porter refers are concerned with the process of bringing raw materials into the organization and then modifying them in some way as a prelude to distribution, marketing and servicing them. The *support* activities, which take place at the same time, are concerned with procurement, technology development, human resource management and the firm's infrastructure (e.g. its management, planning, finance, accounting and legal affairs). The strategist's job therefore involves focusing upon the levels of cost and performance in each of the nine value areas in order to identify any opportunities for improvement. The extent to which this is achieved, relative to competitors, is a measure of competitive advantage. However, in making this comment it needs to be emphasized that different firms operating in the same industry are often capable of creating value in very different ways.

In searching for competitive advantage through the value chain, Porter also gives emphasis to the need to look outside the organization and to consider the value chains of suppliers, distributors and customers, since improvements to each of these will also help in the search for an advantage. As an example of this, a supplier or distributor might be helped to reduce costs, with all or part of the savings then being passed back to the company and used as another means of gaining cost leadership. Equally, an organization might work closely with its suppliers to ensure that particular levels of quality or service are achieved. Marks & Spencer, for example, has traditionally worked very closely with its suppliers to ensure that quality levels are maintained. Similarly, the major food retailers work with their suppliers in areas such as product development and cost control. In each case, the rationale is the same – that of achieving a competitive advantage.

Although the value chain is generally recognized to be a useful framework for searching systematically for greater competitive advantage, its usefulness in practice has been shown to vary from one industry to another. Recognition of this has led the Boston Consulting Group to develop a matrix in which they distinguish between four types of industry (see Figure 10.4).

The two dimensions they identify in doing this are concerned with the *size of the competitive advantage* and the *number of approaches to gaining advantage*. The characteristics of the four types of industry are outlined in Figure 10.5.

It can be seen from this that the scope for benefiting from cost or performance opportunities can vary considerably from one type of industry to another. In some industries, for example, it will be the case that the only opportunities for advantage are small and easily copied. Faced with this, an organization needs to institutionalize the process for searching for new ideas so that, although it is unlikely ever to gain a

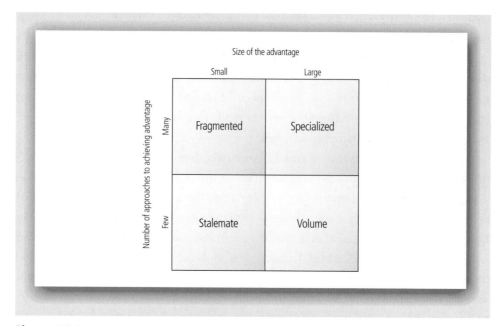

Figure 10.4 The Boston Consulting Group's strategic environment matrix

significant or long-term advantage, it benefits from a whole series of small and constantly updated advantages.

Developing a sustainable advantage

This need to understand that the bases of competition and the way in which competitive advantage is achieved should not be seen in any absolute way can perhaps best be illustrated by recognizing that markets can be viewed in a variety of ways and that a

Volume industry. A volume industry is one in which organizations can typically gain only a few, but generally large, advantages. In the construction equipment industry, for example, firms can pursue either the low-cost position or the highly differentiated position, and succeed in either case. Profitability is therefore a function both of size and market share.

Stalemated industry. Here there are few potential competitive advantages and those that do exist are generally small. An example of this is the steel industry where scope for differentiation is limited, as indeed are the opportunities for significant cost reduction. In these circumstances, size is unrelated to profitability.

Fragmented industry. A fragmented industry is one in which companies have numerous opportunities for differentiation, although each is of limited value. The hairdressing industry typically exhibits this characteristic, where hairdressers can be differentiated in a wide variety of ways but increases in market share tend to be small. Profitability is rarely related to size and both small and large operations can be equally profitable or unprofitable.

Specialized industry. In a specialized industry the opportunities for differentiation are numerous and the payoffs from each can be significant. An example would be the specialist machine tool industry where machinery is made for specific customers and market segments. Here, profitability and size are rarely related.

Figure 10.5 Industry type and the scope for competitive advantage

product can also be used in many different ways. It follows from this that every time the product–market combination changes, so too does the relative competitive strength or competitive advantage. The implications of this are significant and are reflected by the way in which a key element in any strategy revolves around choosing the competitor whom you wish to challenge, as well as choosing the market segment and product characteristics with which you will compete.

The problem faced by many companies, therefore, is not how to *gain* a competitive advantage, but how to *sustain* it for any length of time. Most marketers are, for example, fully aware of the profit potential associated with a strategy based on, say, premium quality or technological leadership. The difficulty that is all too often faced in practice, however, is how to guard against predators and capitalize on these benefits *over the long term*. Business history is full of examples of companies that, having invested in a particular strategy, then fall victim to a larger or more agile organization. The question faced by many marketing strategists at one time or another is therefore how best to sustain a competitive advantage.

A framework for thinking about competitive advantage and how it links to the organization's subsequent performance has been proposed by Cravens (1996). This is shown in Figure 10.6.

A fundamental understanding of competitive advantage and how it is capable of undermining the competition was at the heart of the easyJet strategy. This is discussed in Illustration 10.3, and shows how the low-cost airline developed, leveraged and exploited competitive advantage to become a significant player in the European airlines market.

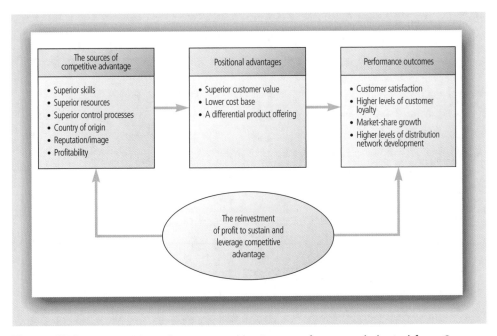

Figure 10.6   Competitive advantage and business performance (adapted from Cravens, 1996, p. 36)

Illustration 10.3 easyJet – competitive advantage through low costs and low prices

In December 1992, the European Union deregulated the airline industry. The implications of this were significant and meant that any European carrier could fly to any European destination and demand landing slots. Recognizing the opportunities that this created, large numbers of new airlines emerged, all of which focused upon offering low prices. However, the majority of these companies quickly encountered problems and, by 1996, sixty of the eighty carriers that had started up after deregulation had gone bankrupt. Given these odds, the success of easyJet is therefore particularly impressive.

The development of the company

Stelios Haji-Ioannou, easyJet's founder, modelled much of his early thinking for the company on the low-cost US carrier, Southwest Airlines. Recognizing that the key to success in this sector of the market was the tight control of costs, he launched the company in 1995, and concentrated upon rethinking and reinventing airline operating practice. An important first step in this was to base the airline at Luton, just north of London, rather than at Heathrow or Gatwick, since it offered lower labour costs and lower airport fees. Whenever possible, he also flew in to the less busy secondary airports in Europe rather than each city's more expensive main airport, which, he calculated, saved £10 per passenger.

This approach to the very tight management of costs was also reflected by the way in which the company focused upon:

➡ One type of aircraft.
➡ Point-to-point short-haul travel.

➡ No in-flight meals (this saved £14 per passenger).
➡ Rapid turnaround times; these averaged 25 minutes.
➡ Very high aircraft utilization – aircraft flew an average of 11.5 hours per day rather than the industry average of six hours. The net effect of this was that two planes could do the work of three.
➡ Direct sales rather than via travel agents, since travel agents and computer reservation systems, it was calculated, added 25 per cent to operating costs.
➡ Booking over the Internet wherever possible. In March 1999, Internet sales accounted for 15 per cent of revenues. By October of that year, it was more than 60 per cent of revenues. By mid-2000, it was more than 70 per cent, a figure that the company aimed to increase yet further by replacing the telephone number livery on its planes with the Internet address.
➡ Ticketless travel. Customers paid by credit card and were given a six-character reference number. This number was the only information needed for passengers to board the plane.
➡ Selling drinks and refreshments.
➡ One class of seating in order to avoid the extra space demanded by business-class passengers.
➡ Yield management in order to sell as large a number of seats as possible. Seats are sold in what could be considered a lottery system – the more people who demand a particular flight, the higher the fare. Put differently, if the load factor (percentage of seats sold) was higher than normal, prices automatically increased. This system worked well for easyJet because it helped to avoid selling out popular flights months

in advance. Yield management also served another purpose – it drew potential customers who were in search of cheap fares. Once they found there were no more cheap seats, they usually bought a ticket anyway, since the next highest fare was still cheaper than easyJet's competitors. Stelios defended his policy vigorously: 'We decided that people who are willing to give us their money early should get a better price, and those who want the flexibility of booking late should pay a bit more.' The net effect of this was that load factors were consistently in excess of 80 per cent.

➡ The outsourcing of as many services as possible, including check-in and the on-site information desk.

This idea of no-frills travel was based on Stelios's belief that 'When someone is on a bus, he doesn't expect any free lunch. I couldn't see why we cannot educate our customers to expect no frills on board.'

But whilst the company aggressively managed costs, it emphasized that it would never compromise on safety, flew new Boeing 737s and only hired experienced pilots who were paid market rates. Stelios commented:

If you advertise a very cheap price, people expect an old airplane. But when they come on board and see a brand new plane, they are impressed. Likewise, many customers expect an unhappy staff because they believe they are not paid well, but they come on board and see the staff are smiling.

The significance of service

In the same way that the company was not prepared to compromise on safety, Stelios believed that low cost and high levels of service and customer satisfaction were not incompatible.

The company saw its principal target market to be people who paid for their own travel. Although they did not target the business market, on some routes, such as London–Amsterdam, London–Glasgow and London–Edinburgh, business travellers typically accounted for 50 per cent of the passengers. However, regardless of whether the passenger was a business or private traveller, punctuality was seen to be important and linked closely to satisfaction. If, therefore, a flight arrived more than four hours late, passengers would receive a signed letter of apology and a full refund.

Taking on the competition

As with many new entrants to a long-established and mature market, the threat posed by easyJet was initially underestimated by some of the major players. When they did begin to recognize that the low-price airlines might possibly be serious competitors, they were initially unsure of how to respond. This was reflected by the way in which, according to easyJet (Rogers, 2000, p. 9):

. . . in 1996, Bob Ayling, British Airways chief, approached Stelios in what appeared to be an offer to buy easyJet. Instead, after a three-month courtship, British Airways abandoned the deal, and one year later, launched Go!, its own budget airline. Still angry over the incident, Stelios got his revenge by buying several rows of seats on Go!'s first flight. He commanded his staff to don orange boiler jackets, and they all boarded the flight like a group of merry pranksters, offering free flights on easyJet to Go!'s passengers. Barbara Cassani, chief executive of Go! airlines, was on the inaugural flight to welcome new passengers. When she saw what was occurring, she lapsed into stunned silence. The publicity stunt paid off for easyJet. Go! Airlines announced losses of £22 million in 1999.

The low-price airlines market grew quickly as the result of the sorts of activities pursued by easyJet and its major competitor Ryanair, with a host of other companies such as Buzz, BMI Baby and Virgin Express entering the market, albeit with varying degrees of success.

In 2002, the company took its next major step by buying its rival Go!, which, through a management buy-out, BA had sold to Cassani and her team.

Source: Rogers (2000).

easyJet: a postscript

The low-cost business model used by companies such as Southwest Airlines, easyJet and Ryanair is one which, if managed properly, can prove to be enormously attractive. It is also one that is fraught with danger. If an organization is to pursue a low-cost strategy successfully, it is essential that costs are continually and ruthlessly driven out of the business, something that the low-price grocery retailers such as Aldi and Netto have long realized. As soon as the management team loses sight of this imperative, the organization is likely to suffer in a dramatic fashion as it falls into the marketing wilderness (see Figure 10.1). This was a lesson learned by the retailer Kwik Save.

The issue of how to develop and sustain a competitive advantage has also been discussed in detail by Davidson (1987a, p. 153). He suggests:

"Competitive advantage is achieved whenever you do something better than competitors. If that something is important to consumers, or if a number of small advantages can be combined, you have an *exploitable* competitive advantage. One or more competitive advantages are usually necessary in order to develop a winning strategy, and this in turn should enable a company to achieve above-average growth and profits."

For Davidson, the ten most significant potential competitive advantages are:

1 *A superior product or service benefit*, as shown by First Direct with its combination of service and value; Pilkington with its self-cleaning glass, Toyota and Lexus with their very high levels of reliability; Disneyland with its overall quality of service; and Samsung initially with its price–performance combination and then more recently with its emphasis upon design, quality and value.

2 *A perceived advantage or superiority*. Marlboro, with its aggressively masculine image featuring cowboys, holds a 22 per cent share of the US cigarette market. The brand is well marketed but there is no reason to believe the cigarettes are objectively superior. Other examples of a perceived superiority advantage include designer label clothing and bottled waters.

3 *Low-cost operations* as the result of a combination of high productivity, low overheads, low labour costs, better purchasing skills, a limited product range, or

low-cost distribution. Amongst those to have achieved this are the low-cost supermarket chains such as Aldi, Netto and Wal-Mart.

4 *Global experience, global skills and global coverage.* Amongst the most effective global operators are Coca-Cola and McDonald's. In the case of Coca-Cola, the brand's coverage has moved from around 2.26 billion people in 1984 to almost 6 billion today, with the result that there are few places in the world where Coca-Cola is not readily available. For McDonald's, its 30 000 outlets worldwide (2002 figures) allow it to serve 46 million customers each day.

5 *Legal advantages* in the form of patents, copyright, sole distributorships, or a protected position.

6 *Superior contacts and relationships* with suppliers, distributors, customers, the media and government, and the management of customer databases.

7 *Scale advantages* that enable costs to be driven down and competitors pushed into a position of competitive disadvantage.

8 *Offensive attitudes* or, as Procter & Gamble label it, an attitude of competitive toughness and a determination to win.

9 *Superior competencies.* Ikea's focus upon developing competencies in product design, warehousing, purchasing and packaging, for example, has allowed it to offer consumers high quality and low prices.

10 *Superior assets*, which may include property or distribution outlets.

Although Davidson's list of the ten bases of competitive advantage is generally comprehensive, there are several other elements that can be added. These include:

➡ The notion of intellectual capital, which embraces the knowledge base of staff across the organization (this is typically the basis for the competitive advantage of management consulting firms and advertising agencies)

➡ Attitudinal issues that give recognition to the idea that creativity and innovation, be it product or process, is ultimately the only really sustainable form of competitive advantage

➡ Sophisticated service support systems

➡ Superior knowledge as a result of more effective market research, a better understanding of costs, superior information systems and a particularly highly skilled workforce

➡ Superior technologies

➡ Complex selling systems

➡ Speed to market (time-based competition)

➡ The brand image and reputation.

In so far as there is a single factor that underpins all eighteen factors listed here, it is that of adding value to the ways in which the organization interacts with the customer, something that is clearly understood within Tesco (see Illustration 10.4). In the absence of this, there is no real competitive advantage.

Illustration 10.4 Tesco and its leveraging of competitive advantage

A fundamental understanding of the significance of competitive advantage was at the heart of Tesco's strategy throughout the 1990s. Their performance outstripped that of the vast majority of retailers and has led not just to the company taking over as the market leader from Sainsbury's in the UK food retailing market, but also to its increasingly successful development of clothes retailing. In doing this, the company has concentrated on developing a series of competitive advantages that, taken together, represent an enormously strong selling proposition, provide consumers with a powerful reason to buy, and put competitors at a disadvantage.

An alternative way of thinking about competitive advantage involves categorizing the bases of advantage under four headings: management, behaviour, staff and the marketing mix.

Management advantages include:

➡ The overall level of management ability
➡ The willingness and ability of the marketing team to redefine the market in order to create market breakpoints
➡ The ability to identify and manage risk
➡ Managerial mindsets
➡ Experience
➡ A focus upon implementation.

Behavioural and attitudinal advantages include:

➡ Offensive attitudes (refer also to the discussion on FUD marketing on p. 442)
➡ Flexibility and speed of response
➡ A willingness to take risks.

Staff resource advantages include:

➡ Levels of creativity
➡ Networks
➡ Staff mindsets.

Marketing mix advantages include:

➡ The nature of each of the elements of the expanded marketing mix
➡ The speed of innovation
➡ Management of the distribution network.

However, irrespective of the type of market in which the organization is operating, competitive advantage must always be looked at from the standpoint of the customer since, unless the customer sees something to be significant, it is not a competitive advantage. Recognition of this leads to a three-part test that the marketing planner needs to apply on a regular basis to any proposed form of advantage:

1 To what extent is the advantage *meaningful* to the customer?

2 To what extent can the advantage be *sustained*? The reality, of course, is that in a fast-moving and competitive market few advantages can be sustained for any length of time. Given this, the planner needs to innovate continuously (refer to the comment above that innovation is ultimately the only sustainable form of advantage) by changing the rules of the game, the boundaries of the market, the value proposition, and so on.

3 How clearly and consistently is the advantage *communicated* clearly and consistently to the market?

In the absence of this, the organization runs the risk of simply being a me-too player.

Gaining, sustaining and exploiting competitive advantage: the problems of self-delusion

One of the themes that has been pursued throughout this book is that of the pivotal importance of competitive advantage. In thinking about how to develop competitive advantage, the marketing planner needs to understand in detail the organization's skills and resources, and then manage these in such a way that the business delivers superior customer value to target segments at a cost that leads to a profit. This can be seen diagrammatically in Figure 10.7.

However, in many cases when thinking about competitive advantage, marketing planners appear to suffer from a degree of self-delusion in that they see something that the organization has or does as being far more important or significant than customers see this to be. In order to overcome this, McDonald argues for the application of the deceptively simple 'So what?' test (see Figure 10.8). Here, the planner begins by identifying the features offered by the product and then – very importantly – translates these into the benefits to the customer. Having done this, the deliberately cynical 'So what?' question is posed. If the benefits that have been identified are essentially the same as those offered by a competitor, then they are of little value. It is only if the benefits pass the test that the advantage can be seen to be at all meaningful.

The problems of sustaining advantage

In developing and, perhaps more importantly, sustaining advantage, the planner needs to recognize that any advantage that an organization or brand possesses that is at all meaningful will be copied or improved upon by competitors sooner rather

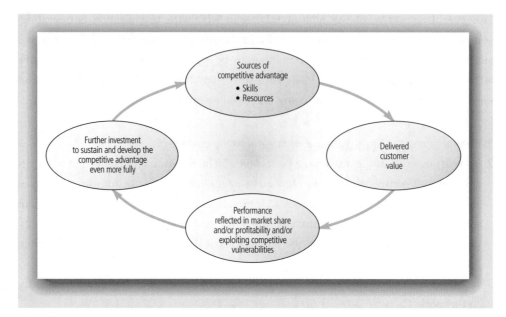

Figure 10.7 The virtuous circle of competitive advantage

than later. Recognizing this, the planner needs to sustain the advantage in one of several ways. These include product and/or process innovation, clever positioning or repositioning (the Co-operative Bank, for example, developed a position as the ethical bank, something that the other banks then found hard to copy), adding value, new forms of delivery (e.g. Amazon.com), and through higher or different levels of service.

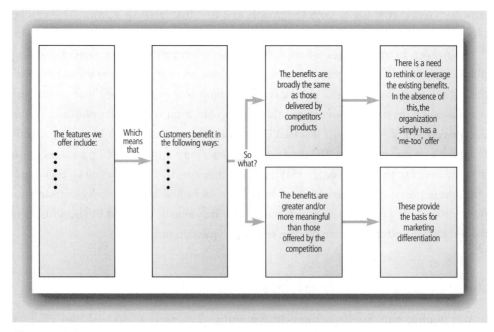

Figure 10.8 The 'So what?' test (adapted from McDonald, 1995)

The idea of service as a (sustainable) competitive advantage has proved to be particularly attractive for organizations in highly competitive and fast-moving markets, where there is a recognition that any product innovation is likely to be copied almost immediately. However, there is a problem in that customers' expectations typically rise over time, with the result that something that is different and an order winner today is seen simply to be an order qualifier tomorrow. Because of this, the planner needs to think about the ways in which the customer can be made to be enthused, excited and delighted by the product and/or service offer.

The ways in which order winners are eroded over time and how the delivery of ever higher levels of customer delight become progressively more important are illustrated in Figure 10.9.

Amongst the implications of this are that the planner needs to think in detail about the nature of order qualifiers (those elements that lead to the customer taking the organization or brand sufficiently seriously to consider buying), order winners (those elements that are significant points of differentiation) and areas of customer delight (those elements that provide the basis for extra value and ever more meaningful bases of differentiation). A framework for thinking about this is shown in Figure 10.10.

Competitive myopia, competitive sclerosis and competitive arrogance: the essentially ephemeral nature of competitive advantage

A fundamental understanding of the significance of competitive advantage was, for a very long time, at the heart of Marks & Spencer's strategies, with the result that the company's performance consistently outstripped the vast majority of retailers and led not just to the company maintaining its position as the market leader in the clothing market, but also to its enormously successful development of food retailing, financial services and household furniture. In doing this, the company concentrated on developing a series of competitive advantages that, taken together, represented a strong selling proposition, provided consumers with a powerful reason to buy, and put competitors at a disadvantage.

However, throughout the 1990s the organization increasingly lost touch with its core markets and began to exhibit all of the characteristics of a fat, lazy and complacent organization that suffered from competitive myopia, competitive sclerosis and competitive arrogance. This arrogance was reflected in a whole series of actions, including their unwillingness to accept credit cards (other than their own store card) as a form of payment as late as 2000, some 30 years after credit cards were introduced to the UK. This managerial arrogance was summarized by a business journalist who, in writing for *The Daily Telegraph* (21 January 2001, p. 133), said:

*"*What other retailer in the world would ask some of the finest designers to produce ranges and then prevent them from putting their own names in them? What the top brass at M & S cannot comprehend is that the Marks & Spencer name, once the group's greatest asset, has become its greatest liability, a Belisha beacon to the clothes buying public that flashes 'Do not shop here! Do not shop here!'*"*

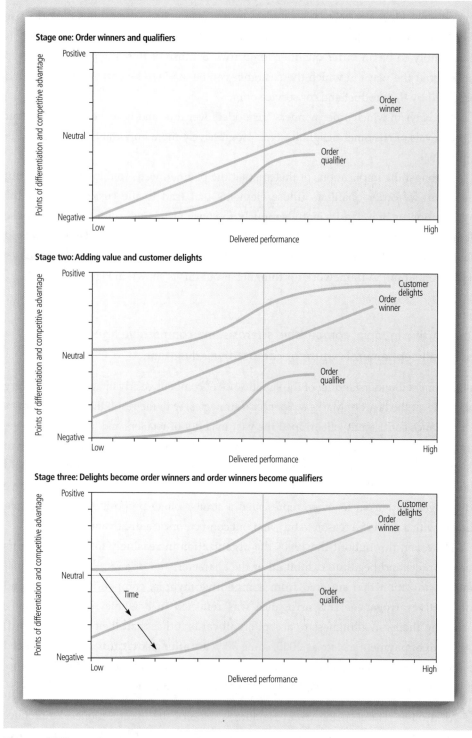

Figure 10.9 Order winners becoming order qualifiers

	Today	Tomorrow
Order qualifiers		
Order winners		
Points of customer delight		

Figure 10.10 Thinking about the order winners and qualifiers of the future

There are several issues that emerge from the Marks & Spencer story, the most significant of which is that it is managerial competencies and attitudes that are the only *real* sustainable competitive advantage. In the absence of these, the organization's position within the marketplace will inevitably suffer.

Subsequently, of course, Marks & Spencer has fought back with a degree of success to regain many of the customers it had lost.

Sustainability of competitive advantage can therefore be seen to depend upon:

➡ A clear understanding by management of a *strategy* for gaining and sustaining competitive advantage
➡ The single-minded pursuit of the strategy
➡ A recognition that some sources of advantage are easier for competitors to copy than others
➡ The continual investment in improving and upgrading sources of advantage.

The speed with which a competitive advantage and strong market position can be eroded was also illustrated in 2003 by the way in which Viagra's dominance of the erectile dysfunction market was attacked by two new drugs, Cialis from Eli Lilly and Levitra from GSK/Bayer. The importance of Viagra to Pfizer was reflected by its sales in 2002 of $1.7 billion and its position as one of Pfizer's three most profitable products. The new entrants to the market based their strategies on a combination of different competitive advantages, including a faster response time to the drug and longer-lasting effects that, together, eroded Viagra's market position.

Competitive disadvantage

Although we have focused so far upon the idea of competitive advantage and the sorts of factors that contribute to this, the reader should not lose sight of the significance of competitive *disadvantage*. This can come about as the result of a series of factors, including a poor brand reputation, the failure to achieve certain service norms within the market, a cost base that is too high, the failure to learn from past experience, the slavish adherence to a previously successful formula, the failure to monitor market conditions, and what might loosely be termed 'country of origin effect'. As an example of the latter effect working against the brand, it is worth thinking back to the way in which many Central and Eastern European products for a very long time – and indeed still today – had a poor reputation for quality, something that has prevented many of these brands penetrating western markets despite low-price strategies.

Creating barriers to entry

Although the development and exploitation of competitive advantage is at the heart of any worthwhile marketing strategy, relatively few organizations prove to be successful at doing this over the long term. Innovators are almost invariably followed by imitators and, because of this, few manage to maintain a truly dominant market position (see the comments above about Marks & Spencer). Tagamet, for example, one of the best-selling and most revolutionary drugs of all time, was quickly eclipsed by an imitator, Zantac. Similarly, Thorn-EMI (with its body scanner) and Xerox (with a series of innovations that helped develop and define the personal computer) are just two companies that, having innovated, failed to capitalize upon their ideas.

The issue that emerges from these and a host of other examples is straightforward: all too often, the resources devoted to *creating* a significant competitive advantage are of little value unless that advantage is subsequently aggressively exploited and sustained. In order to do this and benefit fully from the innovation, Geroski (1996, p. 11) argues that planners need to focus upon understanding two areas:

1 The market's *barriers to entry*, which are the structural features of a market that protect the established companies within a market and allow them to raise prices above costs without attracting new entrants
2 *Mobility barriers*, which protect companies in one part of a market from other companies that are operating in different parts of the same market.

New organizational paradigms and the thirteen commandments for gaining competitive advantage

In 1994, Hamel and Prahalad published their highly influential book *Competing for the Future*. In this, they highlighted the ways in which management paradigms are changing and the nature of the implications of the new paradigm for competitive advantage. Amongst the factors that they suggested would characterize the paradigm of the twenty-first century and how these represent a shift from the 1990s are shown in Figure 10.11.

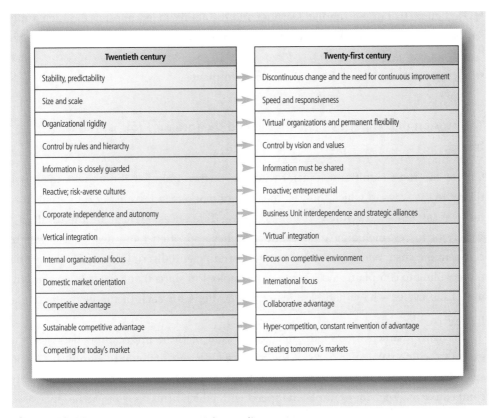

Twentieth century	Twenty-first century
Stability, predictability	Discontinuous change and the need for continuous improvement
Size and scale	Speed and responsiveness
Organizational rigidity	'Virtual' organizations and permanent flexibility
Control by rules and hierarchy	Control by vision and values
Information is closely guarded	Information must be shared
Reactive; risk-averse cultures	Proactive; entrepreneurial
Corporate independence and autonomy	Business Unit interdependence and strategic alliances
Vertical integration	'Virtual' integration
Internal organizational focus	Focus on competitive environment
Domestic market orientation	International focus
Competitive advantage	Collaborative advantage
Sustainable competitive advantage	Hyper-competition, constant reinvention of advantage
Competing for today's market	Creating tomorrow's markets

Figure 10.11 Changing managerial paradigms

The implications of this for competitive advantage and competitive behaviour are obviously significant, and were summarized by Hamel and Prahalad (1994) in terms of the need for marketing planners to:

➡ Stop playing by the industry rules and, instead, create their own, develop a new competitive space and make others follow (e.g. Swatch, Dell and, in the 1960s–1980s, The Body Shop)

➡ Get innovative or get dead – in doing this, the planner needs to avoid believing in the idea of sustainable advantage and to focus instead upon creating a culture of constructive destruction (e.g. Direct Line, 3M, Canon and Sony)

➡ Scrutinize the company for hidden assets, which then need to be leveraged (e.g. Disney and Harley Davidson)

➡ Create a fast action company (e.g. Toyota and CNN)

➡ Create an entrepreneurial and experimental business (e.g. Virgin and easyJet)

➡ Eliminate boundaries within the organization (e.g. Toshiba and Mitsubishi)

➡ Harness the collective genius of staff (e.g. Management consultancies such as McKinsey and Bain & Co)

➡ Globalize or perish (e.g. Ikea and Nokia)

➡ Emphasize the eco-revolution and use environmental efficiency to set standards for the market (e.g. the Co-operative Bank)

➡ Recognize that organizational learning and the ability to learn faster and then apply these ideas more quickly than the competition may be the only real sustainable advantage

➡ Develop real measures of true strategic performance.

The erosion of competitive advantage and the (greater) role of the trust brand

One of the most significant and far-reaching themes pursued throughout this book relates to the ways in which the vast majority of markets today are very different from those of say ten and even five years ago. These differences – which are the result of a variety of forces, including globalization; higher and often more desperate levels of competition; customers who are far more demanding and discriminating, less loyal and more willing to complain; and a series of technological shifts that have led to a shortening of life cycles – have had a series of implications for each of the elements of the marketing mix.

In many markets, one of the most significant of these implications has been the extent to which particular parts of the mix are able to contribute to significant – and sustained – competitive advantage has been reduced. In fast-moving and highly competitive markets, for example, the speed with which firms copy others has increased greatly. As a result, differentiation through the product has all but disappeared. Equally, because many organizations use similar forms of distribution and have broadly similar levels of costs, the ability to differentiate through distribution and price have also been reduced. Faced with this, many marketing planners have shifted their attention to the brand and to the role that it is capable of playing in creating and maintaining differentiation and advantage.

Brands, which are in essence a form of shorthand that creates expectations about purpose, performance, quality and price, are therefore potentially enormously powerful and provide the basis not just for a high(er) profile in the market, but also for higher levels of customer loyalty and the freedom to charge a price premium. Given this, the effective and proactive management of the brand is, for many organizations, essential.

The increasingly important role played by brands is illustrated in Figure 10.12, which shows the three key stages of a market, ranging from commoditization (in which there is little scope or perhaps need for brand identity) through differentiation (in which brand identity becomes increasingly significant) to mass customization (in which the brand values become the basis for differentiation).

However, these ideas can be taken a step further with the development of thinking about 'trust brands'. These trust brands are the brands in which customers have a fundamental long-lasting and deep-seated faith that emerges both from a rational assessment of the product's capabilities ('I know that this product or service will deliver what I want'), and an emotional assessment of the relationship between the organization and the customer ('I know that I will get a fair deal').

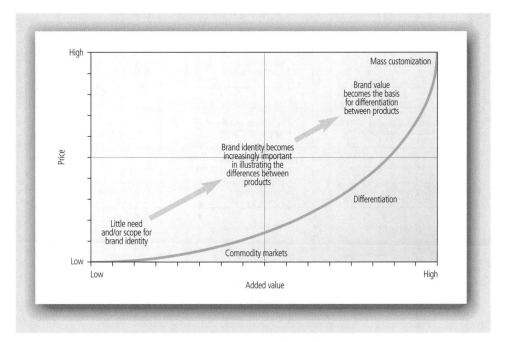

Figure 10.12   The increasing significance of brands and branding

The need for trust brands has grown significantly over the past few years, largely as the result of the privatization of risk within society, something that Edwards (1998) suggests is due to:

❝ . . . the transfer of risk from the state and from the employer to the individual . . . (and) accompanied by a long and steady decline in popular trust for the institutions in society that individuals used to rely on for help in making choices . . . In summary, the privatization of risk in society means that consumers are seeking new partners to help them confront, share and manage that risk. Brands are ideally placed to fill this trust vacuum.❞

These pressures are illustrated in Figure 10.13.

Amongst those brands that have demonstrated high trust credentials are some of the major retailers such as Tesco, and individual brands such as Kellogg's and Nestlé. For Edwards:

❝ . . . the archetypal trust brand is probably still Virgin. Transferring trust apparently effortlessly into new areas, this highly individual conglomerate now takes part in diverse activities ranging from airlines to finance, and soft drinks to cinemas and weddings. The proposition is clear: when you, the consumer, enter an unfamiliar market where you do not trust the current providers then Virgin will be on your side. Virgin's credentials to enter new markets are often unclear in the traditional sense (in fact it often operates in partnership with specialist suppliers) – what it actually brings with it from market to market is the brand name and the consumer trust that resides in it.❞

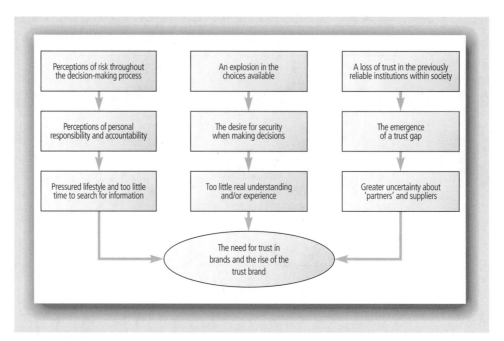

Figure 10.13   The pressure for trust brands (adapted from Edwards, 1998)

The work of Edwards and his colleagues at the Henley Centre suggests that six factors contribute to trust:

1 *Packaging* and the product information that it contains
2 *Provenance* and the country or company of origin (included within this is the country of origin effect, which includes the heritage of the country – e.g. Germany for engineering, Japan for high technology – and the reputation of the company)
3 *Performance* over time that leads to perceptions of dependability
4 *Persistence* – once a brand has gained real consumer trust, it demonstrates long-term resilience even though there may be occasions when things go wrong (Persil, for example, has maintained trust despite problems of enzymes and dermatitis at certain stages in its life)
5 *Portability* – having developed trust, the brand can be moved into new and possibly unrelated areas, something that both Virgin and Tesco have demonstrated with their move into a variety of new market sectors
6 *Praise* – when trust is high, the use and power of word of mouth tends to increase dramatically.

Given that markets are now so much more competitive than even a few years ago, it should be apparent that trust brands can play a pivotal role in achieving differentiation and long-term loyalty. The implications for how brands are managed are therefore significant. Edwards (1998) states:

*"*It has long been axiomatic that competitors can quickly copy product or service innovations in most cases. It is therefore crucial that trust and the infrastructure of trust

are reinforced through all consumer contacts and relationships. In the field of trust management, marketing becomes everyone's job. All stages of the process are relevant in maintaining trust – R&D, product testing, manufacturing, staff training and policies, distribution, pricing and customer service/complaint handling. All consumer interactions are a marketing opportunity. As the banks have discovered – expensive marketing campaigns are quickly negated by poor customer handling at the branch.

Marketing by trust therefore becomes more of a philosophy than simply the responsibility of a single department. The trust brand places the consumer at the centre of its world, it relies more on understanding real consumer needs and fulfilling them than the particular service or product manifestation at any one time. This means it is not merely responsive but also responsible to the consumer knowing the right thing to do or be even when the customer does not.*"*

However, in recent years a number of organizations have been faced with the problem of their brands having been undermined by counterfeit products. In a report published in 2000, the Global Anti-Counterfeiting Group estimated that brand counterfeiting costs European business £250 billion a year. Worldwide, the report suggests that the annual cost is at least £600 billion (*Marketing*, 27 April 2000).

The implications of this for the brand marketer are significant and are reflected not just in a loss of revenue and profits, but also in lower levels of customer loyalty, an erosion in customer confidence and a weakening of relationships throughout the distribution chain.

Although virtually all sectors of the economy have been hit to at least some extent by fakes (one argument is that wherever there is a strong brand name there is scope for counterfeiting), the music, software, videos, toys, watches, cosmetics and perfumes industries have proved to be amongst the most vulnerable.

The third knowledge revolution and the erosion of competitive advantage

With the arrival of the World Wide Web and the third knowledge revolution (the first and second knowledge revolutions were the printing press in 1455 and broadcasting some 500 years later), the competitive advantage that many firms have traditionally enjoyed has either been eroded or has disappeared completely. In discussing this in their book *Funky Business*, Ridderstråle and Nordström's (2000) core argument is that the world is changing ever faster and that the survivors will be those who embrace the changes and modify their corporate behaviour.

Although this is a view that numerous others have expressed over the past few years, Ridderstråle and Nordström focus upon the way in which managers who are accustomed to controlling their environment by the domination of their staff, customers and markets are likely to be faced with major problems as the new world order demands more than technology, production and distribution. Progressive – or 'funky' – companies will attract custom, they suggest, by understanding in much greater detail what customers want and communicating to them the intangible elements (in essence, the brand values) of their product or service. They then take this philosophy to new heights by predicting a scarily harsh business environment where unforgiving consumers and demanding employees will exert a pincer-movement stranglehold on companies that refuse to 'feel the funk'.

The power of knowledge and the growth of commercial freedom make for a better-informed marketplace than the world has ever seen before. But with that freedom, says Ridderstråle, comes the death of corporate loyalty: 'Companies should no longer expect loyalty; they should accept the need to attract and addict people on a continuous basis.' Now that we have moved into a society ruled by over-supply, Ridderstråle believes the future no longer belongs to those who control supply but to those who control demand, 'those who help the customer get the best deal'. Prominent amongst the companies that they believe have come to terms with this ('islands of funk') are Virgin and Nokia.

Competitive advantage and the dangers of benchmarking

In Disney's A Bug's Life, *a moth warns his moth friend not to look at or fly towards the light. 'I can't help it', the doomed insect replies.*

For many organizations, competitive benchmarking – the process by which you identify the best in the sector, determine what it is that has led to such high perform-ance and then copy – has become an integral part of the corporate struggle to stay competitive. But although benchmarking can be of value, it can also lead to problems. Nattermann (2000, p. 20), for example, discusses what he terms 'strategic herding'. This happens, he suggests, when managers forget that benchmarking should only be used as an operational tool rather than the determining framework for strategic development. The effects of herding can be seen by the way in which products and services increasingly become commodities and margins shrink as more and more companies crowd into the same market space.

Amongst the examples he cites to illustrate this is that of the German wireless telecommunications providers between 1993 and 1998. The first two carriers entered the business in 1992 and quickly achieved market share of more than 70 per cent with similar strategies in terms of pricing, selling and advertising. When a third company entered the market in 1994, it differentiated itself by targeting segments that the first two were ignoring – similar to the approach adopted in the UK by Orange, when it attacked the two established players, Vodafone and BT Cellnet. Soon there was little to choose between them as they all frantically copied each other's offerings. By 1998, Nattermann claims, this led to margins 50 per cent lower than at their peak. The same approach has also eroded margins in computers and consumer electronics.

A broadly similar picture began to emerge in Britain when the American retailer Wal-Mart entered the market in 1999. The established players such as Tesco, Sainsbury's and Safeway, all of which had enjoyed profit margins that were far higher than in many other Western European countries, responded in an almost desperate fashion by cutting prices. One of the few to avoid this strategic herding was Waitrose, which continued with its policy of up-market positioning. It also began targeting its e-shopping at people in their offices rather than at home.

The problems of strategic herding are also increasingly being seen in the high street coffee shop market, with Starbucks and numerous other players all fighting for (an ever larger) share of a market, which, although it has grown rapidly, is ultimately of a finite size. In these circumstances, it is not so much a question of *whether* there will be a shake-out in the market, but simply *when* this will happen.

Returning for a moment to the example of Waitrose given above, Nattermann refers to this refusal to follow the pack as a policy of looking for 'white spots' – or those areas that the herd is failing to exploit. Firms such as these, he suggests, may well benchmark, but they then avoid the trap of letting this constrain their strategic thinking.

E-business and competitive advantage

With the development of the Internet and e-commerce, marketing thinking and approaches to marketing planning are having to undergo a number of radical changes. In part, this is being driven by the way in which e-marketing has the potential for changing not just the rules of the game within a market, but also the market space, and in doing so change the bases for thinking about competitive advantage. The ways in which organizations might move from a position in which e-marketing is poorly thought out and reflected largely in the development of web pages that are simply another form of advertising through to the fundamental and strategic integration of e-marketing with the corporate strategy is illustrated in Figure 10.14. Here, organizations move through four stages and, depending upon how proactive they are, are capable of changing the bases of competition in potentially fundamental ways. Those firms that fail to recognize this and continue to focus upon the traditional bases of competition and advantage run the risk of being left behind as the rules of competition and the boundaries of the market develop and change. Amongst the most obvious examples of firms that have done this are Amazon.com, who rewrote the rules of competition within the book-selling market, and easyJet, which took a very different approach to selling airline seats. In both cases, their competitors were put at a disadvantage and forced into a position of copying and catch-up.

The potential implications of the Internet for marketing were outlined in 2000 in a presentation to the Chartered Institute of Marketing by the consultants McKinsey & Co. McKinsey argued that the Internet has the capacity for:

➡ Creating discontinuity in marketing costs
➡ Making new and different types of dialogue with the customer possible
➡ Charging the return on attention equation
➡ Reinventing the marketing paradigm.

In suggesting this, McKinsey were giving emphasis to the way in which the Internet creates a virtual marketplace in which the buyer is unconstrained by the additional

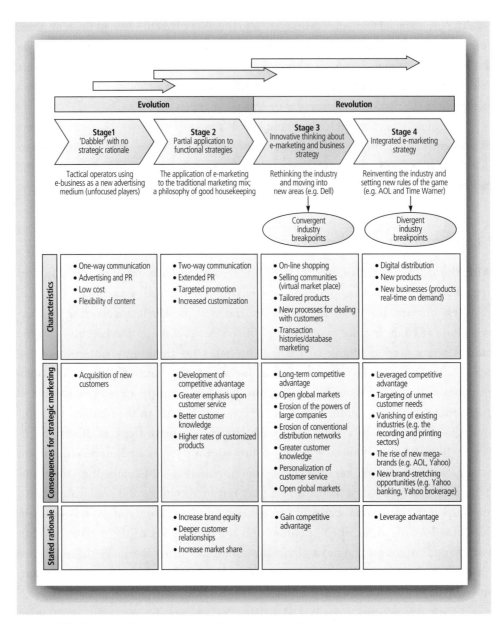

Figure 10.14 E-marketing and the development of strategic thinking and competitive advantage

time and geographic boundaries, and has access to an almost infinite number of potential suppliers. In these circumstances, the seller is no longer (so) constrained by the capability of third parties in the distribution channel and can instead approach the customer in a far more direct fashion. At the same time, of course, the buyer is put into a far more powerful position in that there is far greater and far more immediate access to information, and comparisons between alternatives can be made far more easily and conveniently. Given this, the balance of power between the buyer and seller has the potential for changing in a series of radical and far-reaching ways. The implications of this can be seen most readily in terms of the decline of what may be loosely termed 'interruption marketing' and the emergence of a new approach based on permission marketing. (For a detailed discussion of permission marketing, refer to Godin, 1999.) This is illustrated in Figure 10.15.

The implications of the customer's greater access to information are likely to be manifested in three major ways:

1 A downward pressure on the prices of products and services that lack any real competitive advantage or point of differentiation
2 A greater potential for demand-led markets
3 Increased customer/consumer expectations of higher product and service quality.

However, the picture from the standpoint of the manufacturer/producer is not necessarily negative in that the Internet has the capacity for:

➡ A reduction in the costs of capturing customer information
➡ The scope for far deeper customer/consumer relationships
➡ A greater ability to tailor value propositions
➡ An ability to price differentially
➡ A reduction in the cost of targeting customers/consumers.

The implications of this can then be seen in terms of the ways in which there are far greater opportunities for:

➡ Creating unique value propositions through personalization and customization
➡ More sophisticated segmentation, marketing and pricing
➡ New and possibly smaller and far more geographically dispersed competitors to enter the market.
➡ Developing new barriers to switching.

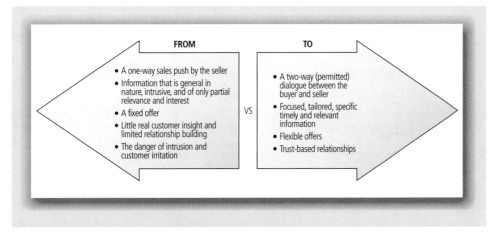

Figure 10.15 Permission marketing: the new paradigm

Given the nature of these comments, it should be apparent that the implications of the Internet for marketing are potentially enormous, and are still misunderstood and often underestimated by many marketing planners (referring back to Figure 10.14, many organizations have still to move beyond Stage 2). Perhaps the greatest danger that many face is that the issue of e-commerce is simply seen to be about selling online rather than about the far broader issue of building relationships with customers. As part of this, there is the need to recognize that the Internet means that, over time, the point of purchase can move and that this requires the marketing planner to have a far greater and more creative insight into the markets served. At the same time, the marketing planner needs to recognize that there are major implications for the organization's speed of response. Because the potential customer has instant access, there is an expectation of a similar speed of response to an enquiry. If this is not done, there is a danger of a deterioration in any relationship that exists or that has begun to emerge.

Recognition of the fundamental significance of the Internet requires the planner to come to terms with the ways in which commercially exploitable relationships might be developed. To do this involves a systematic approach to customer relationship management that has four key characteristics:

1 The need to understand customers in far greater detail
2 The need to meet their needs far more effectively
3 The need to make it easier for customers to do business with the organization than with a competitor
4 The need to add value.

However, underpinning all of this is the need to segment the customer base, since not all customers, be they B2B or B2C, view the development of the Internet and e-marketing in the same way. Recognition of this has led the Henley Centre to identify six principal consumer segments:

1 *Habit die-hards*, who are stuck in their ways and who have little knowledge, interest or access to the Internet
2 *Convenience/frenzied copers*, who are responsive to initiatives that save them time
3 *Experimenters*, who are willing to try new things
4 *Ethical shoppers*, who will purchase provided that the product offering is honest and politically correct
5 *Value shoppers/mercenaries*, who will buy on the basis of value
6 *Social shoppers*, who enjoy the social dimensions of shopping.

Given this, it is possible to identify the level of interest that each segment has in electronic shopping (ES). This is illustrated in Figure 10.16.

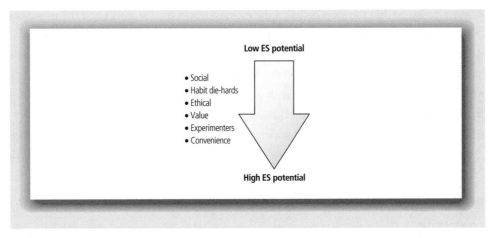

Figure 10.16 Consumer segments and their electronic shopping potential

E-marketing and competitive advantage: a summary

It should be apparent from what has been said so far that the implications of e-marketing for traditional thinking about competitive advantage are potentially significant and can be seen most readily by the way in which some of the traditional bases of advantage can be eroded by a fast-moving and creative e-marketer. It is this that has led Fifield (2000) to suggest that e-failure will emerge from marketing planners seeing the Internet as:

➡ Yet another 'push' activity
➡ A new paradigm that then becomes the 'set' paradigm
➡ Just another form of the same old 'production' mentality.

By contrast, e-success, he believes, will come from:

➡ Understanding the needs of e-customers
➡ Meeting the needs of e-customers
➡ Doing things that can't be done offline
➡ Doing the boring things – well!
➡ Taking a strategic approach.

In discussing the contribution of the Internet to marketing, McDonald and Wilson (1999) argue the case for the six Is model. The model, which is based on the ways in which IT can add value to the customer and therefore improve the organization's marketing effectiveness, is designed to illustrate how the Internet can be used strategically. The model's six dimensions consist of:

1 *Integration*, and the need to ensure that information on customers from across the organization and across the customer life cycle is brought together, evaluated and then used proactively (e.g. First Direct)

2 *Interactivity*, so that the loop between the messages sent to customers and the messages they send back is closed (e.g. Amazon.com)

3 *Individualization* and the tailoring of products and services to meet the customer's specific needs (e.g. Levi's, Dell and the travel company Trailfinders)

4 *Independence* of location and the death of distance (e.g. Amazon.com, again)

5 *Intelligence* through integrated marketing databases

6 *Industry restructuring* and the redrawing of the market map (e.g. Ryanair, easyJet and, again, First Direct).

Rebuilding competitive advantage: the development of the extra value proposition

Amongst the most obvious consequences of markets becoming more competitive and customers more demanding is that many of the traditional bases of competitive advantage have been eroded. One way in which to combat this is for the marketing planner to differentiate the organization from its competitors by focusing upon the delivery of greater customer value. There are several ways in which this can be done, although before identifying some of these, the idea of the extra value proposition (EVP) needs to be put into context.

The basis for a considerable amount of marketing thinking for many years was the idea of strong selling propositions, in which the customer would be presented with one or more good reasons for buying the product – this is reflected in the notion of 'buy this product, receive this benefit'. From here, thinking moved to the idea of the unique selling proposition (USP), in which the strategy was based upon a feature or benefit that was unique to that organization or brand. However, in highly competitive markets, the scope for retaining uniqueness in anything other than the short term is limited unless the product is protected by a patent. The notion of a USP-based strategy has therefore largely been undermined over the past few years. Where there is still scope for USPs, this stems largely from the brand. Although it is often possible for the product itself to be copied relatively easily, a powerful brand is still capable of acting as a powerful differentiator.

At the same time, many marketing planners have recognized that customers who are generally more demanding are likely to respond positively to an extra value-based strategy, something that has led to a focus upon EVPs. Amongst the ways in which these can be delivered is through providing a greater number of benefits to the customer by:

➡ Customizing products and services to meet customers' specific needs

➡ Providing higher levels of customer convenience

➡ Offering faster service

➡ Providing more/better service

➡ Giving customer training

➡ Offering extraordinary guarantees

➡ Providing useful hardware/software tools for customers

➡ Developing membership loyalty programmes

➡ Winning through lower prices

➡ Aggressive pricing

➡ Offering lower price to those customers who are willing to give up some features and services

➡ Helping customers to reduce their other costs by:

   ➡ Showing the customer that the total cost is less despite its initially higher price

   ➡ Actively helping the customer to reduce ordering costs and inventory costs, processing costs and administration costs.

10.6 Summary

In this chapter we have examined Porter's work on generic competitive strategies and how the value chain can be used as a platform for thinking about competitive advantage. Competitive advantage is, as discussed in some detail, a fundamental element of the strategic marketing planning process, and the planner must therefore understand the sources of advantage and how advantage might be leveraged.

With markets currently undergoing a series of radical changes, the traditional bases of advantage are being eroded and there is therefore the need for the planner to think creatively how (new) advantages might be developed and leveraged.

11

The formulation of strategy – 3: strategies for leaders, followers, challengers and nichers

11.1 Learning objectives

When you have read this chapter you should be able to understand:

(a) the influence of market position on strategy;

(b) how organizations might attack others and defend themselves;

(c) how life cycles influence marketing strategy and planning.

11.2 Introduction

In Chapter 10 we focused in some detail upon Porter's generic strategies and the nature and sources of competitive advantage. In this chapter we take the analysis a stage further by examining how the organization's position in the market, ranging from market leader through to market nicher, influences strategy and planning. Finally, we turn our attention to the ways in which market and product life cycles need to be managed.

11.3 The influence of market position on strategy

In discussing how best to formulate marketing strategy, we have focused so far on the sorts of model and approaches to planning that can help to formalize the analytical process. In making use of models such as these, the strategist needs to pay explicit attention to a series of factors, including the organization's objectives and resources, managerial attitudes to risk, the structure of the market, competitors' strategies and, very importantly, the organization's position within the market. The significance of market position and its often very direct influence upon strategy has been discussed in detail by a wide variety of writers, most of whom suggest classifying competitive position along a spectrum from market leader to market nichers:

➡ *Market leader.* In the majority of industries there is one firm that is generally recognized to be the leader. It typically has the largest market share and, by virtue of its pricing, advertising intensity, distribution coverage, technological advance and rate of new product introductions, it determines the nature, pace and bases of competition. It is this dominance that typically provides the benchmark for other companies in the industry. However, it needs to be emphasized that market leadership, although often associated with size, is in reality a more complex concept and should instead be seen in terms of an organization's ability to *determine the nature and bases of competition within the market.*

➡ *Market challengers and followers.* Firms with a slightly smaller market share can adopt one of two stances. They may choose to adopt an aggressive stance and attack other firms, including the market leader, in an attempt to gain share and perhaps dominance

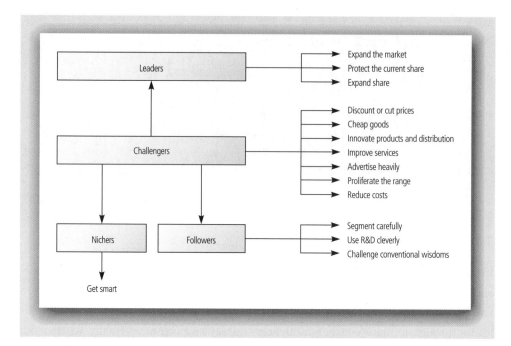

Figure 11.1   Leaders, followers, challengers and market nichers

(market challengers), or they may adopt a less aggressive stance in order to maintain the status quo (market followers).

➡ *Market nichers.* Virtually every industry has a series of small firms that survive, and indeed often prosper, by choosing to specialize in parts of the market that are too limited in size and potential to be of real interest to larger firms. A case in point would be Morgan specializing in traditional sports cars. By concentrating their efforts in this way, market nichers are able to build up specialist market knowledge and avoid expensive head-on fights with larger companies.

This approach to classification has, in turn, led to a considerable discussion of the strategic alternatives for leaders, challengers and nichers, with numerous analogies being drawn between business strategy and military strategy. The idea has been to show how the ideas of military strategists, and in particular Von Clausewitz, Sun-Tzu and Liddell-Hart, might be applied to the alternatives open to a company intent on gaining or retaining a competitive advantage. Within this section we will therefore examine some of these ideas and show how market leaders might defend their current position, how challengers might attempt to seize share, and how followers and nichers are affected by this. An overview of how this might be done appears in Figure 11.1.

11.4 Strategies for market leaders

Although a position of market leadership has undoubted attractions, both in terms of the scope that often exists to influence others and a possibly higher return on investment, leaders have all too often in the past proved to be vulnerable in the face of an attack from a challenger or when faced with the need for a major technological change. If, therefore, a market leader is to remain as the dominant company, it needs to defend its position constantly. In doing this, there are three major areas to which the marketing strategist needs to pay attention:

1 How best to expand the total market
2 How to protect the organization's current share of the market
3 How to increase market share.

A summary of the ways in which leaders might do this appears in Figure 11.2. Of these, it is an *expansion of the overall market* from which the market leader typically stands to gain the most. It follows from this that the strategist needs to search for new users, new uses and greater usage levels of his or her firm's products. This can be done in a variety of ways. In the 1960s and 1970s, for example, Honda increased its sales by targeting groups that traditionally had not bought motorcycles. These groups, which included commuters and women, were seen to offer enormous untapped potential. The company unlocked this by developing a range of small, economic and lightweight machines, which they then backed with a series of advertising campaigns giving emphasis to their convenience and style. Moving into the 1980s, the strategy began to change yet again as the company recognized the potential for selling motorcycles almost as an adjunct to fashion. Styling therefore became far more important. This repositioning was then taken several steps further in the late 1980s as Honda, along

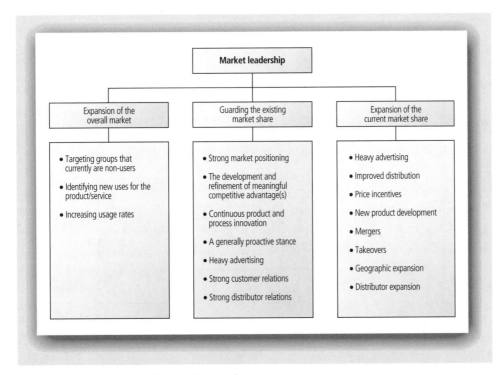

Figure 11.2 Strategies for market leaders

with other manufacturers, began targeting the middle-aged executive market with a series of larger motorcycles that were supported by advertising campaigns giving emphasis to the re-creation of youthful values.

As a second stage the strategist might search for *new uses* for the product. Perhaps the most successful example of this is Du Pont's Nylon, which was first used as a synthetic fibre for parachutes and then subsequently for stockings, shirts, tyres, upholstery, carpets and a spectrum of industrial and engineering uses. A broadly similar approach of market development through a series of new uses has been taken with Teflon. Developed initially as a high-performance lubricant for the American space programme, the product has been reformulated for applications in cooking, motor oils, and as a protection for fabrics, clothing and carpets. This is illustrated in Figure 11.3.

The third approach to market expansion involves encouraging *existing users* of the product to *increase their usage rates*, a strategy pursued with considerable success by Procter & Gamble with its Head & Shoulders brand of shampoo, which was promoted on the basis that two applications were more effective than one.

At the same time as trying to expand the total market, the market leader should not lose sight of the need to *defend its market share*. It has long been recognized that leaders represent a convenient target since, because of their size, they are often vulnerable to attack. Whether the attack is successful is often determined largely by the leader's ability to recognize its vulnerability and position itself in such a way that the challenger's chances of success are minimized. The need for this is illustrated by examples from many industries, including photography (Kodak having been attacked in the film market by Fuji and in the camera market by Polaroid, Minolta, Nikon and Pentax), soft drinks (Pepsi-Cola attacking Coca-Cola), car hire (Avis against Hertz), potato crisps

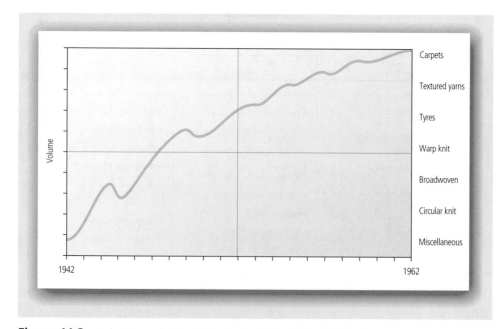

Figure 11.3 Nylon's product cycle (adapted from Yale, 1964)

(Golden Wonder attacking Smiths, and then subsequently both companies being attacked by Walker's), razors (Bic and Wilkinson Sword attacking Gillette), photocopiers (Xerox being attacked by numerous players) and computers (IBM being attacked by, among others, Apple, Compaq, Dell and numerous others).

Although there are obvious dangers in generalizing, the most successful strategy for a market leader intent on fighting off attacks such as these lies in the area of continuous product and/or process innovation, something that involves the leader refusing to be content with the way things are, and leading the industry in new-product ideas, customer services, distribution effectiveness and cost cutting. It therefore needs to keep increasing its competitive effectiveness and value to customer by applying the military principle of the offensive. Typically, this involves setting the pace, exploiting the competitors' vulnerabilities, and generally behaving aggressively and unpredictably. It is this sort of approach that leads to the idea that the best defence comes from a strong offensive posture. However, even when not attacking, the market leader must ensure that it behaves in such a way that it does not allow itself to expose any areas of weakness, something that for many organizations means keeping costs down and ensuring that its prices reflect the value customers see in the brand. An example of the way in which this has been done in the consumer goods sector is by producing a product in several forms (e.g. liquid soap as well as bars of soap) and in various sizes (small, medium, large and economy) to tie up as much shelf space as possible.

Although the cost of 'plugging holes' in this way is often high, the cost of failing to do so and being forced out of a product or market segment can often be infinitely higher. As an example of this, Kodak withdrew from the 35 mm sector of the camera market because its product was losing money. The Japanese subsequently found a way of making 35 mm cameras profitably at a low price and took share away from Kodak's cheaper cameras.

Similarly, in the USA, the major car manufacturers paid too little attention in the 1960s and early 1970s to the small car sector because of the difficulties of making them at a profit. Both the Japanese (Toyota, Mazda and Honda) and the Germans (Volkswagen) took advantage of this lack of domestic competition and developed the small car sector very profitably. The long-term consequence of this has been that the domestic manufacturers, having initially conceded this market sector, have subsequently entered into a series of joint ventures with the Japanese (e.g. Ford with Mazda, General Motors with Toyota, Isuzo and Suzuki, and Chrysler with Mitsubishi).

The third course of action open to market leaders intent on remaining leaders involves *expanding market share*. This can typically be done in a variety of ways, including by means of heavier advertising, improved distribution, price incentives, new products and, as the brewers have demonstrated, by mergers, takeovers, alliances and distribution deals.

It should be apparent from what has been said so far that leadership involves the development and pursuit of a consistently proactive strategy, something which Pascale has touched upon; this is discussed in Illustration 11.1.

Illustration 11.1 Change, transformation and a market focus – reasserting market leadership

Three of the best-known and most successful organizational change programmes in the 1980s and 1990s took place at British Airways ('from Bloody Awful to Bloody Awesome'), Grand Met and SmithKline Beecham. In each case, a slow-moving and increasingly unsuccessful organization was refocused and transformed into a marketing leader. However, the problems of achieving transformation *and maintaining* a successful profile are highlighted by the way in which, only five years after the publication of Peters and Waterman's 1982 bestseller *In Search of Excellence*, all but fourteen of its forty-three 'excellent' companies had either grown weaker or were declining rapidly. Similarly, BA, having been successfully turned around, was then hit very hard by a combination of factors, including the European low-cost airlines such as easyJet and Ryanair (see Illustration 10.3), and was forced into massive restructuring.

In commenting on this, Richard Pascale (1990) argues that too few managers really understand what is involved in transforming an organization. To him, transformation involves not only a discontinuous shift in an organization's capability, but also the much more difficult task of sustaining that shift. Faced with the need for change, he suggests, companies come to a fork in the road. About 80 per cent take the easy route, stripping themselves 'back to basics', searching for the latest tools and techniques, and going on to risk stagnation or decline. Only a fifth of companies take the much tougher, alternative route. This involves three big steps: the first he refers to as 'inquiring into their underlying paradigm' (that is, questioning the way they do everything, including how managers think); attacking the problems systematically on all fronts, notably strategy, operations, organization and culture; and 'reinventing' themselves in such a way that the transformation becomes self-sustaining. It is only in this way that truly intellectual learning is matched by the emotional learning that is needed and transformation truly becomes embedded in the organization.

The PIMS study and the pursuit of market share

The significance of market share, and in particular its influence upon return on investment, has long been recognized, and has been pointed to by a variety of studies over the past 35 years, the best known of which is the PIMS (Profit Impact of Market Strategy) research (aspects of the PIMS research are also discussed on pp. 112–14).

The aim of the PIMS programme has been to identify the most significant determinants of profitability. The factors that have shown themselves to be persistently the most influential are:

1 *Competitive position* (including market share and relative product quality)
2 *Production structure* (including investment intensity and the productivity of operations)

3 The *attractiveness of the served market* (as shown by its growth rate and customers' characteristics).

Taken together, these factors explain 65–70 per cent of the variability in profitability among the firms in the PIMS database. By examining the determinants of profitability it is possible to address a series of strategic questions, such as:

➡ What rate of profit and cash flow is normal for this type of business?
➡ What profit and cash flow outcomes can be expected if the business continues with its present strategy?
➡ How will future performance be affected by a change in strategy?

One of the key notions underlying strategic marketing management is, as already emphasized, that of the relative position of a firm among its competitors, particularly with regard to unit costs, quality, price, profitability and market share.

The respective contribution of each of these factors to overall profitability is estimated by means of a multiple regression model. This allows the impact of weak variables to be offset by strong variables – a low market share might, for example, be offset by high product quality. Once the model has been applied to a given company, it can then be used to assess the relative strengths and weaknesses of competitors in order to identify the best source of competitive advantage. From the viewpoint of the marketing strategist, this has most typically been seen in terms of the organization's relative market share, a factor which has been given considerable emphasis by successive PIMS reports: 'The average ROI for businesses with under 10 per cent market share was about 9 per cent . . . On the average, a difference of 10 percentage points in market share is accompanied by a difference of about 5 points in pretax ROI.' The study has also shown that businesses with a market share of more than 40 per cent achieve ROIs of 30 per cent, or three times that of firms with shares under 10 per cent.

In the light of these findings, it is not at all surprising that many organizations have pursued a goal of share increases, since it should lead not just to greater profits, but also to greater profitability (that is, return on investment).

Although the findings and conclusions of the PIMS study have an initial and pragmatic appeal, the general approach has been subjected to an increasing amount of critical comment in recent years. In particular, critics have highlighted:

➡ Measurement errors
➡ Apparent deficiencies in the model
➡ The interpretations of the findings.

Perhaps the main concern, however, is over the practice of deriving prescriptions about strategy from unsupported causal inferences. It is therefore important in using PIMS data to understand the limitations of the approach. When used as intended, data from the PIMS programme can, its defenders argue, provide valuable insights into effective

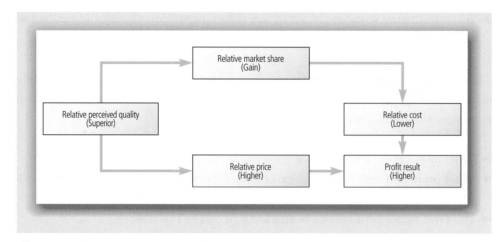

Figure 11.4 Some PIMS linkages (adapted from Buzzell and Gale, 1987)

marketing and corporate strategy. In particular, they point to some of the broad conclusions from the programme, which can be summarized as:

1 In the long run, the single most important factor affecting performance is the quality of an enterprise's products/services relative to those of its competitors.
2 Market share and profitability are strongly related:
 ⇒ ROI increases steadily as market share increases
 ⇒ Enterprises having relatively large market shares tend to have above-average rates of investment turnover
 ⇒ The ratio of marketing expenses to sales revenue tends to be lower for enterprises having high market shares.
 The PIMS programme has demonstrated the linkages among superior relative quality, higher relative prices, gains in market share, lower relative costs and higher profitability. These linkages, which are portrayed in Figure 11.4, indicate the causal role that relative quality plays in influencing business performance.
3 High investment intensity acts as a powerful drag on profitability:
 ⇒ The higher the ratio of investment to sales, the lower the ROI; enterprises having high investment intensity tend to be unable to achieve profit margins sufficient to sustain growth.
4 Many dog and wildcat activities generate cash, while many cash cows do not.
5 Vertical integration is a profitable strategy for some kinds of enterprise but not for others.
6 Most of the strategic factors that boost ROI also contribute to long-term value.

Despite these comments, however, the reader should bear in mind the very real reservations that have been expressed about the study, since the relationship between profit and market share that is claimed as the result of the PIMS study may well be due more to flexible definitions of market boundaries than to market realities (see Baker, 1985, p. 110). Similarly, Porter (1980, p. 44) suggests that:

*"*There is *no single relationship* between profitability and market share, unless one conveniently defines the market so that focused or differentiated firms are assigned high market shares in some narrowly-defined industries and the industry definitions of cost leadership firms are allowed to stay broad (which they must because cost leaders often do not have the largest share in every sub-market). Even shifting industry cannot explain the high returns of firms which have achieved differentiation industry-wide and held market shares below that of the industry leader.*"*

A number of other writers have also argued that the study's findings are generally spurious. Hamermesh et al. (1987), for example, have pointed to numerous successful low-share businesses. Similarly, Woo and Cooper (1982) identified forty low-share businesses with pretax ROIs of 20 per cent or more.

Findings such as these suggest the existence not of a linear relationship between market share and profitability but rather, in some industries at least, of a V-shaped relationship. This is illustrated in Figure 11.5. In such an industry, there will be one or two highly profitable market leaders, several profitable low-share firms, and a number of medium-share, poorly focused and far less profitable organizations. This has been commented on by Roach (1981, p. 21):

*"*The large firms on the V-curve tend to address the entire market, achieving cost advantages and high market share by realizing economies of scale. The small competitors reap high profits by focusing on some narrower segments of the business and by developing specialized approaches to production, marketing, and distribution for that segment. Ironically the medium-sized competitors at the trough of the V-curve are unable to realize any competitive advantage and often show the poorest profit performance. Trapped in a strategic 'No-Man's Land', they are too large to reap the benefits of more focused competition, yet too small to benefit from the economies of scale that their larger competitors enjoy.*"*

Perhaps the most important point to come from this sort of observation is that the marketing strategist should not blindly pursue market share in the expectation that it will automatically improve profitability. Rather it is the case that the return will depend upon the *type* of strategy pursued. In some cases, for example, the cost of achieving a share gain may far exceed the returns that are possible. There are therefore twelve factors that need to be taken into account in deciding whether to pursue a share-gaining strategy:

1 The cost of gaining share and whether this will be higher than the returns that will follow. This is likely to occur in various situations, but most obviously when the market is in or near maturity, since in these circumstances sales (and hence share) can only be gained on the basis of what would typically be a zero-sum game (this would in effect lead to a pyrrhic victory in which the benefits of victory are outweighed by the costs of achieving that victory). In other words, the only way in which a company can gain sales is at the expense of someone else in the market. By contrast, when the market is in the growth stage, sales can be gained without the need to pursue a confrontational strategy.

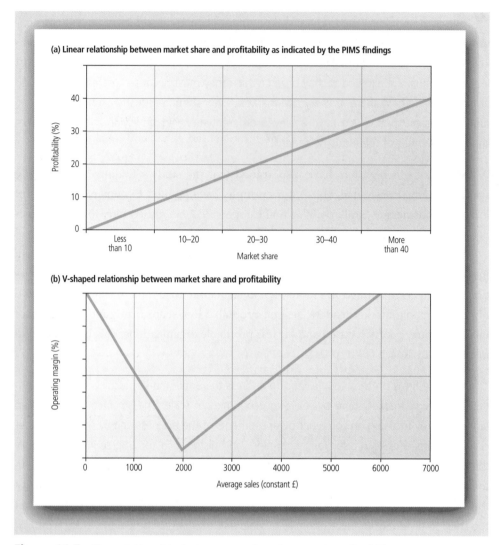

Figure 11.5 The relationship between market share and profitability

2 When the implication of gaining extra share has a knock-on effect to another part of the organization. This might happen when a firm is already operating at full capacity and any increase would involve a heavy investment in new capacity. The likelihood of achieving a positive ROI is then small.

3 There is already a high degree of loyalty to competitors' products among the customer base and this loyalty can only be broken down at a disproportionately high cost.

4 The company intent on gaining share has few obvious or sustainable competitive advantages and hence a weak selling proposition.

5 The future life cycle of the product or market is likely to be short.

6 An increase in share is likely to lead to the firm running foul of anti-monopoly legislation.

7 The increase in share can only be gained by moving into less appealing and less profitable segments.

8 The pursuit of higher share is likely to spark off a major – and potentially unmanageable – competitive fight.

9 It is unlikely that any gain in share can be maintained for anything other than the short term.

10 By increasing share, a larger competitor begins to perceive the organization as an emerging threat and decides to respond when, assuming the organization had not decided to grow, the two firms would have coexisted peacefully.

11 The organization has developed a reputation as a specialist or niche operator and any move away from this would compromise brand values and the brand equity.

12 By growing, the organization would fall into a strategic 'no man's land' in which the firm is too big to be small (in other words, it would no longer be a niche operator), but too small to be big enough to fight off the large players in the market on an equal footing (see Figure 11.5).

In addition, of course, share-gaining strategies can also be argued against when the management team has neither the ability nor the *fundamental* willingness to develop and sustain an appropriate and offensive strategy.

These sorts of points have also been referred to by Jacobson and Aaker (1985), who, in an article entitled 'Is Market Share All That It's Cracked Up To Be?', raised a series of fundamental questions about the value of chasing share gains. It is, however, possible to identify the two conditions under which higher share generally does lead to higher profits. These are: first, when the company offers a superior quality product that is then sold at a premium price, which more than offsets the extra costs of achieving higher quality; and, second, when unit costs fall significantly as sales and share increase.

These two points have been developed by Buzzell and Wiersema (1981), who, by using PIMS data, concluded that companies which successfully achieved gains in market share generally outperformed their competitors in three areas: *new product activity, relative product quality* and *levels of marketing expenditure*. Thus:

1 The successful share gainers developed and added a greater number of new products to their range than their competitors

2 Companies that increased their relative product quality achieved greater share gains than those whose quality stayed constant or declined

3 Those companies that increased their marketing expenditures more rapidly than the rate of market growth gained share

4 Companies that cut their prices more rapidly than competitors rarely – and perhaps surprisingly – did not achieve significant share gains.

In summary, therefore, it is possible to identify the factors that the PIMS researchers believe act as the triggers to profit. These are illustrated in Figure 11.6.

Market share and the definition of market boundaries

Given the importance placed upon market share by the PIMS researchers, it is essential that the marketing planner understands in detail the boundaries of the market in which the organization or the brand is operating. In analysing an organization's market share

Profitability		
• Weak	Relative market share	• High
• Inferior	Relative quality	• Superior
• High	Investment intensity	• Low
• Low	Capacity utilization	• High
• Below par	Productivity	• Above par
• Low or in decline	Market growth	• High
• None	New products	• Some
• High	Market spread	• Low
• Low	Market concentration	• High
• Complex	Logistics	• Simple

Figure 11.6 PIMs and the triggers of profit

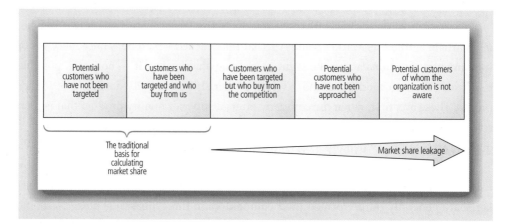

Figure 11.7 Broadening the redefinition of market share

and performance, the marketing planner needs to begin by taking as broad an approach as possible. In doing this, a distinction can be made between that part of the market of which the organization has a share and the broader market, which either has not been approached or has 'leaked' away (see Figure 11.7).

11.5 Marketing strategy and military analogies: lessons for market leaders

*"*It has been suggested in the past that there are, in essence, two sorts of people: those who make change and those who talk about making change. It's better to be in the first group, there is often far less competition.*"*

(Anon.)

The greater intensity of competition that has taken place throughout the world in recent years has led to many managers developing an interest in models of military warfare with a view to identifying any lessons that might be learned and applied to business. From the viewpoint of a market leader intent on defending his position, there are six military defence strategies that can be used: position defence, mobile defence, flanking defence, contraction defence, pre-emptive defence and counter-offensive defence. However, if military history is to teach the marketing or business strategist anything at all, it has to be that some of these strategies are likely to be far less successful than others.

Amongst the best known of the writers on warfare are Basil Liddell-Hart and Sun Tzu. Of the two, it is Sun Tzu who has been the most influential in marketing, with his book *The Art of War (1963)* having been used extensively by marketing strategists (see Illustration 11.2).

Illustration 11.2 Sun Tzu and the art of war

Sun Tzu was a Chinese general who lived around 290 BC. During his life, more than 300 wars were fought between the largely separate Chinese states and it was from these that he learned the principles of warfare that appear in his book *The Art of War*. The essence of the book is that strategy is everything and that preparing for the battle is often more important than fighting it. He argues also that you should never wage war on an army that is deeply committed to its cause. According to Sun Tzu, the art of war is identifying where your rivals are weakest and then exploiting this.

In applying these sorts of ideas to marketing, one lesson that planners have had to learn is that every brand has committed and brand-loyal customers who will only rarely consider changing their brand. Any advertising messages aimed at them will be ignored and, in some cases, may strengthen their commitment to the existing brand. Instead, it is those who are not brand loyal and who are the potential defectors who should be the target.

Although this sort of comment may seem self-evident, the reality is that many marketing campaigns are poorly focused and, as a result, waste resources.

However, in thinking about strategy and what might be learned from looking at other organizations, it is worth remembering a comment made by Sun Tzu:

"All men can see the tactics whereby I conquer, but what none can see is the strategy out of which great victory is evolved.**"**

The issue that emerges from this is that the slavish adoption of another organization's winning strategy is not guaranteed to work. Rather, it is the 'softer' elements of marketing and the mindset of the management team that are of far greater significance.

Position defence

Arguably one of the consistently least successful methods of defence, the position defence or fortress, relies on the apparent impregnability of a fixed position. Militarily, parallels are often drawn between this and the wartime French Maginot and German

Siegfried lines, neither of which achieved their purpose. To overcome a position defence, an attacker therefore typically adopts an indirect approach rather than the head-on attack that the defender expects. Among the companies that have adopted a position defence only to see it fail is Land Rover, which was attacked initially by Toyota, Suzuki and Subaru, and then, more recently, by others such as BMW and Mercedes-Benz. The company, which had developed a strong international reputation for well-made and very rugged four-wheel drive vehicles, did relatively little in the 1960s and 1970s either in terms of product or market development, and subsequently fell victim to an attack based on a lower price and 'fun' appeal. Rather than responding in an aggressive way to this, Land Rover continued with only small modifications to its strategy of selling primarily to farmers and the military, and was then faced with a second-wave attack from Mitsubishi.

There are a series of lessons to be learned from examples such as this, as Saunders (1987a, p. 15) has suggested:

*"*A company attempting a fortress defence will find itself retreating from line after line of fortification into shrinking product markets. The stationary company will end up with outdated products and lost markets, undermined by competitors who find superiority in new products in the marketplace. Even a dominant leader cannot afford to maintain a static defence. It must continually engage in product improvement, line extensions and product proliferations. For instance, giants like Unilever spread their front into related household products; and Coca-Cola, despite having over 50 per cent of the world soft drinks market, has moved aggressively into marketing wines and has diversified into desalination equipment and plastics. These companies defend their territory by breaking it down into units and entrenching in each.*"*

Mobile defence

The second approach, a mobile defence, is based in part on the ideas discussed by Theodore Levitt (1960) in 'Marketing Myopia'; here, rather than becoming preoccupied with the defence of current products and markets through the proliferation of brands, the strategist concentrates upon market broadening and diversification. The rationale for this is to cover new territories that might in the future serve as focal points both for offence and defence. In doing this, the intention is to achieve a degree of strategic depth, which will enable the firm not just to fight off an attacker, but to retaliate effectively. At the heart of a mobile defence, therefore, is the need for management to define carefully, and perhaps redefine, the business it is in. Several years ago, for example, the bicycle manufacturers redefined their business by recognizing that their future was that of leisure and health rather than that of cheap and generally functional transport.

However, in pursuing a strategy of market broadening, the marketing strategist should never lose sight of two major principles – the *principle of the objective* (pursue a clearly defined and realistic objective) and the *principle of mass* (focus your efforts upon the enemy's point of weakness). The implications of these are perhaps best understood by considering for a moment the oil industry. In the 1970s, faced with the likelihood of oil reserves being exhausted in the twenty-first century, the oil companies were encouraged to redefine their business from that of petrol and oil to that of 'energy'. This led several companies to experiment with, and in some cases invest in, nuclear energy, coal, hydroelectric power, solar energy and wind power. In the majority of cases, however, success has at best been limited and in some instances has diluted the company's mass in the markets it is operating in currently. A strategy of market broadening should therefore be realistic and reflect not just the two principles referred to above but also, and very importantly, company capability.

The second dimension of a mobile defence involves *diversification* into unrelated industries. Among those who have done this, in some cases with considerable success, are the tobacco manufacturers, who, faced with a declining market, have moved into industries such as food and financial services, both of which offer greater long-term stability and profits. The net effect of this has been that their vulnerability to predators has been reduced significantly, although there is an irony in the linking of tobacco products with life assurance, which could produce another related net effect.

Flanking defence

It has long been recognized that the flank of an organization, be it an army or a company, is often less well protected than other parts. This vulnerability has several implications for the marketing strategist, the most significant of which is that secondary markets should not be ignored. This lesson was learned the hard way in the 1960s by Smith's Crisps, which, at the time, dominated the UK's potato crisp market. This market consisted primarily of adults, with distribution being achieved mainly through pubs. The children's market was seen by the company to be of secondary importance, and it was therefore this flank that Imperial Tobacco's Golden Wonder attacked with a strategy aimed at children. Distribution to this market then took place through newsagents, sweet shops and the grocery trade. The net effect of this was that, within just a few years, Golden Wonder had taken over as market leader. Subsequently, market leadership was taken over by yet another player, Walker's.

This need to monitor closely the organization's flanks is shown also by the way in which the low-cost airlines deliberately chose not to attack the major airlines such as BA, KLM and Lufthansa head-on, but to pursue a flanking strategy that involved redefining the market (see Illustration 10.3). A similar approach was taken by Dyson, who flanked Hoover and Electrox (see Illustration 11.4).

Contraction defence

There are occasions when, faced with an actual or potential attack, a company will recognize that it has little hope of defending itself fully. It therefore opts for a withdrawal from those segments and geographical areas in which it is most vulnerable or in which it feels there is the least potential. It then concentrates its resources in those areas in which, perhaps by virtue of its mass, it considers itself to be less vulnerable. Militarily, it is a strategy that was used by Russia to great effect in defending itself against Napoleon and, subsequently, Hitler. It was, however, a strategy that was used far less effectively by the British motorcycle industry in the 1960s and 1970s, which, when faced with an attack upon the moped market in South-East Asia by the Japanese, retreated. The rationale for this was explained by the management teams at the time in terms of the way in which they believed that the Japanese development of the small bikes sector would ultimately stimulate demand for large(r) British bikes. In the event, the British manufacturers were forced successively on to the defensive in the 125 cc bikes sector and then the 250 cc and 350 cc sectors. The effect of this was to force out the majority of the British players until only Norton and Triumph were left. Subsequently, even these two were squeezed to such a degree that they became irrelevant. (*Note*: Subsequently, Triumph has come back into the market, albeit as a small and specialist manufacturer.)

Pre-emptive defence

Recognizing the possible limitations both of a position defence and a contraction defence, many strategists, particularly in recent years, have begun to recognize the potential value of pre-emptive strikes. This involves gathering information on potential attacks and then, capitalizing upon competitive advantages, striking first. Pre-emptive strikes can take one of two broad forms: either the company behaves aggressively by, for example, hitting one competitor after another, or it uses psychological warfare by letting it be known how it will behave if a competitor acts in a particular way, a strategy which has been labelled FUD marketing – that is, spreading 'fear uncertainty and despair'.

Among the companies that have successfully used pre-emptive defences are Procter & Gamble and Seiko. In the case of Procter & Gamble, pre-emptive behaviour has been a fundamental element of their strategy for the past few decades and takes the form of consistent and broad-ranging product development, heavy advertising, aggressive pricing and a general philosophy that is sometimes referred to as 'competitive toughness'. A similar philosophy has been pursued by Seiko, which, with more than 2000 different models of watch worldwide, was designed to make it difficult for competitors to get a foothold. The general lesson to be learned from these two companies, and indeed other market leaders, is that the company should never rest even after it has achieved domination, but should instead offer a broad range of products that are replaced frequently and supported aggressively. Any competitor is then faced with a target that is infinitely more difficult to penetrate.

Equally, Tesco, having taken over as the market leader of the UK groceries market, has reinforced its position with a series of astute strategic moves that have seen the business develop into a number of other markets, including books, CDs, computer games, DVDs, brown goods (televisions, vacuum cleaners and so on), finance, flowers, gas and electricity, insurance, travel services, and so on, all of which have been underpinned by speed and agility.

Counter-offensive defence

The final form of defence tends to come into play once an attack has taken place. Faced with a competitor's significant price cut, major new product or increase in advertising, a market leader needs to respond in order to minimize the threat. This response can take one of three forms:

1 Meet the attack head-on
2 Attack the attacker's flank
3 Develop a pincer movement in an attempt to cut off the attacker's operational base.

Of these, it is the first that is arguably the most straightforward; this was seen in the way in which airlines responded in the 1970s to Freddie Laker's attack on prices on the North Atlantic routes. Faced with Laker's price cutting, other airlines flying these routes also cut their prices. Laker's company was eventually forced into liquidation through an inability to service its debts.

As an alternative to this sort of response, market leaders can try searching for a gap in the attacker's armour, a strategy that was used in the USA by Cadillac when faced with a stronger marketing push by Mercedes. Cadillac responded by designing a new model, the Seville, which it claimed had a smoother ride and more features than the Mercedes.

The final counter-offensive move involves fighting back by hitting at the attacker's base. In the USA, for example, Northwest Airlines was faced with a price-cutting attack on one of its biggest and most profitable routes by a far smaller airline. Northwest responded by cutting its fares on the attacker's most important route. Faced with a significant drop in revenue, the attacker withdrew and prices were restored to their original levels.

Defending a position by behaving unconventionally

In defending an organization against its competitors, there is often the need for the marketing planner to behave in a way that at first sight might appear counter-productive, something that was once summed up in terms of 'It's better to shoot yourself in the foot then have your competitors aiming for your head.'

It was this sort of thinking that led Canon, the Japanese camera, copier and printer company, to launch a range of inkjet printers, knowing that it would damage its own dominant position in laser printers. However, in doing this, Canon ensured that it remained the leader in the printer market as a whole rather than dominating just one part of it. But whilst the rationale for this is straightforward, numerous managers have failed to understand this and have responded too late to take advantage of radical shifts within a market or technology.

In discussing this, Loudon (2002, p. 46) has attempted to identify how organizations try to catch what he refers to as 'the next wave of innovations'. The industry's

Goliaths, he says, have been awakened from their slumbers by the new-economy Davids, and the two camps are now getting together in three distinct ways. One is internal venturing, whereby companies promote competition between their divisions, an approach that has long been used by Procter & Gamble and Wal-Mart. Another is corporate venture capital, where companies make investments in third-party operations with a view to eventual pay-off in both financial and strategic terms, something that has been done by Intel and Reuters. The third way involves acquisitions, exemplified by Bertelsmann's buyout of Napster, the online operation. This shows how an old-economy giant can acquire new-technology thinking simply by writing a cheque.

In bringing these ideas together, Loudon has developed the concept of networked innovation. Established companies that want to catch the second (profitable) wave of the Internet revolution need to make sure that they link into the relevant web through networked innovation. In arguing the case for this, Loudon recognizes the potential problems that exist, but cites Volvo as an example of a company that has successfully set up a separate subsidiary to handle this type of innovation.

Market leadership and a customer focus

It should be apparent from what has been said so far that, for an organization to become a market leader and – perhaps more importantly – retain its leadership position over anything other than the short term, the marketing planner needs to develop a clear view of what the future will or can be. As part of this, it is typically argued that there needs to be a strong focus upon the customer and that the organization must, of necessity, be customer-led: indeed, this is a fundamental element of the marketing concept. However, it needs to be recognized that a strong argument can be developed *against* being wholly customer-led in that customers only rarely have a detailed or useful vision of what they will want in the future. (It is important to recognize that, in arguing against being customer-led, we are not arguing against customer satisfaction.) As an example of this, if Sony had relied upon the results of customer research when developing the Walkman, they would have dropped the product at an early stage, since few customers appeared to value the concept. Equally, 3M persevered with its Post-it notes despite initially negative customer research findings.

The lesson that many market leaders have learned from these, and indeed numerous other examples of products that have succeeded in the face of customer myopia, was summed up by Akio Morita, the chairman of Sony:

"Our plan is to lead the public with new products rather than ask them what kind of products they want. The public does not know what is possible, but we do. So instead of doing a lot of market research, we refine our thinking on a product and its use and try to create a market for it by educating and communicating with the public."

This sentiment, which has been echoed by many other consistently innovative companies such as Toshiba, with its Lifestyle Research Institute, highlights the need for the marketing planner to ask – and answer – two questions:

1 What benefits will customers see to be of value in tomorrow's products?

2 How, through innovation, can we deliver these benefits and, in this way, pre-empt our competitors?

In posing the first of these two questions, the marketing planner must, of course, take a very broad view of who the customer is in that, if tomorrow's customers are defined in the same way as those of today, it is almost inevitable that the firm will be eclipsed by others in the market. Recognition of this leads to us being able to identify three types of organization:

1 Companies that insist on trying to take customers in a direction in which they do not really want to go

2 Companies that listen to their customers and then respond by producing products and services that customers are aware they want, but that others in the market are either producing currently or will produce shortly

3 Companies that take their customers where they want to go, even though they may not yet be aware that this is a direction in which they want to go and that the product will deliver value to them.

It is this third type of organization that can be seen to have moved beyond being customer-led and that, as a result, is creating its own future. In doing this, the matrix illustrated in Figure 11.8 is of value in helping managers to focus their thinking (see also Illustration 11.3).

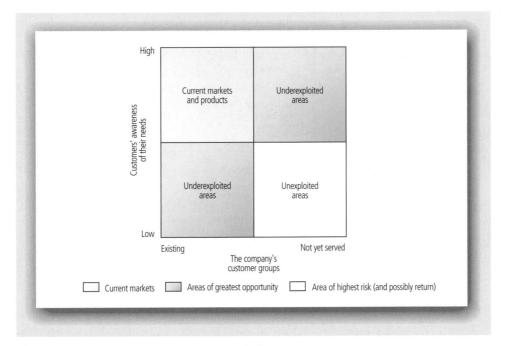

Figure 11.8   The step beyond 'customer-led'

Illustration 11.3 Moving beyond customer-led

Amongst the organizations that have at various stages taken on board the idea of moving beyond being customer-led in the traditional sense are Renault, with its launch in the 1980s of the Espace people carrier; Swatch, with fashionable high-design/low-cost and ultimately disposable watches; and Ryanair and easyJet, with low-cost, no-frills airline travel. Rather than researching customers and tweaking the existing type of service, Michael O'Leary of Ryanair and Stelios Haji-Ioannou of easyJet both identified a need that consumers were not really aware that they had, set about educating them and, in doing this, provided a quantum leap in value.

The move beyond being customer-led and the development instead of a strategy based upon consumer insight and a deeper understanding of changes within society was also at the heart of product and market development within the European car industry in the 1990s. Companies such as Mercedes, BMW and Porsche all identified a series of changes in the profiles of consumers and an often fundamental rethinking of values within this market, and responded by launching sports cars that were lower in price than their traditional products. At the heart of this was the emergence of a sizeable cash-rich ageing baby boomer generation intent on recapturing its youth. The characteristics of this market and the ways in which their values were changing are illustrated in Figure 11.9.

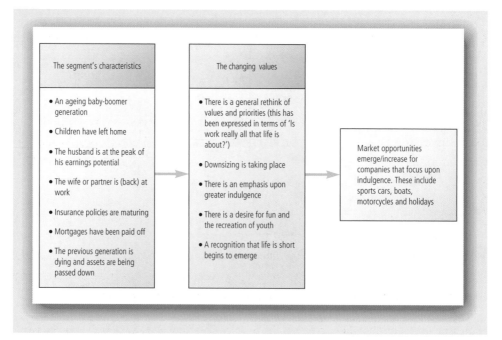

Figure 11.9 Changing markets and marketing opportunities

11.6 Strategies for market challengers

"The Romans didn't build a great empire by organizing meetings. They did it by killing people.**"**

(Anon.)

Companies that are not market leaders are faced with a straightforward strategic choice: either they attack other firms – including perhaps the market leader – in an attempt to build market share and achieve leadership themselves (*market challengers*), or they pursue a far less aggressive strategy and, in doing so, accept the status quo (*market followers*). In deciding between the two, several factors need to be taken into account, the most significant of which are the costs of attacking other firms, the likelihood of success, the eventual probable returns, and the willingness of management to engage in what in most cases will prove to be a costly fight. In commenting on the issue of returns, Fruhan (1972, p. 100) has highlighted the dangers of spending unwisely, arguing that, particularly in mature markets, management can all too easily fall into the trap of chasing market share that proves not to be cost-effective.

This theme has, in turn, been picked up by Dolan (1981), who has suggested that competitive rivalry is typically most intense in industries faced with stagnant demand, high fixed costs and high inventory costs. The implications for a firm in this situation are potentially significant since, while there may well be a need to gain share in order to benefit from greater economies of scale, not only are the costs of doing this high, but the likelihood of the sort of pyrrhic victory referred to above also increases dramatically. Recognition of this should then lead the strategist to a clearer perception of the course of action that is likely to be the most cost-effective. In practice, this means choosing between:

1 Attacking the market leader
2 Attacking firms of similar size to itself, but which are either under-financed or reactive
3 Attacking smaller regional firms.

In making this choice a variety of factors needs to be considered, but particularly the competitive consequences. Picking off a series of small regional players is, for example, often far more profitable than attacking the market leader. This point has been highlighted by Porter (1985b), who suggests that:

"Trying to take business away from the competition that holds the largest share of a market, or makes the most money from that market, may be the most dangerous competitive move a company can make . . . the leader, by virtue of its pre-eminent position, can afford to cut prices, rain down new products on rivals, or bury their offerings under an advertising blitz – in short the big guy can make the business miserable for everyone else.**"**

In making this comment, he highlights the way in which a well-established – and clever – market leader can often afford to slash prices, launch a series of new products and boost levels of advertising spend so that the smaller aggressor is unable to gain share. However, he does recognize that, if the challenger behaves cleverly and strategically, many market leaders are vulnerable. In part, he suggests that this is due to the way in which they become complacent and unwittingly allow the competition to make small inroads that then provide the basis for a more serious attack.

More broadly, he identifies a set of principles that provide a framework for challengers who are thinking of attacking. At the heart of these is the idea that they should never attack head-on with a strategy that simply imitates the leader. Instead, he suggests:

" . . . a successful attack against a strong leader requires that a challenger meet three basic conditions: First, the assailant must have a sustainable competitive advantage, either in cost or in differentiation – the ability to provide the kind of value that commands premium prices. If the challenger's advantage is low cost, the troublemaking upstart can cut prices to lure away the leader's customers or, alternatively, maintain the same price but take the extra money it earns on each product and invest in marketing or R&D. If, on the other hand, the challenger can successfully differentiate itself or its product, then it can invest the proceeds from its premium prices to try to lower its costs or otherwise nullify the leader's cost edge. Whichever advantage the assailant banks on though, must be sustainable – the challenge has to have enough time to close the market share gap before the big guy can come roaring back with his own version of whatever it was that made the challenger successful.

Second, the challenger must be able to partly or wholly neutralize the leader's other advantages, typically by doing almost as well as the leader what the leader does best. An upstart relying on differentiation for example, can't have costs that are hopelessly worse than the leader's – the leader will use his higher returns to bring out a similarly superior product, or will cut prices to make the challenger's offering look pricey indeed.

Finally, there must be some impediment to the leader's retaliating – don't launch an attack without one. The impediment may derive from the leader's circumstances: it's having trouble with the antitrust enforcers, say, or is strapped for cash because of diversification into other businesses. Or the impediment may arise because of the nature of the upstart's challenge, the leader has hundreds of millions of dollars invested in turning out a product based on a particular technology; the challenger attacks with substitute incorporating a new technology which has to be manufactured differently.*"*

At the heart of Porter's ideas is the belief that a challenger must have some kind of strategic insight, something that he or she believes comes from a new or a different way of doing business. The three most common ways of doing this are by:

1 *Reconfiguration*, in which the challenger finds a new and innovative way of performing some of the business's essential activities, such as design, manufacturing, marketing or delivery. An example of this was the way in which Amazon.com used the Internet as the basis of its strategy.
2 *Redefining the market*, either geographically and/or through the product. Federal Express, for example, began by focusing on small packages that required overnight

delivery, and operated its own aircraft. easyJet and Ryanair also redefined the market by offering low-cost, no-frills flights, and in this way avoided attacking head-on the established players such as BA, KLM and Lufthansa.

3 *High spending*. Although this is potentially the most costly and risky of the three approaches, it has been used by firms such as Amazon.com to establish both the technological infrastructure and high levels of brand awareness.

If, however, a company does take on the market leader and succeeds, the rewards both in terms of the power and financial returns that are possible can be considerable. It is largely because of this that many challengers opt for the high-risk/high-return route. For those who do pursue this route, there are several guidelines that emerge from the experience of others. These involve the challenger meeting three basic conditions:

1 It must have a *sustainable* competitive advantage either in terms of cost or differentiation.

2 It must be able to partly or wholly neutralize the leader's advantages, typically by doing almost as well as the leader that which the leader does best.

3 There must be some impediment to the leader's retaliating. Most commonly this might be because the leader will run foul of anti-monopolies legislation or has an enormous and inflexible commitment to a particular technology that the challenger can sidestep.

Whilst ideally the challenger will meet all three of these conditions, fulfilling just one or two can often offset a degree of weakness in meeting the others. In the USA, for example, the no-frills airline People Express began with the benefits of a lower cost base than its competitors – pilots' salaries were lower than the norm, staffing levels were low, and there was little job demarcation – which meant value was passed on to customers in the form of lower prices. Their product, a cramped seat, was sufficiently similar to the cramped seats of other operations for the market leaders to be unable to persuade customers there was a difference. The condition that People Express was unable to meet was the lasting impediment to retaliation, and eventually others in the industry fought back by matching the People Express prices. Having exhausted the growth potential offered on routes that the majors had largely neglected, People Express was forced to look to the more competitive routes if it was to continue growing, and this sparked off a further round of price cutting and retaliation.

A successful attack by a challenger is therefore typically based on a degree of reconfiguration of the activities that make up the business, be it in the form of design, manufacture or delivery; it was this approach that characterized Dyson's attack on the market leader, Hoover (see Illustration 11.4). If the challenger is unable to do this, the safest option is often to ignore the leader and to pursue instead others in the industry who are of equal size or who are smaller and potentially more vulnerable. In this way, any competitive response is likely to be more manageable.

Illustration 11.4 Dyson's reinvention of the vacuum cleaner market

One of the biggest marketing success stories of the 1990s was the launch of the Dyson Dual Cyclone™ Vacuum Cleaner. Following a five-year development period that started in 1978 and involved more than 5000 prototypes, 10 years getting it to the market and grudging retail acceptance, the product took off in a spectacular fashion. Within just a few years of its launch, the company had become the UK's market leader, with more than 52 per cent of the home market in value, and had penetrated some of the most difficult overseas markets in the world, including Japan. By 1999, the company was the fastest growing manufacturer in the UK and had forced companies such as Hoover and Electrolux on to the defensive. Annual sales had grown from £2.4 million in 1993 to £170 million and profits from £200 000 to £22 million. Worldwide, sales were well in excess of £1 billion.

The origins of the market and product

Invented by Hoover at the beginning of the twentieth century, the vacuum cleaner market had, by the final quarter of the century, seemingly reached long-term maturity, with the major players all offering a broadly similar product and fighting desperately for market share. Dyson's approach was very different and involved doing away with the vacuum pump and bag that had been the basis of traditional machines and replacing them with two cyclones, one inside the other, that spun the air at very high speeds and filtered particles as small as cigarette smoke and allergens, which were then collected in a transparent bin.

At the beginning of the 1990s, having developed the product, James Dyson began approaching the leading players of the time, including Bosch, Siemens, Philips, Miele and Electrolux, with a view to their manufacturing and marketing the product in return for a royalty. Having been ignored or rejected by all of them – in part, he felt, because the product would have led to the collapse of the immensely valuable replacement bag market – Dyson decided in 1993 to set up his own manufacturing organization.

Twenty-three months later, and despite selling at twice the price of the conventional vacuum cleaner, the Dyson Dual Cyclone™ had become Britain's best-selling vacuum cleaner.

Niche or mass market product?

In the early stages of the product's life, many commentators focused upon the product's design and colourful style, and suggested that it was 'basically a niche product for technocrats' (Vandermerwe, 1999, p. 6). James Dyson disagreed. The aesthetics were not, he said, 'the defining and differentiating characteristics'. Instead, it was the performance. 'Because everyone has dust, vacuuming is something that everyone has to do.' Despite its technology and its looks, it was in his eyes a product designed not for a niche but for the masses. Everyone, he felt, would want to take advantage of what he saw to be a major leap in performance *and they would be willing to pay for it* (our emphasis). The technology, protected by numerous patents, demanded a high(er) price, which the market would, he believed, pay for if it was convinced it was better than the competition.

The competitive response

The failure on the part of some or all the competitors to respond quickly and aggressively to

Dyson's new technology and entry to the market was seen by some analysts to be surprising. Others saw it to be predictable and a manifestation of the lazy and complacent attitude that often develops in stable and mature markets. Rebecca Trentham, Dyson's Marketing Director, suggested that, even when Dyson was making steady inroads into the competitors' territories, they stayed 'pretty much asleep' and, if pushed, would comment that the product was 'just a fad', 'a gimmick', 'a funny-looking niche product', and 'the Dyson is nothing but a shooting star'.

For James Dyson, this failure to respond was entirely predictable:

> There was a huge opportunity for someone to come along with different and better technology and something which looked different. The market seems impenetrable because it was dominated by big multinationals. I thought it presented a great opportunity because they were all sitting back on their fat market shares without really doing anything. It was all too cosy . . .

The second stage: building upon success

Having established the company as the UK market leader, Dyson reinforced its position with a number of new models, including:

➡ The Dyson Absolute, targeted at asthmatics and others with respiratory problems, the Absolute was the only vacuum cleaner that not only removed pollens but, due to its bacteria-killing screen, killed certain viruses and bacteria such as salmonella and listeria.
➡ The De Stijl, a brightly coloured model that was a homage to the Dutch modernist art movement of the early twentieth century.

The Dyson Antarctica, produced as part of the company's sponsorship of the attempt by Sir Ranulph Fiennes to be the first person to walk across the entire Antarctic continent and, in doing this, raise £5 million for breast cancer research. Dyson donated almost £2 million to the appeal.

In 1999, the company took the product a step further still by launching a new model featuring a filter that did not have to be thrown away, but could instead be cleaned.

By the end of the decade, the competition had come to terms with the inevitable and responded by developing their own products characterized by bright colours, see-through plastic parts and cyclone type design.

The retail and service philosophy

Although the product's performance was, from the outset, far superior to anything offered by the competition, Dyson – in common with many inventors of new and different products – faced difficulties in breaking into the established retail networks. As Vandermerwe (1999, p. 9) commented:

> The first retailers approached by Dyson had been sceptical about stocking a strange looking product with an unknown brand from an unheard-of company – and costing a premium on top of it all. Moreover, several were uneasy with the idea of having this apparatus which graphically showed, as it was being used, the amount of dirt and dust in their stores. Perhaps most importantly, Dyson believed that nobody – be it at the trade or consumer level – really knew that there was anything wrong with the bag – this was part of the educational process.

The Dyson sales force overcame this by focusing upon a variety of techniques to overcome the reluctance, including:

➡ Encouraging the store staff to use the product themselves so that, having been impressed by its performance, this would then sell the product far more enthusiastically and proactively

➡ Giving retailers' sales staff a free 30-day home trial

➡ Offering store staff discounts on the product.

Once anyone bought this precious piece of technology, the company had a responsibility to keep that person happy till the very end. This translated into making the entire process of buying, owning, using and maintaining a Dyson as easy as possible – and, once Dyson had defined its service philosophy, it determined that it couldn't be fulfilled by having any independent, third-party service dealers involved; it would all be done in-house. As Vandermerwe (1999, p. 10) commented:

> One of the first steps in implementing the service philosophy stemmed from a suggestion from one of the people on the Dyson assembly line during the company's early, cottage industry days. 'Why don't we put a helpline number on every machine?' he suggested. The result was that each model in the Dyson range had a prominently displayed label with the Dyson Helpline number on it. The helpline was open seven days a week, from 8.00 am to 8.00 pm, including most bank holidays. By 1999, the company had 100 trained customer service staff manning these helplines.

These helplines led to many day-to-day problems being sorted out over the phone. Where

this was not possible, Dyson would send a courier to the customer's home to collect the machine that day and return the next. This was then followed by an experiment in 1999 whereby a service engineer would go directly to the customer's home to deal with any problems.

The next step

Given the strength of the brand and its market position at the beginning of the twenty-first century, the company faced an interesting set of strategic choices. With only 5 million of the 23 million households in the UK owning a Dyson, there was still scope for significant growth. Similarly, overseas markets offered enormous potential. There was also, Dyson felt, a tremendous opportunity to 'Do a Dyson' within other product categories, such as washing machines, refrigerators and dishwashers. The company was, however, only too aware that the competition, having been hit so hard, was inevitably going to continue to become far more proactive.

Source: Vandermerwe (1999).

Dyson: a postscript

Following on from the enormous success of the Dyson vacuum cleaner, James Dyson launched his next new product – a washing machine – in November 2000. Named the Dyson Contrarotator, the product was the result of an investment of £25 million and four years of research, which involved going back to the first principles of clothes washing and concluding that hand-washing was more effective than even the best of the existing machines on the market. This led to the invention's unique feature: a split drum that rotates in two directions at the same time in order to pummel and flex clothes. When launching the new product, the company claimed that the machine could reduce the time of a family wash by almost two-thirds.

The Dyson Contrarotator featured forty-nine patented improvements, including a 'seal-less' door, a window to retrieve trapped objects such as coins, and a retractable rollerjack to make the machine easy to move. Priced initially at £999 for the basic model with full automatic program-ming (this compares with the £400–580 of the competition), the pricing strategy again reflected Dyson's belief that cus-tomers recognize innovation and higher performance and are willing to pay a pre-mium for them.

Deciding upon who to challenge

Given what has been said so far, the choice of *who* to challenge is fundamental and a major determinant not just of the likelihood of success, but also of the costs and risks involved. However, once this has been done, the strategist is then in a position to con-sider the detail of the strategy that is to be pursued. Returning to the sorts of military analogies discussed earlier, this translates into a choice between five strategies: a frontal attack, a flanking attack, an encirclement attack, a bypass attack and a guerrilla attack. But before choosing among these we need to return for a moment to the more funda-mental issue referred to above of *who* to attack and *when*. In deciding this, the options, as we have suggested, can be seen in terms of an assault on the market leader (a high-risk but potentially high-return strategy), an attack upon companies of similar size, or an attack upon the generally larger number of smaller and possibly more vulnerable firms in the industry. In choosing among these various targets the strategist is likely to be influenced by a variety of factors, including perception of the leader's likely response, the availability of the resources needed to launch an effective attack, and the possible pay-offs. In addition, however, the strategist should also perhaps be influenced by the findings of the military historian, Liddell-Hart. In an analysis of the thirty most important conflicts of the world from the Greek wars up to World War One (this included 280 campaigns), Liddell-Hart concluded that a direct head-on assault suc-ceeded on only six occasions. By contrast, indirect approaches proved not only to be far more successful, but also more economic. This thinking, when applied to business, has led to a series of guidelines for challengers, which are summarized in Figure 11.10.

It has long been recognized that market challengers only rarely succeed by relying on just one element of strategy. Instead, the challenging strategy needs to be made up of several strands that, together, provide the basis for competitive advantage. The eight most commonly used and successful strategic strands are:

1 Price discounting
2 Product and/or service innovation
3 Distribution innovation
4 Heavy advertising
5 Market development

It has long been recognized that market challengers only rarely succeed by relying on just one element of strategy. Instead, success depends on designing a strategy made up of several strands that, by virtue of their cumulative effect, give the challenger a competitive advantage. The ten most commonly used and successful strategic strands used by challengers are:

1 *Price discounting.* Fuji attacked Kodak by offering photographic film and paper that they claimed was of the same quality as the market leader, but 10 per cent cheaper. A similar strategy was pursued by Amstrad in the personal computer market.
2 *Cheaper goods.* Aldi's attack in the grocery retailing market was based on providing a different quality–price combination to that of the other players in the market. Similarly, the coach travel company National Express has based its attack upon the rail industry on a strategy of lower prices.
3 *Product innovation.* By offering a constant stream of new and updated products, a challenger gives buyers a powerful reason for changing their purchasing patterns. Among those to have done this successfully are Polaroid with cameras and, in the 1970s, Apple with microcomputers.
4 *Improved services.* Avis challenged Hertz, the market leader in the car hire market, with a strategy that promised a faster and higher level of service. Its advertising slogan, 'Avis, we're number two, we try harder', is now part of advertising mythology.
5 *Distribution innovation.* Timex watches achieved considerable sales success as the result of a strategy that pioneered a new approach to watch distribution. Rather than selling the product through specialist jewellery stores, the company opted for a far broader approach by distributing through chainstores and supermarkets.
6 *Intensive advertising.*
7 *Market development.* Walker's Crisps achieved considerable success in the 1960s by focusing on the previously ignored market sector of children. The market leader, Smiths, had traditionally concentrated on adults and had distributed through pubs. The attack on such a different front took Smiths by surprise.
8 *Prestige image.* Much of the success achieved in the car market by Mercedes and BMW has been based on the development of an image of quality, reliability and consumer aspiration.
9 *Product proliferation.* The success of Seiko's attack on other watch manufacturers owes much to its strategy of developing some 2400 models designed to satisfy fashion, features, user preferences and virtually anything else that might motivate consumers.
10 *Cost reduction.* Many Japanese companies entered the European and North American markets in the 1960s and 1970s on the back of a cost-reduction, price-led strategy designed to put pressure on domestic manufacturers. Subsequently, a large number of these Japanese companies have modified their approach and repositioned by, for example, emphasizing quality, reliability and prestige. Their place has now been taken by a second wave of companies, this time from Korea, Taiwan and the Philippines, which are emphasizing cost reduction and lower prices.

Figure 11.10 Attack strategies for market challengers

6 Clearer and more meaningful positioning

7 Product proliferation

8 Higher added value.

Frontal attacks

The conventional military wisdom is that for a frontal or head-on attack to succeed against a well-entrenched opponent, the attacker must have at least a 3:1 advantage in firepower; history suggests that broadly similar lessons apply to business.

In launching a frontal attack, a market challenger can opt for either the *pure frontal attack* (by matching the leader product for product, price for price, and so on) or a rather more *limited frontal attack* (by attracting away selected customers). Although the record of success with a pure frontal attack is, as we commented above, generally limited, examples of companies that have adopted this approach and succeeded do exist. Included among these is Xerox, which in the copying market attacked companies such as Gestetner and 3M and, by virtue of a better product, captured the market. (Subsequently, Xerox has itself been attacked by a large number of companies, including Sharp, Canon, Panasonic, Toshiba and Mita.)

A similar frontal attack was used to great effect by the Japanese producers of magnetic recording tape. Having pioneered the market in the 1960s, 3M fell victim to a series of aggressive pricing moves in the 1970s, led by TDK. The effect on 3M was significant and by 1982 it had been forced into the position of a minor player.

More frequently, however, it is the case that a frontal attack proves to be both expensive and ultimately self-defeating, something that both Safeway and Sainsbury's have found in attacking the market leader, Tesco.

Flank attacks

As an alternative to a costly and generally risky frontal attack, many strategists have learned the lesson from military history that an indirect approach is both more economical and more effective. In business terms, a flanking attack translates into an attack on those areas where the leader is geographically weak and in market segments or areas of technology that have been neglected. It was the geographical approach that was used in the late 1960s and early 1970s by Honeywell in competing in the USA against IBM. Quite deliberately, the company concentrated its efforts on the small and medium-sized cities in which IBM's representation, while still high, was not as intense as in the major cities. A similar geographical approach was adopted by the Japanese motorcycle industry, which concentrated its efforts progressively on Asia, the USA and then Europe.

As an alternative, many companies have opted for *technological flanking* or leapfrogging. Among those to have done this with considerable success are the Japanese in the car industry, who rewrote the rules of how to mass produce cars to such an extent that they not only managed to undercut the traditional market leaders, but also reversed the flow of technology transfer in the industry.

Others to have used technological flanking include Michelin against companies such as Goodyear, Firestone and Uniroyal, and the state-owned French helicopter manufacturer, Aerospatiale. Aerospatiale's competitors – Bell Helicopter, Sikorsky and Boeing – worked to full capacity for several years to satisfy the enormous military demand for helicopters in the Vietnam war and had little time for major technological developments. Aerospatiale took advantage of this and in 1980 simultaneously introduced three new-generation fast twin-turbine models designed to cover all conceivable military and civilian needs. These models all featured Aerospatiale-developed fail-safe rotor blades manufactured not from conventional metal but from composite materials.

Segmental flanking has been used to equal effect by numerous companies, over the years, including Hewlett-Packard with mini-computers, Apple with micro-computers, and Toyota and Volkswagen in the USA with small, economical cars. The lesson in each case is straightforward: identify the areas of market need not being covered by the market leader and then concentrate resources on building both size and share. In doing this it is, however, essential that the attacker moves quickly, since the challenge becomes clearer over time and can lead to a sudden competitive response in which the company being attacked regains the initiative. In the majority of cases, however, the company being attacked either fails to recognize the significance of the challenge or is unsure of how best to retaliate and, as a result, responds only slowly. Bic, for example, flanked Gillette in razors by developing the low-priced sector, while Knorr and Batchelor flanked Heinz with the introduction of low-priced soups shortly after Heinz had fought off a head-on attack by Campbells. In both cases, the defender was slow to respond, possibly because of a fear that a stronger reaction would speed up the growth of the low-price sector.

Encirclement attacks

Whereas flanking in its purest form involves an attack on just one front, encirclement has parallels with a blitzkrieg in that it involves launching an attack on as many fronts as possible in order to overwhelm the competitor's defences. In this way, the defender's ability to retaliate effectively is reduced dramatically. Whilst this is an expensive strategy to pursue, and one that is almost guaranteed to lead to significant short-term losses, its record of success in the hands of certain types of company is impressive. Seiko, for example, has made use of a strategy of encirclement not just with the sheer number of models that are changed constantly, but also by acquiring distribution in every watch outlet possible and by heavy advertising that gives emphasis to fashion, features, user preferences and everything else that might motivate the consumer. Similarly, the Japanese motorcycle, audio and hi-fi manufacturers, having started with flanking strategies, quickly developed these into encirclement strategies with an emphasis on rapid product life cycles, frequent and radical new product launches, wide product ranges, aggressive pricing, strong dealer support and, in the case of the motorcycle companies, a successful racing programme. Other companies that have made use of encirclement, admittedly with varying degrees of success, include Yamaha against Honda (see Illustration 11.5) and the Japanese construction machinery manufacturer Komatsu in its attack on the market leader, Caterpillar.

Illustration 11.5 Yamaha and its attack upon Honda

By the early 1960s, Honda had established itself in the USA as the undisputed market leader in the motorcycle market. Its aggressive sales, distribution and product development strategy had had a significant effect on the size and profitability of the market, and led Yamaha to enter the market against Honda. It began by identifying Honda's weaknesses and areas of potential vulnerability. These included a number of successful but complacent deal-ers, a series of management changes, and the discouragement of some new and more aggressive franchise-seeking dealers.

Yamaha offered its own franchises to the best of these dealers and recruited an ambitious sales force to train and motivate them. It then invested heavily in the design of its motorcy-cles so that it could justifiably claim and demonstrate their mechanical superiority. The company capitalized on this with an extensive and costly advertising programme designed to increase buyer awareness and dealer motivation. When motorcycle safety became a significant issue, Yamaha invested in safety features and promoted them extensively.

The combined effect of these strategies led to Yamaha achieving the clear number two position in the market. Yamaha's president, Hisao Koike, then launched a major attack on Honda in order to achieve leadership. With an advertising slogan 'Yamaha take the lead', new models were launched in an attempt to encircle Honda. The plan failed and Yamaha found itself with high inventory levels. This forced the company to reduce its workforce by 2000 employees. Koike resigned, and what was subsequently labelled 'Yamaha's Kamikaze attack' was withdrawn.

In the case of Komatsu and Caterpillar, Komatsu's attack on the market leader was based on the slogan used internally, 'Encircle Caterpillar'. This translated into a series of attacks on market niches, improvements in product quality, extensions to its product range, and pricing at levels 10–15 per cent lower than those of Caterpillar.

Bypass attacks

The fourth approach, a bypass attack, is (in the short-term at least) the most indirect of assaults in that it avoids any aggressive move against the defender's existing products or markets. Instead, the strategist typically concentrates on developing the organization by focusing on *unrelated products* (the Japanese consumer electronics firms developing video recorders and compact discs rather than traditional audio-visual products), *new geographical markets* for existing products and, in the case of the hi-tech industries, by *technological leap-frogging*. Among those to have used a bypass attack successfully are Sturm Ruger and YKK.

Sturm Ruger, a small US gun manufacturer, recognized in the early 1950s that it did not have the resources to develop a product range that would enable it to compete effectively against Colt, Remington and Browning. It therefore concentrated on a bypass strategy by producing a limited range of high-quality and competitively produced guns that earned a reputation for being the best in their class. In this way, Sturm Ruger managed over a 30-year period to capture almost 20 per cent of the US domestic sporting guns market.

A broadly similar strategy was pursued in the zip fasteners market by YKK. The North American market had long been dominated by Talon. YKK therefore concentrated on avoiding a head-on confrontation with the market leader and, by selling direct to fashion houses, managed both to bypass Talon and turn their zip fasteners into a high-fashion item that commanded a premium price. By doing this, YKK captured 30 per cent of the US market. The same strategy was subsequently used in Europe to achieve broadly similar results.

Guerrilla attacks and ambush marketing

The fifth option open to a challenger is in many ways best suited to smaller companies with a relatively limited resource base. Whereas frontal, flanking, encirclement and even bypass attacks are generally broad-based and costly to pursue, a guerrilla attack is made up of a series of hit-and-run moves designed to demoralize the opponent as a prelude to destabilizing and keeping the competitor off balance. In practice, this typically involves drastic short-term price cuts (see Illustration 11.6), sudden and intensive bursts of advertising, product comparisons, damaging public relations activity, poaching a competitor's key staff, legislative moves, and geographically concentrated campaigns. The success of such a strategy has been shown to depend in part upon the competitor's response. In some cases, for example, the competitor chooses to ignore the attack, as has been seen with the way in which the major airlines in the early to mid-1990s chose deliberately not to respond to Virgin's lower prices on the North Atlantic routes. In others, however, the competitor fights back quickly and aggressively in order to minimize any long-term threat. All too often, dealing with guerrilla attacks proves to be difficult.

Illustration 11.6 Safeway and its guerrilla marketing campaign

Guerrilla marketing has also been used by Safeway, the supermarket chain. With its performance having been hit by its traditional competitor such as Tesco, Waitrose and Sainsbury's, as well as a series of discount operators such as Aldi and Netto, which had entered the UK market from continental Europe, the company made radical changes to its strategy in 2000. Having previously run one of the highest profile advertising campaigns in the sector, the decision was taken to focus upon short-term localized campaigns. The rationale for this was straightforward and reflected the view that, as the fourth player in the market, head-to-head battles were unlikely to succeed. Instead, the company needed to concentrate upon the competitors' local areas of weakness and vulnerability, exploit these and then move on.

A variation on guerrilla marketing is the idea of ambush marketing, an approach that was used to enormous effect by Nike and Audi during the 1996 Olympics. The two companies, which were not official sponsors, ran a number of promotions that were tied in with the Olympics and, in so doing, outflanked some of their competitors who were official sponsors. A similar approach was used by the airline Qantas in the period leading up to the Olympics in 2000. Although the company had no official link to the Games, it offered a series of special Olympic deals. The official sponsor, Ansett Australia, fought back by launching a legal challenge against the advertisements, although by this stage Qantas had gained a degree of advantage in the marketplace.

Source: *Marketing*, 25 May 2000, p. 7.

Guerrilla attacks and *No Logo*

The attractions and growth of guerrilla marketing have also been highlighted by Naomi Klein (2000), who, in her book *No Logo*, argues that advertisers are extending their tentacles as never before, commercializing public spaces, branding celebrities and finding new ways to appeal to the traditionally hard-to-reach groups such as the gay market and ethnic minorities. The result has been an enormous upsurge in the volume of advertising and a reduction in the impact of individual advertisements. (Estimates in the USA suggest that each American now sees some 1500 commercial messages a day. Jupiter Communications estimates that, by 2005, wired consumers will be exposed to almost 1000 online advertisements a day, twice the figure for 2000.)

The problems that this has created have, in turn, been compounded by the degree of media fragmentation, with an ever greater number of magazine titles, the growth of cable and innumerable Internet pages. In an attempt to overcome this, a number of organizations have turned to guerrilla marketing, in which the firm adopts either a strategic approach to attacking its competitors (see Illustration 11.6) or resorts to a series of what are essentially gimmicks. Amongst those to have done this are Pizza Hut, which put a 10-metre-high advertisement on a Russian space programme rocket; Mattel, the toy firm that makes Barbie, which painted a street pink to promote its doll; and Jim Thompson, a Canadian, who created interest in medical applications for the Palm Pilot through his 'Jim's Pal pages' site.

However, a problem that has emerged is that guerrilla marketing campaigns often have a relatively superficial appeal and the stunts are neither memorable nor big enough to raise brand awareness and boost sales, something that has led Anita Roddick, the founder of Body Shop, to call most guerrilla campaigns 'the masturbatory indulgences of ad men'.

How challengers defeat the market leaders: lessons from *Eating the Big Fish*

In his book, *Eating the Big Fish*, Adam Morgan (2000) shows how challengers have succeeded against large and well-entrenched brand leaders, and the lessons that emerge from their experiences. Amongst the best of these, he suggests, are:

➡ *Dyson*, who recognized the vulnerabilities of the established players in the vacuum cleaner market and, with a combination of new technology and new marketing thinking, quickly eclipsed companies such as Hoover and Electrolux (see Illustration 11.4).
➡ *Orange*, which overcome people's technological fears by creating a warm and reassuring vision of the future. In doing this, they demonstrated how to build a new technology brand and overtook the established players such as BT.
➡ *Charles Schwab*, the US discount broker, which launched e-Schwab in 1996. Although they knew that the new division would cannibalize their existing business, they recognized how the market was moving and believed that they had to be the first to create a category killer and redefine the market. The result was that they quickly overtook the market leader, Merrill Lynch.

➡ *Bertelsmann Napster.* As the number four player in the media world, Bertelsmann was the first to recognize that the firm that was potentially its greatest threat – Napster, the company that allows consumers to swap music online via MP3 technology – could also provide huge opportunities. Given this, Bertelsmann formed an alliance with Napster and, in doing this, not only neutralized the threat but also redefined the industry.

The single most important lesson to emerge from organizations such as these, Morgan (1999, p. 19) argues, is that of the managerial mindset. The key issue, he suggests, is to think like a challenger rather than to accept the marketing status quo and conventional wisdoms. The ways in which this might best be done include:

1 Forget how the data collectors traditionally define your category. Define it by the way the user thinks of it. Now who is your most dangerous potential competition?
2 Look long and hard at your marketing group's thinking. Be brutal : how much is high interest and how much is low interest? And what are you going to do about the latter?
3 The consumers don't want to know what you think about them. They want to know who you are and what you believe in. Do you know? Honestly? And do they?
4 Everything communicates. How much of your available 'media' – and not just the conventional media you pay for, but the way you act and the way your staff represent you – is projecting your identity?
5 Take away your primary communications medium. How would you build an emotional relationship with people without any television advertising at all?
6 What is the category killer in your market, and what should you risk to create it yourself?

A similar theme has been pursued by Richard Pascale (1990), who, in explaining the success of market challengers and the often relatively poor performance of leaders forced into a defence of their position, has highlighted three areas that need to be considered: resources, the management's concept of the future, and the relationship to the past (see Figure 11.11).

	Leaders forced to defend their position	Challengers and underdogs intent on strengthening their position
Resources	➡ Generally substantial	➡ Often limited
The concept of the future	➡ A focus on protecting what they have already ➡ Growth from the existing base	➡ High aspirations ➡ 'Pioneers of a whole new order'
The relationship to the past	➡ Extrapolation from experience ➡ Fine-tuning of a winning formula	➡ Expediency ➡ Break the rules where possible

Figure 11.11 Leaders and challengers: the significance of mindset

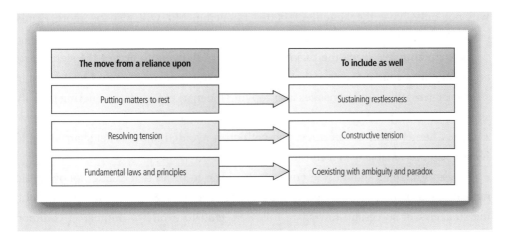

Figure 11.12   The challenger's contextual shift

At the heart of Pascale's ideas of how a challenger can succeed is the development of a particular mindset that requires the sort of contextual shift in management that is shown in Figure 11.12.

11.7 Strategies for market followers

As an alternative to challenging for leadership, many companies are content to adopt a far less proactive posture simply by following what others do. The attractions of this have been pointed to by a variety of writers, including Levitt (1966) and Kotler (1997, p. 393). Levitt, for example, suggested that a strategy of product imitation can often be as profitable as a strategy of innovation. Similarly, Kotler has pointed to the way in which:

*"*An innovator such as Sony bears the huge expense of developing the new product, getting it into distribution, and informing and educating the market. The reward for all this work and risk is normally market leadership. However, other firms can come along, copy or improve on the new products – for example, Panasonic rarely innovates. Rather, it copies Sony's new products, then sells them at lower prices. Panasonic turns a higher profit than Sony because it did not bear the innovation and education expense.*"*

For many firms, therefore, the attractions of being and indeed remaining a market follower can be considerable. This is particularly so when the full costs and risks of challenging an entrenched leader are recognized. If a company is to challenge a market leader successfully, it is essential that the basis for challenging is really worthwhile and meaningful. In practice, this would generally mean a major breakthrough in terms of innovation, price or distribution, something which in relatively long-established and stable industries is often difficult to achieve. Without a major break-through such as this, any attack is almost certain to fail, since most market leaders will not only have the benefit of better financing, but will also be more firmly entrenched.

Recognizing this leads the majority of market followers to accept the status quo, and to pursue a course of action that avoids the risk of confrontation and retaliation. In strategic terms, this often translates into copying the market leaders by offering broadly similar products, prices and levels of service: this is sometimes referred to as a *me-too strategy*. The net effect is that direct competition is avoided and market shares tend to remain relatively stable over a considerable period.

These comments should not, however, be taken to mean that market followers do not have their own distinct strategies. Indeed, as Saunders (1987a, p. 21) has pointed out, the strategies of successful low-share followers tend to exhibit a number of common characteristics, including:

1 Careful market segmentation, competing only in areas where their particular strengths were highly valued.
2 Efficient use of limited R&D budgets – they seldom won R&D battles but channelled their R&D spending into areas that were most likely to generate the greatest financial pay-off, in terms of return on R&D expenditure. Where R&D capabilities were available, they concentrated on truly innovative products.
3 They thought small and stayed small. They tended to emphasize profitability rather than sales growth and market share, concentrating on specialization rather than diversification, high value added rather than mass products, quality rather than quantity.
4 The companies were willing to challenge conventional wisdom – their leaders were often strong willed, committed and involved in almost all aspects of their companies' operations.

It follows from this that the need for a follower to develop a clear and well-formulated strategy is just as great as it is for an infinitely more proactive market leader or challenger. In practice, however, many market followers fail to recognize this and pursue a 'strategy' that is largely implicit and derivative. At the very least a follower needs to recognize the importance of positioning itself so that its customer base is not eroded, that sales increase in line with rates of market growth, and that it is not overly vulnerable to more aggressive and predatory market challengers. This is particularly important when it is remembered that challengers can gain share in three ways, including by taking sales from smaller or equal-sized competitors. A market follower in these circumstances can often prove to be an attractive and vulnerable target.

Followers do therefore need to decide how they intend operating and, in particular, how closely they intend following the market leader. In doing this, it is essential that the firm reduces its vulnerability as much as possible by a combination of tight cost control, an early recognition of developing opportunities, and a clear product and service strategy. This final point is particularly significant, since there is a danger of seeing market followers quite simply as imitators of the market leader. Where this does happen the dangers of confusion among customers increases and the reasons for buying from the follower decrease markedly.

It is possible to identify three quite distinct postures for market followers, depending on just how closely they emulate the leader:

1 *Following closely*, with as similar a marketing mix and market segmentation combination as possible
2 *Following at a distance*, so that, although there are obvious similarities, there are also areas of differentiation between the two
3 *Following selectively*, both in product and market terms, so that the likelihood of direct competition is minimized.

11.8 Strategies for market nichers

The fourth and final strategic position for a firm is that of a market nicher. Although niching is typically associated with small companies, it is in practice a strategy that is also adopted by divisions of larger companies in industries in which competition is intense and the costs of achieving a prominent position are disproportionately high. The advantages of niching can therefore be considerable since, if properly done, it is not only profitable but also avoids confrontation and competition.

The attractiveness of a market niche is typically influenced by several factors, the most significant of which are:

1 It needs to be of sufficient size and purchasing power to be profitable
2 There is scope for market growth
3 The niche is of little immediate interest to the major competitors
4 The firm has the abilities and resources to be able to serve the niche effectively
5 The firm is capable of defending itself against an attack through areas such as customer loyalty.

It is specialization that is at the heart of effective niching, something which has been recognized by retailers such as Ann Summers, and by car companies such as Porsche (the world's most profitable car company in 2002) and TVR.

Specialization can, however, prove dangerous if the market changes in a fundamental way, either as the result of greater competition or an economic downturn, and the nicher is left exposed. For this reason, there is often a strong argument for multiple niching rather than single-sector niching.

The potential profitability of niching has been pointed to by a variety of consultants and authors over the years, including McKinsey & Co. and Biggadike. For example, two of McKinsey's consultants, Clifford and Cavanagh (1985), found from a study of successful mid-size companies that their success was directly attributable to the way in which they niched within a large market rather than trying to go after the whole market. Equally, Biggadike (1977), in a study of forty firms that entered established markets, found that the majority chose to concentrate upon narrower product lines and narrower market segments than the rather better established incumbents.

The supernichers

The potential attractions of market niching have also been highlighted by Hermann Simon (1996), who, in his book *Hidden Champions*, identified a group of what he referred to as 'the supernichers'. These firms, he suggests, typically have a particularly detailed understanding of their markets and have achieved the position of being the largest or second largest player within the world market for their products or the largest in the European market. Amongst these organizations are Hohner (85 per cent of the market for harmonicas), Loctite (80 per cent share of the super-glue market), Swarovski (67 per cent of the cut-cross jewellery market), Tetra (80 per cent of the tropical fish food market) and Steiner (80 per cent of the military field glasses market). Although some of these markets might at first sight seem slightly esoteric, the attractions of being a (successful) market nicher are substantial and include a depth of penetration that makes it difficult for others to attack effectively.

Simon identifies eleven lessons that emerge from the supernichers:

1 Set and then aggressively pursue the goal of becoming the market leader in the chosen market
2 Define the target market narrowly
3 Combine a narrow market focus with a global perspective
4 Deal as directly as possible with customers across the globe
5 Be close to customers in both performance and interaction
6 Ensure that all functions have direct customer contacts
7 Strive for continuous innovation in both product and process
8 Create clear-cut advantages in both product and service, and continually strengthen the selling propositions
9 Keep core competencies in the company and outsource non-core activities
10 Select employees rigorously and retain them for the long term
11 Practice leadership that is authoritarian in the fundamentals and participative in the details.

In terms of how market nichers operate, there are several guidelines that can be identified. These include:

➡ Specializing geographically
➡ Specializing by the type of end-user

→ Specializing by product or product line

→ Specializing on a quality/price spectrum

→ Specializing by service

→ Specializing by size of customer

→ Specializing by product feature.

11.9 Military analogies and competitive strategy: a brief summary

Given the nature of our comments about the parallels between military strategy and business strategy, these can perhaps best be summarized by referring to Von Clausewitz's thoughts, discussed in his book *On War* (1908). In this, he argues for planners to adopt eight principles:

1 Select and maintain the aim

2 Use surprise in the form of originality, audacity and speed

3 Maintain morale

4 Take offensive action

5 Secure your defences and never be taken by surprise

6 Maintain flexibility

7 Use a concentration of force

8 Use an economy of effort.

These ideas are also summarized in Figure 11.13.

The principles of offensive marketing warfare

1. The major consideration is the strength of the leader's position
2. Search for a weakness in the leader's strength, and attack where he is most vulnerable
3. Always launch the attack on as narrow a front as possible

The principles of flanking marketing warfare

1. Flanking moves must be made into uncontested areas
2. Tactical surprise should be a key element of the plan
3. The pursuit is as critical as the attack itself

The principles of defensive marketing warfare

1. Only the market leader should consider playing defence; all others should think more offensively
2. The best defensive strategy involves attack
3. Strong competitive moves should always be blocked; never ignore or underestimate the competition

The principles of guerrilla marketing warfare

1. Find a segment of the market that is small enough to defend (and is worth defending)
2. Regardless of how successful you become, never act like the leader by becoming fat, lazy, complacent and arrogant
3. Be prepared to retreat at short notice when faced with a threat you cannot deal with

Figure 11.13 Military analogies and competitive strategy: a brief summary

Competitive strategy as a game

It has long been recognized that competition between organizations can be seen in much the same way as a game, in that the outcome in terms of an organization's performance is determined not just by its own actions but also by the actions and reactions of the other players, such as competitors, customers, governments and other stakeholders. However, as the pace of environmental change increases and the nature, sources and bases of competition alter, markets become more complex and the competitive game consequently becomes more difficult to win, something that has been illustrated by a spectrum of markets, including colas, films and cameras, airlines, detergents, disposable nappies, tyres, computer hardware and software, and newspapers. In markets such as these, the ever-present danger is of one company taking a step such as a price cut, which then proves to be mutually destructive, as everyone else responds in a desperate attempt to avoid losing customers, volume and share. From the customers' point of view, of course, moves such as these are often attractive, particularly as they can lead to a different set of expectations, which any individual firm then finds difficult to reverse.

It follows from this that the need to manage competition and the competitive process, while often difficult, is essential. Although there are no hard and fast rules, it is possible to identify a number of very broad guidelines that companies might follow. These include:

➡ *Never ignore new competitors*, particularly those who enter at the bottom end of the market, since almost inevitably once a firm gains a foothold it will start targeting other segments of the market. Examples of this include the early manufacturers of calculators, who ignored Casio; IBM, which ignored a series of initially small players such as Apple, Dell and Compaq; the UK motorcycle manufacturers, who underestimated the Japanese such as Honda, Yamaha, Kawasaki and Suzuki; and Xerox, which was hit hard by Canon.
➡ *Always exploit competitive advantages* and never allow them to disappear unless they are being replaced by an advantage that, from the customer's point of view, is more powerful and meaningful.
➡ *Never launch a new product or take a new initiative without working out how the competition will respond* and how you will be affected by this.

Although these three guidelines are in many ways self-evident, the reality is that numerous organizations develop and implement strategies that reflect little real understanding or awareness of the competition. Others, however, do manage to develop competitive strategies in the truest sense. According to Day (1996b, p. 2), there appear to be several factors that set these companies apart, including:

➡ An intense focus upon competitors *throughout* the organization
➡ The desire and determination to learn as much as possible about each competitor, its strategies, intentions, capabilities and limitations

➡ A commitment to using this information and the insights it provides in order to anticipate how they are most likely to behave.

The outcome of this sort of approach is, as Day (1996b, p. 3) comments:

*"*They formulate strategies by devising creative alternatives that minimize or preclude or encourage cooperative competitive responses. They adroitly use many weapons other than price, including advertising, litigation, and product innovation. They play the competitive game as though it were chess, by envisioning the long-term consequences of their moves. Their goal is long-term success, rather than settling for short-run gains, or avoiding immediate losses.*"*

However, in developing a competitive strategy, many managers appear to make the mistake of focusing upon what competitors have done in the past rather than what they are most likely to do in the future. Whilst behaviour in the future is often influenced by what has been done previously, even small changes on the part of a competitor can invalidate the assumptions being made.

At the same time, much thinking about competitors and the interpretation of competitive intelligence is based on mental models that reflect a simplification of reality. Although this simplification is understandable – and may well prove to be adequate in relatively static markets – it is unlikely to be suited to markets in which there is any real degree of competitive intensity. Because of this, competitively successful organizations appear to put a great deal of effort into learning, not just about competitors, but also into developing a detailed understanding of distributors' perceptions and expectations, and the extent to which these are being met. They appear also to devote significant resources to learning from their own experiences so that future strategies can then be built upon this understanding.

Marketing strategy and the search for future competitiveness

We suggested earlier that, if an enterprise is managed a little better than customers expect, and if this is done in a slightly better way than competitors can manage, then the enterprise should be successful (see p. 4). Although the need for a competitively superior approach has long been at the heart of marketing strategy, the search for greater competitive capability has increased dramatically over the past few years. Several factors have contributed to this, a number of which are referred to in the discussion of the strategic challenges facing organizations (p. 120) and the dimensions of the new customer and the new forms of competition (pp. 172 and 223 respectively). Together, these have put pressures on managers to develop strategies that are not only far more clearly focused upon the market, but also infinitely more proactive, flexible and innovative. However, for many managers, the problem is not necessarily that of identifying or gaining an advantage initially, but of *sustaining* it over any length of time. In highly competitive and largely mature markets, for example, an ever greater number of organizations are having to compete directly against competitors who offer almost identical products across 70–80 per cent of the range. Because of this, the focus of competitive advantage is increasingly shifting away from major product and technological breakthroughs to an emphasis upon a series of process improvements. These are illustrated in Figure 11.14.

However, in order to achieve this, it is essential that the interrelationships that exist both internally (between marketing and other functional areas of the business) and externally (between the organization and its suppliers and distributors) are refined – and perhaps rethought – so that the five dimensions of quality, speed dependability, flexibility and cost referred to in Figure 11.14 are operating optimally.

As part of this, the marketing planner also needs to develop a far more detailed understanding of what customers see to be of importance and how the organization's product range compares with those of its competitors. A framework for this is illustrated in Figure 11.15.

This search for competitiveness has been pursued by numerous writers over the years, including Hooley and Saunders (1993) and Hamel and Prahalad (1994). In discussing how to improve performance, Hooley and Saunders focus upon the detail of marketing activity, arguing that there are three areas to which the marketing planner needs to pay attention (these are illustrated in Figure 11.16).

These ideas are taken further by Hamel and Prahalad (1994), who, in *Competing for the Future* (one of the most influential management books of the 1990s), argue that managers need to rethink their strategies in a series of fundamental ways. However, in many organizations they argue that all or most managers have still failed to come to terms with this and are wedded to old patterns of thinking and old formulae. As a test of this, they suggest posing a series of questions (Hamel and Prahalad, 1994, pp. 1–2):

*"*Look around your company. Look at the high profile initiatives that have been launched recently. Look at the issues that are preoccupying senior management. Look at the criteria and benchmarks by which progress is being measured. Look at the track record of new business creation. Look into the faces of your colleagues and consider their dreams and

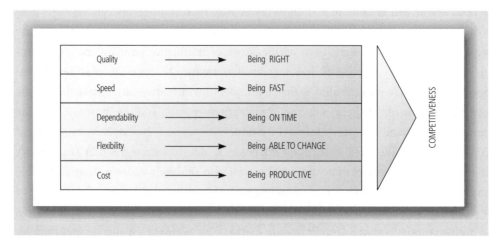

Figure 11.14 The contribution of process improvements to greater competitiveness

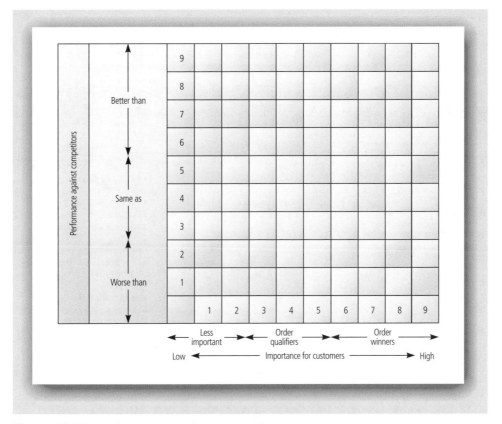

Figure 11.15   Performance against competition

fears. Look toward the future and ponder your company's ability to shape that future and regenerate success again and again in the years and decades to come.

Now ask yourself: Does senior management have a clear and broadly shared understanding of how the industry may be different ten years in the future? Are its 'headlights' shining further out than those of competitors? Is its point of view about the future clearly reflected in the company's short-term priorities? Is its point of view about the future competitively unique?

Ask yourself: How influential is my company in setting the new rules of competition within its industry? Is it regularly defining new ways of doing business, building new capabilities, and setting new standards of customer satisfaction? Is it more a rule-maker than a rule-taker within its industry? Is it more intent on challenging the industry status quo than protecting it?

Ask yourself: Is senior management fully alert to the dangers posed by new, unconventional rivals? Are potential threats to the current business model widely understood? Do senior executives possess a keen sense of urgency about the need to reinvent the current business model? Is the task of regenerating core strategies receiving as much top management attention as the task of re-engineering core processes?

Ask yourself: Is my company pursuing growth and new business development with as much passion as it is pursuing operational efficiency and downsizing? Do we have as clear

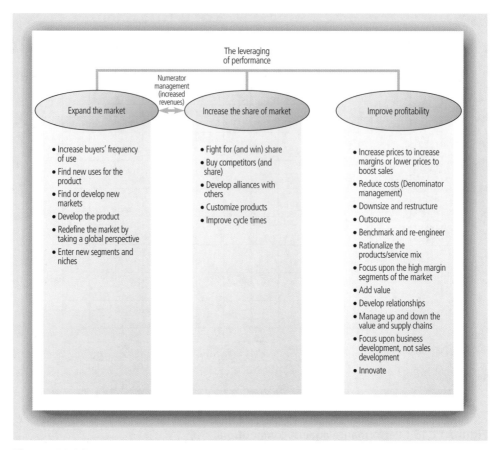

Figure 11.16 Leveraging performance (adapted from Hooley and Saunders, 1993)

a point of view about where the next $100 million or $1 billion of revenue growth will come from as we do about where the next $10 million, $100 million, or $1 billion of cost savings will come from?*"*

The answer to these and a number of other questions, they suggest, is that far too often, far too little really detailed thinking about how best to compete in the future is going on.

As a first step in overcoming this, they suggest that managers focus upon the factors that contribute to greater competitiveness. These are illustrated in Figure 11.17.

They go on to argue that, although many managers have focused upon the first two dimensions in Figure 11.17 (which, it needs to be emphasized, are inward-looking and, in the case of downsizing, if taken to the extreme, can lead to 'anorexia industrialosa', which can best be summarized as the desperate attempt to be ever fitter and ever leaner, leading to emanciation and ultimately death), relatively few have managed to come to terms with the third, even though it is this area that offers the greatest opportunity for an organization to make a major competitive advance. At the same time, of course, it is this area that offers the scope for the greatest competitive disadvantage if a competitor reinvents the industry or strategy first.

Among the organizations that have successfully reinvented the industry and/or regenerated strategy are Xerox, which in the 1970s redefined the document-copying

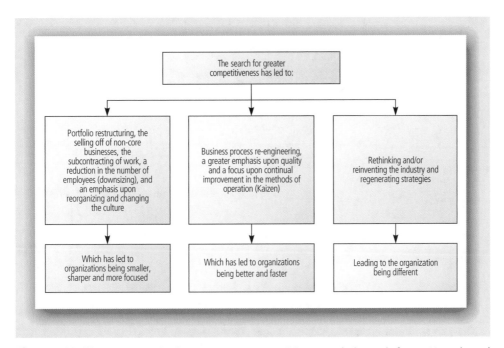

Figure 11.17 The search for greater competitiveness (adapted from Hamel and Prahalad, 1994)

market; Pentax and Canon, which developed highly reliable and low-cost 35 mm cameras; Canon, which, in the 1980s, developed small, low-cost photocopiers and, in so doing, opened up vast new markets that, despite its initial innovatory zeal, Xerox had largely ignored; Compaq, which developed the low-cost PC market; Swatch, with fashion watches; The Body Shop, which pioneered the environmentally friendly health and beauty market; Sony with, among other products, the Walkman; Direct Line, which developed the direct selling of insurance; and Häagen-Dazs, the experiences of which are discussed in Illustration 11.7.

Illustration 11.7 The regeneration of a market – the launch of Häagen-Dazs ice-cream

In 1989, as part of their objective of building the biggest ice-cream brand in the world, Grand Met took the decision to launch Häagen-Dazs into Europe. At the time of the launch, the European market was dominated by three large multinationals: Unilever (which had a worldwide market share of 40 per cent), Mars and Nestlé. However, despite the size, strength and undoubted marketing expertise of their competitors, Grand Met believed that it had identified a number of areas in which the three companies were vulnerable to an attack by a new entrant. The most significant of these was that no real attempt had been made to develop either a global or a Eurobrand.

There were several apparent reasons for this, including the way in which patterns of ice-cream consumption varied significantly from one country to another; taste differences (85 per cent of ice-cream in the UK was non-dairy, whilst almost everywhere else in Europe, except for Portugal and Ireland, it was dairy ice-cream); and buying and eating patterns (in France, the impulse sector accounted for 28 per cent of sales and the take home sector for 72 per cent; by contrast, the impulse sector in Italy accounted for 41 per cent of sales, whilst in the UK and Germany it was 43 and 62 per cent respectively). These differences were then compounded by the product's highly seasonal nature and by the way in which the European ice-cream market had stagnated since 1985. Because of this, the sector was seen generally to be an unexciting market that offered few real opportunities for growth. The majority of consumers were children, the average life expectancy of a brand was around three years, new brands needed heavy advertising support in order to gain national distribution, and the new product failure rate was high.

Despite this, Häagen-Dazs was launched in 1989 and, with only a modest marketing budget, achieved sales in 1990 of $10 million. By September 1991, this had tripled to $30 million and, by 1992, had reached $100 million, making it the European market leader in the premium sector.

So what led to the brand's success?

In a number of ways, Häagen-Dazs illustrates Hamel and Prahalad's thinking on the need for managers to focus upon reinventing their industry and/or regenerating the strategy (see pp. 467–8). At a time when the quality of ice-cream was generally poor (as one commentator remarked, ice-cream had deteriorated to the point at which it was just cheap, cold and sweet) and marketed very largely on the basis of a pull strategy, with heavy television spending supported by trade and consumer promo-

tions, Häagen-Dazs chose to pursue a very different three-pronged marketing push strategy designed to increase the awareness of the brand, achieve a high trial rate, and generate substantial word-of-mouth. One consequence of this was that 'it radically changed the rules of the game in the European ice-cream market' (Joachimsthaler, 1994, p. 4).

The principal dimensions of this strategy involved:

1 The opening of a series of ice-cream parlours in large European cities.
2 Targeting food service accounts in expensive hotels and restaurants.
3 Targeting major retail accounts, including supermarket chains, delicatessens, cinemas and convenience stores. In doing this, Häagen-Dazs opted for extensive sampling and retailer support packages, which included upright freezer display cabinets.

However, underpinning this were four further factors that, for many observers, are the real keys to success:

1 The product's demonstrably superior quality and taste, which stems from the very high dairy (butter) fat content, the use of 100 per cent natural ingredients and the absence of stabilizers
2 A superb product delivery service
3 Premium pricing (in the UK its prices were 30–40 per cent higher than its immediate competitors, whilst in Germany it was twice as expensive as the local premium product)
4 A highly distinctive and provocative advertising campaign, which featured black and white photography inspired by the movie *Nine and a Half Weeks*, a theme of 'The Ultimate Experience in Personal Pleasure', and the ending on every piece of advertising copy, 'Häagen-Dazs – dedicated to pleasure'.

The effect of the Häagen-Dazs strategy upon the market proved to be significant. By taking their competitors by surprise and redefining both the product and the market, the competition was forced to respond. In the event, nearly all did this by launching their own premium-quality and premium-priced products in an almost desperate attempt to capitalize upon the new market. By the end of 1993, however, it was clear that Häagen-Dazs was the winner of what was labelled the ice-cream wars. Not only had it managed to increase its market share yet further, it had maintained a significant price premium.

Source: Joachimsthaler (1994).

Häagen-Dazs: a postscript

Faced with such a radical rewriting of the rules of competition within the ice-cream market, competitors found themselves at a major disadvantage. In essence, they found themselves with three alternatives:

1 To do nothing and let Häagen-Dazs capitalize upon its audacious move
2 To respond quickly by copying
3 To respond rather more thoughtfully by innovating and, hopefully, redefining the market again.

Over the next few years, various competitors responded in all three ways, with the major supermarket chains launching their own-label premium-quality, premium-priced products, whilst others such as Ben & Jerry entered the market from the USA on a platform of environmentalism (a proportion of their profits is donated to environmental courses); amusing product names such as Chubby Hubby, Fish Food, Cherry Garcia (a pun based on Jerry Garcia of The Grateful Dead) and Chunky Monkey; and larger ingredients such as nuts.

However, by the end of the century, the market had begun to stagnate. Faced with this, Häagen-Dazs launched a joint venture with Nestlé, whilst Unilever bought Ben & Jerry.

At the heart of Hamel and Prahalad's thinking on strategy is the idea that, in order to cope with the demands of the future, managers need to make a series of fundamental changes. The starting point in this process, they suggest, involves getting off the treadmill of day-to-day activities and moving away from existing patterns of thought. A fundamental part of this involves managers in 'learning to forget'. In other words, managers need to recognize that, by adhering to the old but possibly successful formulae and to the existing cultural paradigms, failure is almost certain. There needs, therefore, to be an emphasis upon a series of steps, including:

➡ *Competing for industry foresight* by identifying how the market will or can be encouraged to develop. 'The trick', Hamel and Prahalad (1994, p. 73) suggest, 'is to see the future before it arrives.'
➡ Having developed a picture of the future, the emphasis then shifts to *crafting the strategic architecture* or blueprint for developing the skills and structures that will be needed in order to compete in the new environment.
➡ In turn, this leads to the *stretching and leveraging of strategy* so that the organization's resources are focused, developed and exploited to the full.

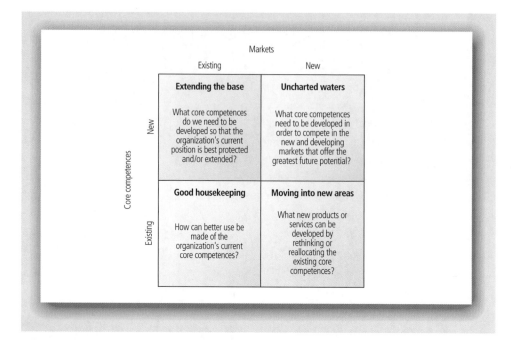

Figure 11.18 Developing the organization's core competences (adapted from Hamel and Prahalad, 1994)

Underpinning all of this is the need for a clear understanding of the core competences or skills that the organization has currently, the nature of the core competences that will be needed in the future and how therefore the organization's competences will need to be developed. A framework for thinking about this appears in Figure 11.18.

11.10 The inevitability of strategic wear-out (or the law of marketing gravity and why dead cats only bounce once)

Regardless of whether the company is a leader, follower, challenger or nicher, the marketing strategist needs to recognize that even the most successful of strategies will, sooner or later, begin to wear out and lose its impact. It is therefore essential that strategies are modified both to anticipate and meet changing competitive challenges and consumer needs. Among the companies that have failed to do this are Polaroid and the large mail-order companies. In the case of Polaroid, its winning strategies of the 1960s and 1970s failed to change sufficiently to come to terms with the radically different markets of the 1980s as non-instant competitors improved product performance and high street witnessed an explosion in the number and reliability of shops offering ur and 24-hour photographic development services.

ly, the mass-market mail-order companies failed in the 1970s to come to changing role of women, their greater spending power, the smaller home during the day, the greater attractions of the high street, and ity of instant credit. The result was a rapid decline in their share of consumer spending, an increasingly tired-looking sales formula and, perhaps more fundamentally, an apparent absence at the time of any real understanding of how to fight back. Subsequently, organizations such as Littlewoods have moved online, whilst new(er) entrants to the market such as Land's End and Next have based their strategies on clearer targeting and a move up the socio-economic scale and down the age scale.

Quite obviously, the vulnerability of a company to a predator in these circumstances increases enormously and highlights the need for regular reviews of strategy. In many cases, however, and particularly when a company has been successful, management often proves reluctant to change what is seen to be a winning strategy. The need for change often becomes apparent only at a later stage, when the gap between what the company is doing and what it should be doing increases to a point at which performance and prospects begin to suffer in an obvious way. It is by this stage that an observant and astute competitor will have taken advantage of the company's increased vulnerability. The argument in favour of regular environmental and strategic reviews is therefore unassailable and reinforces the discussion in the earlier parts of the book. Specifically, the sorts of factors that contribute to strategic wear-out and strategic drift include:

➡ Changes in market structure as competitors enter or exit
➡ Changes in competitors' stances
➡ Competitive innovations
➡ Changes in consumers' expectations
➡ Economic changes
➡ Legislative changes
➡ Technological changes, including in some instances the emergence of a new technology, which at first sight is unrelated or only indirectly related to the company's existing sphere of operations
➡ Distribution changes
➡ Supplier changes
➡ A lack of internal investment
➡ Poor control of company costs
➡ A tired and uncertain managerial philosophy.

These are shown diagramatically in Figure 11.19.

We commented at an earlier stage in this book that, for many companies, strategic development often proves to be a painful and unnatural process. Recognizing this, it is perhaps understandable that, having developed a seemingly successful strategy, many management teams are content either to stick with the strategy or change it only marginally over time.

The law of marketing gravity

The law of marketing gravity states that, regardless of how big or powerful an organization or brand becomes, sooner or later its performance will almost inevitably decline.

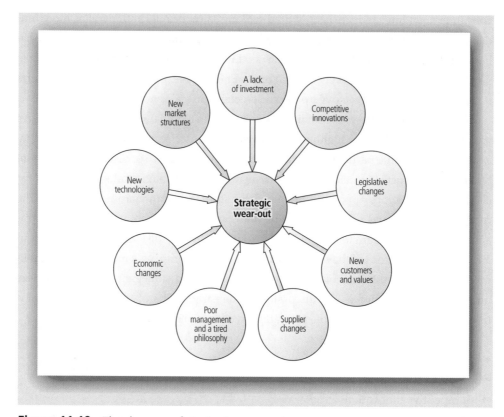

Figure 11.19 The dangers of strategic wear-out

Amongst those to have experienced this are Marks & Spencer in the late 1990s, BA and Hoover.

According to Mazur (2000), the four principal contributors to marketing gravity are:

1 *Marketing myopia*, or the tendency to apply the letter of marketing while ignoring the spirit. BA's decision to redesign the tailfins of its planes, play down the Britishness of the airline and to focus upon premium-paying first- and business-class passengers had an apparent strategic appeal that was lost in the implementation. The new tailfin designs blurred what had previously been a strongly defined and unique image, whilst the focus upon just a small number of passengers failed to recognize the imperfections of market segmentation and that not all business executives fly business class.

2 *Marketing arrogance*, or ignoring the impact of your actions on the brand's success. Amongst those to have fallen victim to this was Marks & Spencer's management team, with its belief for a long time that the company did not really need marketing and that they had an unerring feel for customers' needs. The inward-looking culture that emerged led to a series of mistakes and an unprecedented degree of customer disillusionment and defection. The company's revival only came about once new management was brought in from the outside and a new externally focused culture developed.

3 *Marketing hubris*, or believing your own PR to the detriment of the corporate brand. Amongst those guilty of this have been Bill Gates, with his belief that Microsoft should be free of the sorts of constraints that affect other organizations, and Douglas Ivester (the former head of Coca-Cola), who, for some time, ignored the problems faced by the brand when stories began to emerge in Europe of the possible contamination of the product.

4 *The marketing silliness* that affects the organization when it puts common sense to one side in the interest of decisions that are claimed to be 'creative'. A case in point was Abbey National's choice of the name Cahoot for its Internet bank.

Dead cats only bounce once

Having come to terms with the law of marketing gravity and the apparent inevitability of strategic wear-out, management teams should never lose sight of the investment analysts' management adage that, at best, dead cats only bounce once. In other words, once the organization's strategy loses its impact (this is the idea of strategic wear-out that is referred to above), the management team typically only has one opportunity to recapture its lost position. If it fails to do this, levels of loyalty and the customer franchise rapidly disappear, and market share begins to slide.

Recognizing this, it should be apparent that many organizations run the risk of competitive oblivion, not least because of the way in which the Internet drives margins downwards. Faced with this, the need for the marketing planner to focus upon strategies that create unique value for customers is self-evident, but all too often ignored. Instead, many organizations rely upon friction as a reliable service of profit (friction is defined as customer ignorance or inertia). The banks, for example, have traditionally derived much of their income from customers' perceptions of the difficulties of transferring their account to another bank and/or a belief that, even if they do transfer, the way in which they will be treated will be little different. However, with the development of web-based strategies, a decline in technophobia and generally higher levels of customer promiscuity, the extent to which organizations will be able to rely upon friction is likely to decrease dramatically.

It was the recognition of this that has led companies such as Gateway and First Direct to rethink the ways in which they might interact with customers. In the case of Gateway, having been hit by the economic downturn in the USA in 2001, the company focused upon a two-pronged strategy that involved going 'back to basics' in reducing its product lines and concentrating upon customer satisfaction. As part of the back to basics approach, the company streamlined the number of PC options so that there were fewer chances of things going wrong. The customer strategy concentrated upon satisfaction levels, part of which involved Gateway's employees going to a customer's home or office to guide them through setting up a new PC. The results of this were seen initially in terms of a dramatic reduction in the number of calls to the company's helpline, but then a leap in the number of add-ons that customers bought as the result of a company employee demonstrating their value.

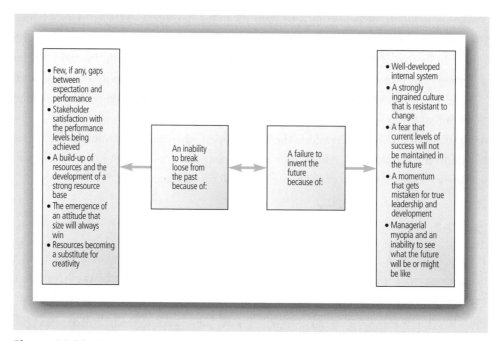

Figure 11.20 The conflicting pressures of the past and the future

A similar approach, in which the organization rediscovered the business benefits of thinking from their customers' point of view, has been adopted by the telephone and Internet banker First Direct, which has encouraged staff to deal with customers in the same way that they would want to be treated.

There is, however, a more fundamental problem that many organizations face as they grow and that stems from past success. Where an organization has been successful, there is an understandable tendency to continue with what appears to be a winning formula (this is a reflection of the idea that only the very brave or the very stupid change things when they are going well). However, in doing this, the management team may well be sowing the seeds of their own destruction, since the alternative view would be that it is when the organization is doing well that it is in the strongest position to take the next (strategic) step. In practice though, and particularly when faced with a challenging and rapidly changing market, a tension develops within organizations in which the management team finds itself unable to break away from the past and is unable to invent its future; this is illustrated in Figure 11.20.

11.11 The influence of product evolution and the product life cycle on strategy

The product life cycle (PLC) is arguably one of the best-known but least understood concepts in marketing. In making this comment, we have in mind the idea that, whilst the concept has an inherent appeal and logic, there is little hard evidence that marketing managers use it in a particularly effective manner when developing strategy. There are several reasons for this, the most obvious being the difficulty in predicting the precise shape of the life-cycle curve and the position of the company on the curve at any particular time. Nevertheless, the idea of the product life cycle has undoubtedly influenced the thinking of many marketing strategists, albeit at a general rather than a specific level.

The rationale of the life cycle is straightforward and reflects the way in which products and services pass through a number of distinct stages from their introduction through to their removal from the market. Recognizing this, the planner needs to develop strategies that are appropriate to each stage of the life cycle.

The strategic implications of the life cycle are thus potentially significant and can be summarized as follows:

1 Products have a finite life
2 During this life, they pass through a series of different stages, each of which poses different challenges to the seller
3 Virtually all elements of the organization's strategy need to change as the product moves from one stage to another
4 The profit potential of products varies considerably from one stage to another
5 The demands upon management and the appropriateness of managerial styles also varies from stage to stage.

In terms of operating practice, the most obvious and immediate implication of a model of product and market evolution such as this can be seen as the need for strategy to change over time and to reflect the particular demands of the different stages. These stages, which are illustrated in Figure 11.21, are typically designated as introduction, growth, maturity and decline, and follow an S-shaped curve.

However, despite the simplicity and apparent logic of the life cycle concept, a series of problems are typically experienced in its use. The most common of these stems from the difficulty of identifying where on the life cycle a product is and where each stage begins and ends. In most cases, the decision is arbitrary, although several commentators have proposed rather more objective criteria. Probably the best known of these is an approach devised by Polli and Cook (1969), which is based on a normal distribution of percentage changes in real sales from year to year. Others, such as Cox (1967), advocate an historically based approach whereby the strategist examines the sales histories of similar products in the industry. If this reveals that in the past the average length of the introductory, growth and maturity periods has been 5, 14 and 48 months respectively, these time scales are, all other factors being equal, assumed to apply to the product in question. The problem, of course, is that other factors almost invariably do intrude, with the result that historical analysis is at best only a vague guide to strategy and at worst misleading. This is particularly so when levels of competitive intensity increase. Moreover, the planner should not lose sight of the way in which life cycles generally are shortening. Other

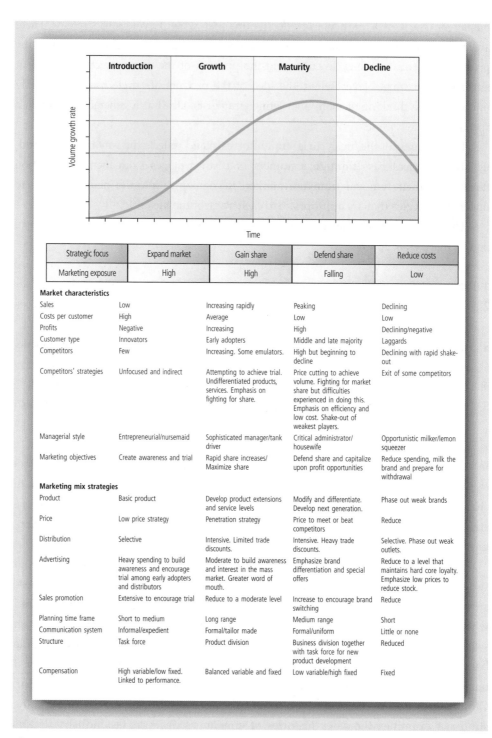

	Introduction	Growth	Maturity	Decline
Strategic focus	Expand market	Gain share	Defend share	Reduce costs
Marketing exposure	High	High	Falling	Low

Market characteristics

Sales	Low	Increasing rapidly	Peaking	Declining
Costs per customer	High	Average	Low	Low
Profits	Negative	Increasing	High	Declining/negative
Customer type	Innovators	Early adopters	Middle and late majority	Laggards
Competitors	Few	Increasing. Some emulators.	High but beginning to decline	Declining with rapid shake-out
Competitors' strategies	Unfocused and indirect	Attempting to achieve trial. Undifferentiated products, services. Emphasis on fighting for share.	Price cutting to achieve volume. Fighting for market share but difficulties experienced in doing this. Emphasis on efficiency and low cost. Shake-out of weakest players.	Exit of some competitors
Managerial style	Entrepreneurial/nursemaid	Sophisticated manager/tank driver	Critical administrator/ housewife	Opportunistic milker/lemon squeezer
Marketing objectives	Create awareness and trial	Rapid share increases/ Maximize share	Defend share and capitalize upon profit opportunities	Reduce spending, milk the brand and prepare for withdrawal

Marketing mix strategies

Product	Basic product	Develop product extensions and service levels	Modify and differentiate. Develop next generation.	Phase out weak brands
Price	Low price strategy	Penetration strategy	Price to meet or beat competitors	Reduce
Distribution	Selective	Intensive. Limited trade discounts.	Intensive. Heavy trade discounts.	Selective. Phase out weak outlets.
Advertising	Heavy spending to build awareness and encourage trial among early adopters and distributors	Moderate to build awareness and interest in the mass market. Greater word of mouth.	Emphasize brand differentiation and special offers	Reduce to a level that maintains hard core loyalty. Emphasize low prices to reduce stock.
Sales promotion	Extensive to encourage trial	Reduce to a moderate level	Increase to encourage brand switching	Reduce
Planning time frame	Short to medium	Long range	Medium range	Short
Communication system	Informal/expedient	Formal/tailor made	Formal/uniform	Little or none
Structure	Task force	Product division	Business division together with task force for new product development	Reduced
Compensation	High variable/low fixed. Linked to performance.	Balanced variable and fixed	Low variable/high fixed	Fixed

Figure 11.21 The characteristics of the product life cycle and the implications for strategy

problems with historical analysis stem from the very different life-cycle curves that products exhibit. One particular piece of research, for example, has identified seventeen different life-cycle patterns (see Swan and Rink, 1982). The combined effect of these few points raises a significant question mark over historical analysis and argues the case for a rather more cautious and individual approach than is normally suggested.

Nevertheless, despite these criticisms, the PLC does offer some scope as a broad planning, control and forecasting tool. As a planning tool its value should be seen in terms of the way in which it highlights the need for marketing strategy to change over time and, indeed, identifies the types of strategy that are best suited to each of the four stages. As a control tool it can be used as a basis for a comparison of a product's performance against broadly similar products in the past, while as a means of forecasting it provides a broad indication of how a product might develop. These are brought together in Figure 11.21, which summarizes the characteristics of the life cycle, and the objectives and strategies best suited to each of the four major stages.

One final word of caution that needs to be uttered here is that life-cycle thinking traditionally revolves around the product. In practice, product life cycles are just one element of life-cycle management, the others being market, brand and technological life cycles, all of which need to be taken into account in the strategic marketing planning process. As an example of this, the development of digital cameras (a significant step on the camera technological life cycle) has implications both for the film processing industry and for the number and type of players within the market, with organizations that previously did not operate within the market but which had digital expertise recognizing the opportunities that were opening up to them.

The influence of market evolution on marketing strategy

The product life cycle is, as we commented earlier, a model of both product and market evolution. In practice, emphasis tends to be placed on the product's life cycle rather than that of the market, with the result that many strategists work to a product-oriented picture rather than to a market-oriented picture. There is, however, a strong argument for the strategist to take a step sideways and to focus periodically upon the market overall in an attempt to identify how it is likely to evolve and how it will be affected by changing needs, new technology, developments in the channels of distribution, and so on. This, in turn, points to the need for the strategist to recognize the nature of the interrelationships between the demand life-cycle curve and the technology life-cycle curve, and how in turn these should be reflected in the management of particular brands.

In doing this, the starting point involves focusing upon the demand life cycle, since it is the demand life cycle that is concerned with the underlying need. The technology life cycle, by contrast, is concerned with the particular ways in which this need is satisfied. One of the most commonly used examples to illustrate this point is that of the need for calculating power. The demand life cycle for this is still growing rapidly and looks as if it will continue to do so for the foreseeable future. The technology life cycle is concerned with the detail of how this need is met. This was done initially with fingers and then subsequently with abacuses, slide rules, adding machines, hand-held calculators and then, most recently, with computers. Each of these has a technology life cycle that exists within the overall framework of the demand life cycle. The strategic implications of this need to be seen in terms of what and who the firm is competing against, something which takes us back to Peter Drucker's questions of 'What business are we in?' and 'What business should we be in?' In practical terms, this can be seen by a manufacturer of slide rules in the 1960s continuing to see its competitors as other manufacturers of slide rules rather than the new and emerging forms of technology such as adding machines and low-priced calculators, which subsequently forced slide rules into decline. For a computer manufacturer today the issues are broadly similar.

The need for a company to identify clearly what type of demand technology to invest in and when to shift emphasis to a new technology has been discussed in some detail by Ansoff (1984), who refers to a demand technology as a strategic business area (SBA), 'a distinctive segment of the environment in which the firm does or may want to do business'. The problem faced by many firms, however, is that, confronted by a variety of different markets and technologies, all of which are changing, there is little scope for mastering them all. The strategist is faced with the need to decide where the firm's emphasis is to be placed. In essence, this involves a choice between investing heavily in one area of technology or less heavily in several. This latter strategy, while offering less risk, has the disadvantage of making it less likely that the firm will either become or retain market leadership. Rather it is the pioneering firm that invests heavily in the new technology that is likely to emerge and remain as the leader.

This line of thought can be taken a step further by relating the development stage of an industry (growth, maturity or decline) to the organization's strategic position (leader, challenger or follower), since the strategic implications of the interplay between these two dimensions is potentially significant. This is illustrated in Figure 11.22.

Managing in mature markets

For many managers, management of the product life cycle on a day-to-day basis is concerned essentially with the management of products and brands that have reached maturity. This stage of the life cycle is typically characterized by high levels of competition and the problems of achieving or sustaining meaningful levels of differentiation. Faced with this, managers have a number of options, the two most obvious of which are to boost promotional spend in an attempt to overcome competitors, and/or to innovate. Although increasing the promotional budget can work, there is an obvious danger of spending levels across the sector escalating and, with few opportunities for market growth, a zero-sum game emerging (see Illustration 11.8). It was the alternative approach of innovation that was used by Lever Brothers in 1998 in an attempt to redefine the fabric washing detergents market.

The UK market, which had a retail value of around £900 million in 1997, was dominated by Lever Brothers and Procter & Gamble, with a combined share of around 30 per cent. The two strongest brands were Persil and Ariel. The introduction by Lever Brothers of Persil Tablets in 1998 represented the biggest revolution in the laundry sector for more than a decade. They were a totally new concept and were

	Stage of industry development		
	Growth	**Maturity**	**Decline**
Strategic position of the firm Leader	Keep ahead of the field Discourage other possible entrants Raise entry barriers Develop a strong selling proposition and competitive advantage 'Lock in' distributors Build loyalty Advertise extensively	Hit back at challengers Manage costs aggressively Raise entry barriers further Increase differentiation Encourage greater usage Search for new uses Harass competitors Develop new markets Develop new products and product variations Tighten control over distributors	Redefine scope Divest peripherals Encourage departures Squeeze distributors Manage costs aggressively Increase profit margins
Challenger	Enter early Price aggressively Develop a strong alternative selling proposition Search for the leader's weaknesses Constantly challenge the leader Identify possible new segments Advertise aggressively Harass the leader and followers	Exploit the weaknesses of leaders and followers Challenge the leader Leapfrog technologically Maintain high levels of advertising Price aggressively Use short-term promotions Develop alternative distributors Take over smaller companies	If the challenging strategy has not been successful, manage the withdrawal in the least costly way to you but in the most costly way to others
Follower	Imitate at lower cost if possible Search for joint ventures Maintain vigilance and guard against competitive attacks Look for unexploited opportunities	Search for possible competitive advantages in the form of focus or differentiation Manage costs aggressively Look for unexploited opportunities Monitor product and market developments	Search for opportunities created by the withdrawal of others Manage costs aggressively Prepare to withdraw

Figure 11.22 Competitive strategies for leaders, challengers and followers

developed in direct response to customers' demands for a more convenient wash product. The launch of the product had a major effect upon the market, with Ariel's concentrated powder slipping from 7.5 to 2.5 per cent of the market, whilst Persil Tablets took almost 9 per cent of the market within just three months of the launch. A year later, the company launched Persil Colour Care Tablets and strengthened their position yet further.

Life cycles and managerial style

Although a considerable amount has been written on product and market life cycles and how strategies need to reflect life-cycle stages, relatively little has been said about the appropriateness of managerial style. There is, however, a strong argument for the

> ## Illustration 11.8 Zero-sum games and negative-sum games
>
> In mature markets, breakthroughs which lead to a major change in competitive positions and to the growth of the market are rare. Because of this, competition becomes a zero-sum game in which one organization can only win at the expense of others. However, where the degree of competition is particularly intense, a zero-sum game can quickly become a negative-sum game, in that everyone in the market is faced with additional costs. As an example of this, when one of the major high street banks in Britain tried to gain a competitive advantage by opening on Saturday mornings, it attracted a number of new customers who found the traditional Monday–Friday bank opening hours to be a constraint. However, faced with a loss of customers, the competition responded by opening on Saturday as well. The net effect of this was that, although customers benefited, the banks lost out as their costs increased but the total number of customers stayed the same.
>
> In essence, this proved to be a negative-sum game.

style of management to be tailored to the particular demands of different stages. In the introductory stage, for example, there is a need for an entrepreneurial style of management in which emphasis is placed upon the rapid identification and seizing of opportunities, flexible structures and a risk-taking culture. In the growth stage this needs to be modified slightly, with greater attention being paid to long-term planning and control. In maturity this needs to change again in order to capitalize on the profit opportunities that exist, something which argues the case for what Arthur D. Little refers to as a critical administrator and is particularly important bearing in mind that the majority of products spend most of their lives in the mature stage. In the final stage of the life cycle the managerial needs change yet again, with the focus tending to shorten, costs being reduced and the need for an increased emphasis upon opportunities milking styles. These ideas have been expressed in a slightly different, albeit more colourful, way by Clarke and Pratt (1985), who argue for four styles of management: nursemaid, tank driver, housewife and lemon squeezer.

11.12 Achieving above-average performance and excellence

*"*The reason no one has ever heard of Alexander the Mediocre is that, unlike Alexander the Great, he was mediocre. So what makes anyone think that mediocre offers are going to reap anything but mediocre results?*"*

(McDonald, 1998)

Throughout this book we have tried to emphasize the importance of internal and external analysis, and for strategy to be based not just on corporate objectives, but also on a fundamental understanding of corporate capability. This theme is a reflection of the paradigm that can be traced back to the work of Mason in the late 1950s and Chandler (1962) in the early 1960s, which 'relates the constructs of strategy, structure, environment and performance in a formulation which verbally states that a firm's performance is a function of its environment, its strategy and its structure'. These ideas have been reflected in a series of empirical studies in recent years by, among others, Peters and Waterman (1982), Goldsmith and Clutterbuck (1988), and Hooley et al. (1983). Of these, it is undoubtedly the work of Peters and Waterman that has had the greatest impact. Their research, which has subsequently provided the basis for a variety of other studies, was designed to identify the organizing characteristics of successful American companies. The characteristics that they suggested led to above-average performance and excellence in ambiguous environments were:

1 A bias for action. Successful organizations showed an ability and desire to try things – to respond to situations rather than to sit back and hope for environments to change in favour of the organization.

2 Closeness to the customer. Success for these firms was founded on understanding customers and in serving them well.

3 Autonomy and entrepreneurship. In order to avoid some of the problems of 'bigness', many successful firms pushed responsibility and authority (autonomy) 'down the line' to product managers and venture teams. In addition, they encouraged staff to be entrepreneurial.

4 Productivity through people. The 'excellent' companies treated their workers as mature people who would respond better to high expectations and peer-group assessment rather than to heavy handed 'boss' control.

5 Hands-on value-driven. This characteristic refers to the way that leaders, through personal example and involvement, have indoctrinated their organizations to accept and adhere to those core values that are essential to the organization's identity and success.

6 'Sticking to the knitting'. According to Peters and Waterman, organizations that branched out into new operating areas that are related enough to benefit from existing 'excellent' skills performed more successfully than the 'out and out' conglomerates.

7 Simple form, lean staff. The successful companies had avoided two dangers that expansion creates – complex organization structures and large numbers of staff personnel. Excellent companies seemed to have few people working at corporate level – most were out 'in the field' getting things done. Despite the hugeness of many of these winning organizations, staff knew their job and their place in the structure – even though jobs and structures might be in a constant state of flux.

8 Simultaneous loose–tight properties. While the excellent firms encouraged autonomy and entrepreneurship, employees knew that discretionary decision-making operated within the constraints of adherence to the organization's core values. Excellence in these areas was often achieved through attention to, and control of, the finest detail.

Although Peters and Waterman's work has had a significant influence on management thinking, a number of critics have pointed out that, by the time their book was published in 1982, several of its 'excellent' firms, including Hewlett-Packard and Caterpillar, had begun to experience difficulties. (Of the forty-three 'excellent' companies that they studied, about one-third were still seen to be excellent five years later. Just under one-quarter were seen to be solid but had lost a position of leadership, 25 per cent were in a much weaker position, and around 18 per cent were 'troubled'.) In the case of Caterpillar, for example, it was, as observed earlier (see pp. 456–7), coming under increasing attack from the Japanese firm Komatsu, and finding it difficult to respond effectively. Peters and Waterman's response was that this did not in any way invalidate their research, but rather it was an illustration of the difficulties of adhering to the characteristics of excellence. This has, in turn, been reflected in a comment by Brownlie (1987, p. 101), who suggested that 'Despite the lessons of Peters and Waterman, the history of many firms reveals that success and excellence remain temporary and elusive phenomena.' Recognition of this highlights the need for constant monitoring of the business's environment and for the results to be reflected in an updating of the assumptions underpinning the firm's strategic thinking.

In the period since the publication of *In Search of Excellence* (1982), Peters has continued to pursue the interrelated themes of excellence and high-performing organizations in a series of books, including *Thriving on Chaos* (1988). In this, as with much of what he has written, he adopts a highly prescriptive and evangelical tone, arguing that for managers to succeed in ever more demanding environments they need to follow certain rules. These involve:

1 Redefining the mundane
2 Listening to and measuring customer satisfaction in order to become a customer-responsive organization
3 Cherishing and empowering front-line people
4 Responding quickly to customers' needs and pursuing strategies of fast-paced innovation
5 Focusing on quality and service
6 Learning to love change.

This general theme has, in turn, been developed by Treacy and Wiersema (1995), who, in the introduction to their book *The Discipline of Market Leaders*, suggest that:

"The challenge facing corporate leaders today is nothing less than the reinvention of their companies. Something is happening to the nature of competition, something fundamental and inevitable. The signs are all around us. Market leadership is increasingly hard to win – and even harder to keep. Customers are more demanding and less loyal than ever before, yet many markets are so saturated that the customer finds it impossible to distinguish between one 'me-too' product and another. In this landscape, the maps and compasses of traditional business strategy will not serve. The navigation charts need to be redrawn.**"**

Because of this, they argue that marketing planners need to ask a number of fundamental questions:

*"*Is your company willing to cannibalize its hottest product with a risky, untested new one? Offer a service at a loss hoping to establish a long-term relationship? Link up with an adversary to drive its costs even lower?

If not – or if you believe the answer isn't of paramount importance – get used to mediocre market performance and to playing competitive catchup continuously. Your company will never be a market leader. Not until it learns discipline.*"*

In a number of ways, these ideas can be seen to be an extension of the sort of thinking that Hammer and Champy (1993) proposed in *Re-engineering the Corporation*. In essence, they suggest, *Re-engineering the Corporation*, which introduced many managers to the ideas of business process re-engineering, was about how to run a competitive race. *The Discipline of Market Leaders* builds upon this in that it is 'about choosing the race to run' (Treacy and Wiersema, 1995, p. xiii). Success, it is argued, is increasingly based on a recognition that no company can succeed by trying to be all things to all people. Instead, it must identify the unique value that it alone can deliver to its chosen markets. In doing this, managers need to come to terms with three essential concepts (Treacy and Wiersema, 1995, p. xiv):

*"*The first is the value proposition, which is the implicit promise a company makes to customers to deliver a particular combination of values – price, quality, performance, selection, convenience, and so on. The second concept, the value-driven operating model, is that combination of operating processes, management systems, business structure, and culture that gives a company the capacity to deliver on its value proposition. It's the systems, machinery, and environment for delivering value. If the value proposition is the end, the value-driven operating model is the means. And the third concept, which we call value disciplines, refers to the three desirable ways in which companies can combine operating models and value propositions to be the best in their markets.*"*

The three value disciplines that Treacy and Wiersema consider to be so important are:

1 *Operational excellence.* Companies that pursue this value and discipline are not product or service innovators, and nor are they concerned with developing deep and long-lasting relationships with their customers. Rather, they offer middle-market products at the best price with the least inconvenience; it is this no-frills approach that characterizes many of the low-price grocery retailers such as Netto, Lidl, Kwik Save, Lo-Cost and Aldi.
2 *Product leadership.* By contrast, this involves focusing upon developing and offering products that consistently push at the boundaries of innovation; both Intel and Nike are examples of this.
3 *Customer intimacy.* This is based on the idea that the organization concentrates upon building relationships and, in many cases, satisfying specialized or unique needs.

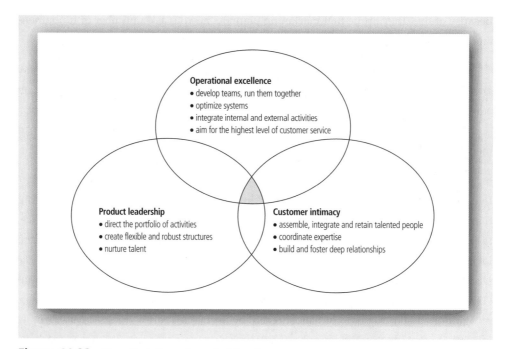

Figure 11.23 The discipline of market leaders

A summary of the bases of each of the three value disciplines appears in Figure 11.23.

It is important to recognize that the choice of which value discipline to pursue cannot be made arbitrarily. Instead, it involves a detailed understanding both of the company and its markets. Equally, Treacy and Wiersema (1995, p. xv) argue, it cannot simply be grafted onto an organization, but is instead 'a central act that shapes every subsequent plan and decision a company makes, coloring the organization from its competencies to its culture. The choice of value discipline, in effect, defines what a company does and therefore what it is.'

Issues of excellence have been addressed by a wide variety of researchers over the past decade, including those at Cranfield School of Management. The team identified what they termed the ten key elements of world class marketing:

1 A profound understanding of the marketplace

2 Creative segmentation and market selection

3 Powerful differentiation, positioning and branding

4 Effective marketing planning processes

5 Long-term integrated marketing strategies

6 Institutionalized creativity and innovation

7 Total supply chain management

8 Market-driven organization structures

9 Careful recruitment, training and career management

10 Vigorous line management implementation.

Other studies that have focused upon excellence include a Bradford University study that distinguished between what they termed 'the winners and the rest'. The comparison of the two highlighted a series of issues, including the importance of a long-term view, a focus upon market share, the clever use of market research (including detailed research on competitors), the adaptation of products and service to merit the *specific* demands of the market, and service excellence.

Given the nature of these comments and the effort that has been put into the identification of the factors that contribute to marketing excellence, it would be comforting to believe that there is indeed a prescriptive formula that the marketing planner might apply. The reality, of course, is that if indeed such a formula exists, it has yet to be found. Nevertheless, it is possible to identify a number of the factors that appear to contribute to success. Included amongst these are the need for:

➡ A fundamental acceptance not just by the Chief Executive but by staff throughout the organization and the delivery chain that customers determine the organization's success or failure

➡ A clarity of purpose that is reflected in a clearly defined mission and set of objectives

➡ A deep understanding of what influences and drives the organization's environment and markets

➡ An honest assessment of the organization's strengths, weaknesses and levels of capability

➡ A detailed understanding of where the company can operate effectively

➡ A detailed knowledge of the competition, its strategies and capabilities, and how it is most likely to develop both in the short and the long term

➡ A creative perception of how to develop and present the product, and how value can be added to the customer experience

➡ An emphasis upon the implementation of strategy and the coordination of activities across the organization

➡ The development of a management team that is committed to leveraging the performance of the organization

➡ The development and exploitation of strong and meaningful selling propositions

➡ A fundamental recognition of the need to differentiate the organization from its competitors.

11.13 Summary

This chapter has focused on the need for a clear statement of marketing strategy and for this strategy to be based on a detailed understanding of corporate capability and competitive advantage. Here, we have examined how the strategic marketing planner, against the background of an understanding of the organization's competitive advantages, needs to begin developing the detail of the strategy. In doing this, explicit consideration needs to be given both to the organization's objectives and to its position within the marketplace.

In part, this position is determined by the competitive stance that has been adopted in the past. Thus, organizations have a choice between a market leader strategy, a market challenger strategy, a market follower strategy and a market nicher strategy. Each of these requires distinct courses of action, and these were explored in some detail, with parallels being drawn between marketing strategy and military strategy.

An important marketing objective for many private sector organizations is the pursuit of market share. The attractions of market share were explored and the findings of the PIMS research examined. Included among these are:

➡ Market share and profitability are strongly related
➡ In the long run the single factor most affecting performance is the organization's relative product/service quality
➡ Most of the strategic factors that boost ROI also contribute to long-term value.

Marketing strategy needs also to take account of the stage of market evolution and the position reached on the product life cycle by the product or brand. Although the product life cycle has been the subject of considerable criticism over the years, recent work has improved our understanding of the ways in which the concept can be used; these were incorporated into a model highlighting the implications of the product life cycle for strategy.

We concluded by making reference to the work done over the past 30 years or so in identifying the characteristics of high-performing organizations. In doing this we made particular reference to the work of Peters and Waterman, who suggested that excellence comes from:

➡ A bias for action
➡ Autonomy and entrepreneurship
➡ A closeness to the customer
➡ Productivity through people
➡ 'Sticking to the knitting'
➡ Hands-on, value-driven
➡ Simple form, lean staff
➡ Simultaneous loose–tight properties.

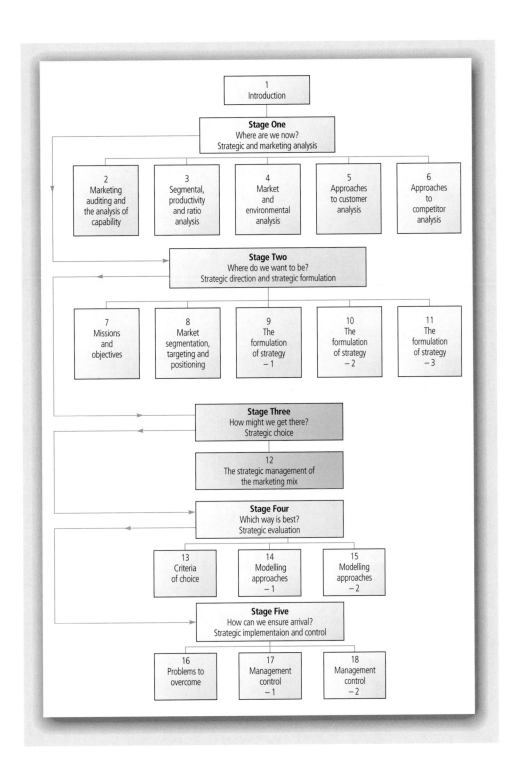

Stage Three: How might we get there? Strategic choice

The principal contribution made by marketing to the achievement of objectives is via the marketing mix. In essence, this entails developing products and services to meet the needs of the target segment(s), communicating their benefits to target audiences and ensuring that they are available in the right place, at the right price and at the right time.

Within this section of the book, we focus upon the marketing mix, how for many organizations it is changing and how the mix needs to be managed both tactically and strategically. However, in doing this, we have recognized that most readers will already be familiar with the components of the mix and how the mix is typically managed in order to gain a competitive advantage. Given this, our treatment of the topic is limited to an overview of the mix, how the focus of the mix has changed – and indeed is continuing to change – and what this means for the marketing strategist.

Chapter **12**

The strategic management of the marketing mix

12.1 Learning objectives

When you have read this chapter you should be able to understand:

(a) the nature and role of the expanded marketing mix;
(b) the issues associated with the strategic management of the individual elements of the mix;
(c) the dimensions of brand strategy;
(d) the need for an integrated approach to the management of the marketing mix.

12.2 Introduction

In this chapter we focus upon the seven principal elements of the marketing mix and discuss how they need to be managed both strategically and tactically. In doing this, we take each of the elements in turn and then, in the final part of the chapter, pull them together to demonstrate the nature of the interrelationships that exist and how, by understanding these interrelationships, the mix might be managed in such a way that a degree of synergy is generated.

Much of the original thinking about the marketing mix emerged from the work of McCarthy (1960), who saw the four principal elements of the mix to be the Product, Price, Promotion and Place (Distribution). Subsequently, the marketing mix has been developed to include the three 'softer' elements of People, Physical evidence and Process management. To a large extent, this is a reflection of the ways in which, in many markets, the nature and rules of competition have changed and some of the traditional bases for competitive advantage have been eroded. However, before we examine the elements of the mix, we need to appreciate the external context within which marketing mix decisions are typically made. This is illustrated in Figure 12.1 and highlights the way in which the management of the mix has as its principal purpose the creation of demand for the product or service, and that this is done against the background of the sorts of factors to which reference was made in Chapters 4–6. Given this, it should be apparent that decisions about the product, price and so on are not made in isolation; they need to take account not just of organizational objectives, but also the competitive, social, political, legal, technological and economic environments. It is the failure to do this effectively that ultimately leads to organizational performance declining.

12.3 Product decisions and strategy

It is commonly acknowledged that the most important single element of the marketing mix is the product, and it is for this reason that our discussion of the mix begins with this. Product policy is, or should be, the principal preoccupation of marketing managers

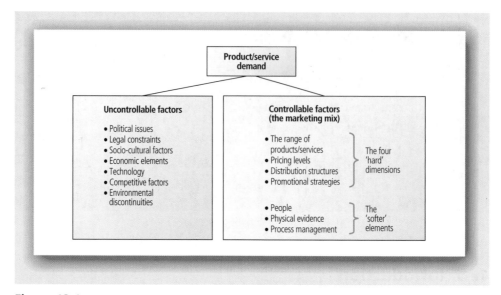

Figure 12.1 The marketing mix and the marketing environment

since it is, as Thomas (1987, p. 238) has pointed out, 'the product or service offering of a company or organization [that] ultimately determines the nature of the business and the marketplace perception of the business. In this sense it is the core of the marketing management function.' In making this comment Thomas gives implicit recognition to the idea that, although in an ideal world marketing management starts with the identification and selection of opportunities, in practice resources have generally already been committed. The principal concern of most organizations is therefore *product* strategy and management rather than *market* strategy and management. Given this, the task faced by the strategist in developing an effective product policy can be seen to consist of three distinct but interrelated elements:

1 The management of the organization's existing range of products or services
2 The development and management of the brand
3 The development of new or modified products or services.

It is to these three areas that we now turn our attention.

12.4 What is a product?

The term 'product' is used throughout this chapter to refer both to physical goods and to intangibles: Dyson, for example, sells vacuum cleaners, which are *goods*; advertising agencies sell ideas, designs and creative approaches, which are *services*; and Weight Watchers sells an *idea* – that of losing weight through changed eating habits and greater self-control. An organization's 'product' may therefore fall into any one of these three categories.

In discussing the nature of the product, there are three distinct elements that need to be considered (see Figure 12.2):

➡ *Product attributes* are associated with the core product, and include such elements as its features, styling, quality, brand name, packaging, and size and colour variants.
➡ *Product benefits* are the elements that consumers perceive as meeting their needs – this is sometimes referred to as the 'bundle of potential satisfactions' that the product represents. Included within this bundle are the product's performance and its image.
➡ *The marketing support services* consist of all the elements that the organization provides in addition to the core product. These typically include delivery, installation, guarantees, after-sales service and reputation.

The relative importance of each of these three elements can of course vary significantly from one product category and brand to another. A consumer buying a watch such as a Rolex, for example, is likely to be more concerned with the intangible attributes, such as image, brand and quality, than with the economic benefits of the watch. The significance of this from the viewpoint of the manufacturer and the dealer needs to be seen in terms of how the product is presented through advertising promotion and then supported by the dealer network.

Recognition of this leads in turn to two distinct views of the product:

1 That the product is simply a physical entity which has a precise specification
2 That it is a far broader concept which consists of anything, be it favourable or unfavourable, that a buyer receives in the exchange process.

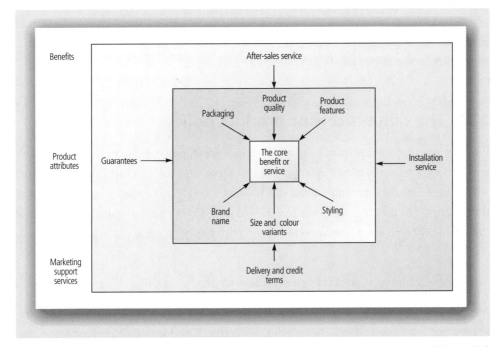

Figure 12.2 The three basic elements of the product (adapted from Kotler, 1988, p. 446)

From the viewpoint of the marketing strategist, it is the second of these two views that is the most meaningful and that is encapsulated in the idea of the product as a 'bundle of potential satisfactions'. This has been elaborated upon by Abbott (1955, p. 9), who has emphasized that 'What people really desire are not the products but satisfying experiences', and expanded upon, in turn, by Levitt (1976), who argues that products need to be seen in terms of the benefits they provide rather than the functions they perform. Thus, he suggests, 'One million quarter-inch drills were sold not because people wanted quarter-inch drills, but because they wanted quarter-inch holes.'

Views such as this provide strong support for the suggestion that, in developing the product strategy, the marketing strategist needs to give explicit recognition both to the objective and the subjective elements of the product. The objective elements (in the form of, for example, the physical specification and price) are often easily copied by a competitor. The subjective element, however (which consists of, among other things, the image and reputation), is generally more difficult to copy and in many markets provides the most effective basis for differentiation, and is the area in which value can most easily be added. In practice, of course, the objective and subjective dimensions are interrelated: a strong image and positive reputation, for example, develop largely as the result of high quality and reliability. It is therefore the recognition of this sort of interrelationship that is at the heart of effective product policy, since it is the combination of the two that delivers 'value' to the customer. This point has been elaborated on in the context of the American car industry by Bennett and Cooper (1982). The success of the Japanese and the Europeans in the 1970s in taking share away from domestic manufacturers was due, they suggest, not simply to lower prices and better fuel economy. Rather, it was the case that:

*"*The European and Japanese car makers have simply been better competitors; they anticipated market needs; they built a better product – one that is more reliable, has better workmanship, and is better engineered; and they did it effectively. In short, these manufacturers delivered better value to the American consumer.*"*

12.5 The dimensions of product policy

Effective product management is, to a very large extent, based on an understanding and application of two major concepts, portfolio analysis and the product life cycle both of which were discussed in some detail in Chapters 9 and 11. The reader should therefore return briefly to the discussion on pp. 367–70 and 478–83 for a detailed discussion of these two concepts, since here we will concentrate simply on some of the key points.

The product life cycle and its contribution to product policy

In our earlier discussion we referred to the product life cycle (PLC) as one of the best-known but least understood concepts in marketing. The ideas that underpin the concept are, as we pointed out, straightforward, suggesting that sales following a product's launch are initially slow but then increase as awareness grows. Maturity is reached when the rate of sales growth levels off and repeat purchasers account for the majority of sales. Ultimately, sales begin to decline as new products and new technologies enter the market, leading eventually to the product being withdrawn.

Although a considerable amount has been written about the product life cycle and how it might or should be used, surprisingly few empirical studies of the concept's real scope for application within an organization's product policy have been conducted. It is perhaps because of this that the literature on the life cycle still tends to lean towards one extreme or the other, with some arguing that life-cycle analysis offers a strong foundation for effective product management, while others dismiss the idea as being conceptually attractive but pragmatically worthless. Prominent among those within this second category are Dhalla and Yuspeh (1976), who, in an article entitled 'Forget the Product Life Cycle Concept', argued that the PLC is conceptually and operationally flawed. The bases of their argument were that:

- The biological metaphors used to suggest that products are living entities is misleading
- Attempts to match empirical sales data to life-cycle curves have proved difficult and the results are largely meaningless
- The life cycle of a product and hence the shape of the curve is determined by how the product is managed over time – it is not an independent variable as is suggested by traditional PLC theory
- The PLC is not equally valid for product class, product form, and brands as is often argued
- The stages of the life cycle are difficult to define
- Identifying where on the life cycle a product is at any particular time is difficult to determine
- The scope for using the concept as a planning tool is limited
- Evidence exists to suggest that where organizations have tried to use the PLC as a planning tool, opportunities have been missed and costly mistakes made.

In the light of these comments, what then is the status of the PLC and what contribution might it be expected to make to product policy? Quite obviously, it is not a model with universal applicability, but rather an ideal type from which insights into the general behaviour of most product forms can be deduced, but which in its application requires a possibly high degree of caution. This is reflected in a comment by Thomas (1987b, p. 242), who suggests that:

❝ . . . as a means to an end – that end being more sensitive management of the product over time – no sensible product manager should ignore the intellectual inheritance represented by the product life cycle literature. Using the product cycle concept is a means to creating an optimal life cycle, rather than being controlled by it. Sales history is a fundamental tool of the product manager, but sales history is not the only variable controlling the future of the product. ❞

This general line of argument has also been pursued by Michael Porter (1980), who has highlighted the significance of the context in which the PLC is applied. Porter argues that the nature of the industry and its evolution from embryonic to declining is at least of equal importance as the stage of the product's life cycle.

The role of portfolio analysis in product policy

The second key contributor to effective product policy is portfolio analysis and management. The techniques of portfolio analysis are discussed in detail in Chapter 9, so here we will limit ourselves to identifying some of the principal elements of its contribution to product policy. The starting point involves recognizing that portfolio analysis provides a firm foundation both for developing and evaluating marketing plans. The data required, for example, for the growth–share and market attractiveness–business position type matrices help not only in the process of allocating resources, but also in deciding upon the current and future mix and balance of the organization's portfolio. This in turn provides the basis for identifying the contribution that each strategic business unit (SBU) is capable of making to short-term and long-term strategy and, where this contribution is perceived to be inadequate, for adjustments to be made.

For Haspelagh (1982), the principal role of portfolio analysis within product policy is that of resource allocation and, subsequently, a series of decisions regarding each product or SBU. These decisions revolve around the issue of how to manage each product and, in particular, whether to adopt a custodial, harvesting, penetration, phased withdrawal, divestment, acquisition, or new product development stance.

In many ways, this view of portfolio analysis represents a neat summary of its potential role and contribution. Portfolio displays are not intended as strategic answers to the resource allocation problem, but are instead designed to help in the process of communication and decision-making at brand management and strategic management levels.

The product as a strategic variable

Because the product is at the very heart of marketing strategy, the need to manage it strategically is of paramount importance, since how well this is done is the key both to the organization's overall financial performance and to the gaining and retaining of market share. The question of *how* to manage the product strategically is not necessarily answered easily, however, and for many firms involves a careful balancing of costs, risks and returns. In doing this, explicit consideration needs to be given to competitors and in particular to the probable implications of any moves that they are likely to make.

In many cases, time is a critical dimension of product strategy and exerts a significant influence on any marketing manager's freedom of movement. In the long term, say five to ten years, products can be changed radically in almost all industries and can therefore make a major contribution to corporate objectives. In the short term, however, the product is often much more inflexible. In the car industry, for example, a period of four years or so is often needed to develop and introduce a totally new model. In the shorter term, the strategist's flexibility is consequently more limited and restricted to a series of minor and often cosmetic changes. For this reason, innovation tends not to be a major element of short-term marketing strategy. Instead, the strategist is limited to a series of package and label changes, new varieties, accessories, options, and combinations of products that inject a degree of newness into the market.

In developing an effective product strategy, a variety of factors need to be considered. The first, and in many ways the most important, is the question of the *type* of product strategy that is to be pursued. Is it, for example, to be broadly offensive or broadly defensive? If it is to be offensive, the strategist needs to consider not just how this is to be translated into action, but also its feasibility and the costs and risks that are associated with it. We can identify four types of product strategy:

1 A market leader product strategy
2 A leadership challenging product strategy, which might translate, initially at least, into 'the strategy of the fast second', whereby the firm allows the existing leader to incur the costs and risks of developing a new product and then moves in rapidly after the launch with a copy or an improved version of the product
3 A product following strategy
4 A me-too product strategy.

The issue of how firms pursue a strategy of leading, challenging or following was examined in detail in Chapter 11, and it may be useful to refer back to Sections 11.4–11.8 for a discussion of the key points. Where, however, an organization is intent either on leading or challenging, the implications for product strategy are considerable and are likely to make heavy demands upon resources. The majority of leaders retain their leadership position by means of a series of small and large innovations, supported by a heavy investment in advertising and distribution. For a challenger to succeed, the implications are straightforward, and in many industries require an even greater level of investment and/or the sort of radical and breakpoint thinking to which reference was made in Section 4.7.

The question of which strategy to pursue cannot be made in isolation, but requires a detailed understanding both of the organization's current position and capabilities, and of each competitor's stance and likely response pattern when challenged. The starting point should therefore be an assessment of the organization's current portfolio. Such an assessment can be carried out in one of several ways, including using the product life cycle and techniques of portfolio analysis, both of which were reviewed briefly earlier in this chapter. Based on this sort of analysis, Drucker (1963) recommends classifying products in one of six ways:

1 Tomorrow's breadwinners
2 Today's breadwinners
3 Products that are capable of making a contribution assuming that drastic action is taken

4 Yesterday's breadwinners

5 Also-rans

6 Failures.

This approach to classification then provides the basis for posing three questions:

1 Should we continue to market the product?

2 If so, should the strategy and level of resource allocation be changed in a minor way?

3 Should there be a major rethink of the product's strategy (e.g. a relaunch, a repositioning, or a major styling change)?

In answering these questions, the strategist needs to consider a variety of factors, but most importantly how the product is perceived by consumers and distributors; its probable future sales pattern; the scope that exists for repositioning or extending the life of the product; the availability of resources; the returns that are being generated currently; the ways in which returns are likely to increase or decrease in the future; possible competitive moves that will affect consumers' perceptions of the product; and the nature of any competing demands for the resources currently being absorbed by the product. In addition, consideration needs to be given to the relative rates of product and market growth, and whether the product is growing at a faster or slower rate than the overall market. Regardless of whether the growth rate is faster or slower, the strategist needs to consider firstly why this is the case and then secondly the strategic implications of this (see Figure 12.3).

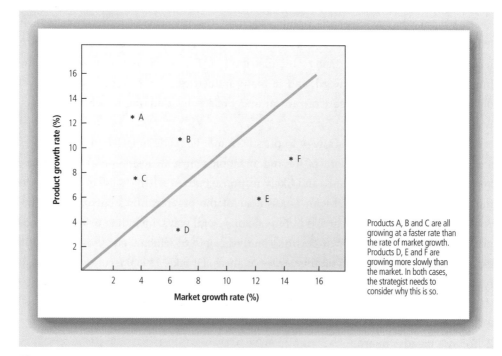

Figure 12.3 Product and market growth rates

Much of the information needed for this should be generated on a regular basis by the organization's marketing information system, although in some instances specific studies of buyers, distributors and competitors will be needed. By studying the product on a regular basis and, in particular, by focusing upon changing consumer needs and competitors' moves, the strategist should be able to identify more readily any inadequacies that exist and the scope or need for product development. As an example of this, having identified that, because of changing lifestyles, ever larger numbers of people were skipping breakfast, the cereals manufacturer Kellogg's responded by developing cereal bars such as Nutri-Grain, which are designed to be eaten on the move and throughout the day.

12.6 Brand strategies

A fundamental element of any product strategy is the role played by the brand. Brands are designed to enable customers to identify products or services that promise specific benefits. As such, they are a form of shorthand in that they create a set of expectations in the minds of customers about purpose, performance, quality and price. This, in turn, allows the strategist to build added value into products and to differentiate them from competitors. Because of this, well-known brand names such as Nike, Microsoft, Nokia, Intel, Disney and McDonald's are of enormous strategic and financial value, and are in many cases the result of years of investment in advertising, positioning and distribution development. The significance of this in the case of Coca-Cola has been highlighted by the suggestion that the company's brand name is now worth far more than the gross national product of many nations. It also helps to explain why pirating of brand names has developed with enormous rapidity over the past decade.

In developing a brand strategy, an organization can pursue one of four approaches:

1 Corporate umbrella branding
2 Family umbrella branding
3 Range branding
4 Individual branding.

The first of these – *corporate umbrella branding* – is used by companies such as Heinz and Kellogg's in which the company's name is attached to the entire product portfolio. In the case of Heinz, for example, the umbrella is used to cover a wide variety of food products, including soups, beans, baby foods and sauces such as Heinz tomato ketchup. For Kellogg's, the corporate brand covers Special K, Corn Flakes, Frosties, Nutri-Grain and many other breakfast cereals.

Family umbrella names, by contrast, are used to cover a range of products in a variety of markets. A case in point is Virgin, with its Virgin brand covering trains, rail travel, mobile phones, music production, and financial services.

Range brand names are used for a range of products that have clearly identifiable links in a particular market. An example of this is Ford's retention of the brand names of companies such as Volvo, Aston Martin and Jaguar that it has acquired. The rationale for this is straightforward in that each of the companies is targeted at distinct market segments and brings with it a brand heritage and set of loyalties that would be eroded if the parent company's name was to replace it.

The fourth approach – *individual brand names* – is typically used to cover one type of product in one type of market, possibly with different combinations of size, flavour and service options or packaging formats. Examples of this include Lucozade, Marmite, Penguin and Dove.

Approaches to brand development

To be truly effective, a brand strategy has to develop over time and reflect environmental conditions. There is therefore a need for brand development, the key elements of which involve a detailed understanding of:

1 Current perceptions of the brand amongst customers and the trade
2 The expectations of both customers and the trade
3 The strengths and weaknesses of each brand within the portfolio
4 The value of each of the brands
5 The links that exist between the different brands owned and the nature and significance of any overlaps and gaps
6 Following on from point 5, the dangers of brand cannibalization
7 When and where new brand names need to be developed
8 The scope that exists for licensing
9 The opportunities for brand stretching
10 Probable competitor moves
11 Corporate expectations of the brand, something that highlights the need for a brand development plan.

The starting point for this involves analysing the brand in order to understand in detail what it means to customers and how much it is worth. In doing this, the strategist needs to identify the core values, the scope that exists for extending the brand name into other product or market sectors, and the areas that must be avoided at all costs. The core values relate to the essential meaning of the brand and can be subdivided into the *inner core values* or intrinsic qualities, which if altered would seriously damage the brand's integrity, and the *outer core values*, which have a greater degree of flexibility.

From here, the strategist needs to move on to consider the interrelationships between the brand names used. In the case of the Volkswagen Golf GTi, for example, Volkswagen is the umbrella name, Golf the model, and GTi the designation for performance. The issue here, therefore, is the extent to which names can be used, how they might be extended and how they might be used in combination with other models in the range.

The third stage involves deciding how far brand names can be stretched and still be meaningful. A company that has done this with considerable success in the 1990s is

Mars, which, having developed a very strong brand name and image with Mars Bars, then stretched the name into a Mars drink and Mars ice-cream. Similarly, Johnson & Johnson, best known for its babycare products, stretched its brand name to cover a range of toiletry products for men, while Marks & Spencer stretched its name for clothes into foods, home furnishings and financial services.

In attempting to stretch a brand, the strategist needs to tread carefully. The obvious danger, of course, is that of moving into an area in which the brand name has little relevance or which detracts from the value of the brand in its core market. The aim should therefore be to operate only in the three cells in the bottom right-hand corner of Figure 12.4.

As an alternative to brand stretching, or indeed in addition to brand stretching, the strategist can opt for the development of new brand names. There are, of course, significant costs associated with this, particularly when put against the background of the traditionally high failure rate of new products. Estimates of the costs of successfully developing a new brand name vary considerably, but as a broad rule of thumb in the food or confectionery market it is unlikely to be much less than £3–4 million. Again, therefore, the strategist needs to tread carefully and consider developing a new brand name only when certain criteria can be satisfied. These include:

➡ The product has a series of distinctive values
➡ The consumer benefits are both strong and obvious
➡ Acceptance of the new product is highly likely
➡ When using an existing brand name would be inappropriate because there is little apparent linkage between the existing and new products
➡ When using an existing name would weaken the novelty impact of the new product.

For those organizations with very strong brand names there is often scope for generating additional profits by means of licensing. Among those to have done this with considerable success are Disney.

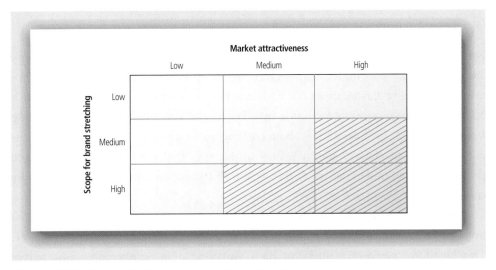

Figure 12.4   Brand stretching and market attractiveness

The final stage of any brand development stems from the need for an explicit brand development plan. There is little real evidence to suggest, despite the growing recognition of the need for planning, that this extends into the area of brand name development. Because of this, and because of the significance of the brand name, the strategist should concentrate upon developing a brand development plan showing how each brand name is to be used over the next five years. In doing this, the strategist needs to consider five key questions:

1 What does the brand mean today and what do we want it to mean in three and five years' time?
2 What line extensions and new products do we wish to develop under this brand name?
3 What changes in market needs and consumer demographics do we foresee that will require us to modify or change the brand meaning?
4 What are the detailed plans by year for achieving these changes in the next five years, and what are the sales, spending and profit implications?
5 Bearing in mind the new markets we wish to enter, which ones can be covered with existing brand names and which need new brand names?

A final issue that needs to be considered at this stage stems partly from the developments taking place in the media as a result of the emergence of the larger pan-European and global media footprints that have emerged as the result of satellite broadcasting, and partly from the growing internationalism of companies. The combination of these factors has led several manufacturers to reconsider their branding policies. Whereas previously different brand names have been used for the same product in different countries, there is now a move towards a greater commonality. Among those to have done this is Mars, which changed the name of its Marathon bar to Snickers.

Developing a brand strategy

For many organizations, branding is a fundamental element of the product strategy and provides the basis for a consumer franchise that, if managed effectively, allows for greater marketing flexibility and a higher degree of consumer loyalty. However, it needs to be recognized that branding involves a great deal more than simply putting a name on a package. Instead, it is about creating, maintaining and proactively developing perceived consumer value. It is only in this way that the organization is able to promise and continue to deliver to the consumer a superior value than that offered by competitors.

It follows from this that any brand strategy is, of necessity, a long-term process that involves an investment in and commitment to the development of the brand over time. This long-term perspective involves the dovetailing of a number of issues, but in essence can be seen to be concerned with the two principal issues that emerge from our discussion above:

1 Where the brand is currently and how it is perceived
2 How the brand is to be perceived in three, five and ten years' time, and how this might best be achieved.

With regard to the first of these, the starting point for any brand strategy involves identifying:

➡ The brand's current market positioning
➡ Competitors' positioning strategies and resource bases
➡ The ways in which the market is likely to develop, and the implications of product, brand and market life cycles
➡ Customers' perceptions of the portfolio of brands in the market
➡ Customers' expectations and the extent to which these are being met both by the brand and its competitors
➡ Levels of customer loyalty across the market
➡ Distributors' expectations and how they are being met by the various players in the market
➡ The financial, managerial and operational resources that can be called upon in managing the brand
➡ The bases of competition
➡ The relative importance of the brand to the organization
➡ Managerial expectations of the brand.

It is only against this background that the strategist is able to develop a vision for the brand. Having done this, attention then turns to the planner, who needs to focus upon issues of detail, including:

➡ The sales, market share and profit objectives that will be pursued.
➡ The geographic markets in which the brand will be sold. Is there, for example, an objective of operating purely in the domestic markets or moving into a series of overseas markets? If the latter, how many markets will be involved, what will be their relative importance, and what timing will be involved?
➡ The competitive stance that is to be adopted.
➡ The segments that are to be targeted and their relative importance to the brand.
➡ The positioning and, in the long term, the repositioning strategy within each of these segments.
➡ The brand values that are to be developed.
➡ Whether the brand is to be developed as an individual name (e.g. the Procter & Gamble policy), under a blanket family name (e.g. the Heinz policy), under a separate

family name, or under the banner of a company trade name combined with individual brand names (e.g. Kellogg's with Rice Krispies, etc.).

➡ The strategy towards brand extensions (e.g. Mars extending its name from chocolate bars to drinks and ice-creams).

➡ The pricing points that the company is aiming for both in the short and the long term.

➡ The brand development policy. Is it the intention, for example, to concentrate upon developing a regular series of (small) modifications to the brand or to make a smaller number of larger modifications on a less frequent basis?

➡ Whether there is scope for licensing the product for sale in other markets and, if so, how, where and over what time period.

➡ The policy towards generics.

Finally, in developing the brand strategy, the planner needs to give consideration to a series of financial issues, including the margins and contribution that the brand is required to generate in both the short and the long term, and the levels of investment that the brand needs if it is to achieve the objectives set.

(*Authors' note*: It may be useful to refer to Chapter 10 (pp. 412–15) for a discussion on the nature and role of trust brands and their contribution to competitive advantage.)

12.7 The development of new products

The third dimension of product strategy revolves around the development of new and modified products. The development and introduction of new products has traditionally been seen to be a costly and risky activity. For an organization intent on either maintaining or improving its position in the marketplace there are, however, few alternatives to new product activity of one sort or another. The issues faced by many marketing strategists therefore revolve around the issue of the type of new product activity that is to be pursued and how best to manage and, hopefully, reduce risk levels.

In the majority of industries, there are two principal ways in which new products can be added to the product range: first, acquisition and, second, internal new product development. Of the two, acquisition is often the faster and involves one of three approaches:

1 The organization can buy other firms
2 The organization can buy a licence or franchise
3 The organization can buy patents.

New product development (NPD) can, in turn, involve two approaches, with products either being developed internally by an in-house R&D team or by means of outside agencies used to develop products that satisfy internally generated criteria. In the majority of firms, of course, both routes are pursued, with a greater or lesser emphasis being placed on one or other activity as environmental conditions and pressures change.

What is a new product?

Definitions of what constitutes a new product have varied greatly over the years. For our purposes, however, the term is used to refer to products that are *totally new to the world*, *product improvements*, *product modifications and new brands*. This issue of definition has been discussed in detail by the American management consultants Booz, Allen & Hamilton (1982). There are, they suggest, two principal dimensions that need to be considered: how new is the product to the company, and how new is it to the marketplace? This led them to propose the six-stage classification that appears below. The figures in parentheses represent the percentage of products appearing in each of these categories in the United States at the beginning of the 1980s, but which are felt by Booz, Allen & Hamilton still to be broadly valid:

1 New-to-the-world products that create an entirely new market. An example would be the launch of Apple's i-Pod (10 per cent).
2 New product lines that are designed to enable a company to enter an existing product sector for the first time (20 per cent). A case in point would be Virgin's entry into the mobile phone market.
3 Additions to existing product lines (26 per cent). This would include Kellogg's launch of Crunchy Nut Corn Flakes and Special K with red berries.
4 Improvements and revisions to existing products (26 per cent). This is simply the idea of 'new, improved . . .'.
5 Repositioning or retargeting existing products in order to appeal to new or untapped market segments (7 per cent), e.g. Skoda's entry into the mass car market.
6 Cost reductions, where products are modified to provide similar performance but at a lower cost (11 per cent).

A slightly different slant on this has been proposed by Robertson (1967), who placed innovations along a spectrum ranging from continuous to discontinuous innovation:

➡ Continuous innovations, which simply involve the modification of existing products and lead to few, if any, changes in consumer behaviour.
➡ Dynamically continuous innovations, which, while more disruptive than the previous category, do not change behaviour patterns in any fundamental way.
➡ Discontinuous innovations, which are dramatically new and which lead to significant changes in patterns of behaviour and usage. Included within this are the jet engine, television, stainless steel, antibiotics, and so on.

The increasing risks of new product development

We commented earlier that new product development has traditionally been seen as a high-risk activity. There are several sources of this risk, the most significant of which represent a mixture of financial, social, psychological and physical elements. For a variety of reasons these risks increased satisfactorily throughout the 1980s, 1990s and into the twenty-first century. There are several explanations for this, the most obvious of which are that buyers are becoming increasingly demanding and discriminating; markets are becoming more fragmented; product life cycles are shortening, with the result that payback periods are reducing; the expectations of distributors and dealers are increasing; the pace of technology is becoming ever faster; and competition generally is increasing. Recognition of this has led to what can be referred to as 'the new product development dilemma' in which, while there is widespread agreement that new products are needed if the firm is to grow, the likelihood of success appears to be getting ever smaller.

The role of new product development

Although organizations have, in the past, demonstrated that they develop new and modified products for a wide variety of reasons, the underlying strategic purpose should always be either to help create and maintain a competitive advantage or to reduce the advantages of a competitor. Recognizing this, the specific role of new product development can be stated in terms of:

➡ Ensuring that the product mix matches changing environmental conditions and that product obsolescence is avoided
➡ Enabling the organization to compete in new and developing segments of the market
➡ Reducing the organization's dependence upon particular elements of the product range or vulnerable market segments
➡ Matching competitive moves – where, for example, a competitor moves into a new and potentially valuable segment there is often a strong argument for following, so that the competitor's advantage is kept to a minimum
➡ Filling excess capacity
➡ Achieving greater long-term growth and profit.

The relative importance of these factors is influenced both by the nature and culture of the organization and by the nature of the market. Where, for example, the organization is either poorly resourced or has a risk-averse culture, the perceived role and importance of new products is likely to be fairly minimal. Where, however, there is a greater availability of resources and the competitive stance is more proactive, new product development is likely to take on a far more important role. At the same time, the nature of the market often exerts a series of pressures that are capable of dictating levels of new product activity. Where, for example, competition is intense, the need both for differentiation and a regular flow of new and modified products increases dramatically. The strategist should nevertheless avoid falling into the trap of seeing the solution purely in terms of new products.

Recognizing that products consist of two interrelated dimensions, an *objective* or *physical* element and a *subjective* or *perceived* element, changes in the product's advertising and packaging can often be achieved with *relatively* low levels of investment in cost and time, but lead to strategically significant different sets of perceptions. These then provide the strategist with a foundation for moving into new sectors of the market both at a lower cost and with a smaller degree of risk.

It should be apparent from this that the parameters for new product development must be set by corporate management. These parameters need to cover the product categories and market sectors in which the organization intends operating in the future, and should be set against the background of the general stance of leader or follower that the organization intends adopting. What the strategist should never lose sight of is that NPD is often a slow process and one that cannot simply be turned on or off as economic conditions dictate. The most successful companies in the field of NPD have tended to be those that recognize its *strategic* role and that allocate resources consistently. Recognizing this, Drucker (1955) has emphasized that not only is innovation a slow process, but that many market leaders owe their position to the NPD activity of earlier generations. The real consequences of cutting back on innovation and new product development are therefore likely to be felt by the next generation of management, who will be faced with a significant reduction in competitive capability.

This question of the strategic role of new product development has been examined in detail by Booz, Allen & Hamilton (1982). Their research highlighted six principal roles. The figures in parentheses below show the proportion of new products in each category:

1 Maintain the organization's position as a product innovator (46 per cent)
2 Defend a market share position (44 per cent)
3 Establish a foothold in a new market sector (37 per cent)
4 Pre-empt a market segment (33 per cent)
5 Exploit technology in a new way (27 per cent)
6 Capitalize on distribution strengths (24 per cent).

Perceptions of the role of NPD have also been examined by Ansoff and by Myers and Marquis. For Ansoff (1968), firms are reactors, planners or entrepreneurs. 'Reactors', he suggested, wait for problems to occur (e.g. the decline of an existing product) before trying to solve them. 'Planners' try to anticipate problems, while 'entrepreneurs' deliberately focus upon and attempt to anticipate both problems and opportunities. The implications for the ways in which new product development is then handled are significant, with reactors typically assigning it a low status. In entrepreneurial firms, by contrast, NPD is seen to be of central strategic importance and allocated resources accordingly. For Myers and Marquis (1969), NPD is broadly either *offensive* or *defensive*. Offensive NPD is designed to open up new markets or enlarge existing ones by a conscious effort to introduce new products. Defensive NPD is, by contrast, often stimulated by competitive forces or other changes in the marketplace and is typically designed to maintain market share or current rates of growth.

These ideas can be taken a step further by categorizing firms as *pioneers* or *imitators*. Firms that are broadly imitative can then be further subdivided into those content to follow at a distance, and those that adopt a deliberate policy of monitoring the leaders (the pioneers) and move in as soon as the market begins to grow or a new product shows signs of success (a wait and see approach). By behaving in this way, it is often possible to capitalize at a relatively low cost on the mistakes made by the pioneer. The attractions of this approach were highlighted by Freeman (1965) in a study of the electronic capital goods market.

The performance of the first laboratory prototypes and early commercial deliveries almost always leaves a great deal to be desired, so that the scope for improvement is very great. For this reason, some entrepreneurs have followed a deliberate policy of being *second* with a new product development rather than first. Success in such a policy often requires a greater capacity for moving fast with new developments once the time is considered ripe.

Proactive and reactive new product strategies

Although for many organizations the idea of a proactive new product strategy has a certain appeal, the reality is that proactive strategies are typically associated with a significant degree of risk and a need for heavy and sustained investment in money, skill and time, not only in the development and launch stages, but also throughout the product's life. If, therefore, an organization is intent on adopting a proactive stance, certain criteria need to be met. Included within these are:

➡ A fundamental and sustained commitment to new product development, and a willingness to accept the associated costs and risks
➡ An ability to protect the new product, possibly by patents, but certainly by a sustained and aggressive investment in marketing
➡ An ability to target high-volume or high-margin markets, and subsequently to capitalize on them
➡ The availability of the financial, staff and time resources needed, as well as a willingness to commit them
➡ A degree of flexibility so that the strategy can be modified to reflect changing environmental conditions
➡ Top management commitment
➡ A previously successful NPD track record (the new product chicken and egg syndrome).

Where these criteria cannot be met, the organization is likely to do far better by opting for a less proactive stance. This typically translates into one of four postures:

1 Rapidly responsive

2 Second but better

3 Imitative (me-too)

4 Defensive.

Overall, therefore, reactive strategies are best suited to an organization when:

➡ Its strengths lie in managing existing products

➡ It is faced with a competitor who has an aggressive and successful new product strategy and who has the capability and willingness to increase the pace of innovation within the industry

➡ There is a lack of specialist NPD skills within the organization

➡ Organizational resources are relatively limited

➡ Only limited protection of an innovation exists

➡ Markets are too small to guarantee the recovery of development costs.

In making these comments, a point that needs emphasizing is that neither a proactive nor a reactive stance is inherently better than the other. Rather it is the case that their suitability is a function of the organization's capability and as such needs to be reflected in the NPD strategy pursued.

12.8 Pricing policies and strategies

The second principal element of the marketing mix – price – is in many ways one of the most visible, and for many organizations price is also potentially the most controllable and flexible element of the mix. It is also in many cases one of the most important elements and, together with the product, a key component of an organization's marketing strategy. At the same time, however, it is generally acknowledged that pricing decisions are among the possibly most difficult that marketing managers are required to make. There are several reasons for this, the most significant of which is the nature and complexity of the interaction that commonly exists between three groups – consumers, competitors and the distribution network – and the need that exists to take this interaction into account when either setting or changing a price. An added complexity is that pricing decisions often have to be made quickly and without testing, but almost invariably have a direct effect upon profit. Largely because of this, many marketing managers work to reduce the relative importance of price by, for example, giving far greater emphasis to the product's distinctive values and to its image. In other cases, the pricing decision is taken out of the hands of the marketing strategist by a combination of market-related factors. Prominent among these is the presence of a large and aggressive competitor, who in effect determines prices for the industry as a whole and who, with the exception of just one or two small niche players, all other organizations are obliged to follow. The issue faced then by the strategist revolves not around the question of what price to set, but rather how to ensure that costs are contained in such a way that profits can still be made.

Price is undoubtedly a significant strategic variable and in many markets, despite a growth in the importance of non-price factors, it is still the principal determinant of consumer choice. Its significance is further emphasized by the fact that price is the only element of the mix that generates revenue – the others produce costs. It is perhaps understandable, therefore, that many marketing strategists treat pricing decisions with an extra degree of caution, which helps to explain why studies on both sides of the Atlantic have suggested that setting prices and dealing effectively with price competition is one of the biggest problems faced by marketing managers. The combination of these factors also goes some way towards explaining why it has often been suggested that relatively few organizations handle pricing well and why a series of mistakes are commonly made. The most common of these are that:

➡ Pricing decisions are often too heavily biased towards cost structures and fail to take sufficient account of either competitors' or customers' probable response patterns
➡ Prices are often set independently of other mix elements and without sufficiently explicit account being taken of, for example, advertising strategies and market positioning
➡ Too little account is taken of the opportunities to capitalize on differentiation
➡ Prices often do not vary sufficiently greatly between different segments of the market
➡ Prices often reflect a defensive rather than an offensive posture.

Taken together, these points suggest that pricing decisions run the risk of emerging largely as the result either of historical factors or of expediency, rather than of detailed strategic thinking. The likelihood of this risk is further increased by the often haphazard way in which the focus of responsibility for pricing is allocated. In many small firms, for example, pricing decisions are often made not by sales and marketing staff, but by senior management. In larger organizations, although the responsibility for price setting is often devolved downwards, senior management typically retains an overseeing brief.

Perhaps the biggest single source of the problems that are typically associated with pricing stems from the question of whether pricing should be the responsibility of marketing or finance. Although writers on marketing have long argued that price is a marketing variable, a substantial body of evidence exists to suggest that in many organizations price is still seen to be the responsibility of the finance department, and that finance staff guard their possession of this with a degree of jealousy that makes it difficult for marketing to do little more than exert a minimal influence. This is, of course, a stance to which we do not subscribe.

12.9 Approaches to price setting

Our earlier comment that, in some industries at least, organizations have little choice other than to follow the prices set by the market leader leads to the hypothesis that there are two types of firm:

1 *Price-takers*, which, by virtue of their size and market position, lack of product differentiation or passive organizational culture, are either unable or unwilling to adopt a proactive pricing stance. As a result, they follow the lead set by one or more larger and more aggressive organizations within the industry.
2 *Price-makers*, which, largely as the result of their size and power within the market, are able to determine the levels and patterns of price that others then follow.

It is the price-makers with which we are principally concerned here.

In setting a price either for a new or modified product, or for an existing product that is being introduced into a new sector of the market, the strategist needs to give explicit consideration to a variety of factors (see Figure 12.5). Of these, the most significant are:

➡ The organization's corporate objectives
➡ The nature and structure of competition
➡ The product life cycle
➡ Legal considerations
➡ Consumers and their response patterns
➡ Costs.

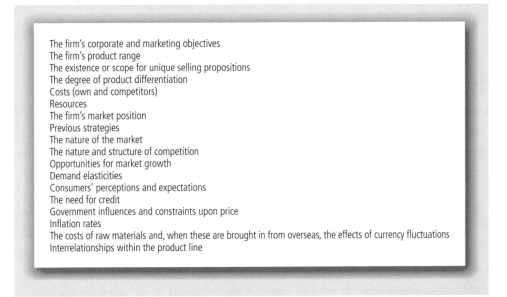

The firm's corporate and marketing objectives
The firm's product range
The existence or scope for unique selling propositions
The degree of product differentiation
Costs (own and competitors)
Resources
The firm's market position
Previous strategies
The nature of the market
The nature and structure of competition
Opportunities for market growth
Demand elasticities
Consumers' perceptions and expectations
The need for credit
Government influences and constraints upon price
Inflation rates
The costs of raw materials and, when these are brought in from overseas, the effects of currency fluctuations
Interrelationships within the product line

Figure 12.5 A summary of the influences on pricing strategy (source: Gilligan and Hird, 1986)

Competition	➡ Who are our direct and indirect competitors?
	➡ What pricing strategies does each pursue?
	➡ Is price competition an important element of their marketing mix?
	➡ How are they likely to behave when faced with price competition?
	➡ What financial resources do they have available to cope with a price war?
	➡ Are competitors' prices related to particular market segments?
Legal	➡ Are there any constraints upon pricing and re-pricing decisions?
	➡ Are there legal constraints upon margins within the distribution network?
	➡ Is there freedom to engage in price promotions?
	➡ Do prices have to be printed on the product and/or package?
	➡ Does retail price maintenance exist?
Customers	➡ How do consumers perceive these types of product?
	➡ How important is the product's country of origin?
	➡ How is our organization perceived?
	➡ Do any social or cultural factors exist that might influence the prices that consumers are willing to pay?
Distribution	➡ What are the implications of the patterns of distribution for costs and subsequent prices?
	➡ What margins typically exist throughout the channel?
	➡ How are price promotions and special offers likely to be received?
Other	➡ Are there any trade associations that might usefully be consulted before setting prices?
	➡ Is there a consumer group (e.g. The Consumers' Association) which publishes comparative analyses of products which might influence consumers' perceptions of prices?
	➡ Will our price strategy be affected by the behaviour of others in the market in the past?
	➡ How is the market as a whole likely to respond to price changes?

Figure 12.6 The dimensions of a market's price profile (source: Gilligan and Hird, 1986)

Taken together, these factors allow the strategist to develop the market's price profile (see Figure 12.6) and, subsequently, to gain a greater insight into the market's pricing dynamics.

12.10 Deciding on the pricing objectives

Having developed the framework within which pricing decisions are to be made, the marketing strategist needs then to decide upon the specific pricing objectives that are to be pursued. Although the nature of these objectives and their implications for the eventual price charged can vary greatly, the ten most commonly pursued are:

1 *Survival*. This is arguably the most fundamental pricing objective and comes into play when the conditions facing the organization are proving to be extremely difficult. Thus, prices are reduced often to levels far below cost simply to maintain a sufficient flow of cash for working capital.

2 *Return on investment*. Here prices are set partly to satisfy the needs of consumers, but more importantly to achieve a predetermined level of return on the capital investment involved.

3 *Market stabilization*. Here, having identified the leader in each market sector, the firm determines its prices in such a way that the likelihood of the leader retaliating is minimized. In this way, the status quo is maintained and market stability ensured.

4 *The maintenance and improvement of market position*. Recognizing that price is often an effective way of improving market share, the marketing strategist uses price partly as a means of defending its current position, and partly as a basis for gradually increasing its share in those parts of the market where gains are most likely to be made and least likely to result in competitive action. Toys 'R' Us is just one example of a company that has used price in this way with considerable success. There are, however, dangers of using price to pursue market share, which include the following:

➡ Gaining market share, particularly in mature markets, is often prohibitively expensive and only rarely cost-effective

➡ Share-gaining price strategies tend to be blunt weapons that do not reflect differences between buyers

➡ At particular stages of the life cycle, market share is an inappropriate goal and can lead to the organization ignoring strategically more important areas, such as distribution.

5 *Meeting or following competition*. Having entered a market in which competitors are firmly entrenched, the firm may decide quite simply to take its lead in pricing from others until it has built up sufficient experience and established a firm reputation on which it can subsequently build.

6 *Pricing to reflect product differentiation*. For a firm with a broad product range, differences between the products can often be made most apparent by means of price variations related to each market segment. The differences in price are not necessarily linked to the costs of product, but are instead designed to create different perceptions of their products' value, and indirectly to increase profits. Among those who do this with a high degree of success and skill are the volume car manufacturers, who offer a variety of derivatives from a basic model.

7 *Market skimming*. With a skimming objective the marketer enters the market with a high price and only gradually lowers it as he or she seeks a greater number of market segments. In this way, profits are likely to be relatively high and, by minimizing the degree of commitment at any one time, the levels of risk are minimized.

8 *Market penetration*. As an alternative to the gradual entry strategy of market skimming, the firm may adopt a far more aggressive approach in which prices are set at a deliberately low level to ensure a high level of sales and to keep competitors at a distance. Among those to have done this consistently and successfully, particularly when entering new markets, are the Japanese.

9 *Early cash recovery*. Faced with problems of liquidity or a belief that the life of the product or market is likely to be short, the firm may opt for a policy designed to generate a high cash flow and lead to an early recovery of cash.

10 *Discouraging others from entering the market*. This is done by deliberately setting a low price so that returns are low, whilst simultaneously sending out signals about a willingness to engage in a price war with any new entrants.

12.11 Methods of pricing

Against the background of our discussion so far, it should be apparent that there are four principal factors that influence the pricing decision:

1 The company's marketing objectives
2 The company's pricing objectives
3 The determinants of demand, including costs, competitors and consumers
4 The product itself and the extent to which it has any distinguishing features.

The relative importance of these varies considerably from one product and market sector to another. All four, however, need to be taken into account in the choice of the pricing method. This is illustrated diagrammatically in Figure 12.7.

Taking account of competitors

One of the recurring themes of this book has been the need for competitive analysis and for the information that is generated through this to be taken into account when developing strategy. In the case of pricing decisions, the need to understand competitors'

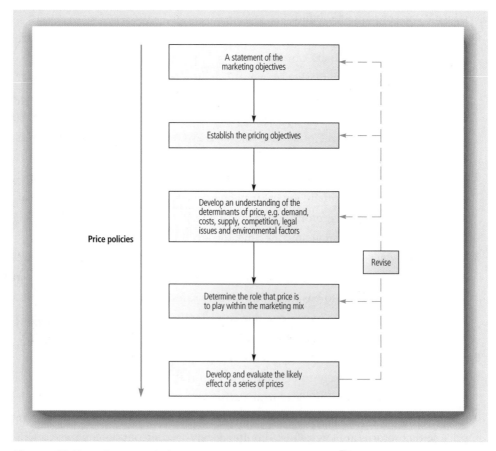

Figure 12.7 A framework for systematic pricing decisions

cost levels and their likely patterns of price behaviour is particularly important, since in many industries a competitive attack can be launched most readily and effectively through the price mechanism. Recognizing this, the strategist should monitor particularly closely each competitor's prices and price movements for any evidence of a possible price offensive. By doing this, it is possible to build a price profile for each competitor that includes a statement of the firm's likelihood and ability to engage in a price war. This involves taking account of nine factors:

1 Each firm's general competitive posture – is it, for example, offensive or defensive and, in Porter's terms (see Chapter 6), a 'good' or a 'bad' competitor?
2 Their cost levels and hence the scope that exists for price cutting
3 The level of resources that would be available in the event of a price war breaking out (see Illustration 12.1)
4 Their relative dependence upon each product and market sector
5 The potential returns from cutting prices
6 The relative importance of each market sector to competitors and hence their probable depth of commitment
7 Their past price history (offensive or defensive)
8 The distinctiveness of each competitor's major products and the apparent degree of brand loyalty that exists
9 The probable response of distributors and any others in the distribution channel.

Illustration 12.1 Price competition and the brand leaders

On 2 April 1993, Philip Morris, USA launched an elaborate integration programme of consumer and retail promotions, which effectively slashed the retail price of its flagship brand, Marlboro, by 20 per cent in the US market. This programme represented a major shift in strategy designed by Philip Morris to reverse the alarming declines in Marlboro's market share that had occurred in the face of severe price competition from discount brands. Given Marlboro's status as one of the world's premier brands and the changing environment of consumer marketing, the date these actions were announced was immediately labelled 'Marlboro Friday' and heralded as a milestone in marketing history.

The Marlboro experience threw into stark relief the vulnerability of even the very strongest of brands to sustained price competition and, in the minds of many brand strategists, raised the question of whether any brand is safe.

Although the information needed under most of these headings is often difficult to obtain with any degree of precision (particularly so in the case of costs), the strategic and tactical need for this information should never be underestimated. The strategist should therefore begin by focusing on the two or three most significant competitors and build the price profile for each firm. The framework can then gradually be developed for the next and less direct level of competition.

12.12 Using price as a tactical weapon

The bulk of our discussion so far has centred around the strategic role played by price. In many cases, however, price is used very largely as a tactical weapon, a role to which, because of its flexibility, it is well suited. There are several ways in which this tactical role can be performed, including:

➡ Varying prices to reflect geographic differences
➡ Offering discounts for early payment, off-season buying, and to encourage high-volume purchases
➡ Trade-in allowances to boost sales when the economy generally is sluggish
➡ Discriminatory pricing in order to capitalize upon the ability or willingness of particular market segments to pay a higher price
➡ Optional feature pricing, which allows the price of the basic product such as a car to be kept low, but for substantial profits then to be made by adding accessories such as a sunroof
➡ Hitting at competitors who appear particularly vulnerable.

Perhaps the most obvious and most important tactical role that can be played by price stems from the periodic need or opportunity to raise or lower prices in order to gain or retain a competitive advantage.

Price cutting, for example, can be used to put pressure on competitors and reverse a falling market share. Equally, it can be used to solve the problem of short-term excess capacity. Raising prices can often be a means of overcoming the problems of excess demand and generating an increase in profits.

However, before making any changes to prices, the strategist needs to consider the impact on the triumvirate to which we referred at the beginning of the chapter – consumers, the trade and competitors – and hence their likely reaction. Faced with a price increase, buyers and distributors may, for example, both respond negatively: buyers by turning to another product and distributors by focusing their attention on competitive products. A price increase might also provide competitors with an opportunity that they then become determined to exploit as far as possible.

Price cutting can, in certain circumstances at least, also create difficulties. Buyers may respond by perceiving the quality to have been lowered, while distributors may feel their margin has been eroded. Even where sales increase, this may simply be as the result of the lower price and does not necessarily lead to any degree of brand loyalty. The implication of this is that when either the price rises at a later stage or when a competitor lowers his price, sales drop. However, perhaps the biggest problem with price cutting is the danger of sparking off a price war.

Faced with a price change that is initiated by a competitor, the strategist has a number of choices:

➡ Follow by increasing prices by the same amount
➡ Keep prices the same in the hope that those who have previously bought from the competitor will be encouraged to shift supplier
➡ Cut prices to increase the price differential.

There are, of course, no hard and fast rules that can be applied. Rather it is the case that the strategist should give full consideration to both the short- and long-term implications of any move that is made.

12.13 Promotion and marketing communications

For many organizations marketing communications represent the most visible face of the organization. The question of how the communications programme is to be managed is therefore a fundamental part of the strategic marketing task. In deciding how best to do this, the planner needs to come to terms with a variety of issues, including the question of how the communications programme can be integrated with the other elements of the marketing mix in order to achieve the greatest degree of synergy; the relationship that exists between the communications or promotions mix and the other elements of the marketing mix is illustrated in Figure 12.8.

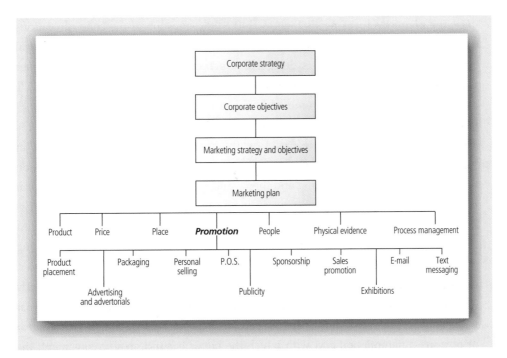

Figure 12.8 The promotions mix and its link with the corporate and marketing strategies

Although eleven elements of the promotions mix are identified in Figure 12.8, it needs to be recognized that this is not an exhaustive list of the communications tools that the marketing planner has available. The area of communications is perhaps the fastest moving element of the marketing mix and, because of this, new ways of communicating with the market are constantly emerging. As an example of this, *product placement*, which involves the deliberate featuring of a product or brand in a film or television programme, was in its infancy even five years ago. Today, however, it represents a useful – if still relatively small – element of the communications programme for many organizations. BMW, for example, has used product placement with a high degree of success in a number of James Bond films. By the same token, *advertorials*, which are print advertisements that have an editorial style and format similar to newspaper or magazine articles, are a small but growing part of the communications mix. Equally, text messaging and e-mail are both becoming increasingly significant communications tools.

Within this part of the chapter it is not our intention to focus in detail upon the individual elements of the communications mix, but rather to highlight the sorts of issues to which the marketing strategist needs to pay attention when developing the guidelines for the communications programme. In doing this, the marketing planner needs to take account of eight areas:

1 *The nature and detail of the target audience(s).* Without this understanding, anything that follows will lack focus. The planner therefore needs to think about how the market might be segmented (refer back to Chapter 8) and then how the messages need to be tailored to fit the needs of each group.

2 *The short- and long-term communications objective(s).* Having identified the target audience, the planner's focus needs then to shift to the question of the communications objectives. In essence, these objectives relate to the cognitive, affective or behavioural responses that the campaign is designed to achieve. In other words, the planner might be aiming to put something into the consumer's mind, change the consumer's attitude or encourage the consumer to behave in a particular way. Labelled *response-hierarchy models*, a summary of the four best known of these appears in Figure 12.9. The four models illustrated are based on the idea of a 'learn–feel–do' process, in which the buyer discovers something in general terms about the product, moves on to a more detailed understanding and then – and only then – takes action in the form of trying the product and possibly becoming a regular user. It is the role of the marketing and communications mixes to move potential buyers through this process. At the same time, of course, there are several elements that have the effect of slowing down or reversing this process; these include competitive action, memory lapses, poor previous experiences with the product or brand, and so on. However, it needs to be recognized that this sequence, although logical, is not necessarily the one that will always be followed. In the case of products in sectors in which there is little real or obvious differentiation and with which the buyer has little real involvement, the sequence may be that of 'learn–do–feel'. In these circumstances, the buyer buys the

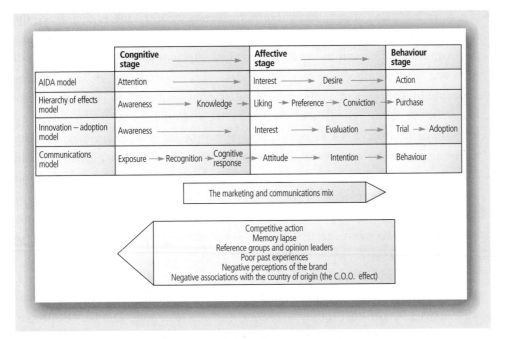

Figure 12.9 Response-hierarchy models and the communications process

product and only after having used it develops a more detailed understanding of it and possibly a degree of brand loyalty. Examples of this would be kitchen rolls and aluminium cooking foil.

3 *The messages that are to be used.* Having developed an understanding of the sort of response that the communications campaign needs to achieve, the planner can then begin to focus upon the design of the message, a task which involves deciding upon four issues:

(i) What to say (the content)

(ii) How to say it logically (the structure)

(iii) How to say it emotionally or symbolically (the format)

(iv) Who should say it (the source).

In deciding upon the first of these – what to say – the planner is faced with a number of choices, including whether to use a highly *rational appeal* (by buying this product you will gain this distinct and tangible benefit) or an *emotional appeal*. Emotional appeals can, in turn, be either positive or negative. In the case of a positive emotional appeal, the planner sets out to associate the product with an especially favourable image; an obvious example would be the ways in which cars, perfumes and expensive watches are advertised. *Negative* emotional appeals include fear, shame and guilt; an example of this would be how the advertisers of toothpastes typically play upon these sorts of emotions by emphasizing bad breath or the fear of tooth decay. However, irrespective of whether the appeal is positive or negative, the planner needs to identify the platform or selling proposition that the campaign is designed to rest upon.

4 *The communication channels that will carry the message.* For the message to reach the target market, the planner needs to select the channels through which contact and communication can be made in the most effective way. These channels fall into one of two categories: *personal influence channels* and *non-personal influence channels*. In turn, personal influence channels can be subdivided into: (a) *advocate channels*, consisting primarily of the sales force and others who are employed by the company; (b) *expert channels*, which consist of those whose views are seen to be independent and respected (these include independent authorities and advisers such as consumer groups, research institutes, *Which?* magazine and other bodies not employed by the company, but which comment on the value of a product); and (c) *social channels*, made up of neighbours, friends, business associates and reference groups. (For a discussion of reference groups, refer to 'social factors'.)

Non-personal influence channels include the mass media, such as newspapers, television, magazines, the cinema and posters, which have the advantage, not generally enjoyed by personal influence channels, of reaching large numbers of people. However, in doing this, they lack any personal element, with the result that the message is more easily ignored and misinterpreted.

5 *The budget.* Although there are various ways in which the communications budget might be set, the most common of these are the *affordable approach, competitive parity*, a *percentage of sales*, and the *objective and task technique,* all of which have been discussed in detail in a variety of other books (see, for example, Wilson and Gilligan, 1997).

6 and **7** *The mix of communication tools that is to be used and how the elements of the promotions mix are to be integrated and how, in turn, the promotions mix is to be integrated with the marketing mix.* In deciding upon which promotional tools should be used, the marketing planner needs to take account of eight elements:

   (i) The degree of control that is needed in terms of how the message is delivered.

   (ii) The financial resources that are available.

   (iii) The credibility of each of the tools in the eyes of the buyer.

   (iv) The size of the target markets and their geographic spread.

   (v) The nature of the product and market and, in particular, whether it is an industrial or a consumer product.

   (vi) Whether a push or a pull strategy is being used. (A *push* strategy, involving a heavy use of the sales force and trade promotions, is best suited to situations where there is a low level of brand loyalty; the choice is generally made at the point of purchase and the benefits are well understood by the buyer. A *pull* strategy, by contrast, is more appropriate when brand loyalty is high, differences between brands are easily perceived and there is a higher degree of involvement in the purchase.)

   (vii) The stage reached by the product in its life cycle.

   (viii) The buyer's readiness stage. Advertising and publicity are generally the most effective tools for raising levels of buyer awareness in the early stages and are more cost-effective than either personal selling or sales promotion. However, as levels of awareness and readiness increase, so personal selling takes on a more direct and valuable role. Closing the sale is also achieved most effectively by personal selling and sales promotion, while advertising then begins to increase in importance again at the re-ordering stage.

8 *How the results of the campaign are to be measured.* An important part of any marketing activity is the measurement of the results that have been achieved. In the case of communications, this can be done using two dimensions: *qualitative measures* and *quantitative measures*. In the case of qualitative issues, the planner is concerned largely with attitudinal changes; quantitative measures relate to changes in sales levels, levels of satisfaction, and trial levels. The extent to which a campaign is successful is, however, influenced by a whole series of factors, many of which are outside the control of the marketing planner.

Although these eight areas are laid out sequentially, it needs to be recognized that, almost inevitably, a degree of iteration will be involved in arriving at a firm decision in at least some of these areas. This is perhaps most obvious in terms of the constraints that might be imposed by the budget. It could well be the case, for example, that having identified the target audience, the communications objectives, the messages and the channels, the costs of implementing the campaign are simply too high for the organization. Given this, the planner is likely to be faced with having to go back and revise the objectives and/or time scales.

Integrating the elements of the promotions mix

Against the background of what has been said so far, the planner needs then to focus upon the ways in which the various communication tools might possibly be brought together in the form of an integrated marketing communications programme. The thinking behind this is straightforward in that by achieving a high(er) level of integration between the individual elements of the communications mix, the planner should achieve a greater degree of clarity and consistency, with the result that there will then be a seamless integration of messages and a correspondingly greater impact in the marketplace. But although there is an obvious logic to the idea of integrating the elements of the communications mix, the reality is that in many organizations too little effort is placed upon achieving this. There are several reasons for this, the most obvious of which is that large organizations in particular often make use of different communications specialists to deal with each of the individual elements of the communications programme. As a result, the focus for integration is the brand or marketing manager, many of whom have little direct experience either of the detail of the individual tools or of the ways in which integration might best be achieved. However, the consequences of *not* achieving a high level of integration are potentially significant, since the messages to the market are then likely to lack the degree of unity and consistency that is needed in an ever more competitive arena.

12.14 Distribution strategies and the distribution plan

Having discussed the process by which orders are obtained, we now need to turn our attention towards the problem of fulfilling these orders.

A significant and increasing part of many organizations' expenditure is that incurred in keeping their products on the move through the channels of distribution to the final consumer. The distribution plan focuses on the set of decisions relating to the processes that are concerned with the flow of supplies, components, products and services between sources of supply, the producer, intermediaries and end-users.

The success of order-getting activities will determine the volume and hence the scale of order-filling activities. This influences distribution planning (and control) in a significant way. Similarly, the level of customer satisfaction engendered by order-filling activities will affect the placing of repeat orders, which again illustrates the interdependency of the elements of the marketing mix.

There are two major areas to consider under the broader heading of order-filling. One relates to channel management decisions, given that few organizations distribute their outputs directly to the final user. The other relates to the management of physical distribution activities, such as transportation, inventory management, warehousing and order-processing (collectively known as logistics). We will deal with each of these aspects of the distribution plan in turn.

12.15 Channel management

Channel management embraces the analysis, planning, organizing and controlling of an enterprise's channel of distribution. This is an increasingly demanding element of the marketing domain due, in part, to pressures from global competition, but also because of a series of other major trends that impact upon channel management:

➡ *An increasing emphasis on the development of channel strategy*. There is a relatively recent recognition that channel strategy can be an important means for achieving competitive advantage.

➡ *The emergence of new retailing concepts*. This includes the Internet and the so-called 'category busters' such as Toys 'R' Us, which operate on a huge scale with very low prices.

➡ *The increasing importance of channel power*. Channel-driven strategies are being employed by an increasing number of companies that seek to develop or acquire products that can be marketed through their existing channels. For example, Gillette acquired Oral-B Laboratories due to the scope for increasing the usage of existing channels (i.e. razors and razor blades are sold through the same intermediaries as toothbrushes and other dental hygiene products).

➡ *The growth of partnerships and strategic alliances*. Every year sees the establishment of close working relationships between producers and key intermediaries with a view to generating competitive advantages.

➡ *The development of direct marketing*. The emergence of database and one-to-one marketing in recent years has resulted in a huge increase in the use of direct mail, the telephone and the Internet as distribution channels. A significant proportion of insurance and banking business, for example, is now conducted by telephone.

➡ *Enhanced distribution productivity.* There has been a considerable increase in the use of information technology (IT) within distribution, along with re-engineering to develop more streamlined organizational arrangements, which have resulted in both cost reduction and better management in distribution channels.

While it is possible to consider channel management from the point of view of, say, the retailer (or other final reseller) by looking 'up the channel' towards the producer, it is much more usual for the perspective to be that of the producer looking 'down the channel' towards the market. This latter perspective will be adopted here.

Key decisions in channel management

Rosenbloom (1995) has identified six major decision areas in channel management. These are illustrated in Figure 12.10. The remainder of this section will deal with those decisions which are of greatest significance to the development of a distribution plan.

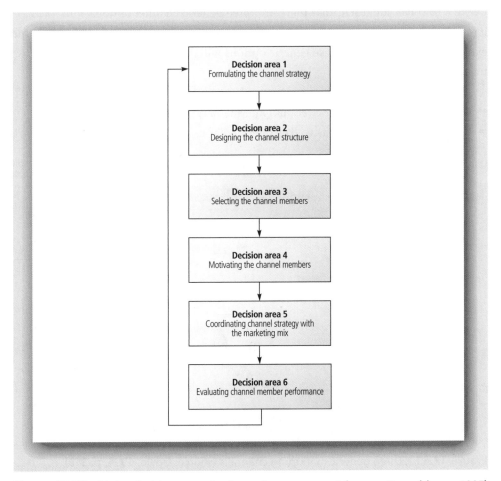

Figure 12.10 Major decision areas in channel management (source: Rosenbloom, 1995)

Formulating the channel strategy

The objectives to be served by a distribution strategy will typically cover how, when and where the enterprise's market offerings should be made available to the targeted markets. The strategy provides a means to these ends. Perhaps the most crucial aspect is the choice of a *level of service* by which an enterprise might seek to secure competitive advantage.

It is also necessary to consider the characteristics of orders: large orders will require different distribution strategies from those which are appropriate for small orders.

As Rosenbloom (1995, p. 554) has pointed out, the importance of channel strategy is likely to depend upon the existence of one or more of the following conditions:

➡ Target markets (or customers) demand a strong emphasis on distribution
➡ Competitive parity exists in other marketing mix variables, with the need for channel strategy to provide some differential advantage (as in the case of McDonald's)
➡ Competitive vulnerability exists because of distribution neglect
➡ Opportunities for synergy exist through channel strategy (e.g. via partnerships and strategic alliances).

Designing the channel structure

Doyle (1994) has suggested that there are three generic channel options: *direct marketing, via a sales force* or *via intermediaries*. These are illustrated in Figure 12.11. To some extent, the choice between these generic options will depend on answers to the following questions:

➡ Can we effect distribution better than intermediaries at an equivalent cost?
➡ Can we effect distribution as well as intermediaries at a lower cost?

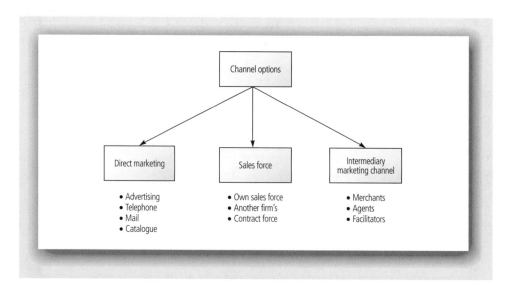

Figure 12.11 Three generic marketing channels (source: Doyle, 1994, p. 318)

If the answer to either of these questions is yes, then the enterprise should consider direct distribution. However, a barrier to direct marketing might exist in the form of *entrenched buying behaviour*. That is, people get used to buying certain products through particular intermediaries and have an inbuilt inertia to change.

In deciding on the most appropriate configuration of distribution channels, it must be decided whether to aim to sell products through all available outlets, through a selection of the available outlets in a particular area, or to limit distribution to one outlet in each area. These three alternative strategies are known as:

➡ *Intensive distribution*, often sought by manufacturers of high-volume, low-value products in mass demand for which the typical pattern of buying behaviour is that of habit and convenience. An obvious example is soft drinks, which are distributed intensively in outlets ranging from vending machines to theatre foyers and fish and chip shops.
➡ *Selective distribution*, used by manufacturers of consumer durables for which the typical pattern of buying behaviour is that of 'shopping around'. Most consumers will make an effort to compare the offerings available in different outlets. For this reason, the manufacturer need not distribute their products through all the available outlets. For example, a dishwashing machine might be distributed via electricity company showrooms and department stores in town centres rather than via all available outlets. Selective distribution involves less communication effort than does intensive distribution and also offers opportunities to develop closer relationships within the channel from which adequate market coverage might be achieved with lower cost and greater control than is possible with intensive distribution.
➡ *Exclusive distribution*, which arises when the producer limits the number of intermediaries more strictly to one per geographical area. The dealer will receive exclusive rights to distribute the producer's offerings in that geographical area in return for agreeing not to carry competing products. The producer will consequently receive a greater commitment from the outlet and more control over image and price. Bang & Olufsen audio equipment is a good example of this type of distribution strategy.

The choice among the alternatives will depend to a large extent on the nature of the market offering, the target market segment and the product positioning. Lancaster and Massingham (1988) suggest that some of the factors that might persuade a company to prefer a more exclusive form of distribution include:

➡ Where the customer needs or expects specialist advice, facilities or service
➡ Where the manufacturer and/or distributor would gain from the enhanced image associated with selective/exclusive distribution
➡ Where potential sales volume would not warrant more intensive distribution
➡ Where the manufacturer wishes to exercise more control over channel members' marketing activities
➡ Where more intensive distribution might result in conflicts between channel members.

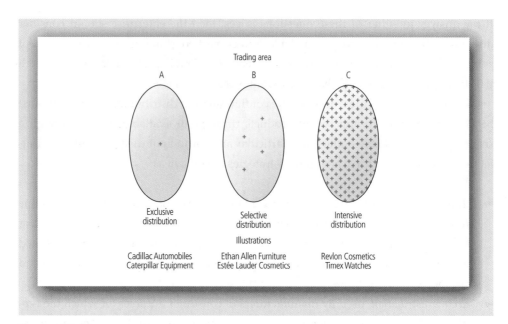

Figure 12.12 Distribution intensity (source: Cravens, 1990, p. 428)

Channels of distribution, once selected and established, involve the enterprise in relatively long-term commitments to other organizations (such as wholesalers and retailers), as well as affecting in a very significant manner every other major marketing decision. It is important, therefore, to ensure that the implications of each alternative choice are carefully evaluated. We now turn to this question.

Selecting the channel members

In developing this part of the distribution plan consideration needs to be given to (see Wilson, 1983, p. 572):

➡ *Economic criteria*, which will reflect the pattern and levels of costs, sales revenue and profit. As each alternative channel configuration is likely to produce different levels of sales revenue and costs, the best alternative is not necessarily that producing the most or the least respectively, but the one which produces the best relationship between the two – i.e. profit.

➡ *Control criteria*, which relate to the degree of influence, motivation and conflict among channel members. For example, an agent who handles many different manufacturers' lines will probably not be seen favourably by manufacturer A because the agent will put his own interests ahead of A's in endeavouring to sell *any* line – not just A's – and this can lead to friction.

➡ *Adaptive criteria*, by which the manufacturer is able to preserve some flexibility in responding to changing conditions. Long-term franchise agreements are antithetical to adaptive behaviour within distribution channels.

To this list Cravens (1990, pp. 429–31) would add:

➡ *End-user considerations*, since it would not be helpful to select intermediaries not favoured by customers further down the supply chain
➡ *Product characteristics*, including the complexity, special application requirements, servicing needs and so forth that channel members must be competent to handle
➡ *Manufacturer's capability and resources*, which are reflected in bargaining power and channel control.

An approach to carrying out an evaluation of alternative channel options has been suggested by Doyle (1994, pp. 319–20). This is illustrated in Figure 12.13, from which it can be seen that a range of criteria has been specified, each accorded a weight to reflect its relative importance, and then weighted scores produced for each channel option. In this example, the vertical marketing system (VMS) produces the highest score. The definition of a VMS is that of 'professionally managed and centrally programmed networks pre-engineered to achieve operating economies and maximum marketing impact . . . through integration, coordination and synchronization of marketing flows from point of production to points of ultimate use' (McCammon, 1970, p. 43). A conventional channel structure (i.e. involving intermediaries but without any attempt at managing the channel as a whole) produces the lowest score. However, the numbers themselves are not the most important feature of this approach. The main aim is to encourage managers to identify the attributes that they consider to be necessary if a channel is to operate effectively. In this way, the strengths and weaknesses of alternative channel options can be highlighted.

Criteria	Importance weight	Channel options			
		Direct	Franchise	Conventional	Vertical
Channel objectives					
1 Goals	0.1	5	2	3	4
2 Resources	0.1	1	2	5	3
3 Positioning	0.1	1	4	2	5
Channel strategy					
4 Target market	0.15	3	3	4	4
5 Differential advantage	0.2	4	4	1	5
Channel reliability					
6 Motivation	0.15	5	4	2	4
7 Control	0.1	5	3	1	4
8 Risk	0.1	2	2	2	3
Weighted scores	**1.0**	**26**	**24**	**20**	**32**

Figure 12.13 Evaluating alternative channel options (source: Doyle, 1994, p. 320)

12.16 The 'soft' elements of the marketing mix

We began this chapter by suggesting that the amount of attention that has been paid to the 'softer' elements of the marketing mix has increased significantly over the past few years. To a large extent, this has been due to the way in which as more markets have become increasingly crowded and competitive, so the traditional bases of competitive advantage of product, price and so on have been eroded. It was the recognition of this that led marketing planners to search for other forms of competitive differentiation and to the development of the expanded marketing mix, with its inclusion of the three 'soft' Ps of:

➡ People
➡ Physical evidence
➡ Process management.

The first of these three elements emerged largely from the service sector, where a firm's personnel play a pivotal role in delivering the product/service and typically have a significant effect on the customer or client's perceptions of quality. The significance of the front-line staff has also been highlighted by a wide variety of studies, and it is these that are reflected in our discussion in Chapter 1 of right-side-up and wrong-side-up organizations (see pp. 22–3).

Given this, *the people or service dimension* needs to be managed both proactively and strategically, with the marketing planner having to decide from the outset on the service levels that are to be achieved. Having done this, staff then needs to be trained, their performance monitored and a series of control systems introduced. Amongst the organizations to have done this well are Dyson (see Illustration 11.4) and Singapore Airlines. In the case of Dyson, the company has used service quality as an integral part of its marketing strategy, whilst Singapore Airlines has astutely used technology to achieve service excellence.

In setting service levels, the planner needs to take account of five areas:

1 Customers' needs and expectations
2 The approaches being taken by competitors
3 The customers' willingness and ability to pay for particular levels of service
4 The ability of the organization to deliver particular service levels *consistently*
5 The cost of delivering different levels of service and the returns that will be generated from this both in the short and the long term.

The second dimension of the expanded marketing mix, *physical evidence*, relates to the environment surrounding the product or service and, as such, embraces buildings, vehicles, colours and anything else that communicates a message about the quality of the product or service, including how the staff are dressed.

The third and final dimension is that of the process by which the product or service is acquired and in particular how this process is managed. Effective *process*

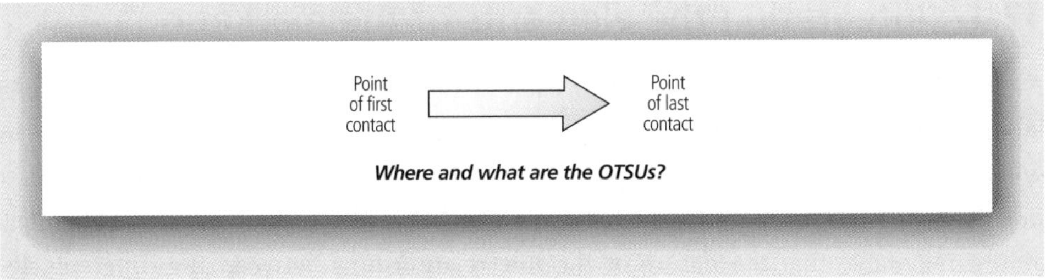

Figure 12.14 Process management and moments of truth

management has proven to be a potentially powerful differentiator, since it relates to how customers are treated from the point of their very first contact with the organization through to the last (see Figure 12.14). We first made reference to this in Illustration 5.8, in which we discussed both Scandinavian Airlines and Jan Carlzon's understanding of the significance of points of contact and David Clutterbuck's ideas about OTSUs (Opportunities To Screw Up); it may be helpful to read this material again (refer to pp. 207–8).

In thinking about process management, the marketing planner needs to develop the strategy and mechanisms against the background of the factors that influence the service level strategy that was discussed earlier. All too often, however, process management is affected by a whole series of seemingly small issues, but which from the customer's standpoint are significant. In order to achieve an effective process management system, the marketing planner needs, therefore, to begin with a detailed audit of the current processes, *looking at each of these from the customer's viewpoint*, with a view to identifying the sorts of factors that are the basis for customer satisfaction and customer dissatisfaction. Having done this, there is then the need to focus upon making the sort of changes that will ensure the customer experience is as smooth as possible. In discussing this, Berry (1987) proposes seven guidelines:

1 Ensuring that *marketing* happens at all levels from the marketing department to where the service is provided

2 Consider introducing *flexibility* in providing the service – when feasible, customize the service to the needs of customers

3 Recruit *high-quality staff* – treat them well, communicate clearly to them and recognize that their attitudes and behaviour patterns are the key to service quality and differentiation

4 Attempt to market to *existing customers* to increase their use of the service, or to take up new service products

5 Set up a *quick response facility* to customer problems and complaints

6 Employ *new technology* to provide better services at lower costs

7 Use *branding*.

12.17 Integrating the elements of the marketing mix

Although the effective management of each of the individual elements of the mix is largely self-evident, the marketing strategist also needs to pay attention to the ways in which the mix as a whole is managed and how the various elements can be integrated in such a way that a (high) degree of synergy is achieved. In the absence of this it is almost inevitable that the nature of the interrelationships between the different elements of the mix will be ignored or misunderstood and conflicting messages will be sent to the market. In discussing this, Jobber (2001) highlights the ways in which an effective marketing mix has four principal characteristics:

1 It matches customers' needs by reflecting the issues of importance to them in the choice process
2 It creates a competitive advantage
3 It matches the resources available to the organization
4 It is well blended in that each of the elements contributes to a single consistent theme.

In order to achieve this, the marketing strategist needs to have a clear understanding not just of what the mix is designed to achieve (what are the short- and long-term objectives?), but also of the spectrum of factors that contribute to and inhibit organizational capability. There are several ways in which this integration can be achieved, but most obviously by being clear about the product's strengths and weaknesses, its current and probable future market positioning, how the competition is behaving, and the role that each element of the mix is capable of playing within the market. Against this background, the marketing strategist can then focus upon the linkages that exist between the mix elements and how they might possibly be leveraged.

12.18 Summary

Within this chapter we have focused upon the individual elements of the mix and shown how, for many organizations, the emphases within the mix are changing. The factors that have led to these changes can be traced back to many of the issues that we have raised at earlier stages of the book, including a very different type of customer, far higher levels of competition, the very different bases of competition, and a generally greater degree of environmental volatility. Together, these factors have led to an erosion of the traditional foundations of competitive advantage and the consequent search by marketing strategists for other elements that will provide the means of differentiation within the marketplace. In giving emphasis to the 'softer' elements of the mix, marketing strategists have learned from organizations in the services sector, where there has long been a recognition that it is people and processes that are capable of providing potentially powerful competitive differentiators.

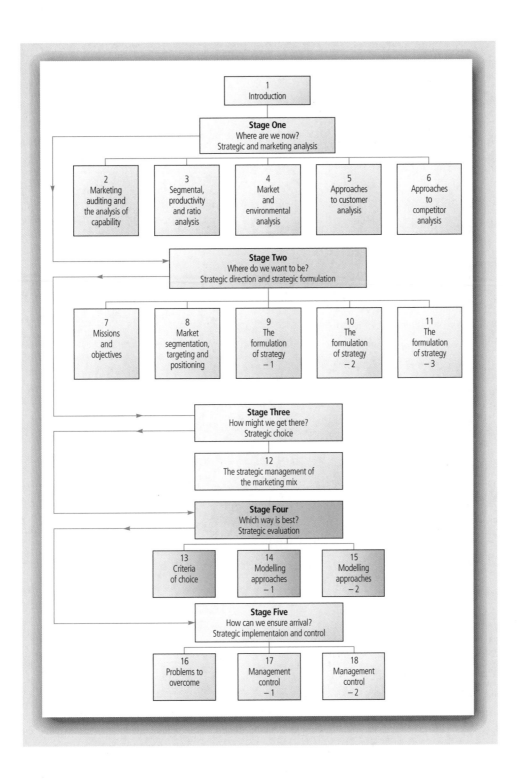

Stage Four: Which way is best? Strategic evaluation

The overall concern within this stage is with the choice among alternative marketing strategies that were suggested in Stages Two and Three. This concern reduces to two principal questions:

1 What criteria of choice should be employed? This is dealt with in Chapter 13.
2 How might alternative marketing programmes be evaluated given the criteria articulated in question 1? This is addressed in Chapters 14 and 15.

Prior to moving on to Chapters 13–15, it may be useful to consider some of the evidence that is available on the effectiveness of marketing activities within the UK. This will provide useful background material as we move through Stages Four and Five of the book.

In their study on the effectiveness of British marketing (Lynch et al., 1988), the Bradford-based research team followed up an earlier study they had undertaken (Hooley et al., 1984). Their main interest was in identifying the characteristics of the more successful organizations across a sample that was broadly representative of British companies in terms of size, sector and business type.

No magic formula was found that might guarantee the success of marketing activities. However, the better performers showed a firmer grasp of the key marketing concepts and a greater consistency in applying those concepts across their range of operations. There was, in fact, a stronger commitment to marketing principles, resulting in a consistent marketing-oriented culture, within the more successful enterprises. In summary, the prevalent attitudes among the better performers were found to be:

➡ A greater emphasis on identifying and meeting customers' needs
➡ The chief executive saw marketing as a guiding philosophy for the whole organization
➡ More aggressive, expansionist objectives
➡ A greater willingness to pursue longer-term marketing goals rather than short-term financial objectives
➡ Great importance was attached to marketing training.

With regard to marketing practices, the better performing companies exhibited the following characteristics:

➡ A greater input was made by marketing to overall strategic planning
➡ There was more evidence of formal, long-term marketing planning
➡ Marketing objectives were more aggressively specified
➡ They were prepared to attack the whole market and take on any competition
➡ They were more prepared to take calculated risks
➡ They adopted superior quality, high-price positioning strategies.
➡ Competitive advantages were built through reputation and quality
➡ They were more active in new product development in order to achieve market leadership.

In overall terms, the more successful enterprises showed impressive consistency in implementation derived from a combination of their clearer marketing grasp and their more focused marketing structures and systems.

Other studies that have examined the success of marketing activities include those by Verhage and Waarts (1988), who looked at Dutch and British companies on a comparative basis, and those by Doyle et al. (1988) and Wong et al. (1988), who looked at the comparative quality of marketing activities in British, Japanese and US companies. Results from the last two studies highlighted significant weaknesses in the marketing effectiveness of British companies that were exacerbated by an excessive emphasis on short-run financial gains. Given that the focus was on comparative performance within UK markets, it was found that US firms were less committed to the UK market than were their Japanese rivals. While the Japanese were working to close the technological gap between themselves and their US competitors, the latter were demonstrating a short-term profit focus. This makes it likely that US market positions will deteriorate, since the Japanese showed themselves to be unmistakably aggressive, single-minded in their pursuit of market share, and undeniably more market-oriented than their US or British counterparts.

In 1994 a report prepared by the Cranfield School of Management for the Chartered Institute of Marketing revealed scepticism about the contribution of marketing to business success (see Simms, 1995, p. 12). The Chartered Institute of Marketing subsequently commissioned a further study (see Parkinson, 1995) to measure marketing's contribution to the competitive performance of British manufacturing industry. The aim was 'to develop and validate a framework which companies could use to assess and improve their competitive performance through effective and efficient marketing'. The Executive Summary of the report *Manufacturing – The Marketing Solution* is reproduced below (with permission of the CIM).

Executive Summary

Objectives

UK manufacturing industry has experienced considerable problems over the last 25 years. From a position of market dominance in the mid-1960s, British companies have steadily lost international market share. Turnover and employment in manufacturing have steadily declined, and overseas competitors have increased their share of world markets.

This report has two objectives:

1 To measure marketing's contribution to the competitive performance of British manufacturing industry

2 To develop and validate a framework that companies in British manufacturing industry can use to assess and improve their competitive performance through effective and efficient marketing.

The excellence framework

Marketing, particularly in a business-to-business setting, involves a much wider range of activities than those typically taking place in the sales or marketing department. These functional areas make an important contribution, frequently providing specialist services such as market research, competitive analysis and business planning services. However, in an effective company, the whole of the organization is market focused. All of its capabilities are focused on the market.

These capabilities include internal processes such as research and development, operations management, and manufacturing. They also include external processes such as supply chain management, customer development, and the management of strategic alliances with suppliers, distributors and other competitors. Effective companies manage this alignment more effectively and more efficiently than their competitors. Such companies are also capable of modifying and developing new ways of meeting market needs to maintain superior market positions.

Improving competitive performance involves managing key marketing processes more effectively. This involves four stages:

1 Defining the processes that influence business performance
2 Measuring performance against these processes
3 Comparing the company's performance with those companies that achieve superior performance
4 Investing in (or redesigning) those processes that are most likely to give competitive advantage.

An increasing number of case histories are now appearing in management literature on how to use business process engineering to improve competitive performance. However, little attempt has been made to date to review the processes that really contribute to competitive success, and there are few practical diagnostic frameworks available to help in the analysis.

Such a framework was developed for this project, and has been used to assess critical marketing processes in over forty companies operating in British manufacturing industry.

The following key processes were seen to be critical:

➡ Marketing strategy development
➡ Quality strategy development
➡ Product and process innovation
➡ Customer development and management
➡ Brand management
➡ Supply chain management
➡ Integration of marketing and operations.

To succeed, organizations should have a clearly defined strategic marketing planning process, in which customer and competitor analysis are major elements. This process

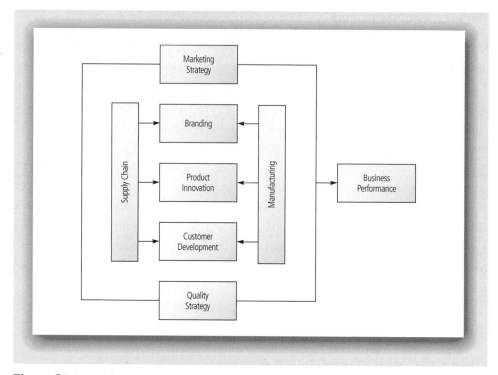

Figure S4.1   Marketing excellence framework

should be driven by a determination to allocate resources in a systematic way to reflect different levels of market opportunity and competitive strengths and weaknesses. Equally importantly, the process should be firmly led, with a clear sense of vision and purpose, and explicit communication of the company's objectives to employees and other stakeholders.

However, having a strategic direction alone is not sufficient. A well worked out strategic marketing plan will flounder if there is no system to ensure that such a plan is effectively implemented. In the framework, the company's quality strategy is the second key enabling factor. If strategic marketing planning is about vision and direction, then quality strategy relates to making things happen in a direct and accountable way.

Five sub-processes have been identified that link together within the broad overall framework of strategic marketing planning and quality strategy. These are product and process innovation, manufacturing and operational support, supply chain management, branding, and customer development. Together, these seven processes make up the marketing excellence framework (see Figure S4.1).

Method

To develop the marketing excellence framework, each of the seven processes was disaggregated into individual components. These components enabled the project team to conduct a detailed analysis of each of the seven elements of the model. They also provided a basis for a company to score itself in terms of competitive marketing performance. A section of the full report discusses how readers can use this approach in their own organizations. These components were derived from the marketing literature, combined with the research team's own experience. In addition, the original framework was piloted to ensure that the main elements made practical sense to the UK manufacturing industry.

The study approach required considerable cooperation from participating companies. Interviews were required with the members of the senior management team responsible for each of the processes in the marketing excellence framework. To implement the research required the participation of up to six managers in each company. At an early stage in the research a decision was taken to build the sample in an incremental way. Considerable negotiation was required with each company to agree participation in the project.

Although the study was focused on individual operating companies, many of these companies had several different divisions. Within each of these divisions there were also potentially many different products and markets. The chief executive of each company was asked to designate the business area within the company where the analysis should be based.

The sample is well distributed, both in terms of industrial sectors and size of companies. In addition, data has been collected at the business unit level, where day-to-day decisions are made about the future of the organization. Perhaps most importantly, the project team interviewed almost 200 managers responsible for different functional areas within each company. Jointly, these managers defined and developed the companies' competitive strategies.

Characteristics of the sample

Of the companies in the sample, 66 per cent (twenty-nine companies) described their major business area as a major cash generator, while 27 per cent (twelve companies) regarded the business as an area to invest in for the future. In only 7 per cent (three companies) was the business regarded as declining. This was consistent with the description of the growth rate of the markets. Fifty-five per cent (twenty-four companies) believed that their major business was operating in a mature marketplace. Approximately one-third (seventeen companies) characterized their markets as new or established and growing.

Over 50 per cent of the sample (twenty-five companies) felt that competition for their core (most important) market was intense and growing. For sixteen companies (36 per cent) it was still moderate and stable. Only three companies (7 per cent) felt that there was little effective competition. Thirteen companies (29 per cent) faced markets where the competition was well established and stable. However, in the majority of cases competition was either gradually changing (nineteen companies) or changing rapidly (twelve companies).

Performance of marketing processes

The companies in this sample do not score highly on any element of the excellence framework (see Figure S4.2). In particular, scores are markedly lower for branding as a business process, reflecting a lack of concern with branding as a strategic process and a potential source of competitive advantage. For most companies, significant changes would need to be made to achieve 'best in class' performance.

Companies were classified into one of four main groupings. Those scoring up to 13 on the excellence framework were termed the *'stragglers'*. Stragglers have been left behind in terms of the use of best-practice techniques. There are twelve such companies in this sample. The second major grouping is the *'copers'*. These companies have adopted some best-practice techniques and are coping with their environment, albeit in an imprecise way. Copers manage some processes effectively, but there is still considerable room for improvement. Copers have been defined as those companies scoring between 13 and 19 on the framework. There are fourteen copers in the sample.

The third grouping includes companies that score heavily on some elements of the framework but not necessarily well everywhere. These companies have been defined as those scoring over 19 and up to 25 on the framework. They are frequently in transition to excellence. Such companies have been termed the *'travellers'*. There are twelve travellers in the sample. The final group is those companies that have already developed 'best in class' practice, defined by scores over 25 on the framework. These companies

Business Process	1	2	3	4	5	Total No. (%)	Average
Marketing Strategy	4 (9)	13 (30)	14 (32)	10 (23)	3 (7)	44 (100)	2.9
Quality Strategy	8 (18)	7 (16)	9 (20)	10 (23)	10 (23)	44 (100)	3.1
Branding	29 (66)	7 (16)	6 (14)	2 (4)	–	44 (100)	1.5
Innovation	6 (14)	9 (20)	13 (29)	9 (20)	7 (16)	44 (100)	3.0
Customer Development	4 (9)	11 (25)	10 (23)	14 (32)	5 (11)	44 (100)	3.1
Supply Chain Management	6 (14)	9 (20)	13 (29)	8 (18)	8 (18)	44 (100)	3.0
Manufacturing	4 (9)	9 (20)	11 (25)	10 (23)	10 (23)	44 (100)	3.3

Figure S4.2   Scores on each business process

have been labelled the *'professionals'*. Professionals manage all of the processes in the framework effectively. Many processes are managed excellently. There are six professionals in the sample.

Stragglers are predominantly smaller companies. Copers, travellers and professionals are increasingly larger organizations, although there is still a significant number of relatively small travellers. The adoption of best-practice techniques increases with size, perhaps reflecting the greater range of skills available. Increasing complexity of tasks and greater resources are available to devote to 'planning rather than doing'. Stragglers are to be found predominantly in the mechanical engineering industry. Automotive supply, aerospace and chemicals have a greater proportion of more sophisticated companies.

A company's customers can have a major impact on the way it manages itself. Companies that are suppliers to the automotive industry have had to respond to increasingly demanding international customers in the last few years. This is reflected in higher overall scores on the excellence framework. Professionals are concerned about the impact of technical change on their business. Moving through to stragglers, each successive category is less concerned about the impact of changing supply market technologies, new products, and changes in manufacturing technology.

Marketing ability and business performance

There is a positive relationship for a significant number of companies between the total score on the marketing excellence framework and return on sales (profit before interest and tax to sales turnover). This is encouraging, since better performance on critical business processes is related to better financial performance. For these companies, getting key processes right makes a difference to financial performance.

Companies that are better at strategic marketing planning, product innovation, customer development, branding, and supply chain management make better return on sales. Funds and time invested in these processes will yield tangible business returns.

Some companies are relatively good at managing business processes, but still show relatively poor return on sales (high scorers/low performers). Better management of critical processes does lead to improved profitability in most circumstances, but not necessarily all.

High scorers/high performers are significantly more likely to operate in markets where there is a high rate of technical change in supply markets. Eight companies out of twenty-two (36 per cent) high performers were in this situation. High scorers/high performers were also experiencing rapid technical changes in their products. Eleven of the twenty-two (50 per cent) high-performing companies operated in markets with high rates of product change. By contrast, only one of the nine high-scoring/low-performing companies (11 per cent) operated in markets with high rates of product change.

Individual case studies show considerable variations in marketing practice across a range of different settings. Analysis of the scores of individual components reveals wide variety in the levels of sophistication with which marketing processes such as strategic planning, quality, product innovation, branding, and customer development are managed.

Application of the findings

There are several ways to use the findings of this survey. These are as follows:

- ➡ To provide an indication of how well the company is managing each element of the excellence framework and enable the company to benchmark itself against the companies in this sample
- ➡ To provide an agenda for action aimed at improving performance on critical processes that can be monitored and evaluated over time
- ➡ To create a debate about critical business processes that is based on a structured approach.

Reviewing the processes requires a degree of objectivity in analysis. The project team defined evidence for each performance dimension that was used in the scoring. Two members of the team scored each company. Readers may not have the time or resources to analyse their own organization to the same level of detail. However, more evidence will lead to greater objectivity in the resultant scores, and greater management consensus about the final result.

Conclusions

One of the most satisfying conclusions from this research is the simple one that the application of marketing processes actually makes a quantifiable difference in the UK manufacturing industry. Companies that scored higher on the excellence framework showed higher levels of return on sales. The study is encouraging to those involved with improving the quality of marketing practice. The depth of analysis and the focus on tightly defined business units in this study gives the project team confidence in the findings.

Considerable effort is required to implement a benchmarking study thoroughly. Amongst the critical problems is the definition of the framework, including main processes, components and individual performance dimensions. The project team is confident in the framework. Statistical tests of the relationship show that the model was a good fit and explained over 65 per cent of the variance in return on sales.

In a few of the best-performing companies the project team found evidence of a genuine attempt to organize the business on a process basis rather than around conventional business functions. In one such company, one job title seemed to the research team to summarize the philosophy of the whole project, namely Director of Customer Satisfaction.

Where companies had begun to focus on key processes, there was greater evidence of awareness of the importance of measurement of market-led performance indicators, such as customer or supplier satisfaction. The positive evidence between process improvement and performance presented in this study should provide encouragement to companies to push ahead with this approach.

The final conclusion from this study is that excellent performance on the framework may be a necessary but not sufficient condition for business success. In some sectors companies were excellent when compared with their peers, but still showed lower profit return on sales. This was due to the intensely competitive markets in which such companies were operating. The simple message for these companies is that it is not sufficient to be excellent in a comparative way with the rest of manufacturing industry. Such companies must continue to set even more demanding targets for process improvement, if they are to stay in business and achieve competitive parity or leadership.

Chapter

13

Criteria of choice

13.1 Learning objectives

When you have read this chapter you should be able to:

(a) understand the role of criteria of choice in the decision-making process;
(b) distinguish between financial and non-financial criteria;
(c) recognize the limitations of using single criteria for making strategic choices;
(d) appreciate the relevance of multiple criteria approaches to strategic choice.

13.2 Introduction

In 1993 a group of chairmen, chief executives and other senior executives from twenty-five of Britain's top businesses came together to form the Royal Society of Arts (RSA) Inquiry 'Tomorrow's Company'. This inquiry was prompted by the recognition that Britain has a long tail of underperforming companies and that the prime responsibility for correcting this situation lay with the business community. The inquiry team has now reported, and a summary of its Inclusive Approach is shown in Illustration 13.1. This contrasts 'tomorrow's company' with 'yesterday's companies'. One of the key means of moving forward successfully is to improve the way in which strategic decisions are made.

Tomorrow's companies (or new products, new markets, new competitors
and new ways of thinking)

In his book *Thriving on Chaos*, Peters (1988) argues that at least ten major forces are at work that are influencing how managers think and how they need to behave. By themselves, each of these forces represents a powerful agent for change. Together, he suggests, they are overturning virtually every well-known precept of corporate management. The ten forces that he highlights are:

1 *Unprecedented uncertainty.* Despite the attention that has seemingly been paid to environmental flux over the past 10 years, the majority of the managerial tools – basic accounting practice, patterns of organization, and approaches to the formulation of strategy – are, he suggests, still predicated on stability.
2 *Time* will increasingly be the main weapon of competition, with speed, flexibility, adaptiveness and information technologies providing enormous scope for the exploitation of opportunities.
3 *The fragmentation of markets* and the consequent need to customize products, services and the marketing effort negates the old ideas of niche markets. Niche marketing is, Peters argues, no longer meaningful, since there are no non-niche markets any more.
4 *Quality, design and service* are the fundamental expectations of customers in virtually all markets. Yet in far too few companies are these areas obsessions.

habit or to others. Yesterday's companies have different messages for different audiences (for example, to providers of capital, employees are costs to be cut, while to the employees 'you are our greatest asset').

Measuring success

➡ Tomorrow's company uses its stated purpose and values, and its understanding of the importance of each relationship, to develop its own success model, from which it can generate a meaningful framework for performance measurement.

➡ Yesterday's companies take it for granted that 'everyone knows' what success is and allow existing systems of measurements to define it for them. They are content to measure returns. Because they have no measures of the value embedded in their

relationships, when hard decisions have to be made they are taken in the dark. They risk destroying value rather than creating it. Yesterday's companies measure what they have always measured in the past.

Relationships

➡ Tomorrow's company values reciprocal relationships and works actively to build them with customers, suppliers and other key stakeholders through a partnership approach and, by focusing on and learning from all those who contribute to the business, will be best able to improve returns to shareholders.

➡ Yesterday's companies are locked in adversarial relationships. They think in terms of zero-sum, imagining that if they were to make customers, employees, suppliers or the community more important, the shareholders would be the losers.

13.3 Financial versus non-financial criteria; effectiveness versus efficiency

In choosing between alternative courses of action or strategies it is, of course, desirable to choose the best, but how is the 'best' to be recognized? The best from the viewpoint of one stakeholder may not be the best from another stakeholder's viewpoint. Similarly, what is best in the short term may not be best in the long term. Specifying the criteria by which choices are to be made among competing alternatives is a crucial step in working towards improved marketing performance.

It has traditionally been the case that financial criteria have dominated choice processes irrespective of the initial emphasis that may have been given to non-financial criteria. Changes in strategic thinking (as reported, for example, by Munro and Cooper, 1989) have suggested that the dominance of financial measures may no longer be appropriate. For instance, the emphasis placed by McDonald's on quality, service, cleanliness and value shows that a financial criterion is insufficient, although there will invariably be one or more financial measures within any enterprise's set of *critical success factors* (see pp. 576–85).

A selection of the most important financial and non-financial criteria is given in Figure 13.1, many of which will be discussed in this chapter.

Figure 13.1 Financial and non-financial criteria

Within the marketing literature there is surprisingly little coverage of effectiveness (i.e. doing the right things) as opposed to efficiency (i.e. doing things right). However, it is implicit in the extensive coverage of efficiency that the results of marketing activities are effective: it is not suggested that effectiveness should be traded off for greater efficiency. Nevertheless, the preoccupation that has existed with inputs rather than outputs tends to mean that outputs such as increased sales revenue, greater market share or higher profits are taken as being self-evident measures of effectiveness.

The various inputs and outputs cited in the literature on marketing efficiency include those shown in Figure 13.2.

If we consider market share to be an appropriate output measure we can relate this back to the discussions of the BCG growth–share matrix and the PIMS approach (see Chapter 9, pp. 367–74 and Chapter 11, pp. 432–7).

The growth–share matrix was developed for use in portfolio planning (i.e. to generate a balanced portfolio of business activities with reference to cash generation and cash use). Relative market share serves as a proxy for cash generation, with market growth acting as a proxy for cash use.

Figure 13.2 Marketing efficiency criteria

Market share as an output measure also features prominently in the PIMS approach (see Abell and Hammond, 1979; Buzzell and Gale, 1987; Day, 1990). ROI is the dependent variable in the PIMS approach (see p. 434), with market share playing a key role in the following sequence:

1 Superior relative quality is established by a business for its products
2 This superiority facilitates the building of market share
3 Greater share brings with it cost advantages due to higher volume and experience curve effects
4 Superior quality allows premium prices to be charged, which, in association with lower costs, ensures higher profits.

Whatever measures of input and output are used in an attempt to assess efficiency – and Figure 13.2 offers only a limited number of each – the overriding emphasis is typically on readily quantifiable factors. This gives a means of both asking and answering the question as to whether the enterprise is getting as much output per unit of input as it should, or whether the efficiency of marketing activities might be improved. As we have seen, however, this concern with 'doing things right' begs the question of whether the right things are being done, which requires a fuller consideration of marketing effectiveness. This is provided in Chapter 14, where we deal with such approaches as the marketing audit (which was also covered in Chapter 2) and Bonoma's approach to assessing marketing programmes.

We will proceed through this chapter by examining a range of individual criteria from both the financial and non-financial categories, and then look at more broadly-based, multiple-criteria approaches to evaluating alternatives.

13.4 Financial criteria

Cash generation

Poor liquidity is a greater threat to the survival prospects of an enterprise than poor profitability; hence it is vitally important in choosing a marketing strategy to consider carefully the cash flow implications of available alternatives. This can be vividly illustrated via the BCG growth–share matrix (as discussed in Chapter 9), which classifies products into four categories (see Figures 9.2 and 9.3):

➡ Stars
➡ Question marks (or wildcats)
➡ Dogs
➡ Cash cows.

Use of the product portfolio as a frame of reference should ensure that all products, business units or profit centres are not treated alike, and that investment decisions are not seen as being independent of continuing business activities. Nevertheless, a strategic success sequence is likely to emerge through following these steps:

1 The cash generated by cash cows (high market share, low market growth) should be invested in building the market share of question marks. If this is done well, sustainable advantage will be provided by which question marks will become stars and then cash cows, and will thereby become capable of financing subsequent strategies.

2 To be avoided is the sequence by which question marks are not supported so that they become dogs when the market matures – low relative share in a low growth market is not the place to find oneself.

3 Also to be avoided is the sequence by which stars lose position and become question marks as market growth slows, with the risk of their becoming dogs.

It should be mentioned that, in focusing on the balancing of operating cash flows, the BCG matrix ignores the existence of capital markets, which also have a role to play in balancing cash flows. Moreover, the BCG matrix fails to allow for differential risk.

Cost leadership

A particular strategy may be more desirable than others if it is likely to secure cost leadership (which is one of Porter's key generic strategies). This notion can be illustrated through the *experience curve*.

In Figure 13.3, the three most offensive price/quality positioning strategies are 4, 7 and 8; it is these that provide the strongest basis for an attack, since each one offers the buyer above-average value for money. By contrast, strategies 2, 3 and 6 all involve

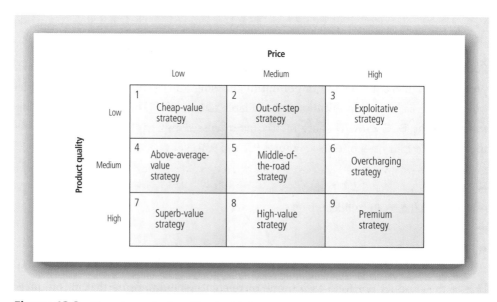

Figure 13.3 The nine price/quality strategies

setting the price above its real value and, particularly in the medium and long term, are unlikely to succeed.

Illustration 13.2 Price cuts and zero-sum games

At the beginning of 1996, Procter & Gamble launched its 'Every Day Low Pricing Strategy', which saw the prices of many of its brands cut by up to 17 per cent. The strategy, which was led by Pampers and Lenor, had a dramatic effect upon the market, forcing competitors such as Kimberly-Clark and Lever Brothers to match Procter & Gamble's lower prices. However, 12 months later, faced with static market share figures and squeezed profit margins, Procter &

Gamble made a dramatic U-turn and began raising prices. Within days, its competitors followed suit.

In commenting on the price war in just one of Procter & Gamble's markets, the disposable nappy sector, a trade buyer commented: 'You cannot grow volumes in the nappy market. The cuts did not help anyone.'

Source: *Marketing*, 13 February 1997, p. 1.

Pricing decisions and portfolio analysis

In our discussion of portfolio analysis in Chapter 9, we commented that cash flow and profitability are both closely related to sales volume. Recognizing, therefore, that products typically follow a well-trodden path through the matrix, portfolio analysis is capable of providing a series of general pricing guidelines. *Question marks*, for example, offer scope either for skimming in order to quickly regain investment (this would be appropriate if the strategist sees the market as having only a limited life), or rapid penetration by means of low prices in order to build share and keep competitors at bay.

In the *star* stage, high prices are appropriate when buyer loyalty is high and/or if a high level of development costs still needs to be recovered. In other markets, a low price may be needed in order to retain share. In the *cash cow* stage, prices are likely to drift down partly because of a general increase in competition as late entrants to the market appear, and partly because the significance of differentiation is often reduced.

For a *dog*, the pricing choice is straightforward. Either price aggressively in order to build share, or where this is felt either not to be possible or worthwhile, raise prices in order to maximize very-short-term profits as far as possible and then withdraw.

The behaviour of costs over time

It has long been recognized that size and market share are primary determinants of profitability. The principal reason for this is that large firms usually have a lower unit cost base. These lower costs are due partly to *economies of scale* in manufacturing, distribution, purchasing and administration, and partly to the *experience effect*, whereby the costs of most products decline by a fixed percentage each time an organization's experience of producing and selling them doubles.

Of the two, the nature and sources of economies of scale are by far the best known, and it is therefore not our intention to do anything more than draw the reader's attention to its significance and to emphasize that these economies can provide a significant input to the pricing decision.

The less well-known *experience effect*, however, is of equal, and in some instances of even greater, strategic significance. The concept is based on the discovery that costs decline with cumulative production and that this decline is measurable and predictable. The origins of the effect can be traced to the idea of the *learning curve*, which recognizes that the time needed to perform a task decreases as workers become more familiar with it. In the 1960s, however, evidence emerged to suggest that this phenomenon was limited not just to labour costs, but applied also to all total value-added costs, including administration, sales, marketing, distribution, and so on. A series of studies by the Boston Consulting Group then found evidence of what was subsequently labelled the *experience effect* in a wide variety of industries covering high-technology to low-technology products, service to manufacturing, consumer to industrial products, new to mature products, and process to assembly plants. The key feature in each case was, as Abell and Hammond (1979, p. 107) have pointed out:

That each time cumulative volume of a product doubled, total value-added costs . . . fell by a constant and predictable percentage. In addition, the costs of purchased items usually fell as suppliers reduced prices as their costs fell, due also to the experience effect. The relationship between costs and experience was called the experience curve.

Sources of the experience effect

The experience effect has a variety of sources, the seven most significant of which have been identified as:

1 Greater labour efficiency
2 Work specialization and methods improvement
3 New production processes
4 Obtaining better performance from existing equipment
5 Changes to the resource mix
6 Greater product standardization
7 Product redesigns.

While these are the principal sources of experience, they do not emerge naturally but are instead, as Abell and Hammond (1979, p. 113) point out:

. . . the results of substantial, concerted effort and pressure to lower costs. In fact, if left unmanaged, costs rise. Thus experience does not cause reductions but rather provides an

opportunity that alert managements can exploit. Consequently strategies resulting from market planning should explicitly address how cost reductions are to be achieved."

The strategic implications of the experience curve are potentially significant, since by pursuing a strategy to gain experience faster than competitors (this would normally mean high market share), an organization lowers its cost base and has a greater scope for adopting an aggressive and offensive pricing strategy. This is illustrated in Figure 13.4, in which three organizations are competing.

In this example, Firm A has the greatest experience and Firm C the least. Firm A therefore has a choice of strategies open to it. By setting the price at level 1, all three firms make a profit. However, by forcing the price down initially to level 2 and subsequently to level 3, Firm A puts ever greater pressure on its two competitors, and forces firstly Firm C and then Firm B into making a loss. Faced with this, the two firms either make a loss that has to be absorbed or they withdraw from the market.

Although the industry prices are shown in Figure 13.4 to fall steadily, in practice they tend to follow a somewhat different pattern. This is illustrated in Figure 13.5.

The essence of the experience curve is that the real costs of generating products and services decline by 20–30 per cent whenever cumulative experience doubles.

The experience curve is derived not from accounting costs but by dividing the cumulative cash inputs by the cumulative output of end products, and the cost decline is shown by the rate of change in this ratio over time. From this rate of change, managers can see how – and why – their competitive costs are shifting. If estimates can be

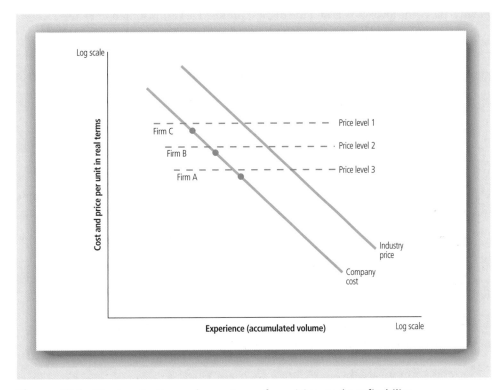

Figure 13.4   The implications of experience for pricing and profitability

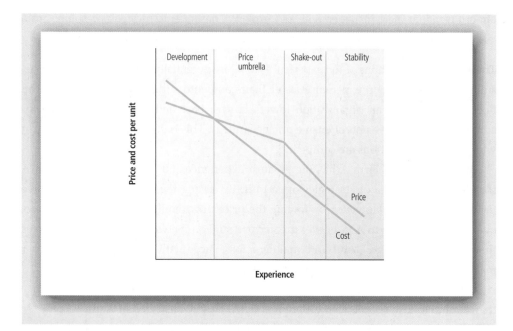

Figure 13.5 The development costs over time (adapted from Boston Consulting Group, 1971, p. 21)

made of competitors' experience curve effects, this should reveal which are the low-cost competitors and which are not, hence which are at risk and from whom.

The main strategic message from the experience curve is that if costs per unit in real terms decrease predictably with cumulative output, then the market leader has the potential to achieve the lowest costs and the highest profits. This is illustrated in Figure 13.4.

Given the empirical existence of the experience curve, it is apparent that the use of cash will be less than directly proportional to a product's rate of growth. Similarly, the generation of cash will be a function of the product's market share, which links back to the BCG product portfolio matrix.

Profitability analysis

Profitability can be defined as the rate at which profit is generated. This may be expressed as profit (i.e. an output measure) per unit of input (e.g. investment, or some measure of effort such as sales calls). Apart from limiting our focus to one output measure (profit) to represent effectiveness, this approach also overlooks such issues as the quality of services rendered, hence its partiality needs to be kept in mind.

As a criterion for strategic decision-making, profitability has been criticized by Robinson et al. (1978) as being insufficient in:

➡ Failing to provide a systematic explanation as to why one business sector has more favourable prospects than another and why one enterprise's position in a particular sector is strong or weak

➡ Not providing enough insight into the underlying dynamics and balance of an enterprise's individual business units and the balance among them.

Other writers (e.g. Chakravarthy, 1986; Day, 1990) have also criticized profitability as a performance criterion due to its remoteness from the actions that actually create value: it represents an outcome rather than a determinant of performance and cannot be managed directly, hence employees are likely to attach limited importance to it on the grounds that their day-to-day actions would appear to have little impact on profitability.

Feder (1965) has defined good marketing performance as existing when investment in each market segment is made to the point where the expenditure of an additional $1 or £1 would produce greater immediate profits if spent elsewhere. This approach reflects the *marginal responsiveness* that is characteristic of marketing experimentation (i.e. where can the greatest response in terms of improved profit be achieved for a marginal increase in effort?). To take an example, if investment of £1 million in advertising within a given market produces sales of £20 million and a gross margin of £10 million, then the *average* response of profit to advertising is 10:1. If an increase in advertising expenditure of £100 000 produced additional sales of £3 million and a gross margin of £1.5 million, then the *marginal* response would be 15:1.

In assessing marketing performance using this approach it would be logical to determine the average response for the existing allocation of marketing effort, segment by segment, which would highlight those areas in which the company has underspent or overspent relative to their profit potential. Improvements can be made by allocating additional effort in accordance with the anticipated marginal response: the greater the anticipated marginal response the more efficient will be the allocation of effort. In considering whether additional effort might be exerted through direct selling, advertising, or improved terms for intermediaries within distribution channels, for example, the need exists to consider the timing factor, since different actions bring results over different time scales.

A less dynamic approach emphasizing profit (rather than profitability) has been suggested by a number of writers. Goodman (1970) and Pyne (1984) both offer modified versions of financial operating statements as bases for assessing marketing performance. These are illustrated in Figures 13.6 and 13.7.

In Figure 13.6, Goodman distinguishes carefully between direct and apportioned costs, which is a more relevant distinction than, say, that between fixed and variable costs if one is concerned to identify the performance of a marketing segment: relevance is given priority over the question of cost behaviour. In principle it makes sense to separate the profit attributable to manufacturing, distribution, and so forth, on a direct cost basis. The operational difficulty in doing this stems from the problems associated with identifying the direct costs of Product 123 within a product range of 10 000 items.

Apart from the quantity of profits as a measure of performance, we might also consider the quality of profits. This depends upon the position of a particular product within its life cycle. It is evident that the profits from products in the growth phase of the cycle are likely to be more valuable than those in the decline phase, since the former have a more promising future.

Pyne's approach is similar in some respects to that of Goodman. For instance, both authors emphasize the need for conventional operating statements (i.e. those having a

	£	£
Proceeds from sales		100.0
Variable cost of goods sold:		
Raw materials	10.0	
Packing	10.0	
Direct labour	5.0	
Variable gross profits (manufacturing contribution margin)		75.0
Other variable expenses:		
Freight	3.0	
Warehousing	2.0	
Spoilage	1.0	
Commissions	5.0	
Discounts	3.0	
Variable profit (distribution contribution margin)		61.0
Direct product costs:		
Advertising	9.0	
Promotion	3.0	
Direct product profits		49.0
Direct division costs:		
Sales management	12.0	
Product management	3.0	
Sales force	2.8	
Sales incentives	1.0	
Market research	0.2	
Division profit contribution (net contribution margin)		30.0
Allocated fixed expense:		
Factory indirect costs	21.0	
Supervision	4.0	
Other indirect costs	19.0	
Corporate administration	5.0	
Net division profit before taxes		(19.0)

Figure 13.6 Marketing-oriented income statement (adapted from Goodman, 1970, p. 38)

legalistic format) to be modified to reflect marketing's circumstances and, in so doing, to highlight direct costs.

In Figure 13.7 we can see that Pyne's approach differs in some significant ways from that of Goodman:

➡ Revenue is analysed more fully
➡ Marketing costs are analysed more fully, with headings that help in distinguishing operating from policy-related costs
➡ The orientation is more radical than that of Goodman in giving a basis for assessing marketing performance in strategic terms.

The amount of profit an enterprise earns is a measure of its effectiveness if that enterprise has a profit objective. (In this sense we can define effectiveness in terms of achieving that which one sought to achieve.) Since profit = revenue (output) − cost (input), it can be seen to be a measure of efficiency also in that it relates outputs to inputs. Thus,

Full revenue sales (at full sale price to end-user)	£
Lost revenue Distributors' mark-ups and margins Mark-downs, offers, deals and allowances Third-party costs of delivery to end-user paid by the purchaser	_____
Sales proceeds Sales taxes and customs duties	£ _____
Net sales proceeds	£

Direct marketing expense
Direct selling – field sales expenses
Sales promotion – merchandising and display
        – samples, point of sales aids
        – cooperative allowances to distributors
Product packaging and branding expense
Product service – installation, warranty and returns
Warehousing – storage, receiving and marking, shipping
Transportation outward – truck, rail, air; cost, insurance,
        freight and delivery	

Direct marketing contribution	_____
Managed marketing expense Order processing Sales and distribution management Brand and product management Marketing direction and administration	£ _____
Marketing policy costs Advertising and publicity Market research and customer relations Product planning, design and development Marketing team training and development	£ _____
Committed marketing costs Inventory carrying – expense and financing Cost of credit – collection and financing Marketing equipment – maintenance, insurance, financing	£ _____
Net marketing contribution	£ _____

Note: where appropriate, lost revenue may be broken down by the marketing channels in use, e.g. wholesalers, stockists, retail chains, stores, direct vending outlets, etc.

Figure 13.7 Marketing-oriented profit statement (source: Pyne, 1984, p. 90)

an organization having revenues of £100 million and costs of £60 million is more efficient than one in the same industry having revenues of £100 million and costs of £70 million, since the former uses less input to produce a given output.

Despite its ability to act as a measure both of effectiveness and efficiency, profit is a less than perfect measure because:

1 It is a monetary measure, and monetary measures do not measure all aspects of either input or output

2 The standards against which profits are judged may themselves be less than perfect

3 At best, profits are a measure of what has happened in the short run, whereas we must also be interested in the long-run consequences of management actions.

Nevertheless, profit measures can still play a distinctly valuable role in the control effort. For example:

➡ A profit measure can provide a simple criterion for evaluating alternatives. (Although it will be necessary to take into account many factors other than profit in making a choice among alternative courses of action, on the face of it, option A is more attractive than option B if A will produce more profit than B.)

➡ A profit measure will permit a quantitative analysis of alternatives to be made in which benefits can be directly compared with costs. (Assuming a market exists for an enterprise's output, these benefits will be measured by the revenue flow from its sale.)

➡ A profit measure can provide a single, broad measure of performance in that it is arrived at after all financial costs and revenues have been taken into account, and it thus subsumes many other aspects of performance.

➡ Profit measures permit the comparison of performance to be made over time for one organization, or comparisons at a point in time to be made for a group of organizational units (e.g. divisions or competing enterprises within an industry), even if they are performing dissimilar functions. This is not possible with other measures, although it may be necessary to standardize accounting practices in measuring profits for this purpose and to ensure that the valuations of assets are made on the same bases.

This all sounds very promising, but we need to bear in mind the limitations of the profit measure. Among these are:

➡ Organizations have multiple objectives and will often forgo profit opportunities in order to avoid conflict over some other objective (or constraint), such as the desired image for the company or some ethical standard.

➡ Social costs and benefits are excluded from corporate profit figures. At best, profit is a measure of an enterprise's success as an economic entity, but this does not measure that enterprise's net contribution (or cost) to society, such as the training programmes it might offer or the pollution it might cause.

➡ As already mentioned, profit measures typically focus on current rather than long-run performance – actions can be taken to improve the former at the expense of the latter (e.g. by cutting advertising, R&D, training and maintenance budgets).

➡ Profit is an inadequate basis for comparing organizations' relative performance or for monitoring one organization's performance over time. The real test is actual versus target profit, but we are really unable to specify this latter figure in any sensible way because it should be based on *profit potential* and a company's profit opportunities are not all identified. It follows that an apparently high profit figure, even when this corresponds with the target figure, may in reality be poor when related to missed opportunities.

➡ Accounting rules are also inadequate, since they often do not permit the recording of economic reality. (Costs should reflect the use of resources, but accounting practice does not allow this to be measured when it values assets on the basis of historical cost rather than their opportunity cost, i.e. current value in an alternative use, which has an impact on the depreciation charge, etc.)

➡ Profit measures are not applicable in certain segments of a business, notably those that incur costs but do not generate revenue (unless a transfer pricing system is introduced to impute revenue flows). Examples of these types of segment are R&D, the legal department, the personnel department and the accounting department.

Creating shareholder value

Perhaps the majority of evaluative criteria advocated in the literature and used in practice focus on the maximization of profit, profitability or sales rather than on the return to shareholders (see, for example, McGuire et al., 1986; Chakravarthy, 1986). The key idea behind *creating shareholder value* (e.g. Rappaport, 1986; Wenner and LeBer, 1989; Reimann, 1989) is that investors only willingly invest in an enterprise when they think that the managers of that enterprise will be able to secure a better return on their funds than they could on their own without additional risk. In contrast to ROI and other short-term measures, the creation of shareholder value emphasizes the market's assessment of the long-term health and wealth of the enterprise. Evidence exists to indicate that movements in an enterprise's share price are due (at least in part) to the impact of management's decisions on the long-term value of the enterprise. This is covered by the *efficient markets hypothesis*, which suggests that financial markets are adept at capturing information and reflecting the significance of that information in changes in share prices. It follows that decision-makers in enterprises having listed shares (which only applies to some 2200 of more than 1 million companies incorporated in the UK) should pay due attention to the impacts of their decisions on share prices.

Day and Fahey (1988) have sought to demonstrate how a value-based approach can be applied to the evaluation of marketing strategies. The starting point is the recognition that value is only created when the financial benefits of a strategic activity exceed its costs. Since strategic activities are carried out over time – often involving several years – it is necessary to apply discounting methods to the relevant cash inflows and outflows. This is equivalent to the long-established practice of applying discounting techniques to new investments in plant and equipment: the extension of the practice to marketing strategies involves dealing with more intangible elements and embracing a series of issues rather than simply the investment in a single item of plant. We will return to this approach in Chapter 16.

13.5 Non-financial criteria

Growth

The importance of growth as a criterion of choice stems from the following:

1 Its relationship to gaining market share. Consider, for example, the sad case of the motorcycle industry in Britain. During the 1960s the level of output of British motorcycles was fairly constant (at 80 000 units per annum) whereas the exports from Japan increased from 60 000 in 1960 to 2.5 million in 1973, with their production volumes tripling over this period. The British manufacturers failed to recognize the strategic importance of market share *on a worldwide basis* for long-term profitability related to the experience curve effect. While UK production during the 1960s ensured that manufacturing facilities were being adequately employed, the significant strategic issue was that Japanese manufacturers' costs were falling whereas those of British manufacturers were not, hence the collapse of the UK motorcycle industry in the early 1970s.

2 The opportunities it provides for investment – as funds are generated they can be reinvested to produce a compound return.

Growth has a significant relevance to an enterprise's relative competitive position. This is most readily measured by relative market share, which is defined as the enterprise's market share divided by that of its largest competitor. Since the stronger the relative competitive position the higher the margins should be (due to the effect of the experience curve), this measure has a strategic importance.

The need for growth is shown in Figure 13.8, in which a gap can be discerned between the enterprise's present position and its preferred future position. (Figure 13.8 is a variation on Figure 7.13.) By continuing with current activities on the same scale, the level of profits will decline (e.g. due to increasing competition, product obsolescence, etc.). By expanding in either existing markets (i.e. larger market share) or by entering new markets with existing products, or by improving existing

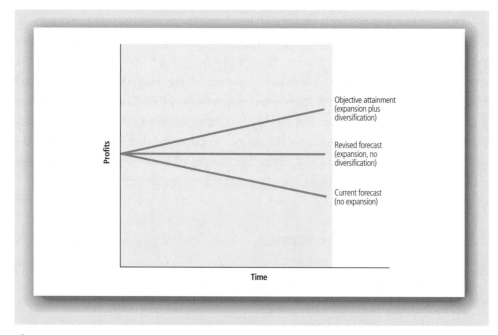

Figure 13.8   Gap analysis

products, it may be possible to maintain the level of profits into the future. (Note: these alternatives employ known technology and, in two out of three cases, known markets.)

By expanding the scale of activity within existing markets, improving existing products *and* diversifying into new markets with new products, a much higher level of profit may result, thereby meeting the desired profit target. The choice of strategy, therefore, will be that by which the gaps in Figure 13.8 might be closed.

Growth will usually involve a move outside the enterprise's existing range of activities. Alternative paths for expansion are shown in Figure 7.10.

➡ *Market penetration* entails an increasing share of existing markets with existing products – this would involve more aggressive promotion and distribution
➡ *Market extension* results from taking existing products into new markets
➡ *Product development* requires that new products be created to replace existing products in present markets
➡ *Diversification* involves the development (or acquisition) of new products for new markets.

The risk levels associated with these strategies tend to increase in the sequence in which they are listed above, so a change in product technology is likely to be riskier than a change in target markets, and a change in markets and products will be riskier than a change in only one of these (see Figures 7.14 and 7.15).

Sustainable competitive advantage (see also Chapter 10)

Wensley (1981), Cravens (1988), and Day and Wensley (1988) argue that the most meaningful guidance for strategic decision-makers is to be found in returning to basics and focusing on the search for *sustainable competitive advantage*. This focus implies that strategic alternatives should be evaluated in terms of the organization's strengths and weaknesses. Sustainable competitive advantage will be found when opportunities are taken to build on an enterprise's unique capabilities. These capabilities reflect the adequacy of the match between the current core activities of an enterprise and the strategic alternatives under consideration. Thus, for example, if we consider Ansoff's growth matrix (see Figure 7.10), an enterprise's greatest competitive advantage is likely to be found in product–market situations that are similar to those of its core activities (i.e. in cell 1).

A clear example is that of Gillette. Razors for men were followed by shaving cream for men and razors for women. Razors – whether for men or women – can be manufactured using the same facilities and the marketing has similarities whether it is razors or shaving cream one is considering. A common brand name helps develop a consumer franchise. The distribution system in use for razors can also be used for shaving cream – the products are bought in the same outlets.

At first sight it may appear odd that Gillette ventured into disposable lighters, since they do not fit synergistically with the marketing of razors, etc. However, Gillette's special capabilities include:

➡ Mass production of low-cost products
➡ Utilization of precision plastic moulded parts
➡ Use of mass distribution
➡ Marketing of low-cost, disposable consumer products under the Gillette brand name.

The manufacturing and marketing capabilities ensured Gillette secured competitive advantage in disposable lighters even if the brand name itself was not particularly useful.

Competitive position

In considering financial criteria it is usually found that a rather introspective approach is adopted (i.e. *this* enterprise's profit or *this* enterprise's cash flow). There is a need to adopt a more strategic perspective in dealing with an enterprise's competitive position.

The strategic dimension emerges when the performance of the business in question is compared with that of its competitors. Viewing the business within its competitive context is possible within the framework suggested by Figure 13.9.

The details from Figure 13.7 would be entered in the rows of Figure 13.9 under the given headings.

A variation on this theme, focusing on the notion of competitive position, has been developed by Simmonds (1986). This is covered in some detail in the following discussion.

The key notion here is that of an enterprise's position *relative to* competitors' positions. In so far as strategy is concerned with competitive position, it has been largely ignored by management accountants, but in a number of papers Simmonds (1981, 1982, 1985, 1986) has proposed how this failing might be overcome. A basic plank in

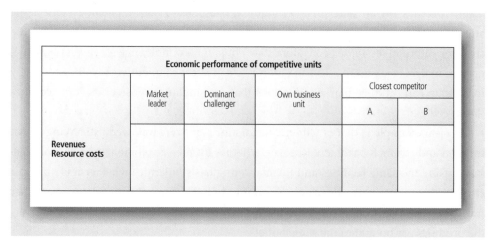

Figure 13.9 Strategic comparisons (adapted from Pyne, 1984, p. 90)

his argument is the preoccupation that accountants have with the recording, analysing and presentation of cost data relating to existing activities. This 'data orientation' begs some fundamental questions, such as why the data is being collected in the first place. An alternative and preferable approach is one of 'information orientation', which starts with the diagnosis of problems, leading to the structuring of decisions, and thence to the specification of information that will help in making appropriate decisions. The focus shifts from the analysis of costs per se to the value of information.

Managers wishing to make decisions that will safeguard their organization's strategic position must know by whom, by how much, and why they are gaining or being beaten. In other words, strategic indicators of performance are required. Conventional measures, such as profit, will not suffice.

Let us take comparative costs as a starting point. It is intuitively the case that organizations having a cost advantage (i.e. lower unit cost for a product of comparable specification) are strong and those having a cost disadvantage are weak. If we relate this to the idea of the experience curve (which was introduced above), it will be appreciated that, if costs can be made to decline predictably with cumulative output, then the enterprise that has produced most should have the lowest unit cost and therefore the highest profits.

Apart from cost, an enterprise may seek to gain strategic advantage via its pricing policy. In this setting, the management accountant can attempt to assess each major competitor's cost structure and relate this to their prices, taking care to eliminate the effects of inflation from the figures being used. Applying cost–volume–profit analysis to one's competitors is likely to be more fruitful than simply applying it internally. As Simmonds (1982, p. 207) states:

" Clearly, competitor reactions can substantially influence the outcome of a price move. Moreover, likely reactions may not be self-evident when each competitor faces a different cost–volume–profit situation. Competitors may not follow a price lead nor even march in perfect step as they each act to defend or build their own positions. For an adequate assessment of the likelihood of competitor price reactions, then, some calculation is needed of the impact of possible price moves on the performance of individual competitors. Such an assessment in turn requires an accounting approach that can depict both competitor cost–volume–profit situations and their financial resources. *"*

After dealing with costs and prices, the next important (and related) variable to consider is volume – especially market share. By monitoring movements in market share, an enterprise can see whether it is gaining or losing position, and an examination of relative market shares will indicate the strength of different competitors. Reporting market share details along with financial details can help in making managerial accounting reports more strategically relevant.

The significance of competitive position has been highlighted by Simmonds (1986) as being the basic determinant of future profits and of the business's value. Moreover, since competitive position can change over time, so can profits and value, but it should not be assumed that an improvement in competitive position will be associated with an improvement in short-run profits. In fact, the opposite is likely to be the case due to the need to incur costs in building up a competitive position, which has the effect of depressing current profits in favour of future profits. This raises the question as to whether competitive position can be measured in accounting terms – not just for a given business, but also for its main competitors, and not just at a point in time, but also over time. Simmonds has attempted to do this by applying strategic management accounting. He makes it clear, however, that it is not possible to express competitive position as a single figure. Instead, it is possible to offer an array of indicators relating to the competitive situation. From these indicators managers can gain insights into the competitive position of a business, which will help them in judging whether or not things are moving in their favour.

Simmonds recommends that competitive data be built up for the market leader, close competitors and laggards rather than for all competitors. The following data (derived from that given in Simmonds (1986) and used with permission) might most usefully be developed.

1 Sales and market share

The sales revenue of each firm relative to the total market is a cornerstone, and changes in market share should be closely monitored. A decrease in market share suggests a loss of competitive position, with unfortunate implications for future profits. Conversely, an increase in market share suggests an improved competitive position, with the prospect of improved future profits. By adding market share details to management accounting reports, managers are able to make much more sense of what is happening.

Figure 13.10 gives sales and market share data for Firm A and the total market for Product X. We can see from Figure 13.10 that, despite an increase in sales revenue of 20 per cent for Firm A, the market share has slipped from 19 to 16 per cent. This is

	Firm A	Total market
Sales (£'000)		
Last year	1,000	5,200
This year	1,200	7,500
% change	+20	+44
Market share (%)		
Last year	19	100
This year	16	100

Figure 13.10 Sales and market share data, Product X

	Sales (£'000s)	Market share (%)	Relative market share
Total market:			
Last year	5,200		
This year	7,500		
Firm A:			
Last year	1,000	19	
This year	1,200	16	
Leading competitor:			
Last year	2,200	42	2.20
This year	3,600	48	3.00
Close competitor:			
Last year	1,200	23	1.20
This year	2,200	27	1.67

Figure 13.11 Relative market shares

explained by the growth in the total market of 44 per cent. It seems probable that the firm's failure to keep pace with the overall market growth will be reflected in a poorer competitive position: not only might competitors have gained market share at the firm's expense, but this is likely to be accompanied by cost advantages – hence improved profits. Some details are given in Figure 13.11.

Relative market share is calculated by dividing each competitor's market share by that of one's own firm, and it indicates any gains or losses. As Figure 13.11 makes clear, Firm A has slipped relative to both the market leader and its closest competitor. The leader's market share has increased to three times that of Firm A, and it will almost certainly have lowered its unit costs.

2 Profits and return on sales

If a competitor has a higher return on sales than Firm A it may well reduce price, or improve quality, or increase its marketing efforts in order to improve its competitive position further.

The data in Figure 13.12 shows sales, market share, relative market share and profit (before tax but after interest) over the last three years for all firms supplying Product X. Over that period the market leader's profit has quadrupled, the closest competitor's has more than doubled, and Firm A's has not quite doubled. In absolute terms, the market leader's profit in Year 3 is almost five times that of Firm A, giving a huge source of funds for expansion, R&D, etc., while in relative terms the leader's return on sales of 22.2 per cent in Year 3 is well ahead of any other competitor.

Firm A's task seems to be to reinforce its competitive position relative to both laggard firms on the one hand, and to develop a defence against the strong competitors on the other.

	Sales (£'000s)	Market share (%)	Relative market share	Profit (£'000s)	(%)
Firm A:					
Year 1	700	17.5		90	12.8
Year 2	1,000	19.2		130	13.0
Year 3	1,200	16.0		170	14.2
Leading competitor:					
Year 1	1,400	35.0	2.0	200	14.3
Year 2	2,200	42.3	2.2	400	18.2
Year 3	3,600	48.0	3.0	800	22.2
Close competitor:					
Year 1	1,000	25.0	1.4	120	12.0
Year 2	1,200	23.1	1.2	170	14.2
Year 3	2,000	26.6	1.7	260	13.0
Laggard 1:					
Year 1	500	12.5	0.71	55	11.0
Year 2	500	9.6	0.50	60	12.0
Year 3	500	6.7	0.42	50	10.0
Laggard 2:					
Year 1	400	10.0	0.57	40	10.0
Year 2	300	5.8	0.30	20	6.7
Year 3	200	2.7	0.17	5	2.5
Total market:					
Year 1	4,000	100.0		505	12.6
Year 2	5,200	100.0		780	15.0
Year 3	7,500	100.0		1,285	17.1

Figure 13.12 Sales, market shares and profits for all suppliers of Product X

3 Volume and unit cost

Details of volume and costs are given in Figure 13.13. Changes in unit costs reveal each firm's relative efficiency: the further a competitor's relative cost falls below unity, the more of a threat this becomes, and vice versa. (Costs are calculated by subtracting profit from sales revenue, and unit costs are obtained by dividing the costs by volume, year by year.)

The market leader has a cost advantage in Year 3 of 69p per unit relative to Firm A, whereas Laggard 2 has a cost disadvantage relative to Firm A of 73p per unit. Perhaps more significant than these figures are those that compare volume and cost changes. Thus, for example, Firm A's two main competitors both increased volume between Years 2 and 3 by more than 70 per cent, yet the close competitor's cost per unit only fell by 3 per cent or so while the market leader's cost per unit fell by more than 9 per cent. Is the explanation to be found in the close competitor's investment in competitive position – such as in R&D, marketing programmes or new plant?

4 Unit prices

Figure 13.14 shows the unit prices charged for Product X by each competitor over the last three years, along with costs and the profits and market shares that

	Volume in units (000s)	Increase (%)	Cost (£'000s)	Cost per unit (£)	Relative cost per unit
Firm A:					
Year 1	100		610	6.10	
Year 2	156	56	870	5.58	
Year 3	192	23	1,030	5.36	
Leading competitor:					
Year 1	200		1,200	6.00	0.98
Year 2	350	75	1,800	5.14	0.92
Year 3	600	71	2,800	4.67	0.87
Close competitor:					
Year 1	140		880	6.29	1.03
Year 2	190	36	1,030	5.42	0.97
Year 3	330	74	1,740	5.27	0.98
Laggard 1:					
Year 1	70		445	6.36	1.04
Year 2	75	7	440	5.86	1.05
Year 3	80	7	450	5.62	1.05
Laggard 2:					
Year 1	56		360	6.42	1.05
Year 2	45	(20)	280	6.22	1.16
Year 3	32	(29)	195	6.09	1.14
Total:					
Year 1	566				
Year 2	816	44			
Year 3	1,234	51			

Figure 13.13 Volume, costs and unit costs

have resulted. (Unit prices are simply calculated by dividing sales revenue by units sold.)

The pattern of price changes reflects the use of price as a competitive variable, and this can be related to cost and market share data to see how competitive positions are changing. For example, the market leader has reduced the price by more than any other firm, but its price reductions have not been as great as its cost reductions, hence profit per unit has increased each year – as has the number of units. This places that firm in a very strong competitive position.

Patterns of price, cost, profit and volume change for Firm A and its closest competitor are less clear, but for the laggards the picture of a downward spiral is clear enough.

5 Cash flow, liquidity and resource availability

Competitive gains and losses will arise over longer periods than the financial year, and the capacity of a competitor to continue in the fray is a function of more than simply profit or market share at a particular point in time. A firm's ability to continue to compete will also depend on its liquidity position and the availability of other resources

	Average price per unit (£)	Average cost per unit (£)	Profit per unit (£)	Market share (%)
Firm A:				
Year 1	7.00	6.10	0.90	17.5
Year 2	6.41	5.58	0.83	19.2
Year 3	6.25	5.36	0.89	16.0
Leading competitor:				
Year 1	7.00	6.00	1.00	35.0
Year 2	6.29	5.14	1.15	42.3
Year 3	6.00	4.67	1.33	48.0
Close competitor:				
Year 1	7.14	6.29	0.85	25.0
Year 2	6.31	5.42	0.89	23.1
Year 3	6.06	5.27	0.79	26.6
Laggard 1:				
Year 1	7.14	6.36	0.78	12.5
Year 2	6.66	5.86	0.80	9.6
Year 3	6.25	5.62	0.63	6.7
Laggard 2:				
Year 1	7.14	6.42	0.72	10.0
Year 2	6.66	6.22	0.44	5.8
Year 3	6.25	6.09	0.16	2.7

Figure 13.14 Unit prices, profits and market shares

over time. For example, a firm with poor cash flow, a high level of debt and out-of-date production facilities is not likely to be able to compete for long.

6 The future

Having analysed the relative positions of each firm supplying Product X over the past three years, the real challenge comes in attempting to make the next move.

The management of Firm A will be able to see that the market leader is controlling the competitive situation with the highest volume and profits, plus the lowest unit costs and price. If that firm reduced its price by, say, 10 per cent, it would force the laggards out of the market and limit the close competitor's profit (assuming it followed suit and reduced its own price). Firm A needs to reduce its costs and strengthen its position against its two main competitors while there is scope for growth in the overall market for Product X.

Using Figures 13.11–13.14 as a basis, various possibilities can be projected for the future, each building on explicit assumptions regarding:

➡ Future market demand
➡ Likely competitive actions
➡ Likely competitive reactions
➡ Competitors' liquidity and solvency.

This takes us a long way from conventional single-entity, single-period management accounting, yet the adaptations that need to be made are not so difficult to comprehend – but the benefits from gaining a clearer picture of one's competitive position and how this is changing should be enormous. Strategic management accounting can help realize these benefits.

After seeing the appeal of the approaches suggested by Pyne and Simmonds, one might wonder how the necessary competitive information might be gathered. Brock (1984), Pyne (1985), Beerel (1986), Jones (1988), Robert (1990) and others offer a variety of ways forward. We will return to this theme in Chapter 18.

Consumer franchise

It has been argued by Mehotra (1984) that market share and profit measures are unsatisfactory for gauging efficiency since they ignore the purpose of marketing, which he sees as being the identification of, and meeting, the needs and wants of end-users. His proposed measure is *consumer franchise*, which he has developed from an approach within General Electric. The basis of this approach is to be found in a continuum, with consumers being arrayed along it in accordance with the probability of their buying a particular brand. An enterprise's core consumer franchise for its brand is represented by consumers having a consistently high probability of buying that brand. Those consumers with a low probability of buying that brand are likely to be either committed to another brand or uncommitted to any brand. It is apparent, therefore, that a brand's sales can be represented by the following equation:

$$\text{Sales} = (P_1 \times N_1) + (P_2 \times N_2)$$

where:

P_1 is probability of buying if committed;
N_1 is number of committed buyers;
P_2 is probability of buying if uncommitted;
N_2 is number of uncommitted buyers.

The level of sales can be increased by increasing the probability of purchasing by a given consumer or by increasing the proportion of high-probability buyers, i.e. the consumer franchise. To achieve the former it is likely that sales promotion methods will be used, whereas advertising and product improvements are more likely for the latter. It can be argued that the use of sales promotions (as inputs) is likely to influence market share, but this may only be temporary. On the other hand, improvements in the consumer franchise are more likely to be lasting, a more desirable output. There is always a risk that some approaches to increasing market share (or sales or profit) may only achieve this in the short term and thereafter actually erode the consumer franchise – this would be reflected in a temporary improvement in efficiency but a reduction in effectiveness. In contrast, a brand's consumer franchise might be enhanced by a more substantive and coordinated improvement in the market offering.

13.6 Multiple criteria

Let us broaden our perspective and consider criteria that go beyond the single-criterion approach we have been focusing on so far in this chapter. The use of a single criterion is inadequate because:

➡ Organizations behave ineffectively from some points of view if a single criterion is used.
➡ Organizations fulfil multiple functions and have multiple goals, some of which may be in conflict. It would be inappropriate to assess strategies purely on the basis of any one criterion.

The difficulty, as will be apparent, lies in identifying those multiple criteria that are necessary and sufficient to ensure corporate well-being and survival. One way is via the application of *Pareto's law*.

Pareto's law (or the 80/20 rule) is widely thought to apply to a range of situations in which most of the behaviour or value of one factor is deemed to depend on only a little of another factor. For example, it is often asserted that 80 per cent of inventory movements within an organization are attributable to 20 per cent of items stocked, 80 per cent of sales volume comes from 20 per cent of customers, or 80 per cent of profits are derived from 20 per cent of product lines. The main point here, of course, is that one can effectively control an inventory if one can focus attention on the critical 20 per cent of active items, or one can control the level of sales if the key customers are properly serviced. This can be greatly beneficial both in terms of cost savings (through eliminating unnecessary control effort on the 'insignificant' 80 per cent of items that only make up 20 per cent of stock issues) and in terms of improved organizational effectiveness (due to better control of the key elements).

The application of Pareto's law is known by a number of different names. Perhaps the most frequently encountered are: key variables, critical success factors (CSFs) and key result areas.

To illustrate the idea further we can consider a generalized example, and then a number of specific industry examples (see Rockart, 1979). Figure 13.15 identifies, for each main sphere of activity, the factors that are likely to be of some major significance to corporate performance. Each factor has financial implications, and if they can be controlled it is probable that the overall company can be controlled.

Within specific industries there is likely to be considerable variation in key variables, as Figure 13.16 illustrates. Johnson (1967), for example, looks in more detail at this key question.

The variables that are critical are those that are causally related to desired outcomes. In seeking to measure the values of variables, great care must be taken to avoid the trap of giving attention to variables that are amenable to measurement and overlooking more important variables that are not amenable to measurement (e.g. quantities are more readily measured than qualities, but it does not follow that the latter are less important than the former). Similarly, variables that reflect a short-run focus, such as reported profit or EPS (earnings per share), should not be allowed to dominate the

Sphere of activity	Critical factors
Environment	Economic – interest rates
	inflation rates
	concentration
	Political stability
Marketing	Sales volume
	Market share
	Gross margins
Production	Capacity utilization
	Quality standards
Logistics	Capacity utilization
	Level of service
Asset management	Return on investment
	Accounts receivable balance

Figure 13.15 A general example of key variables

measurement process when variables with a longer-run focus, such as competitive position, are being ignored in that process.

In a study of more than 250 US organizations, Steiner (1969) sought to determine the factors most likely to influence future success. He did this by asking the senior managers in the chosen companies to rank eighty-five factors. The top ten are shown below:

1 Attract and maintain high-quality top management
2 Develop future managers for domestic operations
3 Motivate sufficient managerial drive for profits

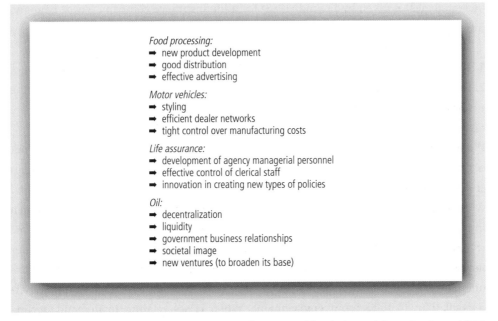

Food processing:
➡ new product development
➡ good distribution
➡ effective advertising

Motor vehicles:
➡ styling
➡ efficient dealer networks
➡ tight control over manufacturing costs

Life assurance:
➡ development of agency managerial personnel
➡ effective control of clerical staff
➡ innovation in creating new types of policies

Oil:
➡ decentralization
➡ liquidity
➡ government business relationships
➡ societal image
➡ new ventures (to broaden its base)

Figure 13.16 Specific industry examples of key variables (adapted from Rockart, 1979)

4 Assure better judgement, creativity and imagination in decision-making at top management levels

5 Perceive new needs and opportunities for products

6 Develop a better long-range planning programme

7 Improve service to customers

8 Provide a competitive return to shareholders

9 Maximize the value of shareholders' investment

10 Develop a better willingness to take risks with commensurate returns in what appear to be excellent new business opportunities in order to achieve growth objectives.

A variety of alternative approaches have been put forward for identifying key variables or critical success factors (see, for example, Leidecker and Bruno, 1984; Hitt and Ireland, 1985; Jenster, 1987; Freund, 1988; De Vasconcellos and Hambrick, 1989; Dace, 1990). Such approaches usually rely on the views of managers and other experts within the particular industries. It is inherent in these approaches that their validity is questionable and that they do not constitute a clear basis for action. Is it helpful in the food processing industry, from the viewpoint of formulating action plans, to know that NPD, good distribution and effective advertising are the prescribed critical success factors (as in Figure 13.16)? However plausible the CSFs might be, it is difficult to know how they will impact upon an enterprise's competitive position.

An alternative approach that Day and Wensley (1988) argue gives more defensible insights is one that relates current *sources* of advantage to the achievement of advantageous competitive *positions* and hence superior *performance*. By relating causes (i.e. sources) to effects (i.e. performance), this approach emphasizes linkages in a more explicit way (see Figure 13.17).

An example of operational linkages between CSFs and actions (in the form of specified strategies) is given by Freund (1988) for a life insurance company. These emerged from a process in which:

1 Top management identified what it considered were the company's CSFs

2 Departmental managers then identified financial strategies that would allow the CSFs to be achieved.

While CSFs can serve as criteria for choosing among competing strategies, they are not equivalent to performance indicators. Figure 13.18 shows CSFs, a selection of strategies and some performance indicators. The performance indicators are designed to show when – and by how much – strategies are not being achieved once they have been implemented.

In a study of US companies, D'Aveni and MacMillan (1991) found that, under normal circumstances, managers in successful enterprises pay equal attention to their internal and external environments, but pay more attention to their output environment than to their input environment. When crises relating to demand decline arise, they focus their attention on the critical aspects of their external environments.

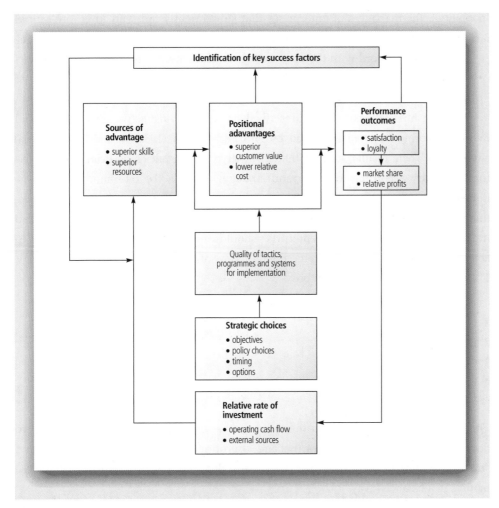

Figure 13.17 Comparing competitors (source: Day and Wensley, 1988, p. 13)

Critical success factor	Strategies	Performance indicators
Ability to achieve critical mass volumes through existing brokers and agents	➡ Develop closer ties with agents ➡ Telemarket to brokers ➡ Realign agents' compensation	➡ Policies in force ➡ New business written ➡ Per cent of business with existing brokers
Be able to introduce new products within six months of industry leaders	➡ Underwrite strategic joint ventures ➡ Copy leader's products ➡ Improve underwriting skills	➡ Elapsed time to introduce ➡ Per cent of products introduced within six months ➡ Per cent underwriters having additional certification
Be able to manage product and product line profitability	➡ Segment investment portfolio ➡ Improve cost accounting ➡ Closely manage loss ratio	➡ Return on portfolio segments ➡ Actual product cost/revenue versus plan ➡ Loss ratio relative to competitors

Figure 13.18 Critical success factors in action (adapted from Freund, 1988, pp. 22–3)

In contrast, the managers of enterprises that subsequently fail tend to ignore output factors during crises and pay more attention to their input and internal environments.

These results accord with the view that successful enterprises attend to critical success factors that relate to their output environments (e.g. customers' needs and demand growth).

Relationships between CSFs (described as *corporate distinctive competencies*) and overall performance were examined by Hitt and Ireland (1985) in 185 US industrial enterprises. Their results suggest that distinctive competencies associated with performance vary according to the 'grand strategy' used on the one hand, and on the industry in which the enterprise is based on the other. A grand strategy refers to a predominant strategy covering the whole enterprise, and the view put forward by Hitt and Ireland for testing was that an enterprise should develop distinctive competencies in activities that are important from the point of view of implementing the grand strategy. They distinguish four industry types:

1 Consumer durables
2 Consumer non-durables
3 Capital goods
4 Producer goods (e.g. raw materials).

The message that emerges from this work is that managers should be concerned to develop distinctive competencies that are appropriate for implementing their grand strategies within the context of their particular industries. It is important to match these matters in a balanced way.

A particular approach to balance that has been enthusiastically received in recent years is Kaplan and Norton's *balanced scorecard framework* (1992, 1993), which 'provides executives with a comprehensive framework that translates a company's strategic objectives into a coherent set of performance measures, thereby providing a powerful tool for decision-making'.

Within their framework, Kaplan and Norton specify four sets of goals and associated performance measures that focus attention on the following basic questions:

1 How do customers see us? (i.e. customer perspective)
2 At what must we excel? (i.e. internal business perspective)
3 Can we continue to improve and create value? (i.e. innovation and learning perspective)
4 How do we look to our shareholders? (i.e. financial perspective).

These elements of the scorecard are illustrated in Figure 13.19, from which it will be apparent that this approach has the potential to overcome two of the most pervasive problems associated with, on the one hand, univariate performance measures and, on the other, linking goals and measures of performance.

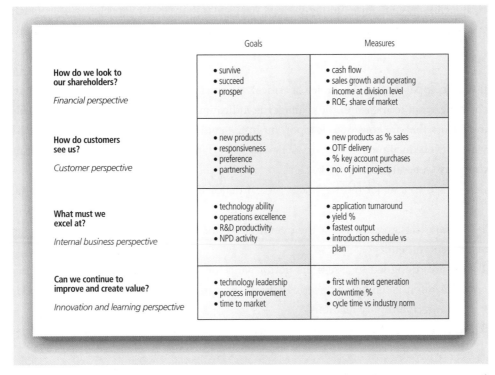

Figure 13.19 The balanced scorecard (adapted from Kaplan and Norton, 1992, p. 76)

To implement the balanced scorecard approach it is necessary that senior managers address four further questions regarding:

1 Their vision of the future
2 The ways in which they will be seen to differ in shareholders' perceptions, customers' perceptions, internal management activities, and their ability to innovate and grow if their vision succeeds
3 The specification of CSFs from financial, customer, internal and innovating perspectives
4 The critical measurements that should be used for each of the four goal and performance areas shown in Figure 13.19.

As Murray and O'Driscoll (1996, p. 386) point out, the balanced scorecard framework improves on traditional approaches in some significant ways. For example:

➡ It is based on the company's strategic objectives and competitive demands; by demanding that managers select a small number of critical indicators, it promotes greater focus on strategic vision
➡ By including financial and non-financial measures, it provides a basis for managing both current and future success
➡ It balances external and internal goals, and measures and reveals trade-offs that managers should or should not make

➡ It facilitates coherence among various strategic initiatives and special projects (such as re-engineering, total quality and empowerment initiatives) by providing a goal-related context and an approach to integrated measurement.

It will be apparent that the choice of critical variables is neither neutral nor objective: in choosing what to measure, the manager is indicating his or her personal view regarding factors that are considered important in the control process. This can be illustrated via the well-documented case (e.g. Lewis, 1955; Greenwood, 1974) of the American company General Electric (GE).

GE set up a major measurement project that had three principal component parts:

1 Measures designed to assess the overall performance of a department or division as an economic entity

2 Measures designed to assess the performance of the functional activities within the organization (such as engineering, production, marketing, finance, employee relations and community relations)

3 Measures designed to assess the performance of departmental or divisional managers.

The overall measurement project was based on the following principles:

➡ Measures should be designed to provide factual inputs to support judgements in appraising the performance of departments or divisions

➡ Measures should be designed so as to provide performance indicators relating both to short-run and long-run goals

➡ A minimum number of measures should be used at each level within an organization.

In order to determine whether or not a variable qualified as a key success factor (which would require it to be measured), the following question was asked: 'Will continued failure in this area prevent the attainment of management's responsibility for advancing General Electric as a leader in a strong, competitive economy, even though results in all other key result areas are good?' A range of eight key success factors emerged from this project (see Figure 13.20).

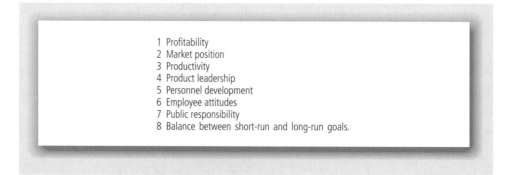

1 Profitability
2 Market position
3 Productivity
4 Product leadership
5 Personnel development
6 Employee attitudes
7 Public responsibility
8 Balance between short-run and long-run goals.

Figure 13.20   General Electric's key results areas

While these eight factors might seem to be generally applicable, it is their precise definition within the context of a particular company's activities that determines how critical they are. This highlights a fundamental aspect of designing any control system: it must be highly 'situational' if it is to be effective. In other words, it must be tailored to the specific characteristics of the situation, which means *this* company's objectives, *this* company's operations, *this* company's managers and *this* company's environment.

The General Electric approach seeks to balance two conflicting tendencies: on the one hand, the diffusion of effort over multiple goals and the failure to perform as well as might be expected in any one area; and on the other hand, the tendency to emphasize one particular goal with the result that other goals are not attained.

The most common tendency in commercial enterprises is to focus on the short-run maximization of net profit (or sales) without considering the damage that this might do to the long-run position (e.g. by postponing repairs or maintenance work; by cutting back on advertising or on research, training or quality control expenditure; by deferring capital investment outlays; or through exhortations to employees to increase productivity). Short-term 'gains' achieved in this way tend to be illusory, because the subsequent need to make up lost ground (e.g. via heavier advertising or training in later periods) more than outweighs short-term gains.

Saunders (1987b) has observed that an enterprise only has two basic ways of increasing wealth: it can do this by innovating to increase its volume or by seeking to improve its productivity via production of the same output but at lower cost. It is much simpler to look inwards and seek to cut costs rather than to look outwards and seek to innovate, compete more effectively or increase margins through better marketing planning. Cost cutting is referred to by many Europeans as 'a British solution', since it is easy to do in the short term but with unfortunate long-term consequences (as suggested in the previous paragraph). Figure 13.21 summarizes the alternative approaches to improving long-run returns.

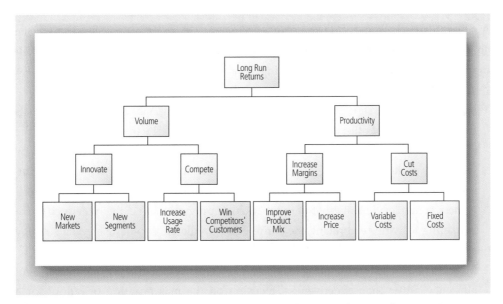

Figure 13.21 Strategic alternatives (source: Saunders, 1987b, p. 174)

Success			
OBJECTIVES	Short-Term Profit	Medium-Term Profit	Innovation
FOCUS	Productivity	Beat Competition	New Product (Market)
TARGET MARKET	Own Customers	Competitors' Customers	New Customers
TARGET COMPETITION	Own Staff	Competition	The Unknown
DIFFERENTIAL ADVANTAGE	Cost Control	Segmentation	Differentiation
MIX	Price	Promotion/Place	Product
ORGANIZATION	Financial	Marketing	Entrepreneurial

Figure 13.22   Routes to success (source: Saunders, 1987b, p. 176)

As is apparent from Figure 13.22, a preoccupation with short-term profit reflects an introspective concern with aspects of productivity. A longer-term perspective requires a shift of focus from internal productivity improvement to external factors – such as beating the competition and innovating (by developing new markets, new products or both).

To the extent that effectiveness is a multifaceted criterion, we must avoid the trap of focusing too sharply on one contributing factor. It would be a mistake to assume that effectiveness would be assured simply through selecting and training the right people. Given our definition of effectiveness in Chapter 1, effectiveness may be assessed in terms of a system's capacity:

1 To survive, adapt, maintain itself and grow – regardless of the functions it fulfils
2 To achieve the aims in point 1 above through its bargaining position with its environment in relation to the acquisition of resources.

Against this background of criteria for effectiveness at an enterprise level, it can be argued that any attempt to deal with the effectiveness of individual elements of marketing, such as advertising or personal selling, is problematic for two major reasons:

1 It is not possible to separate the impact of, say, advertising on the attainment of goals from the impacts of other elements of the marketing mix. The interdependence of the elements of the mix ensures that the selling task is influenced by advertising and by the nature of the product, the price and the channel decisions, all on a *mutatis mutandis* basis. It would not be sensible, therefore, to attempt to consider marketing effectiveness at any level below that of the marketing programme (i.e. the integrated set of marketing activities embracing the entire mix formulated to pursue a given strategy directed at a particular segment).
2 Most criterion measures relating to individual elements of marketing are measures of efficiency rather than effectiveness, focusing on the maximization of output for a given input or the minimization of input to achieve a given level of output. One

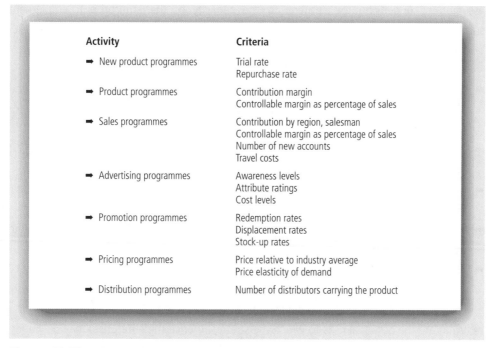

Activity	Criteria
➡ New product programmes	Trial rate Repurchase rate
➡ Product programmes	Contribution margin Controllable margin as percentage of sales
➡ Sales programmes	Contribution by region, salesman Controllable margin as percentage of sales Number of new accounts Travel costs
➡ Advertising programmes	Awareness levels Attribute ratings Cost levels
➡ Promotion programmes	Redemption rates Displacement rates Stock-up rates
➡ Pricing programmes	Price relative to industry average Price elasticity of demand
➡ Distribution programmes	Number of distributors carrying the product

Figure 13.23   Criteria for functional activities

exception to this is the use of sales quotas, which represent output measures, performance being assessed by reviewing how close each salesperson came to achieving his or her quota. We can see that this is a measure of effectiveness, albeit on a small scale relative to the overall scheme of things.

With these caveats in mind it is possible to identify criteria that are regularly applied in choosing among alternative plans for specific elements of the mix (see, for example, Guiltinan and Paul, 1988, pp. 396–8; McNamee, 1988, pp. 131 and 143). Examples are given in Figure 13.23.

13.7 Summary

In this chapter we have looked at a range of possible criteria for assessing marketing strategies as a basis for making choices. Distinctions have been made among:

➡ Short-term versus long-term criteria
➡ Financial versus non-financial criteria
➡ Single versus multiple criteria
➡ Criteria focusing on overall strategies versus criteria focusing on specific activities
➡ Criteria focusing on efficiency versus criteria focusing on effectiveness.

Apart from the variety of input and output measures that have been discussed, there are additional approaches that deal with factors ranging from the degree of realism in the assumptions underlying the strategy to the capacity of the enterprise to implement successfully the chosen strategy. To take specific examples, Tilles (1963) and Day (1990) both outline sets of criteria that might be applied in assessing strategies. These include:

➡ Is there an effective matching of the enterprise's competences with the threats and opportunities from the environment? (If not, then there is unlikely to be a basis for achieving sustainable competitive advantage.)

➡ Will the strategy place the enterprise in a position to counter known threats, exploit opportunities, enhance current advantages or provide new sources of advantage?

➡ Is the strategy robust enough to adapt to a broad range of anticipated environmental events or is it only likely to work under very specific conditions?

➡ Will it be difficult for competitors to deal with the expected advantages to be gained from the strategy?

➡ Are the assumptions underlying the formulation of competing strategies realistic? (Such assumptions might relate to price levels, relative market share, market growth, cost levels, timing aspects, competitive reactions, and so on.)

➡ What are the potential risks to which the strategy (hence the enterprise) may be vulnerable? (These may be internal – in the form of resource availability or implementation factors – as well as external.)

➡ Is the strategy feasible from the viewpoint of the enterprise having the necessary skills and resources? (These would include access to technology, markets and servicing facilities, as well as adequate managerial capabilities.)

➡ Is the strategy capable of being effectively communicated, so that those who will be responsible for its implementation can understand what is required of them?

➡ Will the strategy challenge and motivate key personnel? (This implies that strategies must be accepted by those who are charged with their implementation.)

➡ Are the elements within the strategy internally consistent, so that it hangs together in a coherent way?

➡ Will the expected results from the strategy be acceptable relative to the anticipated risks? (This will require evidence of a clear competitive advantage, from which enhanced value to shareholders and other stakeholders' gains will flow.)

➡ Does the strategy have an appropriate time frame? (Strategies cannot be achieved overnight, so sufficient time must be allowed for their effective implementation.)

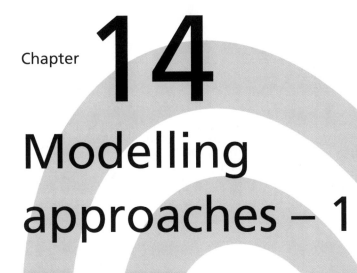

Chapter 14

Modelling approaches – 1

14.1 Learning objectives

When you have read this chapter you should be able to:

(a) understand more fully the role of modelling approaches;
(b) apply financial models to the short-run and long-run evaluation of marketing plans;
(c) appreciate the contribution that cost–volume–profit analysis can make;
(d) carry out appraisals of marketing programmes using discounting methods.

14.2 Introduction

In broad terms a model is anything that is used to represent something else, and models may be classified as descriptive (those that aim to describe real-world processes), predictive (describing both objectives and events, as well as attempting to predict future events) and control models (describing current events, predicting future events and providing a basis for choice among alternative courses of action).

Management science models are typically mathematical in nature, being sets of equations or other expressions that specify the significant variables in a particular situation and indicate the relationship among them. A variable can be defined as any factor that can take on different values under different circumstances, such as:

$$y = a + bx$$

where:

y represents sales turnover (the effect);
x represents consumer income (the cause);
a and b are constants (or parameters), one of which may, for instance, be a time lag.

This shows that management science models are symbolic and are based on the axioms of mathematics. The axioms of probability theory, for example, as one branch of mathematics, will be briefly stated (see pp. 629–30). Furthermore, most mathematical models are based on a small number of highly aggregated factors that are of overriding importance in explaining the way a system works and determining the outcome of different actions.

Models are useful in that they facilitate conceptions of reality that allow the effects of alternative courses of action to be more readily anticipated and measured. Such conceptions, however, are necessarily simplifications of the real situation because this is usually so complex that it could not possibly be explained by a model. The danger is always present that models may be *over*-simplifications of reality, and this renders them useless. Over-simplification is often a trait of corporate model building.

The balance sheet is a form of simplified corporate model governed by the principles of financial accounting, but the annual budget is a better operational example of a corporate model. Such models can be used to examine how the workings of a system affect the flow of inputs and outputs, and are being used with increasing frequency.

Budgeting, as a means of modelling, is limited in its traditional application by:

➡ The inclusion of too few alternative possibilities from which the most satisfactory is to be selected
➡ The difficulty of adjusting traditional operating budgets to rapidly changing conditions – they are at best 'flexible' with respect to changing sales or production levels (see Chapter 8).

It follows that a model permitting the calculation of a larger number of alternatives (based on a larger range of flexible variables and changing parameters) should yield a closer approximation to the ideal solution.

This can be achieved via simulation models, the idea of which is to handle relationships that are too complex to be reduced to simple conclusions by means of mathematical or statistical analysis. These models can then be used to generate predictions about the future course of events.

Two types of simulation are readily identifiable:

1 Analogue simulation, which tends to be a physical representation – such as the use of a model aircraft to predict the behaviour of a full-scale version
2 Symbolic simulation via mathematical modelling, in which the manipulation of the variables within the model simulates the interaction process and is thereby able to predict the outcomes of particular courses of action.

Sensitivity analyses can be performed in the symbolic simulation model by varying the inputs to the system (e.g. time, quantities, funds, etc.) and observing the outputs from each alternative combination of inputs. In this way a pattern of responses can be built up to permit predictions to be made of likely future outcomes.

Probability theory is important in any form of simulation since, for instance, the application of probabilities allows the manipulator to estimate the risk of predictions proving to be wrong. This and related techniques show that the value of simulation to management is in its providing the equivalent of a laboratory in which past or proposed strategies can be examined and experimental evidence produced concerning the probable future outcomes of present decisions.

The building of any model should be carried out by following a *systematic method* such as the following:

1 Specify the objectives to be achieved
2 Formulate the problem to be solved

3 Determine the relationships and major variables in the problem situation, including constraints

4 Construct a model to represent the system under review in such a way that it expresses the effectiveness of the system as a function of the variables isolated in step 3, with at least one of these variables being subject to direct manipulation

5 Derive a solution from the model

6 Test both the solution and the model to ensure that the effects of changes in the system are accurately predicted in the system's overall effectiveness

7 Establish controls over the solution to allow for variations in the relationships among the variables, otherwise the solution may become invalid

8 Implement the tested solution by translating it into a set of operating procedures capable of being understood and applied by the personnel who will be responsible for this use

9 Appraise the results.

Within marketing, many models have been developed that have general application in such areas as brand share and loyalty determination, media selection, measurement of message effectiveness, competitive strategies, transportation and warehouse location, pricing and the determination of competitive bids. However, these models are usually more complex and less precise than those developed for production and administration purposes. This is due to two major factors:

1 The ease of model construction will generally depend on the number of variables involved and the accuracy with which the costs associated with these variables can be measured. The general absence of well-developed costing systems for marketing means that marketing models must handle less precise data than is desirable.

2 The sheer number of variables in the typical marketing decision is huge, many of which are beyond the decision-maker's influence. This results in complex models, as well as the need to make a large number of simplifying assumptions.

In many marketing decisions it is behavioural relationships that are of the essence rather than more easily measured physical or economic factors and, along with other environmental variables, behaviour is difficult to measure in order to accommodate it into a mathematical model. The nature of a behavioural model is shown in Figure 14.1 for predicting sales in the convenience food industry.

This is a *black-box* model that aims to show which given inputs result in a particular output rather than attempting to explain exactly how this occurs.

Decision models (as illustrated in Figure 14.2) permit a higher degree of explanation than is possible with *black-box* models because the variables contained within them are more readily quantified, and the interrelationships contained within these models are less tenuous than in behavioural models.

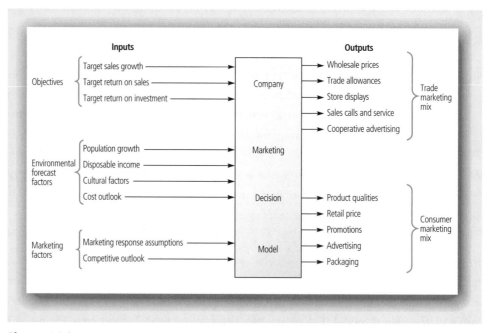

Figure 14.1 Buyer behaviour model

Figure 14.2 Decision model

Analytical decision models (based on the programming techniques discussed later in Chapter 15) can result in the selection of the best marketing mix to adopt for both the trade and the consumer. Simulation models, on the other hand, can start from a different point and attempt to evaluate the effect of alternative marketing mix combinations on the company's sales and profits, as shown in Figure 14.3.

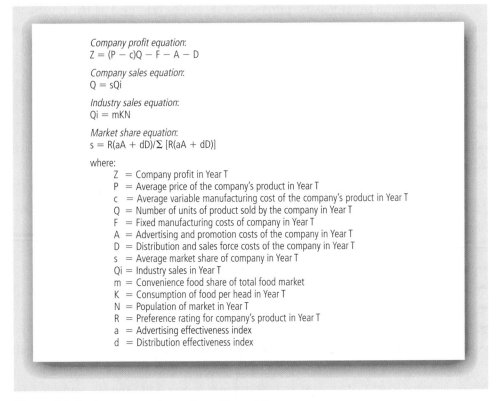

Company profit equation:
$$Z = (P - c)Q - F - A - D$$

Company sales equation:
$$Q = sQi$$

Industry sales equation:
$$Qi = mKN$$

Market share equation:
$$s = R(aA + dD)/\Sigma [R(aA + dD)]$$

where:
Z = Company profit in Year T
P = Average price of the company's product in Year T
c = Average variable manufacturing cost of the company's product in Year T
Q = Number of units of product sold by the company in Year T
F = Fixed manufacturing costs of company in Year T
A = Advertising and promotion costs of the company in Year T
D = Distribution and sales force costs of the company in Year T
s = Average market share of company in Year T
Qi = Industry sales in Year T
m = Convenience food share of total food market
K = Consumption of food per head in Year T
N = Population of market in Year T
R = Preference rating for company's product in Year T
a = Advertising effectiveness index
d = Distribution effectiveness index

Figure 14.3 Company sales and profit model

There can be little doubt that models can assist considerably in marketing planning and control, but this will only happen if models are developed and used properly.

Models must be designed on a systematic basis to ensure that they are geared to the decision-maker's objectives and requirements. In addition, models must function as part of the management process, which means that they should not be developed in isolation of an appreciation of the changes in the balance of power that they can produce: political implications are a significant feature of management science applications.

Once developed, the risk exists that models will be incorrectly used. This does not mean that the decision-maker must become a specialist in the development of models, but he or she should understand the essential features of model building and how to apply a model that has been built.

14.3 Cost–volume–profit analysis

In deciding on future courses of action, management pays a great deal of attention to the alternatives that are available. However, in the case of alternatives that involve changes in the level of business activity with no changes in scale itself, it is generally found that profit does not vary in direct proportion to changes in the level of activity. This is due to the interactions of costs, volume and profits.

For short-run decision-making purposes, costs can be classified as fixed, variable and mixed. In a marketing context, the costs that are typically fixed in relation to the level of activity (within a specified time span) are:

➡ Salaries
➡ Sales administration costs
➡ Advertising appropriations
➡ Market research allocations
➡ Establishment costs of premises.

Many costs depend very much on the level of activity (e.g. volume of business) and are often computed on a per unit basis. Such variable costs include:

➡ Commissions, which may vary with sales revenue
➡ Delivery costs, which may vary with weight shipped
➡ After-sales service costs, which may vary with units sold
➡ Cost of credit, which may vary with debtors' balances
➡ Order processing/invoicing costs, which may vary with number of orders received.

Mixed costs are those that are neither constant over a period nor directly variable on a per unit basis. An example could be the cost of additional sales staff: a particular level of business may require thirty sales staff to service the relevant outlets, but a rise in business of, say, 10 per cent that involves new outlets will probably require additional sales staff. The patterns that emerge are shown in Figure 14.4.

Sales revenue is an increasing function of the level of activity and therefore has the behavioural characteristics of the variable cost curve (see Figure 14.4(b)). Profit is a residual that depends on the interaction of sales volume, selling prices and costs. The non-uniform response of certain costs to changes in the level of activity can have

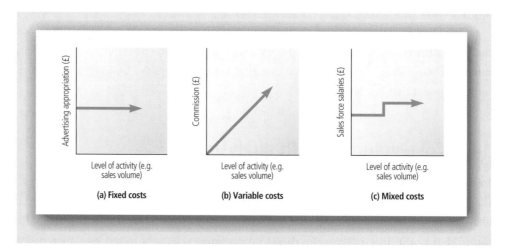

Figure 14.4 Cost behaviour patterns

a serious impact on profit in companies having a high proportion of fixed costs, with the result that a seemingly insignificant decline in sales volume from the expected level may be accompanied by a major drop in expected profit. (This is particularly prevalent in capital-intensive companies producing expensive but specialized industrial equipment.)

On account of the difficulties involved in many industries in accurately predicting the volume of business that may be expected during a forthcoming planning period, it is a wise policy to consider the cost–volume–profit picture for each likely level of activity. This can be done by means of a profitgraph (or break-even chart), which illustrates the profit emerging from different cost/revenue combinations.

The simple profitgraph in Figure 14.5 is compiled by combining the cost and revenue curves. The total revenue curve is simply the expected unit sales multiplied by price for each level of activity, whereas the total cost curve is made up by splitting mixed costs into their fixed and variable costs elements, and superimposing the total fixed cost curve on to the variable cost curve, as shown in Figure 14.6.

It is characteristic of this modelling technique that significant simplifying assumptions underlie its application. For example:

1 It is assumed that fixed costs are constant and that variable costs vary at a constant rate
2 It is assumed that all costs can be broken into either fixed or variable categories
3 It is assumed that only one selling price applies.

Any of these (and other) assumptions underlying cost–volume–profit analysis can be modified in order to produce a more realistic model that is better suited to specific

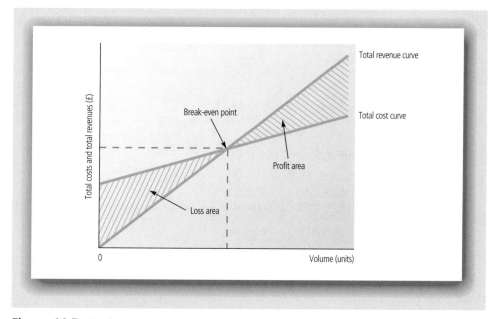

Figure 14.5 Profitgraph

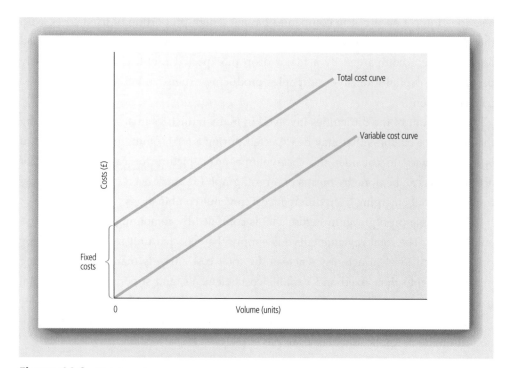

Figure 14.6   Total cost curve

circumstances. This can be demonstrated by reference to Figure 14.7, in which assumption 3 above is relaxed.

Fixed costs are given at £200,000, the unit variable cost is £2.50, and demand forecasts are shown for a number of different prices: £5, £10, £15 and £20. The greatest profit is generated by the £15 price and can be confirmed by the following calculation:

Sales Revenue (SR) (45,000 units at £15.00)	£675,000
Variable Costs (VC) (45,000 units at £2.50)	£112,500
Contribution	£562,500
Fixed costs	£200,000
Profit	£362,500

The break-even volume is derived from the formula:

$$\frac{\text{Fixed costs}}{\text{Unit contribution (i.e. SR/unit } - \text{ VC/unit)}}$$

$$= \frac{£200,000}{£15.00 - £2.50} = 16,000 \text{ units}$$

At £15.00 per unit, the break-even point (i.e. the point at which Total Revenue (TR) = Total Costs (TC), hence Profit (P) = 0), expressed in terms of revenue, is:

$$16,000 \times £15 = £240,000$$

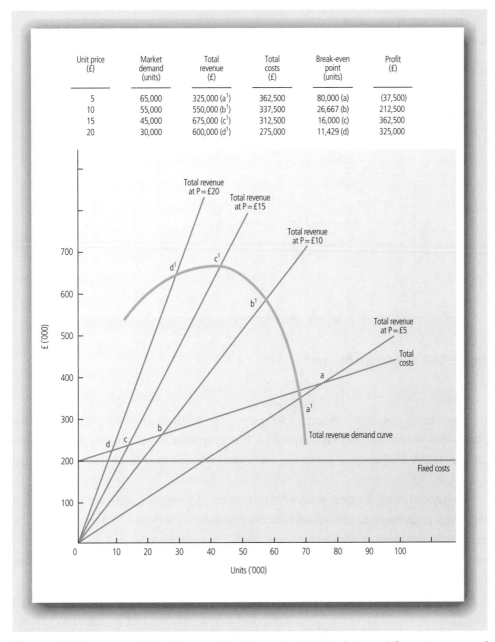

Unit price (£)	Market demand (units)	Total revenue (£)	Total costs (£)	Break-even point (units)	Profit (£)
5	65,000	325,000 (a¹)	362,500	80,000 (a)	(37,500)
10	55,000	550,000 (b¹)	337,500	26,667 (b)	212,500
15	45,000	675,000 (c¹)	312,500	16,000 (c)	362,500
20	30,000	600,000 (d¹)	275,000	11,429 (d)	325,000

Figure 14.7 CVP analysis with a market demand schedule (adapted from Cravens and Lamb, 1986, p. 31)

This gives a margin of safety of:

$$\frac{£675,000 - £240,000}{£675,000} \times 100 = 64\%$$

In other words, sales could fall by 64 per cent before a loss would be incurred.

In Figure 14.7, the line connecting the points a¹, b¹, c¹ and d¹ constitutes the market demand curve for the product in question.

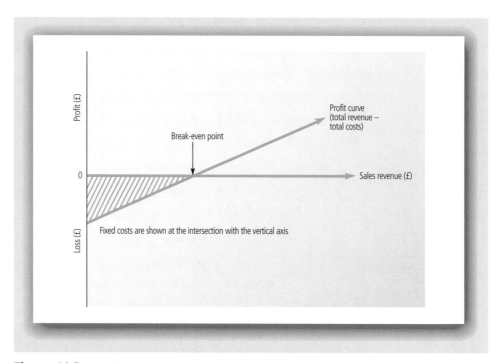

Figure 14.8 Profit–volume chart

An alternative form of presentation to the profitgraph is the profit–volume chart. This shows the same relationships, but simplifies the picture by netting costs and revenues to show the profit for each level of activity. Figure 14.8 shows such a chart.

The reason why the total cost curve of Figures 14.5 and 14.6 does not pass through the origin is the same as the reason why the profit curve of Figure 14.8 cuts the vertical axis below the point of zero profit: even when there are no sales, the fixed costs must still be paid, and consequently the area below the break-even sales volume represents one of loss, being at its greatest at zero sales.

When constructed, the profitgraph represents, in essence, a wide range of profit statements for various levels of activity. As such, it can be used as a benchmark for judging the adequacy of actual performance or it can be used in the planning phase to portray alternative courses of action. The graphical analysis described above is a simple means of illustrating cost–volume–profit interrelationships, but the managerial applications can also be facilitated by algebraic analysis.

The basic equation is simple once mixed costs have been split into their fixed and variable elements and shown as such:

Sales revenue = variable costs + fixed costs + profit

The break-even (BE) equation is even simpler since, at the break-even point, there is no profit:

BE sales revenue = variable costs + fixed costs

In physical volume terms, the break-even point can be calculated as follows:

$$\text{BE volume} = \frac{\text{Fixed costs}}{(\text{Sales revenue} - \text{variable costs})/(\text{units sold})}$$

Thus if a firm has fixed costs of £10 000, variable costs of £15 000, and sells 5000 units for £30,000, the break-even volume is:

$$\frac{10,000}{(30,000 - 15,000)/5000} = 3333 \text{ units}$$

In monetary terms, the break-even volume can be derived by applying the formula:

$$\frac{\text{Fixed costs}}{1 - (\text{Variable costs}/\text{sales revenue})} = \frac{\text{Fixed costs}}{\text{Contribution margin ratio}}$$

Using the data referred to above, the break-even volume is equal to:

$$\frac{10,000}{1 - (15,000/30,000)} = \frac{10,000}{0.5} = £20,000$$

The proof is simple: unit price is £6.00 (i.e. £30 000/5000) and the unit variable cost is £3.00 (i.e. £15 000/5000). The unit contribution towards fixed costs and profit is therefore £6.00 − £3.00 = £3.00, and sufficient units must be sold to cover the fixed costs of £10 000. The solution is thus 3333 units, and at a unit price of £6.00 the break-even revenue is £20 000.

Reference was made in the above example to the contribution margin ratio. This is an important concept that expresses the percentage of a volume change that is composed of contribution to profit. In the example, the revenue from an additional sale is £6.00 and the additional variable cost is £3.00. The contribution margin ratio is therefore 1−[3/6] = 0.5 or 50 per cent. In other words, half the revenue from a change in volume is sufficient to cover the variable costs and the other half contributes to fixed costs and profits. (The slope of the curve in Figure 14.8 is given by the contribution margin ratio.)

The application of this ratio is based on the assumption that other factors remain constant and it should be evident that this is a somewhat unrealistic assumption. Nevertheless, to continue the above example, if a change in sales of £10 000 takes place, the change in profits will be as shown in Figure 14.9.

Figure 14.9 shows that with a contribution margin (or profit–volume) ratio of 50 per cent, the profit variation for an upward move is the same as that for a downward move, with the former being positive and the latter negative, and with both being equal to one-half of the change in sales revenue.

A further equation can be devised to measure the excess of actual (or budgeted) sales over the break-even volume. This is known as the *margin of safety* and is given by the equation:

(Actual sales − sales at break-even point)/actual sales

	Original volume	Increase in volume	Decrease in volume
Sales	(£) 30,000	(£) +10,000	(£) −10,000
Variable costs	15,000	+5,000	−5,000
Fixed costs	10,000	Unchanged	Unchanged
Total costs	25,000	+5,000	−5,000
Profits	5,000	+5,000	−5,000

Figure 14.9 Profit–volume variations

Again, taking data from the earlier example, in monetary terms the margin of safety is:

$$(£30,000 - £20,000)/£30,000 = 1/3 \text{ or } 33^1/_3\%$$

In physical terms it is:

$$(5,000 - 3,333)/5,000 = 1/3 \text{ or } 33^1/_3\%$$

This ratio means that sales can fall by one-third before operations cease being profitable – assuming that the other relationships are accurately measured and remain constant.

The combination of cost–volume–profit analysis with budgeting enables alternative budget figures to serve as the basis for profit graphs. If a particular budget is shown to be unsatisfactory, then the parameters can be recast until a more suitable budget results. It is not surprising that cost–volume–profit analysis has been compared to flexible budgeting in being able to show what the cost and profit picture should be at different levels of sales, but flexible budgets are essentially concerned with cost control whereas cost–volume–profit analysis is more concerned with the predictions of profit.

As with other techniques, cost–volume–profit analysis has its strengths and weaknesses. In its favour is its value as a background information device for important decisions – such as selecting distribution channels, make or buy, and pricing decisions. In this role it offers an overall view of costs and sales in relation to profit requirements.

If simplicity is a virtue, then cost–volume–profit analysis has this virtue, since it is easily understood. However, this very simplicity points the way to the weaknesses and limitations of cost–volume–profit analysis. As suggested earlier in this section, the major weakness is in the underlying assumptions: profit varies not only in relation to changes in volume, but also with changes in production methods, marketing techniques and other factors. Cost–volume–profit analysis is unable to allow for these possibilities, and at best indicates the profit that may be expected under a single set of assumed conditions regarding external factors as well as managerial policies. Thus, it is a static representation of the situation it purports to illustrate: a different set of circumstances would obviously result in a different series of cost–volume–profit relationships.

Furthermore, cost–volume–profit analysis can only accommodate objectives that relate to profits, costs and sales levels/revenues, and it tends to treat costs, volume and profit as if they were independent of each other.

These limitations do not outweigh the value of cost–volume–profit analysis provided that the user is aware of the assumptions and limitations. It is necessary, of course, to supplement the assistance given by any technique with managerial judgement, and cost–volume–profit analysis is no exception to this principle.

The roles of budgeting and cost–volume–profit analysis are illustrated below in further examples.

Examples

1 ABC Ltd

This is a single-product company with a profit objective that is expressed as 10 per cent of net sales revenue.

For the next planning period the total market potential is estimated to be 500 units. Figure 14.10 indicates the cost and profit outlook at each level of sales that ABC Ltd can expect to achieve.

The behaviour of marketing costs is shown in Figures 14.11 and 14.12 for fixed and variable costs respectively.

The unit costs from Figure 14.12 can be extended to show the variable marketing costs of each anticipated sales level:

Market share	10%	12%	14%	16%
Variable marketing cost	£5,000	£6,000	£7,000	£8,000

The combination of Figures 14.10–14.12 gives the total cost–volume–profit situation shown in Figure 14.13.

Forecast percentage share of market	10%	12%	14%	16%
Unit sales	50	60	70	80
Average net price per unit	£1,500	£1,500	£1,450	£1,400
Forecast net sales revenue	£75,000	£90,000	£101,500	£112,000
Variable manufacturing costs at £300 per unit	£15,000	£18,000	£21,000	£24,000
Contribution	£60,000	£72,000	£80,500	£88,000
Fixed manufacturing costs	£20,000	£20,000	£20,000	£20,000
Gross profit	£40,000	£52,000	£60,500	£68,000

Figure 14.10   Manufacturing costs and revenues

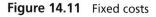

Fixed costs	10%	12%	14%	16%
Sales force (excluding commission)	£6,000	£6,000	£9,000	£9,000
Sales administration	£10,000	£10,000	£12,000	£12,000
Advertising appropriation	£5,000	£5,500	£8,000	£12,000
Establishment costs	£10,000	£10,000	£12,000	£12,000
Marketing research costs	£2,000	£2,000	£2,000	£2,000
Office services	£3,000	£3,100	£3,200	£3,300
Totals	£36,000	£36,600	£46,200	£50,300

Figure 14.11 Fixed costs

Delivery	£10
Order processing/invoicing	£2
Commission	£10
Average cost of credit	£30
After-sales service	£48
	£100

Figure 14.12 Variable cost per unit

Net profit statement	10%	12%	14%	16%
Gross margin (Figure 14.10)	£40,000	£52,000	£60,500	£68,000
Marketing costs (Figures 14.11 and 14.12)	£41,000	£42,600	£53,200	£58,300
Net profit (loss)	£(1,000)	£9,400	£7,300	£9,700
Net profit as percentage sales revenue	−1.33%	10.44%	7.19%	8.66%

Figure 14.13 Net profits

The profit objective of 10 per cent of net sales revenue is only achieved if ABC Ltd secures a 12 per cent market share, but control effort must be rigorously applied because the margin for error is very small.

This gives the basic budget for the forthcoming period, and this can be illustrated in a profitgraph (Figure 14.14).

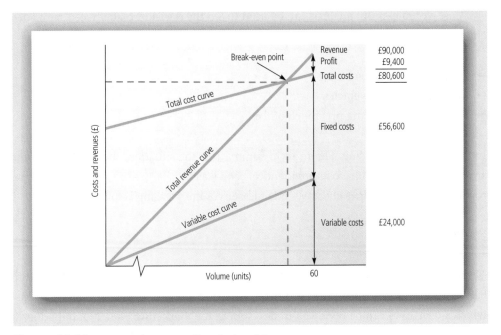

Figure 14.14   Cost–volume–profit relationships

For the selected course of action (i.e. that aiming for a 12 per cent market share), the total cost make-up is:

Variable manufacturing costs	£18,000	
Variable marketing costs	£6,000	
		£24,000
Fixed manufacturing costs	£20,000	
Fixed marketing costs	£36,600	
		£56,600
Total costs		£80,600

The break-even point is computed by applying the formula given earlier in this section:

$$\frac{£56,000}{(£90,000 - £24,000)/60} = 51 \text{ units}$$

This gives a margin of safety of only 15 per cent, calculated thus:

$$(60 - 51)/60 = 15\%$$

A clear and concise summary is given in this way of one particular course of action that provides a standard for management purposes. Separate charts and analyses can easily be drawn up for other alternative courses of action prior to making a choice.

Cost–volume–profit analysis can be used to aid the decision-maker faced with such choices as:

➡ Leasing or buying premises
➡ Leasing or owning vehicles
➡ Using agents or setting up branch offices.

In the case of warehousing, Figure 14.15 summarizes the situation, showing the storage space at which ownership costs are identical with leasing charges (B). At greater volume requirements ownership is cheaper, and at lesser volumes leasing is to be preferred.

2 Product line

The product mix is a major part of the overall marketing plan, and the relationship between the mix and the level of profit can be seen to be one of the basic areas against which alternatives can be reviewed in developing the marketing plan. Not only does it involve the consideration of the roles of single products and product groups, but it also involves considerations of the related effects of decisions bearing on, for example, the choice and emphasis of alternative sales areas.

However, very few companies appear to be aware of the actual gross profit contributions of either individual products or product groups. Furthermore, large variations would probably be found in gross contributions in most cases, and this could suggest different courses of marketing action if only the gross margins were properly computed. Figure 14.16 gives the example of a six-product mix analysed to show how each product contributes to sales and to profit. Product F has a negative contribution of 5 per cent of profit and would thus appear to be a candidate for deletion, while Product C especially,

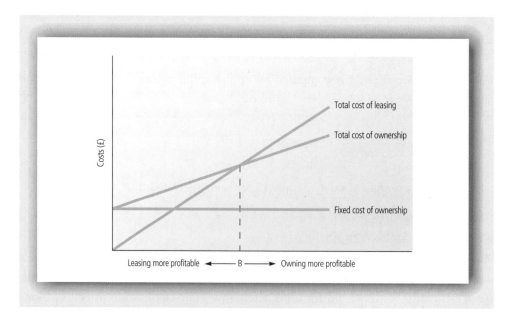

Figure 14.15 Break-even chart for warehousing

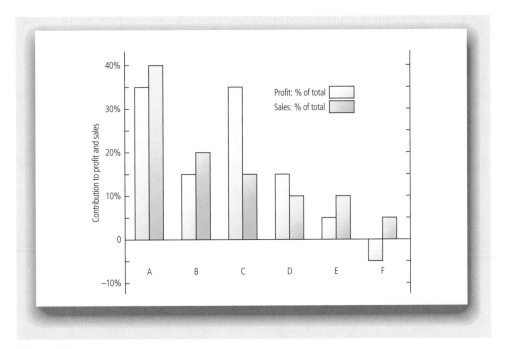

Figure 14.16   Product mix analysis

and to a lesser extent Product D, appear to deserve special marketing emphasis because they both have a proportionately greater profit than their relative volume.

When management adopts direct product costing and distribution cost analysis, it can compute the gross contribution of each item in the product range so that the tactical significance of the mix in relation to profit objectives becomes apparent. This can reveal cases of under-recovery of direct costs (as for Product F in Figure 14.16) that could possibly be corrected by modifications in price or cost reduction if it is decided that the product should be retained to fill out the product line. Direct costing requires the separation of fixed and variable costs, with the latter being treated as 'period costs' (i.e. they are charged to the profit and loss account on a periodic basis rather than being apportioned to units of output). An example should make the picture clear. LMN Ltd markets four products, the most recent financial data for which is shown in Figure 14.17. For each £1 of sales of the existing product mix, therefore, 24.8p is profit contribution. If the fixed costs of LMN Ltd amount to £50 000 and total sales are £250 000, then profit (P) is equal to:

$$(Sales \times 24.8/100) - \text{fixed costs}$$
$$\therefore P = £62,000 - £50,000 = £12,000$$

If it is decided to vary this mix it will be necessary to forecast the costs and sales for the modified mix. For instance, Product E may be launched to replace Product B, having the following characteristics:

Selling price per unit	£7
Variable cost per unit	£5.6
Percentage contribution	20%
Increase in fixed costs	£1000

The effects on the product mix are, for a new total sales level of £275 000:

Product	Former % of sales	Forecast % of sales
A	10%	25%
C	30%	30%
D	40%	30%
E	–	15%
		100%

The total contribution picture then becomes:

A: $20 \times 25/100 = 5\%$
C: $25 \times 30/100 = 7.5\%$
D: $30 \times 30/100 = 9\%$
E: $20 \times 15/100 = 3\%$
$$24.5\%$$

$$\therefore P = (275{,}000 \times 24.5/100) - (50{,}000 + 1{,}000)$$
$$P = £67{,}375 - £51{,}000 = £16{,}375$$

The profit improvement is thus £4357 (i.e. £16,375 − £12,000) on additional sales of £25 000 and this gives ROS of 17.6 per cent.

This example emphasizes the fact that product decisions should be made on the basis of their contribution to fixed costs and profit, and on the basis of their percentage share of total sales, rather than being considered in isolation.

Future planning and control are both aided by studying the progress of each product over its life cycle, since no product can hold its market position indefinitely in the face of changing conditions. The typical curves of Figure 14.18 show the lagged profit curve and the sales revenue curve for a product over the phases of its life. Rates of technological change, market acceptance, and ease of competitive entry will collectively determine the lifespan of the product. However, it may be possible to extend the

Product	Selling price (SP)	Variable cost (VC)	% contribution (SP − VC)/SP × 100	% of total sales	Contribution as % of total sales
A	£5	£4	20%	10%	2.0%
B	£6	£5	16.6%	20%	3.3%
C	£8	£6	25%	30%	7.5%
D	£10	£7	30%	40%	12.0%
				100%	24.8%

Figure 14.17 Product costs and contributions

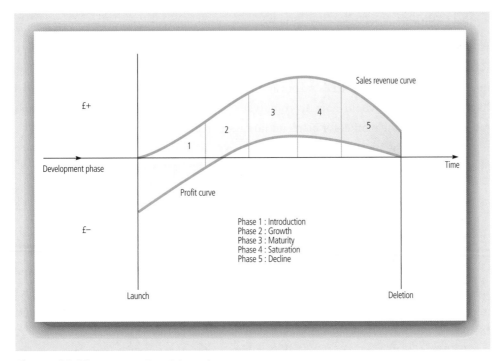

Figure 14.18   The product life cycle

lifespan by either modifying the product, changing its image to appeal to new market segments, or finding new uses for it. Generally, it will be necessary to adapt the marketing effort in each phase, and the ideal situation is one in which new products are introduced at such a rate that optimum profits can be maintained by some products reaching maturity at the time when others are beginning to decline, and so on.

In Figure 14.18 the product in question is deleted at the time when it ceases to be profitable, even though it is still generating sales revenue. But any deletion decision should be preceded by serious consideration of the areas in which it may be possible to improve the product's performance. In particular, areas to consider are selling methods, channels, the advertising message, promotions, the brand image, the pack, the quality and design of the product, and the adequacy of the service offered.

Under no circumstances should a declining product be allowed to continue in decline without evaluation, because it may be consuming resources that could more fruitfully be employed elsewhere. A declining product will tend to take up a disproportionate amount of management time, may require frequent price adjustments, will involve short – hence expensive – production runs, and may damage the company's image. Pareto's law will often apply in that 80 per cent of sales will come from 20 per cent of products and the weakest 20 per cent of products may absorb 80 per cent of management's attention.

Reviewing the product line should not be a rare action but should rather be undertaken in a regular and planned manner. For example, all products could be reviewed every three months and any that are less profitable than, say, the average for the range should be the subject of revised plans to improve their performance.

3 SRD example

Heskett (1976, pp. 410–18) gives the example of a marketing proposal from the Safety Razor Division (SRD) of the Gillette Company for a line of blank audio cassettes. The market penetration of the SRD's razors and blades was such that no further increase was likely; thus, growth would have to come via diversification. Estimates of the size and rate of growth of the market for blank audio cassettes made it particularly attractive.

In the USA the most popular tape was the 60-minute version, available as follows:

Type	Price ($)
Budget quality	1.00
Standard quality	1.75–2.00
Professional quality	2.98

Competition was fierce and price-oriented: some 50 per cent (by value) of tape sales were of budget quality, typically unbranded, with well-known companies supplying standard and professional quality tapes under such brand names as Sony, 3M and Memorex.

If SRD used 10 per cent of its existing sales force's effort to sell cassettes via existing outlets with the 50 per cent discount off retail price that was customary for cassettes, and if an advertising budget for Year 1 was set at $2 million (and $1.2 million per annum thereafter), and if unit costs were as follows:

Cassette case (bought out)	$0.159
Standard quality tape (60 minutes)	$0.214
Professional quality tape (60 minutes)	$0.322
Assembly labour	$0.200

and if the fixed annual costs of an assembly plant with capacity to handle 1 million cassettes per month were $500 000, there is the basis for an economic appraisal of alternative marketing programmes.

Figure 14.19 shows an outline programme offering standard quality cassettes at a price that is a little higher than that applicable to budget cassettes. The break-even volume is almost 40 million units per annum, which is greatly in excess of the capacity of the assembly plant. It also represents 85 per cent of the total retail market of budget-priced cassettes (totalling $65 million). On grounds of feasibility this does not appear to be a viable proposition.

Alternative marketing programmes to allow SRD to enter the cassette market might entail:

➡ Raising list price (with or without an increase in quality)
➡ Reducing trade margins
➡ Using a small sales team and only selling via wholesalers
➡ Reducing the proposed advertising budget
➡ Investing in manufacturing facilities (rather than just assembly).

Item		Computation
Price to final consumer		$1.30 per tape
Price to retailer or wholesaler (50% of list price)		$0.650
Variable costs per tape:		
cassette case	$0.159	
standard quality tape	$0.214	
assembly labour	$0.200	
Total		$0.573
Contribution		$0.077
Fixed costs per annum:		
assembly plant	$500,000	
sales force costs (10%)	$550,000	
advertising	$2,000,000	
Total		$3,050,000

Break-even sales volume: $\dfrac{\$3,050,000}{\$0.077}$

$$= 39,600,000 \text{ tapes}$$

$$39,600,000 \times \$1.30 = \$51.5 \text{ million retail value}$$

Figure 14.19 Economic appraisal of marketing strategy – standard quality at budget prices (adapted from Heskett, 1976)

These alternatives might be considered individually (on a *ceteris paribus* basis) or interactively (on a *mutatis mutandis* basis) and there would also be knock-on effects for other elements of the marketing mix.

Significant effort would need to be applied (via market research) to define the market, its segments, growth rates, etc., in order to determine the viability of alternative marketing programmes. Relevant factors would include:

➡ The quality of forecasts
➡ The rate at which market conditions favourable to entry might change
➡ Alternatives to blank cassette tapes as vehicles for SRD's growth
➡ Assumed buyer behaviour patterns within the cassette market
➡ Assumptions about other elements of the marketing mix.

Three alternative marketing programmes have been developed by SRD. The steps through which they were developed are shown in Figure 14.20 and the evaluated alternatives are shown in Figure 14.21. These alternatives are the marketing of budget cassettes, the marketing of standard cassettes at a low price, and the marketing of professional cassettes. Only the last two would use the Gillette brand name, although all three would have to generate an equivalent profit to Gillette's overall level (at 20 per cent of sales revenue). It is clear from Figure 14.21 that alternative 3 is non-viable and that alternative 1, while viable, is more challenging than alternative 2.

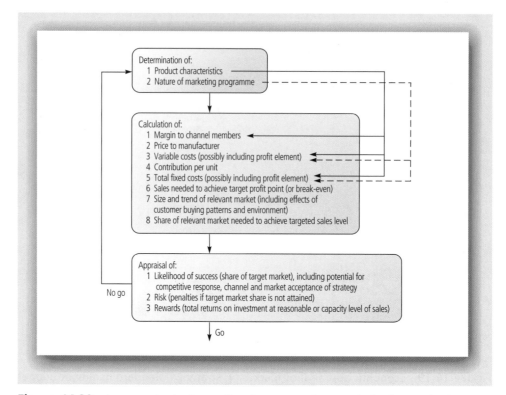

Figure 14.20 A conceptual scheme for the economic appraisal of a marketing programme (source: Heskett, 1976, p. 415)

14.4 Investment appraisal

Any investment involves the outlay of resources at one point in time in anticipation of receiving a larger return at some time in the future. This return must repay the original outlay as well as providing a minimum annual rate of return (or interest) on that outlay. If an individual invests £100 in a building society he will expect to receive that £100 back at some future time, along with compound interest. This is a typical investment situation. The aim will usually be to secure the maximum net cash flow (after tax) from the investment, and this will be achieved only from investments having the highest rate of return of those available.

Characteristically, an investment decision involves a largely irreversible commitment of resources and is generally subject to a significant degree of risk. Such decisions have far-reaching effects on an enterprise's profitability and flexibility over the long term, thus requiring that they be part of a carefully developed strategy that is based on reliable forecasting procedures.

Typical examples of investment projects are:

1 Expansion projects
2 Replacement projects
3 Buy or lease decisions.

	Alternative 1	Alternative 2	Alternative 3
Determination of product characteristics	Budget cassette, sold under a name other than Gillette	Standard cassette, sold under Gillette name	Professional cassette, sold under Gillette name
Elements of marketing programme			
Price (list) to ultimate buyer	$1.20/cassette	$1.50/cassette	$2.50/cassette
Channels	Current Gillette retail outlets, wholesalers; total margin = 25%	Current Gillette retail outlets, wholesalers; total margin = 30%	Audio shops, wholesalers; total margin = 60%
Promotion	Advertising = $2.0 million per year; personal selling = $0.5 million per year	Advertising = $2.0 million per year; personal selling = $0.5 million per year	Advertising = $1.0 million per year; personal selling = $0.2 million per year
Relevant target market	Teenagers for pop music; 50% of total dollar value	Young adults, business people for dictation, letter writing; 40% of total dollar value	Serious audiophiles for convenient high-fidelity recording of music; 10% of total dollar value
Calculation of			
Price to ultimate buyer	$1.20/cassette	$1.50/cassette	$2.50/cassette
Price to SRD	$0.90	$1.05	$1.00
Variable costs and profit per tape			
Unloaded cassette	$0.159	$0.159	$0.159
Tape of each quality	0.214	0.214	0.322
Assembly	0.200	0.200	0.200
Profit (20% of sales)	0.180	0.210	0.200
Total	$0.753	$0.783	$0.881
Contribution to fixed costs	$0.147/cassette	$0.267/cassette	$0.119/cassette
Fixed costs for			
Assembly plant (per year)	$500,000	$500,000	$500,000
Sales force salaries	500,000	500,000	200,000
Advertising	2,000,000	2,000,000	1,000,000
Total	$3,000,000	$3,000,000	$1,700,000
Target sales level (units)	$3,000,000/0.147 = 20,408,163	$3,000,000/0.267 = 11,235,955	$1,700,000/0.119 = 14,300,000
Value to ultimate customers of target sales level	$24,489,795	$16,853,932	$35,800,000
Estimated 1970 target market size ($ and % of $130 million)	$38,000,000 (50%)	$32,000,000 (40%)	$13,000,000 (10%)
Appraisal of			
Likelihood of success (share of target market), including potential for competitive response, channel, and market acceptance of strategy	38% share of target market required to break even	32% share of target market required to break even	275% share of target market required to break even
Potential risk	High fixed investment	High fixed investment	Moderate fixed investment
Potential return on investment of capacity operations	Would require expanded investment in manufacturing facilities	Would require expanded investment in manufacturing facilities	Would require expanded investment in manufacturing facilities

No go

Figure 14.21 An economic analysis of three alternative strategies for designing and marketing SRD cassettes (adapted from Heskett, 1976, pp. 416–17)

Projects for analysis and appraisal do not just appear – a continuing stream of good investment opportunities results from hard thinking, careful planning, and often from large outlays on R&D. Replacement decisions are ordinarily the simplest to make, as the enterprise will have a very good idea of the cost savings to be obtained by replacing an old asset along with the consequences of non-replacement. (A central problem is that of accurately predicting the revenues and costs associated with particular projects for many years into the future.)

Over-investment in capital projects will result in heavy fixed costs, whereas under-investment may mean:

➡ An enterprise's activities are not sufficiently modern to enable it to operate competitively, or
➡ It has inadequate capacity to maintain its share of a growing market.

Investment is one of the main sources of economic growth. The application of reliable means of appraising investment proposals brings out more systematically and reliably the advantages of investing where it will improve performance and thus help to secure faster growth.

Various criticisms have been put forward in relation to the methods of appraisal that many companies employ. Among the most important are:

➡ Although most companies only make investment decisions after careful consideration of the likely costs and benefits as they see them, these decisions are often reached in ways that are unlikely to produce the pattern or level of investment that is most favourable to economic growth – or even most profitable to the company
➡ Many companies apply criteria for assessing investment projects that have little relevance to the measurement of the expected *rate of return on investment* (ROI) by which subsequent performance will be gauged
➡ Even when a calculation of the anticipated ROI of each project is made, the methods used vary widely and are sometimes so arbitrary as to give almost meaningless results – for instance, a failure to assess returns *after* tax is a frequent weakness of many widely used methods, since alternative opportunities can only be effectively compared and appraised on an after-tax basis.

This faulty use of (or use of faulty) means of investment appraisal may result in over-cautious investment decisions in which too high a rate of return is demanded before a proposal is accepted. This will cause delay in economic growth. Alternatively, faulty methods may mean that investment decisions are made that result in the selection of projects that yield an unduly low return. This causes a waste of scarce capital resources, which is also unfavourable to economic growth.

From an information flow point of view, the use of inadequate means of investment appraisal results in a damaging restriction in the flow of information to top management, since these methods are incapable of fully exploiting relevant data. Because a company's future is inextricably linked to its investments, poor appraisal methods that give poor information that leads to poor decisions are likely to result in many mistakes.

Realistic investment appraisal requires the financial evaluation of many factors, such as the choice of size, type, location, and timing of investments, giving due consideration to the effects of taxation and alternative forms of financing the outlays. This shows that project decisions are difficult on account of their complexity and their strategic significance.

No matter which technique is adopted for investment appraisal the same steps will need to be followed. These steps are:

1 Determine the profitability of each proposal
2 Rank the proposals in accordance with their profitability
3 Determine the cut-off rate (e.g. minimum acceptable rate of return)
4 Determine which projects are acceptable and which unacceptable in relation to the cut-off rate
5 Select the most profitable proposals in accordance with the constraints of the company's available funds.

Cash flows

In considering investment decisions, it does not matter whether outlays are termed 'capital' or 'operating', nor whether inflows are termed 'revenue', 'tax allowance' or whatever. All outlays and inflows must be taken into account in cash flow terms.

Cash flow in this context is not the same as the cash flow through a bank account, nor is it identical to accounting profit, since changes in the latter can occur without any change taking place in the cash flow. For purposes of investment appraisal, the cash flow is the incremental cash receipts less the incremental cash expenditures solely attributable to the investment in question.

The future costs and revenues associated with each investment alternative are:

1 *Capital costs.* These cover the long-term capital outlays necessary to finance a project, and working capital. (Since residual working capital is recoverable at the termination of a project's life, this leads to the investment having a terminal value that should be taken into account.) Typically, additional working capital will be required to cover a higher inventory, or a larger number of debtors, and to be worthwhile the project must earn a return on this capital as well as on the long-term capital.
2 *Operating costs.*
3 *Revenue.*
4 *Depreciation.* In the case of the discounting methods of appraisal (discussed below), the recovery of capital (i.e. depreciation) is automatically allowed for from the net cash flow, so depreciation need not be included as an accounting provision. This has the important advantage that the discounted profitability assessment is not affected by the pattern of accounting depreciation chosen.

5 *Residual value*. As with working capital, the residual assets of the project may have a value (as either scrap or in an alternative use or location). This residual value (net of handling costs and tax allowances or charges) should be included within the net cash flow.

An investment decision implies the choice of an objective, a technique of appraisal, and a length of service – the project's life. The objective and technique must be related to a definite period of time. In a static world that period would quite naturally be taken as being equal to the commercial life of the plan that is the purpose of the investment, which may be known with a good deal of certainty on the basis of past experience. However, in a dynamic world the life of the project may be determined by:

➡ Technological obsolescence, or
➡ Physical deterioration, or
➡ A decline in demand for the output of the project – such as a change in taste away from the market offering.

No matter how good a company's maintenance policy, its technological forecasting ability or its demand forecasting ability, uncertainty will always be present because of the difficulty of predicting the length of a project's life.

Time value of money

To permit realistic appraisal, the value of a cash payment or receipt must be related to the time when the transfer takes place. In particular, it must be recognized that £1 received today is worth more than £1 receivable at some future date, because £1 received today could be earning interest in the intervening period. This is the concept of the *time value of money*.

To illustrate this, if £100 was invested today at 5 per cent per annum compound interest, it would accumulate to £105 at the end of one year (i.e. £100 × 1.05), to £110.25 at the end of two years (i.e. £100 × 1.05 × 1.05, or £105 × 1.05), and so on. In other words, £110.25 receivable in two years' time is only worth £100 today if 5 per cent per annum can be earned in the meantime (i.e. £110.25/(1.05 × 1.05) = £100).

The process of converting future sums into their present equivalents is known as *discounting*, which is simply the opposite of *compounding* (see Figure 14.22). Compounding is used to determine the *future value* of present cash flows.

Another example will clarify this further. An investor who can normally obtain 8 per cent on his investments is considering whether or not to invest in a project that gives rise to £388 at the end of each of the next three years. The present value of these sums is:

$$\frac{£388}{1.08} + \frac{£388}{1.08 \times 1.08} + \frac{£388}{1.08 \times 1.08 \times 1.08} = £1000$$

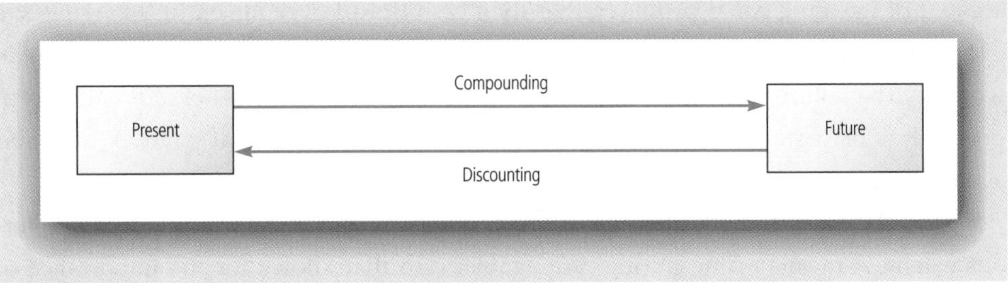

Figure 14.22   Discounting and compounding

If the investment's capital cost is less than the present value of its returns (say £800), then it should be accepted, since the present value of the return on this outlay is a larger amount (i.e. £1000 − £800 = £200 gain from the investment). The gain is the *net present value* of the investment.

The interest rate does not always relate to an outlay of borrowed cash, as the concept of interest applies equally to the use of internal funds. The reason why interest must be considered on *all* funds in use, regardless of their source, is that the selection of one alternative necessarily commits funds that could otherwise be invested in some other alternative. The measure of interest in such cases is the return foregone by rejecting the alternative use (i.e. the opportunity cost).

Financial evaluation

The techniques of financial evaluation fall into two categories, as shown below.

Traditional methods of evaluation

The payback period is the most widely used technique and can be defined as the number of years' net cash flow required to recover the initial cash outlay on the investment. By definition, the payback period ignores cash flows beyond this period and it can thus be seen to be more a measure of liquidity than of profitability. In addition, it fails to take account of the time value of money, and these limitations make it seriously defective in the aim of reflecting the relative financial attractiveness of projects.

Projects with long payback periods are characteristically those involved in strategic planning and that determine an enterprise's future. However, they may not yield their highest returns for a number of years and the result is that the payback method is biased against the very investments that are likely to be most important to long-term success.

The accounting rate of return is defined as the average profit from the project (after allowing for accounting depreciation but before tax) as a percentage of the average required investment. This method is fundamentally unsound. While it does take account of the anticipated profits (rather than cash flows) over the entire economic life of a project, it fails to take account of the time value of money. This weakness is made worse by the failure to specify adequately the relative attractiveness of alternative proposals. It is biased against short-term projects in the same way that payback is biased against longer-term ones.

These traditional methods of investment appraisal can be misleading to a dangerous extent. A means of measuring *cash* against *cash* that allows for the importance of time is needed. This is provided by the discounting methods of appraisal, of which there are basically two, both of which meet the objections to the payback period and accounting rate of return methods.

Discounting methods of evaluation

Both the main discounting methods relate the estimates of the initial cash outlays on the investment to the annual net after-tax cash flows generated by the investment. As a general rule, the net after-tax cash flows will be composed of profit less taxes (when paid), plus depreciation. Since discounting techniques automatically allow for the recoupment of the capital outlay (i.e. depreciation) in computing time-adjusted rates of return, it follows that depreciation implicitly forms part of the discounting computation and so must be added back to profit in specifying cash flow.

The *internal rate of return* (IRR; or discounted cash flow) method consists of finding that rate of discount that reduces the cash flows (both inflows and outflows) attributable to an investment project to zero – this being, in principle, the true rate of return. (In other words, this 'true' rate is that which exactly equalizes the discounted net cash proceeds over a project's life with the initial investment outlay.)

If the IRR exceeds the minimum required rate (or *cost of capital*) then the project is prima facie acceptable.

Instead of being computed on the basis of the average investment, the IRR is based on the funds in use from period to period.

The actual calculation of the rate is a hit-and-miss exercise because the rate is unknown at the outset, but tables of present values are available to aid the analyst. These tables show the present value of future sums at various rates of discount, and are prepared for both single sums and recurring annual payments (i.e. annuities).

The *net present value* (NPV) method discounts the net cash flows from the investment by the minimum required rate of return, and deducts the initial investment to give the yield from the funds invested. If this yield is positive, then the project is prima facie worthwhile, but if it is negative the project is unable to pay for itself and is thus unacceptable. An index can be developed for comparative purposes by relating the yield to the investment to give the yield per £1 invested. This is the *present value index* and facilitates the ranking of competing proposals in order of acceptability. (It is not important in their evaluation in terms of present value that competing proposals require widely different outlays, since the index reduces alternatives to a common base.)

Comparison of discounting methods

In ordinary circumstances the two discounting approaches will result in identical investment decisions. However, there are differences between them that can result in conflicting answers in terms of ranking projects according to their NPV or IRR.

In formal accept/reject decisions both methods lead to the same decision, since all projects having a yield in excess of the minimum required rate will also have a positive net present value. Figure 14.23 shows that this is so.

Example: Projects A and B both require an outlay of £1000 now to obtain a return of £1150 at the end of Year 1 in the case of A, and £1405 at the end of Year 3 in the case of B. The minimum required rate of return is 8 per cent.

Both projects have rates of return in excess of 8 per cent *and* positive net present values, but on the basis of the IRR method Project A is superior, while on the basis of the NPV method Project B is superior.

Confusion arises because the projects have different lengths of life and if only one of the projects is to be undertaken (i.e. they are mutually exclusive), the IRR can be seen to be unable to discriminate satisfactorily between them. As with any rate of return, there is no indication of either the *amount* of capital involved or the *duration* of the investment. The choice must be made either on the basis of net present values or on the return on the *incremental investment* between projects. (In the above example, of course, the same amount of investment is required for each; thus, Project B is to be preferred on the strength of its higher net present value.)

The two methods make different implicit assumptions about the reinvesting of funds received from projects – particularly during the 'gaps' between the end of one and the end of another.

Considering the example further, if it is explicitly assumed that the funds received from Project A can be reinvested at 10 per cent per annum between the end of Years 1 and 3, the situation will be as shown in Figure 14.24.

All three formulations clearly show Project B to be superior, illustrating the importance of project characteristics when only one can be undertaken.

The NPV approach assumes that cash receipts can be reinvested at the company's minimum acceptable rate of return, thereby giving a bias in favour of long-lived projects.

| Internal rate of return: | A = 15%
B = 12% |
| Net present value | A = (1,150 × 0.926) − 1,000 = £65
B = (1,405 × 0.794) − 1,000 = £115 |

Note: 0.926 is the factor that reduces a sum receivable one year hence, at a discount rate of 8 per cent, to its present value; and 0.794 is the discount factor that reduces a sum due three years hence to its present value. These discount factors are derived easily from published tables.

Figure 14.23   Ranking comparisons – 1

IRR	A = (15 + 10 + 10) ÷ 3	= 11.667%
	B (as Fig. 14.23)	= 12%
NPV	A = [(150 × 0.926) + (115 × 0.857) + (1126 × 0.794)] − 1,000 =	£32
	B (as Fig. 14.23)	= £115
Terminal value:	A = (1,150 × 110% × 110%)	= £1,391
	B (as given)	= £1,405

Figure 14.24 Ranking comparisons – 2

In contrast, the IRR approach assumes that cash receipts are reinvested at the same rate (i.e. a constant renewal of the project), giving a bias in favour of short-lived projects.

It follows that the comparison of alternatives by either method must be made over a common time period, with explicit assumptions being made about what happens to funds between their receipt and the common terminal date.

Aspects of application

Alternative proposals

The selection of a particular proposal should follow a careful appraisal of both alternative uses for funds and alternative means of performing a particular project. For instance, a company may wish to double the capacity of its production line and determine three means of accomplishing this, namely:

1 Introduce double-shift working
2 Install a second production line
3 Scrap the existing production line and build a new line with double the initial capacity.

The choice of a particular alternative will depend on how it accords with the enterprise's established investment objectives, and the choice of projects will depend on both corporate objectives and the availability of funds. But the fact remains that if the most advantageous alternative has been overlooked, no amount of technical evaluation and appraisal can overcome this basic omission.

Capital rationing

In terms of financing investment projects, three essential questions must be asked:

1 What funds are needed for capital expenditure in the forthcoming planning period?
2 What funds are available for investment?
3 How are funds to be assigned when the acceptable proposals require more than are currently available?

The first and third questions are resolved by reference to the discounted return on the various proposals, since it will be known which are acceptable and in which order of preference.

The second question is answered by a reference to the *capital budget*. The level of this budget will tend to depend on the quality of the investment proposals submitted to top management. In addition, it will also tend to depend on:

➡ Top management's philosophy towards capital spending (e.g. is it growth-minded or cautious?)
➡ The outlook for future investment opportunities that may be unavailable if extensive current commitments are undertaken
➡ The funds provided by current operations
➡ The feasibility of acquiring additional capital through borrowing or share issues.

It is not always necessary, of course, to limit the spending on projects to internally generated funds. Theoretically, projects should be undertaken to the point where the return is just equal to the cost of financing these projects.

If safety and the maintaining of, say, family control are considered to be more important than additional profits, there may be a marked unwillingness to engage in external financing, and hence a limit will be placed on the amounts available for investment.

Even though the enterprise may wish to raise external finance for its investment programme, there are many reasons why it may be unable to do this. For example:

➡ The enterprise's past record and its present capital structure may make it impossible, or extremely costly, to raise additional debt capital
➡ Its record may make it impossible to raise new equity capital because of low yields – or even no yield
➡ Covenants in existing loan agreements may restrict future borrowing.

Furthermore, in the typical company, one would expect capital rationing to be largely self-imposed.

Post-audit

Each major project should be followed up to ensure that it conforms to the conditions on which it was accepted, as well as being subject to cost control procedures.

An example

The following example illustrates the importance of accurate forecasts of cash flows (representing sales value, cost of sales, operating costs, and initial investment). Taxation is deliberately ignored. (The example is adapted from Winer, 1966.)

A proposal has been put forward in the form of a marketing plan to launch a new line of toys. Cash flow forecasts are shown in Figure 14.25. Note that depreciation is not, in fact, a cash cost. It is shown here simply as a footnote to indicate that there will be no cash inflow at the end of Year 5 from the sale of the equipment, since that equipment is not expected to have any residual value at that point in time.

The evaluation of the plan is shown in Figure 14.26, which is largely self-explanatory. Cost of capital is shown as being 18 per cent. This can be taken to be the minimum required rate of return from the plan (thus reflecting equivalent returns from alternative plans of comparable risk). The plan's net present value is £447 000,

Proposal	Add a new line of toys
Cash investment (£'000s)	
Production equipment	1,000
Recruiting and training salesmen	100
Promotional material	10
Inventory and debtors	190
	1,300
Projected sales volume (£'000s)	
Year 1	600
Year 2	1,000
Year 3	1,200
Year 4	1,000
Year 5 (final year)	800
Cost of sales	30% of sales value
Direct operating costs	£100,000 per annum
Depreciation of equipment	£200,000 per annum. No salvage value.

Figure 14.25 Cash flow projections (adapted from Winer, 1966)

			Year			
(£'000s)	0	1	2	3	4	5
1 Cash investment	(1,300)					
2 Sales revenue		600	1,000	1,200	1,000	800
3 Cost of sales		(180)	(300)	(360)	(300)	(240)
4 Operating costs		(100)	(100)	(100)	(100)	(100)
5 Recovery of investment in inventory and debtors						190
6 Cash flows	(1,300)	320	600	740	600	650
7 Discount factor at 18%	1.00	0.847	0.718	0.609	0.516	0.437
8 Discounted cash flow	(1,300)	271	431	451	310	284
9 NPV	447					

Figure 14.26 Cash flow analysis and evaluation (adapted from Winer, 1966)

which results when the discounted inflows and outflows are summed and the initial investment deducted from the total:

Total discounted value of inflows and outflows from Year 1 to year 5	£1,747,000
Initial investment	£1,300,000
Net present value	£447,000

From these figures it is also possible to calculate the PV index:

$$\frac{£1,747,000}{£1,300,000} = 1.34$$

In other words, the plan promises to generate £1.34 for every £1.00 invested in it, expressed in terms of current £s. Since the PV index exceeds unity (hence the NPV is positive), the plan appears to be economically viable. However, various additional questions need to be raised, such as:

➡ Is there sufficient funding available to meet the initial investment requirements of £1 300 000?

➡ Can the plan be modified to earn even more than £1.34 per £1.00 of investment?

➡ Are there alternatives available that may be more attractive?

➡ How sensitive is the plan's NPV to changes in flow estimates, including their timing?

From the data given in Figure 14.26, it is possible to calculate the payback period of the plan and the accounting rate of return, as outlined below.

Payback period is the length of time it takes to recover the initial investment.

		£'000s
	Year 1	320
	Year 2	600
380/740	Year 3	380
		1,300

It will be two years and 187 days (assuming an even pattern of inflows). The investment is exposed, therefore, over half of the anticipated life of the plan.

The accounting rate of return is an accounting (rather than cash flow) measure of the average profitability of the plan.

➡ Average profits will be (in £'000s):

$$\frac{£(320 + 600 + 740 + 600 + 460)}{5} - £200$$

$$\frac{£2,720}{5} - £200 = £344$$

It is necessary to deduct depreciation as an expense in calculating the average accounting profit.

➡ Average investment will be (in £'000s)

$$\frac{£1,300 - £190}{2} = £555$$

➡ The ARR will be:

$$\frac{£344}{£555} \times 100 = 62\%$$

Valuing market strategies

Mention was made in Chapter 13 of the criterion of enhanced shareholder value. This has been adopted by Day and Fahey (1988) in their approach to strategy evaluation. Since the basic premise of this approach is that shareholders' interests should be maximized, it will be apparent that it is a partial approach that ignores other stakeholders' interests. Moreover, since maximizing the current market value of shareholders' interests presumes that the shares themselves are listed, this restricts Day and Fahey's approach to a little over 2200 of the total of more than 1 million limited companies incorporated within the UK.

Value is created whenever the financial gains from a strategy exceed its costs. The use of discounting methods allows for both the timing of cash flows and the inherent riskiness of marketing strategies in measuring the value of the latter. A potential shareholder will only invest in an enterprise if it is his or her expectation that the management of that enterprise will generate a better return than he could obtain himself, at a given level of risk. The minimum expected return is the cost of capital (i.e that rate used in discounting); hence, shareholder value is only created when activities are undertaken that generate a return in excess of the cost of capital.

The usual approach adopted in assessing the shareholder value of an enterprise is to discount the anticipated cash flows by the risk-adjusted cost of capital. If a new strategy is in prospect then the shareholder value will be the sum of the value to be derived from the new strategy plus the 'baseline' value, reflecting the value that is expected to result from continuing the existing strategy. This gives a basis for comparing strategic alternatives in a way that highlights their respective contributions to value. Thus:

Estimated shareholder value if strategy X is selected	=	Estimated value contributed by strategy X	+	Baseline shareholder value
∴ Estimated value of strategy X	=	Estimated shareholder value if strategy X is selected	−	Baseline shareholder value

When several competing strategies are being evaluated in a situation where there are insufficient resources to undertake all available strategies that meet the specified economic criterion (e.g. offer a positive net present value when discounted at the risk-adjusted cost of capital), the recommended basis for ranking acceptable strategies is by use of the PV index. This shows how much value is created per £1 of investment:

$$\text{PV index} = \frac{\text{Present value of strategy}}{\text{Investment required}}$$

In using this approach to evaluating strategies, there needs to be available:

➡ Cash inflow and outflow forecasts relating to each alternative strategy
➡ Cash flow forecasts relating to the baseline strategy
➡ A suitable discount factor (i.e. the risk-adjusted cost of capital)
➡ Alternative scenarios to allow the sensitivity of the outcomes to changes in the inputs to be tested.

Even if all these information requirements can be met, there is inevitably a large element of subjectivity involved; in part this will be included within the estimates of cash flows, etc., and in part it will reflect both the specification of the strategy and the interpretation of results from the analysis. It is suggested that all assumptions involving judgements be specified explicitly in order that their appropriateness can be gauged by others.

The steps to follow in carrying out a strategic evaluation to enhance shareholder value are:

1 Derive cash flow forecasts from the managerial judgements relating to competitive and market responses to each strategic alternative
2 Adjust the forecasts from point 1 for risk and timing prior to calculating the NPV of each strategy and relating these NPVs to baseline expectations in order to gauge the increase in shareholder value from each alternative
3 Select the strategy that offers the greatest increase in shareholder value and implement it.

It is implicit in this sequence of steps that:

➡ The value creation potential of each strategic alternative relative to the baseline strategy can be accurately predicted
➡ The shareholder value criterion is applicable to all strategic alternatives having cash flow implications
➡ The stock market will recognize and reward strategies that enhance shareholder value.

Each of these matters raises fundamental questions. For example, our ability to predict accurately is limited for reasons of uncertainty as well as personal bias, and the stock market is not a perfect market (and so does not have perfect information on which to base its reactions). Nevertheless, by focusing on cash flows rather than accounting data, and by taking a long-term perspective rather than a short-term one, the approach advocated by Day and Fahey has distinct benefits as well as limitations.

Support for variations on this 'economic value' approach has come from a range of sources. Buzzell and Chussil (1985), for example, have argued that it is rare for managers to evaluate strategies in terms of their effects on future value. This suggests that many enterprises are failing to achieve their full potential by using inappropriate methods for strategic evaluation, and by emphasizing short-run financial results at the expense of long-term competitive strength.

14.5 Summary

Given the specification of marketing programmes in Chapters 11 and 12, and the specification of choice criteria in Chapter 13, this chapter has sought to show some of the ways in which marketing programmes might be evaluated by using financial modelling approaches embodying the appropriate criteria.

The principles of modelling were reviewed and developed via a consideration of short-run financial modelling (using cost–volume–profit analysis) and long-run financial modelling (using investment appraisal methods).

A model is, in essence, a simplified representation of a situation or process that needs to be analysed, evaluated or controlled. The representation can be symbolic, mathematical or physical. In using financial models such as those dealt with in this chapter, it is necessary to bear in mind the limitations of such models. In particular, financial systems measure those things that can be measured by financial systems, and in a marketing context there are typically many additional issues that cannot be adequately reflected in financial models.

Chapter **15**

Modelling approaches – 2

15.1 Learning objectives

When you have read this chapter you should be able to:

(a) understand more fully the role of modelling approaches;
(b) recognize and handle the problems of allowing for risk and uncertainty in carrying out evaluations;
(c) appreciate the contribution that non-financial modelling approaches – such as matrix models and Bonoma's MPA model – can make to evaluating marketing plans;
(d) see the applicability of programming approaches to the evaluation of marketing plans.

15.2 Introduction

In Chapter 14 we looked at the nature of models and modelling, with particular reference to short-run financial modelling (via cost–volume–profit analysis) and long-run financial modelling (using investment appraisal methods). In general, little attention was paid to the problems of risk and uncertainty. These will be dealt with in this chapter.

In addition, matrix models of a non-financial type will be covered as an extension of the discussion in Chapter 9. For example, the directional policy matrix, multifactor portfolio matrix, product positioning matrix and Bonoma's marketing performance assessment (MPA) model will be discussed and illustrated.

We will also extend the discussion (see Chapter 1) on marketing experimentation and introduce aspects of programming and network analysis that can be used to evaluate marketing programmes.

15.3 Allowing for risk and uncertainty

In dealing with risk and uncertainty we will draw heavily from management science. Management science is a method or approach to management problem solving rather than a discipline within its own right. The various techniques of management science offer managers an analytical, objective and (usually) quantitative basis for making better decisions.

The basic requirement in decision-making is information and a major branch of management science is concerned with the provision of information under conditions of risk and uncertainty. This is the role of *decision theory*.

Information should preferably be in quantitative form, and this presupposes some means of measurement. Furthermore, the information presented should relate to the objective of the decision – it is easier to make the correct decision when one keeps in mind what one is trying to achieve. If there exists more than one objective, the decision-maker must balance one against the other by making a *trade-off*. For example, the decision-maker may trade speed for quality in deciding on a particular means of distribution if this appears to reflect accurately the relative importance of multiple objectives.

Decisions are made in relation to objectives and they are well made if the objectives are achieved. However, doubts about the future mean that a choice can be wrong, and it also means that a single choice can have several possible outcomes. The sales of a new product, for instance, may be at any one of several levels estimated at the time of its launch. The systematic approach of decision theory allows good decisions to be made even in the presence of severe doubts about what the future may hold in store.

Views of the future are of four types:

1 *Ignorance*, where the future is seen as a blank
2 *Assumed certainty*, which is a pretence, for all practical purposes, that the future is known exactly and estimates become deterministic
3 *Risk*, where it is not known exactly what will happen in the future but the various possibilities are weighed by their assumed probability of occurrence
4 *Uncertainty*, where a variety of outcomes is possible but probabilities cannot be assigned.

There is little that can be done in cases of ignorance, other than following a systematic approach and attempting to delay making the decision until further information has been gathered. In cases of certainty, of course, there is no such need for delay. This covers situations in which the decision-maker has full knowledge.

In relation to decision-making under conditions of risk and uncertainty, the purpose of expressing an opinion about the likelihood of an event occurring is to facilitate the development of decision-making procedures that are explicit and consistent with the decision-maker's beliefs (see Illustration 15.1).

Illustration 15.1

Lou Gerstner, the chief executive of IBM, when asked about his vision of the company, said: 'The last thing IBM needs now is a vision for the future. What is required is to take control of the immediate problems before we can even consider what lies ahead.'

Allowing for risk

Risk describes a situation in which there are a number of actions or strategies that may be taken, a number of conditions or events that may be experienced (known as *states of nature* because they are beyond the decision-maker's control) and consequently a number of possible outcomes, each of which will depend on a particular combination of strategy and state of nature.

In the risk situation, *probability theory* is central in rational decision-making. The probability of a particular outcome of an event is simply the proportion of times this outcome would occur if the event were repeated a great number of times. Thus, the probability of the outcome 'heads' in tossing a coin is 0.5, since a large number of tosses would result in 50 per cent heads and 50 per cent tails.

By convention, probabilities follow certain rules, such as:

→ The probability assigned to each possible future event must be a positive number between zero and unity, where zero represents an impossible event and unity represents a certain one
→ If a set of events is mutually exclusive (i.e. only one will come about) and exhaustive (i.e. covers all possible outcomes), then the total of the probabilities of the events must add up to one.

The probability of an outcome is a measure of the certainty of that outcome. If, for instance, a sales manager is fairly confident that his division will be able to sell 10 000 units in the forthcoming period, he may accord a probability of 0.8 to this outcome (i.e. he is 80 per cent certain that 10 000 units will be sold). By simple deduction, there is a 20 per cent probability that the outcome will be something other than 10 000 units (i.e. $100 - 80 = 20$ per cent).

A development of this approach gives rise to the concept of *expected value*. This results from the multiplying of each possible outcome of an event by the probability of that outcome occurring, and this gives a measure of the *pay-off* of each alternative. An example should make this clear: Company XYZ has two new marketable products but only sufficient resources to manufacture and market one of these. The relevant estimates of sales, costs and profits are shown in Figure 15.1 for the various anticipated levels of sales activity.

	Sales £	Costs £	Profit £	Probability	Expected value £
Product A	1,000	500	500	0.1	50
	1,250	600	650	0.4	260
	1,500	700	800	0.3	240
	1,750	800	950	0.2	190
				1.0	£740
Product B	2,000	800	1,200	0.2	240
	2,300	950	1,350	0.4	540
	2,500	1,050	1,450	0.2	290
	2,700	1,150	1,550	0.1	155
	3,000	1,300	1,700	0.1	170
				1.0	£1,395

Figure 15.1 Decision information

The calculations are very simple. If sales of Product A amount to £1000, the associated costs – as shown in Figure 15.1 – are £500, and thus the profit is also £500. But there is only a probability of 0.1 that this outcome will eventuate, giving an *expected value* of £50 (i.e. £500 × 0.1).

This procedure is followed for the other possible outcomes of Product A sales, costs and profits, and the expected values of each outcome summated to give an expected pay-off of £740. (This is nothing more than a weighted arithmetic average of the data given in Figure 15.1.)

In contrast, Product B has an expected pay-off of £1395 and this choice is therefore the better one of the two, provided that profit is the desired objective, as measured by the pay-off computation.

Apart from the externally given economic and physical conditions surrounding a decision (i.e. the 'states of nature'), the decision-maker's own attitudes towards the alternatives must also be taken into account. His or her scale of values will determine the *desirability* of each possible course of action, whereas the conventional prediction systems merely assign probabilities. Desirability has connotations of 'best' that are unrelated to profit and may be measured in terms of utility, thus:

Expected utility = (Probability of success × value of success) −
(Probability of failure × value of failure)

As a result of their sense of values, decision-makers will have a general attitude towards risk that may cause them to act as either a *risk acceptor* or a *risk averter*. In the latter case, decision-makers will tend to request more and more information before they attempt to make a decision, and this will often mean that decisions are made too late to be optimal, whereas the risk acceptor makes rapid decisions that may not be the correct ones.

Risk attitudes are one of four essential elements to be ascertained in any decision, these being:

1 What are the available courses of action?
2 What are the relevant states of nature?
3 What are the possible outcomes?
4 What is important to the decision-maker?

Applying risk analysis

The application of simple risk analysis is best illustrated by means of an example. Let it be assumed that RST Ltd has two new products, A and B, but only has the resources to launch one of these. The relevant states of nature relate to competitive activity – no matter which product is launched, it may be assumed that the competition will:

➡ Do nothing, or
➡ Introduce a comparable product, or
➡ Introduce a superior product.

On the basis of past experience and current knowledge, the management of RST Ltd attach probabilities of 0.25, 0.5 and 0.25 respectively to these states of nature. In the light of these alternative conditions, the profit of each strategy can be shown in a *pay-off matrix* (Figure 15.2).

This matrix shows that if Product B is launched and a comparable competitive product is introduced, a profit of £20 000 will be made, and so forth for the other five possible outcomes. The best decision would *appear* to be to introduce Product B and *hope* that competitive action does not change. But is this so?

By using the concept of expected value it is possible to calculate the expected profit (or pay-off) from each strategy by multiplying the probability of each outcome by the profit from that outcome. Thus, for strategy A (the introduction of Product A), the expected pay-off is given by:

$$(40{,}000 \times 0.25) + (30{,}000 \times 0.5) + (20{,}000 \times 0.25) = £30{,}000$$

Similarly, for strategy B the expected pay-off is:

$$(70{,}000 \times 0.25) + (20{,}000 \times 0.5) + (0 \times 0.25) = £27{,}500$$

This analysis clearly shows that strategy A is to be preferred as it has a larger expected profit or pay-off. It is vital, however, that the distinction between the *expected* pay-off and the *most probable* pay-off is understood and attention focused on the former rather than the latter. The most probable pay-off for strategy A is that with the competitive introduction of a comparable product, which has a probability of 0.5 and a profit estimated at £30 000. The most probable pay-off for strategy B has the same state of nature, and a profit estimate of £20 000. But the most probable outcome cannot be used as the basis for decision-making because it ignores the other possible outcomes. It is thought to be 50 per cent certain that a comparable competitive product will be launched, which means that it is also 50 per cent *uncertain* that this will occur, and allowance for this eventuality should accordingly be made. The use of expected pay-off allows for this.

From the information contained in the above example, a *decision tree* can be constructed as in Figure 15.3.

Strategies and states of nature are represented by the branches of the decision tree, and at each fork there are as many branches as there are identified possibilities. Only if all of the possible courses of action have been observed and included will the tree be

| Strategy | State of nature | | |
	Do nothing	Introduce comparable product	Introduce superior product
Launch A	£40,000	£30,000	£20,000
Launch B	£70,000	£20,000	£0

Figure 15.2   Pay-off matrix

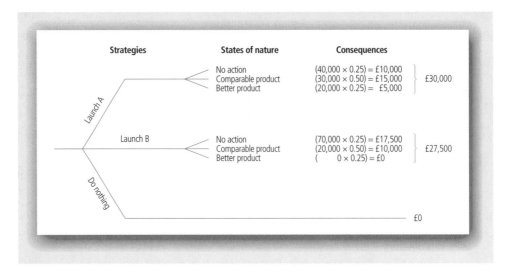

Figure 15.3 Decision tree

complete. For each alternative combination of strategy and state of nature the outcome can be computed, and the expected pay-off for each strategy derived.

A decision tree is a diagrammatic representation of the relationships between decisions, states of nature and pay-offs (or outcomes) that helps in structuring problems in a way that allows risk to be assessed at each stage. Further examples will show how a decision tree can be used. Imagine a research project that is in progress with a view to developing a new product for commercial launch. There are several aspects to this issue:

➡ The project may be aborted or it may be allowed to continue
➡ If it is continued it may or may not result in a potentially marketable new product
➡ If it does result in a marketable product, the organization may choose to launch it immediately or to postpone the launch
➡ Competitors may or may not be able to match the organization's endeavours.

Figure 15.4 spells out these aspects and specifies the two major decisions that need to be made. (The squares represent points at which decisions need to be made, while the circles represent subsequent events.) It can be seen that each decision, combined with the states of nature that are assumed to prevail, produces distinct outcomes.

The next step is to introduce quantitative data, so let us assume the following:

1 It will cost an estimated £50 000 to continue the project (which is itself probabilistic)
2 If the company decides to postpone the launch of the product (assuming the project is successful) and competitors enter the market, there will be a loss of current business amounting to £125 000
3 If the project is successful and an immediate launch is undertaken, the company will generate incremental cash flows of £450 000 if competitors stay out of the market but only £250 000 if competitors enter the market.

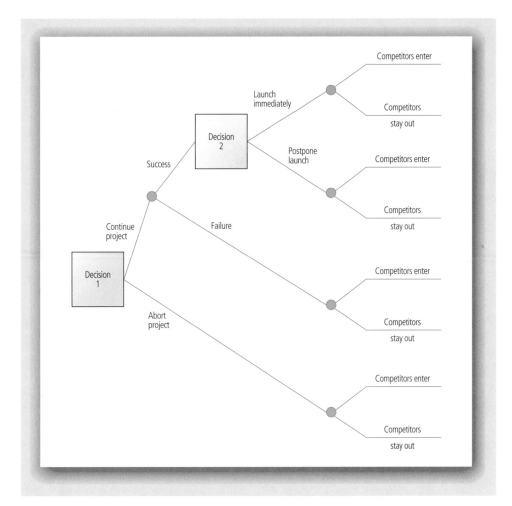

Figure 15.4 A basic decision tree

These figures are shown at the end of each branch of the decision tree in Figure 15.5. We now need to incorporate the probabilities of the events leading to the various possible outcomes, and these are also shown in Figure 15.5. By working back from the right-hand side of the decision tree, it is a simple matter to compute expected values. Taking the branch dealing with the immediate launch of a successful project as an example, the expected value is derived as follows:

£250,000 × 0.7 = £175,000
£450,000 × 0.3 = £135,000
Expected value   £310,000

The figures show that an immediate launch is the better alternative if the project is successful than is postponing it (which has an expected value of −£112 500). But this only gives part of the picture, so the expected values need to be worked through to the next event in the tree (moving across from right to left). The logic in doing this is straightforward: if the project is successful and the launch is immediate, there will be a larger pay-off than if the

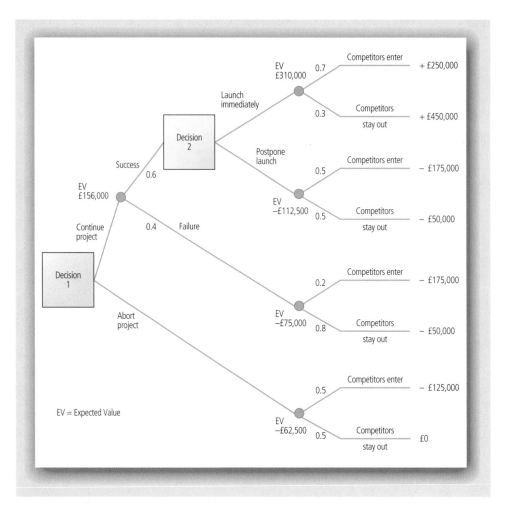

Figure 15.5 Decision tree with quantified outcomes

launch is postponed, so the latter branch can now be ignored. This gives an expected value for continuing the project of £156 000, calculated thus:

$$
\begin{aligned}
£310,000 \times 0.6 &= £186,000 \\
-£75,000 \times 0.4 &= -£30,000 \\
\text{Expected value} &\quad \underline{£156,000}
\end{aligned}
$$

A comparison of this pay-off with the expected value of aborting the project (−£62 500) shows the desirability of continuing with the project.

Risk analysis is applicable to most pricing decisions, such as the situation in which a company can adopt one of three pricing policies for a new product:

1 Skimming pricing – P_1
2 Intermediate pricing – P_2
3 Penetration pricing – P_3

and in which three estimates of demand are available:

1 Optimistic forecast – Q_1
2 Most probable demand – Q_2
3 Pessimistic forecast – Q_3

and in which two sizes of plant are available:

1 Small plant – F_1
2 Large plant – F_2.

The various interrelationships of price, demand and capacity are illustrated in a decision tree format in Figure 15.6.

The pay-off is computed by taking the probability of each level of demand and multiplying it by the forecast level of demand, and then multiplying this by the price. Thus, for a penetration pricing policy (P_3) with a small factory (F_1) and a pessimistic sales forecast (Q_3), the pay-off is given by multiplying the P_3F_1 price of £4 by 0.2, which

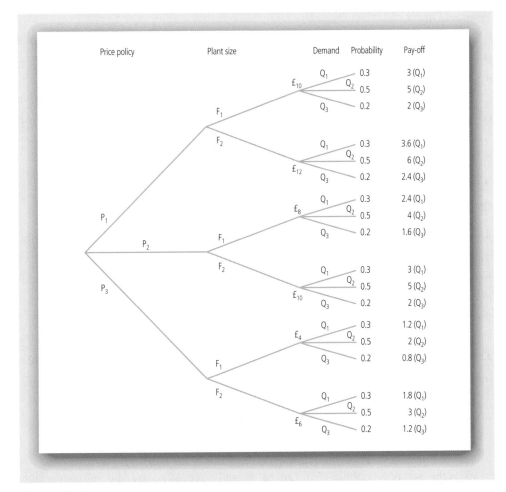

Figure 15.6 Pricing decision tree

3.0 × 50,000	=	150,000	3.0 × 50,000	=	150,000
5.0 × 40,000	=	200,000	5.0 × 40,000	=	200,000
2.0 × 30,000	=	60,000	2.0 × 30,000	=	60,000
Expected pay-off P_1F_1		£410,000	Expected pay-off P_2F_2		£410,000
3.6 × 50,000	=	180,000	1.2 × 50,000	=	60,000
6.0 × 40,000	=	240,000	2.0 × 40,000	=	80,000
2.4 × 30,000	=	72,000	0.8 × 30,000	=	24,000
Expected pay-off P_1F_2		£492,000	Expected pay-off P_3F_1		£164,000
2.4 × 50,000	=	120,000	1.8 × 50,000	=	90,000
4.0 × 40,000	=	160,000	3.0 × 40,000	=	120,000
1.6 × 30,000	=	48,000	1.2 × 30,000	=	36,000
Expected pay-off P_2F_1		£328,000	Expected pay-off P_3F_2		£246,000

Figure 15.7   Expected pay-offs

is the probability of Q_3 occurring, and expressing this in terms of Q_3. If values of 50 000, 40 000 and 30 000 are ascribed to Q_1, Q_2 and Q_3, the pay-off column in Figure 15.6 becomes Figure 15.7.

Clearly, strategy P_1F_2 has the highest expected pay-off because it has the highest price, but each expected pay-off must be related to objectives in order to select the most appropriate in a given situation.

There are several alternatives to the basic decision tree approach to allowing for risk that can be employed. It is not possible within the limits of this volume to cover them, but there is space to refer to *sensitivity analysis*. In its applied organizational setting, this has been broadly defined by Rappaport (1967, p. 441) as:

" . . . a study to determine the responsiveness of the conclusions of an analysis to changes or errors in parameter values used in the analysis.*"*

Sensitivity analysis seeks to test the responsiveness of outcomes from decision models to different input values and constraints as a basis for appraising the relative risk of alternative courses of action. It is also possible to use sensitivity analysis for helping determine the value of information in addition to its role in strategic decision-making.

In effect, what sensitivity analysis allows management to do is to experiment in the abstract without the time, cost or risk associated with experimenting with the organization itself. This can be seen symbolically in the following expression:

$V = f(X,Y)$

where:

   V = a measure of the value of the decision that is to be made;
   X = the set of variables that can be directly regulated by the decision-maker (i.e. the decision variables);

Y = the set of factors (variable or constant) that affects outcomes but is not subject to direct regulation by the decision-maker (i.e. the states of nature);

f = the functional relationship amongst V, X and Y.

One can manipulate any element within X or Y and see the consequent impact on V.

Reference has been made in earlier chapters of this book to balancing the cost and value of information. The broad picture is given in Figure 15.8, from which it will be seen that the optimum amount of information in a given situation (OM) is to be found when the difference between the value and cost curves is greatest. For a number of reasons (including overload), the value of information starts to decline as more is made available, whereas the cost of providing information increases at an accelerating rate as more is made available (due to increasing accuracy, faster transmission, etc.).

In operational terms, how can we assess the value of information? We can readily grasp the principle that by evaluating the consequences of a particular decision based on a given amount of information on the one hand, and then evaluating the consequences of the same decision made with additional information on the other, the difference (in consequences) reflects the value of the extra information. This value gives the maximum sum that should be spent on generating the extra information. To apply this principle requires that we:

1 Enumerate the possible outcomes of future information collection efforts
2 Compute the probabilities of these outcomes
3 Indicate how the information will change the decision-maker's view of this choice.

These are demanding requirements!

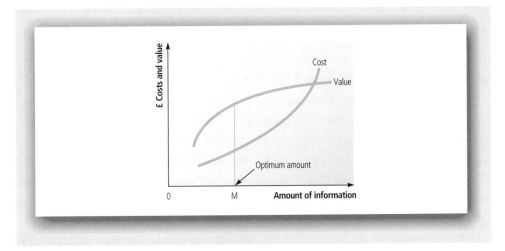

Figure 15.8   Cost and value of information

Allowing for uncertainty

Uncertainty arises from a lack of previous experience and knowledge. This results in the decision-maker's inability to assign probabilities to the elements within alternative strategies.

Inevitably, decision-making under conditions of uncertainty is more complicated than is the case under risk conditions. In fact, there is no single *best* criterion (such as expected pay-off) that should be used in selecting a strategy. Of the various available techniques, company policy or the decision-maker's attitude will determine that which is selected. Four possible criteria are given below.

1 Maximin – criterion of pessimism

The assumption underlying this technique is that the worst outcome will always come about and the decision-maker should therefore select the largest minimum pay-off. Referring back to Figure 15.2, this would mean that strategy A should be adopted; the worst outcome for A is £20 000 and the worst for strategy B is £0, which means that strategy A maximizes the minimum – hence maximin. The philosophy is that the actual outcome can only be an improvement in the majority of instances – the probabilities accorded to strategy A suggest that there is a 75 per cent chance that a better result than £20 000 will be obtained and a 25 per cent chance of its being £20 000.

2 Maximax – criterion of optimism

This is the opposite of maximin and is based on the assumption that the best pay-off will result from the selected strategy. Referring again to Figure 15.2, the highest pay-offs are £40 000 and £70 000 for A and B respectively. Strategy B has the highest maximum pay-off and will be selected under the maximax criterion.

3 Criterion of regret

This criterion is based on the fact that, having selected a strategy that does not turn out to be the best one, the decision-maker will regret not having chosen another strategy when he or she had the opportunity.

Thus, if strategy B had been adopted (see Figure 15.9) on the maximax assumption that competitors would do nothing, and competitors actually did nothing, there would be no regret; however, if strategy A had been selected the company would have lost £70 000 − £40 000 = £30 000. This measures the *regret*, and the aim of the regret criterion is to minimize the maximum possible regret. A regret matrix (Figure 15.9) can be constructed on the above basis.

The maximum regret for strategy A is £30 000 and that for strategy B £20 000. The choice is therefore B if the maximum regret is to be minimized.

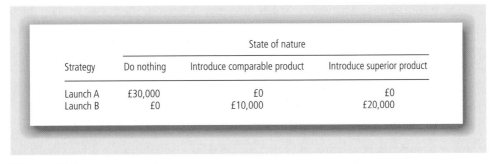

	State of nature		
Strategy	Do nothing	Introduce comparable product	Introduce superior product
Launch A	£30,000	£0	£0
Launch B	£0	£10,000	£20,000

Figure 15.9 Regret matrix

4 Criterion of rationality – Laplace criterion

The assumption behind this criterion is that, since the probabilities of the various states of nature are not known, each state of nature is equally likely. The expected pay-off from each strategy is then calculated and the one with the largest expected pay-off selected.

For strategy A the expected pay-off under this criterion is:

$$(40,000 \times 0.33) + (30,000 \times 0.33) + (20,000 \times 0.33) = £30,000$$

For strategy B it is:

$$(70,000 \times 0.33) + (20,000 \times 0.33) + (0 \times 0.33) = £30,000$$

By chance neither strategy in this example is preferable under this criterion, with the result that the choice must be made on another basis (e.g. in terms of desirability) or under another criterion (e.g. minimax).

Under conditions of risk or uncertainty the decision may appear to be to select one of the available courses of action or to accept none of them. However, another alternative is to postpone the decision and gather more information to aid in the selection process.

Perfect information is rarely available, so the decision-maker must be satisfied with imperfect data, which will reduce even if it does not eliminate the uncertainty. But there comes a point when it is unnecessary or pointless collecting further information, and at this point a decision must be made. An increasingly popular approach to determining this point is given by the Bayesian approach to statistical decision theory.

The theory of Bayesian inference is one that provides the basic rules whereby one set of probabilities can be mathematically (i.e. logically) determined from another. For example, the probability of heads in tossing a coin is 0.5, and Bayesian inference puts the probability of there being 10 heads in a row as 0.5^{10} (about 0.001). Bayesian inference is not restricted to accepting the input of observed data only: it will also accept the decision-maker's subjective probabilities.

The most common form of Bayesian inference is prior–posterior analysis, which involves the derivation of probabilities posterior to evidence by reweighing prior probabilities according to likelihoods indicated by this evidence. This procedure is an important one. However, since it is beyond the scope of this book to present a detailed exposition of Bayes' theorem, the interested reader is referred to Day (1964).

In general, the benefits of decision theory are that it requires the decision-making manager to make uncertainties and other judgements explicit in such a way that they can be incorporated into a formal analysis that will lead to the best decisions being made. This process need not be time-consuming, but it does prevent the hurried selection of the most obvious course of action and encourages creative thinking in seeking new solutions to problems.

This is the best way to determine the value of information prior to carrying out research. It differs from traditional statistical techniques by allowing the assignment of numerical probabilities to *unique* rather than to repetitive events, with probabilities being subjectively determined by the decision-maker. For example, in relation to a new product launch, Bayesian analysis argues that the manager has some idea of how well it will do based on his experience with other products, and that these expectations can be translated into quantitative terms by assigning probabilities to the various sales levels that may be achieved. The key concept is the 'opportunity loss', which represents either:

➡ The actual financial loss due to the new product failing to reach its break-even sales volume, or
➡ The potential loss of profit from failing to introduce the product when sales would have been profitable.

In Figure 15.10 the probabilities of the expected sales levels are shown in columns (1) and (2), and the profit/loss consequences are shown in column (3), with the break-even point being 1 400 000. At a sales level of 1 800 000, a profit of £450 000 is expected, and the opportunity loss of *not* introducing the product (if this level of sales could be achieved) is £450 000 (i.e. the profit of launching the product is foregone by not launching it). The *expected* opportunity loss is given by the product of the estimated probability and the opportunity loss. For a sales level of 1 800 000 the expected loss is (0.10 × £450 000) = £45 000. The same analysis can be applied to all the other possible sales levels, as shown in columns (4)–(7). The sums of columns (6) and (7) show the overall expected opportunity loss of each course of action – introduce the product on the one hand, or do not introduce it on the other. Since the 'introduce' choice has the lowest expected opportunity loss, it should be the chosen course of action, and £67 500 is the maximum value of research expenditure.

Although analytical methods can be applied to the evaluation of risk and uncertainty, management may prefer to take other courses of action to reduce these factors. Perhaps the best method is to increase the information available to the

Unit sales (1)	Estimated probability (2)	Profit/loss (3)	Opportunity loss		Expected opportunity loss	
			Introduced (4)	Not introduced (5)	Introduced (6)	Not introduced (7)
1,800,000	0.10	450,000	0	450,000	0	45,000
1,600,000	0.25	200,000	0	200,000	0	50,000
1,400,000	0.35	0	0	0	0	0
1,200,000	0.15	−150,000	150,000	0	22,500	0
1,000,000	0.10	−250,000	250,000	0	25,000	0
800,000	0.05	−400,000	400,000	0	20,000	0
Totals	1.00				£67,500	£95,000

Figure 15.10   Bayesian analysis for product launch

decision-maker prior to making a decision. For instance, marketing research can supply further information prior to new product launches via product testing or test marketing.

Alternatively, the scale of operations may be increased, or product diversification pursued. Figure 15.11 illustrates the case of two products, with Product A having a seasonal demand pattern that is the opposite of the pattern of Product B.

However, in combination, Figure 15.12 shows that the overall result is one of continuous profitability, whereas either product in isolation would result in a loss during part of its demand cycle.

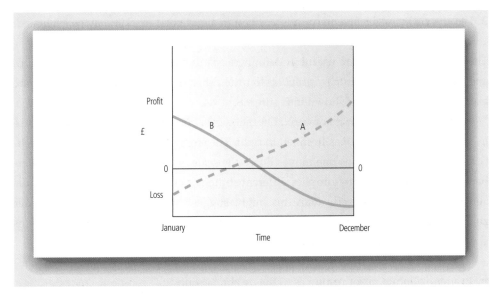

Figure 15.11   Diversified products

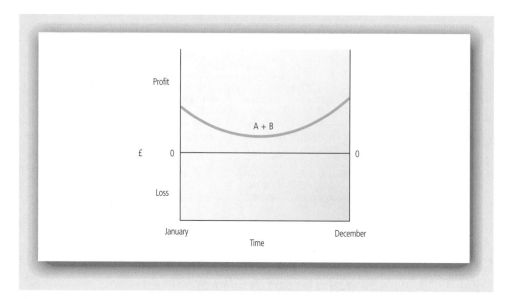

Figure 15.12 Combined profitability

15.4 Matrix models

A number of analytical matrix models were discussed in Chapters 9 and 10. In this section we will focus on three available models: the directional policy matrix, the multifactor portfolio matrix and the product positioning matrix.

Directional policy matrix

This was developed to help in identifying:

1 The principal criteria by which a business unit's prospects may be assessed
2 The criteria by which an enterprise's position in a particular market may be evaluated.

The criteria that emerge are useful in defining *business sector prospects* on the one hand, and the *enterprise's competitive capabilities* on the other. These can be used to label the axes of the matrix itself, as shown in Figure 9.8.

There are nine cells in this matrix. On the x-axis, business sector prospects increase in attractiveness as one moves from left to right. The strength of the enterprise's competitive capabilities increases as one moves down the scale on the y-axis. Locating an enterprise in any cell of the matrix implies different strategic actions, although the boundaries between cells are less precise than this might suggest: it is more helpful to consider zones rather than cells – even though the zones may be of irregular shapes. Strategies appropriate to the zones shown in Figure 9.8 are (after Cohen, 1988, pp. 36–7):

➡ Leader – allocate major resources to the product group
➡ Try harder – acceptable in the short run but may be vulnerable over the longer run

➡ Double or quit – major future sources of competitive advantage and profitability should be developed from this zone

➡ Growth – sufficient resources should be allocated to match market growth

➡ Custodial – maximize cash generation without any further commitment of resources

➡ Cash generator – a cash generator with little further need for finance or expansion

➡ Phased withdrawal – resources can be reallocated to better uses by withdrawing gradually

➡ Divest – withdraw immediately and redeploy resources elsewhere.

Among the criteria by which business sector prospects might be assessed are:

➡ Market growth rate – market growth is needed if profits are to grow

➡ Market quality, reflected in such factors as:
  ➡ Whether profitability is high and stable
  ➡ Whether or not margins can be maintained when demand falls below the level of normal capacity
  ➡ Whether the market is supplied by a few or by many enterprises
  ➡ Whether a small group of powerful consumers dominates the market
  ➡ Whether the market offering is free from risks of substitution.

➡ Environmental aspects (e.g. regulations applying to distribution, marketing or manufacturing).

The criteria for assessing an enterprise's competitive capabilities include:

➡ Its market position (usually specified in terms of market share)

➡ Production capability (including location, number of plants, capacity, access to supplies, technological state of facilities)

➡ Product R&D (as a complete technological package to cover product range, quality, developments in applications, competence of technical service).

It is probably most beneficial if the enterprise in question reviews its competitive capabilities relative to those of significant competitors. Ratings are best determined by a team of relevant personnel attempting to reach a consensus. Alternatively, a more complex set of weights (see multifactor portfolio matrix below) may need to be devised when some criteria (or critical success factors) are deemed to be more important than others.

Multifactor portfolio matrix

This was developed jointly by General Electric and the consulting firm of McKinsey & Co. in order to overcome the limitations of the BCG's growth–share matrix. Like the directional policy matrix it has nine cells with the axes relating to similar notions: industry attractiveness (rather than business sector prospects) and business strengths (rather than the enterprise's competitive capabilities). Figure 9.7 illustrates the multi-factor portfolio matrix. There are three zones dealing with strategies relating to:

➡ Invest
➡ Manage selectively for earnings
➡ Harvest or divest

and these are more clearly defined than are the zones within the directional policy matrix.

Criteria that might be used in establishing industry attractiveness include:

➡ Market size
➡ Size of key segments
➡ Market growth rate
➡ Diversity of market
➡ Demand seasonality
➡ Demand cyclicity
➡ Sensitivity of market to price
➡ Opportunities
➡ Competitive structure
➡ Entry and exit barriers
➡ Extent of integration
➡ Degree of concentration
➡ Bargaining power of suppliers
➡ Bargaining power of distributors
➡ Capital intensity
➡ Capacity utilization
➡ Raw material availability
➡ Inflation vulnerability
➡ Environmental aspects
➡ Profitability
➡ Value added.

Measures that reflect business strength include:

➡ Market share
➡ Enterprise (or SBU) growth rate
➡ Breadth of product line
➡ Distributive effectiveness
➡ Sales effectiveness
➡ Price competitiveness
➡ Promotional effectiveness
➡ Facilities (location, age, capacity, etc.)

➡ Experience curve effects

➡ Investment utilization

➡ Raw material cost

➡ Relative product quality

➡ R&D capabilities

➡ Personnel skills

➡ Relative market position

➡ Relative profitability

➡ Value added.

An enterprise can select whichever measures of industry attractiveness or business strength best suit its circumstances when evaluating plans. The relative importance weightings of the selected measures will need to be determined in order to locate a plan within the matrix. This can be carried out in the following way (after Cohen, 1988, pp. 32–5):

1 Identify the major measures of industry attractiveness that are applicable. Let us suppose these are:

➡ Size of market

➡ Growth of market

➡ Ease of entry

➡ Favourable position in PLC.

2 Weights must be assigned to the chosen measures to indicate their relative importance. If the weightings are 0.30, 0.30, 0.25 and 0.15 respectively for the criteria shown in step 1 above, we can see the overall picture in Figure 15.13.

3 Figure 15.13 also shows the points that might be awarded to any given marketing plan in relation to the extent to which the selected criteria are seen to be met by that plan. Points might be awarded on the following basis:

➡ Very attractive   9

➡ Attractive   7

➡ Fair   4.5

➡ Unattractive   3

➡ Very unattractive   0

Industry attractiveness criteria	Relative importance weightings	Point ratings	Weighted scores
Size of market	0.30	9	2.70
Growth of market	0.30	4.5	1.35
Ease of entry	0.25	9	2.25
Favourable PLC position	0.15	0	0
Total weighted score			6.30

Figure 15.13   Weighted score for industry attractiveness

Business strength criteria	Relative importance weightings	Point ratings	Weighted scores
Image	0.40	9	3.60
Productivity	0.30	7	2.10
Product synergy	0.15	3	0.45
Price competitiveness	0.15	4.5	0.675
Total weighted score			6.825

Figure 15.14 Weighted score for business strength

4 A weighted score relating to industry attractiveness can be calculated for each alternative marketing plan – this is equal to 6.30 for the plan covered by Figure 15.13.

5 Steps 1–4 need to be repeated for business strength in relation to each marketing plan. Let us assume that the applicable criteria are image, productivity, product synergy and price competitiveness, with weights of 0.40, 0.30, 0.15 and 0.15 respectively. The assessment of points to indicate the extent to which any given plan meets the applicable criteria would be carried out as outlined in step 3 above, with the results being shown in Figure 15.14.

6 Having calculated weighted scores of 6.30 for industry attractiveness and 6.825 for business strength, it is now possible to locate these scores within the matrix. Using the scales shown in Figure 9.7 it is apparent that the coordinates interesect in the top left-hand cell within the *invest* zone of the matrix.

7 Similar plots can be made for alternative marketing plans and an appropriate choice made in accordance with strategic priorities.

It will be evident that the weightings and scoring within this procedure involve considerable subjective judgement. This makes it important that all underlying assumptions should be made explicit to facilitate peer review.

Product positioning matrix

Among the many other available matrix approaches that can be used for evaluating marketing programmes is that of Wind and Claycamp (1976). This focuses on product line strategy and is comprehensive in that it deals with all the major measures (sales, market share, profitability) that are essential in positioning products by segment.

The first step involves defining:

1 The product (including its subcategories at both the enterprise and industry levels)

2 The strategic market for the product and the key segments within it

3 The appropriate forms of measurement (e.g. sales in value or volume terms, sales per capita, quarterly time periods).

Following the establishment of suitable definitions the analysis can be undertaken. This will involve the generation of:

➡ Sales position for the given product within the strategic market, showing enterprise and industry sales along with an indication of when the product is expected to reach each stage within the product life cycle. For this purpose the PLC can be characterized as having three stages:
  ➡ Growth (when sales are expected to increase by more than 10 per cent year on year)
  ➡ Maturity (where sales are expected to increase in the range of 0–10 per cent year on year)
  ➡ Decline (when sales growth is expected to be negative).
➡ Market share position, which can also be characterized by means of a set of decision rules such as:
  ➡ Marginal (if market share is likely to be less than 10 per cent)
  ➡ Average (if market share is likely to be within the range 10–24 per cent)
  ➡ Leading (if market share is expected to be over 25 per cent).
➡ Profit position, which can be characterized by distinguishing among:
  ➡ Above par (where profit from a given segment is expected to be greater than from the rest of the enterprise's business when expressed as a rate of return)
  ➡ Par (where the profitability expected from the segment is comparable to that from other segments)
  ➡ Below par (where the profitability of the segment is expected to fall below that of other segments).

The expectations relating to product sales, industry sales, market share and profitability can then be plotted on to the comprehensive product evaluation matrix, as shown in Figure 15.15.

It is possible to plot the anticipated positions of the product in question under different assumptions regarding sales, market share and profitability. A time dimension can be built in as suggested in Figure 15.15.

Figure 15.15 shows for two products – A and B – the current position (i.e. A as at 20×1 and B as at 20×1) and projections into the future. Such projections are built up from estimates of each constituent element (sales, market share, profit outcome) for each alternative marketing programme. We can see, for example, that Product A is a poor performer as at 20×1: it is in a declining industry with declining sales, has only an average market share and is achieving a profit performance that is below par. If no change occurs it is anticipated that Product A's position will get worse. In an attempt to improve the position of Product A, two alternative marketing plans are proposed: plan A[1] is predicted to reposition Product A in an improved situation in 20×2 by moving it from its 20×1 position to a position offering stable sales and profits at par, although it is not expected that the decline in industry sales can be changed.

An alternative to plan A[1] is given by plan A[2], which anticipates an improvement in the profit performance but a continuing decline in sales and also in market share between 20×1 and 20×2.

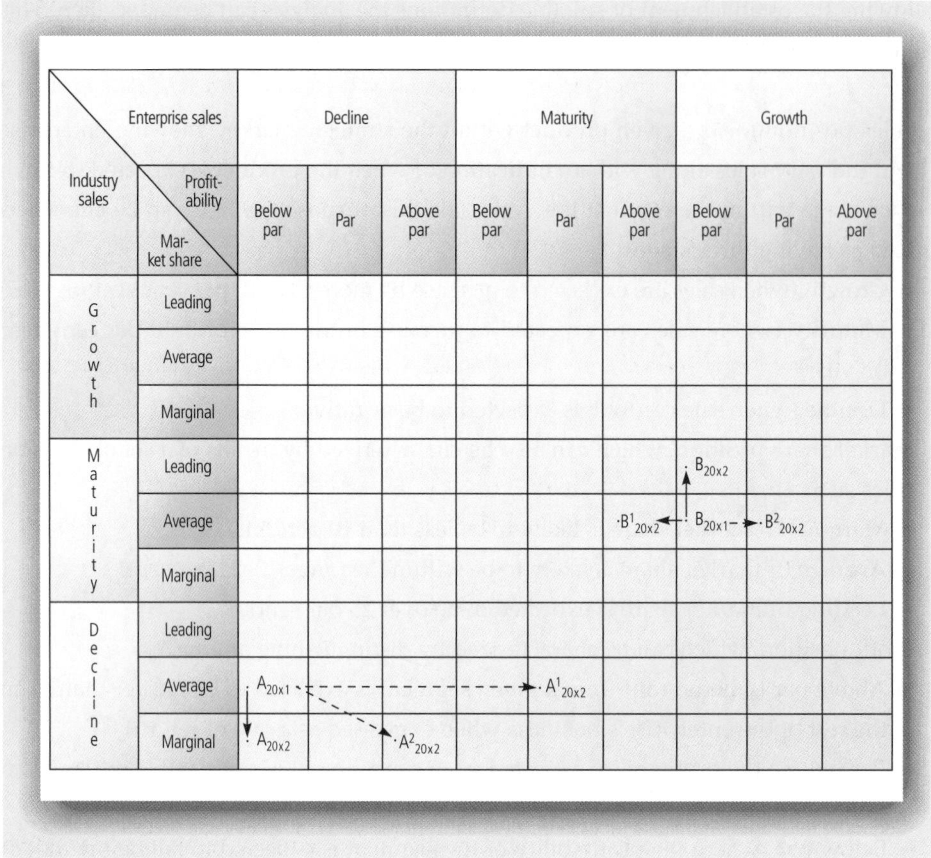

Enterprise sales		Decline			Maturity			Growth		
Industry sales	Profit-ability / Mar-ket share	Below par	Par	Above par	Below par	Par	Above par	Below par	Par	Above par
G r o w t h	Leading									
	Average									
	Marginal									
M a t u r i t y	Leading							B_{20x2}		
	Average					$\cdot B^1_{20x2} \leftarrow$	$B_{20x1} \rightarrow$	$\cdot B^2_{20x2}$		
	Marginal									
D e c l i n e	Leading									
	Average	A_{20x1}				A^1_{20x2}				
	Marginal	A_{20x2}	$\cdot A^2_{20x2}$							

Figure 15.15 Product positioning matrix (adapted from Wind and Claycamp, 1976)

Product B is in a much stronger position in 20×1. It is increasing its sales level within a mature market, thereby increasing its market share, but showing poor profit performance. If no changes occur in the marketing plan for B, the expectation is that, by 20×2, it will have achieved a leading market position with profit performance continuing to be below par. Two alternative marketing plans are proposed for Product B. The first, B^1, will lead to a stable level of sales and an improvement in profit performance from below par to above par. Plan B^2 is expected to produce continuing growth and a better profit position.

For Product A, management must consider the trade-off between a modest improvement in profit with an increase in sales, and a large improvement in profit with a decrease in sales. In the case of Product B, the choice is between taking profits in the near future (plan B^2) or investing for the longer term in increased market share.

15.5 The marketing performance assessment model

Bonoma and Clarke (1988) set out to develop a means of assessing the performance of marketing programmes in a way that avoids the limitations of measures that focus narrowly on either economic issues or efficiency. They do this by relating programme results to management's expectations, thereby focusing on effectiveness via a measure of satisfaction. Efficiency is assessed by means of the effort that needs to be expended to achieve a given level of satisfaction. The effort comprises the skills that must be exercised by a marketing programme's managers and the support structures that are provided for the programme.

Finally, Bonoma and Clarke allow for those factors that are beyond the enterprise's control but that affect the performance of the marketing programme – such as competitors' actions, changes within distribution channels, or in legal, economic or demographic variables. It is possible to determine programmes that succeed (or fail) on the basis of luck rather than effort by utilizing these factors.

In summary, they seek to offer an approach to marketing performance assessment that measures:

1 The degree to which a marketing programme satisfies strategic requirements
2 The effort that is necessary to produce the satisfaction in point 1 above
3 The effect of uncontrollable variables on the programme.

The approach is operationalized via a testable model of *marketing performance assessment* (MPA), which is defined as the adjudged quality of marketing programmes, directed by strategy, as these programmes are executed in the marketplace. The model seeks to combine elements of efficiency and effectiveness in assessing marketing performance. In addition, it incorporates managers' judgements in an explicit way.

The motivation behind this work was a concern to identify whether a set of principles exists that explains 'quality marketing practice' (i.e. the *doing* of marketing in an effective and efficient way rather than just the *planning* of marketing). In part, this motivation stemmed from the following dissatisfactions that Bonoma felt with the literature on marketing practice:

➡ There is a widespread tendency to ignore the role of managers, and hence their values, etc., which implies that all managers act in similar ways – something we know is not the case
➡ It is implicit in the advice offered to guide marketing practice that the causal link is strategy–causes–practice, whereas there is good reason to believe that the reverse causal link exists (i.e. practice–causes–strategy) in some circumstances, which is akin to ex post-rationalization.

Bonoma conceives of marketing practice as an attempt by managers with particular skills (relating to organizing, allocating, interacting and monitoring), values and expectations to achieve specified results. The managers in question operate within an organizational context characterized by particular ways of doing things – whether through particular programmes, systems or policies – which collectively represent a structure for guiding marketing actions. In turn, the organization is located within its environment, with its array of threats, opportunities and constraints, and the link between the organization and its environment is found via the marketing strategy of the organization.

These relationships are portrayed in Figure 15.16, which represents a rudimentary model of marketing implementation.

It is suggested by Figure 15.16 that:

Quality marketing practice = f(market results)

and

Market results = f(environment, strategy, structure, skills)

The combination of structure (in the form of programmes, systems and policies) and skills on the part of individual managers allows strategies to be implemented – within the organization's environment – and results achieved. The extent to which

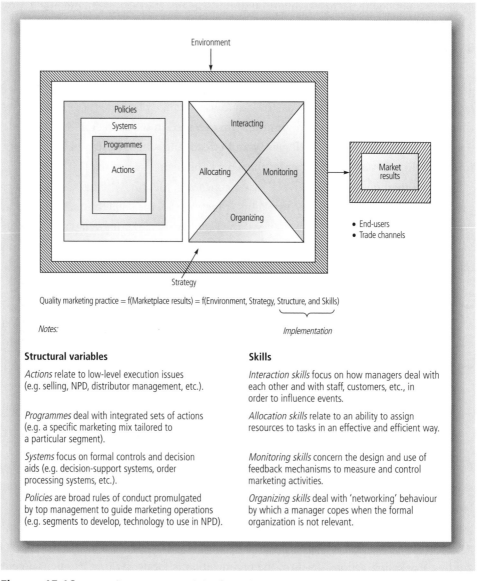

Quality marketing practice = f(Marketplace results) = f(Environment, Strategy, Structure, and Skills)

Notes:

Structural variables

Actions relate to low-level execution issues (e.g. selling, NPD, distributor management, etc.).

Programmes deal with integrated sets of actions (e.g. a specific marketing mix tailored to a particular segment).

Systems focus on formal controls and decision aids (e.g. decision-support systems, order processing systems, etc.).

Policies are broad rules of conduct promulgated by top management to guide marketing operations (e.g. segments to develop, technology to use in NPD).

Skills

Interaction skills focus on how managers deal with each other and with staff, customers, etc., in order to influence events.

Allocation skills relate to an ability to assign resources to tasks in an effective and efficient way.

Monitoring skills concern the design and use of feedback mechanisms to measure and control marketing activities.

Organizing skills deal with 'networking' behaviour by which a manager copes when the formal organization is not relevant.

Figure 15.16 A rudimentary model of marketing implementation (source: Bonoma and Clarke, 1988, p. 59; notes adapted from Bonoma and Crittenden, 1988)

the results represent an effective level of marketing performance will depend on managerial expectations, but Bonoma's contribution is significant in that he builds into his model the idea of effort expended in achieving results as well as the level of satisfaction that managers derive from the results of their efforts, plus an explicit recognition that results are influenced by events outside the enterprise, over which managers have no direct control. These elements are brought together in the following expression:

$$MP = \frac{SAT}{EFF} \times EXT$$

where:

MP = marketing performance;

SAT = managers' satisfaction with the results of effort expended in marketing programmes;

EFF = effort expended to achieve the results;

EXT = the impact of external events on marketing effort.

A variety of implications concerning the relationship between satisfaction and effort stem from the discussion above. These are summarized in Figure 15.17 and indicate

	Management's perceived effort is	
Management's perceived satisfaction with results is	**Low**	**High**
High	Maximum performance	Adequate performance
	Achieving the most results with the least effort, in complete contravention of the Protestant ethic. By definition, low effort is more easily achieved through systematized or routinized procedures than through 'exception management'.	High satisfaction is the 'due consequence' of high effort. Effort, however, is costly, resulting in only adequate performance because much was expended to produce the results. Usually, effort is high when routinized systems and procedures cannot be delegated to do the job 'automatically'.
Low	Adequate performance	Low performance
	There is little to be satisfied with, but little effort was expended in achieving the low performance. The lack of effort is seen as justifying or explaining the lack of performance.	Much effort was expended to little avail in terms of results. This is the worst possible state.

Figure 15.17 Marketing performance: satisfaction and effort (source: Bonoma and Clarke, 1988, p. 65)

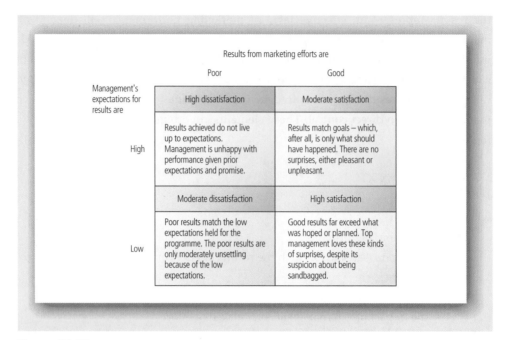

Figure 15.18 The determinants of satisfaction: results and expectations (source: Bonoma and Clarke, 1988, p. 66)

how the MPA model predicts optimal marketing performance when a low level of effort is associated with a high level of satisfaction.

The determinants of satisfaction are seen as being expectations and results: if expectations are not met, the consequences can be high satisfaction (when expectations are exceeded) or high dissatisfaction (when expectations are not realized). Figure 15.18 shows how the lowest level of satisfaction occurs when poor results and high expectations interact, and the highest level of satisfaction arises when low expectations interact with good results.

Within any organization the quality of marketing skills will depend on the availability of suitably trained and motivated staff. The application of marketing skills through the organization's marketing structure (i.e. programmes, systems, policies) will determine the effort that is to be expended in order to achieve results. Skills might be strong or weak, and structures might be flexible or rigid. As shown in Figure 15.19, there are various combinations of skills and structure that determine the effort available, and the way in which that effort might be applied.

15.6 Some other approaches to modelling

In this section we will reinforce earlier coverage of marketing experimentation as a modelling approach by which marketing plans might be assessed. In addition, we will look at programming and networking as further approaches to modelling by which alternative plans can be evaluated.

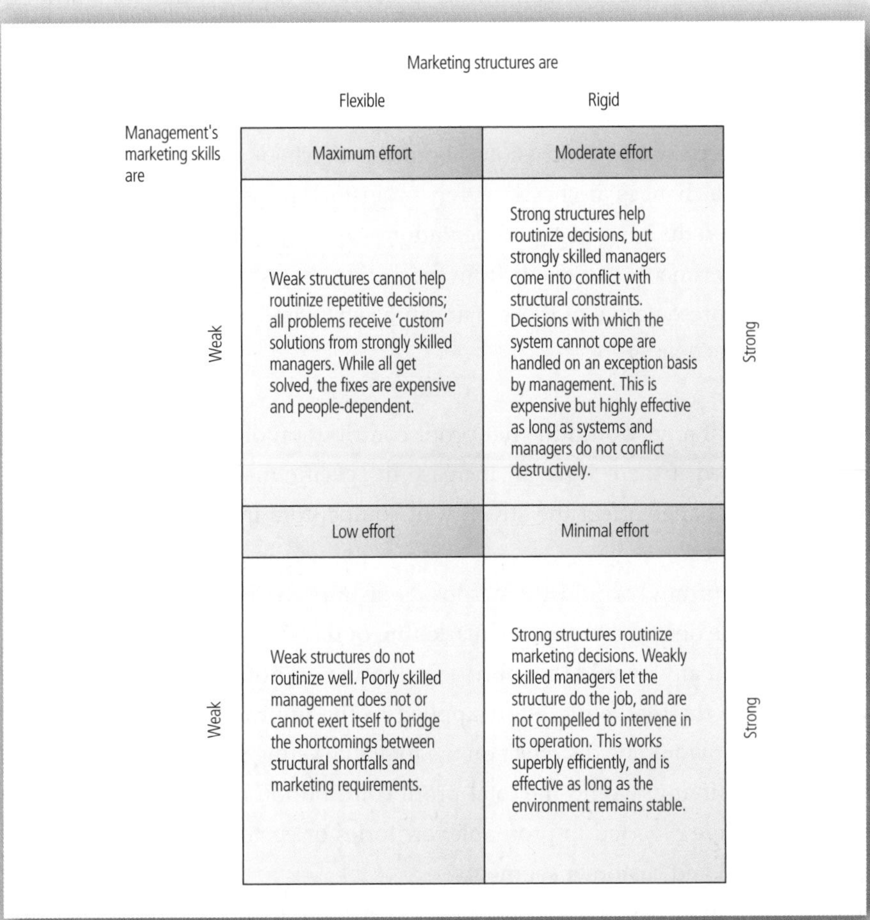

	Marketing structures are	
	Flexible	Rigid
Management's marketing skills are	Maximum effort	Moderate effort
Weak	Weak structures cannot help routinize repetitive decisions; all problems receive 'custom' solutions from strongly skilled managers. While all get solved, the fixes are expensive and people-dependent.	Strong structures help routinize decisions, but strongly skilled managers come into conflict with structural constraints. Decisions with which the system cannot cope are handled on an exception basis by management. This is expensive but highly effective as long as systems and managers do not conflict destructively.
	Low effort	Minimal effort
Weak	Weak structures do not routinize well. Poorly skilled management does not or cannot exert itself to bridge the shortcomings between structural shortfalls and marketing requirements.	Strong structures routinize marketing decisions. Weakly skilled managers let the structure do the job, and are not compelled to intervene in its operation. This works superbly efficiently, and is effective as long as the environment remains stable.

Figure 15.19   The determinants of effort: management skills and marketing structures (source: Bonoma and Clarke, 1988, p. 70)

Marketing experimentation

In an experiment, attempts are made to identify all the factors that affect a particular independent variable, and these factors are then manipulated systematically (in so far as it is within the firm's power to do so) in order to isolate and measure their effects on the performance of the dependent variable.

It is not possible to plan or control all the conditions in which an experiment is conducted – for example, the timing, location and duration of an experiment can be predetermined, but it is necessary to measure such conditions as the weather and eliminate their effects from the results.

The independent variable that is the subject of marketing experimentation may be the demand for one of the company's various products or one of the environmental factors it faces, and the dependent variable may be one of the company's objectives. Profit is a dependent variable of both the particular marketing strategy adopted and of the external conditions prevailing at the time that strategy is executed.

Because experiments are concerned with the deliberate manipulation of controllable variables (i.e. such variables as prices and advertising effort), a good deal more confidence can be placed in conclusions about the effects of such manipulation than if the effects of these changes are based purely on historical associations or vague projections rather than on the basis of experimentation.

Ideas for experiments can result from marketing cost studies. The following questions are fairly representative of those that can be answered as a result of experimentation (as we saw in Chapter 3):

1 By how much (if any) would the net profit contribution of the most profitable products be increased if there were an increase in specific marketing outlays, and how would such a change affect the strategy of competitors in terms of the stability of, say, market shares?

2 By how much (if any) would the net losses of unprofitable products be reduced if there were some decrease in specific marketing outlays?

3 By how much (if any) would the profit contribution of profitable products be affected by a change in the marketing effort applied to the unprofitable products, and vice versa, and what would be the effect on the total marketing system?

4 By how much (if any) would the total profit contribution be improved if some marketing effort were diverted to profitable territories or customer groups from unprofitable territorial and customer segments?

5 By how much (if any) would the net profit contribution be increased if there were a change in the method of distribution to small unprofitable accounts or if these accounts were eliminated?

Only by actually carrying out properly designed marketing experiments can management realistically predict with an acceptable degree of certainty the effects of changes in marketing expenditure on the level of sales and profit of each differentiated product, territory or customer segment in the multi-product company.

Experiments must be conducted under conditions that resemble the real-life conditions of the marketplace in so far as this is possible. It is pointless, for example, carrying out an experiment to prove that the sale of £1's worth of Product X in Southampton through medium-sized retailers contributes more to profit than does the sale of £1's worth of Product Y through small retailers in Leeds, if the market for Product X is saturated and no reallocation of marketing resources can change the situation. This points to the danger of confusing what is happening now with what may happen in the future – ascertaining that Product X is more profitable than Product Y may be the right answer to the wrong question.

The style of question should be 'What will happen to the dependent variable in the future if the independent variables are manipulated now?' If the concern is with the allocation of sales effort, the aim of an experiment may be to show how changes in the total costs of each sales team can be related to changes in the level of sales. In such a simple case, where only one type of marketing effort is being considered, this effort should be reallocated to those sales segments where an additional unit of effort will yield the highest contribution to profits.

The experiment can be designed to show which sales segment produces the highest value when the following equation is applied to each:

(Additional sales − additional variable costs)/additional expenditure

If an additional budget allocation of £1000 to the London sales force results in extra sales of £5000 with additional variable costs amounting to £2000, then the index of performance is $(5000 − 2000)/1000 = 3$. It may happen that the same index computed for the Midlands sales force has a value of 4, in which case selling effort should be reallocated to the Midlands *provided* due consideration has been given to the expected level of future demand.

As a result of the high costs involved, experiments must usually be conducted with small samples of the relevant elements. This is generally valid so long as the samples are properly determined and representative. However, it is believed by some that marketing experimentation is not a feasible means by which information can be obtained as a basis for making important decisions.

There are certainly a lot of difficulties to be overcome in planning and executing experiments, and the need to keep special records and make repeated measurements is both expensive and time-consuming. The risk is always present that the results of an experiment will not be of any value because they may not be statistically significant. A further risk is that even temporary and limited experimental variations in the marketing mix may damage sales and customer relationships both during and after the experiment.

Other problems that are involved in marketing experimentation include:

→ The measuring of short-term response when long-term response may be of greater relevance
→ Accurate measurements are difficult to obtain – apart from the high expense involved
→ It is almost impossible to prevent some contamination of control units by test units, since it is difficult to direct variations in the marketing mix solely to individual segments
→ Making experiments sufficiently realistic to be useful is hindered by such difficulties as the national media being less flexible than may be desired, and the fact that competitors may not react to local experimental action in the same way as they would to a national change in policy.

These problems and difficulties, while discouraging, are insufficient to discount completely the use of experimentation as a valuable means of obtaining information to increase the efficiency of marketing operations. Indeed, it is likely that the use of experimental techniques will become increasingly widespread, as has been the case with test marketing, which is the best-known form of experimentation in marketing.

Programming

Programming is a form of analytical modelling that is useful in allocation problems. The most widely-used technique is *linear programming*, which aims to determine the optimum allocation of effort in a situation involving many interacting variables: in other words, it produces that solution which maximizes or minimizes a particular outcome in accordance with given constraints (e.g. how should sales effort be allocated among regions to maximize the level of sales subject to a maximum availability of 10 000 units of product per period, or what product mix should be sold – subject to demand – in order to give the maximum profit?). Other forms of programming include integer programming, which is concerned with optimizing subject to the constraint that the solution must be in the form of whole numbers, and dynamic programming, which is applicable to problems involving a series of interdependent decisions.

In all cases the marketing manager will be interested in making the best use of his limited resources and the constraints that exist will set the upper limit to the level of performance that is possible. The company cannot spend more on advertisng each product than it has in its advertising appropriation, thus:

$$a_1(W) + a_2(X) + a_3(Y) + a_4(Z) \leq A$$

where:

$\leq$ means 'equal to or less than';

A is the total advertising appropriation;

$a_1(W)$ is the amount spent on advertising Product W;

$a_2(X)$ is the amount spent on advertising Product X;

$a_3(Y)$ is the amount spent on advertising Product Y;

$a_4(Z)$ is the amount spent on advertising Product Z.

Similarly, a constraint exists in relation to every fixed budget or limited resource, such as sales force time and warehouse space:

$$b_1(W) + b_2(X) + b_3(Y) + b_4(Z) \leq B$$

where:

B is the total available sales force time;

$b_1(W)$ is the time devoted to selling Product W, etc.

And:

$$c_1(W) + c_2(X) + c_3(Y) + c_4(Z) \leq C$$

where:

C equals the available warehouse space;

$c_1(W)$ is the space occupied by the inventory of Product W, etc.

The basis on which resources are allocated is the *marginal response*. If the expenditure on advertising of £100 000 produces sales amounting to £500 000, then the *average response* is 5/1; and if an increase in advertising expenditure of £1000 produces additional sales totalling £10 000, this gives the measure of marginal response, which is equal to 10/1. Marginal response can thus be seen to be a measure of the value of opportunities presented.

If a company's advertising budget is set at £100 000 for a period, the optimal allocation to each of the company's products (A, B and C) is given by equating the marginal responses, because this gives the situation where it will not be beneficial to reallocate funds from one product to another. The requirement is to find the best solution to the equation:

$$a_1(A) + a_2(B) + a_3(C) = £100,000$$

where $a_1(A)$ is the advertising budget for product A, $a_2(B)$ that for product B and $a_2(C)$ that for product C. This is given when:

$$dYA/dXA = dYB/dXB = dYC/dXC$$

where dYA/dXA is the marginal response for product A measured as change in sales/change in advertising outlay, and so on for products B and C.

Linear programming must be applied in the absence of uncertainty, which means that uncertainty must be eliminated before variables are incorporated into a linear programme. Moreover, all the relationships of problems put into a linear programming format are assumed to be linear, and this may not apply under all possible conditions. For example, costs rarely rise in direct proportion to increases in sales. But even with this discrepancy linear programming is able to indicate the best direction for allocating resources to segments. This technique can be used to determine the best (i.e. optimal) solution to allocation decisions in the following circumstances:

1 Where there is a clear, stated objective
2 Where feasible alternative courses of action are available
3 Where some inputs are limited (i.e. where constraints exist)
4 Where conditions 1 and 2 above can be expressed as a series of linear equations or inequalities.

Let us consider the application of linear programming to a short-run product selection problem in which the decision-maker's objective is to maximize profits (this illustration is adapted from Dev, 1980). The products in question both offer positive contributions, and market demand is buoyant and likely to be sustained, but there are insufficient resources in prospect to allow for unlimited output. The problem is therefore to choose that allocation of available resources which leads to maximized profits.

Boam Brothers produce two products, M and S, and the following data reflects estimated prices, variable manufacturing costs, and contributions for each product for the following financial year:

	Product M			Product S	
Selling price per unit		£22.20			£14.00
Less avoidable costs:					
Material A @ £1.00 per kilo					
12 kilos	12.00		4 kilos	4.00	
Labour @ £3.00 per hour					
1 hour	3.00		2 hours	6.00	
		15.00			10.00
Contribution per unit		£7.20			£4.00

It is assumed that the material and labour input requirements per unit and the contribution per unit are constant no matter what the level of output. This emphasizes the 'linear' aspect of linear programming.

Available inputs for next year are expected to be subject to possible constraints, as suggested below:

Material A	1,200,000 kilos
Labour	400,000 hours

Fixed costs have been budgeted at £560 000. Assume that there are no opening or closing inventories of M, S or A, and that the selling price will stay constant irrespective of the level of sales.

Three possible situations can be envisaged:

1 *No resource constraints*, in which case Boam Brothers would produce as much of M and S as they are able (since both make a positive contribution).

2 *One resource constraint*, which we might take as material A being limited to 1 200 000 kilos. The solution is derived via the limiting factor – priority will be given to the product generating the highest contribution per unit of the limiting factor. We can see that this is product S from the following computation:

	Product M	Product S
Contribution per unit	£7.20	£4.00
Kilos of A per unit	12	4
Contribution per kilo of A	£0.60	£1.00

With the available amount of A the maximum output would be:

$$\frac{1,200,000}{12} = 100,000 \text{ units M}; \quad \frac{1,200,000}{4} = 300,000 \text{ units S},$$

and the maximum contribution would be:

M: 100,000 × £7.20 = £720,000
S: 300,000 × £4.00 = £1,200,000
(or 1,200,000 × £0.60 = £720,000 for M; and 1,200,000 × £1.00 = £1,200,000 for S)

The optimal choice is to produce 300 000 units of S and to give up producing M. If, on the other hand, the scarce resource was labour hours, the analysis would show the following:

	Product M	Product S
Contribution per unit	£7.20	£4.00
Labour hours per unit	1	2
Contribution per labour hour	£7.20	£2.00

The maximum output with 400 000 labour hours available would be:

$$\frac{400,000}{1} = 400,000 \text{ units M}; \quad \frac{400,000}{2} = 200,000 \text{ units S}$$

and their respective contributions would be:

M: 400,000 × £7.20 = £2,880,000
S: 200,000 × £4.00 = £800,000

The optimal output is to produce 400 000 units of M and no units of S.

3 *Two resource constraints.* This is a more difficult situation than point 2 above, since the material constraint favours production of S and the labour constraint favours the production of M. Four logical alternatives present themselves:

➡ Produce M but no S
➡ Produce S but no M
➡ Produce some combination of M and S
➡ Produce neither M nor S.

The last alternative can be discarded because the contributions of both products are positive. A choice from the remaining alternatives can be made by formulating the problem as follows:

Maximize $C = 7.20Q_m + 4.00Q_s$
Subject to $12Q_m + 4Q_s \leq 1,200,000$
$\qquad\qquad Q_m + 2Q_s \leq 400,000$
$\qquad\qquad Q_m \geq 0; Q_s \geq 0$

where:

C = total contribution;
Q_m = units of product M to be produced;
Q_s = units of product S to be produced.

The resource constraints are expressed as inequalities (i.e. 'less than or equal to') because it may not be necessary to use all 1 200 000 kilos of A or all 400 000 labour hours. In addition, a non-negativity constraint is included in the problem formulation to show that negative quantities of either M or S are not desired.

A solution can be derived either by algebraic or graphical methods (and can easily be handled by standard computer programs). Figure 15.20 shows a graphic approach to the solution. Units of M and S are shown on the x- and y-axes respectively, with line AB showing the maximum output of each under the labour constraint and line CD showing the maximum output of each under the material constraint. AB connects all the possible combinations of M and S within the labour constraint, while CD connects all the combinations that are feasible within the material constraint. However, when we take both constraints into account the combinations of M and S within the triangles ACE and DBE are not feasible because they require more labour and material respectively than is available. This leaves OAED as a *feasible region* within which all the combinations of M and S can be achieved. But which is the best combination (in terms of maximizing profit)?

To determine the answer we need to move from quantities to relative contributions. Let us take a contribution figure of, say, £1 800 000. This can be generated by:

$$\frac{1,800,000}{7.20} = 250,000 \text{ units M} \quad \text{or} \quad \frac{1,800,000}{4.00} = 450,000 \text{ units S}$$

A curve showing these limits is superimposed on the graph in Figure 15.20, but none of the possibilities suggested by this line is within the feasible region. By moving back towards the origin with parallel contribution lines we arrive at point E, which is

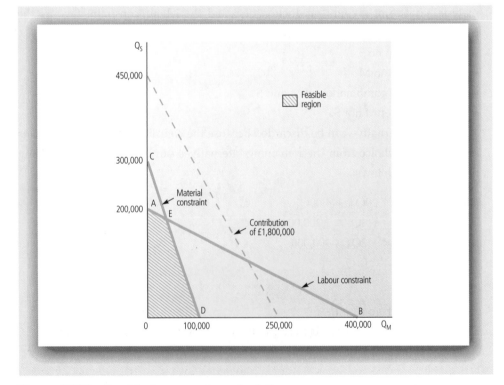

Figure 15.20 Graphical presentation of solution

within the feasible region, and this gives us the optimal combination of M and S. (The lines will be parallel because the contribution per unit of M and S will be the same regardless of the level of output.) It should be apparent that the closer the contribution line is to the origin, the lower will be the total contribution (since the smaller will be the output), so the best point is at a tangent to the feasible region: point E.

The output levels at this point (from the graph) are 40 000 units of M and 180 000 units of S, with the following financial outcome:

Contribution:

M	40,000 × £7.20	288,000
S	180,000 × £4.00	720,000
Total contribution		1,008,000
Fixed costs		560,000
Net profit		£448,000

You may care to manipulate the combination of M and S represented in this solution to see if any marginal change could improve the profit outcome. (For example, if five units less M were produced, this would free 60 kilos of A and five hours of labour, which could be used to produce two more units of S – with one hour of labour and 52 kilos of A left over. However, the contribution gained from S would only be £8.00, whereas the contribution lost by M would be £36.00, so it would be a suboptimal change.)

Networks

Network analysis is a method of problem solving that is based on analysing systematically and logically the relationships and time factors involved in carrying out a particular project. An appropriate project is any activity that can be considered as having a definable beginning and end, and this includes:

→ Developing and launching a new product, which involves coordinating many complex and interrelated factors, along with the need to be able to assess quickly the effects of changes in order to show where corrective action can best be taken
→ Product modification
→ Large-scale promotional campaigns
→ Many smaller activities that would benefit from a more rigorous approach, such as catalogue preparation; planning exhibitions, sales conferences and training courses; carrying out market research studies; and the building of models.

Network analysis is made possible by two techniques developed during the late 1950s: critical path analysis (CPA) and the programme evaluation and review technique (PERT). Networks developed by these techniques show the relationships among all the activities that must be performed in terms of time in completing the project in question. Three estimates of time are characteristically used for each activity – an optimistic, a pessimistic and a 'most likely'. The expected time for each activity can then be calculated on a probability basis, and since some activities must be completed before others can be commenced, the various activities can be laid out along a diagrammatic time scale.

Figure 15.21 relates to the launching of a new washing-up liquid and shows that a network diagram is a graphical representation of a project, indicating how the activities are linked. It is drawn by using three basic symbols:

1 A solid line represents an *activity*
2 A circle represents an *event* or intersection between activities
3 A dashed line represents a *dummy* activity, which is a means of showing logical relationships that are not physical activities – they may be thought of as transfers of information between events.

When the network is first drawn it is usual to omit duration times for reasons of simplicity in ascertaining the correct sequences and dependencies. After times have been incorporated it is possible to find the overall project time that is determined by those activities in sequence – the critical path. A certain amount of time ('float') will usually be available on those activities that are not on the critical path to permit flexibility in executing the project.

Basic networks only cover the time dimension, so further analysis requires the introduction of a cost dimension. This is the role of the PERT/cost technique. Both PERT and PERT/cost are designed for use in single large-scale projects, and resource allocation and multi-project scheduling (conveniently abbreviated to RAMPS) has been

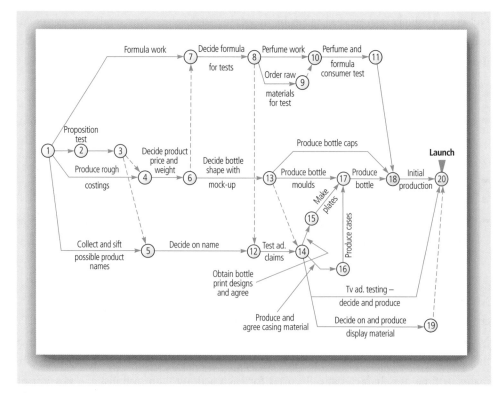

Figure 15.21 Network for launching a new product

developed to deal with the problem of allocating resources to several projects when a number of projects are being undertaken simultaneously but there is a restriction in the availability of resources.

Although drawing up a valid network for a project is difficult, the procedure demands thorough and systematic analysis, and this discipline means that relationships that might otherwise have been overlooked are included. Furthermore, it specifies the decisions that must be made and thus provides a framework for control, as well as permitting planning and scheduling.

Network analysis can fail in practice for such reasons as lack of top management support, the use of excessive detail, bad presentation, a failure to update, and the absence of feedback.

A different type of network is shown in Figure 15.22. This relates to the development of new products, which was discussed in Chapter 11.

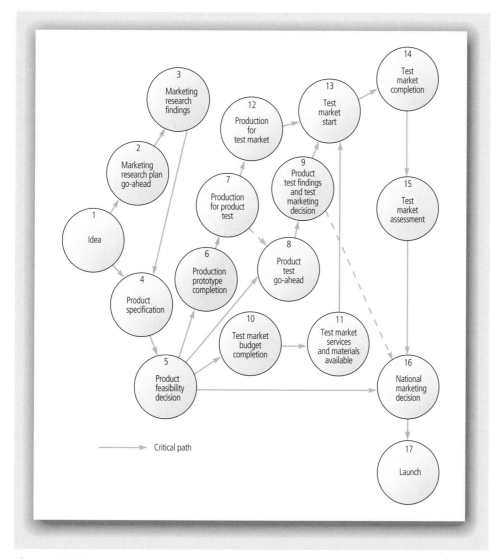

Figure 15.22 New product development network

15.7 Summary

Risk and uncertainty are inevitably present whenever choices need to be made among alternative claims on scarce resources. A variety of ways of accommodating risk and uncertainty have been discussed and illustrated, including probability analysis, sensitivity analysis, decision trees and, briefly, Bayesian analysis.

Some alternative matrix models were covered – the directional policy matrix, the multi-factor portfolio matrix and the product positioning matrix – and their application to evaluating marketing plans illustrated.

Bonoma's MPA (marketing performance assessment) model warranted special attention as the most ambitious approach considered. It is still in the development phase, but holds great promise for the future. Finally, brief coverage was given to some further modelling approaches that can be used to test the robustness, feasibility and desirability of marketing plans: marketing experimentation, networking and programming.

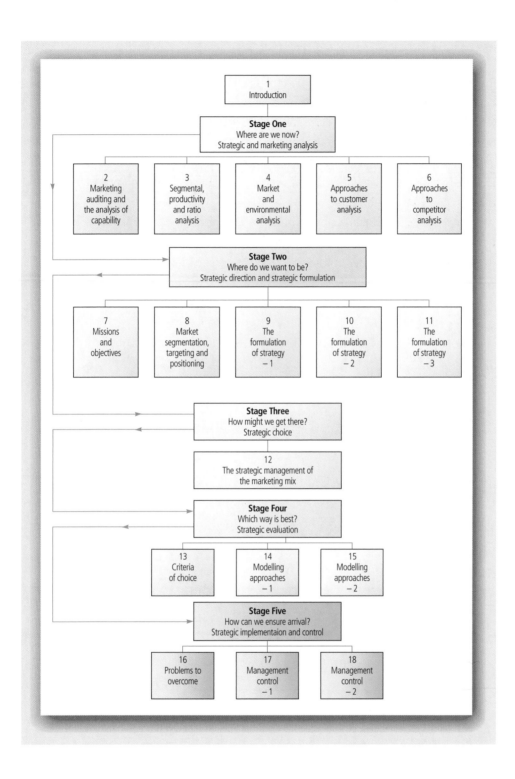

1
Introduction

Stage One
Where are we now?
Strategic and marketing analysis

| 2 Marketing auditing and the analysis of capability | 3 Segmental, productivity and ratio analysis | 4 Market and environmental analysis | 5 Approaches to customer analysis | 6 Approaches to competitor analysis |

Stage Two
Where do we want to be?
Strategic direction and strategic formulation

| 7 Missions and objectives | 8 Market segmentation, targeting and positioning | 9 The formulation of strategy – 1 | 10 The formulation of strategy – 2 | 11 The formulation of strategy – 3 |

Stage Three
How might we get there?
Strategic choice

12
The strategic management of
the marketing mix

Stage Four
Which way is best?
Strategic evaluation

| 13 Criteria of choice | 14 Modelling approaches – 1 | 15 Modelling approaches – 2 |

Stage Five
How can we ensure arrival?
Strategic implementaion and control

| 16 Problems to overcome | 17 Management control – 1 | 18 Management control – 2 |

Stage Five: How can we ensure arrival? Strategic implementation and control

This stage of the book focuses on implementation and control. In this endeavour there are many problems to be overcome (e.g. relating to organizational as well as to environmental matters), which are discussed in Chapter 16.

Management controls to help in ensuring arrival are dealt with in Chapters 17 and 18. Some of these are social/behavioural in character, while others are analytical.

The successful implementation of strategy is neither easy nor widely discussed in the marketing literature. If implementation is left to compete with the internal pressures of coping with crises, reacting to competitors' actions, company politics, personal career needs, and so forth, it is likely to be swamped or disrupted.

The implementation of plans poses a fundamental dilemma, since to be effective it requires the reconciliation of two opposing forces: forces leading to organizational integration must be reconciled with forces leading to organizational segmentation (see Lawrence and Lorsch, 1967). In seeking to achieve this balance, it is helpful if:

1 The messages contained in the plan are communicated so that there is clear recognition of what the plan says
2 The plan is understood, so that all who need to play a role in its implementation are aware of what their roles are
3 There is consensus about the wisdom of pursuing the plan in order to secure commitment to its accomplishment.

A flow chart showing how a strategic marketing plan might be implemented is shown in Figure S5.1. This suggests that a number of key elements within the organization need to be matched with the plan. These elements are:

➡ Leadership
➡ Organizational culture
➡ Organizational structure
➡ Functional policies
➡ Resources
➡ Evaluation and control procedures.

There is a logical sequencing of the key elements, although in practice some may occur simultaneously or in a different order. Feedback loops are shown linking the elements in an iterative process (see McNamee, 1988, pp. 323–35).

No matter how competent the analysis behind the formulation of plans and strategies, it is only possible to outperform one's competitors if those plans and strategies are executed effectively.

This requires, inter alia, an overriding concern for quality. Japanese success in the post-war period is a clear testimony to the pursuit of quality, as reflected in the

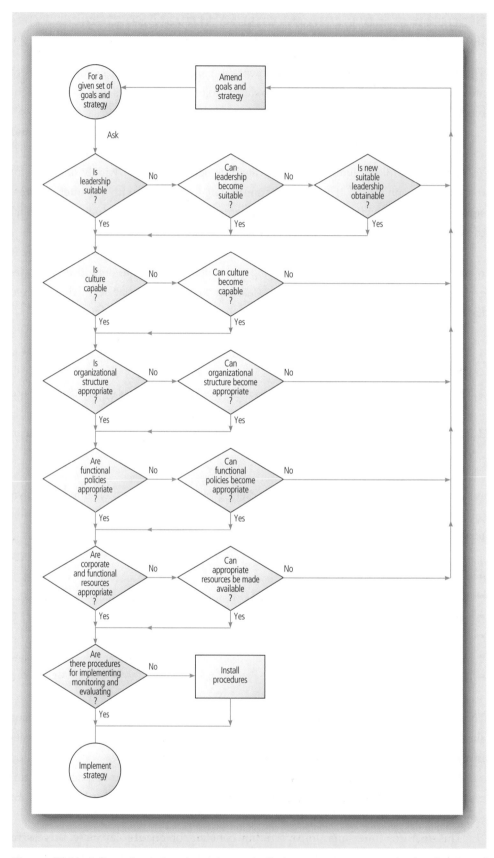

Figure S5.1 A flow chart showing schematically how a strategy may be implemented (source: McNamee, 1988, p. 323)

pioneering work of W. Edwards Deming (see, for example, Mann, 1989). This success is built upon the notion of being 'right first time', which is much more than a catchy slogan: it implies providing exactly what is required by those using an organization's outputs. The *total quality management* (TQM) approach is built around this ideal.

Oakland (1989, pp. 14–15) defines TQM as:

" . . . an approach to improving the effectiveness and flexibility of businesses as a whole. It is essentially a way of organizing and involving the whole organization; every department, every activity, every single person at every level. For an organization to be truly effective, each part of it must work properly together, recognizing that every person and every activity affects, and in turn is affected by, others.*"*

A slightly different emphasis is offered in the definition put forward by Atkinson and Naden (1989, p. 6). They see TQM as being:

" . . . a strategy which is concerned with changing the fundamental beliefs, values and culture of an organization, harnessing the enthusiasm and participation of everyone . . . towards an overall ideal of 'right first time'.*"*

As Figure S5.2 shows, a variation on TQM can be used in a marketing context to attain BS 5750: Marketing Quality Assurance (or MQA).

In the task of implementing plans, it is helpful to consider the core skills that are needed if sustainable competitive advantage is to be achieved. These core skills are the critical capabilities that the organization must possess as distinct from the skills of individuals within the organization. This is not a trivial distinction, since individuals may come and go, but the organization needs to have core skills (such as effective training programmes, clear performance guidelines, well-designed information systems, and incentive schemes that generate high levels of motivation) to link planning and the successful implementation of plans.

A vivid example is that of Marriott Hotels. As with many hotel chains, the basic strategy is to go after business travellers with a level of service that is consistently excellent. However, the success of Marriott (as reflected in an occupancy rate that is some 10 points above the industry average) is to be found in its ability to implement the strategy in a superior way. This is achieved by institutionalizing among its 200 000 employees a fanatical eye for detail (e.g. maids follow a 66-point guide in making up bedrooms). The outcome is that Marriott Hotels is invariably at the top in customer surveys: the core organizational skill of excellent service gives a sustainable competitive advantage.

Another example can be taken from the fast-food sector. In 1968, both Burger King and McDonald's had less than 1000 outlets. By 1990, despite backing from its parent company, Burger King had increased its outlets to a total of only 5500 or so, while McDonald's had emerged as the clear industry leader with over 10 000 outlets and with sales growing at 13 per cent per year. The explanation is to be found in the core skills (see Figure S5.3). McDonald's had the competitive edge on all counts.

There are good examples to be found in the manufacturing sector as well as in the service sector, such as the VF Corporation (which makes Lee and Wrangler jeans,

Marketing needs new sales pitch

British companies need to wake up to what the customer wants. Staying ahead when hundreds of others are going under means taking a new look at quality and service, says **Ian Griffith**. ●

AT A TIME when the newspapers are full of stories about companies closing, there are two developments that encourage optimism.

First, there is a call from a number of chief executives for better performance in the market-place. This is a clear sign that the improvement of marketing and sales is accepted as a priority for business.

Second, quality is shaping up as one of the most important ways of staying ahead of competitors in the 1990s. Many leading companies are already on the road to total quality, where the need to identify and satisfy customer needs is given the highest priority.

The customer has not always been paramount in British business. Products have failed, not necessarily because they were poorly made but because they were not what people wanted.

The Japanese, on the other hand, have understood only too well for the past 20 years that the customer comes first. Before entering a market, they take pains to make sure they have a full understanding of customer needs and expectations. They also weigh up the competition. The Americans and the Germans have not ignored the Japanese lesson; they too are customer-conscious. If Britain is to maintain healthy businesses after 1992, it will also have to become much more market and customer focused.

The only way that this can be achieved is for companies to concentrate on improving marketing and sales effectiveness. Responsibility for this should lie with marketing departments, which not only have to represent the needs of the customer but also ensure that the company has the capability and commitment to satisfy demand with quality goods and services.

How well prepared are marketing and sales people to meet this challenge? In my experience, they are often not. Marketing is still treated by too many companies as a tactical discipline that is involved with publicity and promotion as opposed to a business philosophy that is concerned with how the whole company deals with its customers.

When competition is intensifying, this is a serious issue. Marketing must represent the customers' viewpoint as well as interests in the company boardroom.

However, reforming attitudes, ideas and quality within companies raises the questions of how people achieve such goals, how they measure that achievement and how they can maintain those standards.

The British Standard BS 5750 set out the principles for product quality a decade ago, but it did not lay down how companies should identify and meet customer needs and expectations. Could those standards, which have attracted about 12,000 registrations from British companies, be applied to marketing? It was with all this in mind that the concept of Marketing Quality Assurance (MQA) was developed.

MQA, launched last October, is a third-party certification body that assesses the quality of marketing, sales and customer service in companies. It awards a certificate of excellence, and the right to use the MQA mark, if companies achieve the required standard. This is a way of signalling that the certified company is one that has independent recognition, and is a sign of marketing excellence to customers, competitors, employees and potential employees.

The specification, which is an international first and based on good practice, took five years to research and develop. An important consideration in drafting the 58 requirements in the specification was to ensure that companies were aware of the need for high-quality marketing and sales people and also understood their aspirations.

Findings showed that the most successful people are those who are able to provide a disciplined and well-planned approach based on a real understanding of the market-place and competition. They are good communicators who are able to co-ordinate the work of all parts of the organisation concerned with meeting and satisfying customer needs.

Perhaps most important, they are people who can provide a creative and innovative approach, which has become vital in differentiating one organisation from another.

MQA has captured all of these needs through its specification which covers: business plans; review of market needs; marketing and sales planning; marketing and sales operations; customer assurance; purchasing of marketing and sales services; resources, personnel, training and organisation structure; quality policy, systems, control and procedures, records and audit.

MQA's specification is an associated document to the International Quality Standard ISO 9000 and therefore – as a third-party certification organisation – can grant registration to ISO 9001, EN 290012 and BS 5750 Part 1 for a company's marketing, sales and customer-assurance activities.

So the stage is set for another big step forward as the marketing enlightenment of the 1980s becomes the quality assured marketing of the 1990s.

Early indications would suggest that many chief executives acknowledge the considerable extent to which MQA registration moves their companies towards the ultimate goal of total quality, as well as providing improved marketing effectiveness.

More than 25 companies have applied for registration, with organisations such as Kodak, Sorbus, Newcastle Breweries and Southern Electric already well down the track.

There are those, however, who imagine that a formal set of standards would bring too much bureaucracy to the essentially creative business of marketing. This is not so, for marketing is more than coming up with bright ideas; it is putting those ideas into practice and making sure they work.

● *Ian Griffith is the managing director of Marketing Quality Assurance, Park House, Wick Road, Egham, Surrey TW20 OHW. Telephone: 01784 430953*

Figure S5.2 Marketing quality assurance (source: *The Sunday Times*, 7 July 1991, p. 4.13)

Core skills	McDonald's	Burger King
Site selection	'Penchant for finding the *plum*'	'Generally good locations'
High-quality service	'*Unparalleled* consistency'	'Suffers from operational sloppiness'
Product innovation	'A *knack* for product development'	'Spotty record with new products'
Communications	'Surrogate man'	'Comes off as aggressive, masculine and distant'

Figure S5.3 Contrasting execution of core skills (source: Irvin and Michaels, 1989, p. 7)

Jantzen swimsuits and Vanity Fair lingerie). The strong position of this company over the last 10 years is largely due to:

➡ High quality at competitive prices, thus offering superior value to consumers;

➡ Accurate forecasting, which means lower inventories, fewer stockouts and less plants than most competitors

➡ Managing the risk that is inherent in the clothing industry by means of a focused and disciplined approach to the development of new lines.

It is important to recognize that identifying and creating core skills is far from easy. Both organizations and individuals develop particular ways of doing things, and managing the process of change may require that the behaviour of thousands of people be changed in dozens of different locations. If success depends on it, then this nettle must be grasped. The approach adopted in grasping it will influence how effective the outcome is likely to be. For example, employees are more likely to show a willingness to accept change if they have a clear understanding of what is required of them, coupled with the assurance that there is some latitude for them to exercise judgement. This can be built in to the following steps en route to developing core skills:

1 Establish a clear link between the chosen strategy and the required core skills, such as quick delivery requiring excellent distribution facilities

2 Be specific as well as selective in defining core skills, so that employees will know what to do and how to do it, but in a focused way (e.g. covering no more than five core skills)

3 Clarify the implications for pivotal jobs (hence recruitment and training requirements, support systems, reward schemes, etc.)

4 Provide leadership from the top, since the single most powerful discriminating factor between success and failure in developing core skills is the degree of top management involvement

5 Empower the organization to learn, which requires that individuals within the organization have scope for learning by doing – thereby seeing what works and what fails to work in building core skills through which strategies can be successfully implemented.

While a number of authors have written on the implementation of strategy (e.g. Lorange, 1982; Bourgeois and Brodwin, 1984; Nutt, 1987, 1989; Reed and Buckley, 1988; Reid, 1989), or more specifically on the implementation of marketing strategy (e.g. Spekman and Grønhaug, 1983; McTavish, 1989; Piercy and Morgan, 1989a, b, 1990), as pointed out earlier there is relatively little guidance available on this important theme. Outstanding strategies are worthless if they cannot be put into effect, as Piercy and Morgan (1990, p. 20) state:

*"*In short, the . . . reality the marketing executive faces is that implementing plans and strategies successfully is often dependent on managers and employees who are far removed from the excitement of creating new marketing strategies – people like service engineers, customer service units . . . field sales personnel, and so on.*"*

The same authors (1989a) give examples of a museum failing to deliver a theme park strategy because employees cannot change from being 'policemen' to 'entertainers'; marketing strategies that rely on customer service failing because of employees' negative attitudes at the point of sale; and strategies based on integration and divisional cross-selling foundering because nobody recognized the human costs of change. It is not enough to develop marketing plans by focusing exclusively on customers, competitors and distributors (all *outside* the company) and ignoring those *within* the company. Almost all plans involve substantial human and organizational change: this requires 'internal marketing', which has goals such as to:

→ Gain the support of key decision-makers and facilitators
→ Change attitudes among those employees who deal with customers
→ Obtain employees' commitment to making the marketing plan work by involving them in the 'ownership' of the plan and by rewarding them on the plan's attainment
→ Train staff to allow them to develop new skills that will contribute to the effective implementation of plans.

Training (or management development) has been enthusiastically promoted (e.g. Hussey, 1985; Brache, 1986) as a means of implementing plans. It was suggested by Hussey (1985, p. 32) that training can contribute to some of the problems of strategy implementation identified by Alexander (1985). Of the ten most frequently encountered strategy implementation problems in US organizations, training can probably help with the top six (Figure S5.4).

Bonoma and Crittenden (1988) have put forward a well-considered case showing that the successful implementation of marketing plans results from the interaction of structure and skills. In this context, *structure* is seen to consist of:

→ Actions
→ Programmes

Problem	Percentage of enterprises reporting problem
1 Implementation took more time than originally allocated.	76
2 Major problems surfaced during implementation that had not been identified beforehand.	74
3 Coordination of implementation activities was not effective enough.	66
4 Competing activities and crises distracted management from implementing decisions.	64
5 Capabilities of employees involved were insufficient for the task.	63
6 Training and instructions given to lower-level employees were inadequate.	62

Figure S5.4 Implementation problems (adapted from Alexander, 1985)

➡ Systems
➡ Policies

as portrayed in Figure 15.16. Managerial *skills* embrace:

➡ Interacting
➡ Allocating
➡ Monitoring
➡ Organizing.

Through a series of discussions with managers involved in implementing marketing plans, Bonoma and Crittenden derived an interesting set of propositions concerning the relationship between structure and skills. These propositions are as follows:

1 There is normally a tension rather than a synergy between the enterprise's marketing structures and the skills of its managers. Whether this tension is productive or harmful depends on environmental factors.

2 The interaction between marketing structures and management skills is partially predictable using the rate of market change.

3 In low-change markets, structures and their associated systems dominate skills. Quality marketing practices result more often, and more cheaply, when strong systems and weak management skills are combined.

4 In high-change markets the reverse is true. Enterprises with weak structures and highly skilled managers get more desirable marketplace results, more cheaply, than do enterprises having strong structures.

5 The complexity of tasks that marketing faces suggests whether structure or skills should dominate.

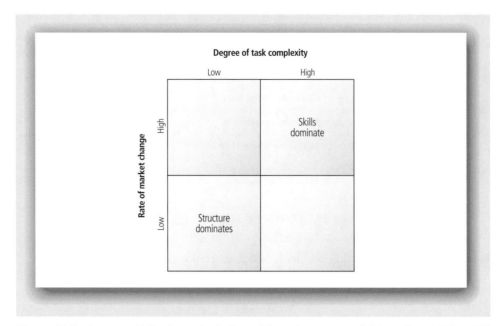

Figure S5.5   Structure/skills dynamics (adapted from Bonoma and Crittenden, 1988, p. 12)

6 Routine, repetitive tasks (i.e. low complexity) are done more efficiently under strong structures with less strong execution skills.

7 Highly complex tasks require stronger execution skills and a weaker structure.

Propositions 1–7 can be portrayed diagrammatically (see Figure S5.5). If strong structures exist in circumstances characterized by rapidly changing markets and complex tasks, it is likely that the enterprise's ability to adapt quickly to market needs will be constrained by rules and procedures. Conversely, if skills are dominant in a situation involving low market change and low task complexity, the enterprise will be unable to increase its efficiency by relying on standard operating procedures.

Propositions 2–4 can be linked to phases of the PLC via a further proposition:

8 In the turbulent periods of the PLC (e.g. introduction, rapid growth and, subsequently, maturity/decline), management skills will dominate execution structures in

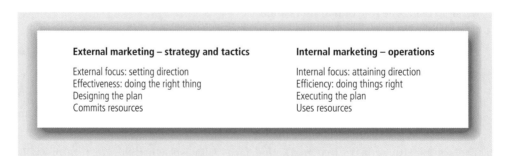

Figure S5.6   Strategy/tactics and operations (adapted from Kotler et al., 1985, p. 245)

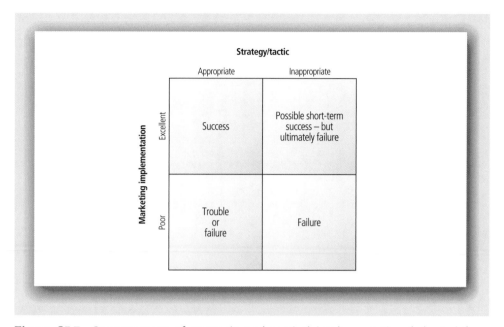

Figure S5.7 Consequences of strategic and tactical implementation (adapted from Bonoma, 1984, p. 72)

those enterprises performing better than average. In the more stable phases of the PLC, structures will dominate skills.

The idea of balancing 'external' and 'internal' marketing in the implementation of marketing plans is portrayed in Figure S5.6. This shows the distinction between strategy and tactics (developed with an external focus) and their implementation (via operations). However, part of the strategic thinking must be to ensure that those who will be responsible for carrying out operations are properly equipped for their tasks. If this is not the case then implementation will be poor, and failure is likely to result. Figure S5.7 offers the logical possibilities. Failure will follow whenever either the strategy/tactics are inappropriate or the implementation is poor.

Chapter **16**

Problems to overcome

16.1 Learning objectives

When you have read this chapter you should be able to:

(a) understand the importance of implementation as part of the overall process of marketing planning and control;

(b) recognize the problems that need to be addressed in implementing marketing plans and controlling marketing activities;

(c) appreciate the need for marketing orientation and a positive approach to planning if marketing objectives are to be achieved;

(d) identify the organizational design issues that are relevant to marketing planning, implementation and control.

16.2 Introduction

Of the two major operating functions, production and marketing, the former has lent itself to rigorous analysis over many years, with the result that it has been studied in great detail. Marketing, however, has not lent itself so much to critical examination until relatively recently, and for this reason it has received an unjustifiably low proportion of analytical attention. The marketing function is the most difficult area to plan and control, since it is the source of sales forecasts and revenue estimates that can rarely be predicted accurately, and there is the further need to plan and control expenditure in addition to dealing with the human dimensions.

The scale of operations is determined by the sales forecast, but it may be found that the level of projected sales exceeds the short-term productive capacity of the enterprise. In such an event it may be necessary to:

1 Expand the productive facilities
2 Raise prices in an attempt to ration the available output
3 Subcontract production to outside suppliers
4 Rely on inventories.

On the other hand, it may be that the projected level of sales is insufficient to produce the desired return on investment (i.e. profitability objective). Apart from increasing the overall level of sales activity, it may be appropriate to reconsider the means of distribution to ensure that it is the most cost-effective, or the existing sales effort may not be properly allocated (e.g. consider exporting – see Pilcher, 1989) or individual product profit margins may be subject to adjustment by product modifications, or an analysis of credit losses may cause credit extension policies to be amended to improve profitability (see, for example, Bass, 1991).

The study, and to a lesser extent the practice, of financial management has been reduced almost to a science in parallel with the study of production. The importance of human rather than technical factors in the marketing subsystem, coupled with the complexity of the marketing interfaces with internal and external subsystems, have been the causes of the delays in rigorous marketing analysis (see Wilson, 1994). This chapter considers some of the problems that must be overcome in controlling marketing activities along the lines suggested in Chapters 17 and 18. Problem areas that are discussed include business pressures, problems in the marketing subsystem, problems of marketing feedback and information adequacy, cost problems, problems relating to marketing orientation, and problems relating to planning. Consideration is also given to the organizational problems associated with the implementation and control of marketing plans.

16.3 Pressures

King (1991, p. 3) has pointed out that the pressures on marketing organizations during the 1980s were formidable and it is likely that these pressures will intensify. Similar views are offered by Hussey (1989) and Buckley (1991) – see also Brown (1995).

The range of external factors impacting on organizations is shown in Figure 16.1, although this is not intended to be an exhaustive portrayal. Many of these factors were discussed in Chapter 7. Pressures that are expected to have an increasing significance include:

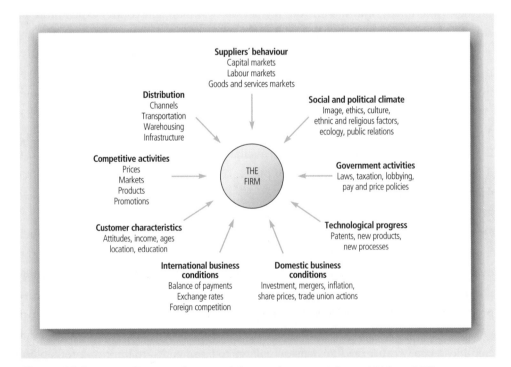

Figure 16.1 The influence of external factors (source: Wilson, 1983, p. 209)

1 More confident customers due to increasing consumer awareness via consumerism, a greater willingness to experiment, more readiness to trust their own judgement, less tolerance of products that fail to contribute to their own values, higher levels of disposable income, and increased individualism.

2 New concepts of quality that reflect *real* values rather than superficial styling, plus personal added values and a requirement for increased customer care.

3 Changing demographic and social patterns, such as fewer school leavers and a higher proportion of retired people, a shortage of skills relative to point 2 above, demands for improved social conditions, and the continuing importance of 'green' issues.

4 An intensification of competition via increased global marketing, the fragmentation of markets, and the risk of excess capacity in many markets.

5 The formation of joint ventures and strategic alliances when outright acquisition is neither feasible nor desirable, or when organic expansion is not possible (see, for example, Clarke and Brennan, 1988; Devlin and Biggs, 1989) and the growing use of shared services.

6 Political changes, including deregulation, political, economic and financial integration, and change in trade policies (see, for example, Quelch et al., 1990; Lynch, 1992; Brown and McDonald, 1994; Bennett, 1995).

7 Technological imperatives in product and process innovations, the acceleration of technological change with an emphasis on new product development, hence shorter PLCs, and changes in the provision of service (e.g. via EFTS) – especially in retailing.

8 The harnessing of information technology in ways that build competitive advantage, which places a greater responsibility on managers both to understand the meaning of the results from the use of analytical techniques and to ensure that the quality of information in use is high.

9 Restructuring of the world economy and restructuring at a micro-economic level due to mergers, management buy-outs, leveraged buy-outs, building, unbundling, etc.

10 More market-focused organizations (i.e. increasing marketing orientation – see below), and an acceleration in the shift from a manufacturing to a service economy.

11 Short-termism. On the question of short-termism, Heller (1990) observed that it has been argued that the spectre of the City of London has cast a shadow over British managers that makes them so uneasy they tend to concentrate on short-term financial goals to the detriment of long-term results. However, the core of Heller's argument is that the short-term demons are, in fact, lurking within the managers themselves rather than within the City institutions (which are rarely inclined to act on a short-term basis). Managers who attach more importance to this year's results than to the organization's likely situation in the twenty-first century, or whose rewards are wholly related to current performance, are not acting in the best interests of the organization as a whole.

The CBI set up a task force to report on the phenomenon of short-termism: the resulting report (entitled *Investing for Britain's Future*) also showed short-termism to be a myth in so far as it is attributable to City institutions. To the extent that it does exist it is attributable to poor management on the one hand and to underlying economic and political factors (such as high interest rates) on the other. Ferguson (1989, p. 68) has observed that share prices typically react well to announcements of strategic commitments but that 'British companies have a curious reticence about heralding their grand schemes'. The fact that there is good empirical support underlying the efficient markets hypothesis was pointed out in Chapter 13 (see also Puxty and Dodds, 1991, pp. 69–86).

If only a few of these pressures were to occur there would be significant implications for marketing planning and control. Since most (if not all) of them are already occurring it is evident that managers must develop understanding, commitment and skills to deal proactively with new situations.

Lewis (1989) has grouped the pressures for change into four main areas, as shown in Figure 16.2. The axes range from task-focused to people-focused pressures on the horizontal plane and from external to internal pressures on the vertical plane. Within the resulting cells we have:

1 Market pressures – with keywords being change, variety and complexity
2 External – people pressures involving increasing liaison with customers and developments such as the Green movement
3 Internal – task pressures for cost reduction and systems development as well as R&D activities
4 Internal – people pressures, including increased autonomy among employees and demands for more flexibility in the way in which staff are treated in the face of reduced job security.

There are no blanket formulae for structuring organizations or motivating staff in order to cope with the problems of constant change. It is evident, however, that not all managers or their subordinates are equally amenable to change. Figure 16.3 gives one approach to assessing resistance to change.

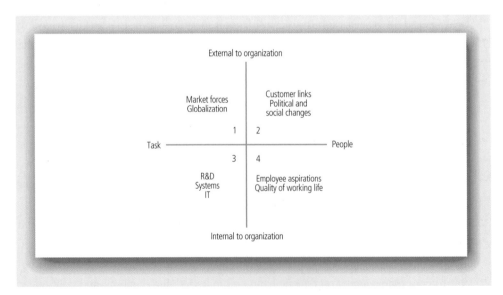

Figure 16.2 Pressures for change (source: Lewis, 1989)

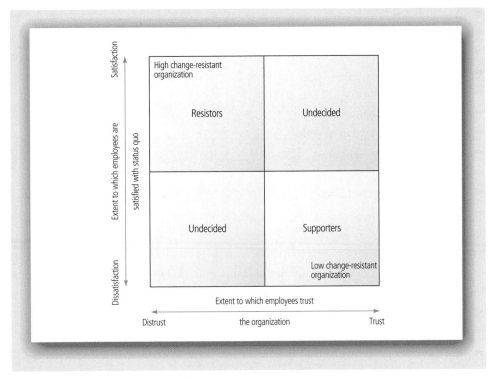

Figure 16.3 Change resistance grid (adapted from Witte, 1990, p. 30)

An organization that is highly resistant to change will exhibit characteristics such as the following:

➡ Large
➡ Established
➡ Centralized
➡ Hierarchic management structures
➡ Predictable tasks
➡ Manufacturing base
➡ Paternal orientation
➡ Vertical information systems
➡ Autocratic management style
➡ Unskilled workforce
➡ Non-professional
➡ Undifferentiated product lines
➡ Immobile workforce.

In contrast, an organization that has a low resistance to change will have characteristics as follows:

➡ Small
➡ New

➡ Decentralized

➡ Flat management structures

➡ Unpredictable tasks

➡ Service base

➡ Fraternal orientation

➡ Horizontal information systems

➡ Participative management style

➡ Skilled workforce

➡ Professional

➡ Differentiated product lines

➡ Mobile workforce.

The ideal environment in which to initiate change is one in which employees trust the organization but feel dissatisfied with the status quo. A classic example of this is to be found in the Virgin Group: it is a relatively young, decentralized, fast-growing service organization with diverse and innovative product lines. The workforce is skilled and mobile, the management structures are flat, and the management style is both participative and fraternal, with an ethos that is virtually synonymous with change.

Innovation is clearly more likely in low-resistance organizations provided that they do not attempt too much too quickly or fail to carry through the changes that are initiated.

It has been contended (see Ulrich and Lake, 1991) that the 'traditional' means of securing competitive advantage (i.e. via financial, strategic and technological capabilities) cover only part of what managers will need to do to build sustainable competitive advantage in the future. Existing capabilities must be supplemented by *organizational capability* – which can be defined as the enterprise's ability to manage people to gain competitive advantage by establishing internal structures and processes that influence its members to create organization-specific competences. This entails more than simply recruiting good people; it requires the deliberate development of competences by which employees will act to ensure the enterprise stays ahead of its competitors (see Hamel and Prahalad, 1994). Two outstanding examples of where this is being done are the Marriott Corporation (covering hotels and food), and Borg-Warner (which deals with chemicals, automotive components and financial services).

16.4 Problems in the marketing subsystem

Several facets of the marketing subsystem that give rise to problems of control have been highlighted by Kotler (1972). These include the following:

➡ The outputs of the marketing function have repercussions on the outputs of other corporate functions, such as credit collection having a significant bearing on the controller's cash flow situation

➡ These outputs of other functional subsystems in turn affect subsequent outputs of the marketing subsystem, so that a poor cash flow may lead to a need to cease extending credit and hence to a lower level of sales and profit

➡ The interface of the marketing subsystem with the subsystems formed by external agents is fraught with difficulty, since the marketing manager must attempt to exercise some degree of control over advertising agents, PR consultants, wholesalers and shipping companies

➡ The human factor that is at the heart of marketing creates problems of control because of the difficulties involved in coordinating the activities of salespeople, product managers, advertising agents and marketing researchers, all of whom are essentially creative and individualistic

➡ The usual problems associated with any corporate project, such as launching a new product, entering a new territory or executing a major promotional campaign are especially noticeable in marketing as a result of the human element and the external interfaces.

To these we can add the problem of assessing performance.

Defining marketing performance has proved to be a difficult task due to a number of problems, including (as suggested by Bonoma and Clarke, 1988):

➡ The nature of marketing as a complex discipline having many dimensions and interfaces (e.g. internally with functions such as production, and externally with intermediaries, agencies, etc.), each of which has an impact on performance

➡ The need for marketing to behave in an adaptive way in the light of environmental changes (such as competitive activities or shifts in the pattern of consumer demand), which renders performance benchmarks perishable

➡ The tendency to focus on inputs rather than outputs, with the presumption being that the desired outputs (such as increased market share) are 'obvious', thereby playing down the importance of both marketing performance and the implementation of marketing plans.

The marketing manager must find means of securing better coordination among the various functional subsystems that are not directly under his or her control, including production, purchasing and materials control. This may be achieved by improving communications and interorganizational understanding about what is in the interest of the enterprise as a whole.

In addition, the marketing manager must strive to influence external agents, as well as to motivate internal staff to carry out their respective duties in the enterprise's best interests. This requires both flexibility in terms of tactics and adequate feedback from operations.

A coordinated approach requires that marketing plans are developed alongside production plans, staffing plans, financial plans, and so forth. The need for this close coordination is due to elements of one plan being the starting point for others: thus, a sales forecast (as an element of the marketing plan) is the cornerstone of the production plan – see Chapter 15 of Fisk (1967) and Chapter 9 of Schaffir and Trentin (1973).

Systems theory provides a conceptual framework within which management can effectively integrate the various activities of the organization, including the marketing function (see, for example, Churchman, 1968; Schoderbek et al., 1975; Emery, 1981). The major benefit of the systems approach lies in the facility it gives to management in recognizing the proper place and function of subsystems within the whole, thereby focusing attention on broader issues than those contained in a single department. With particular reference to marketing, the application of systems thinking (Lazer, 1962b; Wilson, 1970b) should result in at least three developments of significance to improved management:

1 A more concerted emphasis on marketing planning and control
2 Better systems of marketing intelligence to provide management with a clearer perspective for its marketing actions
3 Following on from both of the above items, a better understanding of marketing as an adjustment mechanism that is able to employ corporate resources to meet changing market conditions successfully.

With particular regard to functional coordination, the common flows through all departments are information, physical resources and funds, so one or more of these can be a vehicle for integration. Let us consider some examples.

Production – marketing interface

A failure to control this interface effectively can lead to such problems as the sales force promising early delivery to secure an order that then causes difficulties in both production programming and delivery scheduling. Such behaviour could easily jeopardize future orders. Plant capacity and flexibility, standardization, and quality requirements must all be taken into account by planners attempting to integrate production and marketing operations.

Purchasing – marketing interface

Effective cooperation here should prevent material shortages from appearing and should also help to avoid the holding of excessive raw material/component stocks due to marketing management's failing to inform the purchasing department of reduced requirements. Such failure causes funds to be tied up unnecessarily in an unprofitable use, which is very inefficient.

Personnel – marketing interface

Although selection procedures are imperfect, this in itself is an insufficient cause to ignore the methods that are available and to rely on wholly personal judgement. Those who are to be responsible for recruiting, training and inducting marketing personnel must have a sound knowledge of the work done in, and skill requirements of, the marketing area.

Accounting – marketing interface

The question of coordination and communication between marketing and the financial control function is of fundamental importance (e.g. Wilson, 1970, 1975, 1981, 1998, 1999b, 2001; Ratnatunga, 1983, 1988; Ward, 1989; Shaw, 1998; Ambler, 2003). Our present interest is not with the keeping of books of accounts and the subsequent reporting to outside parties (e.g. via the statutory annual balance sheet and profit and loss account). This is but one decreasingly important function of the financial controller generally referred to as the *stewardship function*. (It is so called because the controller acts as the shareholders' steward in keeping records, paying bills, collecting debts and safeguarding the assets of the business.)

In contrast with stewardship is the controller's *service function*, through which he or she aims to develop information flows and reporting systems to facilitate improved planning, decision-making and control.

Marketing controllership is concerned with the controller's service to marketing management, and this will become increasingly important as the marketing concept is more widely adopted and as marketing becomes more dominant within the typical company.

To offer the best service to marketing involves the controller studying the company's marketing organization and its problems. One approach to this is shown in Figure 16.4.

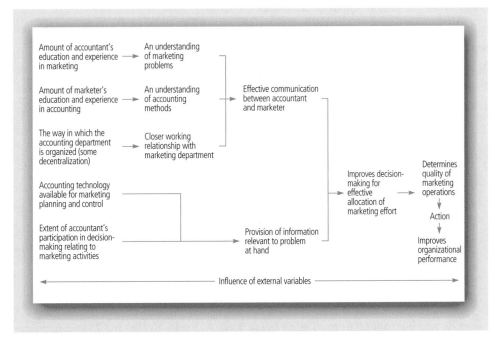

Figure 16.4 A framework for improved management accounting – marketing interaction (source: Bancroft and Wilson, 1979, p. 29)

A greater mutual understanding between marketing managers and management accountants, coupled with the greater involvement of members from both groups in the decision process, should lead to more effective outcomes. The most effective communication, and the best information flows, tend to occur where members of the controller's staff are located within the marketing function with line responsibility to the controller but with a close working relationship with the marketing staff. In their pioneering US study, Schiff and Mellman (1962) found this arrangement in very few companies, and in their UK study Wilson and Bancroft (1983) found a similar situation, but a deeper interest in analysing the costs of marketing seems to have developed since then, along with the spread of the marketing concept. Nevertheless, comparatively little attention has been given to marketing costs as opposed to the extensive attention given to production costs despite the very substantial scale of the former.

16.5 Problems of marketing feedback

The importance of feedback is paramount, since unbalanced and unstable conditions, along with an inability to exercise effective control, can develop within the marketing area if prompt, adequate and undistorted feedback is not present.

However, the marketing manager can rarely benefit from the advantages of statistical feedback to provide an automatic corrective control over marketing activities in the same way that the production manager can use such control over much of his plant. It is necessary for marketing managers frequently to base their decisions on experience alone, and control by relying on their ability to motivate staff and external agents after they have personally received the feedback.

The two major reasons for the rare use of pure automatic feedback in marketing are simple to discern:

1 The fact that performance deviations can arise from a multitude of different causes. For example, a drop in sales volume may be caused by a price increase with elastic demand, as a result of competitive products or promotions, or as a result of a decline in the level of business activity over the trade cycle, and so forth.
2 The plans and standards used in the control process may be as much at fault as the apparent performance. The inability, say, of a sales representative to achieve his or her quota may be due to poor quota setting or unrealistic sales forecasting as well as poor performance. An investigation into such matters may result in a revision of standards or plans, but a feedback mechanism can hardly be expected to deal with mistakes in the basis of performance measurement.

All these problem areas demand that flexibility be maintained in relation to both the planning and controlling of marketing operations. Accordingly, the marketing manager must be able to redeploy the sales force, adapt the advertising campaign, or change the various aspects of the market offer (price, packaging, product features, etc.) to meet changing conditions. This means that he or she is charged with the almost impossible tasks of knowing the changes to make and being able to make them.

Of the greatest importance in this setting is the suitability of the information system in enabling the marketing manager to be flexible in devising alternative plans as a matter of contingency rather than necessity. As in all such matters, the costs and benefits should be balanced in the securing of fuller control.

In considering feedback it is inevitable that delays of one kind or another will be experienced. To a large extent delay is inevitable since feedback is, by definition, *ex post*, thus only arising after the event. However, we can break delays down into their constituent categories, as shown in Figure 16.5.

If a competitor introduces a significant change in their market offering, there is a delay until this information is relayed to the marketing team. It takes time to devise a suitable response, involving revisions to marketing plans. Once the revisions are decided upon there will be a lag until they are implemented. Finally, at least for this iteration, there will be a delay following implementation before it becomes apparent what the impact of the revised course of action is on the competitive change. By the time these delays have been incurred, it is quite possible that the competitor may have established a clear competitive advantage; hence feedback delays must be minimized in responding to competitive threats – or to any other relevant change. This latter situation is illustrated in Figure 16.6, which shows positive and negative feedback loops relating to the sales growth pattern of a newly launched product.

The rate of sales of the new product (i.e. the point of intersection of the positive and negative feedback loops in Figure 16.6) is a function of sales effort on the one hand and sales effectiveness on the other. If the sales rate generates a profitable level of sales revenue, this is likely to lead to an increase in the sales budget and thus to further increases in the amount of sales effort. These linkages are shown in the left-hand

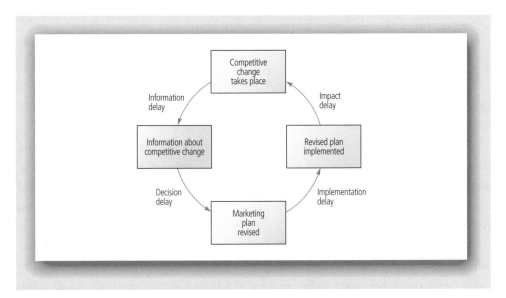

Figure 16.5 Major delays in a feedback system (adapted from Kotler, 1972a, p. 770)

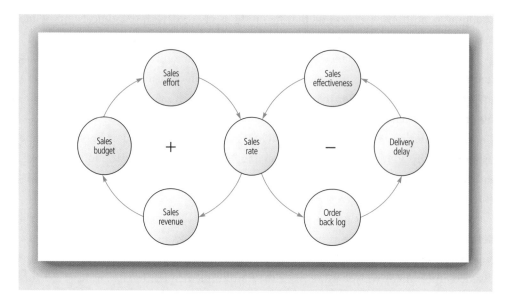

Figure 16.6 Feedback effects on sales growth (adapted from Forrester, 1965, pp. 357, 358 and 361)

(positive feedback) loop, and it would appear that continuous sales growth is in prospect. However, if there is insufficient productive capacity to meet the increased sales rate, an order backlog will build up, along with delays in delivery. This will almost certainly cause a decrease in sales effectiveness that, in turn, will dampen the sales rate, as shown in the right-hand (negative feedback) loop.

As the two loops interact, it becomes clear that sales will grow when there is available productive capacity to ensure that order backlogs are avoided. Whenever the sales rate exceeds full capacity, the result is that sales will then decrease due to the order backlogs, etc. This rather simplified example highlights not only the lack of synchronization in terms of timing, but also the importance of functional coordination.

16.6 Information adequacy

How effective managers are in their jobs will depend on how much, how relevant and how good their information is, and how well they interpret and act upon it.

Nevertheless, one hears frequent complaints from management that information is too late, of the wrong type, unverified, or even suppressed. It is evident, therefore, that if information is to be of value it must be clear, detailed, timely, accurate and complete – and must not consist of vague figures thrown out by an unplanned system.

It is not enough, for example, to observe that the purpose of a particular set of procedures is to provide the information required for planning and controlling the company's marketing operation. The information requirements must be made more explicit, and the aim of a marketing analysis system defined. The aim may be to produce the internal data needed for effective planning and control of marketing activities and the requirements specified as follows:

Marketing planning:

➡ Establishing sales quotas by territory, product, industry and channel
➡ Developing the advertising budget and planning the allocation of funds amongst specified media
➡ Evaluating the character and size of the product line
➡ Developing additional outlets and new channels of distribution
➡ Determining the need for, and location of, additional warehouses.

Measurement and control of results by:

➡ Salesperson
➡ Geographic area
➡ Distribution channel
➡ Customer group
➡ Product.

Management must decide what needs to be done, who is to do it, ensure that it is done, and evaluate the success with which it was done. None of these functions can be performed without the necessary information. But *all* the available information may not be helpful, so the marketing manager must pay great attention to the quality, quantity and relevance of the information that he or she seeks.

It is characteristic of decision-making that in selecting one particular course of action the manager thereby prevents himself from moving in another direction. This constitutes a major difficulty in making decisions, and it follows that the manager's ability to make better decisions involves relying upon information that:

➡ Reduces the uncertainty associated with following one particular course of action
➡ Improves the power to act in the right direction.

The sources of such improvement lie in the methodical selection, collection, processing, analysis and communication of relevant information, along with the ability to formulate sound assumptions as a basis for making more accurate forecasts and decisions on the basis of that information.

However, while to manage a business is to manage information, it may be that either too much or too little information is presented. The economic wastage that results from an excess of information is *not* the incremental clerical cost of producing it, but rather the loss of executive effectiveness that it causes. This comes about in two major ways:

1 The manager may ignore the great volume of information that is presented to him or her, thus missing the vital as well as the irrelevant
2 The manager may become overburdened, or even enslaved, by the excess.

On the other hand, should there be insufficient information presented for good decision-making, it may be wise to postpone the decision until more information is available. A similar situation involving delay is that in which sufficient information is presented but its accuracy is in doubt and extra time must be spent if this accuracy is to be improved. In either situation the loss of control that results from delay must be weighed against the value of improved information in reducing the uncertainties implicit in the making of most decisions.

Only a limited amount of the information that flows through the typical organization is of real management significance. That which is of value, therefore, must be identified and developed in line with organizational requirements – observing the important information qualities of impartiality, validity, reliability and internal consistency.

The organizational structure of an enterprise and its information requirements are inextricably linked. In order to translate a statement of his duties into action, the manager must receive and use information. This involves using all the relevant data and intelligence – quantitative and qualitative, financial and non-financial – that is available, instead of merely relying on an existing system and the reports it produces.

As frequently happens, the manager may not know precisely what information he or she requires or, alternatively, what information is available. Consultants can help by observing the types of decisions made, testing the adequacy of existing information, suggesting alternative information flows, and indicating the means (and costs) of collection.

The aim, then, is to provide the right information to the right people in the right quantity at the right time, and at minimum cost. The purpose of collecting, analysing and using information is essentially the same in any size of business, whether for routine purposes or for special projects. The difference is in the relative employment of manual as opposed to computer-based systems. The increasing adoption of networked computer systems should ensure that fewer managers have cause to complain about insufficient, inaccurate or delayed information. This depends, of course, not only upon accurate information flows, but also upon systematic storage in order to facilitate rapid retrieval. The need to react quickly to a changing environment demands fast and accurate retrieval, as facts that take too long to find and compile are often useless when time is of the essence.

Discussions about information systems can usefully be considered against the background of the *theory of communication*. Relative to the broad subject of communication, there are three major problems:

1 The accuracy with which the symbols of communication can be transmitted – the technical problem
2 The precision with which the transmitted symbols convey the desired meaning – the semantic problem
3 The effectiveness with which the received meaning affects behaviour in the desired manner – the effectiveness problem.

Figure 16.7 illustrates how these problems can arise in the process of selecting a message and transmitting it (i.e. in the usual decision-making process of using an information system).

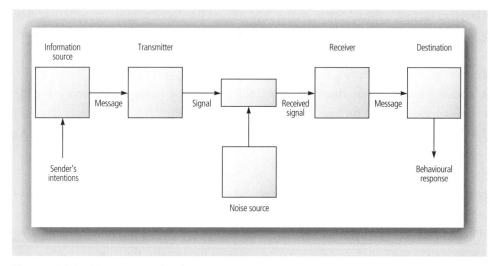

Figure 16.7 The communication system

In the process of being transmitted, it is unfortunately characteristic that certain things are added to (or omitted from) the signal that were not intended by the information source. Such errors, distortions and changes are collectively termed 'noise'.

The transmitter could take a written message and use some code to encipher it into, say, a sequence of numbers (e.g. binary digits), which could then be sent over the channel as the signal. The general purpose of the transmitter thus becomes that of encoding, and the purpose of the receiver that of decoding. However, as one makes the coding more and more nearly ideal, one is forced into longer and longer delays in the process of coding, and this requires the establishing of balance. But no matter how careful one is in the coding process, it will always be found that, after the signal has been received, there remains some undesirable uncertainty (noise) about the precise nature of the message.

It is emphasized throughout this book that managers need information to assist them in decision-making, to indicate performance and to help in making plans, setting standards and controlling outcomes. In this light, the key to developing a dynamic and usable management information system is to move beyond the limits of conventional reporting and to conceive of information as it relates to the two vital elements of the management process – planning and control.

A great deal of information, while useful for planning and control, is primarily raised for some other purpose that is only tangentially related to planning and control. This covers much of the output of the accounting routine in many companies. Such information is derived from:

1 Payroll procedures
2 The order-processing cycle, beginning with the receipt of an order and ending with the collection of accounts receivable
3 The procurement and accounts payable cycle.

The adequacy of these information flows as a basis for decision systems is highlighted by the omission of:

1 Information about the future

2 Data expressed in non-financial terms, such as market share, productivity, quality levels, adequacy of customer service, etc.

3 Information dealing with external conditions as they might bear on a particular enterprise's operations.

Effective business planning requires three types of information – environmental, competitive and operating. Accounting alone, therefore, is insufficient, but if the controllership function exists within a company it should ensure that economic and marketing research and forecasting are closely integrated with the systems function.

Information is the medium of control, but the flows required for planning are not necessarily the same as those required for control. Figure 16.8 outlines the general nature of information flows for planning and control. Their uses in control revolve around communication, motivation and performance, whereas forecasting,

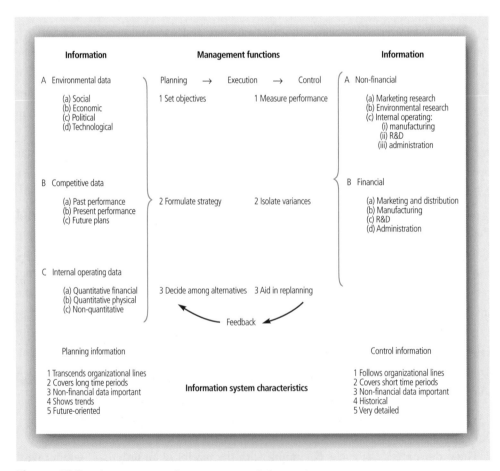

Figure 16.8 The anatomy of management information

establishing objectives and deciding among alternatives are more important in planning.

In summary, a management information system is the means of bringing to each level of management the necessary and complete information that is accurate, timely and sufficient (but not in excessive detail), so that each manager can fulfil his or her responsibilities to the organization. The central purpose, then, is to aid decision-making, and the system should be based on sound data, be sufficiently flexible to allow new techniques to be used and be operated at minimum cost commensurate with the overall system results.

The three basic information flows in marketing are:

1 The inflow of environmental data
2 Internal operating data
3 Communication (usually of a persuasive nature) directed to external audiences.

The effectiveness of each flow should be continually tested by the posing of questions such as:

→ Does the procedure for developing delivery quotations to customers produce the information required to ensure that delivery promises are realistic?
→ Does the procedure for handling customers' enquiries regarding the status of their orders provide for rendering a superior form of customer service?
→ Do the sales statistical procedures produce the best internal data required to plan sales strategy, to control selling effort and to spotlight opportunities for major improvements in the distribution programme?
→ Do the clerical-support activities provided for the sales force help to increase each salesperson's productivity by maximizing the amount of time spent in direct selling work?

These representative questions point to the main uses of a marketing information system in the control effort, and these fall into the following groups:

1 To spot things that are going wrong and to take corrective action before serious loss results, which constitutes the most fruitful and constructive use of control information
2 To highlight things that have actually gone wrong and guide marketing management in either cutting the losses of failure or turning apparent failure to future advantage
3 To determine exactly how and why failures or deviations from plan have arisen and to suggest steps that should be taken to prevent their recurrence, which is another highly constructive application, since mistakes need not be repeated even if they cannot be avoided
4 To find out who is to blame for failure, which, if not done in the proper way and followed up by corrective action, is the least constructive of uses.

Careful consideration must always be applied to deciding which elements of information to include in a marketing information system if cost is not to be a prohibitive factor. The types of decisions that must be made will obviously determine the types of information that the system should provide. A few examples are given below.

Pricing

Before any decision on price can be made, information should be available on:

1 Competitive pricing policies and product prices
2 Consumer attitudes to price
3 The relative profit contribution of the company's products at various prices
4 Distribution and production costs as a basis for point 3 above
5 Volume factors (covering both market share and potential along with capacity details).

Product management

This function depends completely on adequate flows of information from a variety of sources if it is to be successfully carried out. Information should be related to the PLC, since this indicates when to launch new products, when to phase out declining products, and when to revitalize the marketing effort behind other products. The life cycle must be viewed in terms of total sales and market penetration on the one hand, and costs and profit outcomes on the other. Forecasts of costs and revenues will follow from forecasts of total market size and the share that is to be achieved.

Sales operations

Up-to-date details of each live account should be an essential part of a marketing information system because this facilitates analyses that are invaluable to sales planning and control. In addition, accurate customer records mean that new sales staff can be assigned to territories or customer groups and learn a good deal about the accounts before visiting them: this avoids the situation when a poor salesperson is kept on because he or she is the only person knowing about his or her accounts in the absence of proper records, and the total sales job can be smoothly transferred to the case of promotion, transfer or departure only if such records exist.

Analyses from sales records will give essential information to marketing management on product profitability, customer-group profitability and regional profitability, and actual performance can be compared to the requirements of the profit plan. The extent to which variances arise from volume changes, variations in price or adjustments in the mix of products sold can be analysed, and the usual budgetary procedures will provide information on selling expenses.

The role of the salesperson as an information intermediary between the enterprise and its outlets and customers must not be overlooked, since a salesperson who appreciates the importance of rapid information dissemination and feedback can help his or her organization to promote new products as well as adapting quickly to environmental change.

16.7 Cost problems

The essence of control in marketing, as in any other activity, is measurement. In relation to marketing costs, however, this measurement is not as straightforward as it may seem.

Figure 16.9 illustrates the basic elements of financial marketing performance that need to be controlled. The importance of marketing as the 'revenue generator' is made clear, but the other aspect of the financial sphere – cost incurrence – requires further consideration (see the discussion of definitions in Chapter 3, Section 3.3).

It is invariably found that the costs stemming from marketing activities are difficult to plan and control. The lowest costs are not necessarily to be preferred, since these may not result in the effective attainment of the desired sales volume and profit. Most order-getting costs are 'programmed' (i.e. determined by management decision) rather than variable and tend to influence the volume of sales rather than being influenced by it.

The characteristics of marketing costs lead to problems in analysis. Such characteristics include (after Wilson, 1979, 1988a, 1999b; but see also Kjaer-Hansen, 1965; Wilson, 1992):

➡ Long-run effects (e.g. the effect of an advertising campaign lasts longer than the campaign, and is usually lagged).
➡ The difficulty in measuring productivity, since standards are not easily determined. (Standards can be set for sales activities, e.g. cost to create £1 of sales, average costs of each unit sold, cost to generate £1 of profit, cost per transaction, cost per customer

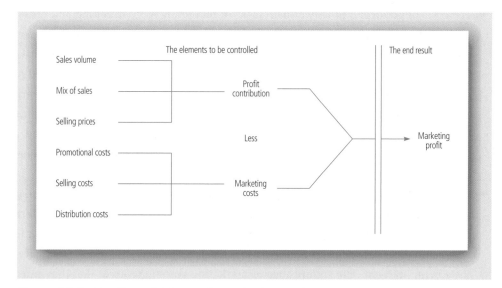

Figure 16.9 Key financial factors in marketing performance

serviced. However, in product decisions, levels of performance may be expressed in terms of the minimum required level of sales per product or the minimum profit contribution required.)

➡ The non-symmetrical nature of costs. (For example, costs increase more in changing from regional to national distribution than would be saved by changing from national to regional distribution.)

➡ Costs are frequently indivisible or joint costs, often intended to support a product group.

➡ Some costs have discontinuities, or a stepped character shape. The special structure of marketing costs raises problems. The cost structure of every activity is related to the interaction of fixed costs (that do not vary with the level of sales activity) and variable costs (such as shipping costs that do vary with the level of activity), and is reflected in the cost per unit produced or sold at different rates of activity. However, a large number of marketing costs are semi-fixed, including, for example, sales force costs – when a salesperson is appointed, his or her salary is a fixed cost, but the number of salespeople and the level of commission and expenses are variable, thus giving rise to a semi-fixed expenses category. In the case of marketing, which accounts for a considerable proportion of total expenditure, these stepped costs of a semi-fixed nature determine the behaviour of many other costs.

Planning in the light of these characteristics must be based to a significant extent on past experience, knowledge of competitive activities, test marketing exercises, and the estimated expenditure that desired profits at various levels of activity will permit. Accounting data in the more conventional form provides a point of departure for marketing cost analyses, but these data must be reworked on the basis of units that are subject to management control. (The relevant control unit will depend on the purpose of the analysis, but may be a product, product line, sales territory, marketing division, customer group, etc.).

➡ The costs of performing the two main tasks of marketing – order-getting and order-filling – have different effects and must be treated differently. The minimization principle should be applied to distribution activities, whereby a given quantitative target is aimed for at the lowest possible cost. But this principle cannot be applied to promotion, since the relationship between promotion and sales means that a variation in promotional expenditure will affect turnover, so minimal promotion may mean minimal sales. Consequently, a predictive approach must be applied and a balance struck between the desired level of sales and the level of promotional expenditure necessary to achieve that level of sales.

➡ The allocation of indirect marketing costs raises questions that require solutions. Along with a general increase in the proportion of fixed costs that exists in modern businesses, there has been an increasing adoption of direct costing systems (i.e. in which indirect costs are not allocated to products), which can result in indirect costs being ignored. The significance of marketing costs is so great that they must necessarily be subjected to detailed control via responsibility centre accounting (see Chapter 17) rather than be left uncontrolled as inevitable indirect outlays.

➡ Further cost problems relate to the greater number of essentially different marketing conditions that have to be controlled continually and rationally. Financial control in marketing is complicated because a number of factors are influenced by the costs incurred – the product, the territory, the customer group and the salesperson's profitability, in contrast to the product alone, which is the centre of attention in production accounting. The addition of varying conditions to a series of control bases makes it difficult to know which costs are to be controlled and in relation to which base.

➡ Special cost control problems arise in attempting to evaluate the results of each element of the marketing mix. It is almost impossible to isolate the role played by, say, direct selling in the marketing operation from the roles played by promotion, price and product features. Measures of individual parameter effectiveness must be related to detailed market analyses on a before and after basis, but this requires a more comprehensive system of marketing intelligence and information than is found in the typical company.

➡ The enormous range of strategic possibilities makes it impossible to include all of them in a formal analysis. Any particular marketing strategy will involve a particular combination of the elements of the marketing mix, with particular assumed environmental conditions. The number of different possible combinations is vast. This does not mean that quantitative techniques are useless, but it does mean that major measurement problems arise to complicate the issue.

➡ The ever-changing environment – including the impacts of competitive activities, developments in technology, changes in consumer tastes, government action and the other factors depicted in Figure 16.1 – makes planning difficult. As a result, control is made more difficult since it is no longer clear which variances were avoidable and which unavoidable.

➡ In considering the range of possible strategies, the uncertainty that any one constituent factor may change at almost any time makes the question of choice even more difficult.

➡ The effectiveness of costs (i.e. productivity or efficiency) is not easy to measure. The interdependent variety of elements involved and their varying long- and short-run effects are the cause of this difficulty.

➡ The tendency towards 'conglomeration', with its attendant diversification of activities and sheer size, results in an increasing complexity that challenges the best efforts in securing control.

In addition, there is the problem relating to the setting up and operating of decision models that strictly require a knowledge of the substitution or supplementation of the elements of the marketing mix. As with the major problem areas discussed above, the latter one (i.e. understanding substitution and supplementation) is concerned with evaluating the efficiency of the marketing effort and rationalizing the pattern of expenditure. In every case it is helpful to relate marketing costs to a profit base, since this is both a measure of efficiency and of goal attainment.

Essentially, costs are incurred in marketing to obtain a sufficient level of sales to give the desired profit. The necessary sales volume can be expressed as either a particular market share or a desired depth of market penetration, in which event the interrelationships are as illustrated in Figure 16.10.

The important point made by Figure 16.10 is that increasing profit is not necessarily a function of increasing market share, nor necessarily of increasing marketing expenditure. A frequently met obsession with sales managers is that of maximizing *sales volume*, whereas the action that they should be recommending is the optimizing of profits. The relationship between sales and profitability should follow one of the following patterns:

1 An increase in sales with a proportionately lower increase in costs should lead to improved profitability
2 An increase in sales with constant costs should improve profitability
3 An increase in sales with a decrease in costs should improve profitability
4 The maintaining of sales at a constant level with a decrease in costs should improve profitability.

The outcome of these various matters in operational terms is that, in order to improve the effectiveness of control in marketing, the following requirements must be met:

➡ A frequent and accurate monitoring of the three main constituents discussed – costs, sales volume and profit

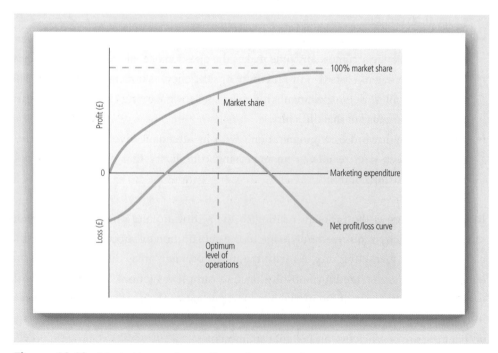

Figure 16.10 Marketing costs, profits and penetration

➡ A regular monitoring of the total market environment in order to detect movements and aid in evaluating the effectiveness of marketing expenditures

➡ A detailed breakdown of marketing effort (expressed in financial terms) into functional/managerial responsibility centres.

In many manufacturing enterprises the costs of marketing greatly exceed the costs of production, yet very little attention has been given to the analysis of marketing costs compared to the extensive attention given to production costs.

It is instructive to consider some of the reasons for this state of affairs, and these include the following:

➡ While the costs of productive labour and materials can be associated with specific machines, processes and products, the costs of the elements of the marketing mix cannot be associated so readily with outputs (such as sales and profit levels).

➡ Marketing activities tend to be less routine and repetitive than is the case with many standardized production activities.

➡ The dependency of marketing activities on outside agencies distinguishes them further from the more internally regulated and predictable manufacturing activities.

➡ Marketing activities tend to be performed in many locations, often distant from each other, rather than on one site.

➡ Within manufacturing there is the relatively simple choice to be made between using the product or the process as the cost object. In contrast, within marketing there are many more possible cost objects – such as the product line, product range, customer, customer/industry group, salesperson, sales territory, size of order, channel of distribution, etc.

➡ The cost behaviour patterns of many marketing activities are the reverse of those for manufacturing activities in the sense that order-getting costs tend to determine sales volume (hence manufacturing costs). Order-getting costs are committed in anticipation of sales. Whereas manufacturing costs *necessarily* increase as sales volume rises, order-getting costs must be *permitted* to increase. Thus, for a given level of activity, the lower the manufacturing costs the better, while the right level (and mix) of marketing costs is a matter of judgement. It can be argued that the 'best' approach is to focus on *technical efficiency* in relation to order-getting outlays (i.e. to maximize the outputs for a given level of input) and on *economic efficiency* in relation to manufacturing outlays (whereby one aims to minimize the inputs for a given level of output). This indicates the analytical complexity inherent in accounting for marketing costs.

➡ Since marketing costs are rarely included in inventory valuations (being treated instead as period costs), financial accounting principles, etc., provide little incentive for detailed analysis.

➡ Manufacturing activities typically have a short-run focus, whereas marketing operations must pay attention to long-run considerations. This also produces a conflict over financial accounting practice in that promotional outlays in a particular period are invariably matched with the sales achieved during that period, notwithstanding the fact that much promotional expenditure (and other order-getting outlays) are in the nature of capital investment intended to stimulate sales over several time periods.

➡ Personnel in manufacturing roles often have a greater cost consciousness and discipline than their marketing colleagues.

➡ The risk of suboptimization (whereby one particular aspect is maximized to the possible detriment of the whole) is much greater in a complex marketing context than it is in manufacturing.

➡ Many marketing activities have an intangible quality that distinguishes them from the tangible characteristics of production activities. Among the intangible factors is the psychological dimension of purchase predisposition.

Although these problems are many, they do not mean that no attempts should be made to plan and control marketing activities successfully. However, there is evidence to show that most accountants are not yet in tune with marketing thinking. First, accountants lack the knowledge and understanding of the information requirements necessary for the marketing function. Second, accountants in general do not accept marketing as a distinct and separate managerial function. This seemingly blind attitude was found in a survey (reported by Williamson, 1979) to be well ingrained and is an appalling indication of the failure of accountants to see the real essence of business activity (i.e. product–market interactions) and of a misplaced arrogance in looking down on a group whose purpose and function they so clearly misunderstand. Lastly, organizational design may impede adequate communications between functions. This could (and does) happen to such an extent that the accounting and marketing departments may be geographically distant from one another, although marketing *activities* are geographically dispersed in any event.

A long-established organizational design could also hinder a new pattern of resource allocation. It may be such that available resources are channelled towards the order-filling production and distribution functions rather than to the order-getting processes such as advertising, sales promotion and personal selling. Allocating to the former in preference to the latter is tantamount to saying that a firm can sell what it can make – the old sales concept – rather than the marketing concept of making what the consumers want.

The practical consequences of these inhibitions manifest themselves in the ways described below.

Schiff and Mellman, as long ago as 1962, in an almost isolated empirical study, noted deficiencies of the accounting function in supplying marketing with sufficient information in certain areas, such as:

➡ Lack of effective financial analyses of customers, channels of distribution and salespeople

➡ An overemphasis on net profit-based reporting (or the full cost allocation approach)

➡ Inadequacies in marketing cost classification (e.g. little distinction was made between fixed and variable costs or between controllable and non-controllable costs)

➡ Return on investment was rarely used

➡ There was a general lack of integration between the accounting and marketing functions.

Goodman (1970), in a later study, found that accounting did not appear to have made much progress in satisfying the needs of marketing planning. These areas of failure he saw as being:

➡ Non-use of sufficient return-on-investment criteria

➡ Insistence on using the traditional full costing for decision analyses

➡ Inability to separate the reporting obligation of accounting from the service function

➡ Imperfect understanding of the marketing concept

➡ Lack of minimum acceptable goal criteria

➡ Disregard for the implications of working capital.

As various authorities have observed, there are fundamental differences between accounting and marketing. For example, accounting builds from an analysis of internal financial data, whereas marketing builds from the diagnosis of external market situations. The respective perspectives are literally poles apart (see Simmonds' Foreword in Wilson, 1981). Thus, the marketing view that profit stems from an enterprise's position relative to its competitors (i.e. reflecting its differential advantage) and is not a function of arbitrary financial periods is not likely to meet with full-blooded approval – or even understanding – on the part of the average accountant, who invariably fails to link his own profit measures either to market share or to changes in market size.

16.8 Marketing orientation

In the absence of marketing orientation it will be difficult to implement and control marketing activities effectively, since there will be no marketing plan. (The following discussion draws heavily from Wilson and Fook (1990).)

The well-documented and long-run decline in Britain's industrial competitiveness has often been attributed to a lack of adequate marketing orientation on the part of UK firms. It is widely felt that the more successful enterprises demonstrate a higher level of marketing orientation than their less successful rivals, although hard evidence to support this is rather rare. Nevertheless, despite a minority view that a preoccupation with marketing orientation is a cause of competitive decline when the former is focused on the short-run requirements of customers, there is a strong case for arguing that marketing

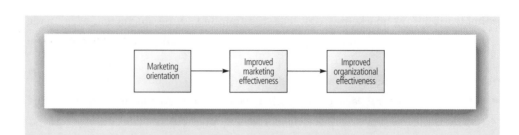

Figure 16.11 The role of marketing orientation (source: Wilson and Fook, 1990, p. 22)

orientation leads to improved marketing effectiveness, which in turn leads to improved corporate effectiveness (see Figure 16.11).

If a business is to seek to improve its effectiveness in this way, it needs to ask the following questions:

➡ What is marketing orientation?
➡ How can marketing orientation be recognized?
➡ How can marketing orientation be developed?

In this section we will address these three questions and suggest how an enterprise might develop its marketing orientation in order to improve its effectiveness.

What is marketing orientation?

A business can exhibit any one of a number of different orientations, such as:

➡ Production orientation
➡ Cost orientation
➡ Engineering orientation
➡ Sales orientation
➡ Marketing orientation.

The last of these is the broadest and highlights the concern the enterprise has with satisfying its customers via the adoption of the marketing concept.

Marketing orientation is concerned with implementing the marketing concept and, as such, is action oriented. However, rather than seeing it as a set of activities, it is more helpful to think of marketing orientation as a process by which an enterprise seeks to maintain a continuous match betwen its products/services and its customers' needs. With a little elaboration we can build this into a formal definition:

"Marketing orientation is the process by which an enterprise's target customers' needs and wants are effectively and efficiently satisfied within the resource limitations and long-term survival requirements of that enterprise."

Doubt has been expressed by many marketing authorities on the extent to which the philosophy underlying the marketing concept has been adequately implemented – hence upon the extent to which marketing orientation really exists. Given that the practical manifestations of marketing orientation are not well known prompts our next question.

How can marketing orientation be recognized?

While it should not be assumed that the following items are in order of priority, it is intended that they should be seen as constituting a reasonably comprehensive listing of the requirements that must be met if marketing orientation is to be effective:

1 Is there a good understanding within the enterprise of the needs, wants and behaviour patterns of targeted customers?
2 Is the enterprise profit-directed rather than volume-driven?
3 Does the chief executive see him- or herself as the enterprise's senior marketing strategist or 'marketing champion'?
4 Does the enterprise have a market-driven mission (for example, a cosmetics company should see itself as being in the beauty business and the Post Office should see those in its market as users of communications)?
5 Do the enterprise's strategies reflect the realities of the marketplace (including the competitive situation)?
6 Is marketing seen as being more important by managers within the enterprise than other functions and orientations?
7 Is the enterprise organized in such a way that it can be more responsive to marketing opportunities and threats than its less successful competitors?
8 Does the enterprise have a well-designed marketing information system?
9 Do managers within the enterprise make full use of marketing research inputs in their decision-making?
10 Are marketing costs and revenues systematically analysed in relation to marketing activities to ensure that the latter are being carried out effectively?
11 Is there a strong link between the marketing function and the development of new products/services?
12 Does the enterprise employ staff in the marketing area who are marketing professionals (rather than, say, sales oriented in their approach)?
13 Is it understood that marketing is the responsibility of the entire organization if it is to be effective?
14 Are decisions with marketing implications made in a well-coordinated way and executed in an integrated manner?

These points can be linked to McKinsey & Co.'s 'Seven S' framework to show what is required in an effective, marketing-oriented enterprise (see Figure 16.12).

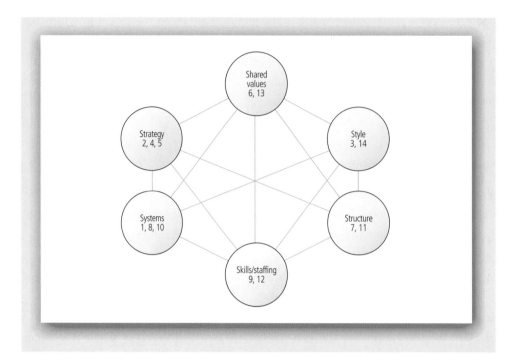

Figure 16.12 Requirements of marketing orientation (adapted from Wilson and Fook, 1990)

If an enterprise's responses to the points listed above contain a lot of negative answers, the next question becomes important if matters are to be improved.

How can marketing orientation be developed?

Developing marketing orientation is a long-term process and needs to be thought of as a form of investment. To a large extent this investment is in changing the organization's culture so that common values relating to the need to highlight service to customers, a concern for quality in all activities, and so forth are shared throughout the organization. This is not an appropriate target for the 'quick fix'.

Steps to be taken in order to enhance an enterprise's degree of marketing orientation are:

1 Secure top management support, since a bottom-up approach would be doomed from the outset given the company-wide implications of marketing orientation.
2 Specify a mission relating to the development of marketing orientation. This should have a plan associated with it, and the necessary allocation of resources to enable it to be executed.
3 A task force should be set up as part of the plan to bring together managers from across the company (and consultants who can help considerably) to carry out tasks such as:
   → Identifying the current orientation of the company

- ➡ Carrying out a training needs analysis as a basis for a management development programme to change the company's culture in a desired way
- ➡ Advising on structural changes within the company to support marketing activities
- ➡ Ensuring commitment to change via the system of rewards (such as bonuses and promotion) that will apply to facilitate change.

4 Maintain the momentum of change by means of continuous monitoring of marketing performance to ensure that inertia does not set in. Progress towards improved marketing orientation can be measured by regularly asking questions of the following type:

- ➡ Are we easy to do business with?
- ➡ Do we keep our promises?
- ➡ Do we meet the standards we set?
- ➡ Are we responsive?
- ➡ Do we work together?

These elements of a process for developing marketing orientation are shown in Figure 16.13.

Developing marketing orientation requires a focus on customers, competitors, the changing environment, and company culture. Achieving it is an expensive and time-consuming endeavour. However, those companies that really make the effort are likely to have a higher level of marketing effectiveness and greater organizational effectiveness than their competitors.

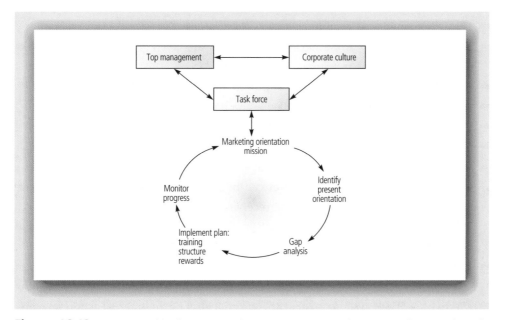

Figure 16.13 Steps in developing marketing orientation (source: Wilson and Fook, 1990, p. 23)

Developing an internal marketing programme

We suggested at an earlier stage in the text that the marketing concept is based upon three principal lines of thought:

1 A market focus
2 A customer orientation
3 Coordinated marketing.

However, in the case of the third of these – coordinated marketing – a problem that is experienced all too frequently is that not all employees are trained or motivated to work together sufficiently closely. The net effect of this is that the organization then works less than optimally. The implications of this are, in turn, exacerbated as markets become more competitive and the difficulties of achieving – and sustaining – a meaningful competitive advantage become ever greater. A programme of internal marketing in which there is a heightened emphasis upon staff training, motivation, empowerment and working in teams is therefore a potentially powerful contributor to organizational performance and, in particular, to the achievement of customer satisfaction. An effective internal marketing programme is therefore likely to be characterized by:

➡ A fundamental acceptance of its strategic significance by senior management
➡ A willingness on the part of senior management to change the structure of the organization so that the importance of front-line staff is recognized and reflected in the structure of the organization – it is this which was referred to earlier in our discussion of the right-side-up organization
➡ The development and communication of clear values
➡ The empowerment of front-line staff so that they are given greater freedom to make decisions that will solve customers' problems
➡ A commitment to staff development and training
➡ A system that recognizes staff excellence and rewards it accordingly
➡ The development of strong teams
➡ The identification of what Jan Carlzon of Scandinavian Airlines referred to as 'moments of truth' (these are the points of contact between the customer and a member of staff where the customer can be won or lost by the quality of service and personal contact that he or she receives) and the conscious thinking through of the ways in which these can best be capitalized upon by staff training and behaviour
➡ The setting of particular standards, a fundamental commitment to their achievement and a total lack of willingness to compromise in doing this, and the development of effective feedback systems so that the effectiveness of the internal marketing programme can be monitored (see Illustration 16.1).

Illustration 16.1 The AA and Unisys and their use of internal marketing

Customer care and satisfaction are fundamental and long-standing elements of the Automobile Association's marketing strategy. However, having positioned itself in the 1990s as 'the country's fourth emergency service' and recognizing that customers generally have ever higher levels of expectation of the organizations they deal with, the AA recognized that there was a need within the organization to re-evaluate how they might best deliver this. The answer, they felt, lay in a greater emphasis upon staff motivation and that the recognition of the achievements of its workforce could often be as effective as financial rewards. This led to the development of a number of reward schemes, with staff being nominated by their supervisors when it was felt they had 'gone the extra mile' to improve customer care and quality.

Although the AA has traditionally been characterized by a family-type atmosphere, something which in many ways made internal marketing a relatively straightforward exercise, Unisys, in common with many large multinationals, was forced to reinvent itself in the 1980s in order to focus upon customers rather than being product-driven. It chose to do this by putting customer service and quality ahead of price, but in the process was forced to make major cultural changes. Staff were retrained and taught to develop completely new mindsets. An important part of this involved a greater degree of staff empowerment, which, for Unisys, meant explaining to staff what they *could not* do and then letting them decide how they wanted to run the business. At the same time, they developed a rewards system designed to recognize staff initiatives to improve quality and customer care.

Underpinning all of this is the belief that to understand customer service means first thinking like a customer. Unisys therefore encourages staff to imagine life on the other side of the desk and, where necessary, to take the unprompted action that can make or break customer satisfaction. However, doing this involves creating the appropriate culture rather than simply emphasizing training.

Source: *The Sunday Times*, 11 June 1995, p. 13.

It follows from this that internal marketing should precede external marketing. This can be illustrated by the way in which, although it is relatively easy for an organization to commit itself to high levels of service, these are unlikely to be achieved until and unless the staff understand the real importance of service excellence and have been trained to deliver this. It is because of this that an increasing number of organizations, such as the AA and Unisys, are restructuring so that the typical organizational chart is inverted and a right-side-up organization created (the right-side-up and wrong-side-up organizations were discussed in Chapter 1). In this way, the pivotal importance of front-line staff to the delivery of customer satisfaction is highlighted (see Figure 16.14 and Illustration 16.2).

Illustration 16.2 The rise and rise of internal marketing

A survey of delegates at the 1996 Marketing Forum revealed that 78 per cent of their organizations were 'fairly' or 'very seriously' committed to internal marketing. This was reflected by the way in which budgets for internal marketing were being raised, some- times dramatically, to ensure that the corpor- ate message was being effectively communi- cated to employees and the corporate identity was being maintained at all levels.

Source: *Marketing*, 12 December 1996, p. 4.

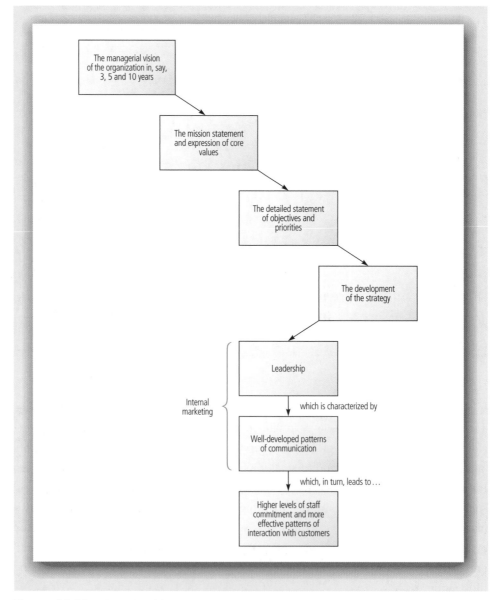

Figure 16.14 The role of internal marketing

16.9 Planning orientation

What benefits does planning offer? Among the most important are the following:

➡ Planning requires effective communication, which improves the functional coordination of efforts throughout the organization (see below). In part this will be due to the clearer definition of objectives and policies that planning presupposes (see Porter and Roberts, 1977).

➡ Planning motivates by showing what is expected of each member of the organization, and if plans have been agreed between superiors and subordinates in an appropriate way, there should be a high degree of commitment to their attainment.

➡ Planning should lead to the making of better decisions by requiring an explicit statement of assumptions underlying choices, as well as the enumerating of alternative courses of action and relevant states of nature. In other words, systematic thought needs to be given to the future, thereby ensuring that effort is not wholly absorbed in the present.

➡ Planning encourages a favourable attitude towards change, which is due in part to a better state of preparation for sudden variations (anticipated and otherwise) so that they can be turned to the organization's advantage, but which is also due to constantly striving to create a desired future. As pointed out by Charles St Thomas (1965, p. 9):

" . . . the manager who successfully undertakes his planning work must begin by recognizing that the primary key to his effectiveness lies in his capability to adapt.*"*

➡ Planning enables standards of performance to be established, and these in turn allow the control process to be effective.

Despite the obvious appeal of planning there are those who believe that any attempt to lay out specific and rational plans is either foolish, dangerous or downright evil. Churchman (1968, pp. 14 and 215–26) refers to these individuals as anti-planners:

" . . . there are all kinds of anti-planners, but the most numerous are those who believe that experience and cleverness are the hallmarks of good management.*"*

It is easy to see what a contrast there is between the 'practical' approach based on intuition and experience and the more analytical approach being recommended in this book. Particular arguments against the adoption of planning in any given organization might include the fear that it will take power away from the chief executive, or make excessive demands on line managers, or consume time and other resources for results that cannot be guaranteed, or be a waste of effort because market forecasts are never wholly correct, and so on (see Hussey, 1971, pp. 9–10).

Failings in strategic marketing planning may arise as a result of:

1 A chief executive who is not committed to planning, or who makes every decision of significance alone.

2 A planner who is too narrow in his view, or too restricted in his ability, to consider all the essential aspects of marketing planning and their impacts throughout the organization.

3 Small-scale operations that are unable adequately to support a planning function.

4 A state of corporate decline that is progressing too rapidly for planning to arrest it (see Stonich, 1975).

5 Too much emphasis being placed on *where* to compete and not enough on *how* to compete given that the latter rather than the former secures sustainable competitive advantage (see Simmonds, 1985).

6 Too little focus on uniqueness and adaptability with a tendency in many industries (e.g. security dealing, semi-conductors, biotechnology, retailing) towards a herd instinct that encourages sameness on the one hand and a limited adaptive capability on the other.

7 Inadequate emphasis on *when* to compete – such as being first into new markets or first with new products as opposed to being fast followers.

8 Too much attention being paid to competing organizations rather than focusing on individuals as competitors (e.g. chief executives' pronouncements in annual reports, etc., effectively lock their organizations into specified courses of action that highlight opportunities for others).

9 Using the wrong measures of success – especially when these favour short-term results to the detriment of long-term performance. Assessing marketing performance is difficult due to problems of both definition and measurement. The traditional approach has been to attempt to measure outputs relative to inputs (e.g. marketing productivity analysis – see Chapter 3). While this is feasible in broad terms, e.g. for an entire organization, it becomes more problematic as one looks in more detail at specific activities or marketing programmes. Much in marketing is unquantifiable and it follows that inputs and outputs cannot be adequately measured and manipulated if some are qualitative. Moreover, the typical result of relating inputs and outputs is the assessment of efficiency, whereas effectiveness is of much greater significance.

10 Planning becoming a mindless ritual rather than an opportunity for sound strategic thinking.

11 Senior staff get involved in 'us versus them' battles with lower-level colleagues.

12 Information that is held in one part of the organization is withheld, or only begrudgingly provided, to those who need it elsewhere in the organization.

13 Key information on which plans are based (such as sales estimates) is biased to justify a particular position rather than providing a sound basis for comparing alternatives (see Lowe and Shaw, 1968).

14 The results of the planning process are ignored when actual decisions with strategic consequences for marketing are made (such as acquisitions).

(See Bleeke (1988) for a fuller discussion of points 5–9. Further coverage of points 10–14 can be found in Chapter 9 of Abell and Hammond (1979).)

16.10 Organizational issues

Introduction

Suggestions have been made, for example by Hayhurst and Wills (1972), that changing organizational needs may lead to the disintegration of a corporate marketing organization. This could be achieved by the separation of operational activities on the one hand and planning activities on the other. Selling and distribution might fall into the former category.

It is clear (e.g. Hooley et al., 1984) that the increasingly competitive environment in which marketing is undertaken has created a recognition that organizational flexibility is a necessary element of marketing orientation.

To a large extent the successful implementation of marketing strategies relies upon an appropriate structure. As Hughes (1980) has pointed out:

"Many marketing plans fail because the planner did not consider the fact that the organization was not capable of implementing the plan. Short-range plans will require adaptation to the existing organization, whereas long-range plans may require redesigning the organization.**"**

There is thus an interdependence between strategy and structure, and this warrants our considering the issue of organizational structures in marketing. For example, organizing marketing around products or markets – rather than around functional tasks – can give an important source of competitive advantage (see Levitt, 1980). Moreover, many writers have argued that organizational structure is a key determinant of marketing effectiveness, marketing failures and the successful implementation of the marketing concept (see, for example, Cascino, 1967; Tookey, 1974; Hakansson et al., 1979).

Organizational design

Apart from serving as a means of linking the organization to its environment, thereby ensuring that the outputs and activities are compatible with the external milieu in which the organization is operating, planning also serves as a means of integrating the goal-striving activities of the organization into a coordinated whole. This latter role is facilitated by effective organizational design, as Nathanson et al. (1982, p. 93) point out:

"Organization design is conceived to be a decision process to bring about a coherence between the goals or purposes for which the organization exists, the pattern of division of labor and interunit coordination and the people who will do the work.**"**

Organization design has similarly been defined by Pfeffer (1978) as:

" . . . the process of grouping activities, roles or positions in the organization to coordinate effectively the interdependencies that exist . . . the implicit goal of the structuring process is achieving a more rationalized and coordinated system of activity.**"**

In considering a framework for organizational design (OD) we can be guided by Child's 1977 classification of the major issues within the domain of OD:

➡ Allocating task responsibilities to individuals
➡ Designating formal relationships leading to hierarchical levels and spans of control
➡ Grouping individuals into departments, departments into divisions, etc.
➡ Designing systems for integration and communication
➡ Delegating authority and evaluation
➡ Providing systems for appraisal and reward.

Galbraith has developed a conceptual framework in which a number of organizational variables over which choices must be made by managers in creating an organization design are identified. These are task, structure, information and decision processes, reward systems and people. In choosing how to balance these elements, top management has considerable scope for varying and influencing all five. However, the organization design that emerges should be one that fits the product – market strategy of the enterprise. If a consciously developed strategy is to be effectively implemented, this needs to be done via a properly designed organization: the process of organization design is the link between strategy formulation and implementation.

Nathanson et al. (1982, p. 110) have proposed a series of 'fit' relationships that indicate the best 'fit' between particular strategies and structures. The main choices consist of:

1 A single business with a functional structure
2 A business having related products (which implies common technology and possibly common manufacturing facilities) with a multidivisional structure
3 A business having unrelated products (hence no technological commonalities) with a holding company structure.

An enterprise's chosen strategy is a key determinant of its relationship with the environment, which in turn places particular information-processing requirements on the management of the enterprise. Different strategies help in defining different environmental settings, thus giving rise to different information-processing requirements. (As an example, consider the different circumstances of an enterprise choosing a strategy taking it into a high-technology sector and another enterprise adopting a strategy that focuses on a traditional, labour-intensive sector.) A good fit is found when the structure – which includes information processing among its elements – matches the strategy and produces the desired outcomes.

Figure 16.15 illustrates the best combinations of strategy and structure ('product relatedness' refers to common technology and 'market relatedness' to common customers).

Piercy (1985) has put forward a very powerful case for viewing the marketing organization as an information-processing structure. His basic model is shown in

Strategic situation Product–market strategy	Operating organization Structure	Planning process
1 High product relatedness with high market relatedness	Functional structure: necessary because of product market and geographic relatedness. No need to divisionalize.	Business-level planning focus on: competition, competitive advantage, distinctive competences, product–market segmentation, stage of product–market evolution. Synergy-integration of different functional areas. Market share, production efficiencies, technological innovation.
2 High product relatedness with low market relatedness	Functional structure: necessary because of product relatedness.	SBUs to deal with the market or geographic diversity, to focus attention on each market and allocate the functional resources to markets in most efficient manner, and to keep abreast of each market's opportunities and threats.
3 Low product relatedness with high market relatedness	Divisionalized structure: necessary because of different technologies and manufacturing processes inherent in the product.	SBUs to provide strategic approach to the market and eliminate counterproductive competition within the marketplace.
4 Low product relatedness with low market relatedness	Multidivisional or holding company structure: the high degree of diversity calls for much decentralization.	SBUs, because of the large size of most of the firms in this category, the focus is primarily on goal formulation and setting on a financial basis, to place emphasis on the 'stars' that are small and might otherwise be overlooked, to serve as a span of control reducer, and to overlap any interdependencies (relatedness) that might exist.

Figure 16.15 Fit relationships (source: Nathanson et al., 1982)

Figure 16.16. In developing this model, Piercy reviewed major approaches to organization theory. His most significant point of departure from the traditional approach lies in his examination of information-processing models of structure and the implications of such models for organizational power and political behaviour.

Such an approach focuses on the processes required to cope with task and environmental uncertainty (Piercy, 1985, p. 38):

" . . . in the sense both that uncertainty imposes an information-processing burden that a given structure may or may not be able to cope with, and that coping with these uncertainties critical to the organization provides a source of power and political strength to certain subunits or individuals."

The link between marketing structures and the environment, and hence to marketing decision-making, is provided by the idea of information processing. The question follows as to which organizational structure is best suited to processing the information

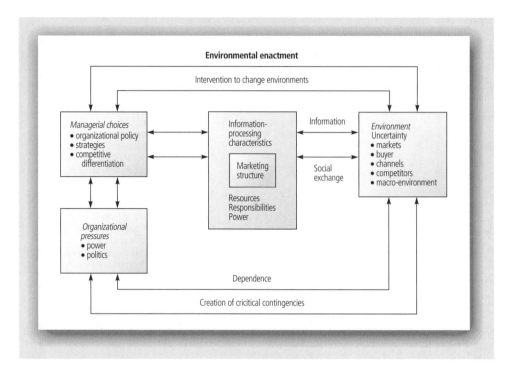

Figure 16.16 The organizational dimensions of marketing (source: Piercy, 1985, p. 17)

required by marketing tasks, but this question has been largely ignored by marketing experts.

One approach to dealing with some aspects of the question is provided by Weitz and Anderson (1981). They suggest that the environment may be analysed in terms of:

➡ *Complexity* – which refers to the number of elements relevant to the organization (such as the number of product markets served)
➡ *Interconnectedness* – which is concerned with the interdependence of key elements within the environment
➡ *Predictability* – which relates to the degree to which the environment is stable or unstable, hence to the degree of uncertainty.

See Figure 16.17, which relates these aspects of the environment to marketing organizations.

The tendency towards increasingly unpredictable and discontinuous change implies that organizational forms need to be considered as being short term and subject to adjustment in response to frequent changes in the contingencies that underpin them. Doyle (1979) points to such factors as an increased focus on integration, a change from volume to productivity orientation and a move towards portfolio management as indicating that a traditional functional structure is becoming less and less appropriate. A more complex and ambiguous set of alternatives is to be found in divisional and matrix forms of organization, but these too may be transitory.

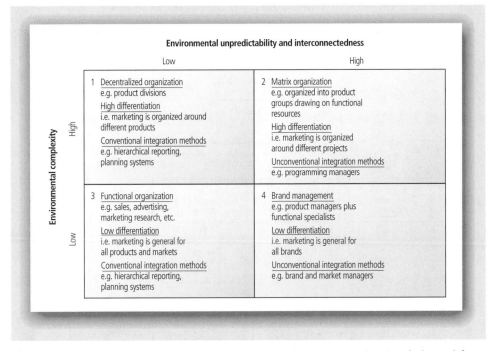

Figure 16.17 Environmental dimensions and marketing organization (adapted from Weitz and Anderson, 1981)

An extreme view has been put forward by Haller (1980a, b) and Wills (1980a, b) to suggest that marketing – as a unified function – will disappear either as a result of its being subsumed within strategic management (see Figure 16.18), or as a result of marketing planning being taken under the wing of a corporate planning department and a sales director on the one hand and a distribution director on the other emerging to take over the operational activities, with no marketing director.

Such views contrast sharply with the traditional approach to marketing structures, where the primary concern has been with differentiation within the marketing department. The basis of this differentiation may be products, functions, markets, geographical regions or customer groups, each of which allows some degree of specialization via the division of labour (see Figure 16.19).

It has been argued that the functional structure is likely to be abandoned in favour of a product-based structure as the number of products in the range increases (Hughes, 1980), or in favour of a market-based structure as the number of markets served increases (Ames, 1971). A further variation is to adopt a hybrid approach, in which product and market structures are combined in a form of matrix organization.

Centralization versus decentralization

We need to recognize that in the context of large, complex organizations it is not simply the creation of a single marketing department (along with its status and integrative

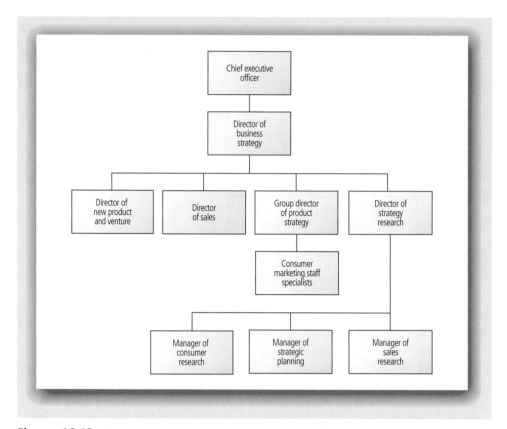

Figure 16.18 A strategic management organizational structure (adapted by Piercy (1985) from Haller (1980a, b))

characteristics) that is of concern, but rather the allocation of marketing responsibilities and activities among different levels in the organizational structure.

In the study that was cited in the introduction to Stage Four, Lynch et al. (1988) found that the better performing British companies exhibited the following organizational characteristics:

➡ More likely to have a marketing department
➡ More likely to have marketing represented directly at board level
➡ More likely to adopt a market-based organizational structure
➡ Work more closely with other functional areas.

The study of large organizations has consistently emphasized the process of divisionalization beyond the point at which a traditional organizational structure (i.e. of a functional form) becomes incapable of effectively coping with such issues as geographic expansion, volume growth, vertical integration and product diversification (e.g. Chandler, 1962).

Buell (1966) suggested a fourfold categorization of divisionalized marketing organization:

Form	Advantages	Disadvantages	Situational indicators
Functional	Specialization in task activities to develop skills. Marketing tasks and responsibilities clearly defined.	Excess levels of hierarchy may reduce unity of control. Direct lines of communication may be ignored. Conflicts may emerge. Integration problem for CME*.	Simple marketing operations. Single primary product/ market.
Product/brand	Specialization in products/brands. More management attention to marketing require- ments of different products/brands. Fast reaction to product-related change.	Dual reporting. Too much product emphasis. More management levels and cost. Conflict.	Wide product lines sold to homogeneous groups of customers, but sharing pro- duction/marketing systems, i.e. proliferation of brands and diversified products requiring different skills/ activities.
Market/customer/ geographical	Specialization in a market entity – focus on customer needs. Fast reaction to market-related changes.	Duplication of functions. Coordination problems. More management levels.	Limited, standardized homogeneous product line sold to customers in differ- ent industries, i.e. prolifer- ation of markets each meriting separate efforts.
Product/market overlay	Advantages of func- tional product and market specialization and integration.	Allocation of respon- sibilities is difficult. Duplication inefficiencies.	Multiple products and multiple markets.

* Chief Marketing Executive

Figure 16.19   Comparison of marketing structures (source: Piercy, 1985)

1 *Divisionalized companies with self-sufficient divisions.* At the corporate level of market- ing (if it exists) policy guidelines and advice are provided, and the marketing per- formance of divisions is evaluated, but no marketing services are provided.

2 *Divisionalized companies with corporate marketing services.* Divisions are responsible for production and selling, but central marketing services deal with advertising, market- ing research, etc.

3 *Geographically divisionalized companies.* Divisions provide some marketing activities for their areas, but central marketing services are also provided, along with national/international coordination.

4 *Centralized manufacturing/decentralized marketing.* All manufacturing is centralized and marketing is undertaken through divisions.

There are benefits from both centralization and decentralization. For example, Heskett (1976) has identified the following.

Centralized control

➡ Facilitates the coordination of marketing
➡ Makes up for low management expertise in some areas
➡ Can lead to better control.
➡ Ensures the transfer of ideas among marketing groups
➡ Avoids duplication of effort.

Decentralization

➡ Encourages more effective local performance
➡ Improves management development opportunities
➡ Favours the development of marketing programmes that are more sensitive to local needs.

Deciding whether centralization is to be preferred to decentralization will depend on the specific circumstances of a given enterprise. For example, an enterprise having a complex and dynamic environment on the one hand and a variety of product groups on the other might be better suited to a decentralized structure. As Nonaka and Nicosia (1979) put it:

❝A simple centralized organization of a marketing department is sufficient to process environmental information that is homogeneous and certain. But a complex, decentralized organization for a marketing department is required to process environmental information that is heterogeneous and uncertain . . . only organisms with high internal variety can cope with and survive high variety in the environment.❞

See Figure 16.20.

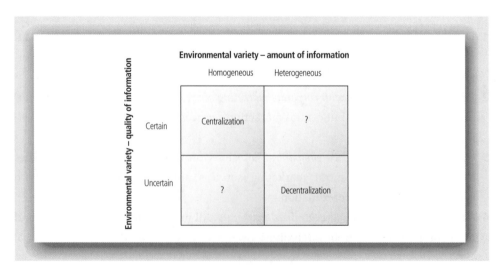

Figure 16.20 Environmental variety and marketing centralization (adapted from Nonaka and Nicosia, 1979)

Whether or not the marketing organization should be centralized is likely to be a function of uncertainty, which in turn reflects environmental turbulence. A centralized structure is able to cope with a relatively stable (hence predictable) environment, whereas a decentralized structure is more appropriate when the environment is unstable (hence more uncertain).

16.11 Summary

In this chapter we have reviewed an array of problems that need to be addressed if marketing plans are to be properly developed, adequately implemented and the outcomes effectively controlled. The origins of problems include:

➡ Pressures from a variety of sources (embracing consumer behaviour, economic conditions, technology, societal expectations, politics), all of which are associated with change and the imperative for enterprises to adapt to change if they are to be successful
➡ The marketing subsystem with its interdependencies
➡ The nature of marketing feedback
➡ The adequacy of information
➡ Cost issues and the analysis of marketing costs as a means of establishing the effectiveness – in financial terms – and efficiency of marketing activities
➡ The degree of marketing orientation that exists within the enterprise
➡ The resistance to planning that is still to be found.

Successful implementation and control will be facilitated by:

➡ A balance between short-run programme-related measures and longer-term performance criteria
➡ The attainment of synergy among the various elements of the marketing mix
➡ The use of appropriate criteria for assessing performance within segments
➡ The use of appropriate criteria for allocating resources to segments, coupled with flexibility in adaptive reallocations
➡ Executing product–market decisions in the broader context of business-level considerations relating to strategic marketing.

The need to balance strategy with a suitable structure was discussed in some detail. An emphasis was given to the principles of organizational design and the view (put forward most strongly by Piercy) of the marketing organization as an information-processing structure within an uncertain environment.

The control structure of an organization embraces the organization structure, responsibility centres, performance measures and the system of rewards. This structure needs to be properly designed if resources are to be allocated effectively in decentralized decision-making.

There is a clear need for the control structure to be coordinated with the organization's planning system if desired behaviour is to be achieved. In assessing the adequacy of results it would be too limiting to rely solely on traditional measures such as costs, profits and profitability (e.g. return on investment), since these are partial on the one hand and emphasize a relatively short-term orientation on the other. It is better to relate short-term measures to strategic performance measures, including changes in market share, changes in growth and changes in competitive position.

Chapter 17

Management control – 1

17.1 Learning objectives

When you have read this chapter you should be able to:

(a) understand the nature of control and the control process;

(b) appreciate some different approaches to control;

(c) appreciate the importance of the behavioural aspects of control;

(d) design basic control systems.

17.2 Introduction to control

Since control is a process whereby management ensures that the organization is achieving desired ends, it can be defined as a set of organized (adaptive) actions directed towards achieving specified goals in the face of constraints.

To bring about particular future events, it is necessary to influence the factors that lie behind those events. It is the ability to bring about a desired future outcome at will that is the essence of control. In this sense it can be seen that control itself is a *process* and not an event. Moreover, the idea of control can be seen to be synonymous with such notions as adaptation, influence, manipulation and regulation. But control is *not* synonymous with coercion in the sense in which the term is used in this book. Nor does it have as its central feature (as so often seems to be thought) the detailed study of past mistakes, but rather the focusing of attention on current and, more particularly, on future activities to ensure that they are carried through in a way that leads to desired ends.

The existence of a control process enables management to know from time to time where the organization stands in relation to a predetermined future position. This requires that progress can be observed, measured and redirected if there are discrepancies between the actual and the desired positions.

Control and planning are complementary, so each should logically presuppose the existence of the other. Planning presupposes objectives (ends), and objectives are of very limited value in the absence of a facilitating plan (means) for their attainment. In the planning process, management must determine the organization's future courses of action by reconciling corporate resources with specified corporate objectives in the face of actual, and anticipated, environmental conditions. This will usually involve a consideration of various alternative courses of action and the selection of the one that is seen to be the best in the light of the objectives.

In seeking to exercise control it is important to recognize that the process is inevitably value laden: the preferred future state that one is seeking to realize is unlikely to be the same for individual A as for individual B, and that which applies to individuals also, within limits, applies to organizations.

In seeking to exercise control the major hindrances are uncertainty (since the relevant time horizon for control is the future, which cannot be totally known in advance) and the inherent complexity of socio-economic and socio-technical systems (such as business organizations). If one had an adequate understanding of the ways in which complex organizations function, and if this facilitated reliable predictions, then the information stemming from this predictive understanding would enable one to control the organization's behaviour. In this sense it can be seen that information and control have an equivalence.

Behind the presumption, therefore, that we can control anything there is an implied assertion that we know enough about the situation in question (e.g. what is being sought, how well things are going, what is going wrong, how matters might be put right, etc.).

17.3 Control defined

There are as many different definitions of control, and of management control, as there are authors.

Maciariello (1984, p. 5), for example, offers the following definitions of management control (MC) and a management control system (MCS):

*"*Management control is the process of ensuring that the human, physical, and techno-logical resources are allocated so as to achieve the overall purposes of an organization. An MCS attempts to bring unity of purpose to the diverse efforts of a multitude of organizational subunits so as to steer the overall organization and its managers toward its objectives and goals. An MCS consists of a structure and a process.*"*

A control system's structure has relative permanence and focuses on what the system is (i.e. the designated responsibility centres, delegated authority, performance measures, etc.). Its process focuses on the way in which decisions are made to establish goals, allocate resources, evaluate performance, revise strategies, etc., in a purposive manner.

Itami (1977) emphasized the fact that management control is control within an organizational context, which implies that it is of a multi-person nature. This is also evident in Tannenbaum's (1964, p. 299) definition of control as being:

". . . any process in which a person (or a group of persons or organization of persons) determines or intentionally affects what another person or group or organization will do.*"*

However, the idea of interpersonal influence was broadened by Hofstede (1968, p. 11) to embrace impersonal control also:

*"*Control within an organizational system is the process by which one element (person, group, machine, institution or norm) intentionally affects the action of another element.*"*

The interpersonal nature of control within organizations needs to be recognized in order to relate to motivation, goal congruence and the reward system. In Figure 17.1 there is no explicit recognition of this requirement, whereas Figure 17.2 allows for it via 'nesting'. Within the nested model the superior exercises control by influencing the subordinate's

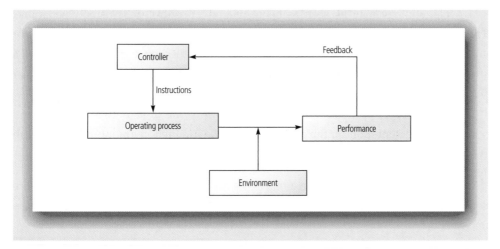

Figure 17.1 The control process

behaviour – largely through the assessment of the subordinate's performance against agreed plans.

The behavioural aspect is highlighted by Merchant (1985, p. 4; 1998), who also refers to the strategic aspects of control:

❞Control is seen as having one basic function: to help ensure the proper behavior of the people in the organization. These behaviors should be consistent with the organization's strategy . . .*❞*

The need for control arises because individuals within the organization are not always willing to act in the organization's best interests.

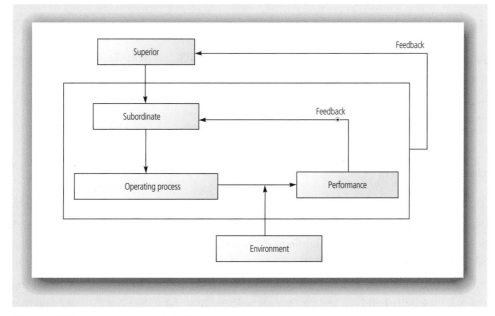

Figure 17.2 A nested model of control systems

Whilst strategy may be seen as being related to control, it is usually separable. Thus, it is possible for an enterprise having good strategies to fail because it has a poor control system, and vice versa. In general, however, the better the formulation of a strategy, the greater will be the number of feasible control alternatives and the easier their implementation is likely to be.

Anthony (1988, pp. 7 and 10) also refers both to the links between control and strategic implementation on the one hand, and the interaction among individuals on the other:

❝ *Control* is used in the sense of assuring implementation of strategies. The management control function includes making the plans that are necessary to assure that strategies are implemented. **❞**

❝ Management control is the process by which managers influence other members of the organization to implement the organization's strategies. **❞**

Merchant (1985, p. 1) has pointed out a number of problems that have inhibited a greater understanding of control:

1 The lack of a comprehensive and generally accepted control framework with supporting terminology
2 Control problems and solutions are discussed at different levels of analysis
3 The solutions that are proposed also differ in accordance with the orientation of their proposers
4 Some authors argue that control should deal with (historical) facts, whereas others argue that control should be future-oriented.

17.4 Basic control concepts

In this section, which draws on Wilson and Chua (1993), we will distinguish between *open-loop control* and *closed-loop control*.

We shall also distinguish between two main forms of closed-loop control: *feedforward control* and *feedback control*.

Open-loop control

This form of control exists when an attempt is made by a system (for example, an organization) to achieve some desired goal, but when no adjustments are made to its actions once the sequence of intended acts is under way. A very simple example is that of a golfer hitting a golf ball: his aim is to get the ball into the hole, and with this in mind he will take into account the distance, the hazards, and so forth, prior to hitting the ball. Once the ball is in the air there is nothing that the golfer can do but hope that he did things right.

Two possible refinements to the basic open-loop model are:

1 To introduce a monitoring device for the continual scanning of both the environment and the transformation process of the system (that is, the process by which the organization converts inputs into outputs). This will provide a basis for modifying either initial plans or the transformation process itself if it appears that circumstances are likely to change before the plan has run its course and the goal realized. This is *feedforward control* and is illustrated in Figure 17.3.

2 To monitor the outputs achieved against desired outputs from time to time, and take whatever corrective action is necessary if a deviation exists. This is *feedback control* and is illustrated in Figure 17.4.

Both feedback and feedforward control entail linking outputs with other elements within the system, and this explains why they are termed *closed-loop* control systems.

Closed-loop control

In an open-loop system errors cannot be corrected as it goes along, whereas likely errors can be anticipated and steps taken to avoid them in a feedforward control system, and actual errors along the way can be identified and subsequent behaviour modified to achieve desired ends in a feedback control system.

The inadequacy of open-loop systems as a basis for organizational control (and hence for the design of MCS) largely stems from our limited knowledge of how

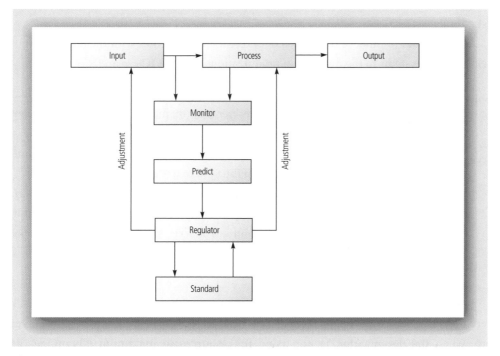

Figure 17.3 A feedforward control system

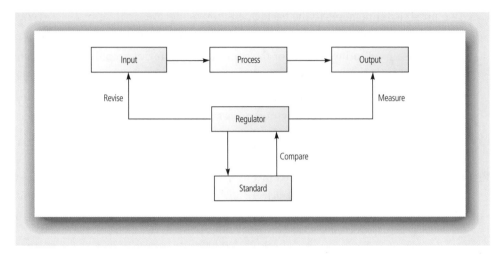

Figure 17.4 A feedback control system

organizational systems operate, which in turn reflects the complexity of organizations and their environments, plus the uncertainty that clouds the likely outcome of future events. If we possessed a full understanding of organizational processes and had a perfect ability to predict the future, then we would be able to rely on open-loop systems to achieve the ends we desire, since we would be able to plan with the secure knowledge that our plans would be attained due to our perfect awareness of what was going to happen, and how, and when (i.e. control action would be independent of the system's output).

In our current state of awareness we must rely on closed-loop systems, whether feedforward or feedback, in which control action is dependent upon the actual or anticipated state of the system.

It is helpful to think of four types of outcome in connection with the application of closed-loop systems to the problem of organizational control. These are:

S_0 = Initial *ex ante* performance (e.g. a budget based on a set of expectations that might include: inflation at 5 per cent per annum; market growth of 10 per cent per annum; no labour disputes).

S_1 = Revised *ex ante* performance (e.g. an updated budget that has taken into account the experience of operating the system to date).

S_2 = *Ex post* performance (e.g. a revised budget based on what should have been achieved in the circumstances that prevailed during the period in question, say: inflation at 7 per cent per annum; market growth of 12 per cent per annum, and a strike lasting three weeks).

A_0 = Observed performance (i.e. that which actually occurred).

An organization's forecasting ability is shown by $A_0 - S_0$ (under feedback control) and, more precisely, by $A_0 - S_1$ (under feedforward control). The extent to which the organization is not using its resources to maximum advantage (its opportunity cost of operating) is given by $A_0 - S_2$.

A feedforward control system will function in a way that keeps revising S_0 as events are proceeding, with a view to producing an eventual outcome in which $A_0 = S_1$. On the other hand, a feedback control system will, from time to time, compare $A_0 - S_0$, and S_0 will only be revised if a discrepancy has been experienced.

It is apparent that feedforward control tends to be:

➡ *Ex ante*
➡ Proactive
➡ Continuous

and seeks to predict the outcomes of proposed courses of action, while feedback control tends to be:

➡ *Ex post*
➡ Reactive
➡ Episodic.

Let us look at each a litle more closely.

Feedforward control

A feedforward system can be defined as:

*"*A measurement and prediction system which assesses the system and predicts the output of the system at some future date.*"*

(Bhaskar and Housden, 1985, p. 199)

This differs from a feedback system in that it seeks to anticipate, and thereby to avoid, deviations between actual and desired outcomes. According to Cushing (1982, p. 83), its components are:

1 An operating process (which converts inputs into outputs)
2 A characteristic of the process (which is the subject of control)
3 A measurement system (which assesses the state of the process and its inputs, and attempts to predict its outputs)
4 A set of standards or criteria (by which the predicted state of the process can be evaluated)
5 A regulator (which compares the predictions of process outputs to the standards, and which takes corrective action where there is likely to be a deviation).

For a feedforward control system to be effective it must be based on a reasonably predictable relationship between inputs and outputs (i.e. there must be an adequate degree of understanding of the way in which the organization functions).

Guidelines for developing feedforward control systems are as follows:

1 Thorough planning and analysis are required (reflecting as much understanding as possible about the links amongst inputs, process and outputs)

2 Careful discrimination must be applied in selecting those variables that are deemed to have a significant impact on output

3 The feedforward system must be kept dynamic to allow for the inclusion of new influences on outputs

4 A model of the system to be controlled should be developed and the most significant variables (along with their effects on process and outputs) defined within it

5 Data on significant variables must be regularly gathered and evaluated in order to assess their likely influence on future outcomes

6 Feedforward control requires action focused on the future (rather than on the correction of past errors).

Feedback control

Feedback control should ensure self-regulation in the face of changing circumstances once the control system has been designed and installed. The essence of feedback control is to be found in the idea of *homeostasis*, which defines the process whereby key variables are maintained in a state of equilibrium even when there are environmental disturbances.

As a hypothetical illustration let us consider a company planning to sell 100 000 cassette players during the next 12 months. By the end of the third month it finds that the pattern of demand has fallen to an estimated 80 000 units due to the launch by another company of a competing product. After a further three months the competitor puts up the price of its product while the original company holds its own price steady, and this suggests that the level of demand may increase to 150 000 units. Feedback signals would ensure that the company is made aware, e.g. by monthly reports, of the actual versus planned outcomes (in terms of sales levels). The launch of the competitive cassette player would be identified as the reason why sales levels were below expectations in the early months, and the competitor's price increase would be identified as the reason why sales levels subsequently increased. In response to deviations between actual and desired results (i.e. feedback), an explanation needs to be found and actions taken to correct matters. Amending production plans to manufacture fewer (or more) cassette players, allowing inventory levels to fall (or rise) to meet the new pattern of demand, modifying promotional plans to counter competitive activities and so forth, could all stem from a feedback control system.

If deviations (or *variances* to give them their usual accounting name) are minor it is probable that the process could absorb them without any modifications, and inventory control systems, for example, are normally designed to accommodate minor variations between expected and actual levels of demand, with buffer stocks being held for this purpose. But in the case of extreme variations – such as the pattern of demand shifting from 100 000 units to 80 000 and then to 150 000 – it will be necessary to amend the inputs in a very deliberate way once the causes of the variations have been established. Inevitably there are costs associated with variances, and these will tend to be proportional to the length of time it takes to identify and correct them.

Some principles for the proper functioning of a feedback control system can be suggested (e.g. Cushing, 1982, p. 80), and might include:

➡ The benefits from the system should be at least as great as the costs of developing, installing and operating it. This is the problem of 'the cost of control'. It is often difficult to specify precisely either the benefits (other than in broad terms – e.g. 'better customer service', 'increased efficiency') or the costs relating to different system designs, but it should be possible to make approximate assessments of both.
➡ Variances, once measured, should be reported quickly to facilitate prompt control action. This is analogous to the feedback – known as *knowledge of results* – in psychological learning theory: if one has been tested on what one has learnt, it is important to be told quickly whether one is right (to reinforce the learning) or wrong (to facilitate remedial learning).
➡ Feedback reports should be simple, easy to understand, and highlight the significant factors requiring managerial attention.
➡ Feedback control systems should be integrated with the organizational structure of which they are a part. The boundaries of each process subject to control should be within a given manager's span of control.

Feedforward versus feedback control

The most significant features of feedforward and feedback control are shown in Figure 17.5. Feedback systems are typically cheaper and easier to implement than are feedforward systems, and they are more effective in restoring a system that has gone out of control. Their main disadvantage, however, is that they can allow variations to persist for as long as it takes to detect and correct them. Feedforward control systems, as we have seen, depend critically for their effectiveness on the forecasting ability of

Characteristic	Feedforward	Feedback
Low cost		✓
Ease of implementation		✓
Effectiveness		✓
Minimal time delays	✓	
Self-regulation	✓	✓

Figure 17.5 Relative strengths

those who must predict future process outputs. Both feedforward and feedback systems lend themselves to self-regulation.

The most effective approach to control comes from using the two approaches as complements, since few (if any) processes could be expected to operate effectively and efficiently for any length of time if only one type of control was in use. (For example, in controlling inventory, feedback data can be used in connection with stock-outs, rates of usage, etc., while feedforward data needs to be generated in gauging the raw material requirements for predicted levels of demand and the ability of suppliers to deliver on time.)

Both types of control are fundamentally intertwined with the design of MCS. In a feedback control system the functions that the system will carry out are:

➡ Standard setting
➡ Performance measurement
➡ Reporting of results.

Within a feedforward control system the role of the MCS will encompass:

➡ Standard setting
➡ Monitoring process inputs
➡ Monitoring operations
➡ Predicting process outputs.

The degree of overlap is modest relative to the degree of complementarity.

17.5 Responsibility accounting

In analysing organizations with a view to securing control over them, there are five key variables to which one must pay attention. A change in any one of these will have consequences for one or more of the others. These variables are:

1 The task of the organization (i.e. the purpose to be served by the outputs from the organization)
2 The technology of the organization (i.e. the means whereby the inputs are converted into outputs)
3 The structure of the organization (i.e. the roles, rules, etc.)
4 The people of the organization (including their expectations, career development, etc.)
5 The environment of the organization (i.e. those factors beyond the organization's boundary).

In this section we will be concerned with aspects of variable 3 – the structure, as reflected through individuals' assigned responsibilities.

If an enterprise is organized in such a way that lines of authority are clearly defined, with the result that each manager knows exactly what his or her responsibilities are and precisely what is expected of him or her, then it is possible to plan and control costs, revenues, profits, etc., in order that the performance of each individual may be evaluated and, one hopes, improved. In addition, a meaningful basis can be given to the design of the reporting system if it is geared to areas of responsibility.

That is the essence of responsibility accounting, which is a system of accounting that is tailored to an organization so that costs, revenues, profits, etc., can be planned, accumulated, reported and controlled by levels of responsibility within that organization. Responsibility accounting requires that costs, revenues and profits – as appropriate – be classified by:

➡ Responsibility centre
➡ Their degree of controllability within their responsibility centre (on the premise that each responsible individual in an organization should only be held accountable for those costs, revenues and profits for which he or she is responsible and over which he or she has control)
➡ Their nature.

This approach to classification will facilitate:

➡ Self-appraisal by lower and middle management
➡ Subordinate appraisal by top management
➡ Activity appraisal (by which top management might evaluate the performance of the overall range of corporate activities).

See Figure 17.6.

However, it is essential to the success of any control system that individuals are only held responsible for results when the following conditions prevail:

1 That they know what they are expected to achieve
2 That they know what they are actually achieving
3 That it is within their power to influence what is happening (i.e. that they can bring points 1 and 2 together).

When all these conditions do not occur simultaneously it may be unjust and ineffective to hold an individual responsible, and it will be impossible to achieve the desired level of organizational performance.

From the above comments it will be apparent that targets or results should be compiled in a way that reflects one individual's 'uncontaminated' performance. Thus, Manager A's budget should contain a clear set of items that are deemed to be controllable at his or her level of authority and a further set of items that are either fixed by company policy or are otherwise beyond Manager A's influence. These latter items are

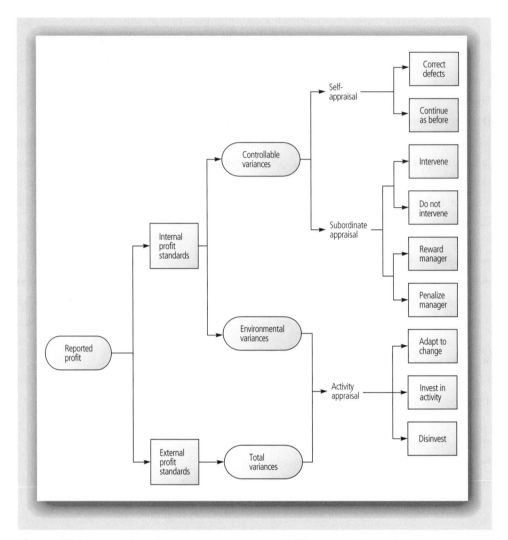

Figure 17.6 Appraisal of performance (source: Shillinglaw, 1964, p. 158)

uncontrollable from A's viewpoint, and his or her performance should not be assessed in relation to costs, etc., over which he or she has no control.

Costs (as well as revenues, profits, and so forth) can only be controlled if they are related to the organizational framework: in other words, costs should be controlled in accordance with the concept of responsibility – a cost should be controlled at whatever level it is originated and initially approved by the individual who did the initiating and approving. In this way it will be clear that certain costs are the responsibility of, and can only be controlled by, the chief executive of a company (such as corporate public relations expenditure), whereas others are controllable by responsible individuals at lower levels of the organizational hierarchy (e.g. a departmental manager will be responsible for the salary expense of those who work within his or her department). It is important to distinguish between costs that are controllable at a given level of managerial authority within a given period of time and those that are not. This distinction is not the same as the one between variable costs and fixed costs. For example, rates are a fixed cost that are uncontrollable, for a given time period, by any managerial level, whereas the annual road licence fee for a particular vehicle is a fixed cost that is controllable by the fleet manager, who has the power to dispense with the vehicle. In the same way the insurance premium payable on inventories is a variable cost (fluctuating with the value of the inventory from month to month) that is not controllable at the storekeeper level, but it is controllable at the level of the executive who determines inventory policy (subject, of course, to the environmental vagaries of such factors as consumer demand, which can never be removed).

Controllability is affected by both managerial authority and the element of time – a short-run fixed cost will be a long-run variable cost. (Thus, the managing director's salary is fixed for 12 months but variable thereafter.) All costs are controllable to some extent over the longer term, even if this involves a change in the scale of operations or a relocation of the company.

The problem of distinguishing between controllable and uncontrollable costs is more difficult in relation to indirect as opposed to direct costs. It is vitally important that costs be regulated at source, and this means that for many indirect items the beneficiary of cost incurrence is very often not the person to be charged with the cost. Obvious examples are central services – maintenance, the personnel department, post room/switchboard facilities – from which all members of the company derive benefits but for which cost responsibility is accorded to the respective supervisors and managers of these service functions.

To sum up so far, the approach to control that is based on the concept of responsibility accounting involves designing the control system to match the organizational structure in order that it reflects realistically the responsibilities of departmental managers, supervisors, etc. (This method of tackling control permits the collecting and reporting of data in such a way that the performance of organizational subunits can be evaluated.) In devising a control system for securing control that accords with the organizational structure, it will usually be found necessary to define more closely the duties of responsible individuals, and various responsibilities will have to be reassigned in order to give a logical structure to an organization that may have grown in a haphazard manner. All subsequent organizational changes that lead to changes in individual responsibilities should be accompanied by suitable modifications to the control system.

Organizational charts are useful if properly detailed. Apart from showing the chain of command (i.e. who reports to whom), such a chart should also include a schedule defining the duties of those individuals and any limitations to their authority. In this way responsibilities can be unambiguously assigned, and this knowledge clearly communicated to all concerned. Figure 17.7 represents a possible marketing organization structure, giving details of duties within each functional area.

The implications of fixing responsibility and of implementing control via responsibility centres are:

➡ The organizational structure must be clearly defined and responsibility delegated so that each person knows his or her role
➡ The extent and limits of functional control must be determined

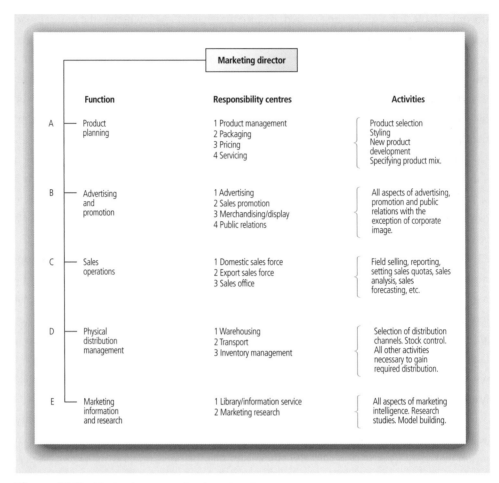

Figure 17.7 Marketing organization structure

➡ The responsible individuals should be fully involved in preparing plans if they are to be held responsible for results

➡ Responsible individuals must be serviced with regular performance reports

➡ Means must be established to enable plans to be revised in line with actual performance in such a way that responsible individuals are involved

➡ Every item should be the responsibility of some individual within the organization.

The ability to delegate is one sign of a good manager and responsibility accounting facilitates this. The act of passing responsibility down the line to the lowest levels of supervision gives these advantages:

1 It helps to create an atmosphere of cost consciousness throughout the organization

2 It tends to get control action quickly without delays resulting from the need for a senior executive to receive a monthly report before decisions can be made

3 It helps to give all levels of management a sense of team spirit with a common purpose.

A central notion in considering control is the evaluation of performance – whether *ex ante* (as in feedforward control) or *ex post* (as in feedback control). This can be undertaken at several levels: at the societal level, at the level of the enterprise as a whole, at the level of a division or other segment – such as activities, or at the levels of the group or individual. In essence, what is required is a comparison of desired outcomes with expected or actual outcomes, an assessment of any divergences, and proposals for future courses of action. Putting this another way, three questions need to be posed:

1 What has happened?
2 Why has it happened?
3 What is to be done about it?

The need to view performance evaluation within a control context is highlighted by our posing all three questions, rather than just the first two.

The concept of performance measurement is a simple one to comprehend but it can only be put into practice if plans are carefully prepared before decisions are made. In the absence of a plan (expressed in terms of standards and budgeted levels of performance), there is no benchmark for evaluating the performance of segments of an enterprise, individuals in responsible positions or the organization as a whole, and attempting to improve upon it. The existence of standards of performance eliminates many of the opportunities and excuses for poor performance, and provides a reference point for improvements.

Measuring the performance of the various types of responsibility centre (i.e. cost, profit and investment) will usually focus on financial aspects of an organization's activity. This will not always be appropriate, although it tends to be the general case that managers are held accountable in terms of quantifiable performance rather than performance that is qualitative (such as employee morale or public relations). It is necessary to know from time to time how actual performance compares with desired performance, and this chapter focuses on this issue.

This comparison answers the question about *what* is happening, and responsibility accounting ensures that managers know *who* is to be accountable. Establishing *why* divergences occur is problematic, as is the question of deciding *how* to apply corrective action in order that control may be effective.

Individuals learn through assessing their experience and organizations learn through their members. However, the extent to which individuals – and thus organizations – can learn is constrained by the rules of the organization (governing decision-making, delegation, membership and other restrictions). Dery (1982) has pursued this question by focusing on the links between erring (e.g. when variances arise) and learning. His argument is as follows:

1 The recognition of errors is a function of interpretation rather than simply an observation of events – it requires that desired and actual outcome be compared and interpreted before one can assert that an error exists

2 The interpretation of events is influenced by organizational rules, etc., which also serve to constrain the extent to which learning can take place

3 It is insufficient to assume that better learning at the organizational level can stem from the learning ability of individual members, since the latter is constrained by the rules of the former; hence an additional factor is required that will change the organization's rules.

The level of performance of a responsibility centre from a control viewpoint can be evaluated by obtaining answers to three pairs of questions:

Quantity
➡ How much was accomplished?
➡ How much should have been accomplished?

Quality
➡ How good was that which was accomplished?
➡ How good should it have been?

Cost
➡ How much did the accomplishment cost?
➡ How much should it have cost?

Performance measurement presupposes a standard of comparison. An obvious example comes from the comparison of actual results with budgeted results – the latter being the predetermined standard of performance. Standards can be compiled for almost every business activity, such as:

➡ Number of customer complaints
➡ Production costs
➡ Unit costs of handling and transporting products
➡ Market share
➡ Employee turnover
➡ Downtime
➡ Unfilled orders
➡ Return on investment
➡ Percentage of late deliveries of orders
➡ A variety of cost/revenue/profit ratios.

Any standard can only be an effective aid to control if it is seen to be equitable: those who are being judged (i.e. the responsible individuals whose performance is being measured) must be consulted in the setting of standards, otherwise no attempt may be made to reach them if they are considered to be either too high or too low. This ruins any attempt to control.

Luck and Ferrell (1979) have portrayed the links among marketing strategy, plans and standards as shown in Figure 17.8.

Control reports should be suited to the various areas of individual responsibility and as one moves further up the managerial hierarchy more items will be contained, albeit in summary form, in reports prepared for each level, since more items are controllable as the scope of managerial responsibility increases. Top management will therefore receive a summary of all items of income and expenditure.

Such summary reports can do little to rectify past mistakes, but by indicating exceptions to plans they can ensure that causes are investigated and appropriate corrective actions are taken to help in preventing future mistakes. The appropriate orientation should clearly be to the future rather than to the past.

A *responsibility centre* is made up of the various cost, revenue and investment items as appropriate for which a given individual is responsible. It is consequently a personalized concept that may be made up of one or more of the following:

➡ A cost centre
➡ A profit centre
➡ An investment centre.

Let us look at each of these in turn.

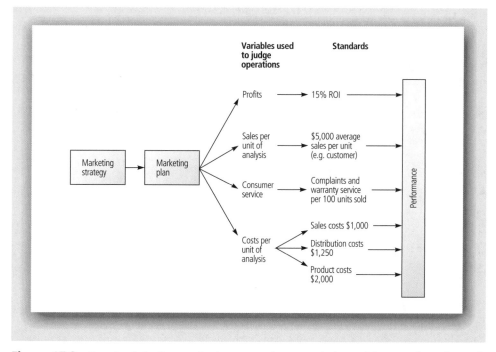

Figure 17.8 Standards in the marketing control process (adapted from Luck and Ferrell, 1979, p. 421)

A cost (or expense) centre

This is the smallest segment of activity, or area of responsibility, for which costs are accumulated. In some cases the cost centre may correspond with a department, but in others a department may contain several cost centres.

A cost centre may be created for cost control purposes whenever management feels that the usefuless of accumulating costs for the activity in question justifies the necessary effort.

Only input costs are measured for this organizational unit: even though there is some output this is not measured in revenue terms. Thus, a distribution team may deliver X units at a given total (or unit) cost, with the output being expressed either as a quantity or in terms of input costs.

A profit centre

This is a segment, department or division of an enterprise that is responsible for both revenue and expenditure. This is the major organizational device employed to facilitate decentralization (the essence of which is the freedom to make decisions). See Illustration 17.1.

Illustration 17.1 BR to split national network into local areas

British Rail is to embark on one of the most far-reaching changes in the organization of the rail network since nationalization in 1948, John Welsby, British Rail's chief executive, said yesterday.

From the end of April, the five regions, inherited from the days of private ownership, London Midland, Eastern, Western, Southern and Scottish, will be progressively abolished and replaced by about twenty smaller units, or profit centres.

The Railways Board will retain responsibility for strategic matters, such as investment programmes, financial targets and railway safety, but most aspects of the day-to-day running of the railway will be devolved to the profit centres.

British Rail's three passenger sectors, InterCity, Network SouthEast and Regional Railways, will be subdivided into several profit centres, run by a director, who will effectively own all the rolling stock, track and signalling equipment needed.

Malcolm Rifkind, the Transport Secretary, has pledged to introduce a bill to privatize British Rail after the next general election. Transport officials are still examining the options, which include privatization of BR as a single unit, the creation of a track authority and its break-up into regional companies.

Under the reorganization, Network SouthEast, which provides rail services in London and the South-East region, will be divided into nine semi-autonomous divisions. Some of these

divisions will be substantial businesses. South West, for example, which embraces all services from Waterloo, has an income of £252 million a year, employs about 8000 staff and covers 500 route-miles. Others, such as the London, Tilbury and Southend division, with an income of £65 million, employing about 1500 and covering 70 route-miles, will be considerably smaller.

InterCity will be divided into five route divisions. Regional Railways, which provides commuter, passenger and cross-country services, will also be split into five subdivisions.

In an effort to make each profit centre more cost conscious, charges will be levied on trains from one profit centre using the tracks of another. Directors will know exactly what they are responsible for and accountability for shortcomings will be instant. 'There will be no more alibis', Mr Welsby said.

The division of the national rail network into what is effectively twenty semi-autonomous railways is the final phase of the radical reorganization of the rail network introduced in the early 1980s by Sir Robert Reid, the former British Rail chairman.

By reorganizing British Rail's passenger sectors around the markets rather than the regions they serve, Mr Welsby is determined to bring about a substantial improvement in the quality of services. 'I'm not changing the organization for the fun of it', he said. 'The changes are vital to improve the quality of service to passengers.'

The move is being watched closely by continental rail organizations, particularly those in France and Germany, which are already following the example set by British Rail with the introduction of the five sectors in the 1980s.

The reorganization is expected to take about a year to complete, and is likely to cost in the region of £50 million. Mr Welsby said that British Rail was not trying to facilitate or impede government plans to privatize the railways.

Source: *The Times*, 11 April 1991, p. 24.

Among the arguments favouring decentralized profit responsibility are:

➡ Divisional managers are only in a position to make satisfactory trade-offs between revenues and costs when they have responsibility for the profit outcome of their decisions (failing which it is necessary for many day-to-day decisions to be centrally regulated)
➡ Managers' performances can be evaluated more precisely if they have complete operating responsibility
➡ Managers' motivation will be higher if they have greater autonomy
➡ The contribution of each division to corporate profit can be seen via divisional profit reports.

The advantages of profit centres are that they resemble miniature businesses and are a good training ground for potential general managers.

When it comes to defining profit measures, several alternatives are available. An example built up from the data in Figure 17.9 will help to illustrate some of them.

Sales revenue generated by Division A	£100,000
Direct costs of Division A:	
Variable operating costs	£45,000
Fixed operating costs under control of manager of Division A	£25,000
Fixed costs not under the control of manager of Division A	£10,000
Indirect costs of Division A:	
Apportioned central costs	£15,000

Figure 17.9 Division A's operating data for July

This data can be analysed in ways such as those suggested in Figure 17.10. One can identify strengths and weaknesses relating to each alternative measure of profit. The *contribution margin* is useful for short-run decision-making since it is not clouded by the inclusion of costs that do not respond to short-run volume changes. From a performance evaluation point of view, however, it is unsatisfactory in that it excludes all non-variable costs.

Controllable profit is a much better measure of the divisional manager's performance because it includes all the costs – whether fixed or variable – that are within his or her control. When non-controllable fixed costs are taken into account we have the *direct profit* of the division. This is more a measure of the division's performance than it is of the divisional manager's performance, so one needs to consider what it is that one is seeking to assess before one chooses a measure.

	Division A contribution margin £	Division A controllable profit £	Division A direct profit £	Division A net profit £
Sales revenue	100,000	100,000	100,000	100,000
Direct costs:				
Variable	45,000	45,000	45,000	45,000
Contribution margin	£55,000			
Fixed controllable		25,000	25,000	25,000
Controllable profit		£30,000		
Fixed non-controllable			10,000	10,000
Direct profit			£20,000	
Indirect costs				15,000
Net profit				£5,000

Figure 17.10 Analysis of Division A's operating data

Finally, *net profit* (as pointed out in Chapter 3) helps us in assessing a division's performance in full cost terms, but this is not a relevant means of gauging the divisional manager's performance on account of the categories of cost that he or she is unable to influence either directly or indirectly. It could be argued that divisional managers benefit from seeing the full cost of their division's operations, but if the controllable elements are dwarfed by the uncontrollable (at the divisional level) it may not be highly motivational!

From the above we can reasonably conclude that controllable profit is the best of the specified measures for assessing a divisional manager's performance – at least in principle. In practice it may be found that the manager of a division acts in ways that improve his or her short-run profit position at the expense of both the division's long-run profit potential and the best interests of the organization as a whole. Examples might include:

➡ Eliminating training and management development activities
➡ Cutting back on advertising, routine maintenance or R&D.

Countering these ways of 'playing the system' must be devised by top management in the form of policy guidelines, etc. But any measure of profit is inevitably sub-optimal as an index of divisional performance for at least one of the following reasons:

1 It typically includes items (such as interest and taxation) that are not under the control of divisional managers
2 It only tells part of the story – something needs to be said about the investment that is needed to generate profit (the next subsection picks up this point).

An investment centre

This is a segment, department or division of an enterprise under an accountable manager who is not only responsible for profit (i.e. for revenue and expenditure), but also has his or her success measured by the relationship of profit to the capital invested within the division (i.e. profitability). This is most commonly measured by means of the rate of return on investment (ROI).

The logic behind this concept is that assets are used to generate profits, and the decentralizing of profit responsibility usually requires the decentralization of control over many of an enterprise's assets. The ultimate test, therefore, is the relationship of profit to invested capital within a division. Much of its appeal lies in the apparent ease with which one can compare a division's ROI with earnings opportunities elsewhere – inside or outside the company. However, ROI is an imperfect measure and needs to be used with some scepticism and in conjunction with other performance measurements.

The value of the controllable/uncontrollable cost split is primarily found in fixing responsibility and measuring efficiency. Time is an important ingredient in this context, since all costs are controllable at some organizational level if a sufficiently long time span is taken. Controllable costs are those that can be directly regulated by a given individual within a given time period.

The division of costs into controllable and uncontrollable categories is important in order that performance levels may be evaluated and also for securing the cooperation of managers at all levels. Managers who are involved in planning their performance level in the knowledge that those controllable costs for which they are responsible will be monitored, accumulated and reported are likely to be motivated towards attaining their predetermined level of performance. In this way it can be seen that the collecting of controllable costs by responsibility centres serves as a motivating force as well as an appraisal mechanism.

While the ideal procedure is for each responsibility centre to be assigned those costs over which its manager has sole control and for which he or she is therefore responsible, in practical terms this cannot usually be achieved. It is rare for an individual to have complete control over *all* the factors that influence a given cost element.

Apart from those costs over which responsible individuals actually have control, their responsibility centre may be charged with costs that are beyond their direct control and influence, but about which management wishes them to be concerned. A good example is the cost of companies' personnel departments: operating managers may be charged with a proportion of the personnel department's costs on the grounds that either:

➡ They will be careful about making unnecessary requests for the services of the personnel department if they are made to feel somewhat responsible for its level of costs, or
➡ They may try to influence personnel managers to exercise firm control over their department's costs.

Allocating general overheads to responsibility centres is done by many companies that practise responsibility accounting (and that therefore recognize that such costs are beyond the control of those to whom they are allocated) on the grounds that each responsible individual will be able to see the magnitude of the indirect costs incurred to support this unit. There is a major disadvantage that should be seriously considered: managers of small responsibility centres incurring directly controllable costs at their level in a given time period of, say, £10 000 may be allocated £45 000 of general overhead costs. In relation to the overall level of overhead costs, managers may feel that those costs for which they are responsible are so insignificant that they may give up trying to control them. The point to note is that each cost must be made the responsibility of whoever can best influence its behaviour, and allocating costs beyond this achieves at best very little from a control viewpoint and may be distinctly harmful to the cost control effort. (Since a specific example of uncontrollable costs has not been given so far, the general overheads of £45 000 referred to above can be used as a suitable example. For control purposes the costs that are being considered are the costs that can be directly influenced at a given level for a specified time span.)

While heads of responsibility centres may not have sole responsibility for a particular cost item, this item may reasonably be considered to be controllable at their level if they have a significant influence on the amount of cost incurred, and in this case their responsibility centre can properly be charged with the cost. This is one aspect of the wider problem that arises because few (if any) cost items are the sole responsibility of just one person. Guidelines that have been established for deciding which costs can appropriately be charged to a responsibility centre are, in summary:

➡ If individuals have authority over both the acquisition and the use of a cost incurring activity, then their responsibility centre should bear the cost of that activity

➡ If individuals do not have sole responsibility for a given cost item but are able to influence to a significant extent the amount of cost incurred through their own actions, then they may reasonably be charged with the cost

➡ Even if individuals cannot significantly influence the amount of cost through their own direct action, they may be charged with a portion of those elements of cost with which management wishes them to be concerned in order that they may help influence those who are more directly responsible.

That which applies to costs also, in essence, applies to revenues and assets.

17.6 Approaches to control

Anthony's approach to control

The views of Robert Anthony of Harvard on management control have been very influential. They are stated in Anthony (1965, 1988).

When Anthony published his 1965 framework, the management control function was not generally recognized as a discrete activity. This has changed.

Management control is one of three types of planning and control activities that occur within organizations; the other categories are strategic planning (SP) and task control (TC). Anthony's definition of management control, given earlier (p. 728), presumes that goals and strategies exist, but that these do not arise automatically, hence:

❝ Strategic planning is the process of deciding on the goals of the organization and the strategies for attaining these goals. **❞**

(1988, p. 10)

Authors often distinguish between *planning* (i.e. deciding what to do) and *control* (i.e. ensuring that desired results are obtained). Anthony argues that both planning and control are undertaken at different organizational levels, hence it is more helpful to look at the mix (as shown in Figure 17.11):

❝ Strategies are the courses of action that an organization has adopted as a means of attaining its goals. They include the assignment of overall responsibility for implementation . . .

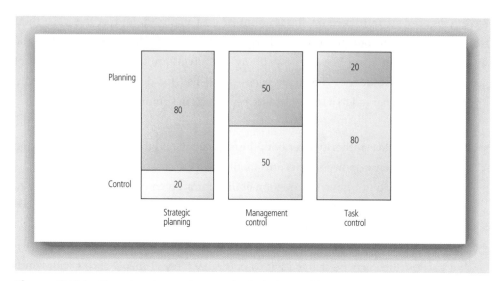

Figure 17.11 The planning and control mix (adapted from Anthony, 1988)

Strategies are big plans, important plans. They state in a general way the *direction* in which the organization is supposed to be headed. They do not have a time dimension: that is, they exist until they are changed."

(1988, p. 31)

"The purpose of the MC process is to carry out the strategies arrived at in the SP process and thereby to attain the organization's goals."

(1988, p. 34)

The 1988 approach links MC to the implementation of strategies in a direct way rather than to the attainment of objectives, which is an indirect purpose of MC.

The key difference between MC and strategic planning is that the latter is unsystematic: the need for strategic decisions can arise at any time – whether in response to a threat or an opportunity. Another difference is that SP is undertaken by top management and it involves a great deal of judgement. In contrast, MC is systematic, done at all levels, and involves considerable personal interaction but less judgement than SP. SP sets the boundaries within which MC takes place.

The third element in Anthony's approach is task control:

"Task control is the process of ensuring that specific tasks are carried out effectively and efficiently."

(1988, p. 12)

Anthony's framework is shown in Figure 17.12. While dealing with SP and TC, Anthony's 1988 book focuses primarily on MC, which can be described in terms of a process and the environment within which it takes place. The environment is partly external and partly internal, with the latter comprising:

→ The organization's structure
→ A set of rules, procedures, etc.
→ A culture.

The external environment contains influences that affect the level of uncertainty faced by the organization. At a highly uncertain extreme are:

→ Newly developed products
→ Differentiated products
→ Aggressive competition
→ Uncertain sources of inputs
→ Uncertain political circumstances.

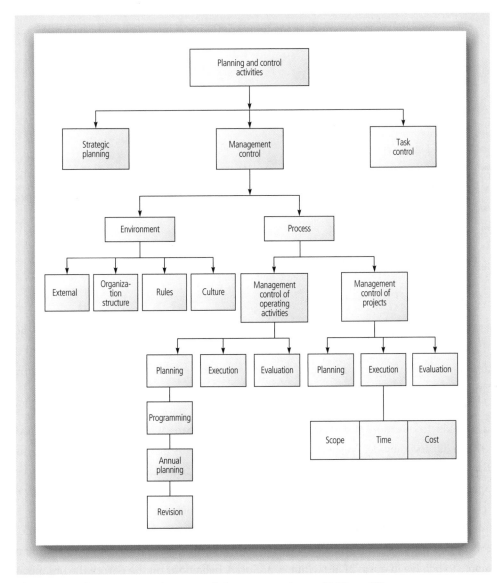

Figure 17.12   Anthony's framework (source: Anthony, 1988, p. 19)

At a less uncertain extreme are:

➡ Mature products
➡ Commodity products
➡ Price competition
➡ Secure sourcing of inputs
➡ Political stability.

Within a highly uncertain setting an organization is likely to pay great attention to programming; to make broad budget estimates; to revise budgets frequently; to set limits to discretionary costs; to permit a good deal of management latitude; to insist on a rapid flow of information; to evaluate performance subjectively in terms of results rather than process; and to have a high proportion of bonus within the reward package.

The opposite characteristics are likely to apply in a relatively certain environment.

Merchant's approach to control

An organization's control system is comprised of a variety of mechanisms, including:

➡ Personal supervision
➡ Job descriptions
➡ Rules
➡ Standard operating procedures
➡ Performance appraisal
➡ Budgets
➡ Standard costing
➡ Incentive compensation schemes.

However, it would be wrong to think of 'controls' – such as the above – as being the plural of 'control', and it would also be wrong to assume that more 'controls' would automatically give us more 'control', since this would assume that they meant the same thing, which they do not.

'Controls' has the same meaning as measurement, or information, whereas 'control' is more akin to direction. 'Controls' is concerned with means while 'control' is concerned with ends, and they deal respectively with facts (i.e. events of the past) and expectations (i.e. desires about the future). From this it will be appreciated that 'controls' tend to be analytical and operational (concerning what was and is) and 'control' tends to be normative (concerning what ought to be). A summary of key differences is shown in Figure 17.13.

The increasing ability to develop 'controls' has not necessarily increased our ability to 'control' organizations. If controls are to lead to control, they must encourage human actors to behave in a way that facilitates adaptive behaviour on the part of the organization as a whole.

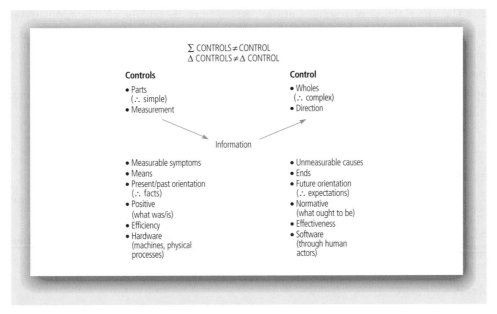

Figure 17.13 The different focus of control and controls (source: Wilson, 1983, p. 57)

The complexity and uncertainty of the control problem are apparent when, for example, controls reveal that 'profits are falling'. But this does not indicate how one might (or should) respond – indeed, it would not be possible even to identify the whole array of potential responses. What is needed, therefore, if control is to be effective is a basis for forming expectations about the future as well as understanding about the past that will enable us to combine these, in order that we might behave in an adaptive way by either anticipating external changes and preparing to meet them, or by creating changes.

From this arises the basic question: how do we control? In large part this is resolved by the answer to another question: what do we measure in order to control? Care must be taken in measuring the key elements in any situation rather than those elements that lend themselves to easy measurement. ('Controls' are only helpful in 'control' if they are designed in the context of the overall control problem.)

Merchant (1985, 1998) offers some valuable advice on a range of controls, but with a control perspective. He classifies these controls under the headings given below.

Results controls

Reward systems – in which an individual's pay, promotion prospects, etc., depend on his or her performance – are a good example of results control. It is not unusual for desired results to be expressed in quantitative terms – whether financial (e.g. ROI, EPS) or not (e.g. growth rate, market share) – which gives a benchmark for exercising results control. At senior management levels this form of control predominates, since it is compatible with decentralized organizational structures. At middle-management levels, where financial goals may be less dominant, results control can be exercised through MbO (management by objectives) systems.

The effectiveness of results controls derives from the ability of this approach to address some key control problems. In particular, motivational problems are eased since individuals are influenced to produce the results that will enhance both the organization's performance and their own rewards. By focusing on future expectations the results approach to control can be useful in informing managers as to what is expected of them. This emphasizes a feedforward orientation.

Three conditions need to be fulfilled before results control can be employed:

1 It is known what results are desirable
2 The desired results can be controlled to some extent by those whose actions are being influenced
3 The controllable results can be measured.

Action controls

Action controls are used:

" . . . to ensure that individuals perform (or do not perform) certain actions that are known to be beneficial (or harmful) to the organization.*"*

(Merchant, 1985, p. 29)

Categories of action controls are:

➡ Behavioural constraints (whether physical or administrative)
➡ Pre-action reviews
➡ Action accountability
➡ Redundancy (in which more resources are allocated to a task than is strictly necessary, which increases the likelihood of its accomplishment).

Two conditions need to be fulfilled if action controls are to be effective:

1 Knowledge must exist as to which actions are desirable (or undesirable)
2 The ability must be present to ensure that the desirable actions occur (or that the undesirable ones do not).

Personnel controls

There are two categories of personnel control that can be usefully harnessed as part of the management control endeavour:

1 Individual self-control, which, as a naturally present force, motivates most people to want to do a good job
2 Social control, which is exerted by other members of a group on those individuals who deviate from group norms and values.

If these two categories are insufficient, they can be augmented by:

➡ Selection and placement
➡ Training
➡ Cultural control.

There are several advantages that personnel controls have over results controls and action controls:

➡ Feasibility is not a serious constraint
➡ There are fewer harmful side-effects
➡ Their cost is typically lower.

Financial controls

Financial controls are a form of results control that constitute the single most important type of control used in organizations of any size. The reasons favouring financial controls are fairly obvious:

➡ Financial objectives are very important in commercial life
➡ Financial performance indicators are easy to derive
➡ Since financial results can be achieved via various routes, the use of financial controls allows for some managerial discretion
➡ Using financial measures is relatively inexpensive, since accounting systems exist within all enterprises.

Inevitably there are negative effects that can outweigh the advantages of using financial controls. The most serious are:

➡ Behavioural displacement – especially when the control system encourages managers to be overly concerned with short-term profits rather than longer-term strategic ends, or when it causes excessive risk aversion
➡ Gamesmanship.

It has been argued that there is a tendency for financial measures to drive out non-financial measures (see, for example, Munro and Cooper, 1989) within MCS design, which, given the partiality of financial measures (i.e. they measure those things that can be measured in financial terms), is unfortunate.

The approach of Johnson and Scholes

Strategic marketing involves strategic change. Johnson and Scholes (1993) have argued that there are two ways in which an organization can cope with strategic change:

1 Make use of control and regulatory systems to ensure that the tasks of implementation are clear, that their execution is monitored, that individuals and groups have the capabilities to implement change, and that they are rewarded for so doing

2 Ensure that those charged with implementing change understand and work within the social, political and cultural systems that regulate organizational behaviour, and which can give rise to a resistance to strategic change.

Their approach to dealing with these issues is reflected in Figure 17.14. If we take the information and control systems first, it is widely recognized that quantitative measures are needed to see if desired results are being achieved. Such measures will typically include:

➡ Financial analysis
➡ Market analysis
➡ Sales and distribution analysis
➡ Physical resource analysis
➡ Human resource analysis.

A set of guidelines for ensuring the effective design and operation of control systems would deal with such aspects as:

➡ Distinguishing between various levels of control (as proposed by Anthony, 1965, 1988), since different levels will require different information
➡ Creating responsibility centres as a means of delegation and motivation, ensuring information is provided in a suitable form for each responsible manager
➡ Identifying the critical success factors and supplying information relating to these in a way that highlights their interrelationships

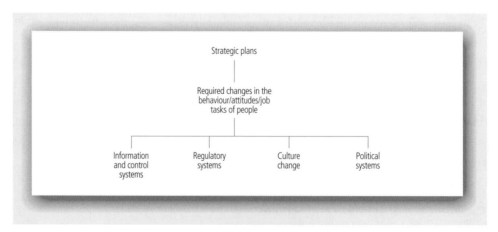

Figure 17.14 The influence of organization systems on strategy implementation (adapted from Johnson and Scholes, 1988, p. 292)

➡ Avoiding misleading measurements by accepting that quantitative indicators of performance are not available for every activity and it is not helpful to use a measurable index as a surrogate for an unmeasurable characteristic

➡ Being wary of negative monitoring in which only poor performance is reported, since this can lead to risk-averse behaviour or a tendency to 'pass the buck'.

The next means for ensuring the implementation of strategic change is via regulatory systems. These might range from training to the management style of an organization:

➡ Training and development to ensure staff are capable of implementing change, which involves both new skills and attitudes

➡ Incentive and reward systems to encourage compliance with required change, whether in the form of pay increases or non-monetary rewards (such as promotion)

➡ Organizational routines by which tasks are carried out may exhibit inertia, so deliberate steps need to be taken to redesign them in order to facilitate change

➡ Management style, which embodies the organization's culture, its circumstances and the characteristics of its managers, needs to be appropriate to the task of strategic implementation.

Moving on from regulatory systems brings us to culture change. At its most basic, this focuses on the need for change to be recognized within the organization in a way that ensures those responsible for bringing change about believe in what they are doing. This can be achieved in two stages, both of which are concerned with cognitive change:

1 The beliefs and assumptions underlying the way in which the organization's members make sense of their organizational world need breaking down

2 A reformulated set of beliefs needs to be put in their place to reorientate the culture from the past to the future. For cultural change to be meaningful, it must impact upon the day-to-day experiences of individuals within the organization.

Finally, there is the political system to consider. The overlaps among control systems, regulatory systems, culture and political systems is largely self-apparent, but it is important to emphasize that planning and control are inherently political rather than neutral. This will be illustrated later when we discuss the notion of entrapment.

The approach of Luck and Ferrell

Once the plan/strategy has been determined and steps taken (e.g. via a suitable organization) to put this into effect, the control process exists to ensure that the plan will be achieved (in so far as this is feasible).

Control can operate at different levels. For example, Figure 17.15 shows *tactical* control, which focuses on the implementation of plans on the right, and *strategic* control,

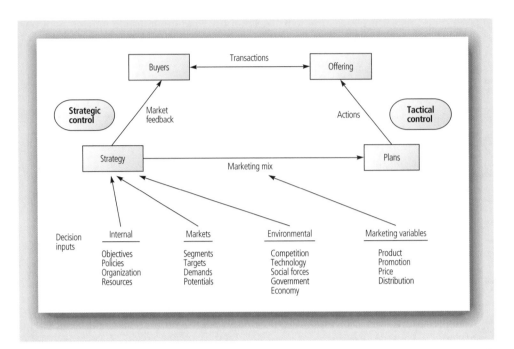

Figure 17.15 A basic control model for marketing (adapted from Luck and Ferrell, 1979, p. 15)

which focuses on the possible revision of strategy on the left. This is developed further in Figure 17.16.

Tactical control typically relates to adjustments in the execution of an established marketing plan – such as fine-tuning on pricing or advertising schedules.

Strategic control deals with the reformulation of the plans themselves. For example, actual buyer behaviour patterns may indicate that a plan has been based on false premises.

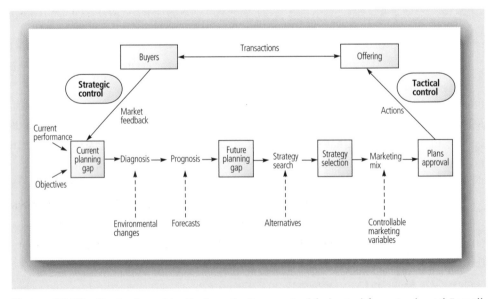

Figure 17.16 Strategic and tactical marketing control (adapted from Luck and Ferrell, 1979, p. 416)

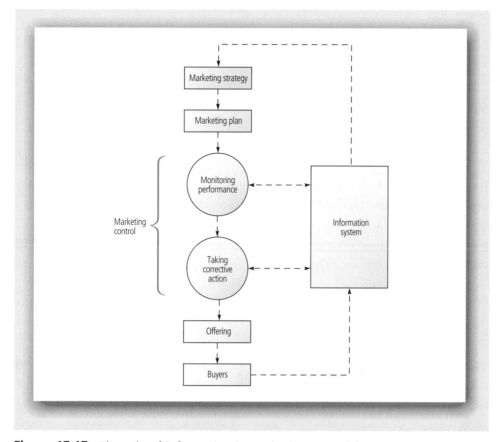

Figure 17.17 The role of information in marketing control (source: Luck and Ferrell, 1979, p. 418)

Strategic rethinking will thus be necessary in developing a new marketing plan (as shown in the lower half of Figure 17.16).

The role of the information system needed to facilitate tactical and strategic control is indicated in Figure 17.17.

17.7 Some behavioural factors

Management control (MC) is based on interactions between an organization's members, hence the control process must reflect how individuals behave, as well as their knowledge, skills and personality traits.

In participating in organizations, individuals are seeking to satisfy various needs, some of which are extrinsic (i.e. satisfied by the actions of others) while others are intrinsic (i.e. satisfied by the feelings individuals have about themselves and their achievements).

The extent to which a given individual might be motivated to engage in organizational activities has been argued to be a function of:

1 Beliefs regarding the outcomes that are likely to result from this individual's actions
2 How attractive these outcomes are in relation to satisfying the individual's needs.

In designing and operating control systems, therefore, it is necessary to consider:

→ The actions that individuals are motivated to take in their perceived self-interest
→ The best interests of the organization.

*"*MC is a blend of rational and behavioral considerations, and neglecting either type leads to erroneous generalizations.*"*

(Anthony, 1988, p. 22)

It can also lead to harmful side-effects. Some side-effects stemming from the design and implementation of control systems are inevitable and an inherent characteristic of certain types of control. On the other hand, some harmful side-effects are avoidable – such as those stemming from poor design, the implementation of the wrong type of control system for a given situation, or both.

The major side-effects of a negative nature are as follows.

1 Behavioural displacement

This arises when the behaviours encouraged by the control system are inconsistent with the strategy the organization seeks to pursue. In the case of results controls, displacement can occur when there is a poor understanding of desired results or an excessive reliance on easily quantified results. In the case of action controls there is the risk of displacement due to means – ends inversion when individuals are (wrongly) encouraged by the control system to pay more attention to what they are doing (the means) rather than to what they should be accomplishing (the ends). Displacement in the context of action controls can also arise when rules and standard operating procedures are followed in a rigid, non-adaptive manner.

There is also the risk of behavioural displacement when social controls (such as group norms) induce a degree of routinized conformity that stifles any form of creative adaptation.

2 Gamesmanship

This refers to the tendency among managers to 'play the system' by means of actions intended to improve their measures of performance without producing any positive economic effects. It is particularly prevalent when either results or action controls are in use. In both, it is possible for data to be manipulated, thus rendering the control system ineffective.

3 Negative attitudes

Such negative effects as job tension, frustration, conflict and resistance can arise even when control systems are well designed. This is most likely to be the case with poor performers, since their limitations become more apparent the better the control system. However, negative attitudes can also arise in the case of potentially good performers if the control system is poorly designed.

Potential consequences of negative attitudes include gamesmanship, sabotage or turnover, all of which can impede the achievement of strategic ends.

4 Short-termism

" . . . if long-term growth of profits is the aim then rewards based on short-term achievement of sales targets are not likely to be helpful."

(Johnson and Scholes, 1988, p. 298)

An organization's reward system is supposed to encourage goal congruence. However, control systems tend to focus on short-term results even though managers are expected to achieve both short- and long-run objectives. The reason for this is simple: the control system tends to report what has happened (e.g. over the past month) and is less capable of specifying what might happen in the long-term future.

"Our lack of knowledge about how best to measure a manager's performance is probably the most serious weakness in MCS."

(Anthony, 1988, p. 74)

For example, performance in a given period may not reflect the manager's real performance. Reasons for this may be that:

➡ Outcomes (hence performance) in that period will be influenced by the actions taken in earlier periods, as well as by actions of managers in other responsibility centres

➡ Current actions will have a lagged impact on future outcomes and it is virtually impossible to eliminate these effects from the measurement of current performance.

Dent (1990, p. 3) has commented on the way in which accounting practices have been drawn into the argument over short-termism:

"The extensive use of short-run financial calculations to appraise managerial performance is deemed to have diverted managerial attention away from fundamental value-creating activities, motivating instead opportunistic behaviours with less permanent benefits . . ."

5 Entrapment and escalation

Anthony's framework (see Figure 17.12) distinguishes between MC of operating activities and MC of projects. Our focus so far has been on the former, but there are some aspects of the latter that warrant our attention.

A project can be defined as a set of activities intended to accomplish a specified end result of sufficient importance to be of interest to management.

❝In a project, the focus of control is on the project itself, rather than on activities in a given time period in individual responsibility centres, as is the case with the management control of ongoing operations.**❞**

(Anthony, 1988, p. 16)

There are three aspects of particular interest within a project:

1 Its scope (i.e. the specifications for the end-product)
2 Its schedule (i.e. the time required)
3 Its cost.

Trade-offs among scope, schedule and cost are usually possible in projects. For example, costs might be reduced by decreasing the project's scope, or the schedule might be reduced by increasing the cost. This is not always easy to plan, since performance standards are likely to be less reliable for a one-off project than for ongoing activities. Moreover, projects tend to be influenced to a greater extent by the external environment than is the case with continuing operations.

The prospect of being assessed as part of the control endeavour – whether in relation to projects or ongoing activities – typically affects the behaviour of individuals, often with dysfunctional consequences. Control activities are far from neutral in their impact, as can be shown by means of a phenomenon of recent interest: entrapment. This occurs when a responsible individual increases his or her commitment to an ineffective course of action in order to justify the previous allocation of resources to that task. Entrapment is seen as being one example of a broader psychological process that focuses on commitment. The commitment of an individual to a particular course of action is likely to depend on, inter alia (see Brockner et al., 1986, p. 110):

➡ Responsibility for the action
➡ Responsibility for the consequences of the action
➡ The salience of the action
➡ The consequences of the action.

While entrapment is not easily explained in terms of economic rationality, there are various plausible explanations reflecting psychological rationality. For example (after Wilson and Zhang, 1997):

➡ There is a need for decision-makers to assert themselves and reaffirm the wisdom of their initial decision
➡ The initial commitment was made as a result of the decision-maker's belief in the goodness of the course of action, hence self-justification, justification to others, and the norms of consistency are served by continuing; continuing avoids the waste of the investment already made (which is known as the sunk-cost fallacy)

➡ Further investment gives further opportunities for the project to come good; negative feedback is treated as a learning experience (i.e. a cue to revise the inputs rather than cancel the project)

➡ Negative feedback, alternatively, may be seen as a chance variation

➡ A state of inertia has been created by which a project's financial past cannot be divorced from its future – prior investment then motivates the decision to continue

➡ Decisions are not made in a social vacuum, hence social costs and benefits must be considered relating to self-image, organizational image, reputation and face saving – continue so long as the social and psychological benefits are greater than the economic costs

➡ Information processing has behavioural underpinnings, such as selective perception, in which we see what we want to see

➡ An organization's reward system may work to encourage the decision-maker to overlook short-term setbacks and continue with the original project through bad times.

Prospect theory (Kahneman and Tversky, 1984) has been used to explain the phenomenon of entrapment (see Figure 17.18). A value function (i.e. the curve in Figure 17.18) shows the relationship between objectively defined gains and losses, and the subjective value placed on these by the decision-maker.

At the outset the decision-maker is at point A, but if the decision is unsuccessful he or she will be at point B, where further losses do not result in large decreases in value. On the other hand, any gains will result in large increases in value; thus, at point B, the decision-maker will risk further losses in the hope of making gains. Despite the sunk costs, risky behaviour is much more likely at point B than it was at point A.

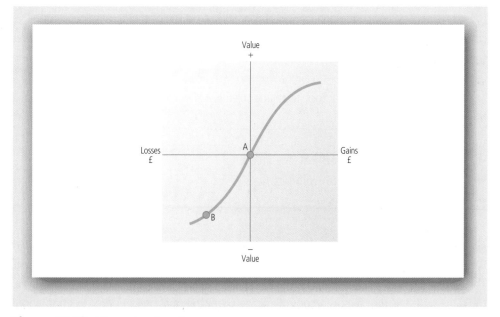

Figure 17.18   The value function

STRATEGIC MARKETING MANAGEMENT

A variation on the theme of entrapment is that of escalation (e.g. see Staw and Ross, 1987a, b). These two phenomena are often related but are analytically separable: entrapment may exist in the absence of escalation. Vivid examples of escalation have been experienced in many major projects when the cost out-turns prove to be much greater than anticipated: the Sydney Opera House, Chicago's sewage system, Concorde, the Channel Tunnel.

17.8 Summary

Many commentators (e.g. Lamb and Shrivastava, 1986) have observed that the study of strategy implementation and control has received far less attention than its importance warrants. No matter how brilliant the formulation of strategy, it is quite useless if it cannot be effectively implemented and the subsequent performance of the organization controlled.

An array of approaches to control that focus in part on social/behavioural issues and in part on analytical techniques has been considered. Feedforward and feedback control, formal and informal controls and the approaches of authorities such as Anthony, Merchant and others were discussed. Some relevant techniques, including ratio analysis, marketing audits and networking, have been dealt with in earlier chapters. The importance of social and behavioural issues is that analytical control techniques function only in an organizational context: social and analytical controls are complements rather than substitutes.

It can be argued (e.g. Maciariello, 1984, p. 54) that the hierarchical structure of an organization is a response to the limited information-processing ability of decision-makers. At each level within the hierarchy it is desirable, from the viewpoint of coordination and control, to identify the responsibilities that need to be undertaken if successful outcomes are to be achieved. One approach to this task is to define the *key success factors* over which each organizational unit has control and to assign responsibilities in accordance with these factors. The basic idea behind this approach is a simple one: if a manager's cognitive limitations constrain the amount of information that can be processed at any time, it makes sense to be deliberately selective by focusing on the information that is most important in terms of fulfilling the manager's designated responsibilities.

Selecting key success factors that adequately reflect these responsibilities gives a basis for:

➡ Establishing appropriate performance measures
➡ Determining resource allocation procedures
➡ Specifying reward systems.

The identification of key success factors gives focus to the control process. In essence, the following question is being posed: to which factors are desired outcomes most sensitive? The greater the degree of sensitivity (or responsiveness) between a factor and an outcome, the more critical is that factor in controlling the organizational unit in order to bring about the desired outcome.

It is inevitable that some critical factors (such as macro-economic variables, government actions, competitive behaviour and suppliers' behaviour) cannot easily be influenced by a given organization, while other critical factors (which might include product design, quality, price and level of customer service) are more readily influenced by the organization's managers. However, in control terms the point to note is that the outcome that is desired (e.g. sustained competitive advantage) can be achieved if the manager understands how the key variables behave (i.e. how they change over time and why those changes occur), since this gives the manager the ability to make future predictions. Through the ability to make accurate predictions of each key variable's future value, the manager is in a position to control the outcome of events. In part this will require the manipulation of those variables that can be directly influenced, and in part it will require an awareness of the anticipated future values of variables that the manager is unable directly to influence. Control is achieved when desired outcomes are realized; hence it is possible to be in control even though one is unable to manipulate the values of all variables. It is worth repeating the major elements underlying the above discussion:

➡ An understanding of the behaviour of key variables gives a basis for making predictions about their likely future values
➡ On the basis of good predictions it is possible to bring about desired outcomes by manipulating the variables over which one has influence in the knowledge of the expected behaviour of those variables over which one has no direct influence.

In seeking to control marketing activities, the requirements of effective control systems are:

➡ They must provide timely information
➡ They must measure the essential nature of the activity being assessed
➡ They should provide information on trends
➡ They must facilitate action
➡ They must be economical
➡ They must be meaningful.

Two developing fields which are likely to increase in importance are those of expert systems (see McDonald and Wilson, 1990) and strategic control (see Wilson, 1997).

Chapter **18**

Management control – 2

18.1 Learning objectives

When you have read this chapter you should be able to:

(a) understand the nature of controls;

(b) design and operate marketing budgeting systems;

(c) carry out variance analyses in a marketing context;

(d) recognize how to use competitive and environmental intelligence in devising corrective responses.

18.2 Introduction

Having considered in Chapter 17 the nature of control and control systems, along with a range of approaches to control, this chapter looks in more detail at the operation of some of the more widely used control systems (such as marketing audits, budgeting and variance analysis). It then goes on to consider how corrective action might be taken if outcomes are not in accordance with plans.

18.3 Controls

Forms of control

In large organizations there are a number of insidious and unobtrusive controls to be found. These are all the more dangerous and powerful because they are so deceptive. Their deceptiveness is shown in their *not* causing participants to feel their presence – there is no feeling of being oppressed by a despot. Instead, there is perhaps just the experience of conforming to the logic of a situation, or of performing in accordance with some internalized standard.

Beyond this source of 'control' there are other sources. To the extent that the behaviour of members of organizations is controlled (i.e. appears to be regular and predictable), such regularity may derive from the norms and definitions of subcultural groups within the organization rather than from official rules and prescriptions. The idea that organizational rules constitute the blueprint for all behaviour within organizations is not a tenable one.

Nevertheless, the most significant form of power within organizations is the power to limit, guide and restrict the decision-making of organizational personnel, such that even when they are allowed (or obliged) to use their own judgement they do not deviate from official expectations. In part this is due to the organization's structure, which can be seen as a series of limitations and controls over members' decision-making, and which results from powerful, senior organizational personnel choosing what the structure should be (and hence determining who is allowed to do what).

It is something of a paradox that the modern individual is free from coercion through the power of command of superiors than most people have ever been, yet individuals in positions of power today probably exercise more control than any tyrant ever did. This is largely due to contemporary forms of power exercised within organizations and by organizations in society. There is a distinct trend that places less reliance on control through a fixed chain of command while placing more reliance on indirect forms of control. Let us pursue this in greater detail.

Forms of control have changed with the passage of time, and these forms have had impacts not only within organizations, but also through them, on contemporary society.

Organizations have taken advantage of a variety of control mechanisms from time to time, ranging from ones that are obviously bureaucratic in nature (e.g. command authority and discipline) to ones that are quite unbureaucratic (such as the controlling power that is rooted in expert knowledge).

We can consider the following range of control mechanisms:

➡ The prototype (bureaucratic control) is the authority exercised through a *chain of command* in which superiors give subordinates instructions that must be obeyed. This coercive form of control has strong military overtones, and an essential element is rigorous discipline that must be enforced through coercive sanctions. Such discipline is not usually a characteristic of contemporary industrial life.

➡ The establishing of explicit regulations and procedures to govern decisions and operations gives a programmed form of control. Discipline is involved in this mechanism also, and close links can be seen between the idea of a set of rules that must be followed and the idea of following orders via a chain of command. However, explicit rules do restrict the arbitrary exercise of power by superiors because they apply to rulers as well as to the ruled.

In specifying rules on how to behave in particular circumstances, it is unlikely that all possible situations will be catered for. It follows that rules should ideally be related to the principles underlying decisions rather than to particular decisions – thus, specifying *criteria* for decision-making will be less restrictive than the stipulating of *how* specific decisions should be made.

➡ Incentive systems constitute a further control mechanism. Salaries and career advancement clearly make individuals dependent to a large extent on the organization that employs them, thereby constraining them to submit to the authority exercised within that organization.

Incentives are often tied directly to performance, with piece-work rates and sales commissions being the most obvious examples. However, performance measures can be developed for most organizational roles, and adjustments in salary levels and promotion decisions will depend at least to some extent on measured achievements.

➡ Technology provides a control mechanism in two forms:
  ➡ Production technology constrains employees' performance, thereby enabling managers to control operations (e.g. the speed of an assembly line can be used to regulate productivity).

➡ The technical knowledge possessed by an organization's 'technocrats' gives them the ability to understand and perform complex tasks and thereby maintain control of a situation. Management is thus able to control operations, albeit indirectly, by hiring staff with appropriate professional/technical skills to carry out the required responsibilities.

This reduces the need to use alternative mechanisms, such as detailed rules or close supervision through a chain of command.

➡ Expert knowledge is a vital requirement in managing organizations. (It could even be argued that successful management comes about through the exercising of control over the basic knowledge.) It follows that recruiting suitable technocrats is a key mechanism for controlling the organization. If technically qualified individuals are selectively recruited and if they have the professional ability to perform assigned tasks on their own, then if the organization gives such individuals the appropriate discretion to do what needs to be done within the broad framework of basic policies and administrative guidelines, it should be possible for control to be effective.

➡ The allocation of resources (including personnel) is the ultimate mechanism of organizational control, since this facilitates certain actions and inhibits others.

Within most organizations one will find several of these mechanisms of control in operation, yet there seems to be a trend towards a decreasing reliance on control through a chain of command and an increasing reliance on indirect forms of control, e.g. via recruitment policies. Incentive systems and machine technologies are perhaps the most prevalent mechanisms of contemporary organizational control: control via recruitment and resource allocation is indicative of the likely future pattern.

Controls may be informal as well as formal. The former are unwritten mechanisms that can influence either individual or group behaviour patterns within organizations in profound ways. A distinction can be made among different types of informal control by means of the level of aggregation (i.e. from individual through small groups to large groups) chosen (see, for example, Jaworski, 1988). Three categories are:

1 Self-control, in which individuals establish their own personal objectives and attempt to achieve those objectives by monitoring their own performance and adapting their behaviour whenever this is necessary. This can lead to high levels of job satisfaction, but it may fail to achieve the outcomes sought by top management (i.e. those relating to the organization rather than specific individuals). In order to motivate individuals to act in accordance with top management's wishes, a system of incentives will be needed.

2 Social control is applied within small group settings by members of the group. It is typically found that groups (e.g. marketing teams) set their own informal standards of behaviour and performance with which group members are expected to conform. These standards represent values and mutual commitments towards some common goal. Whenever a member of the group behaves in a deviant way by

violating a group norm, the other members of the group will attempt to use subtle pressures – such as humour or hints – to correct the deviance. If this fails and violations are repeated, the group's reaction is likely to be to ostracize the deviant individual. In a marketing context there may be group norms for, say, expenses and sales volumes within a sales team.

3 Cultural control applies at a corporate (or divisional) level, and stems from the accumulation of rituals, legends and norms of social interaction within the organization. Once an individual has internalized the cultural norms, he or she can be expected to behave in accordance with those norms. This gives reason to see cultural control as being the dominant control mechanism for senior management positions involving non-routine decision-making – the judgemental factor will reflect the manager's cultural conditioning.

In contrast to informal controls there are formal controls – written management-initiated mechanisms that influence the probability that individuals, or groups, will act in a manner that is supportive of marketing objectives. Three categories of formal controls can be identified, with timing being the distinguishing factor (i.e. these controls echo the sequence of managerial processes):

1 Input controls consist of measurable actions that are taken prior to the implementation of plans, such as specifying selection criteria for recruiting staff, establishing recruitment and training programmes, and various forms of resource allocation. The mix of these inputs can be manipulated in an attempt to secure control.

2 Process control relates to management's attempts to influence the means of achieving desired ends, with the emphasis being on behaviour and/or activities rather than on the end results – such as requiring individuals to follow established procedures. There is no clear agreement in the literature as to whether the organization's structure represents a control mechanism or not. Since it can be seen to influence and shape individual and group behaviour, it is not unreasonable to think of structure as being part of process control.

3 Output controls apply when results are compared with performance standards, as in feedback control.

In considering control in marketing one might emphasize the control of marketing activities in a relatively detached and impersonal way, as is done by strategy formulation (feedforward control) and variance analysis (feedback control). Alternatively, one might emphasize the control of marketing personnel, which involves finding ways to influence the behaviour of those engaging in marketing activities in order that desired ends might be achieved. Since it seems likely that marketing activities can only be controlled through marketing personnel, the best way forward would seem to be a balanced combination of both approaches: in other words, feedforward and feedback need to be combined with marketing activities by those who devise and execute marketing activities.

The ultimate test of any control system is the extent to which it brings about organizational effectiveness, and it is fair to say that there is little rigorously formulated evidence to demonstrate clear linkages between any approach to control and organizational effectiveness.

Audits

One approach towards assessing marketing effectiveness is the marketing audit (dealt with in detail in Chapter 2).

The marketing audit exists to help correct difficulties and to improve conditions that may already be good. While these aims may be achieved by a piecemeal examination of individual activities, it is better achieved by a total programme of evaluation studies. The former approach is termed a 'vertical audit', as it is only concerned with one element of the marketing mix at any one time. In contrast, the latter approach, the 'horizontal audit', is concerned with optimizing the use of resources, thereby maximizing the total effectiveness of marketing efforts and outlays. As such, it is by far the more difficult of the two, and hence rarely attempted.

No matter which form of marketing audit is selected, top management (via its audit staff) should ensure that no area of marketing activity goes unevaluated and that every aspect is evaluated in accordance with standards that are compatible with the total success of the marketing organization and of the firm as a whole. This, of course, requires that all activities be related to the established hierarchy of objectives.

The distribution audit

In the planning and control of costs and effectiveness in distribution activities the management audit can be of considerable value. Not surprisingly, however, it entails a complex set of procedures right across the function if it is to be carried out thoroughly. The major components are the channel audit, the PDM audit, the competitive audit and the customer service audit. Each of these will be considered briefly in turn.

1 The channel audit

Channels are made up of the intermediaries (such as wholesalers, factors, retailers) through which goods pass on their route from manufacture to consumption. The key channel decisions include:

➡ Choosing intermediaries
➡ Determining the implications (from a PD point of view) of alternative channel structures
➡ Assessing the available margins.

It follows from the nature of these decisions that the main focus of a channel audit will be on structural factors on the one hand and on cost/margin factors on the other.

2 The PDM audit

There are three primary elements within this audit: that of company profile (which includes the handling cost characteristics of the product range and the service level that is needed in the light of market conditions); PDM developments (both of a technological and contextual nature); and the current system's capability.

Cost aspects exist in each of these elements, but operating costs loom largest in the latter, since it is predominantly concerned with costs and capacity. For example, some of the items that will be subjected to audit will include those shown in Figure 18.1.

3 The competitive audit

Through this phase it should be possible to ascertain the quality of competitors' distribution policies, etc., and especially the level of service that competitors are able to offer (and maintain). Within the competitive audit, regard should also be given to channel structures, pricing and discount policies, and market shares.

4 The customer service audit

Given that the level of service is at the centre of physical distribution management, it is essential to monitor regularly its cost and quality characteristics.

A very thorough approach to the distribution audit is that developed at the Cranfield School of Management by Christopher and colleagues (see Christopher et al., 1977).

Kotler (1984) has offered the view that auditing is the ultimate control measure, although it can be seen as a means of linking the notions of efficiency and effectiveness. It achieves this latter purpose not only by evaluating performance in terms of inputs used and outputs generated, but also by evaluating the assumptions underlying marketing strategies. The fact that audits are expensive and time-consuming – especially when undertaken in a comprehensive, horizontal manner – may appear to contradict the striving for efficiency. However, by focusing on doing the right thing they should help in ensuring effectiveness, which is of greater importance.

Selecting the right person to carry out the audit has been addressed by Kling (1985). He observed that a balance of experience and objectivity is needed, which tends to favour outside auditors who have a broader range of experience than insiders and who can stand back in a reasonably impartial way from policies and procedures that they were not involved in either formulating or implementing. The range of possible auditors includes:

1 Self-audit
2 Audit from across (i.e. by a colleague in another function but at the same level as the manager whose activities are being audited)
3 Audit from above (i.e. by the manager's superior)
4 Company auditing office
5 Company task-force audit (i.e. a team set up specifically to conduct the audit)
6 Outside auditors.

Capacity utilization	➡ Warehouse
	➡ Transportation
	➡ Flexibility and expansion scope
Warehouse facilities	➡ Total costs
	➡ Age and maintenance costs
	➡ Flexibility throughput/period
	➡ Total throughput/period
	➡ Returns handled – number
	– recovery time
	➡ Picking accuracy
	➡ Service levels/back orders
	➡ Cube utilization
	➡ Cost of cube bought out
Inventory	➡ Total inventory holding costs
	➡ Product group costs
	➡ Service levels – total
	– plant
	– field
	➡ Field inventory holding costs
	➡ Transfers – number
	– volume
	➡ Stock-out effects – loss of business
	– rectification costs
Transportation	➡ Total costs
	➡ Production to field units
	➡ Field units to customers
	➡ Vehicle utilization
	➡ Vehicle cube utilization
	➡ Total volumes shipped
	➡ Cost per mile – volumes shipped
	– cases/pallets shipped
	➡ Costs of service bought out
	➡ Costs by mode/comparisons
Communications	➡ Total costs
	➡ Order communication times – method
	– cost
	➡ Time and costs per line item per order method for:
	– order processing and registration
	– credit investigation
	– invoice and delivery note preparation
	– statement preparation
	➡ Number and cost of customer queries
	➡ Salesmen's – calls/day
	– calls/territory/day
	– calls/product group/day
	– calls/customer group/day
	➡ Salesmen's use of time – selling
	– inventory checking
	– merchandising
	– order processing
Unitization	➡ Total costs
	➡ Volumes shipped
	➡ Unitization method/proportions of
	– pallets
	– roll pallets
	– containers
	➡ Costs of assembly and handling by load type
Service achieved (by market segment)	➡ Total costs
	➡ Service levels operated/costs
	➡ Delivery times
	➡ Delivery reliability
	➡ Order processing and progressing
	➡ Order picking efficiency
	➡ Claims procedure/time/cost
Volume throughput	➡ Total throughout – volume
	– weight
	– units
	➡ Total costs
	➡ Throughput/field locations – volume
	– weight
	– units
	➡ Throughput fluctuations
	➡ Flexibility (capacity availability/time)

Figure 18.1 Distribution audit

It may be better to have a combination of category 6 with one of categories 2–5, thereby bringing together an external view with the perspective of insiders in a joint endeavour. There is little evidence of support for category 1, although it exists as a possibility in the absence of any alternative.

In carrying out a marketing audit it will be evident that the enterprise needs to exhibit adaptive behaviour if it is to remain goal striving in a dynamic environment. Effectiveness is concerned with this ability to achieve goals in an ever-changing context.

Budgeting

Budgeting (or profit planning) is perhaps the widest-ranging control technique in that it covers the entire organization rather than merely sections of it (see Wilson, 1999a).

A budget is a quantitative plan of action that aids in the coordination and control of the acquisition, allocation and utilization of resources over a given period of time. The building of the budget may be looked upon as the integration of the varied interests that constitute the organization into a programme that all have agreed is workable in attempting to attain objectives.

Budgetary planning and control work through the formal organization viewing it as a series of responsibility centres and attempting to isolate the performance measurement of one module from the effects of the performance of others.

Budgeting involves more than just forecasting, since it concerns the planned manipulation of all the variables that determine the company's performance in an effort to arrive at some preferred position in the future. The agreed plan must be developed in a coordinated manner if the requirements of each subsystem are to be balanced in line with company objectives. Each manager must consider the relationship of his or her responsibility centre (or department, or subsystem) to all others and to the company as a whole in the budgetary planning phase. This tends to reduce departmental bias and empire building, as well as isolating weaknesses in the organizational structure and highlighting problems of communication. Furthermore, it encourages the delegation of authority by a reliance on the principle of management by exception.

Having determined the plan, this provides the frame of reference for judging subsequent performance. There can be no doubt that *budgeted* performance is a better benchmark than past performance on account of the inefficiencies that are usually hidden in the latter and the effect of constantly changing conditions.

There are essentially two types of budget: the long term and the short term. Time obviously distinguishes one from the other, and this raises the point that users of budgets should not be unduly influenced by conventional accounting periods – the budget period that is most meaningful to the company should be adopted. For example, the life cycle of a product from its development right through to its deletion is in many ways a more natural budgetary period than calendar units, because it links marketing, production and financial planning on a unified basis. The actual choice of a budget period will tend to depend very much on the company's ability to forecast accurately.

Typically, however, budgets tend to be compiled on an annual basis, with this time span being broken down into lesser time intervals for reporting, scheduling and control

reasons (i.e. half years, quarters, months and even weeks in the case of production and sales activities).

Within this framework of one year the *operating budget* is prepared. This is composed of two parts, with each part looking at the same things in a slightly different way, but both arriving at the same net profit and return on investment. These two parts are:

1 The programme (or activity) budget, which specifies the operations that will be performed during the forthcoming period. The most logical way to present this budget is to show, for each product, the expected revenues and their associated costs. The result is an impersonal portrayal of the expected future that is useful in ensuring that a balance exists amongst the various activities, profit margins and volumes – in other words, this is the plan.

2 The responsibility budget, which specifies the annual plan in terms of individual responsibilities. This is primarily a control device that indicates the target level of performance, but the personalized costs and revenues in this budget must be controllable at the level at which they are planned and reported.

The significance of these two ways of dealing with the operating budget is of importance as the programme budget is the outcome of the planning phase, whereas the responsibility budget is the starting point for the control phase. The former need not correspond to the organizational structure but the latter must. Consequently, the plan must be translated into the control prior to the time of execution and communicated to those involved in order that no one will be in any doubt as to precisely what is expected of him or her.

Given these two complementary aspects of the operating budget, there are two basic ways in which the budget may be prepared:

1 Periodic budgeting, in which a plan is prepared for the next financial year with a minimum of revision as the year goes by. Generally, the total expected annual expenditure will be spread over the year on a monthly basis on the strength of the behaviour of the elemental costs. Thus, 'salaries' will be spread over the months simply as one-twelfth of the expected annual cost per month, but seasonal variations in sales will require a little more attention to be paid to marketing and production costs and their behaviour over time.

2 Continuous (or rolling) budgeting, in which a tentative annual plan is prepared with, say, the first quarter by month in great detail, the second and third quarters in lesser detail, and the fourth quarter in outline only. Every month (or perhaps every quarter) the budget can then be revised by adding the required detail to the next month (or quarter), filling in some of the vagueness in the other remaining months (or quarters), and adding on a new month (or quarter) in such a way that the plan still extends one year ahead. Such a budgeting procedure attempts to accommodate changing conditions and uncertainty, and is highly desirable in that it forces management constantly to think in concrete terms about the forthcoming *year* regardless of where one happens to be in the present *financial* year.

Periodic budgeting will often be satisfactory for companies in stable industries that are able to make relatively accurate forecasts covering the planning period. Conversely, rolling budgeting is of greater value in the more usual cases of somewhat irregular cyclical activity amid the uncertainties of consumer demand.

Whether the concern is with long-term or short-term budgeting, or with continuous or period budgeting, there are certain fundamental requirements that must be met if budgeting is to be of maximum value. Briefly, these requirements are:

1 Established objectives
2 Top management sponsorship and support
3 A knowledge of cost behaviour
4 Flexibility
5 A specified time period
6 Adequate systems support
7 An effective organizational structure
8 A sufficient level of education in budgetary practice.

If these prerequisites exist, then budgeting should enable the company to improve its effectiveness by planning for the future and controlling the execution of the plan by comparing actual results with the desired level of performance.

Deviations between actual and budgeted results will be of managerial concern for such reasons as the following:

➡ To highlight errors in budgeting procedures
➡ To indicate the need for budget revision
➡ To pinpoint those activities requiring remedial attention.

The principles of management by exception should be applied to this process of comparison with the focusing of attention on *significant* variations. However, if the budgeted level of activity differs from the actual level of activity, it will be apparent that variances of an artificial nature arise – such variances are based purely on volume rather than efficiency. This emphasizes the need for flexibility within the budgeting system: it should be able to allow for varying circumstances by recognizing and adapting to significant changes in the fundamental operating conditions of the firm. Such adaptability can be achieved by a *flexible budget*.

In a flexible budgeting system the budgeted cost is adjusted in accordance with the level of activity experienced in the budget period. For example, a budget that is based on sales of 10 000 units during a particular period is of little value for control purposes if 12 000 units (or 8000 units) are actually sold. The sales manager will be necessarily held responsible for the volume variance, but the level of commission, order processing/invoicing, freight and similar cost-incurring activities will tend to depend on the actual level of activity, which requires that the budget be adjusted in order to show the efficient budgeted level of expenditure for the achieved level of activity.

A simple way of building a flexible budget is to start with a budget for the most likely level of activity and then to derive budgets for 5, 10 and 15 per cent above and below this level.

The major advantage of the flexible budget is its ability to specify the budgeted level of costs, revenues and profits *without revision* when sales and production programmes are changed. It achieves this by distinguishing between those costs that vary with changes in the level of activity and those that do not. In other words, it is based on a thorough knowledge of cost behaviour patterns.

A static budget (i.e. a fixed budget that relates to a single level of activity) can result in misleading actions. An example should make this clear. Figure 18.2 shows the comparison of a budgeted level of 10 000 units with an actual sales level of 11 000 units. It appears that profit has improved by £300, *but* not all costs vary in the same way, so a flexible budget analysis is called for. This is shown in Figure 18.3 and indicates clearly that the comparison should be between the actual level of activity and the budgeted costs, revenue and profit for that level. While profit was higher than the budgeted figure, the difference was only £20 rather than £300.

	Budget	Actual	Variance
Sales (units)	10,000	11,000	+1,000
Sales revenue	£15,000	£16,500	+£1,500
Expenditure: Direct	10,000	11,000	+1,000
Indirect	4,000	4,200	+200
Profit	£1,000	£1,300	+£300

Figure 18.2   Fixed budget analysis

	Fixed budget	Flexible actual	Actual	Variance
Sales (units)	10,000	11,000	11,000	–
Sales revenue	£15,000	16,500	16,500	–
Expenditure: Direct	10,000	11,000	11,000	–
Fixed indirect	1,500	1,500	1,450	−50
Variable indirect	2,000	2,200	2,240	+40
Mixed indirect	500	520	510	−10
Profit	£1,000	£1,280	£1,300	+20

Figure 18.3   Flexible budget analysis

The need to distinguish fixed costs (which remain constant in total during a period) from variable costs (which remain constant per unit of output) is of paramount importance, and any costs that are neither one nor the other (i.e. semi-fixed or semi-variable expenses) can usefully be classified as mixed costs. Apart from showing the cost breakdown in some detail, Figure 18.3 shows the target level of activity (i.e. the fixed budget) as well as the efficiency with which the actual level of activity was attained. This information is vital to effective control.

It is important to appreciate that budgeting cannot take the place of management, but rather forms a vital aid to management. Indeed, budgets are based on estimates, and judgement must be applied to determine how valid the estimates are and, consequently, how significant deviations are from those estimates. The adequacy of planning and controlling operations hinges critically upon the adequacy of managerial judgement.

In the light of the need for judgement it is clear that budgeting should not introduce unnecessary rigidity into the management process. A budget should be a flexible framework that is capable of accommodating changing circumstances, but care must be exercised lest the budgetary targets come to supersede the objectives of the company. The budget is a means to an end, not an end in itself.

In its traditional application, budgeting has a major weakness in planning and another in control: in the planning phase there is usually consideration of too few alternative courses of action from which the best is to be selected, and in the control phase it is difficult to adjust operating budgets to reflect rapidly changing conditions – they are at best flexible with respect to changing sales or production levels.

Nevertheless, these weaknesses should not outweigh the general role of budgeting in drawing attention to problem areas, encouraging forward thinking and developing company-wide cooperation.

Other approaches to budgeting: ZBB and PPBS

In order to accommodate the particular needs of non-profit organizations (such as government agencies), as well as providing a focus for more rigorous thinking in relation to *programmed* or *discretionary costs* (i.e. those which are determined purely by managerial discretion – such as R&D, training and many marketing outlays), a number of recent developments in budgeting techniques are worthy of mention. In particular, zero-base budgeting (ZBB) and output budgeting (which is also known as a planning–programming–budgeting system, hence the initials PPBS) have generated considerable interest, so we will take note of them at this point.

Zero-base budgeting (ZBB)

Among other failings it is generally agreed that traditional budgeting (or *incremental budgeting* as it is often known due to the tendency to add on a bit more – an increment – to last year's budget level in order to arrive at a figure for next year) is number-oriented, fails to identify priorities, and starts with the existing level of activity or expenditure as an established base, whereas it might be more useful to managers to have a technique that was decision-oriented, helped in determining priorities, and sought to reassess the current level of expenditure.

It will be appreciated from this last point that in taking as given the current level of expenditure, and the activities that this represents, the traditional approach to budgeting – by looking only at desired increases or, occasionally, decreases – is ignoring the majority of the organization's expenditure. This is rather myopic.

The zero-base budgeting alternative is to evaluate *simultaneously* existing and new ways of achieving specified ends in order to establish priorities among them, which could mean that there are trade-offs between existing and new activities. For example, a new Project A that is considered to be more desirable than an existing Project B may be resourced by terminating Project B. In essence, the approach is carried out in two stages:

1 Decision packages are identified within each decision unit. These decision units are essentially discrete activities that can be described in a way that separates them from other activities of the organization. The decision packages cover both existing and projected incremental activities, and the organizational units responsible for carrying them out are much akin to the responsibility centres that were discussed earlier in the chapter. The object is to define for each decision unit the basic requirements that are needed if it is to perform the function for which it was established. Any costs in excess of this basic level are deemed incremental. (It will be seen, therefore, that the title 'zero base' is something of a misnomer, since the base is certainly greater than zero!) In considering what is needed in order to fulfil a particular purpose, over and above the base level, it is probable that alternative ways of achieving the same end will be identified, and these should be described and evaluated as they arise – these are the decision packages.

2 Once the manager of a decision unit has submitted his or her statement of evaluated decision packages to his or her superior, it is the latter's job to assign priorities to the various submissions from all subordinates, and to select the highest-ranking decision packages that come within the available budget limit. There are a number of ways in which priorities can be determined, all of which presuppose some explicit criterion of effectiveness in order that competing packages may be ranked.

This approach is logical and has much to commend it in relation to discretionary outlays.

Output budgeting

In the traditional approach to budgeting there tends to be an overall emphasis on the functional areas of an organization. Thus, one has the budget for the marketing function and that for the data processing department. However, no organization was ever established in order that it might have these functions as a definition of what it exists to achieve, so it is helpful to look at the situation from another angle.

In a typical business organization there will be functions such as those shown in Figure 18.4, but the organization really exists in order to achieve various purposes, which have been simplified in the 'missions' of Figure 18.5. In developing a business plan, the major concern is with the 'missions', subject to the resource limitations within

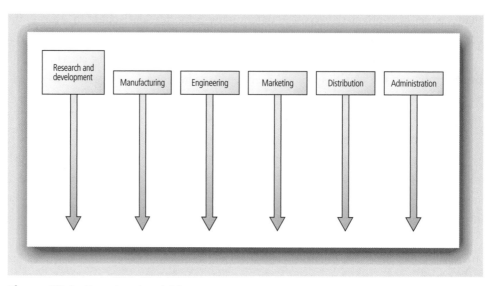

Figure 18.4 Functional activities

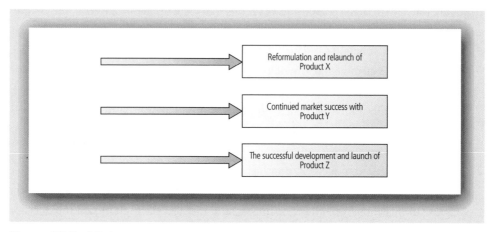

Figure 18.5 Missions

the functions, etc., whereas the development of controls will usually be via the responsibility centres that are contained within the functions.

If we now superimpose the (horizontal) missions over the (vertical) functions, we have the crux of the output budgeting approach. What this does is to focus attention on the purposes to be served by the organization, as shown by the missions, and the contribution that each function must make to each mission if the missions are to be successful. Figure 18.6 suggests this in the most simplified manner.

Variance analysis

When actual selling prices differ from standard selling prices, a *sales price variance* can be computed. Standard selling prices will be used in compiling budgets, but it may be necessary to adapt to changing market conditions by raising or lowering prices, so it

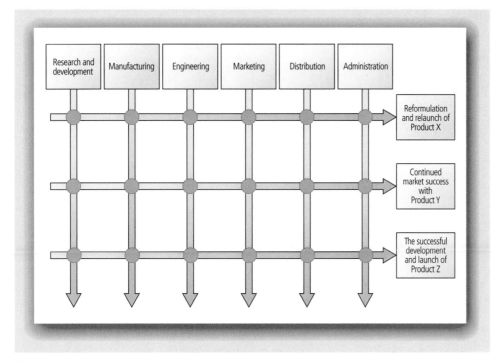

Figure 18.6 A simplified output budgeting format

becomes desirable to segregate variances due to price changes from variances due to changes in quantity and product mix.

Quantity and mix are the two components of *sales volume variances*, and variations in profit can be explained to some extent by analysing sales quantity and sales mix.

The formulae for computing sales variances are:

Sales price variance   = actual units sold × (actual price − standard price)

Sales volume variance = sales quantity variance + sales mix variance

Sales quantity variance = budgeted profit on budgeted sales

                      − expected profit on actual sales

Sales mix variance   = expected profit on actual sales

                      − standard profit on actual sales.

'Expected profit on actual sales' is calculated as though profit increases or decreases proportionately with changes in the level of sales. 'Standard profit on actual sales' is the sum of the standard profit for all units sold. (For a single product enterprise, or in one where the profit per unit of sales is constant over the product range, the standard profit on actual sales is equal to the expected profit on actual sales, and the sales mix variance will necessarily be nil.)

Let us clarify the approach with an example. Assume budgeted sales of a company's two products for a forthcoming period were as follows:

Product A 500 units at £2.00 per unit

Product B 700 units at £1.50 per unit

and budgeted costs were:

Product A £1.75 per unit
Product B £1.30 per unit

Actual costs were in line with the budgeted costs, and actual sales for the period were:

Product A 560 units at £1.95 per unit
Product B 710 units at £1.40 per unit

Budgeted sales revenue	$= £[(500 \times 2.00) + (700 \times 1.50)]$	= £2,050
Actual sales revenue	$= £[(560 \times 1.95) + (710 \times 1.40)]$	= £2,086
Budgeted profit	$= £[(500 \times 0.25) + (700 \times 0.20)]$	= £265
Actual profit	$= £[(560 \times 0.25) + (710 \times 0.10)]$	= £211
Total sales variance		−£54

Sales price variance	$= £[560 \times (1.95 - 2.00)] +$	
	$[710 \times (1.40 - 1.50)]$	= −£99

Sales volume variance:

Quantity variance	$= £265 - [2,086/2,050 \times 265]$	= −£4
Mix variance	$= £269 - [(560 \times 0.25) + (710 \times 0.20)] =$	−£13
Sales volume variance		−£17
Total sales variance		−£116

Standards can be developed for repetitive activities, and it is possible to determine standards in a marketing context for the following illustrative activities:

➡ Cost per unit of sales
➡ Cost per sales transaction
➡ Cost per order received
➡ Cost per customer account
➡ Cost per mile travelled
➡ Cost per sales call made.

The degree of detail can be varied to suit the particular requirements. Thus, 'cost per unit of sales' may be 'advertising cost per £ of sales revenue for Product X' and so on.

It is clearly more difficult to establish precise standards for most marketing activities than is the case in the manufacturing or distribution functions. Physical and mechanical factors are less influential; psychological factors are more prominent; objective measurement is less conspicuous; tolerance limits must be broader; and the range of segments for which marketing standards can be developed is much greater. But the discipline of seeking to establish standards can generate insights into relationships between effort and results that are likely to outweigh any lack of precision.

It is possible for an organization to develop marketing standards by participating in an interfirm comparison scheme (such as the one run by the Centre for Interfirm

Comparison). As Westwick (1987) has shown, integrated sets of ratios and standards can be devised to allow for detailed monitoring of performance (see Sections 3.10–3.12, in Chapter 3).

When budget levels and standards are being developed it is vitally important to note the assumptions on which they have been based, since it is inevitable that circumstances will change and a variety of unanticipated events will occur once the budget is implemented. Bearing this in mind, let us work through an example. Figure 18.7 illustrates an extract from a marketing plan for Product X (column 2), with actual results (column 3) and variances (column 4) being shown for a particular operating period.

The unfavourable contribution variance of £150 000 shown at the foot of column 4 is due to two principal causes:

1 A variance relating to contribution per unit, and
2 A variance relating to sales volume.

In turn, a variance relating to sales volume can be attributed to differences between:

3 Actual and anticipated total market size, and
4 Actual and anticipated market share.

Therefore, a variation between planned and actual contributions may be due to variations in price per unit, variable cost per unit, total market size and market penetration.

In the case of Product X we have:

1 Profit variance:

$$(C_a - C_p) \times Q_a = £(0.35 - 0.40) \times 11,000,000$$
$$= (£550,000)$$

Item (1)	Plan (2)	Actual (3)	Variance (4)
Revenues:			
Sales (units)	10,000,000	11,000,000	1,000,000
Price per unit (£)	1.00	0.95	0.05
Total revenue (£)	10,000,000	10,450,000	450,000
Market:			
Total market size (units)	25,000,000	30,000,000	5,000,000
Share of market (%)	40.0	36.7	(3.3)
Costs:			
Variable cost per unit (£)	0.60	0.60	–
Contribution:			
Per unit (£)	0.40	0.35	0.05
Total contribution (£)	4,000,000	3,850,000	(150,000)

Figure 18.7 Operating results for Product X

2 Volume variance:

$$(Q_a - Q_p) \times C_p = (11,000,000 - 10,000,000) \times £0.40$$
$$= £400,000$$

3 Net variance:

	£
Profit variance	(550,000)
Volume variance	400,000
	£(150,000)

where:

C_a = actual contribution per unit;

C_p = planned contribution per unit;

Q_a = actual quantity sold in units;

Q_p = planned quantity of sales in units.

Figure 18.8 illustrates the relations.

However, variable 2 can be analysed further to take into account the impact of market size and penetration variations.

4 Market size variance:

$$(M_a - M_p) \times S_p \times C_p = (30,000,000 - 25,000,000) \times 0.4 \times 0.4$$
$$= £800,000$$

5 Market share variance:

$$(S_a - S_p) \times M_a \times C_p = (0.367 - 0.40) \times 30,000,000 \times 0.4$$
$$= £(400,000)$$

6 Volume variance:

	£
Market size variance	800,000
Market share variance	(400,000)
	£400,000

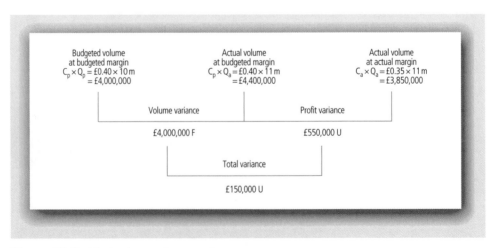

Figure 18.8 Marketing variances – 1

where:

M_a = actual total market in units;

M_p = planned total market in units;

S_a = actual market share;

S_p = planned market share.

See Figure 18.9, which illustrates these relationships.

In summary, the position now appears thus:

	£	£
Planned profit contribution		4,000,000
Volume variance:		
Market size variance	800,000	
Market share variance	(400,000)	400,000
Profit variance		(550,000)
Actual profit contribution		£3,850,000

But this is not the end of the analysis! Variances arise because of unsatisfactory performance and unsatisfactory plans. It is desirable, therefore, to distinguish variances due to the poor *execution* of plans from those due to the poor *establishing* of plans. In the latter category are likely to be found forecasting errors reflecting faulty assumptions,

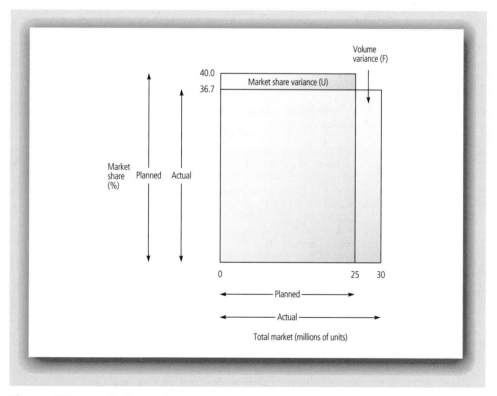

Figure 18.9 Marketing variances – 2

and the estimates of total market size may constitute poor benchmarks for gauging subsequent managerial performance.

It is difficult to determine categorically whether market share variances are primarily the responsibility of forecasters or of those who execute the plans based on forecasts. On the face of it, the primary responsibility is likely to be attached to the latter group.

In interpreting the variances for Product X it can be seen that the favourable volume variance of £400 000 resulted from two variances relating to market size and market share. Both of these are undesirable, since they led to a lower contribution than intended. Had the forecasting group correctly anticipated the larger total market, it should have been possible to devise a better plan to achieve the desired share and profit contribution. The actual outcome suggests that competitive position has been lost due to a loss of market share in a rapidly growing market. This is a serious pointer.

Lower prices resulted in a lower level of contribution per unit, and hence a lower overall profit contribution. The reasons for this need to be established and future plans modified as necessary.

As an approach to improved learning about the links between effort and results – especially in the face of active competitive behaviour – it is helpful to take the above analysis further and to evaluate performance by considering what *should have happened* in the circumstances (which is akin to flexible budgeting, as discussed on pp. 776–8 above).

At the end of the operating period to which Figure 18.7 refers it may become known that a large company with substantial resources made an aggressive entry into the marketplace using lots of promotions and low prices. Furthermore, an unforeseen export demand for Product X may have arisen due to a prolonged strike in the USA's main manufacturer. On the basis of these details, it becomes possible to carry out an *ex post* performance analysis, in which the original plans are revised to take account of what has since become known.

A clearer distinction can be made via *ex post* performance analysis along these lines, since a distinction can be made between:

➡ Planning variances due to environmental events that were foreseeable or unforeseeable, and
➡ Performance variances that are due to problems in executing the plans.

The situation is summarized in Figure 18.10.

This example has focused on a single product line (Product X), but multi-product companies will typically have product lines with differing cost structures, prices and hence profit characteristics. It will be apparent, therefore, that the *mix* of products sold will have an impact on the overall profit outcome. For example, an enterprise may offer three product lines with budgeted characteristics relating to the next operating period, as given in Figure 18.11.

Each product line has a different contribution per unit, so the total contribution from all lines is dependent upon the particular mix of sales across all product lines. If

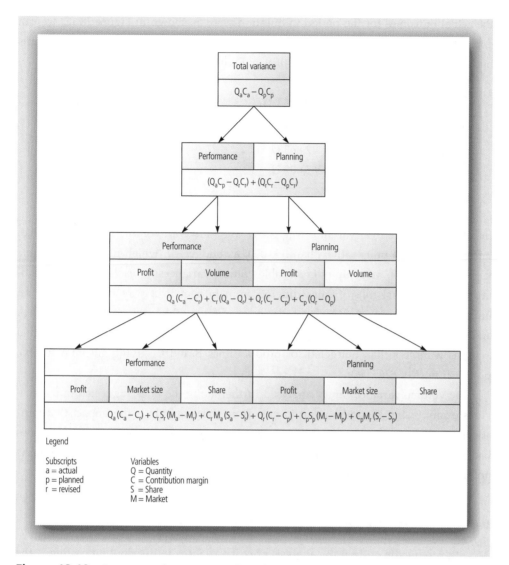

Figure 18.10 *Ex post* performance analysis (adapted from Hulbert and Toy, 1977)

	Product A	Product B	Product C	Total
Budget sales (units)	100,000	200,000	50,000	
Budgeted unit selling price	£12.00	£10.00	£20.00	
Budgeted unit variable cost	£6.00	£4.50	£8.00	
Budgeted unit contribution	£6.00	£5.50	£12.00	
Budgeted contribution	50%	55%	60%	
Budgeted contribution	£600,000	£1,100,000	£600,000	£2,300,000

Figure 18.11 Budgeted operating results by product line

the actual outcomes for the period in question were as shown in Figure 18.12, we can explain the total variance of £275 000 U (i.e. actual profit contribution £2 025 000 minus budgeted profit contribution £2 300 000) as in Figure 18.13.

In summary we have:

	£
Volume variance	32,863 F
Mix variance	42,863 U
Profit variance	265,000 U
Total variance	£275,000 U

In other words, the total variance was partly due to overall volume being higher than budgeted (355 000 units rather than 350 000, as budgeted), which gives a favourable variance of £32 863, made up of favourable volume variances for each individual product line. The actual mix of sales differed from budget in a way that produced an unfavourable variance of £42 863, made up of unfavourable variances for Products A and C, which were partly offset by a favourable variance for product line B. The actual margins were less than budgeted for product lines B and C, giving an unfavourable profit variance of £265 000.

The volume variance can be analysed further along the lines suggested in the previous example, but the main point to note from this example is the impact that variations in the mix of products sold can have on the profit outcome. If all product lines had the same percentage margin there would be no mix variance, but this situation is not normal, so we need to be aware of the impact of mix changes.

Variance analysis for distribution cost control

As with production costing the analysis of cost variances in distribution costing is the first step towards the goal of identifying the factors that caused the difference between the standard and actual costs so that any inefficiencies can be eliminated. To do this, each enterprise will have to decide what specific variance analyses it may want to use. Often, companies only compute a net variance for their distribution costs and do not

	Product A	Product B	Product C	Total
Actual sales (units)	90,000	220,000	45,000	
Actual unit selling price	£12.00	£9.00	£20.00	
Actual unit variable cost	£6.00	£4.50	£9.00	
Actual unit contribution	£6.00	£4.50	£11.00	
Actual contribution	50%	50%	55%	
Actual contribution	£540,000	£990,000	£495,000	£2,025,000

Figure 18.12 Actual operating results by product line

Product	Budgeted volume at budgeted margin for budgeted mix		Volume variance	Actual volume at budgeted margin for budgeted mix*		Mix variance	Actual volume at budgeted margin for actual mix		Profit variance	Actual volume at actual margin for actual mix	
		£	£		£	£		£	£		£
A	100,000 × £6.00 =	600,000	8,580 F	101,430 × £6.00 =	608,580	68,580 U	90,000 × £6.00 =	540,000	0	90,000 × £6.00 =	540,000
B	200,000 × £5.50 =	1,100,000	15,703 F	202,855 × £5.50 =	1,115,703	94,297 F	220,000 × £5.50 =	1,210,000	220,000 U	220,000 × £4.50 =	990,000
C	50,000 × £12.00 =	600,000	8,580 F	50,715 × £12.00 =	608,580	68,580 U	45,000 × £12.00 =	540,000	45,000 U	45,000 × £11.00 =	495,000
Total		£2,300,000	£32,863 F		£2,332,863	£42,863 U		£2,290,000	£265,000 U		£2,025,000

*The budgeted mix was 100,000/(100,000 + 200,000 + 50,000) = 100,000/350,000 = 28.57% for Product A, and so on. Applying this proportion to actual sales units gives 0.2857 (90,000 + 220,000 + 45,000) = 101,430 for Product A, and so on for B and C.

Figure 18.13 Marketing variances – 3

attempt to break the variance down into causal factors. This practice is not to be encouraged, however, since it tends to hide inefficiencies. If the analysis is to be meaningful the variance must be further explained in terms of price and efficiency components. Such price and quantity or efficiency variances can be computed for distribution activities. The price variance is given by:

(standard price − actual price) × actual work units

and the quantity (or efficiency) variance is given by:

(budgeted work units − actual work units) × standard price.

A variance reporting example

The distribution costs of the Hill Company are analysed by territories: data for the southern territory is shown in Figure 18.14. The warehousing and handling function's standards are:

	Total standard for direct and indirect costs (£)
Variable costs:	
Receiving	21 per shipment
Pricing, tagging and marking	6 per unit handled
Sorting	5 per order
Handling returns	10 per return
Taking physical inventory	0.50 per unit warehouse unit
Clerical handling of shipping orders	2 per item
Fixed costs:	
Rent	600 per month per territory
Depreciation	450 per month per territory

The following units of variability were budgeted and recorded for the month of January 1998:

	Budgeted	Actual
Shipments	400	420
Units handled	200	223
Orders	110	108
Returns	70	71
Warehouse unit	1,600	1,630
Item	750	780

The southern territory's actual direct costs for the month of January 1998 were as follows:

Receiving	£6,400
Pricing, tagging and marking	1,115
Sorting	565

HILL COMPANY – SOUTHERN TERRITORY
Expense variance report – warehousing and handling
January 1998

	Units of variability	(1) Actual cost (actual @ actual price)	(2) Actual units @ standard price	(3) Budgeted costs (budgeted units @ standard price)	(2 – 1) Price variance	(3 – 2) Efficiency variance	(3 – 1) Net variance
Detailed function:							
Receiving:	Shipment						
direct costs		£6,400					
indirect costs	$\frac{420}{500} \times £2,500$	2,100					
Total		£8,500	£8,820 (420 × £21)	£8,400 (400 × £21)	£320 F	£420 U	£100 U
Pricing, tagging and marking:	Unit handled						
direct costs		1,115	1,338 (223 × £6)	1,200 (200 × £6)	223 F	138 U	85 F
Sorting: direct costs	Order	565	540 (108 × £5)	550 (110 × £5)	25 U	10 F	15 U
Handling returns:	Return						
direct costs		680	710 (71 × £10)	700 (70 × £10)	30 F	10 U	20 F
Taking physical inventory	Warehouse unit	880	815 (1,630 × £0.50)	800 (1,600 × £0.50)	65 U	15 U	80 U
Clerical handling of shipping orders:	Item						
direct costs		£ 500					
indirect costs	$\frac{780}{900} \times £1,223$	1,060					
Total		£1,560	1,560 (780 × £2)	1,500 (750 × £2)	0	60 U	60 U
Total variable expense		£13,300		£13,150	£483 F	£633 U	£150 U
Fixed expense:							
rent		650		600			50 U
depreciation		445		450			5 F
Total warehousing and handling		£14,395		£14,200			£195 U

F = favourable; U = unfavourable

Figure 18.14 Distribution cost variances

Handling returns	680
Taking physical inventory	880
Clerical handling of shipping orders	500
Rent	650
Depreciation	445

The company allocates the following actual indirect costs to its southern and northern territories:

| Receiving (allocated on actual shipments: southern 420, northern 80) | £2,500 |
| Clerical handling of shipping orders (allocated on actual items: southern 780, northern 120) | 1,223 |

➡ *Efficiency variance.* Shipments received is the unit of variability chosen for the receiving function. There were a total of 420 shipments made, while only 400 shipments were budgeted. This results in an unfavourable efficiency variance because actual shipments exceeded those budgeted. (It should be noted here that care must be used in analysing distribution cost variances, because it is easy to misinterpret the results associated with such costs. Each cost variance is considered favourable or unfavourable as far as that individual detailed function is concerned, not for its effect on the overall company.) The efficiency variance in this case is unfavourable because twenty more shipments were made than planned. Hence, orders of larger quantities should be encouraged to save costs in receiving.

➡ *Price variance.* The actual cost of £20.238 (i.e. £8500 total actual cost of receiving as shown in Figure 18.14 ÷ 420 actual units) for each shipment received is less than the standard price of £21.00, which results in a favourable price variance. This difference in price is multiplied by the actual shipments to give a total favourable price variance of £320. It is not necessary to compute the actual cost per unit using the format illustrated in Figure 18.14, since the price variance can be determined by comparing total actual cost to the actual units at standard price shown in column 2.

Efficiency and price variance are computed for variable costs only. Only a net variance is computed for the two fixed expenses shown in Figure 18.14. This measures the difference between budgeted costs (budgeted units at standard price) and actual costs (actual units at actual price).

Other models

A useful model for assessing product line performance has been proposed (and tested) by Diamantopoulos and Mathews (1990). The model is based on the need to evaluate product performance in a multi-product setting using readily available product information and widely used performance indicators in a systematic way. Not least, it was deemed essential that the model be clearly understood by its intended users (product managers), otherwise, from an implementation point of view, it would not have been worthwhile. Figure 18.15 shows the model.

Gross profit is used as the primary performance indicator since this measure is easily provided without additional analysis. If the gross profit being generated is below par this may be due to:

➡ Insufficient sales volume
➡ High unit cost
➡ Prices that are too low.

Investigation should reveal which of these possible causes applies. If the *unit* gross profit is satisfactory, for example, but the product line's *overall* gross profit is unsatisfactory, the remedy may be to increase volume by revising the marketing mix in a suitable way. There may be products having unsatisfactory gross margins that are not amenable to corrective action. In this case their continued role in the range needs to be questioned.

Areas in which the model is particularly useful are:

1 Pricing (especially the effectiveness of existing pricing policies in terms of profit and volume results)
2 New product introductions (by using previous introductions to set realistic benchmark expectations for new products)
3 Product deletions (using warning signals as the stimulus to further investigations).

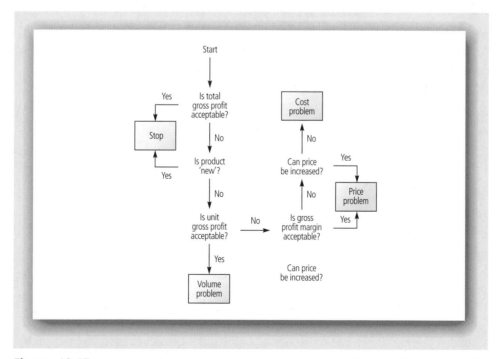

Figure 18.15 A model for product performance analysis (source: Diamantopoulos and Mathews, 1990, p. 9)

Despite the need to specify target values for each element of the model (i.e. total gross profit, unit gross profit, newness of product, gross profit margin, and price), this does not take away the importance of managerial judgement in arriving at an overall assessment of each product's performance. Indeed, judgement is needed in specifying the quantified target values themselves, as well as in interpreting any given product's standing relative to those targets. When a particular product's performance is considered satisfactory it is not self-evident that it should be ignored: in order to ensure *sustained* satisfactory performance, it may be necessary to take action in anticipation of future environmental changes (i.e. feedforward control).

A variation on the product line model that deals with sales deviations from plan is shown in Figure 18.16. This protocol follows a series of logical steps. Having identified a variance that is deemed to be significant (i.e. is unlikely to have arisen by chance), the question is raised as to whether this may be due to controllable or uncontrollable factors. ('Uncontrollable' is used here in the sense of being beyond the influence of managers in the given enterprise, or beyond the forecasting ability of relevant personnel, which might cover changing market conditions leading to a decline in industry sales, or unanticipated competitive actions.)

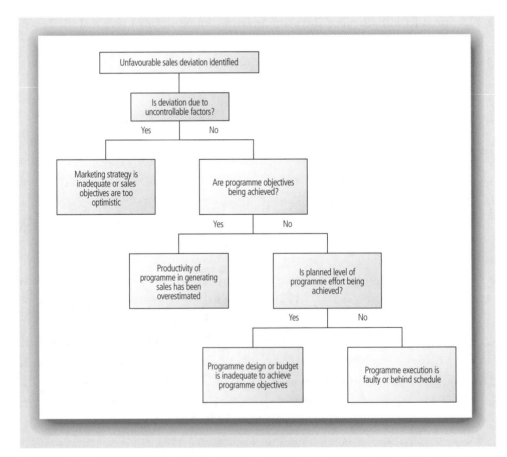

Figure 18.16 Analysing sales deviations (source: Guiltinan and Paul, 1988, p. 399)

If the explanation for the variance is not found at this first stage, the next stage raises the question of the performance of marketing programmes. This can be addressed at two levels:

1 The degree to which programme objectives are being achieved
2 The degree to which planned programme effort is being achieved.

If the degree of effort (as represented by actual sales levels, or advertising coverage) is not as planned, it is unlikely that either programme objectives or sales objectives are being achieved. On the other hand, if the planned input of effort is being achieved but programme objectives (such as brand awareness levels or the number of new accounts) are not, it is probable that either the budget is inadequate or the design of the programme (e.g. sales appeal, pricing level, advertising copy) is ineffective.

It may be found that the sales variance is not attributable to faulty programmes or lack of effort, but is due to the sales productivity of the programme being overstimulated or the implementation of the programme being behind schedule.

In so far as sales variances reflect revenue generation, there is a corresponding need to examine the variances among the costs incurred and budget figures to secure control over the profit consequences of sales activities.

The variance investigation decision

A major inhibiting factor in seeking to control via feedforward systems is our limited ability to make reliable estimates of the outcomes of future events. (This reflects our modest understanding of causal relationships both within the subsystems of the enterprise and between the enterprise and its environment.) All planning is based on estimates (e.g. of prices, costs, volumes) and actual outcomes will rarely be precisely in line with these estimates – some variation is inevitable. Should we expect a manager to investigate every variance that might be reported when we know that some deviation between actual outcomes and budgeted outcomes is bound to occur? On the other hand, if no variances are investigated the control potential of this form of managerial control system is being ignored. An appropriate course of action lies somewhere between these two extremes.

Causes of variances (or 'deviations') can be categorized in the following broad way (after Demski, 1980), with particular variances often being due to one or more deviations:

1 Implementation deviation results from a human or mechanical failure to achieve an attainable outcome, e.g. if the mileage rate payable to employees using their own vehicles for business trips is 35p per mile, but due to clerical error this is being paid at only 25p per mile, the required corrective action is easy to specify. The cost of correction will be exceeded by the benefits.
2 Prediction deviation results from errors in specifying the parameter values in a decision model, e.g. in determining overhead absorption rates *ex ante* predictions must be

made of, inter alia, the future level of activity. If the predictions are wrong, then the overhead absorption rate will be wrong and variances will result.

3 Measurement deviation arises as a result of error in measuring the actual outcome – such as incorrectly adding up the number of calls made in Region X, or the number of units sold of Product P.

4 Model deviation arises as a result of an erroneous formulation in a decision model. For example, in formulating a linear programme the constraints relating to the availability of input factors may be incorrectly specified.

5 Random deviations due to chance fluctuations of a parameter for which no cause can be assigned. These deviations do not call for corrective action, but in order to identify the causes of variances it is helpful to separate random deviations from deviations 1–4 above, in order that the significance of the latter might be established.

While these five categories of deviation appear to be mutually exclusive, their interdependencies should not be underestimated. The traditional view is to assume that variances are due to implementation deviations, but this is patently simplistic. It is also potentially inequitable, since it may deem individual managers to be responsible for variances that arise from reasons beyond their control (such as deviations 3 and 5 above).

In setting up benchmarks (e.g. budget targets or standard costs) it is important to recognize that a range of possible outcomes in the vicinity of the benchmark will usually be acceptable. In other words, random variations around the benchmark are to be expected, and searching for causes of variances within the acceptable range of outcomes will incur costs without generating benefits. Only when variances fall outside the acceptable range will further investigation be desirable.

This prompts the operational question of how one actually determines whether a variance should be investigated. As Figure 18.17 suggests, if it was known in advance that a variance arose on a random basis it would not be necessary to investigate it, since

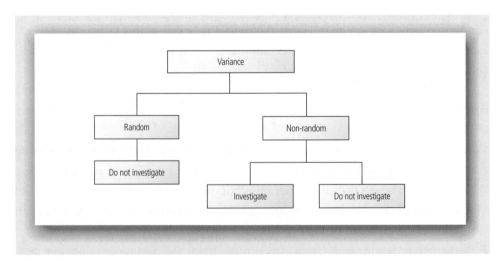

Figure 18.17 The variance investigation decision

there will be no assignable cause. On the other hand, if a variance is of a non-random nature it would not pay to ignore it if it was significant.

How can significance be determined? This boils down to a statistical question, and the technique that is of proven help is that developed for use in quality control situations, to which we will turn very shortly.

A more conventional approach to evaluating the significance of variances is either to:

1 Look at the absolute size of the variance (i.e. actual − standard) such that all variances greater than, say, £1000 are investigated, or
2 Compute the proportionate size of the variance (i.e. variance/standard) and investigate all those exceeding, say, 10 per cent.

Both alternatives 1 and 2 must depend upon the manager's intuition or some arbitrary decision rule when it comes to deciding whether or not to investigate a given variance.

The advantages of options 1 and 2 above are their simplicity and ease of implementation, but both fail to deal adequately with the issues of significance (in statistical terms) and balancing the costs and benefits of investigation. We can resolve these issues with the help of the approach adopted in *statistical quality control*.

Statistical quality control (SQC) is based upon the established fact that the observed quality of an item is always subject to chance variability. Some variability in the observed quality of an item will be due to assignable causes that exist beyond the boundaries due to chance cause. (Assignable causes are, by definition, identifiable and steps can be taken to remove them.) The major task of SQC is to distinguish between assignable and chance causes of error in order that the assignable causes may be identified, their causes discovered and eliminated, and acceptable quality standards maintained.

These basic principles of SQC can be applied in areas other than production. An example of a control chart for monitoring advertising expenditure as a percentage of sales is given in Figure 18.18.

The standard of performance that is expected is that advertising expense will be 8 per cent of sales revenue, but random causes (i.e. chance) can make this figure vary from 6 to 10 per cent of sales revenue. If the range of 6–10 per cent represents three standard deviations on either side of a mean of 8 per cent (i.e. $\overline{x} = 8$, with confidence limits of $\pm 3\theta$), then observations would be expected to fall within this range in 998 out of 1000 cases.

However, when an observation falls outside these limits, two opposing hypotheses can be put forward to explain the situation:

1 The observation is the freak one out of 1000 that exceeds the control limits by pure chance, and the company still has the situation under control
2 The company has lost control over the situation due to some assignable cause, such as a new competitor entering the market.

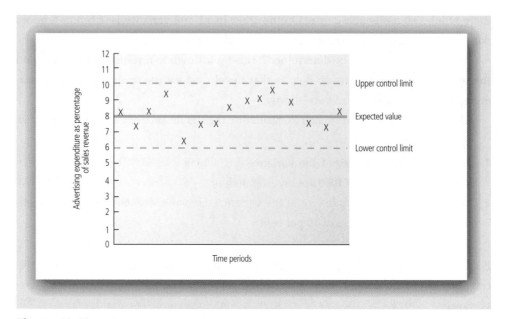

Figure 18.18 Advertising control chart

If hypothesis 1 is accepted, it is unnecessary to investigate – with the risk that something has actually happened to cause the situation to fall out of control. On the other hand, if hypothesis 2 is accepted and investigations are begun into assignable causes, there is always the risk – albeit very small – of the first hypothesis being correct and hence investigation being unecessary.

Investigations to identify the causes of variances – even when the latter are deemed to be significant – involve costs, so we must again reflect on the cost-benefit issue: if the likely penalty from *not* identifying and correcting the cause of the variance is less than the likely cost of the investigation, it hardly seems worth the trouble.

Consider a hypothetical case in which the cost of investigating a reported variance is estimated at £200, while the penalty for not identifying a correctable cause is likely to be £600 (which could be the value of cost savings – or extra profit – that will arise once the cause of the variance is removed). If an investigation is undertaken and no cause is discovered, the enterprise will be £200 worse off, whereas it will be £400 better off (i.e. £600 − £200) if a cause is ascertained and corrected.

18.4 Taking corrective action

Having implemented plans, monitored performance and analysed significant variances, the next step is to decide on the corrective action that is needed. In this section we will concentrate on responding to environmental changes – especially those of a competitive nature.

How should an enterprise respond to environmental changes? There are many ways, and Barrett (1986) has pointed out two opposing possibilities. On the one hand, there is the *deterministic approach*, in which it is felt that the enterprise's environment determines its actions, hence strategies and even its structure. This takes the idea of adaptation to environmental change to an extreme: changes in the environment – whether in the form of opportunities or threats – will result in changes in competitive strategy and the implementation of these changes may well bring about changes in organizational structure.

In contrast there is the *strategic approach*, in which the environment is seen as constraining the enterprise's freedom of action rather than determining it. This concentrates more on the enterprise's strengths (and weaknesses) and its ability to influence its environment rather than simply being influenced by it. One example is the strategy of raising barriers to entry, which modifies the environment against the interests of potential competitors.

Marketing intelligence has a role to play in both these approaches by identifying environmental change as a basis for reactive or proactive responses. The response process is reflected in the model portrayed in Figure 18.19.

Various response stages are highlighted, with any given one being triggered when the intelligence signals pass thresholds. Thus, for example, a strong signal indicating a significant change in the environment will cross a number of thresholds and activate an appropriate high-level response. Weaker signals will cross fewer thresholds and hence prompt lower-level responses. Barrett sets his model within a framework of power relationships – especially those involved in the allocation of resources via the budgeting process. This leads to the building in of 'slack' (i.e. a greater amount of resource than is strictly needed to carry out a given task) in certain parts of the enterprise in accordance with the distribution of power. Figure 18.20 indicates in some detail the links between stages in the response process and thresholds. The sequence of stages presumes that each subsequent stage consumes more slack resources than prior stages, thereby reducing the power given from the existence of slack resources.

How should an enterprise respond to environmental changes that manifest themselves either through the gathering of environmental data (e.g. by means of a competitor intelligence system (see Cvitkovic, 1989), or environmental scanning (see Sanderson and Luffman, 1988)) or via variance analysis? Help is available from the technique of *competitor profiling*. The steps in this technique, developed by SRI International, are:

1 Identify the industry's four key competitive strengths. Figure 18.21 shows one set of possibilities applicable to a manufacturing situation. It is implicitly assumed that both current and future success in the industry is a function of a competitor's ability to:
- ➡ Meet customers' needs and communicate products' attributes
- ➡ Understand and control relevant technology
- ➡ Make superior products in a cost-effective way
- ➡ Manage the coordination of human, financial and technological resources.

2 Select a single specific measure of success for each of the four key competitive strengths identified in step 1 above. See Figure 18.22 for some proposals: sales level, investment in R&D, capacity utilization and ROI are suggested for marketing, technology, manufacturing and management respectively.

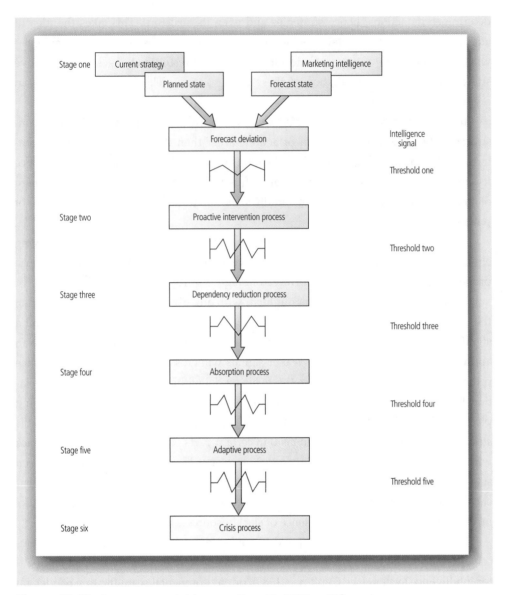

Figure 18.19 Response model (source: Barrett, 1986, p. 37)

3 Define linkages between adjacent pairs of competitive strengths to demonstrate their interdependence. In Figure 18.23, price has been used to link marketing and technology; quality to link technology and manufacturing; integration to link manufacturing and management; and growth to link management and marketing.

4 Determine average performance scores for the measures specified in step 2 and the linkages defined in step 3. This has the effect of setting up an 'average competitor' to use as a yardstick in assessing competitors' relative positions. In Figure 18.24, average performance for the industry is shown as a circle. Above-average performance for any competitor would be plotted outside the circle and below-average performance on any aspect would be plotted inside the circle. Scoring can be done by using a scale of 1 (= excellent) to 5 (= inadequate) to assess a competitor's standing on each

Stage one
The first stage of the model suggests that the organizational plan, or budget, is based on a forecasted state of the market environment. Market intelligence provides a constantly updated forecast of the environment in which the organization operates. Differences between the original planned state of the environment on which the organization is acting, and the revised forecasted state provided by the intelligence function, gives a 'forecast deviation'.

Stage two: the proactive intervention process
If the market intelligence report indicates that the budget allowance will be exceeded, the second stage of the model is entered. In this stage the market executives may be motivated to act to prevent the forecast deviation. This proactive intervention is an attempt to engineer the market into an acceptable state. In its simplest form it may merely necessitate a minor market push. This proactive intervention in the market will, however, consume at least some of the slack resources available to the marketing executive. Successful proactive intervention may, however, require resources in excess of the slack available. In this case the intelligence report will be used to support a plea for additional marketing resources, e.g. to undertake an unabridged campaign to protect a product's position against the anticipated attack of a competitor.

Stage three: the dependency reduction process
This process is an attempt by the organization to reduce its dependency on the market in question and so reduces the significance to the organization of the perceived market adversity. This decoupling may be achieved in a number of ways – diversification, the switching of resources, adapting plant previously devoted to the market to service other markets, and so on. Dependency reduction may, however, require a long lead time and for this reason organizations are likely to engage in diversification as a policy rather than awaiting detailed intelligence reports. However, market signals which cross threshold two are likely to spur this activity. The dependency reduction process, e.g. diversification, requires the use of slack resources.

Stage four: the absorption process
This process is an attempt by the organization to sit out the market change, or at least that proportion of the change which has not been dampened by proactive intervention or dependency reduction processes. Such an absorption process consumes the stock of slack resources available to the organization. 'Belt tightening' and 'shedding' indicate the extent of the rundown of slack. All members of the organizational coalition are likely to be affected if the absorption process continues for any extended period.

Stage five: the adaptive process
In the adaptive process the organization seeks to realign its strategy and/or structure to the perceived changed environment in which it operates. It engages the organization in a 'change mode' and requires the ability by the organizational executives to adapt or react to the forecast market change. Their ability to do so is dependent on the slack resources available and the ease with which such resources can be marshalled to implement strategy/structure changes.

Stage six: the crisis process
In this, the final process, the organization is dependent on a market which is changing. It has insufficient slack to absorb the change, and both proactive intervention and adaptive response are perceived to be ineffective. Such organizations now face the possibility of being 'selected out' by the market change. The perception that such is the case is likely to induce organizational crisis leading to trauma and the termination of the organization at least in the form in which it existed prior to the onset of the market change.

Threshold one
In setting market budgets, marketing executives may build in slack, most of which will usually be cut back in the budget setting process. It is possible that not all the slack will be removed and the marketing revenue budget will be artificially high. Unless market intelligence indicates that this budget allowance is likely to be exceeded no action will be taken on the basis of the market intelligence report. The market signal will not then cross the first threshold.

Threshold two
Should the power elite within the organization be unwilling or unable to make available sufficient resources to allow successfully proactive intervention, the second threshold is crossed and the third stage of the model is entered.

Threshold three
If the organization cannot, or chooses not to, utilize its slack resources in proactive market intervention, or in dependency reduction, the market signal indicating market change will pass over the third information threshold and the fourth stage of the model is entered.

Threshold four
For organizations which do not have sufficient slack to endure the forecast market change, the intelligence signal traverses the fourth threshold and stage five of the model is entered.

Threshold five
Should the organization be unable or unwilling to adapt to the change signalled by the market intelligence report and if the lower order processes cannot effectively be engaged, the intelligence signal will cross the fifth threshold and the sixth stage is entered.

Figure 18.20   Signal thresholds and response stages (source: Barrett, 1986, p. 38)

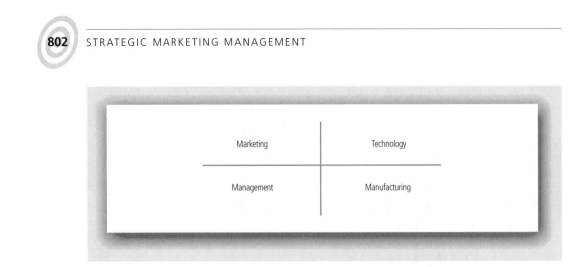

Figure 18.21 Key competitive strengths (source: Cvitkovic, 1989, p. 28)

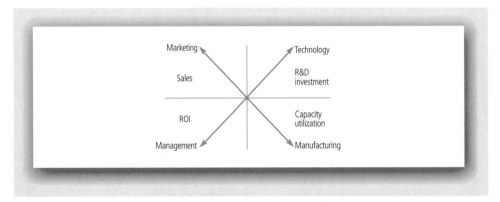

Figure 18.22 Measures of success (adapted from Cvitkovic, 1989, p. 28)

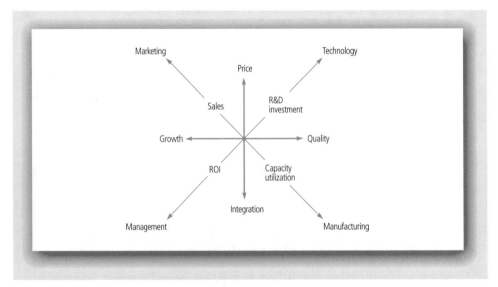

Figure 18.23 Linkages between competitive strengths (adapted from Cvitkovic, 1989, p. 29)

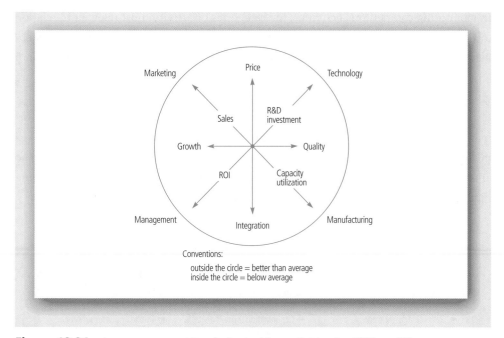

Figure 18.24   Average competitor (adapted from Cvitkovic, 1989, p. 29)

dimension shown in Figure 18.23 and then plotting these scores and joining them up (as shown in Figure 18.25).

5 Generate competitors' profiles in order to identify relative strengths and weaknesses as a basis for taking action. The strengths and weaknesses are shown (as in Figure 18.25) relative to the 'average competitor'.

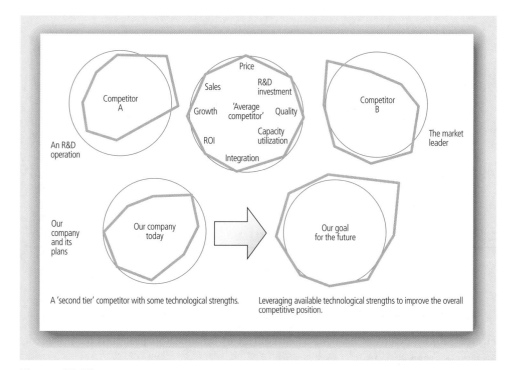

Figure 18.25   Competitive profiles (adapted from Cvitkovic, 1989, p. 30)

In monitoring competitors' activities, the categories of activity most relevant in relation to the strategic needs of the user must be determined. Once the categories are established, frequency of monitoring must be set. Prescott and Smith (1989) reported on a study they undertook in the USA to identify categories and frequencies. Details are given in Figure 18.26.

A further aspect of the study was the extent to which different categories of information were subjected to analysis (see Figure 18.27). Three levels of analysis were used in the questionnaire sent out by Prescott and Smith – extensive, basic and little/no analysis – with the extent to which implications were drawn from the analysis being limited to the first two levels.

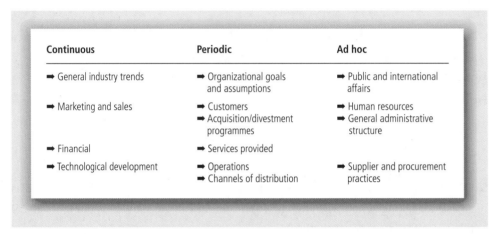

Figure 18.26 Competitive information categories and their frequency of monitoring (adapted from Prescott and Smith, 1989, p. 10)

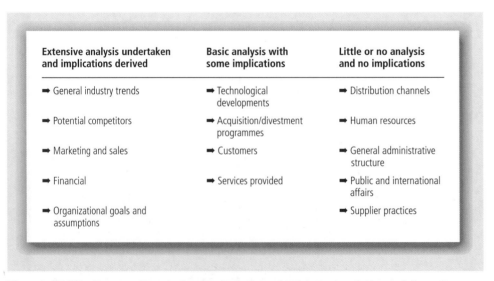

Figure 18.27 Extent of analysis of categories of information (adapted from Prescott and Smith, 1989, p. 11)

Competitor cost analysis methods have been proposed by a number of authors (e.g. Brock, 1984; Pyne, 1985; Beerel, 1986; Jones, 1988; and most notably Porter, 1980, 1985). Brock (1984, p. 226) has related his discussion to the *strategic triangle* (Ohmae, 1983). See Figure 18.28.

The focal points of the triangle were initially customers, competitors and the company in question, but Brock has emphasized the cost differences between one's own company and competitors as a potential source of competitive advantage. Cost differentials stem from the asset bases of competing companies coupled with the way in which assets are utilized. The importance of being cost-effective is evident when one considers the need to deliver value to customers at prices that are competitive while generating an adequate rate of reward to shareholders. As an example, let us take a comparison between an integrated steelmaker (Maxi) and a small competitor (Mini), with the latter using scrap steel and electric furnace technology. A detailed examination of annual reports, public statements of Mini's chief executive (who was a promoter of the mini-mill within the industry) and general trade literature gave sufficient information to allow the comparative profile shown in Figure 18.29 to be compiled.

It is evident that Mini's manufacturing costs are only 59 per cent of those relating to Maxi per ton of hot rolled steel ready for finishing. With a price set at £425 (as opposed to Maxi's £500), Mini not only has a clear price advantage of £75 per ton, but also a gross margin advantage of £175 versus £70, which will allow for even more aggressive pricing. Maxi can see from this type of analysis that its position is being eroded, and appropriate decisions need to be made to avoid a forced decline.

Without this type of information Maxi would not be able to see how the strong strategic position it has held hitherto is being undermined by Mini. Detailed guidance on carrying out this type of cost analysis can be found in Jones (1988).

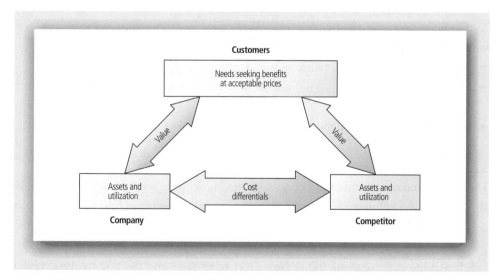

Figure 18.28   The strategic triangle (source: Brock, 1984, p. 226)

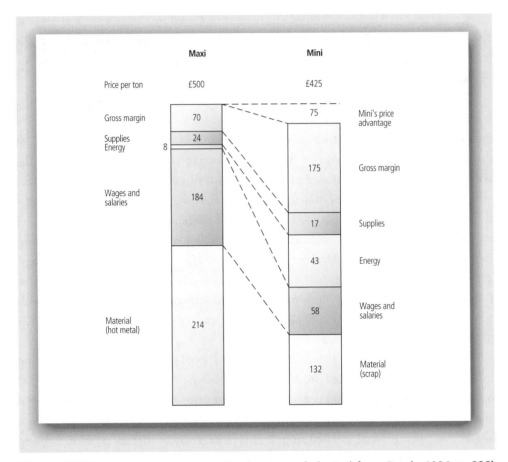

Figure 18.29 Cost advantages and disadvantages (adapted from Brock, 1984, p. 228)

Benchmarking

This is an analytical process through which an enterprise's performance can be compared with that of its competitors. It is used by organizations such as Xerox and Ford in order to:

➡ Identify key performance measures for each business function
➡ Measure one's own performance as well as that of competitors
➡ Identify areas of competitive advantage (and disadvantage) by comparing performance levels
➡ Design and implement plans to improve one's own performance on key issues relative to competitors.

Furey (1987) offers a number of US case studies showing benchmarking in use. One of these concerns a company (Company Y) that is a major vendor of telecommunications equipment in which the senior management was curious about the cost and productivity of its sales force. The comparisons shown in Figure 18.30 were developed through a benchmarking exercise using the largest direct competitor and the best-in-class vendor of data processing equipment.

	Company Y	Direct competitor	Best-in-class competitor
Cost benchmarks			
Average total sales rep. compensation	$38,000	$44,000	$55,000
% compensation earned from commission	10%	15%	30%
Revenue per sales rep.	$835,000	$900,000	$1,200,000
Compensation as % of revenue	4.6%	4.9%	4.6%
Performance benchmarks			
Average number of calls per week per rep.	16–18	13–16	20+
Revenue quotas	Yes	Yes	No
New account quotas	Informal	No	Yes

Figure 18.30 Sales force benchmarking (adapted from Furey, 1987)

The cost of sales representatives (as a percentage of revenues) was found to be very competitive in Company Y (at 4.6 per cent), but the low commission paid by the company relative to that paid by its main competitors was matched by low productivity (in terms of revenue generated). Moreover, the direct competitor's sales force was generating more revenue with fewer calls in the absence of new account quotas than was the case in Company Y. The best-in-class competitor was paying a high rate of commission to its sales force and aggressively pursuing new customers via numerous sales calls and quotas for new accounts.

Company Y's response to this situation was to restructure the sales team's compensation and split the team into two. By raising the rate of commission substantially, and by having one part of the sales force dealing with existing accounts and the other part dealing with new accounts, Company Y's relative market share improved within six months.

Benchmarking is applicable in other functional areas and has the potential, when properly communicated throughout the enterprise, to help change the corporate culture. In the case of benchmarking products or services offered by customers but not by itself, an enterprise's senior managers can gain insights to guide its decisions: by keeping abreast of new developments in this way, it will be easier to assess how to respond (see, for example, Schmid, 1987; Fifer, 1989).

In considering how to take corrective action, it is important to make some assessment of the probable response of competitors to any action that might be taken. This is a vital aspect of strategic behaviour. It is assumed that the identities of the enterprise's competitors – both actual and potential – are known, although this should not be taken for granted. Once the competitors' identities are known, they can be profiled (see Chapter 6) and possible responses can be explored, taking into account conjectures regarding the beliefs that competitors have of one's own enterprise (including its resources, capabilities and strategies).

Let us look further at this, drawing on the approach of Amit et al. (1988). In a simple situation involving an Enterprise X and its sole competitor, Y, there are four possible price policies available. In Figure 18.31, these possibilities for X are shown as the headings for the rows; the column headings show competitor Y's likely reactions. The figures in the cells represent the changes in X's profits that are expected to result from the various interactive outcomes contained in the matrix. Thus, if X reduces its price by 10 per cent and Y responds by reducing its price by 20 per cent, then X's profits will fall by 25 per cent. If the data in the figure is valid, the optimal course of action for X will depend on the likelihood of Y responding in a particular way. For example, if it is felt to be most likely that Y will react to a price reduction on the part of X by reducing price by half as much as X, then the optimal choice for X is to reduce its price by 10 per cent, giving an increase in profits of 15 per cent. It will be apparent that additional information is needed on Y's likely reaction. This can be provided via *conjectural variations*, which are beliefs about competitors' views of one's own enterprise and of their likely reactions to actions taken by one's own enterprise.

In order to gauge a competitor's likely reactions, it is necessary to have information on:

➡ The structural characteristics of the industry and the technical ability plus desire of competitors to respond

➡ Competitors' conjecture about one's own behaviour.

Figure 18.32 illustrates a hypothetical situation involving different conjectural possibilities relating to a price reduction of 10 per cent. The derivation of conjectural variations is explored in detail elsewhere (see Amit et al., 1988), but we need to note here that it ranges from zero (when the competitor believes that the enterprise in question will not respond to changes in the competitor's strategy) to unity (when the competitor expects the enterprise in question to match any changes in strategy on the part of the competitor).

From Figure 18.32 it can be seen that when the competitor's conjectural variation is near to unity it believes the enterprise in question will respond aggressively to a shift in pricing policy. The obvious consequence of this will be a price war if the competitor were to match a reduction in price. As a result of this belief, the competitor is unlikely to match the price reduction for fear of the consequences. The opposing situation (i.e. when the conjectural variation is near zero) is likely to have the opposite result.

Enterprise X's price policy (% change in price)	Competitor Y's reaction (% change in price)			
	0%	−5%	−10%	−20%
0%	0	−10	−15	−20
−5%	+7	−5	−12	−22
−10%	+30	+15	−8	−25
−20%	+12	+8	+5	−30

Figure 18.31   Reaction function (adapted from Amit et al., 1988, p. 432)

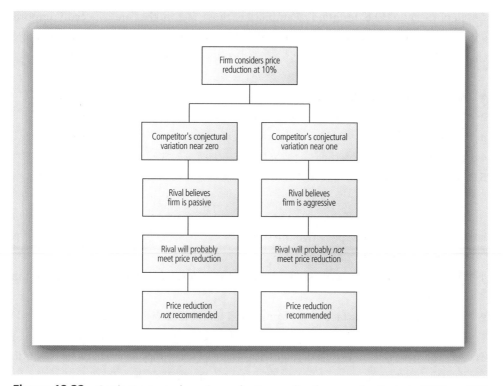

Figure 18.32 Conjectures and a price reduction policy (source: Amit et al., 1988, p. 433)

18.5 Management reports

An effective management reporting system is one that uses the available information flows to control the company's activities in accordance with objectives and plans. The process of controlling business operations depends in no small part on the devising, compiling and constant revising of an adequate and up-to-date system of reports. This should result in better decision-making, faster action, greater management flexibility and vastly improved coordination.

The controller must be aware of the types of decisions made at each managerial level, and the related information needs, if the best reports are to be compiled at the appropriate frequencies. In developing reports, the controller must assess their ultimate utility to their recipients, which requires that they be designed specifically for the individuals who are to receive them, with due consideration being given to the conditions that govern the business and the way in which it is managed. Reports should supply information that is considered important, and this should be arranged and analysed in such a way that it is most convenient and immediately useful to those who must make decisions on the basis of it. To achieve the aim of successfully communicating the essential facts about the business to those who manage it, controllers must have a clear idea of the purposes, possibilities and limitations of the many different types of statement and report. They must, therefore, understand the problems and viewpoints of those who receive their reports and ensure that these people understand the true meaning and limitations of the information contained in those reports.

Reports should be designed to emphasize those factors that are especially important in determining success: the critical success factors. Such factors have the following characteristics:

1 They are important in explaining success or failure
2 They are volatile (i.e. they can change quickly)
3 Prompt action is needed when a significant change occurs
4 Change is not easy to predict
5 They can be measured.

In specifying what is to be reported at each level of management, especially at lower levels, the controller must pose two questions:

1 What are the necessary and controllable factors relevant to the level of authority in question?
2 In what form are these factors best presented to aid in decision-making at this level?

The level of management in question will determine whether reports are to relate results to long-range objectives expressed in aggregate terms, or whether they should relate results to standard costs in great detail. The principles of control are the same for these extremes of top management and supervisory management, but the form of report is different.

The adoption of a structured approach to reporting, with results being reported by areas of responsibility, will enable top management to view the results and efficiencies of individual departments in the light of their contribution to overall performance and objectives. It may be, however, that the need for control action on the part of top management indicates a failure to achieve control at a more appropriate but lower level.

Similarly, a long delay between actual events and the reporting of these events via the top management control system may create the need for corrective action that is more drastic, more complex and involves more people than if such action had been initiated at a lower level of control more closely associated with the actual events.

Within the control framework the characteristics of good reports are that they should:

➡ Be oriented towards the users, taking into account both their level and their function
➡ Give as much information as possible in quantitative terms, and flow both ways in the organization (i.e. up and down)
➡ Be based on a flexible system that allows quick changes to meet new conditions
➡ Be oriented towards action rather than towards curiosity.

On a tangible plane succinctness is a great virtue in reporting, while on an intangible plane a major contribution made by an adequate reporting system is that the recipient of a report is made to pause and think over the contents of that report and its implications for the enterprise.

18.6 Summary

In this chapter we have built on the basic ideas of control and control systems that were introduced in Chapter 17, and looked in some detail at control methods that can be employed to advantage in a marketing context.

Audits are one such control method (discussed in detail in Chapter 2). This highlights the fact that there is not a watertight distinction between the use of marketing audits for *taking stock* (i.e. in addressing the question 'Where are we now?') and dealing with the *flow* issue of 'How might we ensure arrival?'

Budgeting, as the most widely used form of management control, with variants such as zero-base budgeting and output budgeting, was discussed, as was variance analysis, which is a diagnostic device to help explain why discrepancies between desired outcomes and actual outcomes have emerged. It was pointed out that the existence of a variance should not be taken as prima facie evidence that the budget level (or standard) is correct and the actual outcome is incorrect; it is often the case that the existence of a variance points to a poorly set budget target.

One straightforward refinement to a basic variance analysis approach enables a distinction to be made between *planning* variances on the one hand and *operating* variances on the other. The former are the primary responsibility of those engaged in making forecasts and setting targets, whereas the latter are the responsibility of those charged with implementing marketing plans. No matter how detailed the diagnosis of what went wrong and why, the crucial point is for this to be a prelude to action: diagnosis should be followed by prognosis. The chapter covered the importance of *responding* in a way that realigns strategic actions as a step towards achieving corporate missions.

Bibliography

Aaker, D.A. and Day, G.S. (1972), 'Corporate Response to Consumerism Pressures', *Harvard Business Review*, Vol. 50, No. 6, November–December, pp. 114–24.

Aaker, D.A. and Day, G.S. (eds) (1974), *Consumerism*, New York: Free Press, 2nd edition.

Abbott, L. (1955), *Quality and Competition*, New York: Columbia University Press.

Abell, D.F. (1980), *Defining the Business: The Starting Point of Strategic Planning*, Englewood Cliffs, NJ: Prentice-Hall.

Abell, D.F. and Hammond, J.S. (1979), *Strategic Market Planning: Problems and Analytical Approaches*, Englewood Cliffs, NJ: Prentice-Hall.

Abrahams, T. (1999), *The Mission Statement Book: 301 corporate mission statements from America's top companies*, Ten Speed Press, 2nd edition.

Abratt, R. (1986), 'Industrial Buying in High-Tech Markets', *Industrial Marketing Management*, Vol. 15, pp. 293–8.

Ackoff, R.L. (1970), *A Concept of Corporate Planning*, New York: Wiley.

Adler, L. (1960), 'Phasing Research into the Marketing Plan', *Harvard Business Review*, Vol. 38, No. 3, May–June, pp. 118–21.

Adler, L. (1967), 'Systems Approach to Marketing', *Harvard Business Review*, Vol. 45, No. 3, May–June, pp. 105–18.

Aguilar, F. (1967), *Scanning the Business Environment*, New York: Macmillan.

Albrecht, K. (1979), *Stress and the Manager*, Englewood Cliffs, NJ: Prentice-Hall.

Alexander, L. (1985), 'Successfully Implementing Strategic Decisions', *Long Range Planning*, Vol. 18, No. 3, pp. 91–7.

Alexander, R.S., Cross, J.S. and Cunningham, R.M. (1961), *Industrial Marketing*, Homewood, IL: Irwin.

Allen, P. (1989), *Selling: Management and Practice*, London: M & E Handbooks.

Ambler, P.J. (1996) 'Brand Performance and the Product Life Cycle', MBA dissertation, Sheffield Hallam University.

Ambler, T. (2003), *Marketing and the Bottom Line: The marketing metrics to pump up cash flow*, London: FT/Prentice-Hall, 2nd edition.

American Accounting Association (1972), 'Report of Committee on Cost and Profitability Analyses for Marketing', Supplement to *The Accounting Review*, Vol. 47, pp. 575–615.

American Management Association (1959), 'The Marketing Audit: Its Nature, Purposes and Problems', in *Analyzing and Improving Marketing Performance*, AMA Management Report No. 32, New York: AMA.

American Marketing Association (1957), 'The Values and Uses of Distribution Cost Analysis', *Journal of Marketing*, Vol. 21, No. 2, April, pp. 395–400.

Ames, B.C. (1968), 'Marketing Planning for Industrial Products', *Harvard Business Review*, Vol. 46, No. 5, September–October, pp. 100–11.

Ames, B.C. (1971), 'Dilemma of Product/Market Management', *Harvard Business Review*, Vol. 49, No. 2, March–April, pp. 66–74.

Ames, B.C. (1989) 'How to Devise a Winning Business Plan', *Journal of Business Strategy*, Vol. 10, No. 3, May–June, pp. 26–30.

Amit, R. (1986), 'Cost Leadership Strategy and Experience Curves', *Strategic Management Journal*, Vol. 7, No. 3, May–June, pp. 281–92.

Amit, R., Domowitz, I. and Fershtman, C. (1988), 'Thinking One Step Ahead: The Use of Conjectures in Competitor Analysis', *Strategic Management Journal*, Vol. 9, pp. 431–42.

Anandarajan, A. and Christopher, M.G. (1987), 'A Mission Approach to Customer Profitability Analysis', *International Journal of Physical Distribution and Materials Management*, Vol. 17, No. 7, pp. 55–68.

Andreasen, A.R. and Belk, R.W. (1980), 'Predictors of Attendance at the Performance Arts', *Journal of Consumer Research*, Vol. 7, No. 2, September, pp. 112–20.

Ansoff, H.I. (1957), 'Strategies for Diversification', *Harvard Business Review*, Vol. 25, No. 5, September–October, pp. 113–24.

Ansoff, H.I. (1968), *Corporate Strategy*, Harmondsworth: Penguin Books.

Ansoff, H.I. (1984) *Implementing Strategic Management*, Englewood Cliffs, NJ: Prentice-Hall.

Anthony, R.N. (1965), *Planning and Control Systems: A Framework for Analysis*, Cambridge, MA: Harvard University Press.

Anthony, R.N. (1988) *The Management Control Function*, Boston, MA: Harvard Business School Press.

Armitage, H.M. (1987), 'The Use of Management Accounting Techniques to Improve Productivity Analysis in Distribution Operations', *International Journal of Physical Distribution and Materials Management*, Vol. 17, No. 2, pp. 40–50.

Armstrong, J.S. (1982), 'The Value of Formal Planning for Strategic Decisions: Review of Empirical Research', *Strategic Management Journal*, Vol. 3, pp. 197–211.

Arthur Andersen (1997), *Differences and Similarities Between Western and Eastern Managers*, London: Arthur Andersen.

Ashridge Management College (1993), Industrial Buying and Issues of Loyalty.

Ashton, D.J., Hopper, T.M. and Scapens, R.W. (eds) (1995) *Issues in Management Accounting*, London: Prentice-Hall, 2nd edition.

Aspinal, L. (1962), 'The Characteristics of Goods Theory', in Lazer, W. and Kelly, E. (eds), *Managerial Marketing*, Homewood, IL: Irwin.

Assael, H. (1987), *Consumer Behavior and Marketing Action*, Boston, MA: Kent Publishing.

Atkin, B. and Skinner, R.N. (1975), *How British Industry Prices*, London: Industrial Market Research Association.

Atkinson, P.E. and Naden, J. (1989), 'Total Quality Management: Eight Lessons to Learn from Japan', *Management Services*, Vol. 33, No. 3, pp. 6–10.

Baker, K. (1982), quoted in Clark, E., 'Acorn Finds New Friends', *Marketing*, 16 December, p. 13.

Baker, M.J. (1985), *Marketing Strategy and Management*, London: Macmillan.

Baker, M.J. (1987), 'One more time – what is marketing?', in Baker, M.J. (ed.), *The Marketing Book*, London: Heinemann, pp. 3–9.

Bancroft, A.L. and Wilson, R.M.S. (1979), 'Management Accounting in Marketing', *Management Accounting* (CIMA), Vol. 57, No. 11, December, pp. 25–30.

Banks, S. (1964), *Experimentation in Marketing*, New York: McGraw-Hill.

Barclay, I. and Benson, M. (1990), 'Success in New Product Development: Lessons from the Past', *Leadership and Organisation Development Journal*, Vol. 11, No. 6, pp. 4–12.

Barksdale, H.C. and Harris, C.E. (1982), 'Portfolio analysis and the PLC', *Long Range Planning*, Vol. 15, No. 6, pp. 74–83.

Barnard, C.I. (1956), *The Functions of the Executive*, Cambridge, MA: Harvard University Press.

Barrett, T.F. (1980), 'Modular Data Base System', *International Journal of Physical Distribution and Materials Management*, Vol. 10, No. 4, pp. 135–46.

Barrett, T.F. (1986), 'When the Market Says "Beware!" . . .', *Management Decision*, Vol. 24, No. 6, pp. 36–40.

Barrett, T.F. (1987), 'A Surrogate Case Flow Model of Marketing Strategy', *Irish Marketing Review*, Vol. 2, pp. 117–25.

Bartels, R. (ed.) (1963), *Ethics in Business*, Columbia, OH: Bureau of Business Research, Ohio State University.

Bass, R.M.V. (1991), *Credit Management*, Cheltenham: Thornes, 3rd edition.

Bastable, C.W. and Bao, D.H. (1988), 'The Fiction of Sales-Mix and Sales-Quantity Variances', *Accounting Horizons*, Vol. 2, No. 2, June, pp. 10–17.

Baumol, W.J. and Sevin, C.H. (1957), 'Marketing Costs and Mathematical Programming', *Harvard Business Review*, Vol. 35, No. 5, September–October, pp. 52–60.

Beer, S. (1967), *Decision and Control*, New York: Wiley.

Beerel, A. (1986), 'Strategic Financial Control Can Provide Light and Guidance', *Accountancy*, Vol. 97, No. 1114, June, pp. 70–4.

Beishon, J. and Peters, G. (eds) (1972), *Systems Behaviour*, London: Harper & Row.

Bellis-Jones, R. (1989), 'Customer Profitability Analysis', *Management Accounting* (CIMA), Vol. 57, No. 2, pp. 26–8.

Bennett, R. (1995), *International Marketing: Strategy, Planning, Market Entry and Implementation*, London: Kogan Page.

Bennett, R.C. and Cooper, R.G. (1982), 'The Misuse of Marketing: an American Tragedy', *McKinsey Quarterly*, Autumn, pp. 52–69.

Bernard, K.N. (1996), 'Just-in-Time as a Competitive Weapon: The Significance of Functional Integration', *Journal of Marketing Management*, Vol. 12, No. 6, August, pp. 581–97.

Berkowitz, E.N., Kerin, R.A., Hartley, S.W. and Rudelius, W. (1994), *Marketing*, Boston, MA: Richard D. Irwin, 4th edition.

Bernstein, D. (1984), *Company Image and Reality*, Eastbourne: Holt, Rinehart & Winston.

Berry, L.L. (1987), 'Big Ideas in Services Marketing', *Journal of Services Marketing*, Fall, pp. 5–9.

Bhaskar, K.N. and Housden, R.J.W. (1985), *Accounting Information Systems and Data Processing*, Oxford: Heinemann.

Biggadike, R. (1977), *Entering New Markets: Strategies and Performance*, Cambridge, MA: Marketing Science Institute.

Blecke, C.J. (1957), 'The Small-Order Problem in Distribution Cost Control', *NACA Bulletin*, Vol. 38, No. 10, June, pp. 1279–84.

Bleeke, J.A. (1988), 'Peak Strategies', *Across the Board*, Vol. 25, No. 2, February, pp. 45–50.

Blenel, W.H. and Bender, H.E. (1980), *Product Service Planning*, New York: Amacom.

Bliss, M. (1980), 'Market Segmentation and Environmental Analysis', unpublished MSc thesis, University of Strathclyde.

Boag, D.A. (1987), 'Marketing Control and Performance in Early-Growth Companies', *Journal of Business Venturing*, Vol. 2, No. 4, pp. 365–9.

Bonini, C.P., Jaedicke, R.K. and Wagner, H.M. (eds) (1964), *Management Controls: New Directions in Basic Research*, New York: McGraw-Hill.

Bonoma, T.V. (1985a), 'Making Your Marketing Strategy Work', *Harvard Business Review*, Vol. 62, No. 2, March–April, pp. 68–76.

Bonoma, T.V. (1985b), *The Marketing Edge: Making Strategies Work*, London: Collier Macmillan.

Bonoma, T.V. and Clarke, B.H. (1988), *Marketing Performance Assessment*, Boston, MA: Harvard Business School Press.

Bonoma, T.V. and Crittenden, V.L. (1988), 'Managing Marketing Implementation', *Sloan Management Review*, Vol. 29, No. 2, Winter, pp. 7–14.

Bonoma, T.V. and Shapiro, B.P. (1983), *Segmenting the Industrial Market*, Lexington, MA: Lexington Books.

Bonoma, T.V. and Shapiro, B.P. (1984), 'Evaluating Market Segmentation Approaches', *Industrial Marketing Management*, Vol. 13, pp. 257–68.

Booth, J. (1986), 'If You're Not Sure Then Ask', *Accountancy*, Vol. 98, No. 1119, November, pp. 94–5.

Booz, Allen & Hamilton (1982), *New Product Management for the 1980s*, New York: Booz, Allen & Hamilton.

Bork, R. (1996), *Slouching Towards Gomorrah, Modern Liberalism and American Decline*, London: HarperCollins.

Boston Consulting Group (1971), *Perspectives on Experience*, Boston, MA: Boston Consulting Group.

Boston Consulting Group (1982), Annual Report.

Bourantas, D. and Mandes, Y. (1987), 'Does Market Share Lead to Profitability?', *Long Range Planning*, Vol. 20, No. 5, pp. 102–8.

Bourgeois, L.J. and Brodwin, D.A. (1984), 'Strategic Implementation: Five Approaches to an Elusive Phenomenon', *Strategic Management Journal*, Vol. 5, No. 3, pp. 241–64.

Bowersox, D.J. and Closs, D.J. (1995), 'Logistics and Physical Distribution', Ch. 33, pp. 571–587 in Baker, M.J. (ed.), *Companion Encyclopaedia of Marketing*, London: Routledge.

Boyd, S.H. and Britt, J.S. (1965), 'Making Marketing Research More Effective by Using the Administrative Process', *Journal of Marketing Research*, Vol. 2, No. 1, February, pp. 13–19.

Brache, A. (1986), 'Strategy and the Middle Manager', *Training*, Vol. 23, No. 4, April, pp. 30–4.

Brady, J. and Davies, I. (1993), 'The Failure of Marketing', *McKinsey Quarterly*, Vol. 7, No. 3.

Brannan, T. (1993), 'Time for a New Definition of Marketing', *Marketing Business*, November, p. 3.

Brighton, M. (1977), 'Pinning Down the Angels', *Market Research Society Newsletter*, No. 133, April, pp. 8–10.

Brion, J. (1967), *Corporate Marketing Planning*, New York: Wiley.

Broadbent, S. (1979), *Spending Advertising Money*, London: Business Books, 3rd edition.

Brock, J.J. (1984), 'Competitor Analysis: Some Practical Approaches', *Industrial Marketing Management*, Vol. 13, pp. 225–31.

Brockner, J. et al. (1986), 'Escalation of Commitment to an Ineffective Course of Action', *Administrative Science Quarterly*, Vol. 31, No. 1, March, pp. 109–26.

Brown, B. and McDonald, M. (1994), *Competitive Marketing Strategy for Europe*, London: Macmillan.

Brown, S. (1995), *Post-Modern Marketing*, London: Routledge.

Brownlie, D.T. (1983), 'Analytical Frameworks for Strategic Market Planning', in Baker, M.J. (ed.), *Marketing: Theory and Practice*, London: Macmillan.

Brownlie, D.T. (1987), 'Environmental Analysis,' in Baker, M.J. (ed.), *The Marketing Book*, London: Heinemann.

Brownlie, D.T. and Saren, M.A. (1983), 'A Review of Technological Forecasting Techniques and Their Application', *Management Bibliographies and Reviews*, Vol. 9, No. 4.

Brownlie, D.T. and Saren, M.A. (1992), 'The Four Ps of the Marketing Concept: Prescriptive, Polemical, Permanent and Problematic', *European Journal of Marketing*, Vol. 26, No. 4, pp. 34–47.

Buckley, P.J. (1991), 'Development in International Business Theory in the 1990s', *Journal of Marketing Management*, Vol. 7, No. 1, January, pp. 15–24.

Bucklin, L.P. (1978), *Productivity in Marketing*, Chicago: American Marketing Association.

Buckner, H. (1967), *How British Industry Buys*, London: Hutchinson.

Buell, V.P. (1966), *Marketing Management in Action*, New York: McGraw-Hill.

Bureau, J.R. (1981), *Brand Management*, London: Macmillan.

Burnett, L. (1961), *Communications of an Advertising Man*, New York: Leo Burnett.

Burns, T. and Stalker, G.M. (1961), *The Management of Innovation*, London: Tavistock (3rd edition, 1994, OUP).

Burton, P.W. and Miller, J.R. (1990), *Advertising Fundamentals*, Scranton, PA: International Textbook Company.

Business Week (1977), 'The Market Mishandles a Blue Chip', *Business Week*, 20 June, p. 17.

Business Week (1996), 'America, Land of the Shaken', *Business Week*, March.

Button, K. (1994), 'Spies Like Us', *Marketing Business*, March, p. 8.

Buzzell, R.D. and Chussil, M.J. (1985), 'Managing for Tomorrow', *Sloan Management Review*, Vol. 26, No. 4, Summer, pp. 3–13.

Buzzell, R.D. and Gale, B.T. (1987), *The PIMS Principles: Linking Strategy to Performance*, New York: Free Press.

Buzzell, R.D. and Nourse, R.M. (1967), *Product Innovation in Food Processing*, Boston, MA: Division of Research, Harvard Business School.

Buzzell, R.D. and Wiersema, F.D. (1981), 'Successful Share Building Strategies', *Harvard Business Review*, Vol. 59, No. 1, January–February, pp. 135–44.

Buzzell, R.D., Cox, D.F. and Brown, R.V. (1969), *Marketing Research and Information Systems*, New York: McGraw-Hill.

Buzzell, R.D., Gale, B.T. and Sullivan, R.G.M. (1975), 'Market Share: a Key to Profitability', *Harvard Business Review*, Vol. 53, No. 1, January–February, pp. 97–106.

Byars, L.L. (1984), *Strategic Management*, New York: Harper & Row.

Calingo, L.M.R. (1989), 'Achieving Excellence in Strategic Planning Systems', *SAM Advanced Management Journal*, Vol. 54, No. 2, Spring, pp. 21–3.

Campbell, A., Divine, M. and Young, D. (1990), *A Sense of Mission*, London: Pitman/Financial Times.

Cannon, J.T. (1968), *Business Strategy and Policy*, New York: Harcourt, Brace & World.

Cardozo, R.N. (1980), 'Situational Segmentation of Industrial Markets', *European Journal of Marketing*, Vol. 14, No. 5/6, pp. 264–76.

Cardozo, R.N. and Smith, D.K. (1983), 'Applying Financial Portfolio Theory to Product Portfolio Decisions: An Empirical Study', *Journal of Marketing*, Vol. 47, Spring, pp. 110–19.

Carlzon, J. (1987) *Moments of Truth*, New York: Ballinger.

Carson, R. (1963), *Silent Spring*, Boston, MA: Houghton Mifflin.

Carson, and Rickards (1979), 'Structured Creativity and Integrated Modelling for Industry, Technology and Research (SCIMITAR)', cited in Barclay, I. and Benson, M. (1990).

Carter, C.F. and Williams, B.R. (1958), *Investment in Innovation*, London: OUP.

Cascino, A.E. (1967), 'Organizational Implications of the Marketing Concept', in Kelley, E.J. and Lazer, W. (eds), *Managerial Marketing: Perspectives and Viewpoints*, Homewood, IL: Irwin.

Cespeds, F.V. and Piercy, N.F. (1996), 'Implementing Marketing Strategy', *Journal of Marketing Management*, Vol. 12, pp. 135–60.

Chakravarthy, B.S. (1986), 'Measuring Strategic Performance', *Strategic Management Journal*, Vol. 7, pp. 437–58.

Challagalla, G.N. and Shervani, T.A. (1996), 'Dimensions and Types of Supervisory Control: Effects on Salesperson Performance and Satisfaction', *Journal of Marketing*, Vol. 60, January, pp. 89–105.

Chandler, A.D. (1962), *Strategy and Structure*, Cambridge, MA: MIT Press.

Channon, D. (1987), 'Through the Eyes of Customers', *Banking World*, November, pp. 26–9.

Chebat, J.-C., Filiatrault, P., Katz, A. and Tal, S.M. (1994), 'Strategic Auditing of Human and Financial Resource Allocation in Marketing', *Journal of Business Research*, Vol. 31, pp. 197–208.

Chevalier, M. and Charty, B. (1974), 'Don't Misuse Your Market Share Goal', *European Business*, Spring, pp. 43–51.

Child, J. (1977), *Organization*, London: Harper & Row, 1st edition.

Child, J. (1984), *Organization*, London: Harper & Row, 2nd edition.

Chisnall, P.M. (1989), *Strategic Industrial Marketing*, London: Prentice-Hall, 2nd edition.

Christopher, M.G. (1986), *The Strategy of Distribution Management*, London: Heinemann.

Christopher, M.G., Jeffries, J., Kirkland, J. and Wilson, R.M.S. (1968), 'Status Report on Marketing Theory', *British Journal of Marketing*, Vol. 2, No. 3, Autumn, pp. 230–42.

Christopher, M.G., Majaro, S. and McDonald, M.H.B. (1987), *Strategy Search*, Aldershot: Gower.

Christopher, M.G., Payne, A. and Ballantyne, D. (1991), *Relationship Marketing*, Oxford: Heinemann.

Christopher, M.G., Schary, P. and Skjott-Larsen, T. (1979), *Customer Service and Distribution Strategy*, London: Associated Business Press.

Christopher, M.G. and Walters, D.W., with Gattorna, J.L. (1977), *Distribution Planning and Control*, Farnborough: Gower.

Christopher, W.F. (1977), 'Marketing Achievement Reporting: A Profitability Approach', *Industrial Marketing Management*, Vol. 6, pp. 149–62.

Chua, W.F., Lowe, E.A. and Puxty, A.G. (eds) (1989), *Critical Perspectives in Management Control*, Basingstoke: Macmillan.

Churchman, C.W. (1968), *The Systems Approach*, New York: Delacorte Press.

Clarke, C. and Brennan, K. (1988), 'Allied Forces', *Management Today*, November, pp. 128–31.

Clarke, C. and Pratt, S. (1985), 'Leadership's Four Part Progress', *Management Today*, March, pp. 84–6.

Clifford, D.K. and Cavanagh, R.E. (1985), *The Winning Performance: How America's High and Mid-Size Growth Companies Succeed*, New York: Bantam Books.

Clutterbuck, D. and Dearlove, D. (1993), 'The Basic Lessons of Change', *Managing Service Quality*, Vol. 3, No. 1, March, pp. 97–101.

Coates, D., Finlay, P. and Wilson, J. (1991), 'Validation in Marketing Models', *Journal of the Market Research Society*, Vol. 33, No. 2, April, pp. 83–90.

Cochran, E. and Thompson, G. (1964), 'What New Products Fail', *The National Industrial Conference Board Review*, October, pp. 11–18.

Cohen, W.A. (1988), *The Practice of Marketing Management: Analysis Planning and Implementation*, New York: Macmillan.

Cohn, C. (1990), 'Agents of Argent', *Management Today*, March, pp. 97–8, 101.

Coleman, R.P. (1961), 'The Significance of Social Stratification in Selling', in Bell, M. (ed.), *Marketing*, New York: American Marketing Association.

Collins, J.C. and Porras, J.I. (1998), *Built to Last: Successful habits of visionary companies*, London: Random House.

Cook, R. (1992) 'Aspects of Customer Service', *ITC Magazine*, March–April, pp. 10–12.

Cook, V.J. Jr (1985), 'The Net Present Value of Market Share', *Journal of Marketing*, Vol. 49, Summer, pp. 49–63.

Cooper, R.G. (1979), 'The Dimensions of New Product Success and Failure', *Journal of Marketing*, Vol. 43, No. 2, Summer, pp. 93–104.

Cooper, R.G. (1980), 'Factors in New Product Success', *European Journal of Marketing*, Vol. 14, No. 5/6, pp. 277–92.

Coulson-Thomas, C.J. (1983), *Marketing Communications*, London: Heinemann.

Cowley, P.R. (1985), 'The Experience Curve and History of the Cellophane Business', *Long Range Planning*, Vol. 18, No. 6, pp. 84–90.

Cox, K.K. and Enis, B.M. (1969), *Experimentation for Marketing Decisions*, Scranton, PA: Intertext.

Cox, R. and Brittain, P. (1988), *Retail Management*, London: M & E Handbooks.

Cox, R., Alderson, W. and Shapiro, S.J. (eds) (1964), *Theory in Marketing*, Homewood, IL: Irwin.

Cox, W.E. (1967), 'Product Life Cycles as Marketing Models', *Journal of Business*, Vol. 40, No. 4, October, pp. 375–84.

Crainer, S. (1990), 'A Niche for High Performance', *Marketing Business*, Issue 13, October, pp. 14–15.

Cravens, D.W. (1981), 'How to Match Marketing Strategies with Overall Corporate Planning', *Management Review*, Vol. 70, No. 12, December, pp. 12–19.

Cravens, D.W. (1986), 'Strategic Forces Affecting Marketing Strategy', *Business Horizons*, Vol. 29, No. 5, September–October.

Cravens, D.W. (1988), 'Gaining Strategic Marketing Advantage', *Business Horizons*, Vol. 31, No. 5, pp. 44–54.

Cravens, D.W. (1990), *Strategic Marketing*, Homewood, IL: Irwin, 3rd edition.

Cravens, D.W. (1996), *Strategic Marketing*, Homewood, IL: Irwin, 4th edition.

Cravens, D.W. and Lamb, C.W. (1986), *Strategic Marketing Cases and Applications*, Homewood, IL: Irwin, 2nd edition.

Crawford, C.M. (1979), 'New Product Failure Rates – Facts and Fallacies', *Research Management*, September, pp. 9–13.

Crissy, W.J.E. and Kaplan, R.M. (1963), 'Matrix Models for Marketing Planning', *MSU Business Topics*, Vol. 11, No. 3, Summer, pp. 48–66.

Crissy, W.J.E., Fischer, P.M. and Mossman, F.H. (1973), 'Segmental Analysis: Key to Marketing Profitability', *MSU Business Topics*, Vol. 21, No. 2, Spring, pp. 42–9.

Cross, R.H. (1987), 'Strategic Planning: What it Can and Can't Do', *SAM Advanced Management Journal*, Vol. 52, No. 1, Winter, pp. 13–16.

Culliton, J.W. (1948), *The Management of Marketing Costs*, Boston, MA: Division of Research Harvard Business School.

Cunningham, M.I. and Roberts, D.A. (1974), 'The Role of Customer Service in Industrial Marketing', *European Journal of Marketing*, Vol. 8, No. 1, Spring, pp. 15–19.

Cushing, B.E. (1982), *Accounting Information Systems and Business Organizations*, Reading, MA: Addison-Wesley.

Cvitkovic, E. (1989), 'Profiling Your Competitors', *Planning Review*, Vol. 17, No. 3, May–June, pp. 28–30.

Cvitkovic, E. (1993), *Competition: Forms, Facts and Fiction*, London: Macmillan.

Cyert, R.M. and March, J.G. (1963), *A Behavioral Theory of the Firm*, Englewood Cliffs, NJ: Prentice-Hall.

Dace, R.W. (1990), 'Exporting to Japan – Key Factors for Success', *Quarterly Review of Marketing*, Vol. 16, No. 1, October, pp. 1–7.

Dale, E. and Michelon, L.C. (1969), *Modern Management Methods*, Harmondsworth: Penguin.

Daniell, M. (1990) 'Webs We Weave', *Management Today*, February, pp. 81–4.

Darwin, C. (1859), *The Origin of Species by Means of Natural Selection*.

D'Aveni, R.A. (1999), 'Hypercompetition Closes In', in *Financial Times Mastering Global Business*, London: FT Pitman.

D'Aveni, R.A. and MacMillan, I.C. (1991), 'Crisis and the Content of Managerial Communications: A Study of the Focus of Attention of Top Managers in Surviving and Failing Firms', *Administrative Science Quarterly*, Vol. 35, No. 4, December, pp. 634–57.

Davidson, J.H. (1987a), *Offensive Marketing or How to Make Your Competitors Followers*, Harmondsworth: Penguin, 2nd edition.

Davidson, J.H. (1987b), 'Going on the Offensive', *Marketing*, 16 April, pp. 24–9.

Davidson, J.H. (1997), *Even More Offensive Marketing: An exhilarating action guide to winning in business*, Harmondsworth: Penguin.

Davidson, J.H. (1998), 'Building Profitable Growth Through Asset & Competency Based Marketing', *Market Leader*, Spring, pp. 17–21.

Davies, G. (1988), Marks & Spencer UK Case Study, Manchester Polytechnic.

Davies, H.L. (1970), 'Dimensions of Marital Roles in Consumer Decision Making', *Journal of Marketing Research*, Vol. 7, No. 2, May, pp. 168–77.

Davis, J. (1970), *Experimental Marketing*, London: Nelson.

Day, G.S. (1983), 'Gaining Insights through Strategy Analysis', *Journal of Business Strategy*, Vol. 4, No. 1, pp. 51–8.

Day, G.S. (1984), *Strategic Market Planning: the Pursuit of Competitive Advantage*, St Paul, MN: West Publishing.

Day, G.S. (1986), *Analysis for Strategic Marketing Decisions*, St Paul, MN: West Publishing.

Day, G.S. (1990), *Market Driven Strategy*, New York: Free Press.

Day, G.S. (1996a), 'How to Learn about Markets', *Financial Times, Mastering Management*, Part 12, p. 12.

Day, G.S. (1996b), 'Keeping Ahead in the Competitive Game', *Financial Times, Mastering Management*, Part 18, pp. 2–4.

Day, G.S. and Fahey, L. (1988), 'Valuing Market Strategies', *Journal of Marketing*, Vol. 52, No. 3, July, pp. 45–57.

Day, G.S. and Wensley, J.R.C. (1988), 'Assessing Advantage: A Framework for Diagnosing Competitive Superiority', *Journal of Marketing*, Vol. 52, No. 2, April, pp. 1–20.

Day, G.S., Weitz, B. and Wensley, J.R.C. (eds) (1990), *The Interface of Marketing and Strategy*, Greenwich, CT: JAI Press.

Dean, J. (1951), *Managerial Economics*, Englewood Cliffs, NJ: Prentice-Hall.

de Chernatony, L., Daniels, K. and Johnson, G. (1993), 'A Cognitive Perspective on Managers' Perceptions of Competition', *Journal of Marketing Management*, Vol. 9, No. 4, October, pp. 373–81.

De Jouvenal, B. (1967), *The Art of Conjecture*, New York: Basic Books.

De Kare-Silver, M. (1997), *Strategy in Crisis: Why business urgently needs a completely new approach*, Basingstoke: Macmillan Press.

De Kluyver, C.A. and Pessemier, E.A. (1986), 'Benefits of a Marketing Budgeting Model: Two Case Studies', *Sloan Management Review*, Vol. 28, No. 1, Fall, pp. 27–38.

Dempsey, W.A. (1978), 'Vendor Selection and the Buying Process', *Industrial Marketing Management*, Vol. 7, pp. 257–67.

Demski, J.S. (1980), *Information Analysis*, Reading, MA: Addison-Wesley, 2nd edition.

Deng, S. and Dart, J. (1994), 'Measuring Market Orientation: A Multi-Factor, Multi-Item Approach', *Journal of Marketing Management*, Vol. 10, No. 8, November, pp. 725–42.

Dent, J.F. (1990), 'Strategy, Organization and Control: Some Possibilities for Accounting Research', *Accounting, Organizations and Society*, Vol. 15, No. 1/2, pp. 3–26.

Deran, E. (1987), *Low-Cost Marketing Strategies*, New York: Praeger.

Dery, D. (1982), 'Erring and Learning: An Organizational Analysis', *Accounting, Organizations and Society*, Vol. 7, No. 3, pp. 217–23.

Dev, S.F.D. (1980), 'Linear Programming and Production Planning', Chapter 7 (pp. 121–47) in Arnold, J.A., Carsberg, B.V. and Scapens, R.W. (eds), *Topics in Management Accounting*, Deddington: Philip Allen.

De Vasconcellos, J.A.S. and Hambrick, D.C. (1989), 'Key Success Factors: Test of a General Theory in the Mature Industrial-Product Sector', *Strategic Management Journal*, Vol. 10, No. 4, pp. 367–82.

Devlin, G. and Biggs, I. (1989), 'Partners in the Strategic Quickstep', *Accountancy*, Vol. 104, No. 1155, November, pp. 144–6.

Dhalla, N.K. and Yuspeh, S. (1976), 'Forget the Product Life Cycle Concept', *Harvard Business Review*, Vol. 54, No. 1, January–February, pp. 102–12.

Diamantopoulos, A. and Mathews, B.P. (1990), 'A Model for Analysing Product Performance', *Quarterly Review of Marketing*, Vol. 15, No. 3, April, pp. 7–13.

Dibb, S., Simkin, L., Pride, W.M. and Ferrell, O.C. (1991), *Marketing: concepts and strategies*, Boston: Houghton Mifflin.

Dickinson, R.A. (1967), *Buyer Decision Making*, Berkeley, CA: Institute of Business and Economic Research.

Diffenbach, J. (1983), 'Corporate Environmental Analysis in Large US Corporations', *Long Range Planning*, Vol. 16, No. 3, pp. 107–16.

Dolan, R.J. (1981), 'Models of Competition: A Review of Theory and Empirical Evidence', in Enis, B.M. and Roering, K.J. (eds), *Review of Marketing*, Chicago: American Marketing Association.

Dominguez, L.V. and Page, A. (1984), 'Formulating a Strategic Portfolio of Profitable Retail Segments for Commercial Banks', *Journal of Economics and Business*, Vol. 36, No. 3, pp. 43–57.

Doyle, P. (1979), 'Management Structures and Marketing Strategies in UK Industry', *European Journal of Marketing*, Vol. 13, No. 5, pp. 319–31.

Doyle, P. (1985), 'Marketing and ZBB', *Management* (Eire), December, pp. 33–4.

Doyle, P. (1987), 'Marketing and the British Chief Executive', *Journal of Marketing Management*, Vol. 3, No. 2, Winter, pp. 121–32.

Doyle, P. (1992), 'What are the Excellent Companies?', *Journal of Marketing Management*, Vol. 8, pp. 101–16.

Doyle, P. (1994), *Marketing Management and Strategy*, London: Prentice-Hall.

Doyle, P. (2002), *Marketing Management and Strategy*, London: Prentice-Hall, 3rd edition.

Doyle, P. and Newbould, G.D. (1974), 'Advertising Management for Building Societies'.

Doyle, P. the True Profitability of Sales Promotions', *Journal of the Operational Research Society*, Vol. 37, No. 10, October, pp. 955–66.

Doyle, P., Saunders, J. and Wong, V. (1986), 'Japanese Marketing Strategies in the UK: A Comparative Study', *Journal of International Business Studies*, Vol. 17, No. 1, pp. 27–46.

Doyle, P., Saunders, J. and Wright, L. (1988), 'A Comparative Study of British, US, and Japanese Marketing Strategies in the British Market', *International Journal of Research in Marketing*, Vol. 5, No. 3, pp. 171–84.

Driver, J.C. (1990), 'Marketing Planning in Style', *Quarterly Review of Marketing*, Vol. 15, No. 4, July, pp. 16–21.

Drucker, P.F. (1955), *The Practice of Management*, London: Heinemann.

Drucker, P.F. (1959), 'Long Range Planning: Challenge to Management Science', *Management Science*, Vol. 5, No. 3, April, pp. 238–49.

Drucker, P.F. (1963), 'Managing for Business Effectiveness', *Harvard Business Review*, Vol. 41, No. 3, May–June, pp. 53–60.

Drucker, P.F. (1969), *The Age of Discontinuity*, New York: Harper & Row.

Drucker, P.F. (1973), *Management: Tasks, Responsibilities and Practices*, New York: Harper & Row.

Duffy, M.F. (1989), 'ZBB, MBO, PPB, and Their Effectiveness within the Planning/Marketing Process', *Strategic Management Journal*, Vol. 10, No. 2, pp. 163–73.

Düro, R. (1989), *Winning the Marketing War*, New York: Wiley.

Dutton, J.E. and Duncan, R.B. (1987), 'The Influence of the Strategic Planning Process on Strategic Change', *Strategic Management Journal*, Vol. 8, pp. 103–16.

Edwards, P. (1998), 'The Age of the Trust Brand', *Market Leader*, Winter, pp. 15–19.

Eells, R. and Nehemkis, P. (1984), *Corporate Intelligence and Espionage: A Blueprint for Executive Decision-Making*, New York: Macmillan.

Ehrenberg, A.S.C. (1965), 'News and Notes: American Marketing Association – 50th Anniversary Speech', *Operational Research Quarterly*, Vol. 16, No. 3, September, pp. 406–12.

Ellsworth, J. (2000), 'Engineering a Revival for Levi's', *Marketing*, 19 October, p. 25.

Emery, F. (ed.) (1981), *Systems Thinking*, Harmondsworth: Penguin, two vols.

Engel, J.F., Kollat, D.T. and Blackwell, R.D. (1968), *Consumer Behavior*, New York: Holt, Rinehart & Winston.

Evans, F.B. (1959), 'Psychological and Objective Factors in the Prediction of Brand Choice: Ford Versus Chevrolet', *Journal of Business*, Vol. 32, No. 4, October, pp. 340–69.

Fahey, L., King, W.R. and Narayanan, V.K. (1981), 'Environmental Scanning and Forecasting in Strategic Planning – The State of the Art', *Long Range Planning*, Vol. 14, No. 1, February, pp. 32–9.

Farris, P.W. and Reibstein, D.J. (1979), 'How Prices, Expenditure and Profit are Linked', *Harvard Business Review*, Vol. 57, No. 6, November–December, pp. 173–84.

Feder, R.A. (1965), 'How to Measure Marketing Performance', *Harvard Business Review*, Vol. 43, No. 3, May–June, pp. 132–42.

Feldman, W. and Cardozo, R.N. (1968), 'The Industrial Revolution and Models of Buyer Behavior', *Journal of Purchasing*, Vol. 4, November.

Feldwick, P. (ed.) (1990), *Advertising Works – 5*, London: Cassell.

Ferguson, A. (1989), 'Hostage to the Short Term', *Management Today*, March, pp. 68, 70–72.

Fern, R.H. and Tipgos, M.A. (1988), 'Controllers as Business Strategists: A Progress Report', *Management Accounting* (NAA), Vol. 69, No. 9, March, pp. 25–9.

Festinger, L. (1957), *A Theory of Cognitive Dissonance*, Stanford, CA: Stanford University Press.

Fielding, H. (1997), *Bridget Jones' Diary*, London: Picador.

Fifer, R.M. (1989), 'Cost Benchmarking Functions in the Value Chain', *Planning Review*, Vol. 17, No. 3, May–June, pp. 18–23, 26–7.

Fifield, P. (1997), Seminar at the Chartered Institute of Marketing, Cookham, Berks, UK.

Fifield, P. (1998), *Marketing Strategy*, Oxford: Butterworth-Heinemann, 2nd edition.

Fifield, P. (2000), 'Marketing in the Post-Internet Age', A Presentation to the Sheffield Branch of the Chartered Institute of Marketing, October.

Fifield, P. and Gilligan, C.T. (1996), *Strategic Marketing Management: planning and control, analysis and decision*, Oxford: Butterworth-Heinemann, 2nd edition.

Filiatrault, P. and Chebat, J.-C. (1987), 'Marketing Budgeting Practices: An Empirical Study', *Developments in Marketing Science*, Vol. 10, pp. 278–82.

Filiatrault, P. and Chebat, J.-C. (1990), 'How Service Firms Set their Marketing Budgets', *Industrial Marketing Management*, Vol. 19, pp. 63–7.

Fill, C (1995), *Marketing Communications: Frameworks, theories and applications*, Hemel Hempstead: Prentice-Hall.

Fisher, L. (1966), *Industrial Marketing*, London: Business Books.

Fisk, G. (1967), *Marketing Systems*, New York: Harper & Row.

Fisk, G. and Dixon, D.F. (eds) (1967), *Theories for Marketing Systems Analysis*, New York: Harper & Row.

Flamholtz, E.G. and Das, T.K. (1985), 'Toward an Integrative Framework of Organizational Control', *Accounting, Organizations and Society*, Vol. 10, No. 1, pp. 35–50.

Foreman, S.K. and Money, A.H. (1995), 'Internal Marketing: Concepts, Measurement and Application', *Journal of Marketing Management*, Vol. 11, No. 8, November, pp. 755–68.

Forrester, J.W. (1961), *Industrial Dynamics*, New York: Wiley.

Forrester, J.W. (1965), 'Modeling of Market and Company Interactions', pp. 353–64 in Bennett, P.D. (ed.), *Marketing and Economic Development*, Chicago: American Marketing Association.

Fox, H.W. (1986), 'Financial ABCs of Test Marketing', *Business Horizons*, Vol. 29, No. 5, September–October, pp. 63–70.

Foxall, G.R. (1984) 'Marketing's Domain', *European Journal of Marketing*, Vol. 18, No. 1, pp. 25–40.

Foxall, G. (1987), 'Consumer Behaviour', in Baker, M.J. (ed.), *The Marketing Book*, London: Heinemann.

Freeman, C. (1965), 'Research and Development in Electronic Capital Goods', *National Institute Economic Review*, No. 34, November, pp. 40–91.

Freund, Y.P. (1988), 'Critical Success Factors', *Planning Review*, Vol. 16, No. 4, July–August, pp. 20–3.

Frey, A.W. and Halterman, J.C. (1970), *Advertising*, New York: The Ronald Press, 4th edition.

Frey, J.B. (1982), 'Pricing Over the Competitive Life Cycle', speech presented at the 1982 Marketing Conference, New York.

Frey, J.B. (1987), *Pricing Over the Competitive Life Cycle*, New York: The Conference Board.

Fruhan, W.E. (1972), 'Pyrrhic Victories in Fights for Market Share', *Harvard Business Review*, Vol. 50, No. 5, September–October, pp. 100–7.

Fuld, L.M. (1985), *Competitor Intelligence*, New York: Wiley.

Fuld, L.M. (1988), *Monitoring the Competition: Finding Out What's Really Going on Out There*, New York: Wiley.

Fuld, L.M. (1995), *The New Competitor Intelligence*, New York: Wiley.

Furey, T.R. (1987), 'Benchmarking: The Key to Developing Competitive Advantage in Mature Markets', *Planning Review*, Vol. 15, No. 5, September–October, pp. 30–2.

Gabb, A. (1991), 'How the Discovery Took Off', *Management Today*, October, pp. 64–8.

Gable, M., Fairhurst, A. and Dickinson, R. (1993), 'The Use of Benchmarking to Enhance Marketing Decision Making', *Journal of Consumer Marketing*, Vol. 10, No. 1, pp. 52–60.

Gaedeke, R.M. and Etcheson, W.W. (1972), *Consumerism*, New York: Harper & Row.

Galbraith, J.K. (1958), *The Affluent Society*, Harmondsworth: Penguin Books.

Galbraith, J.K. (1977), *The Age of Uncertainty*, London: BBC/André Deutsch.

Gale, B.T. (1994), *Managing Customer Value: Creating Quality and Service that Customers Can See*, New York: The Free Press.

Gale, B.T. and Swire, D.J. (1988), 'Business Strategies that Create Wealth', *Planning Review*, Vol. 16, No. 2, March–April, pp. 6–13, 47.

Gallagher Report (1973), cited in Barclay and Benson (1990).

Garsombke, D.J. (1989), 'International Competitor Analysis', *Planning Review*, Vol. 17, No. 3, May–June, pp. 42–7.

Geroski, P. (1996) 'Keeping out the Competition', *Financial Times, Mastering Management*, Part 16, pp. 11–12.

Gerson, R. (1992), 'Dealing with the Customers who Complain', *The Straits Times*, 27 April, p. 18.

Ghemewat, P. (1986), 'Sustainable Advantage', *Harvard Business Review*, Vol. 64, No. 5, September–October, pp. 53–8.

Gilligan, C.T. and Crowther, G. (1976), *Advertising Management*, Deddington: Philip Allen.

Gilligan, C.T. and Hird, M. (1986), *International Marketing: Strategy and Management*, London: Routledge.

Gluck, F. (1985), 'Big Bang Management', *Journal of Business Strategy*, Vol. 6, No. 1, Summer, pp. 59–64.

Godin, S. (1999), *Permission Marketing: Turning strangers into friends, and friends into customers*, New York: Simon & Schuster.

Gofton, K. (1984), 'The Fed Loses its Reserve', *Marketing*, 2 August, p. 15.

Goldsmith, W. and Clutterbuck, D. (1988), *The Winning Streak*, London, Weidenfeld & Nicholson.

Goodman, S.R. (1970), *Techniques of Profitability Analysis*, New York: Wiley.

Goold, M.C. and Campbell, A.E.C. (1987a), *Strategies and Styles*, Oxford: Basil Blackwell.

Goold, M.C. and Campbell, A.E.C. (1987b), 'Many Best Ways to Make Strategy', *Harvard Business Review*, Vol. 65, No. 6, November–December, pp. 70–6.

Goold, M.C. and Quinn, J.J. (1990), *Strategic Control: Milestones for Long-term Performance*, London: Hutchinson.

Govindarajan, V. and Shank, J.K. (1989), 'Profit Variance Analysis: A Strategic Focus', *Issues in Accounting Education*, Vol. 4, No. 2, Fall, pp. 396–410.

Graf, F. (1967), A speech by the A.C. Nielsen Vice-President to a grocery manufacturers' executive conference, cited by Gerlach, G.T. and Wainwright, C.A. (1968), *Successful Management of New Products*, New York: Hastings House, pp. 125–6.

Grashof, J.F. (1975), 'Conducting and Using a Marketing Audit', in McCarthy, E.J., Grashof, J.F. and Brogowicz, A.A. (eds), *Readings in Basic Marketing*, Homewood, IL: Irwin.

Green, P., Faris, P. and Wind, Y. (1968), 'The Determinants of Vendor Selection: The Evaluation Function Approach', *Journal of Purchasing*, Vol. 4, August.

Greenley, G.E. (1986a), *The Strategic and Operational Planning of Marketing*, London: McGraw-Hill.

Greenley, G.E. (1986b), 'The Interface of Strategic and Marketing Plans', *Journal of General Management*, Vol. 12, No. 1, pp. 54–62.

Greenwood, R.G. (1974), *Managerial Decentralization: A Study of the General Electric Philosophy*, Lexington, MA: D.C. Heath.

Gregory, M. (1994), *Dirty Tricks*, Little, Brown.

Griffith, I. (1986), 'Cost-Cutting Doesn't Move Merchandise', *Financial Decisions*, October, pp. 77, 78, 80, 82.

Griffith, I. (1991), 'Marketing Needs New Sales Pitch', *The Sunday Times*, 7 July, p. 4.13.

Groönroos, C. (1983), *Strategic Management and Marketing in the Service Sector*, Bromley: Chartwell-Bratt.

Grundy, A. (1986), 'Why Accountants and Marketing Men Should Be Friends', *Certified Accountant*, November, pp. 12–15.

Guiltinan, J.P. and Paul G.W. (1988), *Marketing Management: Strategies and Programs*, New York: McGraw-Hill, 3rd edition.

Gummeson, E. (1987), The New Marketing – Developing Long-Term Interactive Relationships, *Long Range Planning*, Vol. 20, No. 4, pp. 10–20.

Hakansson, H. (ed.) (1981), *International Marketing and Purchasing of Industrial Goods: An Interaction Approach*, Chichester: John Wiley.

Hakansson, H. et al. (1979), 'Industrial Marketing as an Organizational Problem', *European Journal of Marketing*, Vol. 13, No. 3, pp. 81–93.

Haley, R.J. (1963), 'Benefit Segmentation: A Decision Orientated Research Tool', *Journal of Marketing*, Vol. 27, No. 3, July, pp. 30–5.

Haller, T. (1980a), 'An Organization Structure to Help You in the 1980s', *Advertising Age*, Vol. 51, No. 36, pp. 45–6.

Haller, T. (1980b), 'Strategic Planning: Key to Corporate Power for Marketers', *Marketing Times*, Vol. 27, No. 3, pp. 18–24.

Hambrick, D.G. and Cannella, A.A. (1989), 'Strategy Implementation as Substance and Selling', *The Academy of Management Executive*, Vol. 3, No. 4, November, pp. 278–85.

Hamel, G. (2001), *Leading the Revolution*, Boston, MA: Harvard Business School Press.

Hamel, G. and Prahalad, C.K. (1994), *Competing for the Future: breakthrough strategies for seizing control of your industry and creating the markets of tomorrow*, Boston, MA: Harvard Business School Press.

Hamermesh, R.G., Anderson, M.J. and Harris, J.E. (1987), 'Strategies for Low Market Share Businesses', *Harvard Business Review*, Vol. 65, No. 3, May–June, pp. 95–102.

Hammer, M. and Champy, J. (1993), *Re-engineering the Corporation*, New York: Harper Collins.

Handy, C. (1991), *The Age of Unreason*, London: Random House.

Handy, C. (1994), *The Empty Raincoat: Making Sense of the Future*, London: Random House.

Harding, M. (1966), 'Who Really Makes the Purchasing Decision?', *Industrial Marketing*, September, p. 76.

Harris, D. (1990), 'British Shoe Exports Shine', *The Times*, 5 March, p. 41.

Hart, N.A. (1978), *Industrial Advertising and Publicity*, London: Associated Business Programmes, 2nd edition.

Hartley, R.F. (1995), *Marketing Mistakes*, New York: Wiley, 6th edition.

Hartman, B.P. (1983), 'The Management Accountant's Role in Deleting a Product Line', *Management Accounting* (NAA), Vol. 65, No. 2, August, pp. 63–6.

Harvey-Jones, Sir J. (1988), *Making it Happen*, London: Collins.

Haspelagh, P. (1982), 'Portfolio Planning: Its Uses and Limits', *Harvard Business Review*, Vol. 60, No. 1, January–February, pp. 58–73.

Hay Management Consultants (1989), *Headlines 2000: The World as We See It*, London: Hay.

Hayhurst, R. and Wills, G.S.C. (1972), *Organizational Design for Marketing Futures*, London: Allen & Unwin.

Head, V. (1981), *Sponsorship: The Newest Marketing Skill*, Woodhead-Faulkner in association with the Institute of Marketing.

Hedley, B. (1977), 'Strategy and the Business Portfolio', *Long Range Planning*, Vol. 10, No. 1, pp. 9–15.

Heller, R. (1990), 'Pinstripe Devils', *Management Today*, September, p. 36.

Henderson, B.D. (1981), 'Understanding the Forces of Strategic and Natural Competition', *Journal of Business Strategy*, Vol. 2, Winter, pp. 11–15.

Henderson, B.D. (1982), *Henderson on Corporate Strategy*, New York: Mentor.

Henderson, B.D. (1984), *The Logic of Business Strategy*, Cambridge, MA: Ballinger.

Hendon, D.W. (1979), 'A New Empirical Look at the Influences of Reference Groups on Generic Product Strategy and Brand Choice: Evidence from Two Nations', pp. 752–61 in Proceedings of the Academy of International Business, *Asia Pacific Dimensions of International Business*, Honolulu: College of Business, University of Hawaii, December.

Henley, D.S. (1976), 'Evaluating Product Line Performance: A Conceptual Approach', pp. II-10 and II-11 in *Multinational Product Management*, Cambridge, MA: Marketing Science Institute.

Henley Centre (2000), *Planning for Consumer Change*, Henley Centre.

Hersey, P. (1988), *Selling: A Behavioral Science Approach*, Englewood Cliffs, NJ: Prentice-Hall.

Hershey, R. (1980), 'Commercial Intelligence on a Shoe-String', *Harvard Business Review*, Vol. 58, No. 5, September–October, pp. 22–4, 28, 30.

Herzberg, F. (1966), *Work and the Nature of Man*, London: Collins.

Heskett, J.L. (1976), *Marketing*, New York: Macmillan.

Heskett, J.L., Jones, T.O., Loveman, G. et al. (1994), 'Putting the Service Profit Chain to Work', *Harvard Business Review*.

Hill, R.W. (1972), 'The Nature of Industrial Buying Decisions', *Industrial Marketing Management*, Vol. 2, October, pp. 45–55.

Hill, S. and Lederer, C. (2002), *The Infinite Asset: Managing brands to build new value*, Boston, MA: Harvard Business School Press.

Hirsch, R. (1990), 'Getting the Ratios Right', *Management Today*, April, pp. 107–8, 110.

Hise, R.T. and Strawser, R.H. (1970), 'Application of Capital Budgeting Techniques to Marketing Operations', *MSU Business Topics*, Vol. 18, No. 3, Summer, pp. 69–75.

Hitt, M.A. and Ireland, R.D. (1985), 'Corporate Distinctive Competence, Strategy, Industry and Performance', *Strategic Management Journal*, Vol. 6, pp. 273–93.

Hlavacek, J.D. (1974), 'Towards More Successful Venture Management', *Journal of Marketing*, Vol. 38, No. 4, pp. 56–60.

Hofer, C.W. and Schendel, D.E. (1978), *Strategy Formulation: Analytical Concepts*, New York: West.

Hofstede, G.H. (1968), *The Game of Budget Control*, London: Tavistock.

Hollingworth, C. (2001), *Future Shock 21st Century Marketing*, London: The Marketing Society.

Holmes, G. and Smith, N. (1987), *Salesforce Incentives*, London: Heinemann.

Hood, P. (1983), 'Sales Promotion and Merchandising', in Hart, N.A. and O'Connor, J. (eds), *The Practice of Advertising*, London: Heinemann, 2nd edition.

Hooley, G.J. (1993), 'Market-Led Quality Management', *Journal of Marketing Management*, Vol. 9, No. 3, pp. 315–35.

Hooley, G.J. and Lynch, J.E. (1985) 'Marketing Lessons From the UK's High-Flying Companies', *Journal of Marketing Management*, Vol. 1, No. 1, pp. 65–74.

Hooley, G.J. and Saunders, J.A. (1993), *Competitive Position: The Key to Market Success*, London: Prentice-Hall International.

Hooley, G.J., West, C.J. and Lynch, J.E. (1983), *Marketing Management Today*, Cookham, Berks: Chartered Institute of Marketing.

Hooley, G.J., West, C.J. and Lynch, J.E. (1984), *Marketing in the UK – A Survey of Current Practice and Performance*, Cookham, Berks: Chartered Institute of Marketing.

Hopkins, D.S. and Bailey, E.L. (1971), 'New Product Pressures', *The Conference Board Record*, June, pp. 16–24.

Howard, J. (1983), 'Marketing Theory of the Firm', *Journal of Marketing*, Vol. 47, No. 4, Fall. pp. 90–100.

Howard, K. (1972), 'Network Analysis and Marketing Decisions', *European Journal of Marketing*, Vol. 6, No. 4, Winter, pp. 270–80.

Howell, S. (1994), *Analysing Your Competitor's Financial Strengths*, London: Pitman Publishing/Financial Times.

Huegy, H.W. (ed.) (1963), *The Conceptual Framework for a Science of Marketing*, Urbana, IL: University of Illinois.

Hughes, G.D. (1980), *Marketing Management: A Planning Approach*, Reading, MA: Addison-Wesley.

Hulbert, J.M. and Toy, N.E. (1977), 'A Strategic Framework for Marketing Control', *Journal of Marketing*, Vol. 41, No. 2, April, pp. 12–20.

Hunter, V.L. (1997), *Business to Business Marketing: Creating a community of customers*, McGraw-Hill.

Hurst, E.G. Jr (1982), 'Controlling Strategic Plans', Ch. 7, pp. 114–23 in Lorange, P. (ed.), *Implementation of Strategic Planning*, Englewood Cliffs, NJ: Prentice-Hall.

Hussey, D.E. (1971), *Introducing Corporate Planning*, Oxford: Pergamon (4th edition 1991).

Hussey, D.E. (1985), 'Implementing Corporate Strategy: Using Management Education and Training', *Long Range Planning*, Vol. 18, No. 5, pp. 28–37.

Hussey, D.E. (1989), 'Management in the 1990s', *Management Training Update*, September.

Hutton, W. (1995), *The State We're In*, London: Jonathan Cape.

Irvin, R.A. and Michaels, E.G. (1989), 'Core Skills: Doing the Right Thing Right', *The McKinsey Quarterly*, Summer, pp. 4–19.

Itami, H. (1977), *Adaptive Behavior: Management Control and Information Analysis*, Sarasota, FL: American Accounting Association (Studies in Accounting Research, No. 15).

Jackson, K.F. (1975), *The Art of Solving Problems*, London: Heinemann.

Jacobson, R. and Aaker, D.A. (1985), 'Is Market Share All That It's Cracked Up To Be?', *Journal of Marketing*, Vol. 49, No. 4, Fall, pp. 11–22.

Jain, S.C. (1990), *Marketing Planning and Strategy*, Cincinnati, OH: South-Western Publishing Company.

James, B.G. (1966), 'Emotional Buying in Industrial Markets', *Scientific Business*, Vol. 3, No. 12, Spring, pp. 326–30.

James, B.G. (1985), *Business Wargames*, Harmondsworth: Penguin.

Jaworski, B.J. (1988), 'Toward a Theory of Marketing Control: Environmental Context, Control Types, and Consequences', *Journal of Marketing*, Vol. 52, No. 3, July, pp. 23–39.

Jaworski, B.J. and MacInnis, D.J. (1989), 'Marketing Jobs and Management Controls: Toward a Framework', *Journal of Marketing Research*, Vol. 26, No. 4, pp. 406–19.

Jefkins, F. (1986), *Planned Press and Public Relations*, Glasgow: Blackie, 2nd edition.

Jefkins, F. (1990), *Modern Marketing Communications*, Glasgow: Blackie.

Jenster, P.V. (1987), 'Using Critical Success Factors in Planning', *Long Range Planning*, Vol. 20, No. 4, pp. 102–9.

Joachimsthaler, E.A. (1994), *Häagen-Dazs Ice Cream: The Making of a Global Brand* (case study), International Graduate School of Management.

Jobber, D. (2003), *Principles and Practice of Marketing*, Maidenhead: McGraw-Hill, 4th edition.

Johnson, G. and Scholes, K. (1988), *Exploring Corporate Strategy*, London: Prentice-Hall, 2nd edition.

Johnson, G. and Scholes, H.K. (1993), *Exploring Corporate Strategy*, Hemel Hempstead: Prentice-Hall, 3rd edition.

Johnson, G. and Scholes, H.K. (2002), *Exploring Corporate Strategy*, Hemel Hempstead: Prentice-Hall, 6th edition.

Johnson, H.G. (1967), 'Key Item Control', *Management Services*, Vol. 4, No. 1, January–February, pp. 21–6.

Johnson, H.G. and Flodhammer, A. (1980), 'Industrial Customer Segmentation', *Industrial Marketing Management*, Vol. 9, July, pp. 201–5.

Johnson, R. and Pound, E.T. (1992), 'Hot on the Trail of Trade Secret Thieves: Private Eyes Fight All Manner of Snakes', *Wall Street Journal*, 12 August, p. 131, B4.

Johnson, R.A., Kast, F.E. and Rosenzweig, J.E. (1973), *The Theory and Management of Systems*, New York: McGraw-Hill, 3rd edition.

Jones, C.M. (1986), 'GTE's Strategic Tracking System', *Planning Review*, Vol. 14, No. 5, September–October, pp. 27–30.

Jones, G.R. and Butler, J.E. (1988), 'Costs, Revenue and Business-Level Strategy', *Academy of Management Review*, Vol. 13, No. 2, April, pp. 202–13.

Jones, L. (1988), 'Competitor Cost Analysis at Caterpillar', *Management Accounting* (NAA), Vol. 70, No. 4, October, pp. 32–8.

Joseph, L. and Yorke, D. (1989), 'Know Your Game Plan', *Quarterly Review of Marketing*, Vol. 15, No. 1, Autumn, pp. 8–13.

Kahaner, L. (1996), *Competitive Intelligence*, New York: Simon & Schuster.

Kahneman, D. and Tversky, A. (1984), 'Choices, Values and Frames', *American Psychologist*, Vol. 39, pp. 341–50.

Kakabadse, A. (1999), 'Art of Visioning', *Management Focus*, Vol. 11, pp. 10–11.

Kanter, R.M. (1989), *When Giants Learned to Dance*, New York: Simon & Schuster.

Kaplan, R.S. and Norton, D.P. (1992), 'The Balanced Scorecard – Measures that Drive Performance', *Harvard Business Review*, Vol. 70, No. 1, January–February, pp. 71–9.

Kaplan, R.S. and Norton, D.P. (1993), 'Putting the Balanced Scorecard to Work', *Harvard Business Review*, Vol. 71, No. 5, September–October.

Kaplan, R.S. and Norton, D.P. (1996), *The Balanced Scorecard*, Boston, MA: Harvard Business School Press.

Kashani, K. (1996), 'A New Future for Brands' *Financial Times, Mastering Management'*, Part 3, pp. 7–8.

Kay, J. (1993), *Foundations of Corporate Success: How Business Strategies Add Value*, Oxford: OUP.

Keiser, B.E. (1987), 'Practical Competitor Intelligence', *Planning Review*, Vol. 15, No. 5, September–October, pp. 14–18.

Kelley, W.J. (1972), *Marketing Planning and Competitive Strategy*, Englewood Cliffs, NJ: Prentice-Hall.

Kelly, J.M. (1987), *How to Check Out your Competition*, New York: Wiley.

Kerin, R.A. and Peterson, R.A. (1993), *Strategic Marketing Problems: Cases and Comments*, Boston, MA: Allyn & Bacon, 6th edition.

Kerin, R.A., Mahajan, V. and Varadarajan, P.R. (1990), *Contemporary Perspectives on Strategic Market Planning*, Englewood Cliffs, NJ: Prentice-Hall.

Kettlewood, K. (1973), 'Source Loyalty in the Freight Transport Market', Unpublished MSc Dissertation, UMIST.

Kight, L.K. (1989), 'The Search for Intelligence on Divisions and Subsidiaries', *Planning Review*, Vol. 17, No. 3, May–June, pp. 40–1.

King, S. (1991), 'Brand-building in the 1990s', *Journal of Marketing Management*, Vol. 7, No. 1, January, pp. 3–13.

King, W. (1968), 'A Conceptual Framework For Advertising Agency Compensation', *Journal of Marketing Research*, Vol. 5, No. 2, May, pp. 177–80.

Kjaer-Hansen, M. (ed.) (1965), *Cost Problems in Modern Marketing*, Amsterdam: North-Holland.

Klein, H.E. and Linneman, R.E. (1984), 'Environmental Assessment: An International Study of Corporate Practice', *Journal of Business Strategy*, Vol. 5, Summer, pp. 66–75.

Klein, N. (2000), *No Logo: Taking aim at the brand bullies*, London: Flamingo.

Kling, N.D. (1985), 'The Marketing Audit: An Extension of the Marketing Control Process', *Managerial Finance*, Vol. 11, No. 1, pp. 23–6.

Klir, G.J. and Valach, M. (1967), *Cybernetic Modelling*, London: Iliffe.

Kohli, A.K. and Jaworski, B.J. (1990), 'Market Orientation: The Construct, Research Propositions and Managerial Implications', *Journal of Marketing*, Vol. 54, April, pp. 1–18.

Kortge, G.D. (1984), 'Inverted Break-even Analysis for Profitable Marketing Decisions', *Industrial Marketing Management*, Vol. 13, pp. 219–24.

Kotler, P. (1971), *Marketing Decision-Making: A Model-Building Approach*, New York: Holt, Rinehart & Winston.

Kotler, P. (1972a), *Marketing Management: Analysis, Planning and Control*, Englewood Cliffs, NJ: Prentice-Hall, 2nd edition.

Kotler, P. (1972b), 'What Consumerism Means for Marketers', *Harvard Business Review*, Vol. 50, No. 3, May–June, pp. 48–57.

Kotler, P. (1977), 'From Sales Obsession to Marketing Effectiveness', *Harvard Business Review*, Vol. 55, No. 6, November–December, pp. 67–77.

Kotler, P. (1980), *Marketing Management: Analysis, Planning and Control*, Englewood Cliffs, NJ: Prentice-Hall, 4th edition.

Kotler, P. (ed.) (1984), *Marketing Management and Strategy: A Reader*, Englewood Cliffs, NJ: Prentice-Hall, 5th edition.

Kotler, P. (1987), *Marketing: An Introduction*, Englewood Cliffs, NJ: Prentice-Hall.

Kotler, P. (1988), *Marketing Management: Analysis, Planning, Implementation and Control*, Englewood Cliffs, NJ: Prentice-Hall, 6th edition.

Kotler, P. (1991), *Marketing Management: Analysis, Planning, Implementation and Control*, Englewood Cliffs, NJ: Prentice-Hall, 7th edition.

Kotler, P. (1997), *Marketing Management: Analysis, Planning, Implementation and Control*, Upper Saddle River, NJ: Prentice-Hall, 9th edition.

Kotler, P., Fahey, L. and Jatusripitak, S. (1985), *The New Competition*, Englewood Cliffs, NJ: Prentice-Hall.

Kotler, P., Gregor, W.T. and Rodgers, W.H. (1977), 'The Marketing Audit Comes of Age', *Sloan Management Review*, Vol. 18, No. 2, Winter, pp. 25–43.

Kotler, P., Gregor, W.T. and Rodgers, W.H. (1989), 'The Marketing Audit Comes of Age', *Sloan Management Review*, Vol. 30, No. 2, Winter, pp. 49–62.

Kuehn, A.A. (1961), 'A Model For Budgeting Advertising', in Bass, F.M. et al. (eds), *Models and Methods in Marketing*, Homewood, IL: Irwin.

Lalonde, B.J. and Zinszer, P.H. (1976), *Customer Service: Meaning and Measurement*, Chicago: NCPDM.

Lamb, R. and Shrivastava, P. (eds) (1986), *Advances in Strategic Management*, Greenwich, CT: JAI Press, Volume 4.

Lambert, D.M. and Sterling, J.U. (1987), 'What Types of Profitability Reports Do Marketing Managers Receive?', *Industrial Marketing Management*, Vol. 16, pp. 295–303.

Lancaster, G. and Jobber, M.D. (1985) *Sales: Technique and Management*, London: MacDonald & Evans.

Lancaster, G. and Massingham, L. (1988), *Essential of Marketing: Text and Cases*, London: McGraw-Hill.

Langrish, J., Gibbons, M., Evans, W.G. and Jevon, F.R. (1972), *Wealth from Knowledge – Studies of Innovation in Industry*, London: Macmillan.

Lawrence, P.R. and Lorsch, J. (1967), *Organization and Environment*, Boston, MA: Harvard University Press.

Lazer, W. (1962a), 'The Role of Models in Marketing', *Journal of Marketing*, Vol. 26, No. 2, April, pp. 9–14.

Lazer, W. (1962b), 'The Systems Concept in the Evolution of Marketing Management Thought', in *Marketing Precision and Executive Action* – Proceedings of 49th Annual Conference of the American Marketing Association.

Lehmann, D.R. and O'Shaughnessy, J. (1974), 'Differences in Attribute Importance for Different Industrial Products', *Journal of Marketing*, Vol. 38, No. 2, April, pp. 36–42.

Lehmann, D.R. and Winer, R.S. (1990), *Analysis for Marketing Planning*, Homewood, IL: Irwin, 2nd edition.

Leidecker, J.K. and Bruno, A.V. (1984), 'Identifying and Using Critical Success Factors', *Long Range Planning*, Vol. 17, February, pp. 23–32.

Leppard, J. and McDonald, M.H.B. (1987), 'A Re-Appraisal of the Role of Marketing Planning', *Journal of Marketing Management*, Vol. 3, No. 2, pp. 159–71.

Levitt, T. (1960), 'Marketing Myopia', *Harvard Business Review*, Vol. 38, No. 4, July–August, pp. 45–56.

Levitt, T. (1966), 'Innovative Imitation', *Harvard Business Review*, Vol. 44, No. 5, September–October, p. 63.

Levitt, T. (1976), 'The Augmented Product Concept', in Ruthberg, R.R. (ed.), *Corporate Strategy and Product Innovation*, New York: Free Press.

Levitt, T. (1980), 'Marketing Success Through Differentiation – of Anything', *Harvard Business Review*, Vol. 58, No. 1, January–February, pp. 83–91.

Lewis, K. (1997), 'World Changing Megatrends', A Presentation to Abbey National, London.

Lewis, R.W. (1955), 'Measuring, Reporting and Appraising Results of Operations with Reference to Goals, Plans and Budgets', in *Planning, Managing and Measuring: A Case Study of Management Planning and Control at General Electric Company*, New York: The Controllership Foundation.

Lewis, R. (1989), 'The Shape of Organisations to Come', *Management Training Update*, December.

Lewis, D. and Bridger, D. (2000), *The Soul of the New Consumer: Authenticity, what we buy and why in the new economy*, London: Nicholas Brearley.

Lieberman, M.B. (1987), 'The Learning Curve, Diffusion, and Competitive Strategy', *Strategic Management Journal*, Vol. 8, pp. 441–52.

Little, Arthur D. (1974), see Patel, P. and Younger, M. (1978), 'A Frame of Reference for Strategy Development', *Long Range Planning*, Vol. 11, No. 2, April, pp. 6–12.

Little, J.D.C. (1966), 'A Model of Adaptive Control of Promotional Spending', *Operations Research*, Vol. 14, No. 6, pp. 1075–97.

Littler, D. and Wilson, D. (eds) (1995), *Marketing Strategy*, Oxford: Butterworth-Heinemann.

Litwin, G., Bray, J. and Brooke, K.L. (1996), *Mobilizing the Organization: Bringing Strategy to Life*, London: Prentice-Hall.

Lorange, P. (ed.) (1982), *Implementation of Strategic Planning*, Englewood Cliffs, NJ: Prentice-Hall.

Loudon, A. (2002), *Waves of Innovation*, Pearson Education.

Lowe, E.A. (1971), 'On the Definition of "Systems" in Systems Engineering', *Journal of Systems Engineering*, Vol. 2, No. 1, Summer, pp. 95–8.

Lowe, E.A. and Machin, J.L.J. (eds) (1983), *New Perspectives in Management Control*, London: Macmillan.

Lowe, E.A. and Shaw, R.W. (1968), 'An Analysis of Managerial Biasing: Evidence from a Company's Budgeting Process', *Journal of Management Studies*, Vol. 5, No. 3, October, pp. 304–15.

Luck, D.J. and Ferrell, O.C. (1979), *Marketing Strategy and Plans*, Englewood Cliffs, NJ: Prentice-Hall.

Luck, D.J., Ferrell, O.C. and Lucas, G.S. (1989), *Marketing Strategy and Plans*, Englewood Cliffs, NJ: Prentice-Hall, 3rd edition.

Lunn, A., Blamires, C. and Browne, P. (1996), 'The Revitalisation of Mothercare', Proceedings of The Market Research Society Annual Conference.

Lyles, M.A. (1987), 'Defining Strategic Problems: Subjective Criteria of Excellence', *Organization Studies*, Vol. 8, No. 3, pp. 263–80.

Lynch, R. (1992), *European Marketing: A Guide to the New Opportunities*, London: Kogan Page.

Lynch, J.E., Hooley, G.J. and Shepherd, J. (1988), *The Effectiveness of British Marketing*, University of Bradford Management Centre.

McCammon, B.C. Jr (1970), 'Perspectives for Distribution Programming', in Bucklin, L.P. (ed.), Glenview, IL: Scott, Foresman.

McCarry, C. (1972), *Citizen Nader*, London: Jonathan Cape.

McCarthy, E. (1960), *Basic Marketing*, Homewood, IL: Irwin.

McCarthy, M.J. and Perreault, W.D. Jr (1990), *Essentials of Marketing: A Global-Managerial Approach*, Homewood, IL: Irwin.

McClelland, D.C. (1961), *The Achieving Society*, New York: Free Press.

McColl-Kennedy, J.R., Yau, O.H. and Kiel, G.C. (1990), 'Marketing Planning Practices in Australia: A Comparison Across Company Types', *Marketing Intelligence and Planning*, Vol. 8, No. 4, pp. 21–9.

McDonald, M.H.B. (1984), *Marketing Plans: How to Prepare Them, How to Use Them*, London: Heinemann.

McDonald, M.H.B. (1989), 'Ten Barriers to Marketing Planning', *Journal of Marketing Management*, Vol. 5, No. 1, pp. 1–18.

McDonald, M.H.B. (1990), 'SMEs – twelve factors for success in the 1990's', *Business Growth and Profitability*, Vol. 1, No. 1, pp. 11–19.

McDonald, M.H.B. (1995), *Marketing Plans: How to Prepare Them, How to Use Them*, Oxford: Butterworth-Heinemann, 3rd edition.

McDonald, M.H.B. (1998), 'A Slice of the Action', *Marketing Business*, July–August, p. 47.

McDonald, M.H.B. and Wilson, H.N. (1990), 'State-of-the-Art Developments in Expert Systems and Strategic Marketing Planning', *British Journal of Management*, Vol. 1, No. 3, September, pp. 159–70.

McDonald, M.H.B. and Wilson, H. (1999), 'Research for Practice: The Internet and Marketing Strategy', *Marketing Business*, June, Special feature.

McGonagale, J.J. and Vella, C.M. (1993), *Outsmarting the Competition*, London: McGraw-Hill.

McGraw-Hill (1963), *How Advertising Affects the Cost of Selling*, London: McGraw-Hill.

McGraw-Hill (1963), *Special Report on the Buying and Selling Techniques in the British Engineering Industry*, London: McGraw-Hill.

McGuire, J., Schneeweis, T. and Hill, J. (1986), 'An Analysis of Alternative Measures of Strategic Performance', pp. 127–54 in Lamb, R. and Shrivastava, P. (eds), Advances in Strategic Management, Greenwich, CT: JAI Press, Volume 4.

McKay, E.S. (1972), *The Marketing Mystique*, New York: American Management Association.

McKenna, R. (1991), *Relationship Marketing*, Reading, MA: Addison-Wesley.

McKinsey & Co. (2000), 'Marketing and Internet', A Presentation to the Chartered Institute of Marketing, Cookham, Berks, UK.

MacLennan, N. (2000), *Financial Times*, 31 July, p. 13.

MacLuhan, M. (1964), *Understanding Media: The Extension of Man*, London: Routledge.

MacLuhan, M. (1968), *The Medium is the Message*, New York: Random House.

McNamee, P. (1988), *Management Accounting: Strategic Planning and Marketing*, Oxford: Heinemann.

MacNeill, D.J. (1994), *Customer Service Excellence*, New York: American Media Inc.

McTavish, R. (1989), 'Implementing Marketing Strategy', *Management Decision*, Vol. 26, No. 5, pp. 9–12.

Machin, J.L.J. (1983), 'Management Control Systems: Whence & Whither?', Ch. 2, pp. 22–42 in Lowe, E.A. and Machin, J.L.J. (eds), *New Perspectives in Management Control*, London: Macmillan.

Maciariello, J.A. (1984), *Management Control Systems*, Englewood Cliffs, NJ: Prentice-Hall.

Madrick, J.G. (1995), *The End of Affluence: The Causes and Consequences of America's Economic Decline*, New York: Random House.

Magrath, A.J. (1988) 'People Productivity: Marketing's Most Valuable Asset', *Journal of Business Strategy*, Vol. 9, No. 4, pp. 12–14.

Magrath, A.J. and Hardy, K.G. (1986), 'Cost Containment in Marketing', *Journal of Business Strategy*, Vol. 7, No. 2, pp. 14–21.

Majaro, S. (1972), 'A Market Strategy for Europe', in Blake, J.E. (ed.), *Design For European Markets: A Management Guide*, London: Design Council.

Majaro, S. (1978), *International Marketing*, London: George Allen & Unwin.

Makens, J.C. (1989), *The 12-Day Marketing Plan*, Wellingborough: Thorsons.

Mann, N.R. (1989), *The Keys to Excellence: The Deming Philosophy*, London: Mercury.

Mansfield, E. and Wagner, S. (1975) 'Organizational and Strategic Factors Associated with Possibilities of Success in Industrial R&D', *Journal of Business*, April, pp. 179–98.

March, J.G. and Simon, H.A. (1958), *Organizations*, New York: Wiley (2nd edition 1993, Cambridge, MA: Blackwell).

Market Research Society (1990), *Occupational Groups: A Job Dictionary*, London: MRS.

Markovitz, Z.N. (1987), 'Hidden Sector Competitor Analysis', *Planning Review*, Vol. 15, No. 5, pp. 20–4, 46.

Martilla, J.C. (1971), '"Word of Mouth" Communication in the Industrial Adoption Process', *Journal of Marketing Research*, Vol. 3, No. 2, pp. 173–8.

Martin, P. (2002), 'Decline of the Turin Empire', *Financial Times*, 14 May, p. 17.

Maslow, A.E. (1954), *Motivation and Personality*, New York: Harper & Row.

Mathur, S.S. (1986), 'Strategy: Framing Business Intentions', *Journal of General Management*, Vol. 12, No. 1, pp. 77–97.

Mazur, L. (2000), 'Past Experience is No Guide to the Future', *Marketing*, 15 June, p. 20.

Mehotra, S. (1984), 'How to Measure Marketing Productivity', *Journal of Advertising Research*, Vol. 24, No. 3, pp. 9–15.

Meldrum, M.J., Ward, K. and Srikanthan, S. (1986), 'Can You Really Account for Marketing?', *Marketing Intelligence & Planning*, Vol. 4, No. 4, pp. 39–45.

Meldrum, M.J., Ward, K. and Srikanthan, S. (1987), 'Needs, Issues and Directions in the Marketing Accountancy Divide', *Quarterly Review of Marketing*, Vol. 12, No. 3–4, pp. 5–12.

Merchant, K.A. (1985), *Control in Business*, Boston: Pitman.

Merchant, K.A. (1988), 'Progressing Toward a Theory of Marketing Control: A Comment', *Journal of Marketing*, Vol. 52, No. 3, pp. 40–4.

Merchant, K.A. (1998), *Modern Management Control Systems*, Upper Saddle River, NJ: Prentice-Hall.

Miles, R.E. (1980), *Macro Organisational Behavior*, Glenview, IL: Scott, Foresman.

Miles, R.E. and Snow, C.C. (1978), *Organizational Strategy, Structure & Process*, New York: McGraw-Hill.

Milton, F. and Reiss, T. (1985a), 'Competitive Strategy', *Accountancy Ireland*, Vol. 17, No. 5, pp. 13–17.

Milton, F. and Reiss, T. (1985b), 'Developing a Competitive Strategy', *Accountancy Ireland*, Vol. 17, No. 5, pp. 19–23, 28.

Mintel Report (1988), 'Retailing: The Non-Store Alternatives – 1987', London: Mintel.

Mintzberg, H. (1987), 'Crafting Strategy', *Harvard Business Review*, Vol. 65, No. 4, pp. 66–75.

Mintzberg, H. (1994), *The Rise and Fall of Strategic Planning: Reconceiving Roles for Planning, Plans, Planners*, New York: The Free Press.

Mitchell, A. (1995), 'Missing Measures', *Management Today*, November, pp. 76–8, 80.

Mitchell, A. (1997), *Marketing Business*, February, p. 18.

Montgomery, D.B. and Urban, G.L. (1969), *Management Science in Marketing*, Englewood Cliffs, NJ: Prentice-Hall.

Montgomery, D.B. and Urban, G.L. (eds) (1969), *Applications of Management Science in Marketing*, Englewood Cliffs, NJ: Prentice-Hall.

Morgan, A. (1999), *Eating the Big Fish*, London: John Wiley.

Morgan, N.A. and Piercy, N.F. (1996), 'Competitive Advantage, Quality Strategy and the Role of Marketing', *British Journal of Management*, Vol. 7, pp. 231–45.

Morrison, A. and Wensley, J.R.C. (1991), 'Boxing Up or Boxed In?: A Short History of the Boston Consulting Group Share/Growth Matrix', *Journal of Marketing Management*, Vol. 7, No. 2, pp. 105–29.

Mossman, F.H. and Worrell, M.L. (1966), 'Analytical Methods of Measuring Marketing Profitability: A Matrix Approach', *MSU Business Topics*, Vol. 14, No. 4, pp. 35–45.

Mossman, F.H., Fischer, P.M. and Crissy, W.J.E. (1974), 'New Approaches to Analyzing Marketing Profitability', *Journal of Marketing*, Vol. 38, No. 2, pp. 43–8.

Mowen, J.C. and Gaeth, G.J. (1992), 'The Evaluation Stage in Marketing Decision Making', *Journal of the Academy of Marketing Science*, Vol. 20, No. 2, pp. 178–88.

Mulvaney, J. (1969), *The Use of Network Analysis in Marketing*, Cookham: Chartered Institute of Marketing.

Munro, R.J.B. and Cooper, P. (1989), 'The Impact of Changes in Strategic Thinking on Management Control Systems: The Selection of Non-Financial Measure in a Functional Structure'. Paper given at the Annual Conference of the British Accounting Association, University of Bath, March.

Murray, J.A. and O'Driscoll, A. (1996), *Strategy and Process in Marketing*, London: Prentice-Hall.

Myers, J.H. and Samli, A.C. (1969), 'Management Control of Marketing Research', *Journal of Marketing Research*, Vol. 6, No. 3, pp. 267–77.

Myers, S. and Marquis, D.G. (1969), *Successful Industrial Innovations: A Study of Factors Underlying Innovation in Selected Firms*, New York: National Science Foundation.

Nagle, T.T. (1987), *The Strategies and Tactics of Pricing*, Englewood Cliffs, NJ: Prentice-Hall.

Naisbitt, J. and Aburdene, P. (1982), *Megatrends: Ten New Directions Transforming Our Lives*, New York: Warner Books.

Naisbitt, J. and Aburdene, P. (1990), *Megatrends 2000*, London: Sidgwick & Jackson.

Narver, J.C. and Savit, R. (1971), *The Marketing Economy*, New York: Holt, Rinehart & Winston.

Narver, J.C. and Slater, S.F. (1990), 'The Effect of a Market Orientation on Business Profitability', *Journal of Marketing*, Vol. 54, October, pp. 20–35.

Nathanson, D.A., Kazanjian, R.K. and Galbraith, J.R. (1982), 'Effective Strategic Planning and the Role of Organization Design', Ch. 6 (pp. 91–113) in Lorange, P. (ed.), *Implementation of Strategic Planning*, Englewood Cliffs, NJ: Prentice-Hall.

Nattermann, P. (2000), 'Best Practice Does Not Equal Best Strategy', *McKinsey Quarterly*, Summer.

Naumann, E. (1995), 'Creating Customer Value: The Path to Sustainable Competitive Advantage', *National Productivity Review*, Vol. 14, No. 1, pp. 16–17.

Neugarten, B. (1968), *Middle Age and Aging*, University of Chicago Press.

Newell, F. (2003), *Why CRM Doesn't Work: How to win by letting customers manage the relationship*, London: Kogan Page.

Nicosia, F.M. (1966), *Consumer Decision Processes*, Englewood Cliffs, NJ: Prentice-Hall.

Nilson, T.H. (1995), *Chaos Marketing: how to win in a turbulent world*, Maidenhead: McGraw-Hill.

Nonaka, I. and Nicosia, F.M. (1979), 'Marketing Management, its Environment and Information Processing: A Problem of Organization Design', *Journal of Business Research*, Vol. 7, No. 4, pp. 277–301.

Nutt, P.C. (1987), 'Identifying and Appraising How Managers Install Strategy', *Strategic Management Journal*, Vol. 8, pp. 1–14.

Nutt, P.C. (1989), 'Selecting Tactics to Implement Strategic Plans', *Strategic Management Journal*, Vol. 10, pp. 145–61.

Oakland, J.S. (1989), *Total Quality Management*, Oxford: Butterworth-Heinemann.

O'Brien, S. and Ford, R. (1988), 'Can We at Last Say Goodbye to Social Class?', *Journal of the Market Research Society*, Vol. 30, No. 3, pp. 289–332.

Ogilvy, D. (1964), *Confessions of an Advertising Man*, London: Longmans Green.

Ohmae, K. (1983), *The Mind of the Strategist*, London: Penguin.

Openshaw, S. (1989), 'Making Geodemographics More Sophisticated' *Journal of the Market Research Society*, Vol. 31, No. 1, pp. 111–31.

O'Shaughnessy, J. (1995), *Competitive Marketing: A Strategic Approach*, London: Routledge, 3rd edition.

Otley, D.T. and Berry, A.J. (1980), 'Control, Organization and Accounting', *Accounting, Organizations and Society*, Vol. 5, No. 2, pp. 231–46.

Ouchi, W. (1983), *Theory Z*, Reading, MA: Addison-Wesley.

Oxenfeldt, A.R. (1973), 'A Decision Making Structure for Price Decisions', *Journal of Marketing*, Vol. 37, No. 1, January, pp. 48–54.

Packard, V. (1957), *The Hidden Persuaders*, Harmondsworth: Penguin Books.

Palin, R. (1985), 'Operational PR', in Howards, W. (ed.), *The Practice of Public Relations*, London: Heinemann.

Parkinson, S. (1995), *Manufacturing – The Marketing Solution*, Cookham: The Chartered Institute of Marketing.

Pascale, R.T. (1990), *Managing on the Edge: how successful companies use conflict to stay ahead*, New York: Simon & Schuster.

Pearson, G.J. (1979), 'Setting Corporate Objectives as a Basis for Action', *Long Range Planning*, Vol. 12, August, pp. 13–19.

Pearson, G.J. (1993), 'Business Orientation: Cliché or Substance?', *Journal of Marketing Management*, Vol. 9, No. 3, July, pp. 233–43.

Peattie, K.J. and Notley, D.S. (1989), 'The Marketing and Strategic Planning Interface', *Journal of Marketing Management*, Vol. 4, No. 3, pp. 330–49.

Peck, H., Payne, A., Christopher, M. and Clark, M. (1999), *Relationship Marketing: Strategy and Implementation*, Oxford: Butterworth-Heinemann.

Peters, T.J. (1988), *Thriving on Chaos*, Macmillan.

Peters, T.J. (1992) *Liberation Management*, New York: Knopf.

Peters, T.J. and Waterman, R.H. (1982), *In Search of Excellence: Lessons from America's Best Run Companies*, New York: Harper & Row.

Pettigrew, A.M. (1975), 'The Industrial Purchasing Decision as a Political Process', *European Journal of Marketing*, Vol. 9, No. 1, pp. 4–19.

Pfeffer, J. (1978), *Organizational Design*, Arlington Heights, IL: AHM.

Piercy, N.F. (1985), *Marketing Organisation: An Analysis of Information Processing, Power and Politics*, London: Allen & Unwin.

Piercy, N.F. (1986), *Marketing Budgeting*, London: Croom Helm.

Piercy, N.F. (1987a), 'Servicing the Needs of Marketing Management', *Management Accounting* (CIMA), Vol. 65, No. 3, March, pp. 42–3.

Piercy, N.F. (1987b), 'The Marketing Budgeting Process: Marketing Management Implications', *Journal of Marketing*, Vol. 51, No. 4, October, pp. 45–9.

Piercy, N.F. (1991), *Market-led Strategic Change*, London: Thorsons.

Piercy, N.F. (1992) *Market-led Strategic Change*, Oxford: Butterworth-Heinemann.

Piercy, N.F. (1997), *Market-led Strategic Change: Transforming the process of going to market*, Oxford: Butterworth-Heinemann, 3rd edition.

Piercy, N.F. (1999), 'Relationship Marketing Myopia', *Marketing Business*, October.

Piercy, N.F. (2002), *Market-led Strategic Change: Transforming the process of going to market*, Oxford: Butterworth-Heinemann, 4th edition.

Piercy, N.F. and Morgan, N. (1989a), 'Good Plans Need Internal Marketing', *The Sunday Times*, 10 September, p. E1.

Piercy, N.F. and Morgan, N. (1989b), 'Learning to Love the Marketing Task', *The Sunday Times*, 12 November, p. E14.

Piercy, N.F. and Morgan, N. (1990), 'Making Marketing Strategies Happen in the Real World', *Marketing Business*, Issue 9, February, pp. 20–1.

Piercy, N.F. and Morgan, N.A. (1994), 'The Marketing Planning Process: Behavioral Problems Compared to Analytical Techniques and Explaining Marketing Plan Credibility', *Journal of Business Research*, Vol. 29, pp. 167–78.

Pilcher, R. (1989), 'Managing Exports Effectively', *Accountancy*, Vol. 103, No. 1148, April, pp. 75–8.

Pilditch, J. (1987), 'Winning Companies Concentrate on Their People and Products', *The Times*, 25 June, p. 29.

Planning Review (1989), Competitive Intelligence Issues: Vol. 15, No. 5, September–October 1987; Vol. 17, No. 3, May–June.

Platchta, J. (1990), 'Does Sweet Talk Pay?', *Management Today*, March, pp. 91–2, 94.

Ploos Van Austel, M.J. (1987), 'Physical Distribution Cost Control', *International Journal of Physical Distribution and Materials Management*, Vol. 17, No. 2, pp. 67–78.

Poczter, A. and Siegel, J.G. (1986), 'How to Finance Your Marketing Strategy', *FE*, Vol. 2, No. 2, February, pp. 41–4.

Polli, R. and Cook, V. (1969), 'The Validity of the Product Life Cycle', *Journal of Business*, Vol. 42, No. 4, October, pp. 385–400.

Popcorn, F. (2001), *Eve-olution: The 8 truths of marketing to women*, Profile Business.

Porter, L.M. and Roberts, K.H. (eds) (1977), *Communication in Organizations*, Harmondsworth: Penguin.

Porter, M.E. (1979), 'How Competitive Forces Shape Strategy', *Harvard Business Review*, Vol. 57, No. 2, March–April, pp. 137–45.

Porter, M.E. (1980), *Competitive Strategy*, New York: Free Press.

Porter, M.E. (1985a), *Competitive Advantage: Creating and Sustaining Superior Performance*, New York: Free Press.

Porter, M.E. (1985b), 'How to Attack the Industry Leader', *Fortune*, Vol. 111, 29 April, pp. 97–104.

Porter, M.E. (1990), *The Competitive Advantage of Nations*, New York: Free Press.

Posner, M. (1986), 'Sales and Finance Staff Should Harmonise', *Accountancy*, Vol. 98, No. 1116, August, pp. 113–14.

Powers, T.L. (1987), 'Breakeven Analysis with Semifixed Costs', *Industrial Marketing Management*, Vol. 16, No. 1, February, pp. 35–42.

Prescott, J.E. (ed.) (1989), *Advances in Competitor Intelligence*, Vienna, VA: Society of Competitor Intelligence Professionals.

Prescott, J.E. and Smith, D.C. (1989), 'The Largest Survey of "Leading Edge" Competitor Intelligence Managers', *Planning Review*, Vol. 17, No. 3, May–June, pp. 6–13.

Prescott, J.E., Kohli, A.K. and Venkatraman, N. (1986), 'The Market Share–Profitability Relationship: An Empirical Assessment of Major Assertions and Contradictions', *Strategic Management Journal*, Vol. 7, No. 4, July–August, pp. 377–94.

Project SAPPHO (n.d.), *A Study of Success and Failure in Innovation*, Science Policy Research-Unit, University of Sussex.

Publicis (2002), *The New Assertiveness*, London: Publicis.

Puxty, A.G. and Dodds, J.C. (1991), *Financial Management: Method and Meaning*, London: Chapman & Hall, 2nd edition.

Pyne, F.G. (1984), 'Better, Operating Statements for the Marketing Director', *Accountancy*, Vol. 95, No. 1086, February, pp. 87–90.

Pyne, F.G. (1985), 'Accountancy that Helps to Meet and Beat Competition', *Accountancy*, Vol. 96, No. 1104, August, pp. 104–7.

Quelch, J.A., Buzzell, R.D. and Salama, E.R. (1990), *The Marketing Challenge of 1992*, Reading, MA: Addison-Wesley.

Rabino, S. and Wright, A. (1984), 'Applying Financial Portfolio and Multiple Criteria Approaches to Product Line Decisions', *Industrial Marketing Management*, Vol. 13, pp. 233–40.

Rafiq, M. and Ahmed, P.K. (1993), 'The Scope of Internal Marketing: Defining the Boundary Between Marketing and Human Resource Management', *Journal of Marketing Management*, Vol. 9, No. 3, pp. 219–232.

Rapp, S. and Collins, T.L. (1987), *Maxi Marketing*, New York: McGraw-Hill.

Rapp, S. and Collins, T.L. (1990), *The Great Marketing Turnaround: The Age of the Individual and How to Profit From It*, Englewood Cliffs, NJ: Prentice-Hall.

Rappaport, A. (1967), 'Sensitivity Analysis in Decision-Making', *The Accounting Review*, Vol. 42, No. 3, July, pp. 441–56.

Rappaport, A. (1986), *Creating Shareholder Value: The New Standard for Business Performance*, New York: Free Press.

Ratnatunga, J.T.D. (1983), *Financial Controls in Marketing: The Accounting – Marketing Interface*, Canberra: Canberra College of Advanced Education.

Ratnatunga, J.T.D. (1988), *Accounting for Competitive Marketing*, London: CIMA (Occasional Paper Series).

Reading, B. (1988), 'Why it's Time for Us to Save', *The Sunday Times*, 11 December.

Reed, R. and Buckley, M.R. (1988), 'Strategy in Action – Techniques for Implementing Strategy', *Long Range Planning*, Vol. 21, No. 3, pp. 67–74.

Reeves, R. (1961), *Reality in Advertising*, New York: Knopf.

Reid, D.M. (1989), 'Operationalizing Strategic Planning', *Strategic Management Journal*, Vol. 10, pp. 553–67.

Reid, D.M. and Hinckley, L.C. (1989), 'Strategic Planning: The Cultural Impact', *Marketing Intelligence and Planning*, Vol. 7, No. 11/12, pp. 4–11.

Reimann, B.C. (1989), *Managing for Value*, Oxford: Basil Blackwell.

Resnik, A.J., Turney, P.B.B. and Mason, J.B. (1979), 'Marketers Turn to Countersegmentation', *Harvard Business Review*, Vol. 57, No. 5, September–October, pp. 100–6.

Rhyne, L.C. (1986), 'The Relationship of Strategic Planning to Financial Performance', *Strategic Management Journal*, Vol. 7, pp. 423–36.

Richards, M. (1978), *Organizational Goal Structures*, St Paul, MN: West Publishing Company.

Richardson, P.R. (1988), *Cost Containment: The Ultimate Advantage*, New York: Free Press.

Richardson, S. (2001), *The Young West: How we are all growing older more slowly*, San Diego, CA: University of California.

Richardson, W. and Richardson, R. (1989), *Business Planning: A Strategic Approach to World Markets*, London: Pitman.

Ridderstråle, J. and Nordström, K. (2000), *Funky Business: Talent makes capital dance*, FT.com.

Ries, A. and Trout, J. (1982), *Positioning: the Battle for Your Mind*, New York: Warner Books.

Ries, A. and Trout, J. (1986), *Marketing Warfare*, New York: McGraw-Hill.

Riesman, D., Glazer, N. and Dinny, R. (1950), *The Lonely Crowd*, New Haven, CT: Yale University Press.

Ritson, M. (2002), 'Wal-Mart: A Shopping Revolution', *Business Life*, March, p. 21.

Rivkin, J. (1995), *The End of Work: The Decline of the Global Labor Force and the Dawn of the Post-Market Era*, New York: G.P. Putnam's Sons.

Roach, J.D.C. (1981), 'From Strategic Planning to Strategic Performance: Closing the Achievement Gap', *Outlook*, Spring, New York: Booz Allen & Hamilton.

Robert, M.M. (1990), 'Managing Your Competitor's Strategy', *Journal of Business Strategy*, Vol. 11, No. 2, pp. 24–8.

Robertson, R.S. (1967), 'The Process of Innovation and the Diffusion of Innovation', *Journal of Marketing*, Vol. 3, No. 1, January, pp. 14–19.

Robinson, P.J., Faris, C.W. and Wind, Y. (1967), *Industrial Buying and Creative Marketing*, Boston, MA: Allyn & Bacon.

Robinson, S.J.Q., Hichens, R.E. and Wade, D.P. (1978), 'The Directional Policy Matrix – Tool for Strategic Planning', *Long Range Planning*, Vol. 11, No. 3, June, pp. 8–15.

Robinson, W.T. and Fornell, C. (1985a), 'Market Pioneering and Sustainable Market Share Advantages', *PIMSletter*, 39, Cambridge, MA: Strategic Planning Institute.

Robinson, W.T. and Fornell, C. (1985b), 'Sources of Market Pioneer Advantages in Consumer Goods Industries', *Journal of Marketing Research*, Vol. 22, No. 3, August, pp. 305–17.

Rockart, J.F. (1979), 'Chief Executives Define Their Own Data Needs', *Harvard Business Review*, Vol. 57, No. 2, March–April, pp. 81–93.

Rodger, L.W. (1965), *Marketing in a Competitive Economy*, London: Hutchinson.

Rogers, E.M. (1962), *Diffusion of Innovations*, New York: Free Press.

Rogers, B. (2000), *easyJet 2000*, Lausanne: International Institute for Management Development.

Rosenbloom, B. (1995), 'Channel Management', Ch. 32, pp. 551–570 in Baker, M.J. (ed.), *Companion Encyclopaedia of Marketing*, London: Routledge.

Rothman, L.J. (1989), 'Different Measures of Social Grade', *Journal of The Market Research Society*, Vol. 31, No. 1, pp. 139–40.

Rothschild, W.E. (1984), *How to Gain (and Maintain) the Competitive Advantage*, New York: McGraw-Hill.

Rothschild, W.E. (1989), *How to Gain (and Maintain) the Competitive Advantage*, New York: McGraw-Hill.

Rothwell, R. (1972), Project SAPPHO: An Interim Report, Working Paper, Science Policy Unit, University of Sussex.

Rothwell, R. (1974), SAPPHO Updated – Project SAPPHO Phase II, *Research Policy*, Vol. 3, pp. 258–91.

Rothwell, R. (1977), 'The Characteristics of Successful Innovators and Technically Progressive Firms', *R & D Management*, Vol. 7, No. 3, pp. 191–206.

Ruekert, R.W., Walker, O.C. and Roering, K.J. (1985), 'The Organization of Marketing Activities: A Contingency Theory of Structure and Performance', *Journal of Marketing*, Vol. 49, pp. 13–25.

St Thomas, C.E. (1965), *Practical Business Planning*, New York: AMA.

Salancik, G.R. and Upah, G.D. (1978), Directions for Interorganisational Marketing, Unpublished paper, University of Illinois, August.

Sanderson, S.M. and Luffman, G.A. (1988), 'Strategic Planning and Environmental Analysis', *European Journal of Marketing*, Vol. 22, No. 2, pp. 14–27.

Saunders, J.A. (1987a), 'Marketing and Competitive Success', in Baker, M.J. (ed.), *The Marketing Book*, London: Macmillan.

Saunders, J.A. (1987b), 'Attitudes, Structure and Behaviour in a Successful Company', *Journal of Marketing Management*, Vol. 3, No. 2, pp. 173–83.

Saunders, J.A., Saker, J.M. and Smith, I.G. (eds) (1996), 'Exploring Marketing Planning', Special Issue of *Journal of Marketing Management*, Vol. 12, Nos 1–3.

Schaffir, K.H. and Trentin, H.G. (1973), *Marketing Information Systems*, New York: Amacom.

Scherer, F.M. (1980), *Industrial Market Structure and Economic Performance*, Chicago: Rand McNally, 2nd edition.

Schiff, M. and Mellman, M. (1962), *The Financial Management of the Marketing Function*, New York: FERF.

Schiffman, L.G. and Kanuk, L.L. (1983), *Consumer Behavior*, Englewood Cliffs, NJ: Prentice-Hall, 2nd edition.

Schmid, R.D. (1987), 'Reverse Engineering a Service Product', *Planning Review*, Vol. 15, No. 5, September–October, pp. 33–5.

Schoderbeck, P.P. (ed.) (1971), *Management Systems: A Book of Readings*, New York: Wiley, 2nd edition.

Schoderbek, P.P., Kefalas, A.G. and Schoderbek, C.G. (1975), *Management Systems: Conceptual Considerations*, Dallas: Business Publications.

Schoeffler, S. (1977), 'Market Position: Build, Hold or Harvest?', *The PIMSletter on Business Strategy*, No. 3, Cambridge, MA: Strategic Planning Institute.

Schwartz, D. (1973), *Marketing Today*, New York: Harcourt, Brace, Jovanovich.

Schwartz, G. (ed.) (1965), *Science in Marketing*, New York: Wiley.

Sevin, C.H. (1965), *Marketing Productivity Analysis*, New York: McGraw-Hill.

Seybold, P. (2001), *The Customer Revolution*, London: Random House Business Books.

Shapiro, S.J. and Kirpalani, V.H. (eds) (1984), *Marketing Effectiveness*, Boston: Allyn & Bacon.

Shapiro, B.P. et al. (1987), 'Manage Customers for Profits (Not Just Sales)', *Harvard Business Review*, Vol. 65, No. 5, September–October, pp. 101–8.

Shaw, R. (1998), *Improving Marketing Effectiveness*, The Economist/Profile Books.

Shell Chemical Company (1975), *The Directional Policy Matrix: A New Aid to Corporate Planning*, London: Shell.

Sheth, J.N. (1969), *The Theory of Buyer Behavior*, New York: Wiley.

Sheth, J.N. (1973), 'Industrial Buyer Behavior', *Journal of Marketing*, Vol. 37, No. 4, October, pp. 50–6.

Shillinglaw, G. (1964), 'Divisional Performance Review: An Extension of Budgetary Control', in Bonini, C.P., Jaedicke, R.K. and Wagner, H.M. (eds), *Management Controls: New Directions in Basic Research*, New York: McGraw-Hill.

Shuchman, A. (1950), 'The Marketing Audit: its Nature, Purposes and Problems', in Oxenfeldt, A.R. and Crisp, R.D. (eds), *Analysing and Improving Marketing Performance*, New York: American Management Association, Report No. 32.

Simkin, L. (1996), 'People and Processes in Marketing Planning: The Benefits of Controlling Implementation', *Journal of Marketing Management*, Vol. 12, No. 5, July, pp. 375–90.

Simmonds, K. (1980), 'Strategic Management Accounting', Paper presented to ICMA Technical Symposium, Oxford.

Simmonds, K. (1981), 'Strategic Management Accounting', *Management Accounting*, Vol. 59, No. 4, April, pp. 26–9. Reprinted in Cowe, R. (ed.) (1988), *Handbook of Management Accounting*, Aldershot: Gower, 2nd edition, pp. 14–36.

Simmonds, K. (1982), 'Strategic Management Accounting for Pricing: A Case Example', *Accounting and Business Research*, Vol. 12, No. 47, Summer, pp. 206–14.

Simmonds, K. (1985), 'How to Compete', *Management Today*, August, pp. 39–43, 84.

Simmonds, K. (1986), 'The Accounting Assessment of Competitive Position', *European Journal of Marketing*, Vol. 20, No. 1, pp. 16–31.

Simmonds, K. (1989), 'Strategic Management Accounting: The Emerging Paradigm', Plenary lecture given at 12th Annual Conference of the European Accounting Association, University of Stuttgart, April.

Simmons, W.W. (1972), 'Practical Planning', *Long Range Planning*, Vol. 5, No. 2, June pp. 32–9.

Simms, J. (1995), 'Market or Die', *Marketing Business*, June, pp. 12–13.

Simon, H.A. (1960), *The New Science of Management Decision*, New York: Harper & Row.

Simon, H. (1996), *Hidden Champions: Lessons from 500 of the world's best unknown companies*, Boston, MA: Harvard Business School Press.

Simons, R. (1987), 'Accounting Control Systems and Business Strategy: An Empirical Analysis', *Accounting, Organizations and Society*, Vol. 12, No. 4, pp. 357–74.

Simons, R. (1990), 'The Role of Management Control Systems in Creating Competitive Advantage: New Perspectives', *Accounting, Organizations and Society*, Vol. 15, No. 1/2, pp. 127–43.

Slack, N., Chambers, S., Harland, C. et al. (1998), *Operations Management*, London: Pitman, 2nd edition.

Slevin, D.P. and Pinto, J.K. (1987), 'Balancing Strategy and Tactics in Project Implementation', *Sloan Management Review*, Vol. 29, No. 1, Fall, pp. 33–41.

Smith, D.C. and Prescott, J.E. (1987), 'Demystifying Competitive Analysis', *Planning Review*, Vol. 15, No. 5, September–October, pp. 8–13.

Sofer, C. (1972), *Organizations in Theory and Practice*, London: Heinemann.

Spekman, R.E. and Grønhaug, K. (1983), 'Insights on Implementation: A Conceptual Framework for Better Understanding the Strategic Marketing Planning Process', AMA Conference Proceedings, Chicago: American Marketing Association.

Srikanthan, S., Ward, K. and Meldrum, M.J. (1986), 'Reducing the Costs of the Marketing Game', *Management Accounting* (CIMA), Vol. 64, No. 10, November, pp. 48–51.

Srikanthan, S., Ward, K. and Meldrum, M.J. (1987a), 'Segment Profitability: A Positive Contribution', *Management Accounting* (CIMA), Vol. 65, No. 4, April, pp. 27–30.

Srikanthan, S., Ward, K. and Meldrum, M.J. (1987b), 'Marketing: The Unrecognised Asset', *Management Accounting* (CIMA), Vol. 65, No. 5, May, pp. 38–42.

Stacey, R. (1991), *The Chaos Frontier: Creative Strategic Control for Business*, Oxford: Butterworth-Heinemann.

Stacey, R.D. (1992), *Managing Chaos: Dynamic business strategies in an unpredictable world*, Kogan Page.

Stacey, R.D. (1994), 'Order from Chaos', *Management Today*, November, pp. 62–5.

Stacey, R.D. (1996), *Strategic Management and Organisational Dynamics*, London: Pitman, 2nd edition.

Stapleton, C. (1991), 'Strategic Alliances', *Management Consultancy*, April, pp. 40, 43.

Starr, M.K. (1971), *Management: A Modern Approach*, New York: Harcourt, Brace, Jovanovich.

Stasch, S.F. (1972), *Systems Analysis for Marketing Planning and Control*, Glenview, IL: Scott, Foresman.

Staw, B.M. and Ross, J. (1987a), 'Knowing When to Pull the Plug', *Harvard Business Review*, Vol. 65, No. 2, March–April, pp. 68–74.

Staw, B.M. and Ross, J. (1987b), 'Behavior in Escalation Situations: Antecedents, Prototypes and Solutions', *Research in Organizational Behavior*, Vol. 9, pp. 39–78.

Steiner, G. (1969), *Strategic Factors in Business Success*, New York: FERF.

Stern, M.E. (1966), *Marketing Planning: A Systems Approach*, New York: McGraw-Hill.

Stone, M. and Young, L.D. (1992), *Competitive Customer Care: a guide to keeping customers*, London: Croner.

Stonich, P.L. (1975), 'Formal Planning Pitfalls and How to Avoid Them', *Management Review*, No. 64, July.

Strauss, G. (1962), 'Tactics of Lateral Relationships: The Purchasing Agent', *Administrative Science Quarterly*, Vol. 7, No. 3, September, pp. 161–86.

Strebel, P. (1996), 'Breakpoint: How to Stay in the Game', *Financial Times, Mastering Management*, Part 17, pp. 13–14.

Sturges, J. (1991), 'Top Marketers', *Marketing Week*, 22 March, pp. 26–33.

Sun Tzu (1963), *The Art of War*, London: Oxford University Press.

Sutton, H. (1988), *Competitive Intelligence* (Research Report No. 913), New York: The Conference Board.

Swan, J.E. and Rink, D.R. (1982), 'Variations on the Product Life Cycle', *Business Horizons*, Vol. 25, No. 1, January–February, pp. 72–6.

Tannenbaum, A.S. (1964), 'Control in Organizations: Individual Adjustment and Organizational Performance', in Bonini, C.P., Jaedicke, R.K. and Wagner, H.M. (eds), *Management Controls: New Directions in Basic Research*, New York: McGraw-Hill.

Taylor, J.W. (1992), 'Competitive Intelligence: A Status Report on US Business Practices', *Journal of Marketing Management*, Vol. 8, No. 2, April, pp. 117–25.

Test, D.L., Hawley, J.D. and Cortright, M.F. (1987), 'Determining Strategic Value', *Management Accounting* (CIMA), Vol. 68, No. 12, June, pp. 39–42.

Thomas, M.J. (1984), 'The Meaning of Marketing Productivity Analysis', *Marketing Intelligence and Planning*, Vol. 2, No. 2, pp. 13–28.

Thomas, M.J. (1986), 'Marketing Productivity Analysis: A Research Report', *Marketing Intelligence and Planning*, Vol. 4, No. 2.

Thomas, M.J. (1987a), 'Does Your Marketing Pay?', *Management Decision*, Vol. 25, No. 4, pp. 41–5.

Thomas, M.J. (1987b), in Baker, M.J. (ed.), *The Marketing Book*, London: Heinemann.

Thomas, M.J. (1993), 'Marketing – In Chaos or Transition?', pp. 114–23 in Brownlie, D. (ed.), *Rethinking Marketing*, Coventry: Warwick Business School Research Bureau.

Thomas, M.J. (1994), 'Marketing's Future as a Profession', Keynote Presentation to the Annual Conference of the Chartered Institute of Marketing, Harrogate.

Thomas, P.S. (1980), 'Environmental Scanning – the State of the Art', *Long Range Planning*, Vol. 13, No. 1, pp. 20–8.

Tilles, S. (1963), 'How To Evaluate Corporate Strategy', *Harvard Business Review*, Vol. 41, No. 4, July–August, pp. 111–21.

Tocher, K. (1970), 'Control', *Operational Research Quarterly*, Vol. 21, No. 2, June, pp. 159–80.

Tocher, K. (1976), 'Notes for Discussion on "Control"', *Operational Research Quarterly*, Vol. 27, No. 2, June, pp. 231–9.

Toffler, A. (1970), *Future Shock*, New York: Bantam Books.

Toffler, A. (1980), *The Third Wave*, New York: Bantam Books.

Tomkins, C.R. (1991), *Corporate Resource Allocation: Financial, Strategic and Organizational Perspectives*, Oxford: Blackwell.

Tookey, D.A. (1974), 'The Marketing Function in its Organisational Context', in *Marketing as a Non-American Activity*, Proceedings, MEG Conference, July.

Treacy, M. and Wiersema, F. (1995), *The Discipline of Market Leaders*, Reading, MA: Addison-Wesley.

Trout, J. and Rifkin, S. (2000), *Differentiate or Die: Survival in our era of killer competition*, John Wiley.

Tschohl, J. (1991) 'Courtesy, Friendliness and Speed: Customer Service Importance', *Supervision*, Vol. 52, No. 2, February, pp. 9–11.

Turnbull, P.W. (1987), 'Organisational Buying Behaviour', in Baker, M.J. (ed.), *The Marketing Book*, London: Heinemann.

Turnbull, P.W. and Cunningham, M.T. (1981), *International Marketing and Purchasing*, London: Macmillan.

Tushman, M.L. and Nadler, P.A. (1978), 'Information Processing as an Integrating Concept in Organizational Design', *Academy of Management Review*, Vol. 3, No. 3, pp. 613–24.

Udell, J.G. (1964), 'How Important is Pricing in Competitive Strategy?', *Journal of Marketing*, Vol. 28, No. 1, pp. 44–8.

Ule, M. (1957), 'A Media Plan for Sputnik Cigarettes', *How to Plan Media Strategy*, American Association of Advertising Agencies.

Ulrich, D. and Lake, D. (1991), 'Organizational Capability: Creating Competitive Advantage', *The Executive*, Vol. 5, No. 1, February, pp. 77–92.

Vandermerwe, S. (1999), *Doing a Dyson (A)*, London: Imperial College of Science, Technology and Medicine.

Vangermeersch, R. and Brosnan, W.T. (1985), 'Enhancing Revenues Via Distribution Cost Control', *Management Accounting* (NAA), Vol. 67, No. 2, August, 56–60.

Veblen, T. (1899), *The Theory of the Leisure Class*, London: Macmillan.

Vella, C.M. and McGonagle, J.J. (1987), 'Shadowing Markets: A New Competitive Intelligence Technique', *Planning Review*, Vol. 15, No. 5, September–October, pp. 36–8.

Venkatesan, M. and Holloway, R.J. (1971), *An Introduction to Marketing Experimentation: Methods, Applications and Problems*, New York: Free Press.

Verhage, B.J. and Waarts, E. (1988), 'Marketing Planning for Improved Performance: A Comparative Analysis', *International Marketing Review*, Vol. 8, No. 5, Summer, pp. 20–30.

Vickers, Sir G. (1965), *The Art of Judgement*, London: Chapman & Hall.

Vickers, Sir G. (1968), *Value Systems and Social Process*, London: Tavistock.

Vickers, Sir G. (1972), *Freedom in a Rocking Boat: Changing Values in an Unstable Society*, London: Penguin.

Vidale, M.L. and Wolfe, H.B. (1957), 'An Operations Research Study of Sales Responses to Advertising', *Operations Research*, Vol. 5, No. 3, June, pp. 370–81.

Von Clausewitz, C. (1908), *On War*, London: Routledge & Kegan Paul.

Walden, G. and Lawler, E.O. (1993), *Marketing Masters: Secrets of America's Best Companies*, New York: HarperCollins.

Walker, O.C. and Ruekert, R.W. (1987), 'Marketing's Role in the Implementation of Business Strategies: A Critical Review and Conceptual Framework', *Journal of Marketing*, Vol. 51, No. 3, July, pp. 15–33.

Wall, S.L. (1974), 'What the Competition is Doing: You Need to Know', *Harvard Business Review*, Vol. 52, No. 6, November–December, pp. 22–4, 28, 30, 32, 34, 36, 38, 162–6, 168, 170.

Walleck, A.S., O'Halloran, J.D. and Leader, C.A. (1991), 'Benchmarking World Class Performance', *The McKinsey Quarterly*, No. 1, pp. 3–24.

Walters, C.G. and Paul, G.W. (1970), *Consumer Behavior: An Integrated Framework*, Homewood, IL: Irwin.

Walton, P. (1999), 'Marketing Rivalry in an Age of Hypercompetition', *Market Leader*, Spring, pp. 33–7.

Ward, A.J. (1968), *Measuring, Directing and Controlling New Product Development*, London: In Com Tec.

Ward, K. (1989), *Financial Aspects of Marketing*, Oxford: Heinemann.

Webster, F.E. (1970), 'Informal Communications in Industrial Markets', *Journal of Marketing Research*, Vol. 7, No. 2, May, pp. 186–9.

Webster, F.E. (1988) 'The Rediscovery of the Marketing Concept', *Business Horizons*, Vol. 31, No. 3, pp. 29–39.

Webster, F.E. (1999), 'Is Your Company Really Market Driven?', *Financial Times Mastering Global Business*, London: Pitman.

Webster, F.E. and Wind, Y. (1972), *Organisational Buying Behavior*, Englewood Cliffs, NJ: Prentice-Hall.

Weigand, R. (1966), 'Identifying Industrial Buying Responsibilities', *Journal of Marketing Research*, Vol. 3, No. 1, February, pp. 81–4.

Weigand, R. (1968), 'Why Studying the Purchasing Agent is Not Enough', *Journal of Marketing*, Vol. 32, No. 1, January, pp. 41–5.

Weihrich, H. (1982), 'The TOWS Matrix: A Tool for Situational Analysis', *Long Range Planning*, Vol. 15, No. 2, pp. 54–66.

Weihrich, H. (1993), 'Daimler-Benz's Move Towards the Next Century', *European Business Review*, Vol. 93, No. 1.

Weinberg, R. (1969), Paper presented at a seminar on Developing Marketing Strategies for Short-Term Profits and Long-Term Growth, sponsored by Advanced Management Research, Inc., Regency Hotel, New York, 29 September.

Weinshall, T.D. (ed.) (1977), *Culture and Management*, Harmondsworth: Penguin.

Weitz, B.A. and Anderson, L. (1981), 'Organizing the Marketing Function', in *AMA Review of Marketing 1981*, Chicago: American Marketing Association.

Wells, W.D. and Gubar, G. (1966), 'Life Cycle Concepts in Marketing Research', *Journal of Marketing Research*, Vol. 3, No. 4, November, pp. 355–63.

Wenner, D.L. and LeBer, R.W. (1989), 'Managing Shareholder Value – From Top to Bottom', *Harvard Business Review*, Vol. 67, No. 6, November–December, pp. 1–8.

Wensley, J.R.C. (1981), 'Strategic Marketing: Betas, Boxes or Basics', *Journal of Marketing*, Vol. 45, No. 3, Summer, pp. 173–83.

Wensley, J.R.C. (1987), 'Marketing Strategy', in Baker, M.J. (ed.), *The Marketing Book*, London: Heinemann.

Wernerfelt, B. (1986), 'The Relation Between Market Share and Profitability', *Journal of Business Strategy*, Vol. 6, No. 4, Spring, pp. 67–74.

West, A. (1967), *Modern Sales Management*, London: Macmillan Education.

Westfall, R. (1962), 'Psychological Factors in Predicting Product Choice', *Journal of Marketing*, Vol. 36, April, pp. 34–40.

Westwick, C.A. (1987), *How to Use Management Ratios*, Aldershot: Gower, 2nd edition.

White, J. (1969), 'Some Aspects of The Marketing of Machine Tools in Great Britain', Unpublished PhD thesis, UMIST.

Williamson, R.J. (1979), *Marketing for Accountants and Managers*, London: Heinemann.

Wills, G.S.C. (1980a), 'Sweeping Marketing Overboard', *European Journal of Marketing*, Vol. 14, No. 4, p. 1.

Wills, G.S.C. (1980b), 'Commercial Phoenix', *European Journal of Marketing*, Vol. 14, No. 6, p. 1.

Wills, G.S.C., Christopher, M.G. and Walters, D.W. (1972a), *Output Budgeting in Marketing*, Bradford: MCB.

Wills, G.S.C., Wilson, R.M.S., Hildebrandt, R. and Manning, N. (1972b), *Technological Forecasting*, London: Penguin Books.

Wilson, A. (1982), *Marketing Audit Check Lists*, London: McGraw-Hill.

Wilson, I. (ed.) (1994), *Marketing Interfaces: Exploring the Marketing and Business Relationship*, London: Pitman.

Wilson, R.M.S. (1970a), 'Accounting Approaches to Marketing Control', *Management Accounting* (CIMA), Vol. 48, No. 2, February, pp. 51–8.

Wilson, R.M.S. (1970b), 'The Development and Application of a Systems Approach', *Marketing Forum*, July–August, pp. 5–28.

Wilson, R.M.S. (1971a), 'The Role of the Accountant in Marketing', *Marketing Forum*, May–June, pp. 21–33.

Wilson, R.M.S. (1971b), 'Implications of Technological Forecasting for Industrial Marketing', Ch. 21 (pp. 326–46) in Wills, G.S.C. (ed.), *Exploration in Marketing Thought*, London: Crosby Lockwood/Bradford University Press.

Wilson, R.M.S. (1971c), 'The Role of Marketing in Conglomerates', *European Journal of Marketing*, Vol. 5, No. 3, Autumn, pp. 116–22.

Wilson, R.M.S. (1972), 'Financial Control of Physical Distribution Management: Some Basic Considerations', *International Journal of Physical Distribution*, Vol. 3, No. 1, Autumn, pp. 7–20.

Wilson, R.M.S. (1973), *Management Controls in Marketing*, London: Heinemann.

Wilson, R.M.S. (1974), *Financial Control: A Systems Approach*, London: McGraw-Hill.

Wilson, R.M.S. (1975), 'Marketing Control: A Financial Perspective', *The Business Graduate*, Vol. 5, No. 2, Summer, pp. 15–20.

Wilson, R.M.S. (1979), *Management Controls and Marketing Planning*, London: Heinemann.

Wilson, R.M.S. (ed.) (1980), *The Marketing of Financial Services*, Bradford: MCB.

Wilson, R.M.S. (compiler) (1981), *Financial Dimensions of Marketing*. London: Macmillan, two volumes.

Wilson, R.M.S. (1983), *Cost Control Handbook*, Aldershot: Gower, 2nd edition.

Wilson, R.M.S. (1984), 'Financial Control of the Marketing Function', Ch. 12 (pp. 130–53) in Hart, N.A. (ed.), *The Marketing of Industrial Products*, London: McGraw-Hill, 2nd edition.

Wilson, R.M.S. (1986), 'Accounting for Marketing Assets', *European Journal of Marketing*, Vol. 20, No. 1, pp. 51–74.

Wilson, R.M.S. (1988a), 'Cost Analysis', Ch. 11 (pp. 150–88) in Lock, D. and Farrow, N.A.E. (eds), *The Gower Handbook of Management*, Aldershot: Gower, 2nd edition.

Wilson, R.M.S. (1988b), 'Marketing and the Management Accountant', Ch. 13 (pp. 255–95) in Cowe, R. (ed.), *Handbook of Management Accounting*, Aldershot: Gower, 2nd edition.

Wilson, R.M.S. (1990), 'Strategic Cost Analysis', *Management Accounting*, Vol. 68, No. 9, October, pp. 42–3.

Wilson, R.M.S. (1991), 'Corporate Strategy and Management Control', Ch. 4 (pp. 115–65) in Hussey, D.E. (ed.), *International Review of Strategic Management*, Chichester: Wiley.

Wilson, R.M.S. (1995a), 'Strategic Management Accounting', Ch. 8 (pp. 159–190) in Ashton, D.J., Hopper, T.M. and Scapens, R.W. (eds), *Issues in Management Accounting*, London: Prentice-Hall, 2nd edition.

Wilson, R.M.S. (1995b), 'Marketing Budgeting and Resource Allocation', pp. 277–300 in Baker, M.J. (ed.), *Companion Encyclopaedia of Marketing*, London: Routledge.

Wilson, R.M.S. (1997), 'The Case for Strategic Control', pp. 152–181 in Lapsley, I. and Wilson, R.M.S. (eds), *Explorations in Financial Control*, London: International Thomson Business Press.

Wilson, R.M.S. (1999a), *Accounting for Marketing*, ITBP/CIMA.

Wilson, R.M.S. (1999b), 'Marketing Budgeting and Resource Allocation', pp. 208–24 in Baker, M.J. (ed.), *IEBM Encyclopedia of Marketing*, London: ITBP.

Wilson, R.M.S. (ed.) (2001), *Marketing Controllership*, Aldershot: Dartmouth/Ashgate.

Wilson, R.M.S. (Forthcoming), *Accounting for Marketing*, London: Academic Press.

Wilson, R.M.S. and Bancroft, A.L. (1983a), 'Management Accounting for Marketing – Some Industry Practices', *Management Accounting* (CIMA), Vol. 61, No. 2, February, pp. 26–8.

Wilson, R.M.S. and Bancroft, A.L. (1983b), *The Application of Management Accounting Techniques to the Planning and Control of Marketing*, London: CIMA.

Wilson, R.M.S. and Chua, W.F. (1993), *Managerial Accounting: Method and Meaning*, London: Chapman & Hall, 2nd edition (1st edition 1988).

Wilson, R.M.S. and Fook, N.Y.M. (1990), 'Improving Marketing Orientation', *Marketing Business*, Issue 11, June, pp. 22–3.

Wilson, R.M.S. and Gilligan, C.T. (1997), *Strategic Marketing Management: Planning, implementation and control*, Oxford: Butterworth-Heinemann, 2nd edition.

Wilson, R.M.S. and McHugh, G.J.P. (1987), *Financial Analysis*, London: Cassell.

Wilson, R.M.S. and Zhang, Q. (1997), 'Entrapment and Escalating Commitment in Investment Decision-making: A Review', *The British Accounting Review*, Vol. 29, No. 3, September, pp. 277–305.

Wind, J. (1996) 'Big Questions for the 21st Century', *Financial Times, Mastering Management*, Part 15, pp. 6–7.

Wind, Y. (1978), 'Issues and Advances in Segmentation Research', *Journal of Marketing Research*, Vol. 15, No. 3, August, pp. 317–37.

Wind, Y. and Claycamp, H.J. (1976), 'Planning Product Line Strategy: A Matrix Approach', *Journal of Marketing*, Vol. 40, No. 1, January, pp. 2–9.

Winer, L. (1966), 'A Profit-Oriented Decision System', *Journal of Marketing*, Vol. 30, No. 2, April, pp. 38–44.

Witcher, B.J. (1990), 'Total Marketing: Total Quality and the Marketing Concept', *The Quarterly Review of Marketing*, Vol. 15, No. 2, Winter, pp. 1–6.

Witte, M. (1990), 'Organising to Make the Most of Change', *Management Consultancy*, March, pp. 29–30, 32–3.

Wolff Olins (1989a), *Corporate Personality – A Enquiry into the Nature of Corporate Identity*, London: Wolff Olins.

Wolff Olins (1989b), *Corporate Identity*, London: Thames & Hudson.

Wong, V. and Saunders, J.A. (1993), 'Business orientations and corporate success', *Journal of Strategic Marketing*, Vol. 1, No. 1, pp. 20–40.

Wong, V., Saunders, J.A. and Doyle, P. (1988), 'The Quality of British Marketing: A Comparison with US and Japanese Multinationals in the UK Market', *Journal of Marketing Management*, Vol. 4, No. 2, pp. 107–30.

Woo, C.Y. and Cooper, A.C. (1982), 'The Surprising Case for Low Market Share', *Harvard Business Review*, Vol. 60, No. 6, November–December, pp. 106–13.

Wright, R.V.L. (1974), *A System for Managing Diversity*, Cambridge, MA: Arthur D. Little.

Yale, J.P. (1964), *Modern Textiles Magazine*, February, p. 33.

Yankelovich, D. (1964), 'New Criteria for Market Segmentation', *Harvard Business Review*, Vol. 42, No. 2, March–April, pp. 83–90.

Young, S. (1972), 'The Dynamics of Measuring Unchange', pp. 61–82 in Haley, R.I. (ed.), *Attitudes Research in Transition*, Chicago: American Marketing Association.

Zakon, A. (1971), *Growth and Financial Strategies*, Boston, MA: Boston Consulting Group.

Index